MARIANNE MOORE

Modern Critical Views

Henry Adams
Edward Albee
A. R. Ammons
Matthew Arnold
John Ashbery
W. H. Auden
Jane Austen
James Baldwin
Charles Baudelaire
Samuel Beckett
Saul Bellow
The Bible
Elizabeth Bishop
William Blake
Jorge Luis Borges
Elizabeth Bowen
Bertolt Brecht
The Brontës
Robert Browning
Anthony Burgess
George Gordon, Lord Byron
Thomas Carlyle
Lewis Carroll
Willa Cather
Cervantes
Geoffrey Chaucer
Kate Chopin
Samuel Taylor Coleridge
Joseph Conrad
Contemporary Poets
Hart Crane
Stephen Crane
Dante
Charles Dickens
Emily Dickinson
John Donne & the Seventeenth-Century Metaphysical Poets
Elizabethan Dramatists
Theodore Dreiser
John Dryden
George Eliot
T. S. Eliot
Ralph Ellison
Ralph Waldo Emerson
William Faulkner
Henry Fielding
F. Scott Fitzgerald
Gustave Flaubert
E. M. Forster
Sigmund Freud
Robert Frost
Robert Graves
Graham Greene
Thomas Hardy
Nathaniel Hawthorne
William Hazlitt
Seamus Heaney
Ernest Hemingway
Geoffrey Hill
Friedrich Hölderlin
Homer
Gerard Manley Hopkins
William Dean Howells
Zora Neale Hurston
Henry James
Samuel Johnson and James Boswell
Ben Jonson
James Joyce
Franz Kafka
John Keats
Rudyard Kipling
D. H. Lawrence
John Le Carré
Ursula K. Le Guin
Doris Lessing
Sinclair Lewis
Robert Lowell
Norman Mailer
Bernard Malamud
Thomas Mann
Christopher Marlowe
Carson McCullers
Herman Melville
James Merrill
Arthur Miller
John Milton
Eugenio Montale
Marianne Moore
Iris Murdoch
Vladimir Nabokov
Joyce Carol Oates
Sean O'Casey
Flannery O'Connor
Eugene O'Neill
George Orwell
Cynthia Ozick
Walter Pater
Walker Percy
Harold Pinter
Plato
Edgar Allan Poe
Poets of Sensibility & the Sublime
Alexander Pope
Katherine Ann Porter
Ezra Pound
Pre-Raphaelite Poets
Marcel Proust
Thomas Pynchon
Arthur Rimbaud
Theodore Roethke
Philip Roth
John Ruskin
J. D. Salinger
Gershom Scholem
William Shakespeare (3 vols.)
  Histories & Poems
  Comedies
  Tragedies
George Bernard Shaw
Mary Wollstonecraft Shelley
Percy Bysshe Shelley
Edmund Spenser
Gertrude Stein
John Steinbeck
Laurence Sterne
Wallace Stevens
Tom Stoppard
Jonathan Swift
Alfred, Lord Tennyson
William Makepeace Thackeray
Henry David Thoreau
Leo Tolstoi
Anthony Trollope
Mark Twain
John Updike
Gore Vidal
Virgil
Robert Penn Warren
Evelyn Waugh
Eudora Welty
Nathanael West
Edith Wharton
Walt Whitman
Oscar Wilde
Tennessee Williams
William Carlos Williams
Thomas Wolfe
Virginia Woolf
William Wordsworth
Richard Wright
William Butler Yeats

These and other titles in preparation

Modern Critical Views

MARIANNE MOORE

Edited and with an introduction by

Harold Bloom
Sterling Professor of the Humanities
Yale University

CHELSEA HOUSE PUBLISHERS ◇ 1987
New York ◇ New Haven ◇ Philadelphia

133 Christopher Street, New York, NY 10014
345 Whitney Avenue, New Haven, CT 06511
5014 West Chester Pike, Edgemont, PA 19028

Printed and bound in the United States of America

∞ The paper used in this publication meets the minimum requirements of the American National Standard for Permanence of Paper for Printed Library Materials, Z39.48-1984.

Library of Congress Cataloging-in-Publication Data
Marianne Moore.
(Modern critical views)
Bibliography: p.
Includes index.
Summary: A collection of critical essays on the poetry of Marianne Moore. Also includes a chronology of events in her life.
1. Moore, Marianne, 1887–1972—Criticism and interpretation. [1. Moore, Marianne, 1887–1972—Criticism and interpretation. 2. American literature—History and criticism] I. Bloom, Harold. II. Series.
PS3525.05616Z689 1986 811′.52 86-17094
ISBN 0-87754-631-2 (alk. paper)

Contents

Editor's Note

This book brings together a representative selection of the best criticism available on the poetry of Marianne Moore. I am grateful to Susan Lasher for her aid in researching this volume.

My introduction centers upon an exegesis of Moore's major poem, "Marriage," possibly the masterpiece of her allusive mode. The sequence of critical essays, arranged in the chronological order of their original appearance, begins with Hugh Kenner's High Modernist account of what he takes to be Moore's tradition. Kenner sees this as a purified version of the procession that goes from the dandy on through a tragic aesthete like Lionel Johnson and culminates with Hemingway.

Pamela White Hadas, in a reading of "Marriage" that contrasts to the one offered in my introduction, analyzes the poem as a dialectic of moral fastidiousness. The best reader of the language of Moore's language, Marie Borroff, brilliantly describes the poet's transformation of the "promotional prose" of journalism and advertising into the image of wholeness and integration that dominates her characteristic poetry.

A moving overview by Helen Vendler rightly emphasizes that Moore's poems are not about nature but concern the poet herself. Bonnie Costello, studying Moore's language, finds its "feminine" quality to be a demonstration that "humility, affection, reserve, are not passive but dynamic and vital modes of response."

In a retrospective review of Moore's achievement, David Bromwich justly leads us to see that her closest affinities, as a poet, were not with W. C. Williams and Pound, but with Stevens and the early Eliot. In a second essay by Bonnie Costello, the personal and poetic relationship between Marianne Moore and Elizabeth Bishop is viewed as one of "nurture," as opposed to any account of the influence process that judges it to be marked always by agonistic elements, however repressed.

The concluding essay, by John M. Slatin, portrays Moore as natural historian, but in the strong sense of analyzing her complex, double, American relationship to the English poetic past. Slatin emphasizes the ways in which Moore's "parodies" of major poets like Keats and Wordsworth work both to establish her own originality, and also to carry the past alive into the present in her own poetry.

Introduction

I

For Plato the only reality that mattered is exemplified best for us in the principles of mathematics. The aim of our lives should be to draw ourselves away as much as possible from the unsubstantial, fluctuating facts of the world about us and establish some communion with the objects which are apprehended by thought and not sense. This was the source of Plato's asceticism. To the extent that Miss Moore finds only allusion tolerable she shares that asceticism. While she shares it she does so only as it may be necessary for her to do so in order to establish a particular reality or, better, a reality of her own particulars.

—WALLACE STEVENS

Allusion was Marianne Moore's method, a method that was her self. One of the most American of all poets, she was fecund in her progeny—Elizabeth Bishop, May Swenson, and Richard Wilbur being the most gifted among them. Her own American precursors were not Emily Dickinson and Walt Whitman—still our two greatest poets—but the much slighter Stephen Crane, who is echoed in her earliest poems, and in an oblique way Edgar Poe, whom she parodied. I suspect that her nearest poetic father, in English, was Thomas Hardy, who seems to have taught her lessons in the mastery of incongruity, and whose secularized version of Biblical irony is not far from her own. If we compare her with her major poetic contemporaries—Frost, Stevens, Eliot, Pound, Williams, Aiken, Ransom, Cummings, H. D., Hart Crane—she is clearly the most original American poet of her era, though not quite of the eminence of Frost, Stevens, Crane. A curious kind of devotional poet, with some authentic affinities to George Herbert, she reminds us implicitly but constantly that any distinction between sacred and secular poetry is only a shibboleth of cultural politics. Some day she will remind us also of what current cultural politics obscure: that any distinction between poetry written by women or poetry by men is a mere polemic, unless it follows upon an initial distinction between good and bad poetry. Moore, like Bishop and Swenson, is an extraordinary poet-as-poet. The issue of how gender enters into her vision should arise only after the aesthetic achievement is judged as such.

Moore, as all her readers know, to their lasting delight, is the visionary of natural creatures: the jerboa, frigate pelican, buffalo, monkeys, fish, snakes, mongooses, the octopus (actually a trope for a mountain), snail, peacock, whale, pangolin, wood-weasel, elephants, race horses, chameleon, jellyfish, arctic ox (or goat), giraffe, blue bug (another trope, this time for a pony), all of La Fontaine's bestiary, not to mention sea and land unicorns, basilisks, and all the weird fabulous roster that perhaps only Borges also, among crucial modern writers, celebrates so consistently. There is something of Blake and of the Christopher Smart of *Jubilate Agno* in Moore, though the affinity does not result from influence, but rather is the consequence of election. Moore's famous eye, like that of Bishop after her, is not so much a visual gift as it is visionary, for the beasts in her poems are charged with a spiritual intensity that doubtless they possess, but which I myself cannot see without the aid of Blake, Smart, and Moore.

I remember always in reading Moore again that her favorite poem was the Book of Job. Just as I cannot read Ecclesiastes without thinking of Dr. Johnson, I cannot read certain passages in Job without recalling Marianne Moore:

> But ask now the beasts, and they shall teach thee; and the fowls of the air, and they shall tell thee:
>
> Or speak to the earth, and it shall teach thee: and the fishes of the sea shall declare unto thee.
>
> Who knoweth not in all these that the hand of the Lord hath wrought this?
>
> In whose hand is the soul of every living thing.

This, from chapter 12, is the prelude to the great chant of Yahweh, the Voice out of the whirlwind that sounds forth in the frightening magnificence of chapters 38 through 41, where the grand procession of beasts comprehends lions, ravens, wild goats, the wild ass, the unicorn, peacocks, the ostrich, the sublime battle-horse who "saith among the trumpets, Ha, ha," the hawk, the eagle, and at last behemoth and leviathan. Gorgeously celebrating his own creation, Yahweh through the poet of Job engendered another strong poet in Marianne Moore. Of the Book of Job, she remarked that its agony was veracious and its fidelity of a force "that contrives glory for ashes."

"Glory for ashes" might be called Moore's ethical motto, the basis for the drive of her poetic will toward a reality of her own particulars. Her poetry, as befitted the translator of La Fontaine, and the heir of George Herbert, would be in some danger of dwindling into moral essays, an impossible form for our time, were it not for her wild allusiveness, her zest for quotations, and her essentially anarchic stance, the American and Emersonian insistence upon seeing everything in her own way, with "conscientious inconsistency." When her wildness or freedom subsided, she produced an occasional poetic disaster like the patriotic war poems "In Distrust of Merits" and " 'Keeping Their World Large.' " But her greatest poems are at just the opposite edge of consciousness: "A Grave," "Novices," "Marriage," "An Octopus," "He 'Digesteth Harde Yron,' " "Elephants," the deceptively light "Tom Fool at Jamaica."

Those seven poems by themselves have an idiosyncratic splendor that restores my faith, as a critic, in what the language of the poets truly is: diction, or choice of words, playing endlessly upon the dialectic of denotation and connotation, a dialectic that simply vanishes in all Structuralist and post-Structuralist ruminations upon the supposed priority of "language" over meaning. "The arbitrariness of the signifier" loses its charm when one asks a Gallic psycholinguistifier whether denotation or connotation belongs to the signifier, as opposed to the signified, and one beholds blank incredulity as one's only answer. Moore's best poems give the adequate reply: the play of the signifier is answered always by the play of the signified, because the play of diction, or the poet's will over language, is itself constituted by the endless interchanges of denotation and connotation. Moore, with her rage to order allusion, echo, and quotation in ghostlier demarcations, keener sounds, helps us to realize that the belated Modernism of the Gallic proclamation of the death of the author was no less premature than it was, always already, belated.

II

Marriage, through which thought does not penetrate, appeared to Miss Moore a legitimate object for art, an art that would not halt from using thought about it, however, as it might want to. Against marriage, "this institution, perhaps one should say enterprise"—Miss Moore launched her thought not to have it appear arsenaled as in a textbook on psychology, but to stay among apples and giraffes in a poem.

—WILLIAM CARLOS WILLIAMS

If I had to cite a single poem by Moore as representing all of her powers working together, it would be "Marriage" (1923), superficially an outrageous collage but profoundly a poignant comic critique of every society's most sacred and tragic institution. As several critics have ventured, this is Moore's *The Waste Land*, a mosaic of fragments from Francis Bacon, the *Scientific American*, Baxter's *The Saint's Everlasting Rest*, Hazlitt on Burke, William Godwin, Trollope, *The Tempest*, a book on *The Syrian Christ*, the Bible, Ezra Pound, and even Daniel Webster (from an inscription on a statue!), and twenty sources more. Yet it is a poem, and perhaps is more ruggedly unified than any other poem of such ambition by Moore.

The poet's own headnote to "Marriage" could not be more diffident: "Statements that took my fancy which I tried to arrange plausibly." The arrangement is more than plausible; it is quite persuasive, though it begins with a parody of the societal *apologia* for marriage:

> This institution,
> perhaps one should say enterprise
> out of respect for which
> one says one need not change one's mind
> about a thing one has believed in,
> requiring public promises
> of one's intention
> to fulfil a private obligation.

No one, I believe, could interpret that opening stance with any exactitude. The substitution of "enterprise" for "institution" qualifies the wryness of "public promises / of one's intention / to fulfil a private obligation," but adds a note both of commerce and of the human virtue of taking an initiative. Who could have anticipated that the next movement of the poem would be this?

> I wonder what Adam and Eve
> think of it by this time,
> this fire-gilt steel
> alive with goldenness;
> how bright it shows—
> "of circular traditions and impostures,
> committing many spoils,"
> requiring all one's criminal ingenuity
> to avoid!

Like nearly every other quotation in this poem, the two lines from Sir Francis Bacon gain nothing for Moore's own text by being restored to their own context. Steel burned by fire does not exactly brighten into a golden bough, so the "gilt" is there partly as anticipation of "criminal ingenuity." Yet "gilt" is in cognitive sequence with "goldenness" and "bright," even if we rightly expect to behold blackened steel. All who have known marriage (as Moore declined to do) will register an unhappy shudder at the force the Baconian phrases take on when Moore appropriates them. Traditions as treasons become circular, and together with impostures can be read here either as performing many despoilments or as investing many gains of previous despoilments. Either way, it might seem as though an ingenuity avoiding this equivocal enterprise could only be taken as criminal by some dogmatist, whether societal or theological.

The poem proceeds to dismiss psychology, since to explain everything is to explain nothing, and then meditates upon the beauty, talents, and contrariness of Eve, a meditation that suddenly achieves Paterian intensity:

> Below the incandescent stars
> below the incandescent fruit,
> the strange experience of beauty;
> its existence is too much;
> it tears one to pieces
> and each fresh wave of consciousness
> is poison.

The detachment of Moore as watcher is not totally lost, but seems (by design) never fully recovered again in the poem. A woman's fine bitterness against the West's endless assault upon Eve is felt in Moore's description of the universal mother as "the central flaw" in the experiment of Eden, itself "an interesting impossibility" ecstatically described by Richard Baxter as "the choicest piece of my life." If Baxter's ecstasy (though not his eloquence) is qualified shrewdly by Moore's contextualizations, Eden is nowhere near so scaled down by her as is Adam, whose male pomp is altogether undermined. He is pretty well identified with Satan, and like Satan is: "alive with words, / vibrating like a cymbal / touched before it has been struck."

Moore's genius at her method allows her the joy of exemplifying her borrowings even as she employs them in a corrective polemic against male slanderings of women:

> "Treading chasms
> on the uncertain footing of a spear,"
> forgetting that there is in woman
> a quality of mind
> which as an instinctive manifestation

is unsafe,
he goes on speaking
in a formal customary strain.

In the first quotation, Hazlitt is praising his precursor Edmund Burke for a paradoxically certain footing: for power, energy, truth set forth in the Sublime style. Burke is a chasm-treader, sure-footed as he edges near the abyss. But men less given to truth than Burke have very uncertain footing indeed, whether they forget or remember their characteristic brutalities in regard to a woman's "quality of mind." The poem's "he" therefore goes on speaking of marriage in Richard Baxter's ecstatic terms, as though marriage itself somehow could become "the saints' everlasting rest." Fatuously joyous, the male is ready to suffer the most exquisite passage in the poem, and perhaps in all of Moore:

Plagued by the nightingale
in the new leaves,
with its silence—
not its silence but its silences,
he says of it:
"It clothes me with a shirt of fire."
"He dares not clap his hands
to make it go on
lest it should fly off;
if he does nothing, it will sleep;
if he cries out, it will not understand."
Unnerved by the nightingale
and dazzled by the apple,
impelled by "the illusion of a fire
effectual to extinguish fire,"
compared with which
the shining of the earth
is but deformity—a fire
"as high as deep
as bright as broad
as long as life itself,"
he stumbles over marriage,
"a very trivial object indeed"
to have destroyed the attitude
in which he stood—.

I hardly know of a more unnerving representation of the male fear and distrust of the female, uncannily combined with the male quandry of being obsessed with, fascinated by, not only the female but the enterprise of marriage as well. Moore imperishably catches the masterpiece of male emotive ambivalence towards the female, which is the male identification of woman and the taboo. Here the nightingale, perhaps by way of Keats's erotic allusions, becomes an emblem of the female, while the male speaker, ravished by the silences of the emblem, becomes Hercules suicidally aflame with the shirt of Nessus. The poor male, "unnerved by the nightingale / and dazzled by the apple," stumbles over the enterprise that is Adam's experiment, marriage:

> its fiddlehead ferns,
> lotus flowers, opuntias, white dromedaries,
> its hippopotamus—
> nose and mouth combined
> in one magnificent hopper—
> its snake and the potent apple.

We again receive what might be called Moore's Paradox: marriage, considered from either the male or female perspective, is a dreadful disaster, but as a poetic trope gorgeously shines forth its barbaric splendors. The male, quoting Trollope's *Barchester Towers*, returns us to the image of Hercules, and commends marriage "as a fine art, as an experiment, / a duty or as merely recreation." I myself will never get out of my memory Moore's subsequent deadpan definition of marriage as "the fight to be affectionate." With a fine impartiality, the poet has a vision of the agonists in this eternal dispute:

> The blue panther with black eyes,
> the basalt panther with blue eyes,
> entirely graceful—
> one must give them the path—.

But this mutual splendor abates quickly, and a rancorous humor emerges:

> He says, "What monarch would not blush
> to have a wife
> with hair like a shaving brush?"
> The fact of woman
> is "not the sound of the flute

but very poison."
She says, "Men are monopolists
of 'stars, garters, buttons
and other shining baubles'—
unfit to be the guardians
of another person's happiness."
He says, "These mummies
must be handled carefully—
'the crumbs from a lion's meal,
a couple of shins and the bit of an ear';
turn to the letter M
and you will find
that 'a wife is a coffin.'

This marvelous exchange of diatribes is weirdly stitched together from outrageously heterogeneous "sources," ranging from a parody of *The Rape of the Lock* (in which Moore herself took a hand) to a women's college president's denunciation of the male love of awards and medals on to a surprising misappropriation of a great moment in the prophet Amos, which is then juxtaposed to a brutal remark of Ezra Pound's. Amos associates the lion with Yahweh:

> The lion hath roared, who will not fear? the Lord GOD hath spoken, who can but prophesy?
>
> Thus saith the LORD; As the shepherd taketh out of the mouth of the lion two legs, or a piece of an ear; so shall the children of Israel be taken out that dwell in Samaria in the corner of a bed, and in Damascus in a couch.

Moore slyly revises the roaring prophet, making the lion every male, and the children of Israel every woman. Pound's dictum, that "a wife is a coffin" is presumably placed under the letter M for "male," and sorts well with Moore's unfair but strong revision of Amos, since the revision suggests that a wife is a corpse. In order to show that her revisionary zeal is savagely if suavely directed against both sexes (or rather their common frailties), Moore proceeds to dissect the narcissism of men and women alike, until she concludes with the most ironic of her visions in the poem:

"I am such a cow,
if I had a sorrow
I should feel it a long time;

> I am not one of those
> who have a great sorrow
> in the morning
> and a great joy at noon";

which says: "I have encountered it
among those unpretentious
protégés of wisdom,
where seeming to parade
as the debater and the Roman,
the statesmanship
of an archaic Daniel Webster
persists to their simplicity of temper
as the essence of the matter:

> 'Liberty and union
> now and forever';

the Book on the writing table;
the hand in the breast pocket."

Webster, hardly unpretentious, and wise only in his political cunning, is indeed the message inscribed upon his statue: "Liberty and union / now and forever." As a judgment upon marriage, it would be a hilarious irony, if we did not wince so much under Moore's not wholly benign tutelage. That Book on the writing table, presumably the Bible, is precisely like Webster's hand in the breast pocket, an equivocal emblem, in this context, of the societal benediction upon marriage. Moore's own *The Waste Land*, "Marriage," may outlast Eliot's poem as a permanent vision of the West in its long, ironic decline.

HUGH KENNER

The Experience of the Eye

Miss Moore has told *viva voce*, and surely more than once, the story of her supervised visit to the zoo. She had consented to be accompanied there by a man from *Life*, to be photographed in acts of guarded friendship with such beasts as might offset, by their bizarre aloofness, her innocent self-sufficient face and cartwheel hat. She had nothing more to say, though *Life* later had a few hundred words to say, about her dealings with the photogenic beasts. What she remembered was a man expounding the snakes to a group of children. She had heard what he said, and noted what he neglected to say: a libel by omission, which she saw it was her duty to correct. So, "You must be sure to tell those children," she said, "that snakes are not cold and not slimy; that they are dry and just as warm as their surroundings. One need not hesitate to touch them." The man from *Life* saw his cue; he caused a large snake to be passed into the hands of Miss Moore. He was obeying the tradition by which journalism was governed as long ago as Boswell's famous question to Dr. Johnson: "What would you do, Sir, if you were shut up in a tower with a baby?" It is the tradition of Pécuchet's laboratory: supply some incongruous reagent, and see what happens. It is the molecular unit in the only American tradition for dealing with genius, which is to write a biography.

Miss Moore did not flinch from her principle, though she had never handled a snake before. She accepted it. She was immediately asked what

---

From *The Southern Review* 1 (October 1965). Originally entitled "The Experience of the Eye: Marianne Moore's Tradition."

it felt like. And then, faithful to a tradition of her own, she consulted her fingers, and the memories to which her fingers gave access, and pronounced simply, "Like rose petals." It was perhaps too poetic a remark to make its point, but she has never allowed a fear of being thought poetic to deter her from accuracy. For she meant the resemblance of snakes to rose petals neither as a fancy nor as a simile, but as a virtual identity of tactile sensation: a species of wit gone into the fingertips: a tactile pun.

In her poems, things utter puns to the senses. These, registered in words, make odd corrugations of the linguistic surface. Thus her words note a certain sleepy cat's "prune-shaped head and alligator eyes," and identify in his whiskers "the shadbones regularly set about the mouth, to droop or rise / in unison like the porcupine's quills," and register him, awake, "Springing about with froglike accuracy": the frog and the cat being two creatures that land where they meant to.

This policy of accurate comparison, bringing, if need be, the prune, the alligator, the shad, the porcupine, the frog to the service of a discussion of a cat, does not worry about congruousness just as Bracque does not worry about perspective, being intent on a different way of filling its elected spaces. Congruity, like perspective, deals in proportions within an overall view. Miss Moore's poems deal in many separate acts of attention: optical puns, seen by snapshot, in a poetic normally governed by the eye, sometimes by the ears and fingers, ultimately by the moral sense. It is the poetic of the solitary observer, for whose situation the usual meanings of a word like "moral" have to be redefined: a poetic whose effort to define itself has for two centuries constituted a tradition of some centrality. To understand that tradition is to perceive Miss Moore's place in the story of the mind of Europe, neither as eccentric nor as peripheral as she is sometimes made to seem.

Not more than two centuries' weight, though two centuries of continuous revolution, lies behind the ideal of describing accurately the thing seen. The art of doing that was developed, so far as it has been developed, almost wholly in the nineteenth century. Hardly anyone had wanted to do it earlier. It was a thing that Boswell felt he wanted to do, when the Hebrides offered ruins, rocks and grandeurs, but the despairing *Journal* note in which he confesses to being very weak at it points less to his private inadequacies than to the fact that there existed no descriptive tradition from which he might have learned. Words can set things seen before the mind only by a system of analogies, and no one had thought to want analogies for the experience of the eye, as it passes along the contours or across the surfaces of the seen world.

This is not a question of what is called "visual imagery." When Shakespeare has Romeo say,

Night's candles are burnt out, and jocund day
Stands tiptoe on the misty mountain-top,

he sets before our minds visual imagery, but imagery that offers no analogy for the experience of the eye; rather, for our iconograms of effortless power. If you commission an artist to draw what Shakespeare is setting before the mind, you get Blake's painting "Glad Day," which looks like a jocund youth but not like the sun rising. In the same way "night's candles" suggests the elation of the mind, but not the experience of the eye with a field of stars. Nature, from the time of Homer to the time of John Donne, had been apprehended according to forms of personal analogies, as a field of wills and forces which, written down as analytically as possible, generated the physics of things seeking their places and vacua abhorred; and written down according to a less exigent discipline, the world of moonlight sleeping on banks, winds cracking their cheeks, and the stars keeping their courses. So pervasive is this tradition that even the austerity that merely names things is apt to commit the things named to fields of mythological force. In the little poem attributed to Sappho which begins *Deduke men a selanna* we are apt to find what no doubt H. D. found, pioneering Imagism:

The moon is gone down,
and the Pleiades,
time passes, and at midnight
I lie in my bed alone.

But most certainly a Greek reader would have thought of the moon going down to sleep with Endymion, and the Pleiades with Ocean. Far from being numbed, as we Copernicans feel, by the heavens' chill otherness, the poet feels deserted while they are fulfilled. Delicate arms enfold the beings of the sky; all things complete their couplings save myself.

In a world which was felt in that way the mere testimony of the eye had negligible power to declare the otherness of the visible; and after the world had ceased to be felt in that way, some time in the seventeenth century, after the New Philosophy had put all in doubt, the eye did not instantly enforce such assertions. Rather poetic diction continued to trace the old paths, informing us that restless Sol had shone his ardent ray, and justifying itself by claims about sublimity and about fancy. Already by the 1720s Pope had sensed that the old language, in enlightened times, could only make fun of itself in a complicated fashion, the real world, as distinguished from the one poetry inhabits, having been created by Sir Isaac Newton. Pope at his most solemn remains a tireless personifer—

Another age shall see the golden ear
Embrown the slope, and nod on the parterre.

It was not until the 1790s that the universe of Newton, about which in detail there is much to record but really little to say, was admitted to English poetry.

Wordsworth, of course, admitted it, Wordsworth whose very model was Newton, the unspeaking sage: not generating utterances (except perhaps afterward, in tranquility), but rather "voyaging through strange seas of thought, alone." And Wordsworth seeking to come to terms with a world where no restless Sol puts forth an ardent ray, but rather people are "Roll'd round in earth's diurnal course / With rocks, and stones, and trees," sensed at once that in the presence of such a universe one's traditional language could register no more than one's feeling about it. And Wordsworth's is the traditional language. His diction, by which he maneuvers himself from one end of a poem to the other, retains the trick of personifying, but a trick now suffused by "as if":

> The city now doth like a garment wear
> The beauty of the morning;

and what is not personified will be merely listed:

> silent, bare,
> Ships, towers, domes, theatres, and temples lie
> Open unto the fields, and to the sky,
> All bright and glittering in the smokeless air.

The Westminster Bridge sonnet is partly about the bare city and partly about the observer's emotions:

> Ne'er saw I, never felt, a calm so deep!

For this universe, as he was to reflect repeatedly, is one whose meaning you half perceive and half create. Moreover, it half creates you; and Wordworth's principal subject became "The Prelude, or The Growth of a Poet's Soul." And there, for some decades, the matter rested.

Or there poetry let it rest. The task of mediating with a universe now merely visible, now merely *there*, was carried on, since no work of the imagination is ever abandoned; but not carried on by poets, who contented themselves with the orchestration of passion. It was carried on by painters and scientists. Wordsworth's immediate successor is John Constable, whose theme is quite simply a drama perceptible in the experience of the eye, experience imitated by the brush. Next, with less drama but much narrative about fieldwork, the art of natural description was pursued by geologists, who had two objectives, both practical. Their first objective was to present in a printed book an array of visual evidence, at a time when getting an accurate picture onto the page involved laborious collaboration between observer, artist and engraver. The observer had maximal control over his discriminations and emphases if he could somehow learn to make his point with unassisted language. Their other objective was to educate the reader's eye, so he could learn to see things for himself. The finest energies of the nineteenth century flowed into teaching people to see what was around them, reading in a new way, intimate, surprising, the Book of Nature. By the time Sherlock Holmes was damning "the great unobservant public, that could hardly tell a weaver by his tooth, or a compositor by his left thumb," the tradition had become accessible for vulgarization in the *Strand* magazine. It was a Scottish geologist, Hugh Miller, who composed the phrase Stephen Dedalus was to draw from his treasure-house, "a day of dappled seaborn clouds." It was a Swiss naturalist, Louis Agassiz, who carried the mimesis by words of the experience of the eye to such a pitch that Ezra Pound, in whose visual world "light shaves grass into emerald," was to set him in the sphere of the fixed stars, and remark that he could teach "even a literatus" to write. And a principal amateur geologist of the nineteenth century, who spent some thousands of pounds on a collection of rocks and gems, and gave his attention by turns to the experience of the eye amid natural things and the experience of the eye amid the painted forms of a Constable or a Turner, was of course John Ruskin.

Two quotations from Ruskin will bring us to the threshold of Miss Moore. Here is what he says about the moral attributes of perception:

> The greatest thing a human soul ever does in this world is to see something, and tell what it saw in a plain way. Hundreds of people can talk for one who can think, but thousands can think for one who can see. To see clearly is poetry, prophecy and religion all in one.

This tells us that Nature does not teach us by dramatic example, as the Renaissance supposed, or by stealing into our hearts in a wise passiveness, as Wordsworth supposed, but by guiding an act of perception and enunciation entered into with the whole being: which act is a moral act, and exfoliates legitimately into moral reflections. Here is Ruskin describing a fir tree:

> The Power of the tree . . . is in the dark, flat, solid tables of leafage, which it holds out on its strong arms, curved slightly over them like shields, and spreading towards the extremity like

> a hand. It is vain to endeavor to paint the sharp, grassy, intricate leafage until this ruling form has been secured; and in the boughs that approach the spectator the foreshortening of it is just like that of a wide hill-country, ridge just rising over ridge in successive distances.

The moral reflection Ruskin derives from this is that painters have an obligation to look. For the passage is specifically an education of the eye for painters, who without Ruskin to instruct them in seeing are apt to paint fir trees constructed like chandeliers. He is tracing the tree's visible gestures. The strong arms his fir tree holds out betoken no act of facile personification, in the manner of the tiptoe posture of Romeo's dawn. They are analogies for the eye retracing the gesture made in three-dimensional space by piney branches. These arms hold out "dark, flat, solid tables of leafage," and these tables curve over the branches "like shields," and spread out toward the extremity "like a hand." They are foreshortened, furthermore, as they approach the spectator, like the ridges of "a wide hill-country." Arms, table, shields, hands, hills are so many analogies for the experience of the eye, by which the painter's eye is to be educated, and the art-critic's also. They do not constitute a recipe for a painter, who if he were to paint what Ruskin names would arrive at surrealism. He is to learn from what Ruskin names, and paint the tree, having learned at last how to see it; and this putting down of what he has learned to see will not be copying but "poetry, prophecy and religion all in one."

This tree of arms, shields, tables, hands and hills, like Miss Moore's cat of porcupine, alligator, shad and prune and frog, is a tree of language, not of painting, existing only on Ruskin's printed page. It got there by an effort of attention, commanding the resources of the whole being, that devised and traversed a half-dozen analogies, analogies not for a tree but for a tree's fancied kinetic act, and the eye's act responding. And Miss Moore's focal discovery, aligning her with Bracque not with Dali, has been simply this, that poetic cats exist only on the page. Ruskin himself did not know this, being content to impersonate Isaiah.

Like prophecy since Isaiah, poetry since Homer has imitated a voice crying, and the literary imitation of the visual was involved, when the problem finally arose, in endless compromises occasioned by the fact that the visual is voiceless. Wordsworth dropped his voice to a murmur without quite availing, and poetry ceded the theme pending the discovery of some poetic medium as physical, as detectable as John Constable's pigments. This medium proved at last to be something as uncompromisingly mute as cats and trees, the printed page itself.

In Miss Moore's time—she was born thirteen years before Ruskin died—the poet found it indispensable to work directly with the printed page, which is where, and only where, his cats and trees exist. Constable in the same way worked directly with his pigments, and not by transmitting directions to an accomplice. We may say that this became possible when poets began to use typewriters. And we may note three of the things that Miss Moore has been in her lifetime: a librarian; an editor; and a teacher of typewriting: locating fragments already printed; picking and choosing; making, letter by letter, neat pages.

Her poems are not for the voice; she senses this in herself reading them badly; in response to a question, she once said that she wrote them for people to look at. Moreover, one cannot imagine them handwritten; for as Ruskin's tree, on the page, exists in tension between arboreal process and the mind's serial inventory of arms, shields, tables, hands and hills, so Miss Moore's cats, her fish, her pangolins and ostriches exist on the page in tension between the mechanisms of print and the presence of a person behind those mechanisms. Handwriting flows with the voice, and here the voice is as synthetic as the cat, not something the elocutionist can modulate. The words on these pages are little regular blocks, set apart by spaces, that have been generated not by the voice but by the click of the keys and the ratcheting of the carriage.

The stanzas lie on the page, one after another, in little intricate grids of visual symmetry, the left margin indented according to complex rules which govern the setting of tabulator stops. The lines obey no rhythmic system the ear can apprehend; that there is a system we learn not by listenting but by counting syllables, and we find that the words exist within a grid of numerical rules. Thus *The Fish* has 27 syllables per stanza, arranged in five lines on a three-part scheme of indentation, the syllables apportioned among the lines 1, 3, 9, 6, 8. And since a mosaic has no point of beginning, the poem is generated from somewhere just outside its own rigidly plotted field: generated not merely by ichthyological reality, but by two words, "The Fish," which are part of the first sentence but not part of the pattern, being in fact the poem's title. Therefore:

The Fish

wade
through black jade.
        Of the crow-blue mussel-shells, one keeps
        adjusting the ash-heaps;
            opening and shutting itself like

an
injured fan.

To begin this sentence we read the title, and to end it we read three words (four syllables) of the next stanza: for the single stanza is a patterned zone specified within, but not coterminous with, the articulation of the sentences. The single stanza exhibits, in fact, an archaic disregard of the mere things human desire does with sentences. The voice shaping sentences is anxious to be understood; the stanzas are cut and laminated in severe corrective to that anxiety, posing against it their authority of number (1, 3, 9, 6, 8) and typography. They even invade the sounds of speech with their rhymes, not performing however the traditional offices of rhymes, not miming a symmetry, clinching an epigram, or caressing a melodic fluid, but cutting, cutting, cutting, with implacable arbitrariness: "like / an / injured fan."

It is a poem to see with the eye, conceived in a typewriter upon an 8½″ × 11″ sheet of paper. If metric is a system of emphases, centered in human comfort, human hope, syllable-count is a system of zoning, implied by the objectivity of the words, which lie still side by side for their syllables to be counted. If the stanzas of "Go, lovely rose" are audible, created by the symmetries of the uttering voice, the stanzas of "The Fish" are visible wholly, created by the arrangement of words in typographical space, the poem made for us to look at. And it is amusing to notice that Miss Moore can revise a poem from beginning to end without changing a word in it. The first three times "The Fish" appeared in print its stanzaic system grouped the syllables not 1, 3, 9, 6, 8, but 1, 3, 8, 1, 6, 8, and in six lines, not five. What we have been looking at since 1930 is a revised version. The poem was twelve years old when the author made this change, and it is not, despite the mechanical ease of retyping with newly set tabulator stops, a trivial change, since it affects the system by which pattern intersects utterance, alters the points at which the intersections occur, provides a new grid of impediments to the overanxious voice, and modifies, moreover, the obtrusiveness of the system itself; the new version actually relents a little its self-sufficient arbitrariness, and consigns more leisurely fish to only half as many winking little quick monosyllabic turns. One can nearly say, putting the first and second versions side by side, that we have a *new* poem, arrived at in public, without changing a word, by applying a system of transformations to an existing poem. One remembers Charles Ives's statement that American music is *already written* (so that he had no need to invent tunes), and his pendant outburst on sound ("What has music to do with sound?"), as who should ask, what has poetry to do with people's anxiety to make themselves understood?

It contains, of course, the rituals generated by that anxiety, as music contains sound. Miss Moore's poems deal with those rituals as music dealt with them before the clavichord's mathematic was supplanted by the throb of the violin. She will not imitate the rising throbbing curve of emotion, but impede it and quick-freeze it. One impediment is the grid of counted formalisms. Another is the heavy system of nouns.

The Fish

wade
through black jade.

The black jade got onto the page by the same process as Ruskin's arms, shields and hills, but without benefit of the syntactic lubricants that slide us past a comparison: simile becomes optical pun. "Black jade" is an optical pun. So are the "ash-heaps" of the "crow-blue mussel-shells." Optical precision has brought these ash-heaps and crows into the poem; a moment later it will bring in a fan, to swell the bizarre submarine population; and before the poem is over we shall have taken stock of spun glass, turquoise, stars, pink rice grains, green lilies, toadstools, an iron wedge, a cornice. Each of these optical puns a moment's thought will assimilate; yet each such moment interrupts the attention (which simply does not expect to encounter such objects under water) and interrupts also the expected mechanisms of the English sentence, which has two places for nouns, before verbs and after them, actor-noun and patient-noun, "John threw the ball" but not "move themselves with *spotlight* swiftness." Miss Moore's sentences, unlike those of Olson or Creeley, are formally impeccable; but that impeccability, like the straightness of the horizontal lines of a graph, takes some searching out, interrupted as it so constantly is by repeated intersections with different systems entirely for dealing with nouns.

Just as idiosyncratically the poems deal with quotations. These lie on the page with as arbitrary a look as the nouns wear, set off by quotation marks yet none of them familiar quotations: not allusions therefore but found objects, slivers of excellence incorporated into the *assemblage*. One function of the notes to these quotations is to persuade us that they are genuine found objects, that Miss Moore has not been fabricating found objects by setting quotation marks around phrases of her own devising. The notes are not, like the notes to *The Waste Land*, part of our education; we are certainly not meant to look up the sources; the author says she hopes that we will "take probity on faith" and disregard them. And it is probity, of course, that these poems most obviously enact, creating, according to rigorous self-imposed rules, a crystalline structure, bristling with internal geometry, which (1) exhibits patent optical symmetries; (2) reassures us, if we take the trouble to trace out its syntax, by rigorously fulfilling any syntactic law we care to apply; (3) maneuvers through this system, with a maximum of surface discontinuity, some dozens of surprising words and phrases, treated as objects, laid end to end; and (4) justifies each of these objects by a triumphant hidden congruity, usually based on some acute visual resemblance. The poem is a system, not an utterance, though one can trace an utterance through it.

The poem is *other* than an utterance, other than what the poet "has to say." And this otherness is doubled by the presence within the poem of some autonomous envelope of energies, a fish, a cat, a ballplayer, to which the poem conforms its oddly depersonalized system of analogies. This autonomous thing is always represented as fulfilling the laws of its own being by minding its own business, which is not ours. It also fulfills laws of the poem's being, serving frequently as a point of departure, left behind. Thus the poem headed "An Octopus" is really "about" a glacier, probably the only glacier in literature that not only exists but behaves, and in a way meant to earn our approbation.

An Octopus

of ice. Deceptively reserved and flat,
it lies "in grandeur and in mass"
beneath a sea of shifting snow dunes;
dots of cyclamen-red and maroon on its clearly defined
 pseudopodia
made of glass that will bend—a much needed invention—
comprising twenty-eight ice-fields from fifty to five hundred
 feet thick,
of unimagined delicacy.
"Picking periwinkles from the cracks"
or killing prey with the concentric crushing rigor of the
 python,
it hovers forward "spider-fashion
on its arms" misleadingly like lace;
its "ghostly pallor changing
to the green metallic tinge of an anemone-starred pool."

The icy octopus has by this time torn up and carried toward us not only the normal detritus of the landscape but five separate quotations, being in this respect as "deceptively reserved" as the poet. And the poem continues to edge forward glacially, picking up and shifting periwinkles, pythons, spiders, lace, anemone. In fact by the time it has drawn toward its close (having incorporated, *inter alia*, the Greek language, Henry James, and numerous citations from the National Parks Rules and Regulations) it appears to be discussing its own decorum as much as that of the glacier-octopus:

> Relentless accuracy is the nature of this octopus
> with its capacity for fact.
> "Creeping slowly as with meditated stealth,
> its arms seeming to approach from all directions."

It resembles, in its "capacity for fact," the capacity of the imaginary garden, in the celebrated example, for real toads. Miss Moore's subjects—better, perhaps, her fields of preoccupation—have these two notable characteristics among others, that they are self-sufficient systems of energy, and that they can appropriate, without hostility, almost anything that comes near. They are generally animals; they feed and sleep and hunt and play; they are graceful without taking pride in their grace. They exemplify, as nearly as possible, the qualities of the poems in which they are found.

This is the point to invoke one last tradition, and make one last discrimination, for we are on treacherous ground. When the moral of a poem is its own aesthetic, aesthetics have become at least continuous with morals, a continuity human experience has recurrently tested and seldom found reliable. Miss Moore, causing her poems to enact with vigor the moral virtues they celebrate, skirts the tradition of the dandy, whose life was a controlled thing and whose norms of conduct were stylistic. The tradition was detached from that of fancy dress and made available to art by the "Tragic Generation" among whom Yeats passed his youth; its principal modern celebrant, a descendant of the nineties in that as in so much else, was Ernest Hemingway, whose bullfights and lion-hunts were aesthetic gestures, and whose descriptions of clear water running over stones were moral achievements. It was Hemingway who most dramatically fulfills, in our time, Ruskin's precept that to see something, and tell what one saw in a plain way, is "poetry, prophecy and religion all in one," though the second word would have made him uneasy. We can see in his career one apotheosis to which the discipline of describing natural objects was tending during many decades.

But Hemingway's conception of style as the criterion of life, which he had from the tragic dandies of whom Lionel Johnson may serve as the type, contains one element totally alien to any poetic effect of Miss Moore: *self-appreciation*. To take satisfaction in one's achievements, and to undertake the achievements in quest of that satisfaction, these are the great temptations by which such a poetic is beset; and the theme of many poems of Miss Moore is precisely the duty to resist such a temptation. Her black elephant utters an opening vaunt not immune from self-congratulation:

> Openly, yes,
> with the naturalness
>   of the hippopotamus or the alligator
>   when it climbs out on the bank to experience the
> sun, I do these
> things which I do, which please
>   no one but myself.

but midway through the poem it is making a crucial discrimination:

> nevertheless I
> perceive feats of strength to be inexplicable after
> all; and I am on my guard: external poise, it
>
> has its centre
> well nurtured—we know
>   where—in pride; but spiritual poise, it has its centre
>   where?

To offer behavior which is "inexplicable after all" is to take no credit for it. The "beautiful element of unreason" has its uses. Another poem in the same way recommends "unconscious fastidiousness," and having surveyed with some astrigency the behavior of a swan and of an ant, asks,

>   What is
> there in being able
>   to say that one has dominated the stream in an attitude of
>   self-defence;
>
>   in proving that one has had the experience
>   of carrying a stick?

These last words delimit our present theme. To "prove that one has had the experience" of playing with a cat, or seeing a fish, or pretending to be an elephant, is just what a poetic of visual experience is likely to find itself engaged upon: even as Ruskin tended to be intent on proving that he alone had ever really seen a fir tree. We have seen some of the formal obstacles Miss Moore lays across the assertions of her sentences, in part to avoid implying that a cat or a fish has never really been looked at before. The remaining problem is how to avoid seeming to assert that one has had the experience of overcoming formal obstacles. It is here that her habitual preoccupation with otherness comes to her aid.

For those autonomous envelopes of energy she so admires are adamantly *other*, in a way that Wordsworth's Nature never was. Where Hemingway imitated bullfighters, she is content to admire ball-players. Her cats, her jerboas, her pangolins and elephants, are not beings she half-perceives and half-creates. Their accomplishments are wholly their own. It is not the poet who notes that the jerboa is sand-colored, but the jerboa that "honors the sand by assuming its color." Similarly the verse, without an excess of mimetic virtuosity, follows the little creature toward its burrow:

> By fifths and sevenths,
> in leaps of two lengths,
> like the uneven notes
> of the Bedouin flute, it stops its gleaning
> on little wheel castors, and makes fern-seed
> footprints with kangaroo speed.
>
> Its leaps should be set
> to the flageolet;
> pillar body erect
> on a three-cornered smooth-working Chippendale
> claw—propped on hind legs, and tail as third toe,
> between leaps to its burrow.

It is the animal that has discovered a flute-rhythm for itself, "by fifths and sevenths / in leaps of two lengths," and to play the flageolet in its presence is not our ingenuity but our obligation. Similarly the formal ingenuities of the poem, each stanza opening with a 5-syllable line and closing with a 7, are a tribute the jerboa earns. So when, as normally, we find that the poem is itself enacting the virtues it discerns in its subject, we are not to say that what it is doing is commenting on its own aesthetic, as in Hemingway's celebrations of the way one works close to the bull; rather that its aesthetic is an offering to the virtuosity of the brisk little creature that changes pace so deftly, and direction so deftly, and keeps intent, and keeps alert, and both offers and refrains from flaunting its agility.

The subject is other, exacting tribute; Miss Moore's descriptions are not feats but homages. She herself, finally, is other; and saying with the elephant, "I do these / things which I do, which please / no one but myself," she is fulfilling a nature of her own, in whose presence the merely curious are meant to be disarmed. For the unclubbable cat she offers this defense:

As for the disposition
invariably to affront, an animal with claws wants to have to use
them; that eel-like extension of trunk into tail is not an
accident. To
leap, to lengthen out, divide the air—to purloin, to pursue.
To tell the hen: fly over the fence, go in the wrong way in
your perturba-
tion—this is life; to do less would be nothing but
dishonesty.

In the same way, a being with an eye wants to have to use it; and so does a being with a memory, and a being with a typewriter. So by a long way round, by way of a poetic that dislocates, seemingly, each nuance of normal utterance, this rendition of the experience of the eye comes to be natural after all, an instance of commendable behavior. It imitates, in Aristotle's strictest sense, without congratulating itself on having thought to imitate, or on having found the means. It compels our minds to move across an opaque and resistant surface, that of the printed language, in emulation of the eye's experience moving across the contours of a pangolin's armor; and it impedes the facilities of the conclusion drawn, the thing said, the instance appropriated into a satisfactory system, on the principle that while psychic experience flows naturally into utterance, optical experience requires to be carefully anatomized before we can too readily allow it to be psychic. For the supreme insult—this is its final claim—the supreme insult to that which is other than we, that which, perceived by the eye, is *therefore* other: the supreme insult we can offer to the other is to have, on too little acquaintance, something to say "about" it.

PAMELA WHITE HADAS

Treading Chasms

Marianne Moore's style and structuring of poems is what provides for her the balance between the fight to be affectionate and the fight not to be. It is for this that the paper nautilus "constructs her thin glass shell." She guards her "eggs," scarcely eating until they are hatched:

> Buried eightfold in her eight
>   arms, for she is in
>   a sense a devil-
> fish, her glass ram's-horn-cradled freight
>   is hid but not crushed.

The poet's "freight" is the substance of her poems; they will hatch as the tentative communications that come from efforts of affection. Feelings, in Marianne Moore's scheme of things, must be hidden but maintained whole in hiding. Their existence, more than any other force, dictates the form and beauty of the shell that holds them. Perhaps this is why the typical man and the typical woman who seek each other and each other's feelings in marriage must use, at least in Moore's poem "Marriage," the careful rhetoric they use, and why the poet must arrange her poem so as neither to express too early an unformed and unprotected feeling nor to deny the loving motives that underly and oversee the finished form.

The poet may have the appearance, in jumping from image to image, of a ship veering in the wind, like the cruising frigate pelican "allowing the

---

From *Marianne Moore: Poet of Affection*. © 1977 by Syracuse University Press. Originally entitled "Fighting Affections."

wind to reverse [his] direction," "quiver[ing] about / as charred paper behaves—full / of feints," but the apparent aimlessness is important; it reflects the true character of wind, wings, and words—an end that is not at all aimless. The poem "Marriage" veers in the wind, so to speak, on both rhetorical and psychological levels; this is one of the things that makes the poem "work." The poet no sooner makes her cynical comments on the lavishness of the false rituals of marriage, when she must be off again, with extraordinary lavishness of her own, describing it with images of eccentric beauty (bracketed lines in 1923 Manikin edition only):

its fiddlehead ferns,
lotus flowers, opuntias, white dromedaries,
its hippopotamus—
nose and mouth combined
in one magnificent hopper—
[its crested streamer—
that huge bird almost a lizard,]
its snake and the potent apple.

Henry James, speaking of "men of largest responding imagination before the human scene," notes that they provide generous mixtures of the two tones or attitudes toward experiencing the world that James calls the romantic and the real. "His current," says James, "remains therefore extraordinarily rich and mixed, washing us successively with the warm wave of the near and familiar and the tonic shock, as may be, of the far and strange." Certainly the poem "Marriage" is evidence of this sort of "largest responding imagination before the human scene." In it we are given the most realistic, not to say prosaic, view of marriage at the outset ("an enterprise . . . requiring public promises / of one's intention / to fulfill a private obligation") and we are given as well the "tonic shock" of strange beauty below incandescent stars and incandescent fruit where "each fresh wave of consciousness is poison." The "real," says James, is composed of "things we cannot possibly *not* know," and the romantic or strange, of "things that can reach us only through the beautiful circuit and subterfuge of our thought and our desire." The word "subterfuge," associated here with desire, seems particularly apt with respect to the work of Marianne Moore, for many of her most beautiful images seem to come, not through the conscious fastidiousness that informs her observations of the "real," but through that unconscious fastidiousness which lets certain "efforts of affection" bloom into real longing. The lavishness of exotic detail in the Persian miniature that she describes at one point in "Marriage," for instance, is a desired extravagance. In the very remoteness of its fantastic animal-figures and jewels from "real" life is hidden the remotest (to common sense) and the nearest (to sensibility) object of the imagination—the "crouching mythological monster" that is seen to be Adam himself. Or Love, or Evil. In "An Octopus" Moore describes the mysterious bear's den "composed of calcium gems and alabaster pillars / topaz, tourmaline crystals and amethyst quartz" where the bear, unseen for all this extravagance, is known to lurk. The danger is not dangerous when it is hibernating in such dreamed beauty. The mythological monster is never fully revealed; what is revealed in Moore's poetry inspired by him is the primal desire for excess and love that escapes her everyday ascetic attitudes toward marriage and life. The greediness that she despises is a greediness that she knows, as we all must know it, from self-inspection.

One finds in Moore's calculated alternations between lavishness and stoicism, "rigid fidelity and the most fanciful extravagance" (to use Hazlitt's words concerning Burke's style), a coincidence of moral and psychological responses to the possible richness of experience. Whether it is called, with moral prejudice, "the garden of earthly delights," or, with psychoanalytic prejudice, the "nurturing other," the reader must have an affection for it, as Marianne Moore herself does. One must have both moral and psychological defenses against the hunger and the affection, however, as well as ways of expressing both. The questions and the statements Moore presents us with by first indulging and then damning material and verbal extravagance embody her method, make up the "story" that almost, but never quite, answers the mythical quest for meaning. When the artistic defenses become too rigid, one begins again "the fight to be affectionate" as in "Marriage." One must begin the fight over and over, as one loses it.

Thus Eve must be introduced, and introduced again, as she loses her original brilliance and, chameleon-like, takes on a new but still transitory brilliance (bracketed lines in 1923 version only).

> "See her, see her in this common world,"
> the central flaw
> in that first crystal-fine experiment,
> this amalgamation which can never be more
> than an interesting impossibility
> describing it
> as "that strange paradise
> unlike flesh, stones,
> gold or stately buildings,
> the choicest piece of my life:

[I am not grown up now;
I am as little as a leaf,]
the heart rising
in its estate of peace
as a boat rises
with the rising of the water."

In this rather long description of Eve describing paradise in Richard Baxter's words, there are actually two descriptions of paradise—the one the poet sees surrounding Eve, surrounding "the central flaw," and the paradise within her. Outside of her it is disaffected, or disinfected, by intellect and abstraction; it is an "experiment," an "amalgamation," and "interesting impossibility" (a good description, incidentally, of the poem "Marriage" itself). Within Eve, Paradise or "marriage" is associated with nostalgia for childhood, "the choicest piece of my life." But there are problems beyond inner and outer paradise in this passage; there is a central flaw deeper than simple Eve.

Eve is "in this common world" describing marriage as a strange "paradise" (an idea she picked up from "mechanical advertising" most probably) or quality of soul that is unlike material wealth. She describes it as "the choicest piece of my life." We have assumed she refers to a real childhood on the basis of the lines later removed, but there is another possible reading, also based on the excised lines but more closely connected with the rest of the poem. Later on the woman, the "she" of the lovers' debate, is described in rather unfavorable circumstances and in a nasty tone by the "he" of the debate as "uniquely disappointing, / revengefully wrought in the attitude / of an adoring child." In the earlier passage we hear only Eve's thoughts on the matter, in which the idea of marriage seems to remind her of being a child. This makes her heart rise exactly as Richard Baxter describes the hearts of ambitious and covetous men rising in the passage from which Moore quotes to supply her Eve with words. Could it be that her "innocent" heart rises with the expectations of what she will get by marriage, by returning to weak dependency? One suspects that Moore certainly thought so. Seen in this cynical light, the loveliness of the passage partakes of the "circular traditions and impostures / committing many spoils" that were part of Moore's initial definition of marriage. If the lines specifying childhood are removed from the passage, the connection is lost. For better or for worse?

In Marianne Moore's own retreat from beauty that "tears one to pieces" (a retreat which is at least partially distinct from Eve's), we note that she first pulls back to the safety of abstraction, in the description of Eve's outward circumstances, then allows a measure of release in giving us her inner perceptions of "paradise." We are, in this reflection of Eve's, still safely removed from the place where consciousness itself is poison. The Eve of this common world needs this safety, for she is

> constrained in speaking of the serpent—
> shed snakeskin in the history of politeness
> not to be returned to again.

Because Eve cannot speak of the serpent, she reminds herself of childhood, when one is "as little as a leaf," free from consciousness that can kill, and ignorant of the potency of the apple. Marianne Moore, however, often speaks of the serpent, which in one poem she describes as

> This animal to which from the earliest times, importance has
> attached,
> fine as its worshippers have said—for what was it invented?
> To show that when intelligence in its pure form
> has embarked on a train of thought which is unproductive, it
> will come back?
> ("Snakes, Mongooses, Snake Charmers, and the Like")

"There is something attractive about a mind that moves in a straight line," as Moore observes in "People's Surroundings," but there is a remedy for, as well as something attractive in, one which does not. The snake was "invented" so that we can, when thinking scatters itself (as it so consistently does in Moore's poems and in the reading of them) come back to snakedom as to a basic premise, a hidden principle of consciousness, of life and evil. For instance, when one sets one's "intelligence in its pure form" a task, such as defining so broad a thing as "marriage," and when one finds oneself talking instead about somebody or other's ability to write in three languages simultaneously and the unproductive paradise of childhood in which you are a vegetable and there is no serpent to speak of, one finds oneself returning to intelligence in a less pure form, a kind of ur-intelligence of images. The dazzling image throughout Moore's work more often than not comes back to a simple and dangerous consciousness of the identity of beauty and evil in the snake or some related animal—the chameleon in "People's Surroundings" for example. Possibly more central than Adam to the various hypotheses of the poem "Marriage" is the serpent that constrains us.

The encounter between Eve and the evil beauty of serpentine intelligence is referred to in the poem as "that invaluable accident / exonerating Adam." This allusion to Eve's seduction is a little resentful, but mostly witty, as is the "shed snakeskin in the history of politeness." The humor relieves the tension underlying Eve's attraction to "the strange experience of beauty" that will tear her to pieces. It begins with Adam:

And he has beauty also;
it's distressing—the O thou
to whom from whom,
without whom nothing—Adam;
"something feline,
something colubrine"—how true!
a crouching mythological monster
in that Persian miniature of emerald mines,
raw silk—ivory white, snow white
oyster white, and six others—
that paddock full of leopards and giraffes—
long lemon-yellow bodies
sown with trapezoids of blue.

Adam is so distressingly beautiful, and Eve's dependence on him so utter, that he must, like a god, be seen in the mystery of creation that surrounds him to be seen at all. We cannot look at him directly. Adam's being swallowed up by this particular Persian miniature characterizes one aspect of all of Marianne Moore's poems; in her the experience of intense beauty inspires both fear (of her own seduction by it) and praiseful wonder, and she summons all creatures here below to help her, to help her conceal and control her feelings through their own artful armorings and their lending of them to her. Animals and the art of others help her praise the origin of an individuality that cannot be explained, but that must be proved. Art provides a necessary retreat from the feline and serpentine beauty of Adam, specifically from his sexual attractiveness. Sublimation is the fate of this poet, whose fate is confused with verse:

Alive with words,
vibrating like a cymbal
touched before it has been struck.

The crash never comes, but the instrument lightly agitated keeps trembling out a message of possibility. It is a possibility that could not help but call attention to itself among the rest of Moore's orchestration, her "tuned reticence with rigor" that belongs to her "Propriety."

The image of vibration in the touched cymbal is attributed to the words of someone who "has prophesied correctly," but the reader is left in doubt about the prophecy itself and the person who made it, and the passage in quotation marks is not acknowledged in the notes.

> Alive with words,
> vibrating . . .
> . . . . .
> he has prophesied correctly—
> the industrious waterfall
> "the speedy stream
> which violently bears all before it,
> at one time silent as the air
> and now as powerful as the wind."

The stream, related to the Pierian spring perhaps, is, in all its violence, the same stream that at another time was quiet. The latent power of the stream is analogous to the latent power of still air, which as wind can be felt. This power is analogous to the latent power of sound in a vibrating cymbal, or the latent power of words that, as prophecy, can become truly enacted. It encompasses possibilities within realities. Verse *can* become fate. "The power of the visible is the invisible" ("He 'Digesteth Harde Yron' "). The associations that these ideas of latent power have with marriage are made clearer by the statements that caught Moore's fancy in presenting the second proposal scene in the poem:

> "Treading chasms
> on the uncertain footing of a spear,"
> forgetting that there is in woman
> a quality of mind
> which as an instinctive manifestation
> is unsafe,
> he goes on speaking
> in a formal customary strain,
> of "past states, the present state,
> seals, promises,
> the evil one suffered,
> the good one enjoys,
> hell, heaven,
> everything convenient
> to promote one's joy."

The first proposal was a simple "Why not be alone together?" This, its "formal customary strain" more apparently calculated and seriously thought about, nevertheless has similar dramatic and ironic elements. We as readers have information about Eve's mental qualities—in the first such scene they were the freak ones of "multiple consciousness" that allowed her to write in three languages with both hands and talk at the same time, and here they are informed by sinister instincts connected with the garden of Eden and a childish greed. Into such hostile or unsafe atmosphere comes the man with his inept proposals. He is persistent here, though his proposal may seem to go off in many different directions at once—heaven, hell, past, present, and everything convenient, coming together. Moore, by quoting Hazlitt on Burke's style in this passage, is commenting on the style of the proposal and on the style of the poem as a whole. Because it contains such an important double commentary, here is the quoted passage and environs from Hazlitt:

> Burke's style is airy, flighty, adventurous, but it never loses sight of the subject; nay, is always in contact with and derives its increased or varying impulse from it. It may be said to pass yawning gulfs "on the unsteadfast footing of a spear": still it has an actual resting place and tangible support under it—it is not suspended on nothing. . . . The principle which guides his pen is truth, not beauty—not pleasure, but power. He has no choice, no selection of subject to flatter the reader's idle taste or assist his own fancy: he must take what comes and make the most of it. . . . It is all the same to him, so that he loses no particle of the exact, characteristic, extreme impression of the thing he writes about, and that he communicates this to the reader, after exhausting every possible mode of illustration, plain or abstracted, figurative or literal. . . . The most rigid fidelity and the most fanciful extravagance meet and are reconciled in his pages.

One can easily see how this praise of Burke can be turned into a rationale for the poem "Marriage," which does proceed by fancy and by "exhausting every possible mode of illustration, plain or abstracted" in offering us its hand. And we have seen how it does not cater to the reader's natural idleness. The man proposing marriage within "Marriage" does not flatter the idle tastes of the woman to whom he speaks, either. He is like the writer who assumes his readers must admire him because of the integrity he knows is inside himself. Marianne Moore makes fun of this, but it is also something which the writer or suitor or reader must believe in order to go on.

In the situation at hand, then, the suitor continues his little lecture without seeming to be aware of the woman's mental state, which is, like his, one of lonely calculation. So he goes on talking to himself, unaware that he is on dangerous ground with respect to her and that there are chasms between them which his rhetoric barely crosses, "speaking / in a formal customary strain" which has to do with customs that are a strain for both of them. We feel it is the woman in the poem—the mental Eve—who appreciates the wit of "everything convenient" in his talk of good and evil, heaven and hell. For her, joy is different than for him. It is from her point of view that his joy is mocked in the following passage:

> In him a state of mind
> perceives what it was not
> intended that he should;
> "he experiences a solemn joy
> in seeing that he has become an idol."

Is this really what he sees or what he is made to think he sees by the "masked ball attitude" (Nothing Will Cure . . .") in her, an attitude that is instinctive and self-destructive.

Marianne Moore abandons this particular irony for a different level of consciousness in this "Adam" in which his mental state is taken much more seriously; and it is, as are all the most emotionally charged insights of the poem, conveyed by image rather than by verbal wit or abstract rhetoric.

> Plagued by the nightingale
> in the new leaves,
> with its silence—
> not its silence but its silences,
> he says of it:
> "It clothes me with a shirt of fire."
> "He dares not clap his hands
> to make it go on
> lest it should fly off;
> if he does nothing, it will sleep;
> if he cries out, it will not understand."

Efforts of affection are efforts of communication and this Everyman has chosen to appeal to a creature who, although she may be able to understand many languages simultaneously, cannot seem to understand or respond to *his* language. The situation is similar to one Moore presents in "Half-Diety," where a butterfly, conscious that a "nymph" is pursuing it, proves to be inaccessible to her efforts of affection toward it; the butterfly is "indifferent to her. Deaf to ap- / proval." The nightingale is, like the butterfly, or the unicorn, a creature of "miraculous elusiveness" ("Sea Unicorns . . ."); it is hidden and silent where visible and affirmative responsibleness is most fervently desired of it. The pursuer of this elusive creature knows that it will be frightened by too obvious a gesture, yet will ignore him if he makes no gesture at all.

Later in "Marriage" the man is described as an "orator," master of rhetoric, skillful but of questionable sincerity; there is no real or personal communication between him and the lady he importunes. Whims and studied effects cannot compose themselves into a whole; perhaps "Marriage" is partly about the divorce of poetry and prose. Both bad poetry and bad prose, or whimsical arbitrariness and sterile rhetoric, are meant to appeal to the psychology of the auditor, as advertisement and cliché do. But calling the prospective or actual husband "orator" looks not just to the ironic scene of private argument or imprecation, but beyond that to the culminating figure of the poem, Daniel Webster, an orator who failed to make a "marriage" work between civil warriors. "Marriage" becomes more and more a poem about political America at the same time as it is a critique of the personal lives of Americans.

The man, despite his being on stage, an "orator," has deep feelings that lessen our possible contempt for him. The following presentation of "Adam" balances Eve's meditation on paradise quoted earlier.

> Unnerved by the nightingale
> and dazzled by the apple,
> impelled by "the illusion of a fire
> effectual to extinguish fire,"
> compared with which
> the shining of the earth
> is but deformity—a fire
> "as high as deep
> as bright as broad
> as long as life itself,"
> he stumbles over marriage,
> "a very trivial object indeed"
> to have destroyed the attitude
> in which he stood—
> the ease of the philosopher
> unfathered by a woman.
> Unhelpful Hymen!

The vision of the nightingale—a creature of myth in its own right—and the apple, which in this context is the apple of dazzling and poisonous consciousness identified with Eve's accident, creates in the aspiring suitor the illusion of an eternal love, "compared with which / the shining of the earth / is but a deformity." It is the highest illusion possible; it defies the precision of a certain woman's freak multiple abilities, of the definitions of paradise as "crystal-fine experiment" and "interesting impossibility," and of the particularization of shades of white in the Persian miniature. It may be the highest possible illusion, but it is still only illusion. It is the shocking irrelevance, or perhaps it is relevance (the issues are so mixed on this level), of this image of desire, of "fire effectual to extinguish fire" that jolts the poem back to the relative clumsiness of wit and verbal precision. The suitor "stumbles" over the reality of marriage, over the realization that it is not a legalization of his affection for his own images of desire but legalization on an earthly plane, "a very trivial object indeed"; and somehow—he cannot understand how—this trivial object is able to destroy the ease of his imaginings and his narcissistic philosophy of eternals. His extravagant desire was "unfathered by a woman." She obviously can "father" nothing. He has fathered his vision himself, plagued by her uncanny silences.

Just as the "O thou / to whom from whom, / without whom nothing—Adam" was at the center of the "emerald mines / raw silk—ivory white, snow white / oyster white, and six others— / that paddock full of leopards and giraffes," Adam is at the center of the ritual of marriage with its ferns, flowers, prickly pears, dromedaries, hippopotamus, crested bird-lizard, snake, and apple. The hippopotamus is described specifically as a huge mouth, a "magnificent hopper," and this is, perhaps, one of the most germane images in "Marriage"—the mouth that needs to be filled—with vows, with irony, but most important, with beauty and love. We have seen how Moore extends and retracts, extends and again retracts the feelings of her poem. She will envision a scene, be filled with it, and make us passive in looking at it (i.e., we do not act upon it intellectually, ask is this true, are giraffes "sown with trapezoids of blue"?); she will then turn against this instinct for beauty and mock it with words that require from us, as well as from her, an active intellectual evaluation.

In the following passage from "Marriage" the Manikin edition is used because it contains lines, indicated by brackets, that the other editions do not possess and that in my reading of the poem are significant. (One might speculate that they were taken out because their private significance was greater than their artistic contribution to the poem; but one can contend, too, that they are poetically justified.)

["When do we feed?"]
We Occidentals are so unemotional,
[we quarrel as we feed;
one's] self [love's labor] lost
the irony preserved
in "the Ahasuerus *tête-à-tête* banquet"
with its small orchids like snakes' tongues,
with its "good monster, lead the way,"
with little laughter
and munificence of humor
in which "four o'clock does not exist,
but at five o'clock
the ladies in their imperious humility
are ready to receive you";
in which experience attests
that men have power
and sometimes one is made to feel it.

"When do we feed?" is a slyly vulgar question at this point in the poem. It is a barbarian talking, surely, or a husband demanding service. The animal-monster and the prospective husband are not always separable, and the gratification of food is not always far from that of the marriage bed. It is a more jocular than affectionate communication, and it leads to the observations which follow, on the prearranged meetings of men and women over food. Dining, which could be an intimate and serious mutual occupation between husbands and wives, is called "feeding," is denied grace and communion. The "quarrel as we feed" is perhaps the only communication, and is engaged in for its own sake. The "quarrel as we feed" may also be a witty but not complicated slur against those whose tastelessness in love is brought to table; or it may be a quarrel with the food itself, fighting against what one knows one needs, as a poet may fight her own images.

The line "one's self love's labor lost," which is shortened in subsequent printings to "self lost," has, in its original willful ambiguity the tone of preoccupation with one's own language that Moore makes fun of in the language of the lovers throughout the poem. One's self is one's greatest labor of love, of course, and it is a labor in vain. There is no real love left, or no self, but there is irony, the irony of having unwittingly made one's efforts of affection in the wrong direction.

The "Ahasureus *tête-à-tête* banquet" is a reference to the story of Esther (chaps. 5–7) and the two banquets she prepares to give Haman his just desserts. Ironically, Haman feels himself to be specially favored by the royal attentions the first night, only to be hanged upon the second. The small orchids with snakes' tongues are Moore's own sinister decoration of the banquet table; we know *her* attitude toward feasting together and betrayal. Esther's story emphasizes the power a wife may have over her husband while he still retains the illusion of freedom. The quotation from *The Tempest*, "Good monster, lead the way," is associated with Esther's banquet by virtue of the scene in which it occurs. In this scene (act 2, scene 2), it will be remembered, Stephano and Trinculo discover Caliban, get him good and drunk, and enlist his services in their scheme. Caliban, poor monster, under the influence of their spirits, thinks mistakenly that he has found new freedom whereas he has merely found new bondage. "O brave monster, lead the way," ends the act, and the next act opens with a love scene between Ferdinand and Miranda wherein she offers to be his wife, or servant, however he is willing to take her—another example of bondage exchanged for a new bondage. The "monster" has led the way; feasting, drinking, loving, one must beware.

The feast is set "with little laughter / and munificence of humor," much as the gems of warning are set into the poem "Marriage." We do not laugh at the ironies, but they have a "quixotic atmosphere of frankness" that makes us smile to ourselves as we imagine the civilized gentlemen and ladies at their tea. The ladies who serve it have "imperious humility" because they know the men have the real power and because they have learned in their own way how to manipulate it. Only sometimes is it felt. The whole passage beginning with the uncivilized "When do we feed?" and progressing through time and literature—from the Bible to Shakespeare to a dissertation on *La Thé* (by the Comtesse de Noailles)—attests to the fact that the obligation to satisfy one's own body and to serve another's are inseparable in life and ritualized by art.

In this passage, as in most of Moore's poems, the conscious fastidiousness of the rhetoric of the sequence and the unconscious fastidiousness of the motives behind it are equally thorough. The close association of the *tête-à-tête* banquet, the drunk monster, and the affectatious tea, is not unlike the "condensation" of dreamwork. Kenneth Burke, in "Freud and the Analysis of Poetry," argues that poetry uses such phenomena as "condensation" and "displacement" as dreams do, and that poetry is therefore susceptible to the kind of analysis that is applied to dreams. "In so far as art contains a surrealist ingredient (and all art contains some of this ingredient), psychoanalytic coordinates are required to explain the logic of its structure." The "psychoanalytic coordinates" of the passage just discussed, and perhaps of the whole poem "Marriage," would seem to be on one hand the desire to be satisfied, to be "fed" and treated royally, as if one had power; on the other hand, we have the coordinate of fear of betrayal, enslavement, and physical injury to which any intimacy with another human being makes one vulnerable. It is summed up in "the spiked hand / that has an affection for one / and proves it to the bone." The "displacement" of this desire and this fear is, as is characteristic in Moore's poetry, raised to the level of art—the Old Testament, the Elizabethan play, and the western tea ceremony—and to the level of occasions where people get especially dressed up and speak in carefully calculated phrases which invariably mean something other than they seem to mean. Sublime sublimation.

Next we overhear a debate between a "he" and a "she" which shows superlative lack of mutual understanding.

He says, "What monarch would not blush
to have a wife
with hair like a shaving brush?"
The fact of woman
is "not the sound of the flute
but very poison."

In other words, if she must be at all, she must be beautiful; but it would be even better if she were invisible and inaudible. This little speech shows Moore characteristically using negatives to introduce associations as extraordinary as possibilities. If she is not getting ready to symbolically castrate him with her shaving-brush hair, she will poison him with her decidedly unflute-like assaults on silence. What he would like is something sublime and artistic, not physically embarrassing and humanly noisy.

She answers his rebuke with one of her own:

"Men are monopolists
of 'stars, garters, buttons
and other shining baubles'—
unfit to be the guardians
of another person's happiness."

This observation, Moore's notes tell us, is taken from a Mount Holyoke Founder's Day address (1921) in which Miss M. Carey Thomas goes on to say that these "baubles" are "so valueless in themselves and yet so infinitely desirable because they are symbols of recognition by their fellow-craftsmen of difficult work well done." This does not seem to convey the insult intended by Moore's woman's statement. The Holyoke address, furthermore, reads, "men practically reserve for themselves," not "men are monopolists of," the latter being much more definitely denunciatory. Moore is outdoing her sister feminist as well as paying tribute to her.

"He" is allowed to rally, though, with a stranger insult than he has received:

> He says, "These mummies
> must be handled carefully—
> 'the crumbs from a lion's meal,
> a couple of shins and the bit of an ear';
> turn to the letter M
> and you will find
> that 'a wife is a coffin,'
> that severe object
> with the pleasing geometry
> stipulating space not people,
> refusing to be buried
> and uniquely disappointing,
> revengefully wrought in the attitude
> of an adoring child
> to a distinguished parent."

The physicality, and it is not a sheer but a dense one, of his perceptions of woman is meant to be appalling. These "mummies" are delicate, for they exist only as the leftovers of a lion's meal. The quotation is from the book of Amos (3:12): "Thus saith the Lord; As the shepherd taketh out of the mouth of the lion two legs, or a piece of an ear; so shall the children of Israel be taken out that dwell in Samaria in the corner of a bed, and in Damascus in a couch." Now what makes Moore think of this particular verse of Amos in connection with marriage? The passage in Amos has nothing in it about marriage, but it is about punishment for transgression, the punishment being to be all but eaten by the metaphorical lion of Assyria. The remains from the lion's meal are moral remains, and they must be retrieved from the beds and couches of the Samarians. One commentator on the Bible suggests that the morally despoiled people are found in the corners of beds because they have grown to love the evil luxury of soft cushions; another suggests that they are there out of cowardice, hiding with only legs and perhaps an ear showing. In the context of Moore's poem we think of the marriage bed, of course, but this is not the sort of bed anybody thinks Amos had in mind—except her.

What is the speaker's interest in "mummies?" Is he simply talking to himself about some archeological interest apart from women, or is he suggesting that these "mummies"—mothers—are like the horribly evil remains of women after the "lion" has satisfied himself? Can we see in the lion a continuance of the animal and monster imagery in the rest of the poem? This would be to see him as the pursuing lover. Can we connect the "meal" with the other references in the poem to feeding? "But questioning is the mark // of a pest!" ("For February 14th"), and these may be too monstrously leading.

If the lion's meal is not enough to convince us that we are on dangerous ground when debating marriage, we can "turn to the letter M"—for Marriage, Murderousness, Moore?—and find Ezra Pound's claim that "a wife is a coffin." She is, in fact, less than two shins and an ear; she is an "object," a "geometry," a "space" unaccommodating of living people. You would like to bury her like a coffin, but unfortunately she is only *like* one, and in reality is a dependent object "wrought in the attitude / of an adoring child." The remains of passionate wickedness, the helplessness of a child—what compliment can the "she" of the debate return?

> She says, "This butterfly,
> this waterfly, this nomad
> that has 'proposed
> to settle on my hand for life'—
> What can one do with it?
> There must have been more time
> in Shakespeare's day
> to sit and watch a play.
> You know so many artists who are fools."

There is "munificence of humor" in this transition, and considerable irony. He speaks of lion's hunger, and death, and ponderous object-worship, with allusion to punishment by an angry God, and she comes back at him with butterflies and waterflies, nomadic and undependable creatures.

The lady is obviously flustered. She is almost muttering to herself when she says "What can one do with it?" "It," not "him"; he is an object to her as she is an object—no more—to him. She goes on to speculate on what two people can do together. Go to a play? One can only guess why she thinks there was more time in Shakespeare's day. Perhaps she believes that if one did have time one would find out enough about the trials of love not to want to try it out oneself. Or that one would find out enough about writing plays to be more than just a *foolish* artist. It does not matter much; she may be stalling for time, filling her part of the conversation with to her, as if she were free-associating. It is practically her l

When the lady criticizes the proposing or imposing gentl so many foolish artist friends, he immediately retorts that friends who are not even artists. I suspect that is one of which took Moore's fancy" that is inserted into the poem merely for the delight of it. We may think of it as an overheard and remembered conversation. Here ends the "debate,"

> The fact forgot
> that "some have merely rights
> while some have obligations,"
> he loves himself so much,
> he can permit himself
> no rival in that love.

He cannot let anyone love him more than he himself does, but it doesn't matter, because she feels the same way about herself: "she loves herself so much, / she cannot see herself enough—." "She" sees herself as an object in a household of objects,

> a statuette of ivory on ivory,
> the logical last touch
> to an expansive splendor
> earned as wages for work done.

She believes she deserves this fate, and she does. Moore caps this little aside on the utter barrenness of narcissistic enchantment with a moral: "one is not rich but poor / when one can always seem so right." One that does not question one's position has no way into the meaning of the myth. These people are poor in their self-satisfied segregation from each other. The "vermin-proof and pilfer-proof integration / in which unself-righteousness humbles inspection" that Moore indicates would be welcome in "Efforts of Affection" would be welcome here.

MARIE BORROFF

Marianne Moore's Promotional Prose

Marianne Moore is unique among poets in the nature and importance of her indebtedness to prose writings. The promotional prose of feature articles and advertisements, which is of special interest in this study, was for her a source not only of subject matter but at times of inspiration. Two of the five articles examined [previously]—"Pangolins" by Robert Hatt and "Golden Fleece of the Arctic" by John J. Teal, Jr.—are responsible for Moore's "Pangolins" and "The Arctic Ox (or Goat)," respectively. . . . The other three figure in her Notes in much the same manner as items in the bibliography of a research theme. Mythological lore from Frank Davis's "The Chinese Dragon" and scientific description from W. P. Pycraft's "The Frilled Lizard" (Moore cites as "The Malay Dragon and the 'Basilisks' ") appear side by side in the opening sections of "The Plumet Basilisk" [Notes, pp. 264, 265; all poetry references are to *The Complete Poems of Marianne Moore* (New York, 1967)]. Berthold Laufer's "Ostrich Egg-Shell Cups from Mesopotamia" is mentioned (p. 277) as a source of certain of the facts about the ostrich incorporated in "He 'Digesteth Harde Yron.' " Other feature articles that gave Moore ideas for poems are "Economies [actually "Economy"] in the Use of Steel," by Waldemar Kaempffert, for "The Icosasphere" (pp. 281–82), and "Festivals and Fairs for the Tourist in Italy," by Mitchell Goodman, for "The Web One Weaves of Italy" (p. 164). "Four Quartz Crystal Clocks" was largely derived from a Bell Telephone Company pamphlet, a hybrid of

From *Language and the Poet: Verbal Artistry in Frost, Stevens, and Moore*. © 1979 by The University of Chicago. The University of Chicago Press, 1979. Originally entitled "Marianne Moore's Promotional Prose: A Poem's Guise at Last."

feature article and advertisement of the sort described [previously]. Elsewhere the Notes acknowledge indebtedness to a variety of newspapers and magazines for information on a variety of subjects: on the diet of the fieldmouse, to the *National Geographic* (p. 264); on the legendary Persian nightingale, to the *New York Sun* (pp. 278–79); on the history of the herb rosemary, to *The Spectator* (p. 288); on the grasshopper-shaped weathervane atop Faneuil Hall in Boston, to the *Christian Science Monitor* (p.293), to cite only a few instances. Advertisements and quasi-advertisements which provided Moore with poetic material include a catalog for "the Karl Freund collection sale" (p. 266), and advertisement for India paper in the *New York Times* (p. 269), an "advertisement entitled 'Change of Fashion' " in the *English Review* (p. 272), and an article in *What's New*, a pamphlet distributed by Abbott Laboratories (p. 287). In view of the prominence of fixed poses and scenes in Moore's descriptions, it is not surprising that some of her promotional sources are pictures. According to its headnote (p. 218), "Blue Bug" was written "upon seeing Dr. Raworth Williams' Blue Bug with seven other ponies, photographed by Thomas McAvoy: *Sports Illustrated.*" Photographs in the *National Geographic* and *Life* are cited in the Notes to "Camellia Sabina" (p. 264) and "Saint Nicholas" (pp. 293–94), respectively. Other visual credits are cinematic. The tuatera described in "The Plumet Basilisk" was "shown by Captain Stanley Osborne in motion pictures" (p. 265), and "Elephants" was written after Moore had attended "a lecture-film entitled *Ceylon, the Wondrous Isle*" (p. 281). There is one reference to a picture in an advertisement: the "bock beer buck" of "Armor's Undermining Modesty" with its "pale-ale-eyed impersonal look" (an animal the author of this study remembers well) was seen by Moore on a "poster unsigned, distributed by Eastern Beverage Corporation" (p.283). (Cf. her allusion in "Style" to "the traditional unwavy / Sandeman sailor," i.e., the angular silhouette wearing a flat-brimmed hat on the label of Sandeman sherry.)

Moore gave us her notes because she honestly, though mistakenly, believed that the "chief interest" of much that she wrote was "borrowed" ("A Note on the Notes," p. 262). They gratify our curiosity in that they tell us the *sort* of reading she got her information from, but they are (fortunately) far from complete. The grasshopper-shaped weathervane in Boston is duly documented, but what of the four dragons with intertwined upright tails over the door of the bourse in Copenhagen (p. 21)? We are assured that Peter, in the poem of that title, is the real "cat owned by Miss Magdalen Hueber and Miss Maria Weniger," but in what zoo did Moore see the cat she celebrates, in "The Monkeys," as "that Gilgamesh / among the hairy carnivora"? We are not told, and it does not matter. Probity was never in question; accuracy can be taken on faith.

The fact in itself is of no importance. What concerns us is the fact chosen for the poem, formulated and verbalized in the poem, imbued with the spirit of the poem. And it is here that we encounter at every turn the resemblances to the feature article and the advertisement which were posited at the outset of this study and which must now be spelled out in detail. But first, lest it should seem that these resemblances are intended to explain the *power* of the poetry, let me concede, nay assert, that Marianne Moore was always true to the conventions of promotional prose—in her fashion. We could not do without the admixture of eccentricity and originality that perfuses her language: the Latinate technical terms; the polysyllabic rarities and neologisms; the free-wheeling images that compare lions' heads to flowers, flowers to the feathers of Andalusian cocks, and the tails of cocks to scimitars; the ellipses and divagations; the sudden flashes of aphorism and satiric wit. Moore's poetry . . . can deceive us into thinking we are reading promotional prose, but not for very long. Deprived of its lineation as verse, the statement in "The Steeple-Jack" that "You can see a twenty-five-pound lobster; and fish nets arranged to dry" may look for all the world like information in a guidebook, but it is immediately followed by a descriptive passage whose final comment, at least, is calculated to confuse the tourist: "The whirlwind fife-and-drum of the storm bends the salt marsh grass, disturbs stars in the sky and the star on the steeple; it is a privilege to see so much confusion." "He 'Digesteth Harde Yron' " leads off in the manner of a feature article about ostriches: "Although the aepyornis or roc that lived in Madagascar, and the moa are extinct . . ." Continued in conventional fashion, the sentence might run, "the ostrich, called 'a large sparrow' by the classical author Xenophon, who saw one walking by the Euphrates when travelling in northern Arabia, has survived in large numbers to the present day." What Moore actually wrote was, "the camel-sparrow, linked with them in size—the large sparrow Xenophon saw walking by a stream—was and is a symbol of justice." Had I started my investigation on the assumption that Moore really was writing promotional prose, I should have had to conclude that she failed. This, of course, is the moral of the bathetic tale of her correspondence with the Ford company after it had engaged her to devise a name for a new car. Much as we may deplore "Edsel," we can understand the rejection, inter alia, of "Mongoose civique," "Turcotingo," and "Utopian Turtletop."

I shall begin my examination of the promotional aspects of Moore's poetic language by discussing visual imagery, an aspect of her style treated [elsewhere] under the heading of syntax. Like those we find in feature articles and advertisements, Moore's word pictures are literally "colorful." Colors themselves are definite and bright, their intrinsic qualities often heightened by contrast. The lizards of the Virgin Islands (described in "People's Surroundings") glitter "like splashes of fire and silver on the pierced turquoise of the / lattices" (p. 56); a sycamore tree is an "albino giraffe" against a "gun-metal sky" (p. 167); a brocade "blaze[s] green as though some lizard in the shade / became exact— // set off by replicas of violet" (p. 189). No poet has ever loved better than Moore to number the streaks of the tulip. Stripes, especially the distinctive markings of animals, are a signature of her imagery. The hairs of the jerboa's tail form a black and white tuft at the tip, "strange detail of the simplified creature" (p. 14); the plumet basilisk has eight green bands on its tail "as piano keys are barred / by five black stripes across the white" (p. 22); the fauna of Big Snow Mountain include "the nine-striped chipmunk" (p. 73); the skunk in "The Wood-Weasel" emerges in "sylvan black and white chipmunk / regalia" (p. 127); the roadrunner in "The Mind, Intractable Thing" is "stenciled in black / stripes all over" (p. 208). The poet's affection extends to spotted creatures as well: the calico horses of "New York" (p. 54); the "paddock full of leopards and giraffes" of "Marriage" (p. 64); the "conspicuously spotted little horses" of "An Octopus" (p. 74); the "snow-leopard wrap" worn by El Greco's possibly fictitious daughter, "the fur widely // dotted with black" (p. 233). Elsewhere, variegation creates a verbal technicolor. The translucent black water beneath the ocean cliff in "The Fish" is populated with blue mussels, pink jellyfish, and green crabs (p. 32); pink nectarines are painted beside "slender crescent leaves / of green or blue or / both" in "Nine Nectarines" (p. 29); in "Rosemary," the leaves of the herb are "green but silver underneath, / its flowers—white originally—turned blue" (p. 168); jet black and pale gray-blue pansies grow beside box hedges within a pink brick border in "Virginia Britannia" (p. 108). All this may remind us of *Natural History* and the *National Geographic*, but bright colors in clearly defined contrastive patterns and variegated arrays are equally characteristic of the descriptive content of advertisements for clothing, accessories, and jewelry. Accounts in Moore's poems of the "white pin-dots on black horizontal spaced- / out bands" on the back of the newt (p. 6), the "pink and black-striped, sashed or dotted silks" of racehorses (p. 162), and the decorations on the uniforms of the palace guards of the Sultan Tipu, "little woven stripes incurved like buttonholes" (p. 241), have their truest counterparts in "cool grey-and-white stripes, white piqué touches" (advertisement for women's suit-dresses, *Times*, 6/7/44, p. 13), "Bare-midriff swim suit accented with bands of navy or red" *(Times* 6/4/44, p. 7), and "skinny streaks of beige, turquoise or licorice sharply drawn on the chalkiest white cotton knit" (advertisement for women's dresses, *Times* 1/1/56, p. 46). A significant pictorial analogue to both sets of passages is the vividly striped apron worn by the figure in the Swedish Travel Bureau advertisement reproduced [elsewhere].

In poems about places, the content of key passages seems chosen as a professional photographer assigned to illustrate a magazine article might choose scenes in a locale. Some "shots" are at close range, some at a distance. Particularly memorable is the sunset panorama that concludes "Virginia Britannia":

> The live oak's darkening filigree
> of undulating boughs, the etched
> solidity of a cypress indivisible
> from the now agèd English hackberry,
> become with lost identity
> part of the ground, as sunset flames increasingly
> against the leaf-chiseled
> blackening ridge of green.

Vividness of color contrast is here enhanced by clarity of line, another recurrent feature of Moore's visual imagery. In some especially striking passages, contour and surface detail are meticulously rendered with the uniformly heavy lineation of a Dürer engraving. The rows of scales forming the armor of the pangolin overlap "with spruce-cone regularity until they / form the uninterrupted central / tailrow" (p. 117); the shell of the paper nautilus has "wasp-nest flaws / of white on white, and close- // laid Ionic chiton-folds / like the lines in the mane of / a Parthenon horse" (p. 122); the spines of the porcupine, in "Apparition of Splendor," are "thistlefine spears, among / prongs in lanes above lanes of a shorter prong" (p. 158).

Visual images of so high a degree of resolution, for all their authenticity, are far from realistic—they do not correspond to the selective and partially focused picture recorded by the seeing eye. The discrepancy between representation and experience is especially apparent when the subject is in motion or only momentarily at rest, as at the end of "The Jerboa" (p. 15). The creature pauses,

> pillar body erect
> on a three-cornered smooth-working Chippendale
> claw—propped on hind legs, and tail as third toe,
> between leaps to its burrow.

Since, as we have just been told, the jerboa moves with "kangaroo speed," neither its method of locomotion nor the shape of its claw could have been as precisely observed as the speaker's words imply, had it been seen running on a single occasion. Such details have their source in the repeated and careful observations of the naturalist or artist in the field, armed with pencil and paper, or in the freezing of motion made possible by the high-speed camera. Other images suggest the "zoom shot" in which the camera eye can approach the subject far more closely than the human eye—for example, the description of the "minute legs" of the Malay dragon "trailing half akimbo" after it has dived from a tree top to a hanging spray (pp. 20–21). Moore's surreal word photographs bespeak an *intellectual* curiosity as readily satisfied by the printed page as by visible phenomena themselves. The minutiae of external appearance serve in the poems as data, pointing toward an apprehension of the object in terms of essential form or emblematic significance.

Facts as well as pictures are dramatized in the poems by such tried-and-true promotional techniques as the heightening of contrasts and incongruities latent in the subject matter. In "Elephants," a "six-foot" mahout lying asleep on his mount is said to be "so feather light the elephant's stiff / ear's unconscious of the crossed feet's weight" (p. 128); while those officiating at the display of the Buddha's tooth are "gnat // trustees" in comparison with the bulk of the white elephant which leads the procession (p. 129). "Moon-vines [are] trained on fishing twine" in the village described in "The Steeple-Jack" (p. 6); early American history is summed up in "New York" as a progression from "the beau with the muff . . . to the conjunction of the Monongahela and the Allegheny' (p. 54); and "tobacco-crop / records" are inscribed "on church walls" in Virginia (p. 110). The poems are populated with creatures that excel: heroes, champions, sole survivors. The frigate bird, outmaneuvering all other birds in flight, is supreme in "the height and in the majestic / display of his art" (pp. 25–26); the ostrich, alone among large flightless birds, has resisted man's depredations (p. 99); the racehorse Tom Fool has "that mark of a champion, the extra / spurt when needed"; his performance reminds the speaker of "the time Ted Atkinson charged by on Tiger Skin— / no pursuers in sight" (p. 163); the Spanish dancer Escudero moves to "tempos others can't combine," while the skill and grace of the jai-alai champion Etchebaster "preclude envy" (p. 169). Moore's cast of heroic characters includes some notorious oddities: the pangolin, who "endures exhausting solitary trips" from dusk to dawn in search of food (p. 177); the ostrich, who guards the eggs at night, "his legs / their only weapon of defense" (p. 99); the paper nautilus, who "scarcely // eats until [her] eggs are hatched" (p. 121).

"Remarkable facts" are made the more impressive by statistics. The extinct wild aurochs, a beast well worth painting, had a "six- / foot horn spread" (p. 27); the elephant must break off enough branches daily to "provide his forty-pound bough dinner" (p. 128); a prickly pear leaf clinging to barbed wire once sent "a root . . . down to grow / in earth two feet below" (p. 125). The intensiveness of the persecution survived by the ostrich in ancient times is brought home by references to "six hundred ostrich brains served / at one banquet" and "eight pairs of ostriches / in harness" (p. 100). Such statements are at times amusingly reminiscent of advertising claims. Moore's description, in "People's Surroundings," of "paper so thin that 'one thousand four hundred and twenty / pages make one inch' " (p. 55) is in part quoted verbatim from an advertisement. The icosasphere is brought to our attention as a money-saving device, "since twenty triangles conjoined, can wrap one // ball or double-rounded shell / with almost no waste" (p. 143). We are informed in "Rigorists" that the reindeer "can run eleven / miles in fifty minutes," much as we might be told about the performance of an automobile, and the speaker's statement, in "The Buffalo," that the Indian buffalo "need not fear comparison" with "any / of ox ancestry" sounds for all the world like an advertisement for an expensive wristwatch. Moore's enthusiastic report on qiviut, "the underwool of the arctic ox," in "The Arctic Ox (or Goat)," concludes:

> Suppose you had a bag
> of it; you could spin a pound
> into a twenty-four-or-five-
> mile thread—one, forty-ply—
> that will not shrink in any dye.

It is not surprising that she was impelled to add,

> if you fear that you are
> reading an advertisement,
> you are.

As in promotional prose proper, the complex noun phrase does yeoman service, conveying much descriptive detail in little space. It tells us, inter alia, of "impassioned Handel— // meant for a lawyer and a masculine German domestic / career" (p. 25); of "the Indian buffalo, / albino- / footed, standing in a mud lake with a / day's work to do" (p. 28); of the reindeer, a "candelabrum-headed ornament / for a place where ornaments are scarce, sent // to Alaska" (p. 96); of elephants that are "ministrants all gray or / gray with white on legs or trunk" (p. 129); and of "Thanatopsis-invoking tree-loving Bryant / conversing with Timothy Cole / in Asher Durand's painting of them / under the filigree of an elm overhead" (p. 242). Some of Moore's more elaborate creations produce effects of drift or digressiveness such as were illustrated [elsewhere] from feature articles and advertisements:

Pacific yet passionate—
for if not both, how
could he be great?
Jerome—reduced by what he'd been through—
with tapering waist no matter what he ate,
left us the Vulgate.
(p.201; italics for emphasis throughout)

Lightness of tone and felicity of rhyme beguile us here; after all, this is a poem we are reading, not a biography. In the following example from "In Lieu of the Lyre," we are willingly led away from the gist of the sentence by the charms, both intrinsic and verbal, of the descriptive details themselves:

To the *Advocate*, *gratia sum*
unavoidably lame as I am, *verbal pilgrim*
like Thomas Bewick, drinking from his hat-brim,
drops spilled from a waterfall, denominated later by him
a crystalline Fons Bandusian miracle.
(p. 206)

Yet at times we may feel that the cargo of the phrase has sunk the ship of the sentence, as in this example from "The Pangolin":

The giant-pangolin-
tail . . .
. . . . .
is not lost on *this ant- and stone-swallowing uninjurable*
artichoke which simpletons thought a living fable
whom the stones had nourished, whereas ants had done
so.

Some especially striking examples of the extended complex noun phrase are found in one of Moore's longest and best poems, "Virginia Britannia." Early in the poem, we are introduced to Captain John Smith, in connection with a comparison between the fur crown of the Indian chief Powhatan, one of whose capitals was at "Werewocomoco," and Smith's coat of arms. A good deal of biographical information, some of it totally irrelevant to the relationship between the men, is given in two successive phrases of which the second is in apposition to the first:

We-re-wo-
co-mo-co's fur crown could be no

odder than we were, with ostrich, Latin motto,
and small gold horseshoe:
arms for *an able sting-ray-hampered pioneer—*
painted as a Turk, it seems— + *continuously*
exciting Captain Smith
who, patient with
his inferiors, was a pugnacious equal, and to
Powhatan as unflattering
as grateful.

(p. 107)

The hedge sparrow whose singing at dawn ushers in the close of the poem is the referent of three phrases linked by apposition within the compass of a single sentence:

The mere brown hedge sparrow . . .

. . . .

even in the dark
flutes his ecstatic burst of joy— + *the caraway*
seed-
spotted sparrow perched in the dew-drenched juniper
beside the window ledge;
+ *this little hedge-*
sparrow that wakes up seven minutes sooner than the lark.

At least one critic has complained in print of the irrelevance of the bit of bird lore contained in the final detail, credited in the Notes (p. 280), without indication of published source, to "the British Empire Naturalists' Association." Other readers may enjoy it, as Moore no doubt did, for its own sake. But in view of the allusion to Wordsworth's Immortality Ode in the last lines of the poem, it seems possible that the comparison between the two species "works" by putting us in mind of Shelley's skylark. The American bird is equally a blithe spirit, equally a spokesman for the poet's imaginative vision, and a touch more ardent in his celebration of the dawn.

Other phrases in other poems bring us down to the terra firma of the documentary advertisment. The Irish grow

flax for damask
that when bleached by Irish weather
has the silvered chamois-leather
water-tightness of a
skin.

(p. 113)

In "Saint Nicholas," the speaker longs for

a chameleon with tail
that curls like a watch spring; and vertical
on the body—including the face—pale
tiger-stripes, about seven.
(p. 196)

And her next two wishes are unmistakably inspired in content and idiom by Madison Avenue itself:

If you can find no striped chameleon,
might I have a dress or suit—
I guess you have heard of it—of *qiviut?*
and to wear with it, a taslon shirt, *the drip-dry fruit*
of research second to none;
sewn, I hope, by Excello.

Premodification in the complex noun phrase is rich and rife. All the distinctive features described [previously] are present. As in promotional prose, the designative modifier is ubiquitous; it is frequently combined with one or more nondesignative (gradable) modifiers which may be either objective or qualitative terms. Each of the following sequences includes at least one designative modifier in its normal position immediately adjacent to the head (line division markers omitted): with two modifiers, "sweet sea air" (p. 5), "white plush dewlap" (p. 27), " 'charming tadpole notes' " (p. 53), "comic duckling head" (p. 99), "fine pavement tomb" (p. 107); with three modifiers, "the true Chinese lizard face" (p. 20), "hollow whistled monkey notes" (p. 22), "innocent wide penguin eyes [of baby mockingbirds]" (p. 105), "exhilarating hoarse crow-note" (p. 160). An odd feature of some of the longer sequences is the placement of a designative modifier out of order, in front of a gradable one; the effect is to heighten our awareness of the individual components. In the phrase describing the ostrich as "an alert gargantuan little-winged, magnificently speedy running-bird" (p. 100), the designative modifier *little-winged* (signifying an ornithological characteristic) precedes the gradable modifier *speedy;* so too with *box-bordered* and *tidewater* in "box-bordered tide-water gigantic jet black pansies" (p. 108), *Indian* in "feminine odd Indian young lady" (p. 109), *left* in "Tom Fool's left white hind foot" (p. 162), and *equidistant* in "the equidistant three tiny arcs of seeds in a banana" (p. 170).

As in promotional prose, the premodifying sequence has three recurrent constituents: the noun used adjectivally, the adjectival compound, and the

As in promotional prose, the premodifying sequence has three recurrent constituents: the noun used adjectivally, the adjectival compound, and the noun in the inflected genitive case. Nominal modifiers and compounds are regularly formed "for the nonce" from the descriptive content of the poems, as in "*grape* holiday" (p. 17), "*bird-reptile* social life" (p. 21), "*Old Dominion* flowers" (p. 109), "*Bell Laboratory* time vault" (p.115), "*giant-pangolin*-tail" (p. 118), *teatime* fame" (p. 121), "*Parthenon* horse" (p. 122), *cork oak* acorn" (p. 151), *hunt-mad* Hubert" (p. 197), and "*Christmas-fire* tale-spinner" (p. 228). Nonce compounds with present and past participles, whose content might alternatively have been expressed by clauses containing finite verbs, include "*gold-defending* dragon" (pp. 23–24, "*sting-ray-hampered* pioneer" (p. 107), "*ant- and stone-swallowing* uninjurable artichoke" (p. 118), "*ram's-horn-cradled* freight" (p. 121), and *Thanatopsis-invoking tree-loving* Bryant" (p. 242), among others. And nouns in the inflected genitive increase the informational density of such sequences as "*philology's* determined, ardent eight-volume Hippocrates-charmed editor" (p. 97), which also contains two striking nonce compounds, "the house-high glistening green *magnolia's* velvet-textured flower" (p. 109), "the gently breathing *eminence's* prone mahout" (p. 128), "its terrorized *thieves'* whole camel-train" (p. 201), and "*China's* very most ingenious man" (p. 219).

The "condensed simile" appears in all the varieties described [previously]. Formations like *-like* as suffix include "maple-leaflike" (p. 38), "froglike" (p. 43), "racoon-like" (p. 45), "parchment-like" (p. 48), "ladyfinger-like" (p. 72), "not unchain-like machine-like" (p. 118), "Iscariot-like" (p. 138), "catlike" (p. 169), and "Fate-like" (p. 209). Past participles and adjectives are preceded by nouns in adjectival compounds in "match-thin hind legs" (p. 14), "porcupine-quilled palm trees" (p. 23), "prune-shaped head" (p. 43), "house-high glistening green magnolia" (p. 109), "mandolin-shaped big and little fig" (p. 110), "hammer-handed bravado" (p. 160), and "pitchfork-pronged ears" (p. 218). The vehicle alone is expressed by a noun modifier in "water-whistle note [of an owl]" (p. 8), "kangaroo speed [of the jerboa]" (p. 15), "quicksilver ferocity" (p. 24), "swan's-down dress [of the young of the frigate bird]" (p. 25), "compass-needle nervousness [of the revolving head of the ostrich guarding his nest]" (p. 99), "bayonet beak" (p. 106), "ostrich-skin warts [on the stem of a climbing rose]" (p. 108), "mirror-of-steel uninsistence" (p. 152), and "puma paw [of a baseball catcher]," (p. 221).

Condensed similes specifying shades of color equal or outdo the language of advertising in dramatic interest, and are of course more recondite. The jerboa is "the sand-brown jumping-rat" (p. 13), camellias have "amanita-white petals" (p. 16), bison have "hematite-black, compactly incurved horns" a "grass-green throat" (p. 103). As in advertising, such color comparisons often appear in groups. The ocean viewed from the fishing village in "The Steeple-Jack" changes from "the purple of the peacock's neck . . . to greenish azure,"

> as Dürer changed
> the pine green of the Tyrol to peacock blue and guinea
> gray.
>
> (p. 5)

Ancient Egyptian civilization presents to the eye of the student "an evident poetry of frog grays, duck-egg greens, and eggplant blues" (p. 12). The maiden who entraps the unicorn, in an echo of the language of advertising innocently reminiscent of medieval piety, wears a dress of "Virgin-Mary blue" (p. 79). The trunk of a sycamore, seen "against a gun-metal sky," is "chamois-white" (p. 167). The subjects of the Indian ruler Tipu, approaching his throne, kiss an "emerald carpet" with "velvet face of meadow-green" (p. 241). Moore is especially resourceful in describing shades of gray and brown; in addition to the above-quoted "guinea gray," "frog gray," "sand-brown" and "Siamese-cat brown," she has "beeswax gray" (p. 29), "lead-gray" (p. 108), "mouse-gray" (p. 128), "buff-brown" (p. 14), "fawn-brown" (p. 19), "snuff-brown" (p. 20), "soot-brown" (p. 27), and "cinnamon-brown" (p. 30).

It would seem that Moore's language outdoes the feature article in the length of the premodifying sequence, without, however, equaling the advertisement. The longest sequences I have observed in Moore contain nine elements; there are three of these, and four with eight, versus the high of eight, exemplified only once, in my sample feature articles. (Each sequence is quoted in italics in the context of the complex noun phrase in which it appears. [I have counted compound formations as two or more words, depending on the number of elements they contain. Where the head of the phrase is a compound, as in *town coat*, *gearbox*, *milk-jug*, I have counted the first element separately, whether or not it is joined typographically to the second.])

With nine elements:

> *The prompt-delayed loud- / low chromatic listened-for down- /* scale which Swinburne called in prose, the / noiseless music that hangs about / the serpent when it stirs or springs
>
> (p. 23)

Business-like atom / in *the stiff-leafed tree's blue- / pink dregs-of-wine* pyramids / of mathematic / circularity

(p. 103)

The fragile grace of *the Thomas- / of-Leighton Buzzard Westminster Abbey wrought-iron* / vine

(p. 117)

With eight elements:

An alert gargantuan / little-winged, magnificently speedy running-bird

(p. 100)

Rare / unscent- / ed, provident- / ly hot, too sweet, inconsistent flower bed!

(p. 109)

The house-high glistening green magnolia's velvet- / textured flower

(p. 109)

A vein // of resined straightness from *north-wind / hardened Sweden's once-opposed-to / compromise* archipelago / of rocks

(p. 131)

With seven elements (a selection):

Émile Littré, / + *philology's determined, / ardent eight-volume / Hippocrates-charmed* / editor

(p. 97)

Their thickly filamented, pale / pussy-willow-surfaced / coats

(p. 105)

A deliriously spun-out-level / frock-coat skirt

(p. 199)

A thirteen / twisted silk-string three-finger solo

(p. 218)

Sequences of six elements or fewer are present in abundance, but limits of space forbid the further multiplication of examples.

At this point, it would be possible to call a halt. There is a sense in which Marianne Moore's poetic language is an idiosyncratic and brilliant version of promotional prose, given an additional dimension of interest by the arbitrary patterns of line and stanza length, the "little intricate grids of visual symmetry," as Hugh Kenner calls them, which interrupt the discursive flow of syntax and sense as traditional metrical patterns do in the language of other poets. And there is a sense in which the poems have the sort of effect on us that successful feature articles and advertisements have: if nothing else, they convince us of the existence of a world full of a number of remarkable things. So much for the real toads; what of the imaginary gardens? Can the factual details assembled in one of Moore's essays in promotional prose be seen as participating in the development of a *dramatic form*—a form that makes a vision of human experience imaginatively accessible to other human beings? If so, the most prosaic of them may indeed wear a poem's guise at last.

Consider "A Carriage from Sweden," a poem featuring, on the one hand, an artifact, the "country cart" of the title, and on the other hand, the country where it was made. We are given a good deal of information about both. Sweden is a rocky archipelago; it has spruce-tree forests through which run paths thickly covered with pine needles; Swedish folkdancers wear white stockings and thicksoled shoes; Swedish men wear Sunday jackets decorated with hanging buttons and frogs—and there is more. As for the carriage, it is described feature by feature with the enthusiasm of an automobile salesman:

> Seats, dashboard and sides of smooth gourd-
>   rind texture, a flowered step, swan-
>   dart brake, and swirling crustacean-
> tailed equine amphibious creatures
> that garnish the axletree!

(Compare "Hand-built coachwork, real leather upholstery, sliding roof, 4 wide (draught-proof) doors, 4-speed (silent 3rd) gearbox, rear safety petrol tank" [advertisement for the Singer Junior Saloon, *ILN*, 1/18/32, p. 111; typography and punctuation have been altered]) Documentation now gives way to lyricism: "What // a fine thing! What unannoying / romance!" . . . The last stanza of the poem describes an ornamental flower bed that in context takes on the look and meaning of a trademark, and the concluding line contains a phrase stamped on imported merchandise:

>   it's a Sweden
>
> of moated white castles—the bed
>   of white flowers densely grown in an S
>   meaning Sweden and stalwartness,
> skill, and a surface that says
> Made in Sweden: carts are my trade.

A notable feature of formulation in these lines is the reiteration of the name *Sweden;* we are made aware of it as of a brand name in advertising copy. (Compare "Regan meets your needs for coordinated furniture, floor coverings, draperies, and accessories. Your Reganized office is planned to take advantage of Regan's free decorating and its 29 years of experience" [*Times,* 1/11/56, p. 7].)

So far, so good. Yet it goes without saying that the poem as a whole is not a feature article about Sweden, or an advertisement for a carriage made in Sweden (which in any case "no one may see"). The sort of "unity, coherence and emphasis" we expect of the professionally written feature article are lacking; instead, we find lacunae and bewildering shifts of topic. The speaker describes the physical appearance of Swedish women but not of Swedish men; contrariwise, she describes the Sunday clothes of men but not those of women; she speaks (twice) about a champion Swedish runner, but ignores other national sports such as skiing. Her train of thought moves from an account of the configuration of the branches of the spruce tree, such as one might find in a tree handbook, to folk dancing, thence to "Denmark's sanctuaried Jews," and on to a list of miscellaneous Swedish items including "puzzle-jugs and hand-spun rugs," with never a connecting link. Toward the end of the poem, she asks rhetorically, as if setting the stage for a conventional promotional encomium,

Sweden,
what makes the people dress that way
and those who see you wish to stay?

The answer is convoluted and engimatic. It begins by referring to a standard tourist attraction, Sweden's "moated white castles," but from these the eye of the camera zeroes in on the aforesaid single bed of white flowers "densely grown in an S." The concluding lines, like "What // a fine thing! What unannoying / romance!" are reminiscent of advertising language in its lyrical aspect. The name *Sweden,* of which the S-shaped flowerbed forms the initial letter, is linked with a series of attributes, two designated by qualitative terms of praise, all alliterating on the letter S. The first, "stalwartness," seems to hark back to the tireless strength of the runner named the Deer, but the second, "skill," points to the making of artifacts rather than to physical performance. The third, "surface," is clearly reminiscent of the cart and its "smooth gourds - / rind texture," while what the surface "says" in the last line of the poem is "Made in Sweden: carts are my trade."

If we now look in the poem for an imaginative order capable of superseding the prosaic order of exposition, a major clue offers itself—not surprisingly—in the image on which the speaker's thoughts finally dwell: the shape of the letter S, present not only in the descriptive content of the poem as the S-shaped bed of flowers we are made to "see" as we read, but literally, there before our eyes on the printed page in both capitals and lower case, repeated eight times in the two next-to-last lines. This shape is most definitely of the *surface*, but it is associated also with the words *stalwartness* and *skill*, which denote qualities invisible to the eye. Though the first of these, as I have said, seems calculated to remind us of the champion runner, it is also an attribute of the cart. And the curved shape of the S has been prefigured in the poem by the "swirling" seahorse decorations on the axletree. The axletree, a crucial structural component of the cart, forms a straight line, and the cart itself has been described as "a vein // of resined straightness" (presumably because it is built of pine boards). The complementary relationship between the curved line and the straight line can thus be understood to represent, on the visible plane, a more deep-seated relationship between appearance and structure, grace and strength, or, to use the language with which the poem concludes, "surface" and "stalwartness." The two qualities are conjoined in the carriage by the "skill" of its maker.

The nature of their conjunction is made clear by the speaker's description of the carriage in the opening stanzas. As "a vein // of resined straightness," it is a welcome reminder, in a "city of freckled / integrity," of the moral rectitude of centuries past, personified by great and pious leaders like King Gustavus Adolphus of Sweden and George Washington of the speaker's own United States of America. The trustworthy "stalwartness" of the carriage bespeaks the care with which it was made, but it is more than merely serviceable: it is a "country cart / that inner happiness made art." Its decorative elaboration is charming, an "unannoying / romance," because it is unpretentious, an authentic and unselfconscious expression of a tradition in which the craftsman takes pleasure. The key attribute of unpretentiousness is stressed by Moore's choice of the word *cart* (three times) in preference to the *carriage* of the title, and by the matter-of-fact tone of the statement that concludes the poem. The maker of the cart thinks of himself not as a "folk artist," still less as a "creative artist," but as a workman: "Carts are my trade."

The letter *s* stands for stalwartness, surface, and skill; it also stands, as the carriage itself does, for Sweden. Once we have grasped the speaker's imaginative definition of "the spirit of Sweden" as grace founded on strength, we can see it exemplified everywhere in the poem; indeed, it explains the selection and ordering of descriptive detail as principles of exposition do not. The lovely Swedish lady for whom the carriage comes to the door has "the natural stoop of the / snowy egret," but she also has a "deer- / swift step"; the branches of the spruce tree fan out gracefully from a trunk which is "vertical though a seedling"; the runner's stride has the "spring" conferred by pine-needle paths and is backed by inexhaustible energy. (He, like the maker of the cart, is motivated by "inner happiness," since "when he's won a race, [he] likes to run / more.") The curved line reappears in "the hanging buttons and the frogs / that edge the Sunday jackets," the straight line in "the sun-right gable- / ends due east and west." And if "the deft white-stockinged dance in thick-soled / shoes" and "Denmark's sanctuaried Jews" are read as exemplars of physical grace and moral strength, respectively, then their odd juxtaposition is not so odd after all.

Trying to formulate the theme in abstract terms, I am reminded of some well-known lines of nineteenth-century verse:

> Straight is the line of Duty;
> Curved is the line of Beauty;
> Follow the straight line, thou shalt see
> The curved line ever follow thee.

Nothing is morally right, says the poet, that is not also beautiful. But the coin has another side: nothing is beautiful that is not also morally right. For human beings, "Duty," the moral imperative, has primacy—"Beauty" pursued for its own sake eludes the pursuer. Viewed retrospectively, *sub specie aeternitatis*, the two are one and the same. In the poetry of Marianne Moore, the expressiveness of outward form or action, whether perceived directly in the symbolic object or at second hand in the emblematic fact, elicits a response in which aesthetic pleasure merges with moral approval. Beauty for Moore is in the last analysis an ethical concept. Another name for it is "integrity"; still another is "genuineness."

One of the exemplars of Swedish integrity mentioned along with the cart toward the end of "A Carriage from Sweden" is "a Dalen / lighthouse, self-lit." The lighthouse with its beam, at once visibly beautiful and helpful to the traveler, is an especially apt embodiment of Moore's conception; it appears not only here but in "Light Is Speech," where it stands for the moral qualities that are "the spirit of France." Two similar emblems contribute to the definitional passage that concludes "The Hero."

> He's not out
> seeing a sight but the rock
> crystal thing to see—the startling El Greco
> brimming with inner light—that
> covets nothing that it has let go. This then you may know
> as the hero.

The poet has just spoken of Moses, who "would not be grandson to Pharaoh." This historical figure is the last of a group of textbook heroes paraded before us in the poem, including Jacob, Joseph, Cincinnatus, Regulus, Christian in *Pilgrim's Progress*, and George Washington. Though the speaker does not deny heroic status to any of them, she looks longest and most appreciatively at one who is not a biblical patriarch, general, or father of his country, but merely a "decorous frock-coated Negro" guide at Washington's tomb. Ignored by the significantly "fearless" lady tourist who "asks the man she's with, what's this, / what's that, where's Martha / buried," he nevertheless carries out his official task with composure, voluntarily answering her questions, "speaking / as if in a play—not seeing her . . . standing like the shadow / of the willow." His behavior fulfills the definition of courage quoted in "In Distrust of Merits":

> "When a man is prey to anger,
> he is moved by outside things; when he holds
> his ground in patience patience
> patience, that is action or
> beauty."

The Negro guide in "The Hero" is one of a number of unprepossessing, humble, little-known, or lightly regarded figures singled out for special commendation in Moore's poems, including the jerboa, "a small desert rat, / and not famous," whose "shining silver house // of sand" surpasses the treasures of the pharaohs (p. 13), the mule, whose "neat exterior / [expresses] the principle of accommodation reduced to a / minimum" (p. 53), the ostrich with its "comic duckling head" and "leaden-skinned back" (p. 99), the freakish pangolin, and that perennial figure of fun, the skunk.

Perhaps the unlikeliest of Moore's unlikely heroes are the plants whose feats are recorded in "Nevertheless" in a kind of "Wonders of Nature" catalog. Among them is a prickly pear leaf clinging to barbed wire which has sent down a root "to grow / in earth two feet below." Another is a carrot; meeting an obstacle in the earth, it has turned back on itself in a coil to form a "ram's-horn root." From these and other examples the speaker draws a general conclusion: "Victory won't come // to me unless I go / to it." Hearing this aphorism out of context, one might think it endorsed an aggressive courage, urging us to go forth and crush the enemy. Actually, it does almost the opposite. "Victory," as we see it dramatized in the poem, comes from acquiescence; it is achieved by yielding to obstacles rather than by shouldering them aside. Even the prickly pear, in sending down its root, has shown a kind of Mohammed-goes-to-the mountain compliance with circumstance.

In the plant protagonists of "Nevertheless," as in the cart of "A Carriage from Sweden," integrity manifests itself visibly as "expressive form." The tenacity of the carrot in continuing to grow while conforming to the obstacles in its way has not only brought about its survival but has given it a graceful shape, as the sap of the cherry tree in passing through the narrow stem has made the cherry red. So too in other poems. The pangolin flattens his scales as a defense against stinging ants and "rolls himself into a ball" when attacked; he is "a thing / made graceful by adversities, con- // versities." The contours of the jerboa have been "simplified" and thus made aesthetically pleasing by the exigencies of life in the desert. And such triumphs bring joy as well. The jerboa "has / happiness," and the caged bird of "What Are Years,"

> grown taller as he sings, steels
> his form straight up. Though he is captive,
> his mighty singing
> says, satisfaction is a lowly
> thing, how pure a thing is joy.

In this passage, the biblical archaism *lowly* is a verbal sign of the Christian affinities of Moore's moral vision, evident especially in poems that celebrate the voluntary meekness of a powerful being. The white elephant, capable of crushing his keepers with one foot, nonetheless quietly holds up his foreleg "for use // as a stair"; he is "a life prisoner but reconciled." The gray elephants who follow him in the procession are "elephant-ear-witnesses-to-be of hymns / and glorias." But the procession itself is a Buddhist ceremony, and the movement of the speaker's thoughts in the latter half of the poem is ecumenical, assimilating the humility of Socrates and the wisdom of the Buddha to Christian meekness and love. The white elephant's "held-up foreleg . . . expounds the brotherhood / of creatures to man the encroacher, by the / small word with the dot, meaning know—the verb bud." The Indian buffalo is eulogized in similar terms. Though capable of killing a tiger on the spot, it allows itself to be "led by bare-leggèd herd-boys to a hay / hut where they / stable it." It willingly carries the Buddha and helps him dismount at the shrine, serving him better than any "white / Christian heathen." The same tranquility in servitude is shown by the Negro guide whose ancestors were slaves; he, like the white elephant, "covets nothing that [he] has let go." A moving passage of "What Are Years?" states the theme with unusual explicitness:

> He
> sees deep and is glad, who
> accedes to mortality
> and in his imprisonment rises

upon himself as
the sea in a chasm, struggling to be
free and unable to be,
    in its surrendering
    finds its continuing.

Imprisonment ultimately becomes a metaphor for the human condition, for mortality itself.

Moore said of art that "it must acknowledge the spiritual forces which have made it" (p. 48). We have seen such forces in action in "The Hero," "Nevertheless," and other poems. In "A Carriage from Sweden," the conjunction of underlying strength and outward grace, both physical and spiritual, reveals itself in a diverse and colorful assortment of "things," from "the split / pine fair hair, steady gannet-clear / eyes and the pine-needled-path deer- / swift step" through "the deft white-stockinged dance" and "Denmark's sanctuaried Jews" to "the table / spread as for a banquet" and "a Dalen / lighthouse, self-lit." Diversity itself is the theme of another travel poem, "The Web One Weaves of Italy," which, as we observed earlier, was inspired by a feature article in the *New York Times*, "Festivals and Fairs for the Tourist in Italy" by Mitchell Goodman. The poem is short. Of the sixty-odd events listed by Goodman in his five-column spread, Moore mentions only six, but these stand for an array of possibilities that becomes overwhelming, "blurred by too much." Overwhelming, yet delightful too.

Are we not charmed by the result?—

quite different from what goes on
at the Sorbonne; but not entirely, since flowering
    in more than mere talent for spectacle.
    Because the heart is in it all is well.

The entertainments offered the tourist at Italian festivals and fairs may not be edifying in the high cultural sense, yet they are not unworthy after all of comparison with "what goes on / at the Sorbonne." Such popular art forms, like those we take more seriously, deserve our admiration if "the heart" is in them—if they manifest what Moore in "Tom Fool at Jamaica" calls *ardeur*, ardor, the mark of the champion. In a significant image borrowed from one of her own translations of La Fontaine, Moore calls Italy a "fount by which enchanting gems are split." For *fount*, we must read *source* in the root sense of that word. The spiritual forces reflected in all valid expressions, humble or exalted, are for Moore a kind of Platonic unity underlying diversity, a One manifest in the Many, jets of a single "fount" beside which lie varicolored gems, all alike enchanting. So, in "Tom Fool at Jamaica," championship is exemplified not only by the horse that wins the race, but by a Spanish schoolboy's drawing, the play of porpoises about the prow of a ship, the jazz performances of Fats Waller, Ozzie Smith, and Eubie Blake, the acrobatics of Lippizan horses, and a monkey riding a greyhound (perhaps in a circus).

In the poem called "Style," the virtuosity shared by the flamenco dancer with the figure skater and the court tennis champion is likened to the spirit (expressed in "a letter") of Pablo Casals, the darting movements of the lizard, the hovering flight of fireflies, and the whorls in water brought about by the skillful manipulation of a canoe paddle. The speaker hesitates among alternative similes. The dancing of Soledad is

like a letter from
Casals; or perhaps say literal alphabet-
S soundholes in a 'cello
set contradictorily; or should we call her
la lagarta?

More images follow: Etchebaster's grace in the court tennis game is "catlike"; Escudero's silhouette resembles that of the Sandeman sherry sailor, and Rosario Escudero's guitar is a "wrist-rest for a dangling hand / that's suddenly set humming fast fast fast and faster." With this last line, the grammatical mode of the passage changes, hovering momentarily between stative and dynamic. The abrupt shift of tempo is characteristic of flamenco dancing, but it also occurs "suddenly," now, at this moment in the train of thought. Overwhelmed as if by an actual display of virtuosity on stage, the speaker throws up her hands and abandons her attempts to find "a suitable simile." There is none, because the only adequate vehicle would be an impossible conjunction, "as though" music could render visual pattern, or an artist could interpret a composer's music by painting the expression of his eyes or face. At the end of the poem, descriptive terminology is abandoned in favor of a series of proper names, each of which "means" only the individual it refers to. Multiplicity has triumphed. And yet the "unsuitable" similes have been expressed, the impossible conjunctions have occurred on the imaginative level, just as the individuals belonging to different realms—dancing, music, sport—have been joined in the intensity of a single invocation.

Unity in diversity, or rather, unity arising from diversity, is the presiding theme of Moore's great poem "Virginia Britannia." The Virginia of the present is conceived of as a cultural amalgam to which each phase of American history has made its contribution: the native Indians, the British colonials, the founders of the Republic, the frontiersmen, the enslaved blacks (Moore incorporates in the poem an idiom they have contributed to the language), and the well-to-do modern Virginians with their fine country homes and their fine horses, their "buckeye-burnished jumpers / and five-gaited mounts." Underlying all the accretions brought about by human settlement, both Indian and white, is the land itself with its indigenous flora and fauna. The poem begins with the "pale sand," the "soft, warm, hot" air, and the "cedar-dotted emerald shore" of the Virginia coastline

known to the redbird, the red-coated musketeer,
the trumpet flower, the cavalier,
the parson, and the wild parishioner.

The musketeer was preceded in Virginia by the redbird, and the cavalier by the trumpet flower; the "wild parishioner" at the end of the series is presumably a deer, since the next detailed mentioned is "a deer- / track in a church-floor / brick." The trumpet flower initiates a catalog of flowers, shrubs, and trees that runs through the poem. The theme of amalgamation—the coalescence of indigenous and alien which has given the state its present form—is epitomized by complementary groups of plants: the native live oak, cotton, and tobacco, on the one hand; the imported white wall-rose, fig, and silkworm mulberry on the other. The subject matter encourages "incongruities" of the sort that characterize the descriptive style of the feature article, leading off with the "deer- / track in a church-floor / brick." The mockingbird, a wild creature native to the state, stands on a "stone- / topped table with lead cupids grouped to form the pedestal"; the Virginian "cavalcade" of horses and mules includes the "witch-cross door" harking back to a superstitious past; the modern lady, played off against a "birdclaw-ear-ringed" Indian princess and a "gauze-and-taffeta-dressed" English lady of colonial times, eats the meat of the native sea turtle from a "crested spoon." She is

mistress of French plum-and-turquoise-piped chaise-
longue;
of brass-knobbed slat front door, and everywhere open
shaded house on Indian-
named Virginian
streams in counties named for English lords.

The poem is strewn with personal and place names that bespeak the history of the state: *Virginia Britannia*, *England*, *Old Dominion*, *We-re-wo- / co-mo-co*, *Captain Smith*, *Powhatan*, *Christopher Newport*, *Daniel Boone*, *Fort Old Field*, *Jamestown*, *Potomac*, *Chickahominy*, *Pamunkey*, *Mattaponi*, *Jefferson*.

Other themes we have noted in Moore appear in passing. Virginia itself is presented throughout the poem as an example of "expressive form," a veritable rebus spelling out its own history. Among the living cast of characters, important parts are played by two outwardly unprepossessing figures. The "meditative" mockingbird who stands for the speaker's train of thought is "lead- / gray" and "lead-legged"; his eye is "as dead / as sculptured marble / eye." He alights noiselessly and holds his head to one side, "standing on tall thin legs as if he did not see" as the Negro guide stands by the lady tourist, "not seeing her," in "The Hero." And the bird who becomes the speaker's emotional surrogate as the poem moves toward its conclusion is a "mere . . . hedge sparrow," a little brown bird with spots like caraway seeds. The theme of acquiescence as moral victory is touched on in the reference to the enslaved Negro, dubbed "inadvertent ally and best enemy of tyranny."

In the last two stanzas, the speaker's thoughts move from the joyous singing of the hedge sparrow in the darkness before the dawn to the coming of darkness at the close of day. Visible disparities are obliterated as live oak, cypress, and English hackberry "become with lost identity, / part of the ground," one silhouette against a flaming sky. I have already quoted the passage in another connection, but it will bear repetition:

> The live oak's darkening filigree
> of undulating boughs, the etched
> solidity of a cypress indivisible
> from the now agèd English hackberry,
> become with lost identity,
> part of the ground, as sunset flames increasingly
> against the leaf-chiseled
> blackening ridge of green; while clouds, expanding above
> the town's assertiveness, dwarf it, dwarf arrogance
> that can misunderstand
> importance; and
> are to the child an intimation of what glory is.

If we are to understand this passage fully, we must understand *arrogance* not only in its usual meaning, but in the Latinate meaning preserved in the modern English word *arrogation:* the preempting of what is not rightfully one's own. The charge of "arrogance" in this sense has already been leveled by the speaker against us and our ancestors:

> not an explorer, no imperialist,
> not one of us, in taking what we
> pleased—in colonizing as the
> saying is—has been a synonym for mercy.

And we have "misunderstood importance" in acting with the arrogance of prejudice, in failing to see that "the redskin with the deer / fur crown, famous for his cruelty, is not all brawn / and animality," or, to quote the quoted conclusion of another poem,

"that the Negro is not brutal,
that the Jew is not greedy,
that the Oriental is not immoral,
that the German is not a Hun."

The sort of behavior Moore calls "arrogance" at the end of "Virginia Britannia" is singled out for reproof also at the end of "Apparition of Splendor," a poem whose literal subject is the porcupine. The speaker defends the animal against the superstitious charge that, when embattled, it shoots its quills, and goes on to commend it for its lack of aggressiveness: "Maine should be pleased that its animal / is not a waverer, and rather / than fight, lets the primed quill fall." In that it is "not a waverer," the porcupine reminds us of the soldier or hero who "stands his ground." In that it "lets the primed quill fall" rather than fight, it reminds us of those powerful but docile creatures, the Indian elephant and the Indian buffalo, and of the pangolin, who "draws / away from danger unpugnaciously, / with no sound but a harmless hiss" (p. 117). The poem ends with a summarizing accolade: "Shallow oppressor, intruder, / insister, you have found a resister." "Intrusion" and "insistence" in personal relationships correspond to "oppression" on the larger scale of relationships within and among societies. All three are expressions of the spiritual "shallowness" or pettiness stigmatized in "In Distrust of Merits":

O alive who are dead, who are
proud not to see, O small dust of the earth
that walks so arrogantly,
trust begets power and faith is
an affectionate thing.
(p. 137)

Just as "arrogance" in Moore manifests itself in a number of forms, so too does the opposite kind of behavior that "makes us who look, know // depth" (p. 136). It appears as self-effacement, tolerance, the encouragement of others, self-sacrifice, charity in the New Testament sense. In "Armor's Undermining Modesty," the speaker muses on the knights of old who sought the Grail: "They did not let self bar / their usefulness to others who were / different" (p. 152). The armor they wore in battle conferred on them "a mirror-of-steel uninsistence" which is the appropriate outer form or "countenance" of inner moral strength or "continence." Paradoxically, the mirror of steel is at once an expressive emblem and an invulnerable disguise, giving back to the aggressor only his own reflected face. Hence the title: the "modesty" of armor "undermines" the antagonistic forces that would penetrate it.

Elaborate diction and syntax combine in the final stanza of "Virginia Britannia"—a peroration made up of a single sentence—to produce an effect of high formality such as we rarely find in Moore. Here are no eccentric Latinate polysyllables, no scientific or quasi-scientific terms, no informative nonce compounds or condensed similes to inhibit the gathering solemnity of the panoramic description. Romance and Latinate words like *filigree*, *undulating*, *flames*, and *chiseled*, become, in context, idealizing qualitative terms. Important meanings are expressed by finite verbs—*become*, *flames*, *dwarf* (twice)—and these verbs are dynamic in the grammatical sense, signifying action in process. The poem ends with an allusion to another poem, Wordsworth's "Ode: Intimations of Immortality," again unusual in a poet who more characteristically alludes to prose. But the rhetorical intensity of the passage diminishes noticeably in the last few lines. The full meaning of the word *arrogance* is operative only if we can penetrate its etymological disguise, and the description of arrogant behavior as capable of "misunderstanding importance" is surely a charitable understatement for centuries of exploitation and prejudice. Even the allusion to Wordsworth comes wrapped in a prosy syntax, including two instances of *to be* as link verb and an awkwardly periphrastic indirect question. (Imagine Wordsworth's poem entitled "Intimations of What Immortality Is.") The sunset continues to flame as the last words of the poem are spoken, but the colors of the language have faded.

We note a similar damping down or withholding of eloquence in the concluding passages of other poems. In "He 'Digesteth Harde Yron,' " the speaker's contemplation of the ostrich's survival of persecution leads to the resonant manifesto beginning, "The power of the visible / is the invisible." But the last two lines, with their final reminder of the ludicrous appearance of the bird, are as flat as they are pat:

> This one remaining rebel
> is the sparrow-camel.

The concluding passage of "The Hero" moves from the vivid evocation of emblems to a Q.E.D. which comes perilously close in form to the "Thus we see" of the undergraduate theme: "This then you may know / as the hero." And the celebration of French ardor and courage in "Light Is Speech" winds up with a definition whose last phrase is quoted from a prose essay:

"The word France means
enfranchisement; means one who can
'animate whoever thinks of her.' "

Here, as in the final allusion of "Virginia Britannia," Moore leaves the last word to someone else. A similar retreat from center stage takes place in other poems in which she allows her subjects to speak for themselves rather than undertaking to speak for them. "The Monkeys" ends with the astringent remarks of the Gilgamesh-cat; "In the Days of Prismatic Color" ends with the words uttered by "truth"; what the captive songbird "says" forms the conclusion of "What Are Years?" The first stanza of "The Pangolin" is similarly stage-managed, with man himself as the designated spokesman:

The prey of fear, he, always
curtailed, extinguished, thwarted by the dusk, work partly
done,
says to the alternating blaze,
"Again the sun!
anew each day; and new and new and new,
that comes into and steadies my soul."

In all these poems, and in others, we see the self-effacement which is a central value in Moore's moral pantheon dramatized as an "uninsistence" enacted on the level of language. In pushing in the stops, in descending from flights of eloquence to the ground of prose, Moore is practicing her own precept, an odd one for a poet: "The deepest feeling always shows itself in silence; / not in silence, but restraint" (p. 91). And the self-effacement of the poet in the poem is also the self-effacement of the real Marianne Moore. In her work, if anywhere, person and persona are one; to distinguish them would be to multiply entities unnecessarily. "One should be as clear," she wrote in a prose essay, "as one's natural reticence allows one to be"; asked in an interview why she had delayed publishing her early poems, she replied "To issue my slight product—conspicuously tentative—seemed to me premature. I disliked the term 'poetry' for any but Chaucer's or Shakespeare's or Dante's . . . What I write, as I have said before, could only be called poetry because there is no other category in which to put it."

But self-effacement in Moore also has a particular significance in relation to the style in which she chose to write much of her poetry: it is in accord with the conventional self-presentation of the "expounding I" in promotional prose. The author of the feature article is "there" to draw our attention to the subject, as the copywriter is there to draw our attention to the product.

(Testimonials in advertisements are of course an entirely different thing.) In adopting the descriptive and verbal techniques of promotional prose, Moore plays the part of a high-minded publicity agent or honest advertiser, one who is giving us information for what he sincerely believes to be our own good. Tirelessly she describes the important accomplishments of others, turns the spotlight on beauties or excellences that might otherwise have remained obscure, vindicates the unjustly maligned by dispelling popular misconceptions. And her habit of quoting serves in similar fashion to publicize the words of other authors. "If I wanted to say something," she explained, "and somebody had said it ideally, then I'd take it but give the person credit for it."

In an essay called "Subject, Predicate, Object," Moore wrote, "One thinks of poetry as divine fire, a perquisite of the gods. When under the spell of admiration or gratitude, I have hazarded a line, it never occurred to me that anyone might think I imagined myself a poet." Yet in acknowledging the spiritual forces that have made them, in expressing a moral vision in which her readers can imaginatively join, Moore's poems too are carriers of the divine fire, whether or not their author thought they were. Moore's promotional prose is at once a "guise" and a "disguise," an outer aspect which, as with armor's mirror-of-steel uninsistence, may all but conceal the soul within. Her poems have the unprepossessing aspect of a number of her chosen subjects: the jerboa, the pangolin, the coiled-up carrot, the mule. And we can see in both the visible effect of constraining circumstances—the poet's acquiescence in what she considered to be her own imaginative limitations. Speaking, as she rarely did in her poems, of her own art, Moore hinted at this in a memorable aphorism: "Ecstasy affords / the occasion and expediency determines the form" (p. 88).

Though she felt duty-bound to leave the quotation marks in, Moore regretted their presence, fearing that they were "disruptive of pleasant progress." For us, her readers, they are a mild distraction, an eccentricity we can find forgiveable, even touching, in view of the self-deprecation that underlies it. On occasion, however, the quoting of a phrase or line has a positive value, adding an expressive nuance to the passage in which it occurs. Here again, we must look to the advertisement for an analogue: the descriptive statement put in quotation marks to simulate a chorus of public enthusiasm for a particular brand of this commodity or that:

> Any place you may elect, you can always Sealect . . . "the milk that tastes like cream!"
>
> (*Sun*, 6/25/34, p. 13)

> When the children join the grown-ups to enjoy a refreshing glass of ginger ale, then, more than ever, "it must be Canada Dry!"
> (*Sun*, 6/28/34, p. 16)

And, without a dramatic matrix, "Just that much better" (*Sun*, 6/27/34, p. 32 [advertisement for Seagram's Gin]). Certain of the quoted phrases in Moore's poems have an oddly similar effect: the word *France* "means one who can / 'animate whoever thinks of her' " (p. 98); what matters about New York City "is not the plunder, / but 'accessibility to experience' " (p. 54); the racehorse Tom Fool " 'makes an effort and makes it oftener / than the rest' " (p. 162).

The quotation in advertising expresses as dramatic "fiction" what the device of the slogan, if successful, achieves in reality: a link in the mind of the consumer between a certain product and a certain descriptive statement or phrase. All the quoted statements in the above examples were in fact slogans in their day, as was another that every American of a certain age, at least, will remember: "Woodbury's Facial Soap for 'The skin you love to touch' " *(Sun*, 6/28/34, p. 14). But the slogan does more than describe what has been; it is also a pledge that the quality of the past will be maintained in the future. We can count on Sealect milk to continue to taste like cream, on Seagram's Gin to be just that much better, on Woodbury's soap to give us the skin we love to touch. In its promissory aspect, the slogan is a humbler analogue of the personal or family motto, especially the visible motto which forms part of the crest of a coat of arms (it is not wholly surprising that the word *slogan* originally meant battle cry, or that the promotion of a product frequently includes the fabrication of a coat of arms complete with crest and motto).

Moore's poems contain a number of phrases and statements, with or without quotation marks, that sound, depending on the subject matter, like slogans or mottoes, from "Carts are my trade" (p. 133) and "Will not shink in any dye" (p. 195) to "Dignity with intimacy" (p. 160) and " 'Diversity; controversy; tolerance' " (p. 173; credited in the Notes to James B. Conant). And a number of her moral aphorisms take on the force of mottoes in that we recognize the speaker's aspiration or determination to behave accordingly: " 'If I do well I am blessed / whether any bless me or not, and if I do / ill I am cursed' " (p. 26; identified in the Notes as a Hindu saying). "Don't be envied or / armed with a measuring-rod" (p. 144); "One need not shoulder, need not shove" (p. 172). There is a scattering of actual mottoes, personal and national, as well: " 'Liberty and union / now and forever' " in "Marriage"; "*Lux et veritas, / Christo et ecclesiae, Sapient / felici*" in "The Student"; " 'By

Peace / Plenty; as / by Wisdom Peace' " in "Smooth Gnarled Crape Myrtle"; " 'rather dead than spotted' " and "*Mutare sperno // vel timere*" in "Then the Ermine." And the poet herself sets her habitual reticence aside on occasion and steps to center stage to make a pledge of her own: "Renouncing a policy of boorish indifference / to everything that has been said since the days of Matilda, / I shall purchase an etymodoligical dictionary of modern English" (p. 59); "Only / wood-weasels shall associate with me" (p. 127); "I vow . . . I am going // to flee . . . the viper's traffic-knot—flee / to metaphysical newmown hay" (p. 231). In "In Distrust of Merits," the speaker joins with "us" to make her commitment, as in a spiritual congregation:

We
vow, we make this promise

to the fighting—it's a promise—"We'll
never hate black, white, red, yellow, Jew,
Gentile, Untouchable."

A retrospective look at "Virginia Britannia" with this recurrent feature of Moore's poems in mind immediately yields an insight: underlying the portrayal of the state is the unspoken motto "E pluribus unum." And as we reread the conclusion of the poem, we can catch an additional nuance in the reference to

the etched
solidity of a cypress indivisible
from the now agèd English hackberry.

On first inspection, *indivisible* may strike us as another instance of Moore's idiosyncratic Latinity; a more idiomatic (though equally Latinate) word for the meaning would have been *indistinguishable.* But it is now possible to see in *indivisible* an allusive value as important (for Moore) as that of *intimation.* The word appears in a text of the utmost solemnity that every American child once knew by heart and recited in school daily, expressing a patriotism now fallen into disrepair. I mean, of course, the Pledge of Allegiance, with its reference to "one nation, indivisible, with liberty and justice for all." Moore, who could without embarrassment use "flying Old Glory full mast" as a symbol of spiritual self-affirmation (p. 157), manages the allusion here with the utmost delicacy, not thrusting it upon us, but allowing us to find and feel it for ourselves.

"Out of many, one." Marianne Moore made her country's aspiring motto come true imaginatively, in her vision of genuineness: the perceived authenticity of aspect or action that can "unite" the deer-fur crown of the Indian chief with the coat of arms of the English colonist, and the singing of the hedge sparrow with the affirmation of human rights in the Preamble to the Declaration of Independence. Her career as a poet was a promotional campaign waged on behalf of that ideal, and we can say of her achievement what she herself said, in her curiously prosaic accents, of that greatest of spiritual forces, a self-effacing love.

> Thus wholeness—
>
> wholesomeness? best say efforts of affection—
> attain integration too tough for infraction.

HELEN VENDLER

Marianne Moore

In 1921 the Egoist Press, in London, published a small volume of twenty-four poems by an American woman named Marianne Moore. She had not submitted the poems to the press. Two of her women friends, both writers—H. D. and Bryher—had taken the poems (all previously published in magazines) and seen them into type. Three years later, enlarged to fifty-four poems (with three of the original twenty-four dropped and others revised), the volume was issued in the United States, under its now famous title *Observations*. Like *Prufrock, and Other Observations* (1917) and *Harmonium* (1923), it was a book to be read whole; like them, it has become in literary history an index of the state of American art after the First World War. Pound, Eliot, and Stevens all liked *Observations*. In 1923, Eliot had written a flattering review of the 1921 *Poems*, and he was later to contribute an introduction to Moore's 1935 *Selected Poems*. Pound displayed, as he often did, the most accurate grasp of a new poet. He saw as early as 1918 that Moore's work belonged with the "utterance of clever people in despair . . . a mind cry . . . 'In the midst of this desolation, give me at least one intelligence to converse with.' "

The despair is the arresting part of *Observations*. For the first thirty years of her life, Marianne Moore had no literary society to speak of; after 1918, when she and her mother moved to New York, she lost her isolation and, with it (though this can only be conjectured), some measure of her gift for despair, dismissiveness, and denunciation. She was born, in 1887, the

---

From *Part of Nature, Part of Us: Modern American Poets*. Harvard University Press, 1980.

younger of two children; her brother, Warner, was seventeen months older. Her father had gone insane; she never knew him. After the father left the family, Mrs. Moore took the children to live in the house of her widowed father, a Presbyterian minister, in Kirkwood, Missouri, a suburb of St. Louis. He died when Marianne was seven. Mrs. Moore then moved to Carlisle, Pennsylvania, where she, Marianne, and Warner lived in an extraordinary and peculiar intimacy of shared reference, which persisted all through their later lives and produced an enormous number of family letters. Warner became a Presbyterian minister, like his grandfather; as soon as he had a parsonage, Mrs. Moore and Marianne moved in with him. When he became, shortly afterward, a Navy chaplain, traveling abroad, Mrs. Moore and Marianne moved to Greenwich Village. Later, when Warner was assigned to the Brooklyn Navy Yard, they moved to Brooklyn. Moore's verse, published in the *Egoist* and *Poetry*, had attracted attention even before she moved to New York. Within a few years after the move, she was writing for *The Dial*. Soon she began serving as its acting editor, and then, for three years, was its editor—until, following Scofield Thayer's nervous breakdown, the magazine (which he had founded with Sibley Watson) was discontinued, in 1929. After the stint with *The Dial*, Moore in effect worked only as a writer. (She had taught for four years in her twenties and was for a while during her thirties a part-time librarian in the branch library across from her house.) Her life became one without public event, lived quietly in Brooklyn, punctuated by various publications and prizes.

The *Selected Poems*, published when Moore was forty-eight, added eight new poems. Subsequent volumes show a falling off, in the judgment of many critics. The *Complete Poems*, published in 1967, is not complete (an "Author's Note" says tightly, "Omissions are not accidents") and revises several well-known poems—notably the celebrated "Poetry— out of all recognition. The reader who wants to know Moore's work in any orderly way has to track down the juvenilia in magazines, to find the 1921 *Poems* in a rare-book room, to disentangle the early poems from the later ones in the 1935 *Selected Poems*, and so on. The state of the prose is no more satisfactory. *Predilections* (1955) is not the *Complete Essays and Reviews* that we need. The early prose has to be found in the review pages of *Poetry* and *The Dial*. As things now stand, anthologists have tended to print the later, easier, more explicit poems, and have thereby—to my mind, at least— done Moore a disservice. (*The New Oxford Book of American Verse* offers one poem from 1921; most are from the later volumes.) As for Moore's letters, they are not yet published. Some are in private hands, some are in restricted library collections, and some, along with a mass of Moore papers, can be read in the Rosenbach Foundation collection in Philadelphia. In short, no complete view of Moore will be easy to acquire for some years to come. A biography is scheduled to be written by Clive Driver, Moore's literary executor.

In the meantime, the poems stand, to the public eye, relatively alone. Few readers today can remember when *Observations* appeared. Most readers, unluckily, are likely to have known Moore first and last through the favorite anthology pieces—a scanty selection, insufficient to give a steady sense of her odd but instinctive rhythm ("a kind of pleasing jerky progress," as she called it) and her biting wit. The biographical fact of first importance to recall in reading Moore is that she spent her college years at Bryn Mawr as a biology major. She had failed Italian and German (though she subsequently passed them) and for a time did not have the grades necessary to take English electives. "I thought, in fact, of studying medicine," she said in an interview with Donald Hall, adding that "precision, economy of statement, logic employed to ends that are disinterested, drawing and identifying, liberate . . . the imagination." In this assertion, Moore set herself firmly against one sort of American writing—the breezy rhetoric of native oratory, the afflatus of romantic sentiment, the optimism of self-help—and just as firmly placed herself in alliance with another American attitude toward words: our pragmatic, taxonomic, realistic conviction that words are useful, practical, and exact; that they can convey the specifications for a bridge, the identifying marks of an animal, the geographical directions for an explorer, and even, in our earliest literature, the path to salvation. To write so that no single word can be misunderstood is a mark of the American pride in accuracy, punctual speech, and laconic completeness; the abstractions of metaphysical dispute are as foreign to this sort of American as are the pleasures of mystification in the service of sentiment.

Moore disliked enigmas and disliked being thought enigmatic; she wanted to be lucid without sacrificing implication. The deliberate (as it seemed) hermeticism of some modern verse repelled her. "Enigmas are not poetry" was the final line, in the truncated version printed in the second edition of *Observations* (1925), of the most famous single poem—the one called "Poetry," which begins, "I, too, dislike it." Moore's balance between lucidity and implication always remained precarious, as she herself knew. Pressed into an unwise explicitness by her horror of the Second World War, she wrote a bad poem called "In Distrust of Merits," which was monotonously anthologized because of its concurrence with popular sentiment. In commenting on it later, she said, "I do like it; it is sincere, but I wouldn't call it a poem . . . [It is] haphazard; as form, what has it? It is just a protest—disjointed, exclamatory. Emotion overpowered me. First this thought and then that." If in that instance emotion overpowered Moore so that implication was sacrificed to banality of outcry, in other instances the factual overwhelmed her so that feeling was sacrificed to baldness of transcription. The early poems visibly skirt both dangers, but are happily preserved from both by their brio and their scornful energy. They are the work of a girl who knows what she likes, and knows even more what she dislikes.

Moore must from childhood have had edge, sharpness, watchfulness, and wit. Bryn Mawr gave her the habit of scientific observation and, perhaps in conjunction with her mother, a sense of justice wronged. She remembered and later quoted a speech given by M. Carey Thomas, the president of Bryn Mawr:

> Men practically reserve for themselves stately funerals, splendid monuments, memorial statues, membership in academies, medals, titles, honorary degrees, stars, garters, ribbons, buttons and other shining baubles, so valueless in themselves and yet so infinitely desirable because they are symbols of recognition.

Not only did men form a self-perpetuating élite, not only did they ignore women, they also categorized and patronized them:

> [You] have heard men say: "There is a feminine
> temperament in direct contrast to
>
> ours which makes her do these things. Circumscribed by a
> heritage of blindness and native
> incompetence, she will become wise and will be forced to
> give in. Compelled by experience, she
>
> will turn back; water seeks its own level."

Supercilious male writers "write the sort of thing that would in their judgment interest a lady; / curious to know if we do not adore each letter of the alphabet that goes to make a word of it." The lady in this instance bites her tongue (or so we imagine, reading these lines), only to have her revenge later in immortalizing the fool who writes for "ladies."

Moore's asperity in the poems written in her twenties and early thirties shows the revengeful impatience of one not suffering fools gladly. The poems display a whole gallery of self-incriminating fools—self-important, illiterate, unimaginative, sentimental, defensive, pompous, cruel. For each of the fools, a portrait. There is the opinionated and conclusive Steam Roller: "You crush all the particles down / into close conformity, and then walk back and forth on them." There is the critic who did not understand that Hebrew poetry had its own compositional rules, and asserted that "Hebrew poetry is / prose with a sort of heightened consciousness." There is the military man of "warped wit": "You use your mind / Like a millstone to grind / Chaff." There is the terrifyingly ornamented woman who speaks only to wound, her scalpels "whetted / to / brilliance by the hard majesty of . . . sophistication." There are the snobbish "high priests of caste . . . kissing the feet of the man above, / kicking the face of the man below"; the conventional poet, "the Coliseum / meet-me-alone-by-moonlight maudlin troubadour"; the humburg who thinks that "*summa diligentia*" means that "Caesar crossed the Alps on the 'top of a / *diligence*' "; the pedants of criticism, "saying it is not for us to understand art; finding it / all so difficult"; the "pedantic literalist" in whom everything once alive and erect has drooped and withered; the "embalmed" statesman who stalks about "with moribund talk, / Half limping and half ladified." The interesting thing about Moore's poems of fools or knaves is that most of them are addressed very cooly to their victims. To the lady of the scalpels, Moore, the former biologist, will say, "Why dissect destiny with instruments which / are more highly specialized than the tissues of destiny itself?" To the pedantic literalist, "You are like the meditative man / With the perfunctory heart." To the moribund politician, "We find / No / Virtue in you—alive and yet so dumb." To the Steam Roller, "As for butterflies, I can hardly conceive / of one's attending upon you." These deadly anatomies, so impossible in well-bred life, are unsparingly uttered in print; Moore tells all her fools to their faces exactly what she thinks of them, finding her own annihilating metaphor for each one. Hers is the aggression of the silent, well-brought-up girl who thinks up mute rejoinders during every parlor conversation. Because Moore showed her work to her mother, and sought her mother's approval before publishing, it seems probable that Mrs. Moore shared her daughter's astringent judgment as well as her intelligence and her gift for a sharp phrase. In a note to the *Selected Poems*, in lieu of a dedication to her mother Moore wrote, "In my immediate family there is one 'who thinks in a particular way'; and I should like to add that where there is an effect of thought or pith in these pages, the thinking and often the actual phrases are hers."

In these early years, Moore showed no inclination to mince matters or to spare the hapless. Her early reviews in *The Dial* display the same short way with fools exercised in the early poems. "Criticism," Moore was to say in 1965, "should stimulate an improved understanding of the subject discussed—'with a truce to politeness' as Montaigne says." She was severe, in the early twenties, on Vachel Lindsay, affronted as much by his improper use of tenses as by his carelessness of phrase. "To speak of 'Christ, the beggar,' is inexact," she wrote in a characteristic sentence, "since it has never been said of Christ that he begged; he did without." Reading her now, we may feel that under her penetrating glance none of us would 'scape whipping, but her moral fervor with respect to language came from her tremor at its every nuance, her princesslike apprehension of every pea-size solecism. Clumsy language was a torture to her: beautiful language was for her a physical experience. Delighted by phrases of others, she copied them down and inserted them, sometimes in quotation marks, in her poems. In the company of someone who used language crudely or unfeelingly she experienced a helpless rage:

> I can but put my weapon up, and
> Bow you out . . .
> Since in your hearing words are mute, which to my senses
> Are a shout.

That poem—suppressed after *Observations*—is called "To Be Liked by You Would Be a Calamity." It must often have seemed to Moore, to whom understatement was the figure of predilection, that most people around her were shouting, and that a brief or dry phrase from her would be "mute" to them. It may be that she gave up hope in later years of reaching a general audience with her fine ellipses; if Eliot and Stevens understood her, they were not instances easily multiplied. Eliot was more forbidding than hospitable in his 1935 introduction: "To the moderately intellectual the poems may appear to be intellectual exercises; only to those whose intellection moves more easily will they immediately appear to have emotional value." If the "moderately intellectual" were not intellectual enough to grasp her intent—and by "moderately intellectual" Eliot meant a group well educated by American standards—Moore might well have despaired of company and broadened her effects.

But the early poems, one senses, were written entirely to please herself, an odd girl in her twenties, turning from her dissections to her verses. Speaking of her early influences, in an interview with Howard Nemerov, she recalled "feeling over-solitary occasionally (say in 1912)—in reflecting no 'influences;' to not be able to be called an 'imagist.' " Her repudiation of that label is just, as is her repudiation of the label "syllabic verse": "I do not know what syllabic verse is. I find no appropriate application for it"—and yet she has so often been described as a poet deriving from Imagism who writes in syllabic verse that the discrepancy between the common view and her own begs some explanation. The prosodic knot is the easier to untie: though she sometimes counted syllables in composing her *lines*, the stanza, and not the line, was for her the poetic unit. Stanzas, she said, came to her first, unplanned: the words clustered "like chromosomes," and she fixed stanzas until the tune sounded right. She was "governed by the pull of the sentence as the pull of a fabric is governed by gravity" (and the pull of the sentence on her mind is as evident in the most commonplace letter of thanks from her—but her letters were never commonplace—as in the densest poem). The rhythm of the stanza and the rhythm of the sentence impelled the poem; the syllabic count imposed some strictness on her procedure, but even in the non-syllabic poems, written in a species of free verse, her rhythms are instantly recognizable. Whatever small formalities she employed—her internal rhymes, her "light" rhymes, her syllable counts—did not define her practice or her originality. Jean Garrigue, so far Moore's best critic, wrote, "Of *Observations* one might say: it is first and last a voice. The voice of sparkling talk and sometimes very lofty talk, glittering with authority." Moore's rightful insistence that the syllabic label did not define her can be ratified by viewing the unpleasant results of the syllabic experimentation of poets lacking her independent and bristly grace.

In his 1923 review of *Poems*, Eliot praised her rhythm without being able to define it:

> Rhythm, of course, is a highly personal matter; it is not a verse-form. It is always the real pattern in the carpet, the scheme of organization of thought, feeling, and vocabulary, the way in which everything ocmes together. It is very uncommon. What is certain is that Miss Moore's poems always read very well aloud. That quality is something which no system of scansion can define.

Since Eliot's truths do not make for easy textbook summary, the syllabic label, being a simple one, persists. The ready coupling of Moore's work to the Imagist movement is even more limiting. She had been brought up, she told Pound, on the minor prophets, on Blake, on Hardy; they, not the Imagists, were her true antecedents.Eliot saw that her use of images was too rapid to be called Imagism: "The second image is superposed before the first has quite faded." But, more important, the Imagist power, such as it was—and it now can be seen to have been, in itself, weak—was photographic, mimetic, perceptual. Moore's early poetry, by contrast, takes as its chief subject states of the soul, not external "reality." Geoffrey Hartman rightly remarks that many of her poems are really "poems of Spiritual Combat, and show in Miss Moore that clear identifying mark of the Puritan: an extreme reverence for created things coupled with an extreme distrust of the self." If in attempting to describe the souls of people who are oppressive like streamrollers, or modestly contractile like snails, or patient and enduring like elephants she needed metaphor, she was not in that need unusual. If Disraeli seemed to her like a chameleon, with his "parti-colored mind"; if

Shaw resembled a "colossal bird . . . [with] brazen claws"; if Kenneth Burke was "a psychologist— of acute, raccoon-like curiosity"; if a conventional diplomat seemed a mummified ibis; if Molière might be thought a peacock unfurling his broad tail for spontaneous delight: surely, though these images may be drawn from a private or restricted code book, they are not the issue of an Imagist creed. They come, rather, from religious usage, as in illustrations of the deadly sins the lustful man sits on a goat and the glutton on a pig. The difference between Moore and the emblem-writers is that she has a much more lively interest than they in real pigs and peacocks; she takes, so to speak, the two sides of the emblem equally seriously.

And this is the other side of her early work, balancing her ridiculings and her repudiations: satirist that she was, she was also, by temperament, affectionate. Her affections went first of all (after her family) to people who were in some way both beautiful—conventionally or unconventionally—and strong. There is no doubt that some of the early poems on animals or objects are also, even principally, about human beings. The one on the elephant is, or ought to be taken as, a poem about Moore herself—her most personal and "lyric" poem, one that she suppressed when compiling the *Complete Poems.* That it could have been dropped on grounds of taste is inconceivable; it surely ranks among her most natural and beautiful pieces. It was called "Black Earth" in *Poems,* in *Observations,* and in *Selected Poems.* The name was changed in 1951, in the *Collected Poems,* to the more obscure "Melanchthon"—a title drawn from the Greek translation of the surname of the sixteenth-century German reformer Schwarzerd (meaning "Black Earth"). Moore may have intended a side-glance at the doctrine of predestination, which she took up in her own way in the poem called "The Monkey Puzzle": "But we prove, we do not explain our birth."

All possible touching things are said in "Black Earth." It belongs with another poem that was published in her first volume but suppressed in the *Complete Poems*—the poem entitled, in an arithmetical proportion, "Diligence Is to Magic as Progress Is to Flight." Flying carpets, says the poem, are the recommended means of travel in the realm of romance, and magic flights are, of course, all very well in their way; but some people progress, if oddly, by simple diligence. "With rings on her fingers, and bells on her toes, elephants to ride upon"—the song made an impression on Moore, and she made a poem about a woman who rides not on flying carpets, those "scarecrows / of aesthetic procedure," but, rather, on the laborious elephant, one of those "tough-grained animals as have outstripped man's whim to suppose / them ephemera." "Black Earth" pursues the analogy of "Diligence," but more inwardly. The elephant here speaks wonderfully for itself: "I do these / things which I do, which please / no one but myself." In spite of this leisured mastery, the elephant has not had an easy past: its skin is "cut / into checkers by rut / upon rut of unpreventable experience." The poem dwells on the need to preserve "spiritual poise" in the midst of all this scarring; the elephant has looked "at electricity and at the earth- / quake and is still here." The poem is agitated by all of Moore's central concerns: the nature of power, the nature of identity, the impassivity of selfhood, the wounds of circumstance, the failures of human perception. "I see and I hear," muses the poet-elephant, who accuses man, seen through his eyes, of self-delusion, of having eyes and seeing not, of having ears and hearing not: that "wand-like body . . . which was made / to see and not to see; to hear and not to hear; / that tree trunk without / roots, accustomed to shout / its own thoughts to itself." Moore was perfectly and inhumanly removed, at such a moment, from her fellow human beings. The removal—her superior amusement and denigration—was the source of her virgin strength.

When the local librarian suggested to Mrs. Moore that Marianne might like to work in the library, since she was so often there, Mrs. Moore said no—that if Marianne joined the staff she would probably feel she had no time to read. In the interview with Donald Hall, Moore continued the anecdote: "When I came home she told me, and I said, 'Why, certainly. Ideal. I'll tell her. Only I couldn't work more than half a day.' If I had worked all day and maybe evenings or overtime, like the mechanics, why, it would *not* have been ideal." The "ideal" has strange ways, however. Moore's intense inner life had been fed by her obsessive family relations, by her schooling at Bryn Mawr, and by her first literary engagements; but the permanent arrest of her life—with her mother, without employment, in the Brooklyn apartment—may ultimately seem a cause for regret. She was protected from vicissitude, but she was also shielded from those irregularities and abasements of life which open new, if darker, chambers of thought. Her life gave less opportunity than some for the worst dilemmas of passion or conflicting loyalties. She took a dim view, even very early, of human attempts at what we would nowadays call "communication": "The I of each is to / the I of each / a kind of fretful speech / which sets a limit on itself." Between the 1921 and 1924 volumes, she wrote her great poem "Marriage," in which she examined, satirized, envied, and dismissed—as a possibility for herself—that institution in which two "I"s attempt a real speech.

I will return to "Marriage," but I must stop for a moment longer on the 1921 *Poems*, in which we can see, besides the satiric impalings, beyond the tenderness of "Black Earth," a prompt and inquisitive lyric gift in poems of a startling independence of thought. I have in mind poems like "England" (stemming from an early two-month trip with her mother; it makes one wish she had traveled more in her first youth), "When I Buy Pictures," "Dock

Rats," and "In the Days of Prismatic Color." These unsentimental poems have always at least one abyss hiding in their neat parterres, some crevasse down which the unwary reader could slip. Moore's most characteristic gesture is a throwaway remark revealing whole horizons explored and rejected. If she calls Greece "the nest of modified illusions," she is asking us to have illusions and to have—stunning word—"modified" them. It is almost the word of a seamstress. To tailor an illusion is already a cataclysmic fall from innocence, but the notion is so innocently slipped in that the careless eye skids over it. It has been said that America is barren because it has no ruins; for Moore it is deficient because it has "no proof readers, no silkworms, no digressions." What is this discontented patriotism that longs for a literate page, a natural fabric, an idiosyncratic learning, and sickens and dies for the lack of them? Can it be the same patriotism that turns on itself and insists that fineness must exist in America? ("It has never been confined to one locality.") Moore's crevasses are for herself, not her audience; like George Herbert, whom she resembles in her self-incrimination, she might say, "My God, I mean my self." When she buys pictures, she wishes to avoid (not surprisingly, given her severity) her own besetting sins:

> Too stern an intellectual emphasis . . . detracts from one's
> enjoyment;
> it must not wish to disarm anything.

"Poetry" is an indirect self-reproach for her painstaking absorption in "all this fiddle." Other early poems utter suspicions about "the passion for setting people right" ("in itself an afflictive disease"); about the wish of human nature to dominate, to "stand in the middle of a thing"; about being diverted by the "mystery of construction" from "what was originally one's / object—substance at the core." Certain excuses for sins are offered: for a cat, it is natural to have "the disposition invariably to affront," since "an animal with claws wants to have to use / them." A poet with an affronting or diverting tongue may want to have to use it, too, and Moore's rebellious outspokenness about herself and others, no matter how disciplined by the angular geometry of her verse, is the chief ornament of the early volumes. It is no accident that when she wrote about the poet, in an essay bearing the name of her two polarities, "Feeling and Precision," she compared the writer to a clawed lion: "The lion's leap would be mitigated almost to harmlessness if the lion were clawless, so precision is both impact and exactitude, as with surgery."

Moore's first ethical impulse was, we might say, an Aristotelian one, interested in the taxonomy of the virtues and vices. The early poems served to set her mind in order about what was virtue, what vice—a question that was for her almost indistinguishable from what was art, what ugliness. She conceded later that Shakespeare's villains were not illiterate, but she added that rectitude "*has* a ring that is implicative." The long process of deciding what she liked, what she disapproved of, whom she admired, whom she found foolish or wicked, how her mind worked, what sort of literary form she should write in, occupied Moore for the classic two decades—from fifteen to thirty-five— of such human search. The poems that resulted *(Observations* came out when she was thirty-seven) represent one of the most individual, private, and conclusive inquiries into identity ever brought into print by an American woman. Her young eye was willing to look even at death (in "A Grave"), but she drew back from dramatizing it; her invariable diffidence of rhythm avoided grand climax. Pound wanted her to rearrange the last line of "A Grave" to gain emphasis, and she did it to please him, but she did not forbear to tell him she preferred the original phrasing. She was right, and later she changed the poem back to suit herself.

One oddity of literary history is that Moore became known, with a peculiar disregard for the brilliant character sketches in *Observations*, as an animal poet, a writer of texts to go beside a *National Geographic* photograph of an ostrich or a pangolin. *(Life*, in 1953, featured her in a story headed "*Life* Goes on a Zoo Tour with a Famous Poet: Marianne Moore Calls on Some Animals She Often Writes About.") In part, Moore was herself to blame for this absurdity: her distrust of emotions made her increasingly submissive to fact; her isolation made her more dependent on books; and the war caused her flexible ethical meditations to rigidify into moral outcries. Animals became an end in themselves, as human beings became more remote or more repellent. The disjunction between her mind and her heart is reflected in two statements made in the same interview (she was then approaching eighty): the first was that now, as always, the "forces which result in poetry" are "irrepressible emotion, joy, grief, desperation, triumph"; the second was that "every day it is borne in on us that we need rigor—better governance of the emotions." To govern the irrepressible is the paradoxical aim of all art, but her governance seems to have become an almost habitual censorship. When the pain of the irrepressible emotion and the pain of governance remain intertwined in the poems, the poetry weighs on us as it did on her. Conversely, when the emotion is a wholly innocent one—usually, in her case, a visual emotion (her religious upbringing seems not to have repressed sight and hearing)—her pure joy brings her closer than any other American poet to the Whitman of Manhattan and the sea. The exhilaration of port activity passes, transfused, unchanged, into "Dock Rats," and even Whitman could not better the description of the fishing boats and the waves in "A Grave":

the blades of the oars
moving together like the feet of water-spiders as if there were
no such thing as death.
The wrinkles progress upon themselves in a phalanx—beautiful
under networks of foam,
and fade breathlessly while the sea rustles in and out of the
seaweed.

That limpid delight appears in all her contemplations of the variety of the natural world. In her pursuit of its stranger forms, she is like the Herbert of the "outlandish proverbs" and natural curiosities:

Most things move th'under-jaw; the Crocodile not.
Most things sleep by lying; th'Elephant leans or stands.

No one is likely to forget Moore's ostrich who digests hard iron, or that human frigate bird compared to Handel, "never . . . known to have fallen in love," or the swan "with swart blind look askance / and gondoliering legs." But the shield of the animal metaphor eventually became almost impenetrable. It was true of Moore, as of her "student" (in the poem of that name), that she was too reclusive for some things to touch her, not because she had no feeling but because she had so much.

It is not sentimental, I hope, to see her great, if confined, poem "Marriage" as her most nearly perfect union of the pain of feeling and the pain of governance. The Marvellian theme that Paradise was Paradise only when Adam was there alone is touched on in the early poem "In the Days of Prismatic Color," which, after beginning in an airy, happy, rainbow-hued atmosphere, quickly darkens into a miserable debate with itself about the value of complexity, darkness, and sophistication. By the time of "Marriage," complexity has inexorably entered, as prelapsarian radiance is intruded on by the worldly cynicism of Bacon and then by Moore's own expostulating humor:

I wonder what Adam and Eve
think of it by this time,
this fire-gilt steel
alive with goldenness;
how bright it shows—
"of circular traditions and impostures,
committing many spoils,"
requiring all one's criminal ingenuity
to avoid!

When, at the age of eighty, Moore published "Marriage" in the *Complete Poems,* she added a prefatory sentence to the "Notes" to the poem, saying that it consisted of "statements that took my fancy which I tried to arrange plausibly." It was a dignified way to rebuke overbiographical readings of the poem; but nothing else she wrote contains nearly so many quotations and references. She had been squirreling away others' remarks on marriage with intense attention: more statements "took her fancy" on this subject than on any other on which she composed a poem. A "plausible arrangement," to a poet, means an arrangement that feels faithful to the emotional force that has given off the poem: in "Marriage," an unmistakable satiric comedy exists in tension with an equally unmistakable longing and admiration. The poem vacillates between thinking that marriage should be the most natural, easy, and companionable of arrangements and thinking it a dangerous enterprise: "men have power / and sometimes one is made to feel it." Both the sweetnesses and the hatreds of marriage enter the poem, which sees both the propriety of human union and its competing narcissistic destructions:

> He loves himself so much,
> he can permit himself
> no rival in that love.
> She loves herself so much,
> she cannot see herself enough.

In herself she clearly did not find that simplicity of temper, as she calls it, which sees in homely rules a natural of things that it easily obeys. People with that simplicity repeat phrases and attitudes in marriage which Moore compares to "the statesmanship / of an archaic Daniel Webster," saying—as though marital government were blissfully easy—"Liberty and union / now and forever," as they pose for their stolid daguerreotypes: "the book on the writing table; / the hand in the breast pocket." If that ending seems to a reader affecting, he will like Moore.

Many of the early poems, all brilliant, remain relatively unpossessed by readers in part because of their peculiar titles, which have nothing to do with their subjects. "An Octopus" is improbably about a glacier and a mountain, "The Fish" is about a scarred cliff and the ocean that batters it—though, of course, neither is really "about" its putative topic. Intellectually speaking, "An Octopus" is about multiplicity, and how it appears from different angles of vision, and "The Fish" is about the interfaces, as we might now call them, between the ocean, its creatures, and the adjacent land. Emotionally speaking, the glacier poem—written about Mount Rainier, and full of compressed detail—may be taken as a poem about America and its nature and its unclassical art, and as a poem about a life journey; while the fish poem reproduces the sliding motions of the sea creatures, the brutal pressure of the water, and the stolid endurance of the cliff, all intermixed in what one might feel to be a transcription of conflicting motions of the nervous system transliterated into earthly symbols.

In the last major poetic effort of her life, Moore spent a decade translating the fables of La Fontaine. Perhaps a flagging of her own inner energies made such a work proper, but the constraints of sense invaded her elegant rhythms and made the translations, in spite of many felicities of phrase, finally unsatisfying as poems by Moore. When they first appeared, Howard Nemerov called them "very jittery as to the meter." Not a great deal should be claimed for them, not even for Moore's affinities with La Fontaine: he was less soulful than she, and his animals have an existence not so much biological or visual as fabular. He was not a naturalist; Moore was.

Moore's poetry has so far not been especially well served by commentary, with the exception of Jean Garrigue's brief pamphplet *Marianne Moore* (1965). The most intimate and attractive short essay on her work was done, under the title "Her Shield," by Randall Jarrell; yet even Jarrell did not quite seem to grasp that her poems are not about "nature," but about herself. His witty remark "She sent postcards to only the nicer animals" falls slightly awry, like the gibes about what Wordsworth would have done if he had grown up among scorpions instead of sheep. It is a tribute to Moore's accuracy of drawing that Jarrell should allow her metaphors the veracity of photographs. He found her early poems too oblique and mannered; now that we are perhaps more accustomed to them, they seem not the "dry glittering expanse, i.e., a desert" that he found them but, rather, descriptions of self, full of candor as well as of reticence. (Even the critiques of knaves and fools are indirections for finding her own direction out.)

Most of her commentators have been men; with the exception of Geoffrey Hartman (who did the notes on the sleeve of the Yale Series recording of Moore reading her work), they have on the whole made Moore more shrinking and squeamish than she is. They bring up Dickinson. Eliot brought up Christina Rossetti. Pound, after his early sponsorship, said in a letter, "Marianne is scarce an exuberance, rather protagonist for the rights of vitrification and petrifaxis." William Carlos Williams, who once called her "our saint," compared her work to a "brittle, highly set-off porcelain garden." Jarrell said some of her poems "have the manners or manner of ladies who learned a little before birth not to mention money, who neither point nor touch, and who scrupulously abstain from the mixed, live vulgarity of life." Words like "tidy," "fussy," "finicking," and "ingenious" turn up. Denis

Donoghue thinks her poems resemble "things like ice-skating, which are hard play." David Perkins says, "She was untouched by existential angst, and the delighted reading of her work among so many highly sophisticated writers resembles Werther's love for Charlotte." There is no doubt something in Moore that elicits this uneasiness in male commentators, no matter how strongly they extol her virtues. Perhaps her work is in fact more "feminine" than it may appear to a woman reader, to whom Moore's angle of vision may seem more congenial. Or perhaps Moore's occasional contempt for the world of male power provokes a counterattack on what may seem to some her miniature version of life.

The book-length studies of her work by male admirers have not in themselves been notable works of literary criticism. A full-length book by a sympathetic reader who is also a woman is consequently a good addition to the available criticism. Laurence Stapleton, a professor of English at Bryn Mawr, is the first critic to write at length about the formidable assemblage of Moore materials in the Rosenbach collection, and her book—*Marianne Moore*—is most interesting in its revelation of Moore's habit of incessant work, and in its description of the reading and conversation notebooks from which poems were quarried. Stapleton writes always as an advocate, and is loath to grant any falling-off in Moore's work, tranquilly defending even the later poems and the translations. (She is admirably informative about the original fables and about the virtues of Moore's solutions to problems of expressive difference between English and French.) Younger readers looking for a reader's companion for their first tackling of Moore could do no better than to have Stapleton's book at hand. She paraphrases concisely, dissolves Gordian knots, and offers unobtrusive factual helps. She knew Moore; she has evidently spent years with the poems and feels wholly at home with them. Although her emphasis veers a little stiffly between the strictly thematic and the strictly technical, she is consistently reliable on both—though she does not, I think, find a more comprehensive ground, subsuming the two. Her argument is embodied in her subtitle, "The Poet's Advance." It is useful to have a lengthy, reasoned case made for the view that Moore got better after *Observations*. (Jarrell and others would agree; still others, like Hugh Kenner, would dissent.) Stapleton's quotations from early drafts (especially revealing in the case of "Marriage") and from letters and family papers enrich the instructive running commentary on the poems.

The fragments of biographical fact which appear now and then equally please and horrify. We might have been happier not knowing that "on a visit to the circus or the zoo [Moore] collected [elephant hairs], seizing an opportune moment to snip some from the tail or the trunk, using a small scissors that she carried with her for this purpose." We may wince at the familiar style she affected in letters, as in one to her brother on a bracelet of elephant charms which he had sent her: "I can't make out what they are standing on . . . I gotta determine this. Well Bible [her brother] as I said to Cub, Badger [her brother] has imagination . . . This here bracelet is not 'cold' . . . so I figure I am gonna wear it pretty much all the time."

Stapleton's commentary always derives from pleasure, and from a conviction of Moore's worth. If Moore could be better served by a book that discriminated more severely between her poetry and her verses, this well-stocked volume, full of hitherto unpublished fact and quotation, nonetheless cannot fail to make Moore's work much better known and more widely appreciated. Even the footnotes are full of interest. We learn from one of them that Bryher offered Moore five thousand dollars "so that she and her mother might spend some time in England," but "the offer was refused." Another note reveals that in 1943 Moore's "combined income from royalties . . . and for reading manuscripts for the Macmillan Co. totaled $310, supplemented by less than a thousand dollars from other sources." It is no wonder the Moores sometimes referred to themselves as field mice. Donald Hall, in his readable book on Moore, quotes a pen portrait by Robert McAlmon in the roman à clef *Post Adolescence* (though the character is called Martha Wullus, she is recognizably the young Marianne Moore): "A Dresden doll thing with those great contemplative Chinese eyes of hers, and that wisplike body with its thatch of carrot-colored hair, so picturesque too in her half-boyish clothes." That this young girl grew up to tell herself, "It is better to be lonely than unhappy," that she took herself in hand and decided to go her solitary way in her delicate but unconventional rhythms, is itself remarkable, since her need to steady herself into satire, security, and peace hints at undertows of fear, anger, and discouragement. Stapleton speaks of Moore's insubordination; it was a quality from which Moore profited, but of which she could scarcely entirely approve. Marguerite Young told, in a festschrift for Moore's seventy-seventh birthday, how the poem "Nevertheless" arose: Moore, seeing in a box of strawberries a misshapen green one, almost to seeds, said, "Here's a strawberry that's had quite a struggle," and found thereby a first line. It is a pity that Moore's own struggle culminated in things like the weaker poems and the preposterous exchanges with the Ford Motor Company over the naming of the Edsel, but it may be true, as Yeats said, that "all great men are owls, scarecrows, by the time their fame has come."

evoted (she has no self). Man has lapsed, since childhood, from eelings, and his mind thus grows apart from woman's (woman childish). Woman does not go to the office (she has the leisure to nd cultivate her tenderness). Woman is set in her "famous attitudes" s mind is full of clichés and household truisms). These assumptions under a gauze of affection, throughout criticism of Moore's poetry. vey Pearce begins by praising Moore's modesty and ease, but his tical criticisms make him sound a little insincere in wishing William Villiams, Conrad Aiken, and E. E. Cummings had Moore's female

prisingly, in her staunchly feminist argument, Suzanne Juhasz ith the men, both in the way they read the poems and in how they them. Rather than reexamining the male standards she assumes priori. Rather than consider the possible complexity of Moore's ions and the original strength of her verse, Juhasz accepts past ations and simply seeks to explain how Moore's social and historical might cause her to "retreat" into the "lesser" qualities of "spinsterly" for self-protection. Because she is looking for something else (confes- oetry), Juhasz completely misses the distinctiveness of Moore's in- . To Juhasz, insofar as Moore's stylistic devices are "feminine" they nses.

ore's art does display much of the taste and manners, the "vanity" as the "nobler virtue" our society ascribes to women. She is a lover mental surfaces; she is fascinated with fashion and wrote several on the subject; she is "gossipy" and chatty, passing on bits of hearsay rowed phrases; she is a collector of knickknacks, her poems are like fed cupboards, full of irrelevancies and distractions. Moore's life l the same tendencies and tastes. Her scrapbooks and library are full ture on women's dress, interior design, jewelry, ornamental art. Her o on for paragraphs describing someone's living room, a new coat, e is caring for. But somehow, when she is describing a friend's hat y bird someone gave her, these particulars seem more important as for imaginative response than for their conventional value.

ore's critics have tended to identify her "feminine" qualities super- taking up her lexicon of virtues but applying their own definitions judices to it. In context, I want to suggest, these qualities take on a powerful meaning, quite inverted in value. Moore purposely assumes litional "household" virtues and attributes in order to redefine them ction of her poems. Moore's "feminine" virtues and manners do not or soften reality, do not trivialize experience or diminish the claims elf, but on the contrary become in various ways the chief sources of

BONNIE COSTEL

The "Feminine" Language of M

Several critics of Marianne Moore's poetry ha indirectly, on its "feminine" quality, although it decide just what they mean by this. T. S. Eliot, 1923 essay on Moore with a statement he either s atory or hasn't really examined: "And there is o compliment: Miss Moore's poetry is as 'feminine' a never forgets that it is written by a woman; but v of this as anything but a positive virtue." What the "restraint" and "humility" that Randall Jarre on Moore, entitled "Her Shield"? Is it the ladyl of taste (a term rarely applied to men) that R. P. virtue and defect of her work? Or perhaps Elio preoccupation with surfaces and objects of sense e experience) which he and others have praised a they have distinguished genuineness from "grea primitive or heroic occasions, women write out his essay about Edna Saint Vincent Millay, "T Crowe Ransom distinguishes Moore for having le ity," that is, (and he is explicit about this) "intell women writers. Yet we feel a reserve of prejudi her, even when his purpose is to applaud, as in Distinction." Woman's love, he says in the Mi natural sense objects (woman can't transcend mun

From *Women and Language in Literature and Society.* ©

love is devoted (she has no self). Man has lapsed, since childhood, from natural feelings, and his mind thus grows apart from woman's (woman remains childish). Woman does not go to the office (she has the leisure to be idle and cultivate her tenderness). Woman is set in her "famous attitudes" (woman's mind is full of clichés and household truisms). These assumptions appear, under a gauze of affection, throughout criticism of Moore's poetry. Roy Harvey Pearce begins by praising Moore's modesty and ease, but his parenthetical criticisms make him sound a little insincere in wishing William Carlos Williams, Conrad Aiken, and E. E. Cummings had Moore's female virtue.

Surprisingly, in her staunchly feminist argument, Suzanne Juhasz agrees with the men, both in the way they read the poems and in how they evaluate them. Rather than reexamining the male standards she assumes them a priori. Rather than consider the possible complexity of Moore's predilections and the original strength of her verse, Juhasz accepts past interpretations and simply seeks to explain how Moore's social and historical situation might cause her to "retreat" into the "lesser" qualities of "spinsterly" writing for self-protection. Because she is looking for something else (confessional poetry), Juhasz completely misses the distinctiveness of Moore's inventions. To Juhasz, insofar as Moore's stylistic devices are "feminine" they are defenses.

Moore's art does display much of the taste and manners, the "vanity" as well as the "nobler virtue" our society ascribes to women. She is a lover of ornamental surfaces; she is fascinated with fashion and wrote several articles on the subject; she is "gossipy" and chatty, passing on bits of hearsay and borrowed phrases; she is a collector of knickknacks, her poems are like overstuffed cupboards, full of irrelevancies and distractions. Moore's life reflected the same tendencies and tastes. Her scrapbooks and library are full of literature on women's dress, interior design, jewelry, ornamental art. Her letters go on for paragraphs describing someone's living room, a new coat, a cat she is caring for. But somehow, when she is describing a friend's hat or a clay bird someone gave her, these particulars seem more important as *occasions* for imaginative response than for their conventional value.

Moore's critics have tended to identify her "feminine" qualities superficially, taking up her lexicon of virtues but applying their own definitions and prejudices to it. In context, I want to suggest, these qualities take on a special, powerful meaning, quite inverted in value. Moore purposely assumes the traditional "household" virtues and attributes in order to redefine them in the action of her poems. Moore's "feminine" virtues and manners do not glass-in or soften reality, do not trivialize experience or diminish the claims of the self, but on the contrary become in various ways the chief sources of

BONNIE COSTELLO

The "Feminine" Language of Marianne Moore

I

Several critics of Marianne Moore's poetry have remarked, directly or indirectly, on its "feminine" quality, although it is sometimes difficult to decide just what they mean by this. T. S. Eliot, for instance, concludes his 1923 essay on Moore with a statement he either seems to feel is self-explanatory or hasn't really examined: "And there is one final, and 'magnificent' compliment: Miss Moore's poetry is as 'feminine' as Christina Rossetti's, one never forgets that it is written by a woman; but with both one never thinks of this as anything but a positive virtue." What can he have in mind? Is it the "restraint" and "humility" that Randall Jarrell talks about in his essay on Moore, entitled "Her Shield"? Is it the ladylike quality, the "chastity" of taste (a term rarely applied to men) that R. P. Blackmur saw as both the virtue and defect of her work? Or perhaps Eliot was thinking of Moore's preoccupation with surfaces and objects of sense experience (especially trivial experience) which he and others have praised as her "genuineness" while they have distinguished genuineness from "greatness." Men write out of primitive or heroic occasions, women write out of everyday occasions. In his essay about Edna Saint Vincent Millay, "The Poet as Woman," John Crowe Ransom distinguishes Moore for having less "deficiency of masculinity," that is, (and he is explicit about this) "intellectual interest" than other women writers. Yet we feel a reserve of prejudice influencing his view of her, even when his purpose is to applaud, as in "On Being Modern with Distinction." Woman's love, he says in the Millay essay, is a fixation to natural sense objects (woman can't transcend mundane experience). Woman's

---

From *Women and Language in Literature and Society*.

energy in her work. Continually in her poetry and in her prose Moore shows a close relationship between moral and technical virtue. As Geoffrey Hartman has observed in a brief note on the poet, "her style does not embody a morality, it is one." The central morality of her style (and the chief source of its vitality) is a resistance to the complacencies of thought and language, to a tendency to accept given forms as descriptive of the world as it is. This is not a passive resistance, for it works in alliance with her mental voracity, continually readjusting the line and pushing against the limits of language. Moore's access to this central concern with the limits of language is through a conventional but redefined femininity. Or, conversely, the breaking up of our assumptions about certain types of virtue and manner is a natural instance of a larger concern for resisting complacencies of thought and language.

This is not, for Moore, an explicitly feminist issue. She nowhere indicates that she thinks of her poems or the values they advocate as particularly "feminine." In fact most of the animal figures that demonstrate these qualities are given male pronouns. But it seems only natural that Moore should select the attributes most readily applied to her as the focus of her efforts to rediscover language. Whether these qualities are a natural or inherited part of her femininity, however, one feels in reading her poems that a man could not have seen the potential in such qualities that Moore has seen and exploited.

One of Moore's favorite categories of virtue, observed throughout her poetry and criticism, is humility, with its analogues, restraint, and modesty. What a nineteenth-century reviewer said of the woman poet Felicia Hemans has been said in other ways (in the quotations above) of Moore: "she never forgets what is due feminine reserve." Indeed, Moore learned well the lesson of Bryn Mawr president Carey Thomas which she quotes in her essay on the "impassioned emancipator": she "behaved not with decorum but with marked decorum." This does not mean that Moore practiced humility without sincerity. Rather, she discovers in it a special value: "humility is a kind of armor." Critics usually take this to mean that by playing down the self, by making few overt claims to authority and power, we avoid subjecting ourselves to envy or attack. Moore's descriptiveness, her extensive use of quotation, her choice of peripheral subject matter, her circumlocution, are all pointed to as technical counterparts of her moral predilections. But what Moore, with Carey Thomas, understood is that strength and power are not necessarily stifled or even contained, but are on the contrary nurtured through acts of self-protection. Aggressive, indecorous, intolerant behavior wastes energy and creativity which can be better sustained and wielded with a certain guardedness. She quotes Thomas' remark: "Bryn Mawr must not be less guarded because it is good." Juhasz and others tend to see nothing but the armor, neglecting what is achieved by its use. Moore compromises nothing in her "self-protective" humility; she gains. Though the idea of "feminine reserve" may conventionally imply an attitude appropriate to inferiority, Moore does not even pretend to weakness. She shows humility to be a reserve, in the sense of a reservoir of power. At the end of "In This Age of Hard Trying," for instance, Moore shows how an apparent "inconsequence of manner" is more effective and durable than aggressive certitude.

In This Age of Hard Trying, Nonchalance Is Good and

"really, it is not the
  business of the gods to bake clay pots." They did not
    do it in this instance. A few
      revolved upon the axes of their worth
  as if excessive popularity might be a pot;

they did not venture the
  profession of humility. The polished wedge
    that might have split the firmament
      was dumb. At last it threw itself away
  and falling down, conferred on some poor fool, a privilege.

"Taller by the length of
  a conversation of five hundred years than all
    the others," there was one whose tales
      of what could never have been actual—
  were better than the haggish, uncompanionable drawl

of certitude; his by-
  play was more terrible in its effectiveness
    than the fiercest frontal attack.
      The staff, the bag, the feigned inconsequence
  of manner, best bespeak that weapon, self-protectiveness.

[All lines quoted from Marianne Moore's poetry are taken from *The Complete Poems of Marianne Moore* (New York: Viking, 1967).]

Humility, a guarded manner, has the advantage of taking the listener off-guard. And Moore practices her point in a number of ways here. The prosaic, conversational tone, the long, meandering, run-on lines and shifts of figurative level, give the impression of nonchalance. She is not, she seems to suggest, writing anything so grand as a poem. But the design is present, though unobtrusive, acting on our imaginations almost without alerting us. We hardly notice, though we subliminally hear, the careful rhymes, the subtly extended metaphor, the logic of the tale, so that the final lines have a special bold effect in their paradoxical clarity.

Moore's feminine humility, then, is designing: she wants to create and sustain an interest which overt self-assertion or pronounced form would snuff out. Moore's humility and restraint are not passive defenses but ways of gathering force, as a bow is pulled back in order to carry the arrow farther when it is finally released. Such motives and strategies are at work in many of her best poems, especially "The Plumet Basilisk," "The Frigate Pelican," "To a Snail," and "The Pangolin," poems about animals she admires for elusive strengths similar to those she displays in her writing. The end of humility is not self-protection for its own sake so much as "gusto," the spark released in the discovery of and enthusiasm for what is out of our control. In language, "humility is an indispensable teacher, enabling concentration to heighten gusto." Whereas humility associated with women usually implies something negative, a withdrawal, a deference, Moore shows its positive outcome. She is one woman for whom humility is not an end but a means of inspiration and expression.

Humility is not armor against the aggressions of the world on the self so much as against those of the self on the world, against the "disease, My Self," as she calls it. To impose the self and its accumulated structures on the world is to narrow the world and trap the self, a self-defeating gesture. "In Distrust of Merits" takes this theme up directly, but it is always present obliquely in Moore's verse. For her, humility "keeps the world large," preserves a place for something beyond the self that keeps us from complacency and satiation, consequently keeping us alive.

"His Shield" is the poem quoted most often in connection with Moore's idea of the armor of humility. She says it directly: "his shield was his humility." The poem warns against "greed and flattery," insisting that "freedom" is "the power of relinquishing what one would keep." Bravado does not please or improve anything, it simply attracts contenders, and wastes energy fighting them off. "Be dull, don't be envied or armed with a measuring rod." Don't attract envy by flaunting your achievement. This is a traditional code of femininity, but it usually implies that feminine achievement is incommensurate with envy or pride. Let us see how Moore understands her message.

The poem contrasts two kinds of armor, as several critics have pointed out. Moore finds that the spiny covering of the "edgehog miscalled hedgehog with all his edges out . . . won't do." Instead, "I'll wrap myself in salamander skin." The armor of "pig-fur" aggressing on the outside would scare things off. Its force is its inadequacy. But "asbestos" armor endures rather than extinguishes fire. It allows the outside world to enclose without annihilating the subject. Furthermore, it keeps the edges inside, keeps a fire alive internally rather than exhausting it in consuming ego. The ideal is "a lizard in the midst of flames, a firebrand that is life," who is, to use a phrase from Moore's critical essays, "galvanized against inertia." Where possession, and its verbal equivalent, singleminded assertion, imply stasis and complacency, survival and freedom require the constant readjustment of thought. At the level of the sentence, "humility" does not mean that one should be silent, but rather that language should continually be revised in the presence of what it cannot accommodate.

The utopia represented in the poem is an "unconquerable country of unpompous gusto." Power is not compromised, it is simply redistributed. Presbyter John, the hero of the poem, "styled himself but presbyter." Gusto is generated less out of self-aggrandizing conquest or consumption than out of awareness, out of a perpetually perceived difference between himself and the world, and the preservation of that difference and of desire. Resources are never used up in such a country.

Self-denial sounds like an odd basis for utopian experience, however. How can untapped wealth and power be considered as such? Moore manages to develop a sense of wealth without conquest through symbols of the potential effects of power. "Rubies large as tennis / balls conjoined in streams so / that the mountain seemed to bleed." The mountain only *seems* to bleed, but in doing so it marks a potential encounter. Emblematized strength is perpetual, exerted strength expires. Indeed, the emblem of external battle is only realized internally in the struggle for self-possession. The stream of blood, as the internalized warfare of humility, is only the blood stream, the "firebrand that is life."

If we think of the poet as presbyter, the vitality of Moore's lines comes from investing her thought in a presentation of the external world, hence so many poems in a descriptive mode which obliquely suggest a personal attitude. The oddity and apparent awkwardness of her lines comes from that sense of the inadequacy of the "measuring rod" to deal honesty with particulars. In language, "to relinquish what one would keep" is to continually resist available form. One way she does this is by having different forms displace each other to create a variegated surface. Images cut across each other to deny any rigid hierarchy. The "I" of the poem is swallowed up in description. Moral and discursive languages do not preside over the poem, but take their place in a range of languages: commercial, conversational, descriptive, metaphoric. While her lines expand and digress in pursuit of what is always posited as indefinable, they also create images of the self's internal activity, thereby steadying the flux of exploration. Thus, as Geoffrey

Hartman has pointed out, "she achieves a dialogue of one, an ironic crossfire of statement that continually denies and reasserts the possibility of a selfless assertion of self . . . the armor she describes is the modesty whereby the self is made strong to resist itself, but also strong to assert its being against voracious dogmatism." The abnegation of self ultimately satisfies the self, for it widens the sphere of response, the self being continually discovered through response to the external world. It declares knowledge a matter of process rather than possession, and it ensures the continuance of that process. The aggressive self is identified in the conquest of one form over another, an impulse to narrow and exclude, which finally entraps the self in the form it has imposed. But the humble self flourishes in the multiplicity of form, identifying with none. It neither narrows its domain nor can be narrowed by the force of others, for it exists in resisting closure. Humility, restraint, paradoxically conduce to freedom.

The armor of humility appears as a recurrent theme and technique in the critical essays as well. "Humility, Concentration and Gusto" opens in the more than metaphorical context of war.

> In times like these we are tempted to disregard anything that has not a direct bearing on freedom; or should I say, an obvious bearing, for what is more persuasive than poetry, though as Robert Frost says, it works obliquely and delicately. Commander King-Hall, in his book *Total Victory*, is really saying that the pen is the sword when he says the object of war is to persuade the enemy to change his mind.

Such talk of persuasion would seem on the side of the porcupine's edgy, aggressive "battle dress." But what is persuasive, it turns out, what has bearing on freedom, is humility.

> We don't want war, but it does conduce to humility, as someone said in the foreward to an exhibition catalogue of his work, "With what shall the artist arm himself save with his humility?". Humility, indeed, is armor, for it realizes that it is impossible to be original in the sense of doing something that has never been thought of before. Originality is in any case a byproduct of sincerity; that is to say, of feeling that is honest and accordingly rejects anything that might cloud the impression, such as unnecessary commas, modifying clauses, or delayed predicates.

One should not speak from ambition, then, but from honest feeling. The work, as one early critic of "female poetry" said, should "come from the heart, to be natural and true." Humility begins in this essay as a principle of simplicity and "quiet objectiveness," the reduction of self-assertion and the elevation of the external "impression." This is what Ransom "admired" in Millay, "a vein of poetry which is spontaneous, straightforward in diction, and excitingly womanlike; a distinguished objective record of a woman's mind." But humility becomes, as the essay goes on, a principle of difficulty standing for "the refusal to be false." When associated with "sincerity," the principle of humility and restraint becomes an agent of "gusto" by continually turning up a difference between the ways things are described and the way things are. "Gusto thrives on freedom," Moore explains, and freedom is preserved by failures of formal closure, by linguistic deviation. Daniel Berkeley Updike, Moore tells us, "Has always seemed to me a phenomenon of eloquence because of the quiet objectiveness of his writing."

> And what he says of printing applies equally to poetry. It is true, is it not, that "style does not depend on decoration but on simplicity and proportion"? Nor can we dignify confusion by calling it baroque. Here, I may say, I am preaching to myself, since, when I am as complete as I like to be, I seem unable to get an effect plain enough.

But this is sophisticated humility on Moore's part. What is persuasive is her preaching to herself. Certainly we would not expect her to be less complete than she would like to be, so what might seem like ornament or excess in her verse is justified as honesty. Humility, which upholds an ideal of quiet objectiveness, of simplicity and proportion, also upholds sincerity, which will not force a perception into a dishonestly neat structure. What results from this ironic conflict is a lively play of impulses through a highly variegated, rebellious surface. Though she will not make public claims to "originality," her poems are certainly idiosyncratic and individual, and invite the interest of a public into the special world of a private enchantment.

Moore often speaks of her "natural reticence" in explaining the disobliging difficulty of some of her work. Conventionally, natural reticence belongs to woman's lesser capacity for logical assertion. As a supposedly intuitive rather than analytical creature, woman naturally has trouble being articulate: language is a system of codification and dissection. Moore herself "feeling at its deepest tends to be inarticulate." But in her verse, once natural reticence gives way to speech it paradoxically causes an overflow of words.

The extreme digressiveness of surface in Moore's poetry has perplexed many critics. Juhasz sees it as deliberate evasiveness, her way "of not talking about what she is talking about and talking about what she is not talking about." Roy Harvey Pearce criticizes her "gossipy" quality and her "uncertainty as to direction." Though Pearce doesn't label these qualities "feminine" he implies as much, and Ransom is explicit. Woman's mind "has no direction or modulation except by its natural health." In other words, women live without purpose or focus beyond their immediate daily cares, to which they respond with inarticulate emotions. Their minds cannot sustain a logical argument or coherent structure because they live in a continuous present.

Moore takes this digressive mode of thought and examines its special advantages. The mind that folows "its natural health" has a capacity for nuance which evades us where there is "too stern an intellectual emphasis." The "steam roller" mind crushes "all the particles down into close conformity." "As for butterflies, I can hardly conceive of one's attending upon you." The "aimless" mind, like "the magic flute" illogically weaves "what logic can't unweave." It is closer to the center of experience, alive to changes of an unconscious voice. It has a greater capacity for discovery, not blinded by its own hypotheses. It is more inclusive; it has more variety. Through her unwieldy, non-hierarchical structures, her elongated, loquacious sentences, Moore achieves a sense of "continuous present," a sense of the poem in process, the mind experiencing and discovering itself. Moore's prosody works to this same end, through inconspicuous syllable measure, through dispersed rhyme and run-on lines. Ransom thinks women are always weak on form "because they are not strict enough and expert enough to manage forms, in their default of the discipline under which men are trained." Moore's form is indeed not uniform or abstractly applied; it depends upon movement and changes inflection, unleashing new impulses as they are called up.

Geoffrey Hartman has been unusually sensitive to the force of Moore's "gossipy" meanderings.

> . . . one reads her poems less for their message (always suffused) than for the pleasure of seeing how style may become an act of the living—the infinitely inclusive and discriminating—mind. This mind, or rather Miss Moore's, is "an an enchanting thing;" it takes us by its very irrelevancies. Here too everything is surface; she talks, so to say, from the top of her mind and represents herself as a gossip on the baroque scale. But secretly she is a magician, and distracts on purpose. While her message eludes us through understatement, the poem itself remains teasingly alive through the overstatement of its many tactics, till we accept the conventional rabbit, glorified by prestidigitation. Yet the magic of language becomes intensely moral on further acquaintance and

> her crazyquilt of thoughts, quotations and sounds resolves into subtler units of meaning and rhythm. The free (but not formless) verse helps break up the automatic emphases of traditional syntax, and respects the more dynamic shifts of the inner, and not merely spoken voice.

Moore's elusive surfaces involve a moral prudence as well as an aesthetic one. She wants to dodge self-consciousness. What male critics have called a certain "fussiness" in Moore, she calls "unconscious fastidiousness" in which she finds "a great amount of poetry." What she seems to describe with the phrase is a kind of impulsive persistence in attempting to manage unmanageable material. Moore sees "unconscious fastidiousness" as an important part of the nurturing process, and imitates the process in her poems. Maternity is the subject of "The Paper Nautilus," and in comparing it to poetry she alters the conventional view of both. We conventionally think of maternal affection as a soft, graceful attitude, and similarly Moore's poetry has been prized, condescendingly, for its "relaxed ease." But the poem describes the process of nurture as a struggle beneath a surface of gentleness, a highly precarious restraint of power. Here unconscious fastidiousness means a high level of attentiveness without the imposition of rigid design which might impede natural development. The health of the eggs somehow depends upon maximum power and maximum restraint. The juxtaposition of "the ram's-horn cradled freight" and "a devil-fish" and her eggs reinforces this tension. Later we are told of the shell's relative delicacy (like a wasp nest) and of its strength (like Ionic columns and the force of Parthenon sculpture). The tension described in holding back Hercules is clarified through a notion of a "fortress of love" but not relieved. We have metaphors of maximum impulse without the expiration of energy in action. The paper nautilus must "hide" her "freight" but not "crush" it. The same goes for poets. They too are "hindered to succeed."

> For authorities whose hopes
> are shaped by mercenaries?
> Writers entrapped by
> teatime fame and by
> commuters' comforts? Not for these
> the paper nautilus
> constructs her thin glass shell.

The poem starts by distinguishing two kinds of form, one which is complacent and commercial, generated by petty ambition, (and the association of mercenaries and commuters suggests a male domain) and another kind which will not "entrap" the writer or the audience. Appropriately, Moore will not "entrap" herself and her subject by restricting the tenor of this other kind. Rather, after an initial reference to writers, she shifts into a metaphor for metaphor itself: the shell in which our impression of the world can take shape without calcifying. But the shell is importantly the source and product of a maternal affection, a desire to nurture, in order finally to release the growing object. Her shell does not contain the eggs, or in terms of poetry, is not "the thing itself."

The feminine code of sacrifice says one must "relinquish what one would keep," and this is often applied to maternal relationships. But Moore changes this idea, in an artistic context, to a mode of freedom, not just a duty. Thus "the intensively watched eggs coming from / the shell free it when they are freed." And the mother is free from her state of tension. Freedom, that is, requires differentiation.

We are curious when we sense something like ourselves yet different. Moore knows that observation is always in a way self-interested. Indeed, language is fundamentally of the self and not of the other, so self-expression is inevitable. Her mind follows likeness and finds difference, and again likeness, in the form of statements that are qualified, images which clash, rhymes that are interrupted, deviating detail, almost any form of verbal differentiation. In the process she does not accomplish "objectification" (curiosity is not satisfied) but something more interesting: a composition which metes out likeness and difference, visual and aural as well as semantic. The composition has the rhetorical power both to make associations and to suggest its own limits, since these verbal differences are made to seem like the difference betwen the world and what we say about it. Moore's compositions are trails of associations which conduct the reader to their source. This identification occurs not only as our vicarious experience of her mental flux, but through her final, subtle self-portraiture. Moore begins by presenting an object apparently for its own sake, but in the process of describing it she borrows the object as a figure of her own activity. This self-portraiture is not the point of arrival of the poet's search for unity or for the thing itself, but a kind of parting embrace of words and things, a form of possession or appropriation that leaves the thing untouched while its ghost performs the function of analogy. Moore pursues the contours of objects for what she can discover of herself, but precisely because she learns about herself through observation of the external world, she can never declare her motive or speak of herself directly. "Imaginary possession" allows her to make associations without assumptions. She never gets to the point at which the idea subverts the observation.

The narcissists and sophisticates in the art world are the constant butt of Moore's satire, though they are "deaf to satire." In "Novices," for instance, she criticizes the "supertadpoles of expression" so attentive to their own egos

> so that they do not know "whether it is the buyer or the seller
> who gives the money"—
> an abstruse idea plain to none but the artist,
> the only seller who buys and holds on to the money.
> . . . .
> they write the sort of thing that would in their judgment interest
> a lady;
> curious to know if we do not adore each letter of the alphabet
> that goes to make a word of it.

These "Will Honeycombs" who "anatomize their work," whose art is highly rational and symmetrical, are "bored by the detailless perspective of the sea," too absorbed in flattering themselves with their intellectual conquests to recognize the irrational power of nature. Moore contrasts their style with "the spontaneous unforced passion of the Hebrew language," which derives its "tempestuous energy" from a complete surrender to the sublimity of nature. In their example Moore shows that the self grows larger by imaginatively embracing something beyond its rational control.

But Moore is not simply advocating unconscious spontaneity or self-annihilation. Moore's is a highly conscious art, its objects derived primarily from books, not wild nature. It is the activity of tracing an "other," of knowing it in relation to oneself, as similar and different, that interests her, and she has called this "imaginary possession." With imaginary possession the mind is free to make associations, but at the same time knows them as such and does not identify them as exclusive truths. The task of "When I Buy Pictures," for instance, is to give both the illusion of a figure in the world who does not affect it, and to make a gesture of possession, to bring what is seen under the control of language.

When I Buy Pictures

> or what is closer to the truth
> when I look at that of which I may regard myself as the
> imaginary possessor,
> I fix upon what would give me pleasure in my average
> moments:
> the satire upon curiosity in which no more is discernible
> than the intensity of the mood;

> or quite the opposite—the old thing, the medieval decorated
> hat-box,
> in which there are hounds with waists diminishing like the
> waist of the hourglass,
> and deer and birds and seated people.

The game of imaginary possession involves discretion and humility, not prohibition:

> Too stern an intellectual emphasis upon this quality or that
> detracts from one's enjoyment.
> It must not wish to disarm anything; nor may the approved
> triumph easily be honored—
> that which is great because something else is small.

Of course these are not "average moments"; they are moments of luminosity, selected for their suggestiveness. The difference is that between selection which reveals a will and transformation which emblematizes a will. Moore does not simply direct her imagery toward a final or overarching intention. Her mind is attentive to the properties of each object and each word as it occurs. Age suggests images of age: hatboxes which bear images of old-fashioned hounds that are shaped like hourglasses whose waists remind her of time's waste and as these waists diminish the imagery narrows its reference to the matter of fact: deer, birds, and seated people. The coherence of a part takes her to the next, without rejecting the influence of the immediate details. But while avoiding "too stern an intellectual emphasis" a surprisingly complex range of associations, built upon the problems of time, distance and complexity, emerges in the movement from one image to the next, at no cost to the surface randomness of local association:

> It may be no more than a square of parquetry; the literal
> biography perhaps,
> in letters standing well apart upon a parchment-like expanse;
> an artichoke in six varieties of blue; the snipe-legged
> hieroglyphic in three parts;
> the silver fence protecting Adam's grave, or Michael taking
> Adam by the wrist.

Parquetry, artichoke, biography, hieroglyphic are all patterns of one kind or another. The range is inclusive and humorous. These orders are mocked, but shown to be natural. "Literal biography" is a contradiction reduced to its formal elements, letters standing well apart. We are directed through meaningless "orders" to consider our desire for possession, and the poem moves to emblems of our fall. These unite the previously separate and random problems of time, distance, and complexity raised in the imagery. Poems suppose a hierarchy of elements, but the rhetoric of the list resists our locating ourselves anywhere in particular in the poem. Moore quite consciously tempts our desire for architectonic, mythic structures, our need to privilege the "heroic" moment. She wants these associations while she restrains them from blocking their natural contexts. One does not forfeit the self, then, one does not resign all "views"; one simply explores them discreetly.

Of course the poem itself is a picture for sale. The satire on curiosity is a picture of ourselves since it is, finally, the intensity of the mood which is at issue. Its "opposite," the picture of receding things, draws the curious figure on until it becomes a mirror ("when I look at that of which I may regard myself"). The self does get expressed, through its own enchantment with something else, and this, I think, is what Virginia Woolf means in *A Room of One's Own* when she speaks of a woman's ability to get close to the fountain of creative energy.

While Moore's poetry is in a way "impersonal," in that the self is not the focus or dominant presence, we feel the movement of a distinct personality throughout. Indeed, Moore's very resistance to formal closure becomes for her a means of self-revelation. The "minor defects" of form, as she called unassimilated elements, are marks of style. And it is in style that we know this poet, not in subject or assertion. Though she never advocates "originality," the ambition to supersede the forms others have created, she is a great defender of "idiosyncrasy," an inevitable expression of "honest vision." Idiosyncrasy is connected with sincerity, a kind of non-competitive, oblique presentation of self; it does not require a personal subject or a show of power; it challenges no one.

Emily Watts, in *The Poetry of American Women*, identifies Moore's verse with a tradition of "feminine realism." What she and other critics are pointing to in the use of this term is the combination of "mundane realities," "simple human and natural situations," and "natural sense objects," with ethical generalizations or "household morality." The feminine mind neatly integrates nature and morality. Randall Jarrell, for one, strongly objects to Moore's poetry on the basis of this integration. In clear sexual categories he challenges what he sees as Moore's domestic falsifications, upholding instead the male vision of amoral nature and its corresponding cosmic ambition.

But Moore has transformed the structure of feminine realism (which links observation to ethical generalization) in a number of ways. While she does detail nature, she celebrates her subjects for their recalcitrance. And the morality that accompanies these pictures is one of resisting the mind's impulse to circumscribe experience. In "Sea Unicorns and Land Unicorns," (about the Unicorn Tapestries) Moore points out that the unicorn remains "a puzzle to the hunters." Only the virgin knows him:

> Thus this strange animal with its miraculous elusiveness,
> has come to be unique,
> "impossible to take alive,"
> tamed only by a lady inoffensive like itself—
> as curiously wild and gentle.

All the poems follow a dictum of resistance even while they move through an apparent structure of observation-moral, for they continually propose definitions only to unravel them. "Integration, too tough for infraction," integration of the mind and the external world, of ethos and nature, is the goal of Moore's poetry, not its claim. And it is based on "efforts of affection" and not on aggression. It is achieved through process, through an open-ended dialectic of observing and making observations, in a continuous present.

While Moore follows the tendency in "feminine realism" to keep an eye on the external object, she is distinctly modern in her awareness of the limits of language to present that object. Moore's "descriptions" break up the conventions of composition, not to protect the self but to bring language into a more adequate relationship to experience, to discover a new realism which resists the habits of mind and eye. But what such resistance to referential conventions does, finally, is bring us into a closer awareness of the surface of language. By blocking the easy transfer from word to picture of meaning, by continually shifting the flow of counters and intruding on conventions which we too readily naturalize, Moore reminds us that we are not actually seeing, but only reading. This technique is especially effective in her poem "An Octopus," a long description of a glacier that concludes with a moral of "relentless accuracy." The extreme difficulty of accurately perceiving the object creates a corresponding difficulty in the words. Often the lengthy and cumbersome sentences lose their syntactic hold on us. We forget the subject or antecedent in the tow of subordinate clauses. Colons and semicolons are suspended between groups without an easy sense of their relation. Appositions become subjects with their own appositions in turn. Participial phrases go on for several lines until we cease even to anticipate their subjects. Where conventional "realism" trusts the parts of speech to represent reality, Moore's language continually demonstrates their failure. In its attempt to circumscribe the viscous presence, the language of "An Octopus," for instance, doubles back on itself with lines that refer outwardly to the objective experience, and inwardly to the experience of reading. "Completing the circle, you have been deceived into thinking that you have progressed." "Neatness of finish! Neatness of finish! Relentless accuracy is the nature of this octopus / with its capacity for fact." Such self-reflective imagery admits that ultimately the "morals" we derive are not natural but represent our efforts to come to terms with nature. In that sense all of Moore's ethical generalizations have to do with her poetic activity.

"Neatness of finish" and "relentless accuracy" sound, in isolation, like mundane lessons. But in the context of this poem they present an enormous challenge to the eye and mind. And Moore proves the point she is making, for instead of rounding off the descriptions with this abstract conclusion, she returns to the particular. She adopts, in the end, a policy of accuracy more relentless than before:

> Is "tree" the word for these things
> "flat on the ground like vines"?
> some "bent in a half circle with branches on one side
> suggesting dust-brushes, not trees;
> some finding strength in union, forming little stunted groves
> their flattened mats of branches shrunk in trying to escape"
> from the hard mountain "planed by ice and polished by the
> wind"—
> the white volcano with no weather side;
> the lightning flashing at its base,
> rain falling in the valleys, and snow falling on the peak—
> the glassy octopus symmetrically pointed,
> its claw cut by the avalanche
> "with a sound like the crack of a rifle
> in a curtain of powdered snow launched like a waterfall."

The breathlessness of the passage pulls us away from the organizing frame of grammar and syntax and hurls us into the midst of detail. Ethical generalization is returned to the level of perception. And yet even in the midst of detail, the mind makes associations. In this case the associations simply remind us of the controlling presence of language. At the end of the mountain is a curtain of snow; at the end of the poem—is a curtain of snow, the page. Her humility denies both the claims of an achieved realist and those of an achieved moralist; but her struggle for integration is vital and rewarding.

Moore transforms and toughens our understanding of familiar virtues when she uses them as stylistic devices. Humility, affection, reserve, are not passive but dynamic and vital modes of response. They do not protect but rather sustain the self in experience. In her redefinition and revaluation of what have been seen as "feminine" modes of identity, Moore displays a larger, encompassing concern to avoid all complacencies of mind. No container will hold her gusto.

> You have been compelled by hags to spin
> gold thread from straw and have heard men say:
> "There is a feminine temperament in direct contrast to ours
>
> which makes her do these things. Circumscribed by a
> heritage of blindness and native
> incompetence, she will become wise and will be forced to
> give in.
> Compelled by experience, she will turn back;
>
> water seeks its own level":
> and you have smiled. "Water in motion is far
> from level." You have seen it, when obstacles happen to bar
> the path, rise automatically.

In describing Ireland, Moore has obliquely celebrated the resilient power of the "feminine temperament." Ireland survives and deepens its identity by a combination of persistence and responsiveness. By rising to meet the shapes experience presents rather than retreating or imposing artificial forms, Moore sustains a vital, creative contact between her self and her surroundings.

DAVID BROMWICH

Emphatic Reticence

A fault of every good criticism of Moore I have ever read is the assumption of a generalized familiarity with the poetry, an atmosphere-of-Mooreishness, which allows the quotations to be copious and admiring and yet seldom anchored in a parent poem. And perhaps we know the poetry well enough; but do we know the poems? Many readers will want to reply: "Oh certainly, I know what they're *like;* whimsical, helter-skelter; odds and ends, all in sharp focus; alive with incidental humor—every word an incident." Because I was tired of giving this answer myself, I made of list of poems. The following groups are neither exhaustive nor mutually exclusive; but they do make room for a different sort of answer.

Riddles, anecdotes, squibs: "To Statecraft Embalmed," "To Military Progress," "To a Steam Roller," "Silence"; with innumerable unrhymed epigrams, and divagations of a too-charitable satirist.

Prayers; calls to fortitude: "What Are Years?", "In Distrust of Merits," "By Disposition of Angels," and the bulk of the later poems (epitomized by "Blessed Is the Man," with its echoes of Eisenhower and Omar Khayyam).

Trials of Ingenuity: "The Plumet Basilisk," "The Fish," "Peter," "England," "When I Buy Pictures," "The Labors of Hercules," "Snakes, Mongooses, Snake-Charmers, and the Like," "An Octopus," "Sojourn in the Whale," "The Student," "Spenser's Ireland," "Four Quartz Crystal Clocks," "Elephants," "His Shield."

From *Poetry* 139, no. 6 (March 1982). Originally entitled "Marianne Moore's Poems."

Far-fetchers: "The Steeple-Jack," "The Hero," "The Jerboa," "The Frigate Pelican," "In the Days of Prismatic Color," "A Grave," "New York," "Marriage," "Virginia Britannia," "The Pangolin;" and, blameless outcast from the 1951 *Collected Poems,* "Melanchthon."

The most searching of her inventions belong to the last two groups. Wit, as *ingenium*, or the reasoning intelligence—as finder of hidden analogies, or master of the sociable challenge and repartee—here delights in testing its object for all uncharted incongruities, and a map showing every turn would be no help. Who, coming to the end of "Four Quartz Crystal Clocks," will say where we forgot the smart touch of the colloquist, and find that we have learned something about science and the morality of play?

The lemur-student can see
that an aye-aye is not

an angwan-tíbo, potto, or loris. The seaside burden should not embarrass
the bell-boy with the buoy-ball
endeavoring to pass
hotel patronesses; nor could a
practiced ear confuse the glass
eyes for taxidermists

with eyeglasses from the optometrist. And as
MEridian-7 one-two
one-two gives, each fifteenth second
in the same voice, the new
data—"The time will be" so and so—
you realize that "when you
hear the signal," you'll be

hearing Jupiter or jour pater, the day god—
the salvaged son of Father Time—
telling the cannibal Chronos
(eater of his proxime
newborn progeny) that punctuality
is not a crime.

[Unless otherwise noted, quotations are from *The Complete Poems of Marianne Moore* (New York, 1981).]

After such beautiful display one may still prefer the extravagant persuasion of the far-fetchers; and to justify the preference there is a decisive aphorism in "Armor's Undermining Modesty": "What is more precise than precision? Illusion." That poem more than any other was Moore's apology for her work, and to her its credo had an obvious application.

She was most satisfied, and hoped we would be, with poems that argued the necessity of some single illusion—poems in which, after enough scruples to disarm the skeptic, she could welcome the believing mind for its strengths, especially strength of sight. Any illusion that assisted life to its ends was perhaps another name for single-mindedness. In "The Steeple-Jack" this quality is what favors the not-native observer of a native place: the citizen for whom the author cares most is the one who may set "part of a novel" in the town she describes. Since Moore dropped the full title, "Part of a Novel, Part of a Poem, Part of a Play"—which covered two further poems in sequence, "The Student" and "The Hero"—"The Steeple-Jack" may now seem a more complacent piece of naturalism than it really is. But her decision was correct for other reasons. The three did not answer each other deeply enough, and "The Hero" had more in common with "The Jerboa" than with its companions. Like "The Jerboa," it bears witness to a personal ideal of ascetic heroism, some of whose elements Moore named in an essay on "Humility, Concentration, and Gusto." As the "Too Much" section of "The Jerboa" concludes with the desert and its real animals, unenvyingly remote from civilization and its toy ones—"one would not be he / who has nothing but plenty"—so "The Hero" moves from the tourist laden with his collected wits to the different figure, rich without plenty, who can follow a personal liking: "He's not out / seeing a sight but the rock / crystal thing to see—the startling El Greco / brimming with inner light—that / covets nothing that it has let go." These poems make as right a pair as "The Frigate Pelican" and "The Pangolin," in which an animal at once upsets and submits to be measured by the human scale of custom and value; or "New York" and "Virginia Britannia," one poem each for the North and South, in which the dream of paradise is close-woven with the dream of plunder. But the foregoing are all well-known or at least much-recognized poems, and this late in the history of Moore's reputation I would rather concentrate on three that seem to me too little read: "A Grave," "Marriage," and "In the Days of Prismatic Color."

"A Grave" is propositional in structure, categorical in mood, shorn of even such heterodox exuberances as Moore sometimes allows to flourish within the parallel rows of a catalogue. It is a poem about death, as dry as life can make it.

Man looking into the sea,
taking the view from those who have as much right to it as you
    have to it yourself,
it is human nature to stand in the middle of a thing,
but you cannot stand in the middle of this;
the sea has nothing to give but a well excavated grave.
The firs stand in a procession, each with an emerald turkey
    foot at the top,
reserved as their contours, saying nothing;
repression, however, is not the most obvious characteristic of
    the sea;
the sea is a collector, quick to return a rapacious look.
There are others besides you who have worn that look—
whose expression is no longer a protest; the fish no longer
    investigate them
for their bones have not lasted:
men lower nets, unconscious of the fact that they are
    desecrating a grave,
and row quickly away—the blades of the oars
moving together like the feet of water-spiders as if there were
    no such thing as death.
The wrinkles progress among themselves in a phalanx—
    beautiful under networks of foam,
and fade breathlessly while the sea rustles in and out of the
    seaweed;
the birds swim through the air at top speed, emitting cat-calls
    as heretofore—
the tortoise-shell scourges about the feet of the cliffs, in motion
    beneath them;
and the ocean, under the pulsation of lighthouses and noise of
    bell-buoys,
advances as usual, looking as if it were not that ocean in which
    dropped things are bound to sink—
in which if they turn and twist, it is neither with volition nor
    consciousness.

One sees the poem just as one hears it—a respectful monochrome, unflattering to man, of something larger than man: but how does it get this consistency of effect? One notes first the use of words at several removes from any lively particular, words like "unconscious," "volition," "characteristic," "contours," "repression," along with the careless drab music of the vernacular, "at top speed," "no such thing," "as much right to it," "the fact that," "as usual." T. S. Eliot would have had in mind words and phrases like these, when he praised Moore for having heard, in "the curious jargon produced in America by universal university education," one of the possible languages of men in a state of vivid sensation. And yet there seems, at a glance, hardly one vivid feature in this poem; it seems almost wrong to call it a poem. Only on the return visit that it somehow compels, and a step or so back from its subject, do certain details emerge from the flat continuous statement; and then it takes on quite suddenly the answering bluntness and unanswerable severity of a Aeschylean chorus: nothing could be more direct, more like words meant to surprise and unenchant, than "it is human to stand in the middle of a thing, / but you cannot stand in the middle of this"; and, "the sea is a collector, quick to return a rapacious look. There are others besides you who have worn that look"; down to the theorem-like and almost affectless "dropped things are bound to sink." It would be hard to imagine any poem that sustained a more uncanny gravity. Under its law we naturally reserve for ourselves the few stage-properties of the sea, to make an interval of elation and release before the end: the sound of the bell-buoys and sight of the lighthouse, the "phalanx" of wrinkles beneath the foam, and birds swimming in the air, "emitting cat-calls as heretofore," with the ghostly tortoise-shell (no tortoise) moving among the cliffs below. Yet, much as these things may please us, the poem absorbs them without pleasure; and the detail we remember most irresistibly, a metaphor powerful enough to survive paraphrase, is also the most disquieting of all: the men, ignorant of death and of the figure they cut beside it, rowing quickly away from the thing they do not know is a grave, their oars "moving together like the feet of water-spiders as if there were no such thing as death." It is a long line without pause in which surely no reader has ever skipped one word. The entire poem must have been a favorite of Elizabeth Bishop's: some of it is still going in the background of "At the Fishhouses"; a smaller borrowing, but as gifted with appreciation and command as Bishop's use of a familiar Moore-genre in "The Man-Moth."

By an impartial observer, "Marriage" might be described as a duel of quotations. But we are none of us impartial; so let it be a male critic who says, In this poem man holds the chains and one woman, the words; yet she is cunning as a whisper and makes it seem, almost to the end, a remarkably equal match. The contestants are Adam and Eve, or the virtues of Adam and Eve. And Moore's Adam is the same as Milton's, though she does not tell us so; he whose first recorded words, to the first of women, are "Sole partner and sole part of all these joys," dull, sententious, and good, the temple of a selfless mastery. Who else could be let down so gently but so finally by Moore's reference to "the ease of the philosopher / unfathered by a woman"? Many unkindnesses as well as (one feels) many liberties and general vexings, were required to move her to this. But steel against satire, Adam—the old and ever-renewed, in marriage—will be heard out; while Eve calmly wonders at "the spiked hand / that has an affection for one / and proves it to the bone, / impatient to assure you / that impatience is the mark of independence, / not of bondage." For, marrying, she has joined that locus " 'of circular traditions and impostures, / committing many spoils,' / requiring all one's criminal ingenuity / to avoid"—and, crushed by his single stroke of wit, his "Why not be alone together," she now dwells in those circles, a listener. The poet comes confusingly near a gesture of sentimental homage, when she speaks of

> This institution,
> perhaps one should say enterprise
> out of respect for which
> one says one need not change one's mind
> about a thing one has believed in,

but the recoils by the end, and transposes even this tentative melody into a more dubious key, with a minefield of sharps and flats:

> What can one do for them—
> these savages
> condemned to disaffect
> all those who are not visionaries
> alert to undertake the silly task
> of making people noble?

But this is not quite the end; we see the wife a last time, still listening to her husband, whose eloquence now has something of "the statesmanship / of an archaic Daniel Webster," proclaiming "Liberty and union / now and forever"; yet another man, husband, orator, in a poem that has featured everyone from Adam to Edmund Burke. There is more bitterness than affection in this wind-up; it is an unexpected tone, for which we are glad: suitable, after all, to a poet whose refusal to be assured about her impatience was the making of her. Besides, in the masterly orchestration of the thing, a great many other voices have been heard—Bacon, Shakespeare, Pound, Richard Baxter, Charles Reade, and at last a voice close to Moore's own, which turns out to be La Fontaine: "Everything to do with love is mystery; / it is more than a day's work / to investigate this science." There is in this more wonder than bitterness; and the quotations generally help Moore to keep her balance. "Psychology which explains everything / explains nothing, / and we are still in doubt." For every Adam there must be an Eve, who listens and smiles, and does not show her smile. The hurtful acuteness of some passages comes, notwithstanding the disclaimer, from the habitual care of a good and disturbing psychologist; and any writer who can describe Satan's investment in the serpent as "that invaluable accident / exonerating Adam," is none the worse for having a *parti pris.*

To square the account, she included in her *Selected Poems*, and reprinted ever after, a poem about Adam before Eve, "when there was no smoke and color was / fine, not with the refinement / of early civilization art, but because / of its originality." The poem, "In the Days of Prismatic Color," is alert to the snares of its myth; it knows that this sort of aboriginal earliness can never exist as its own contemporary; it is not born but comes to be original, when later eyes have seen it so. History alone, with memory, can make those days, and Moore writes out the history that her poem seems to deny, by adopting an idiom she has employed at other times—refined, self-conscious, derivative, *and fine*—and pressing it beyond any known reach of the abstract. We arrive at originality by this curious route; so that she can say, of Adam's solitude and perfect vision, "obliqueness was a variation / of the perpendicular, plain to see and / to account for: it is no / longer that; nor did the blue-red-yellow band / of incandescence that was color keep its stripe." That is science not poetry, we may say, too stupid to read our myths deviously; but the image stops us short: it is the first poetic rainbow in half a century that one can admire without embarrassment. This poem is no friend of complexity, which it admits may not be "a crime, but carry / it to the point of murkiness / and nothing is plain"; nor of sophistication, which it suspects of being "Principally throat," and "at the antipodes from the init- / ial great truths." Yet it is wonderfully aware throughout that our originals though great can never be simple, except in their power to survive. We reduce them only from our need for something uncompounded to serve as the givens of thought and reliables of metaphor. But when they first appeared, before they could be remembered, there was always the stumbling, the obliqueness of the rude assault:

"Part of it was crawling, part of it
was about to crawl, the rest
was torpid in its lair." In the short-legged, fit-
ful advance, the gurgling and all the minutiae—we have the
classic
multitude of feet. To what purpose! Truth is no Apollo

Belvedere, no formal thing. The wave may go over it if it
likes.
Know that it will be there when it says,
"I shall be there when the wave has gone by."

In those lines originality becomes one with the self-confidence of genius anywhere. Seeing the naturalness of the transition, from "the gurgling and all the minutiae" to "the classic / multitude of feet," we are educated in how originals make their way, and incidentally shown a distinction Moore keeps in view all the time, between the precisionist's dreaming with one eye open and the formalist's interrogation with both eyes closed.

So far I have said nothing about Moore's verse forms—and after all, too much has been said by others. To most readers they probably still convey, for a little while, the sense of an absorbing peculiarity, like a friend's matinal fondness for mango juice. But one soon accepts them like any other convention, and once accepted they join the form of life with which the author has linked them permanently in our minds. Beyond that, what does anyone care about their appropriateness? They are uniquely suited, or unsuited, to the person who chose them, just as all poetry is; one can learn nothing more essential about Moore from her syllabic lay-outs than one can about Collins from the English-cucumber-shape of an irregular ode: the important thing about both is that they are products of a given age and climate, streaked by the weather that followed, but undesirable or obsolete only in the dimmest of short runs. Moore herself, in "The Past Is The Present," says this best: "Ecstasy affords / the occasion and expediency determines the form." Yet an audience for whom modernism was never new may pass by her innovations unnoticing and therefore unalarmed; what they will want to have explained is her didactic freedom with aphorisms; for it is this that makes her remote not only from modernist practice but from all that has succeeded it. The causes of her uniqueness are rooted in what can sometimes feel like the land poetry forgot. I mean the Eighteenth Century—one of Moore's cherished haunts, and *not* her idea of the second fall of man, as it was to Pound and Eliot—when critics rashly spoke of "casting one's eye over mankind." Poems could then be praised for their sentiment. By this was generally meant the perfect utterance of a common feeling which no one could know was common until the poet made it so. Apart from poetry governed by the most relentless logical structure, sentiments might easily serve the purpose of classical sententiae: they were simply the best means by which the performer-with-words could recommend himself to the trust of his listeners. Moore's poems abound in wise feelings, which she often appears to set in place with an air of having left room for something of that sort, in case it should ask for admission. The reader who wonders at her daring must remember that among the writers she most admired were Pope, Johnson, Blake—and Shaw, a latecomer not at all strange to this company. She would have agreed with everyone who pointed out that a poem cannot be all poetry: only, she would have added, we ought in that case to change our definition of poetry. She did it more by example than precept, with "the physiognomy of conduct must not reveal the skeleton," and "Denunciations do not affect / the culprit; nor blows, but it / is torture to him not to be spoken to"; with "why dissect destiny with instruments / more highly specialized than components of destiny itself?" and "He can talk but insolently says nothing. What of it? / When one is frank, one's very presence is a compliment" and "The passion for setting people right is in itself an afflictive disease. / Distaste which takes no credit to itself is best."

Statements like these may look planted. But how different are they from those others, obviously at home in one place, which have a hardy existence on almost any soil? One does not need to know the title of the poem, "People's Surroundings," or the topic for discussion, the flats of Utah and Texas, to appreciate Moore's qualified love of "those cool sirs with the explicit sensory apparatus of common sense, / who know the exact distance between two points as the crow flies." In "Elephants," the relevant context can seem almost a pettiness to recall, after she speaks of one creature in particular as "too wise / to mourn—a life prisoner but reconciled." Again, how different are these in turn from the many celebrated passages of "straight" description, in which animal traits, refigured as man-mores, are esteemed as tokens of character and then of virtue?

> Make hay; keep
> the shop; I have one sheep; were a less
> limber animal's mottoes. This one
> finds sticks for the swan's-down-dress
> of his child to rest upon and would
> not know Gretel from Hänsel.
> As impassioned Handel—
>
> meant for a lawyer and a masculine German domestic
> career—clandestinely studied the harpsichord
> and never was known to have fallen in love,
> the unconfiding frigate-bird hides
> in the height and in the majestic
> display of his art. He glides

a hundred feet or quivers about
as charred paper behaves—full
of feints; and an eagle

of vigilance.

The final phrase, tucked into a new stanza, nicely conceals its satisfaction at having found a witty way of obliging man to serve as a middle man—nothing but a German domestic could translate the eagle into a language the pelican understands: this done, the poem is done with Germany, Handel, and harpsichords. The perception starts from and returns to its formative sayings. In the meantime it has made havoc of our pedagogic aids, which read, in a march of progress, "From Abstract to Concrete" of "From General to Particular."

As a composer of words Moore's greatest affinities are with Francis Bacon, and the Baconian essay or prose-amble may be the least misleading analogy for one of her poems. To be curt, undeviating, end-stopped wherever a thought might enter, but at the same time vivid, striking, inventive in the highest degree conscionable, is the ideal of both writers. Like Bacon a despiser of ornament, Moore rejects with equal vehemence the aims of bringing conceit for a matter or matter for a conceit. She will frame no description that has any hint of the superlative, unless she can first set in the middle of it a skeptical gargoyle at least six syllables long: "Rare, unscent- / ed, prov- ident- / ly hot, too sweet, inconsistent flower bed!" She refuses to claim the literary exemption from syllogisms, dependent clauses, subordinate conjunctions, and everything that smacks of the uncraftily sheltered: she will submit with the worst of us, and find her poetry there besides. Bacon's untheatrical rigor would have found nothing wanting in her resolve to be literal, and for range of style he leaves her plenty. "Nature is often hidden; sometimes overcome; seldom extinguished," is a sentence one can imagine her writing, or quoting, as easily as "It is good to commit the beginnings of all great actions to Argos with his hundred eyes, and the ends to Briareus with his hundred hands; first to watch, and then to speed."

But Bacon's essays sometimes trail off in QED's, whereas Moore was born to the stroke they call in tennis *a concluder*. An extraordinary number of her endings are extraordinarily beautiful. In "The Student," "Sojourn in the Whale," "The Hero," the first section of "The Jerboa," she lifts the errant thing to its resting seat, with a parental touch so quick and encircling that we come to rely on her in every playground, including Eden. Nor does she bring a particle of pomp to occasions that need a different sort of authority: "Spenser's Ireland" and "To a Steam Roller" are famous because they close with famous jokes. Yet above all these are the endings carried out in perfect earnest. First, "Elephants," which has warned us hardship makes the soldier, teachableness the philosopher, and then turns to Socrates, who

> prudently testing the suspicious thing, knew
> the wisest is he who's not sure that he knows.
> Who rides on a tiger can never dismount;
> asleep on an elephant, that is repose.

These lines once had and still deserve for company, the last of another elephant-poem, "Melanchthon," with their less reconciled note: "Will / depth be depth, thick skin be thick, to one who can see no / beautiful element of unreason under it?" [*Collected Poems*, 1951]. However, Moore never outdid the description of man in "The Pangolin"—bringing him by chance to the fore ("To explain grace requires a curious hand"), keeping him there till he changed everything—and this she left standing.

> Consistent with the
> formula—warm blood, no gills, two pairs of hands and a few
> hairs—that
> is a mammal; there he sits in his own habitat,
> serge-clad, strong-shod. The prey of fear, he, always
> curtailed, extinguished, thwarted by the dusk, work
> partly done,
> says to the alternating blaze,
> "Again the sun!
> anew each day; and new and new and new,
> that comes into and steadies my soul."

Felicities which here sound accidental the whole poem makes essential: man "curtailed," for instance, which takes us back to the pangolin "strongly intailed," a pun encouraging to all who if they pursue symbolic logic feel that they must do it on four legs.

In a memorable criticism, Kenneth Burke conceived of Moore's "objectivist idiom" as fostering "an appraisal or judgment of many things in and for themselves. They would be encouraged to disclose their traits, not simply that they might exist through the vicarage of words, but that they might reveal their properties as workmanship (workmanship being a trait in which the ethical and the esthetic are one)." Only the first part of this seems to me false. It brings her too much into line with Williams, whose work vaguely resembles hers in matters of the surface, but whose brittler temperament had much to do with his interest in programs like objectivism. Pound, who usually comes next in the effort to triangulate her, is just as wrong for comparison, in spite of their mutual loyalty. Irony like Pound's, of the nervous modern sort, which regards its object from an unsteady point of view but with an advanced degree of scorn, was never part of her armor or weaponry, and she could have written "Mauberley" without the quotation marks. Her intellectual virtues came from the enlightenment and protestantism; from the start, she had the concerns of a genuine moralist, as well as the ambition to be one; and she knew that the gesture of humility was to ask forgiveness from enemies rather than friends. These things helped to make "In Distrust of Merits" a better poem than "Pull Down Thy Vanity."

Of all her contemporaries, the Stevens of *Harmonium* and the early Eliot, who also called his work "observations," seem closest to the spirit of her poetry. In one appreciation of Eliot she mentions "certain qualities" that he shares with Stevens—qualities she supposed would be sufficiently plain to her readers, though they were not so to the authors themselves—"reticent candor and emphasis by understatement" being the two she cares for most. Some lines from "La Figlia che Piange" and "Peter Quince at the Clavier" are quoted as proof: a juxtaposition both strange and right, which it took Moore to imagine. And with those poems in view, one can understand how far she does belong to her generation after all, the generation of "Prufrock," "Le Monocle de Mon Oncle," and "Marriage." Eliot was alluding to their shared enterprise when in a letter to Moore he thanked her for writing poems that forced him to consider each word. Revolutions in taste cannot give us better monuments; but they may force us to work at the new ones slowly. Moore knew what she had done and what she had made possible, and nothing could be more emphatic than the reticence with which she told us so: "Know that it will be there when it says, / 'I shall be there when the wave has gone by.' "

BONNIE COSTELLO

Marianne Moore and Elizabeth Bishop: Friendship and Influence

Marianne Moore and Elizabeth Bishop claimed not to understand the critical inclination to compare them in reviews and articles, and on many occasions dismissed anything more than juvenile and superficial resemblances. Reporting one such conversation with a critic, Moore wrote to Bishop (June 21, 1959):

> You have sometimes asked what I thought, Elizabeth; but even if you ever took my advice, did you ever get to sound like me? or I like you? You sound like Lope de Vega and I sound like Jacob Abbot or Peter Rabbit.

Such remarks ought to be fair warning against elaborate claims of influence. Nevertheless, this was one of the most abiding and significant literary friendships in either woman's career, so that the nature and evolution of that friendship should be of interest to readers of their poetry.

As women and as writers, Moore and Bishop were kindred spirits. But they complemented as much as mirrored each other in their friendship. The Protestant poet of manners and morals, Moore, and the skeptic poet of mysteries, Bishop, approached life and language from separate vantage points, but their enduring friendship centered in the intersection of their angles of vision.

It is tempting to read their relationship within a mother/daughter paradigm. Twenty-two years older than Bishop, unmarried and childless, Moore

From *Twentieth Century Literature* 30, nos. 2/3 (Summer/Fall 1984).

may have found in her young friend an object of maternal affection and concern. Such attention was certainly missing in Bishop's life. Her father died when she was eight months old. Her mother became permanently insane in 1916, when Bishop was seven, and died in 1934, the same year she met Moore. Moore's parental and Bishop's filial attitudes show themselves most often in the letters of the first ten years, later letters demonstrating a growing mutuality, although with continued deference on Bishop's part. But neither poet thought of their relationship in this way. Though fully self-conscious about the obstacles confronting women artists, they did not think of their lives or their art in specifically feminist terms. We may, retrospectively, recognize their aesthetic or personal choices as determined by an inherent feminism, but we should also recognize how multi-faceted their common interests were, addressed to both wider and more specific issues than the experience of women in patriarchal society. The category of mentor and protégée makes a better fit. Moore schooled Bishop in the practice of poetry, not in a visionary stance or a code for living.

Still, art and life, aesthetics and morality, are deeply linked for both poets. If the nouns of family life (mother, daughter, sister, etc.) do not quite fit, the verbs still do, not the oedipal verb "struggle" which dominates our Bloomian notion of literary influence, but the centrally female verb "nurture." Indeed, when the young Bishop made Moore the present of a paper nautilus shell, Moore's gift in return was a poem about mother love and its relationship to writing. While the poem most directly figures an artist's creative gesture (perhaps complimenting Bishop for her care and devotion as a writer), it might also stand for the relation between mentor and protégée.

The Paper Nautilus

For authorities whose hopes
are shaped by mercenaries?
Writers entrapped by
teatime fame and by
commuters' comforts? Not for these
the paper nautilus
constructs her thin glass shell.

Giving her perishable
souvenir of hope, a dull
white outside and smooth-
edged inner surface

glossy as the sea, the watchful
  maker of it guards it
  day and night; she scarcely

  eats until the eggs are hatched.
Buried eight-fold in her eight
  arms, for she is in
  a sense a devil-
fish, her glass ram's-horn-cradled freight
  is hid but is not crushed;
  as Hercules, bitten

  by a crab loyal to the hydra,
was hindered to succeed,
  the intensively
  watched eggs coming from
the shell free it when they are freed—
  leaving its wasp-nest flaws
  of white on white, and close-

  laid Ionic chiton-folds
like the lines in the mane of
  a Parthenon horse,
  round which the arms had
wound themselves as if they knew love
  is the only fortress
  strong enough to trust to.

[All lines quoted from Marianne Moore's poetry are taken from *The Complete Poems* (New York: Viking, 1981).]

The poem describes a careful balance between firmness and gentleness by which the nautilus nurtures her eggs. She is indeed a strong figure, compared to Hercules, to a Parthenon horse and ram's horn, but also a delicate figure. Like the wasp nest she combines the Greek qualities of fortitude and refinement. Her power of love and support surpasses but encompasses the power of force. And this love is not possessive or narcissistic, it is "hindered to succeed" for "the intensively watched eggs coming from the shell free it when they are freed." That mutual freedom meant an acknowledgment of and respect for difference. We see that difference most clearly from the point of view of Bishop's emerging poetic identity.

The partnership between Moore and Bishop is in part that between the gentlewoman and the seeker. I mean no value judgment here, for the gentlewoman looks after the good and the beautiful (or the good as the beautiful) while the seeker looks after the true. Of course in the Platonic realm these three are one, and even in this less perfect realm they often overlap. But each poet defined a point of view in this triadic scheme. Moore approached vision from the point of view of values, Bishop approached values from the point of view of vision, and these points of view carried implicit priorities that sometimes required choice. Our predilection in this doubting age is naturally for the poetry of the seeker, but Bishop was deeply attracted to the high civility, and more profoundly the metamorphic power, of Moore's charmed imagination. Remembering the gentle and gentile qualities of Moore's mind, Bishop quotes Hopkins' letter to Robert Bridges about the ideal of the "gentleman":

> "to be a gentleman is but on the brim of morals and rather a thing of manners than morals properly. . . . [a] chastity of mind which seems to lie at the very heart and be the parent of all good, the seeing at once what is best, and holding to that, and not allowing anything else whatever to be even heard pleading to the contrary."

For Hopkins, it should be noted, where there arises a choice between artist and gentleman the artist must be despised. In her essay "Efforts of Affection," from which this quotation is taken, Bishop presents an amused but also deeply affectionate and admiring portrait of her friend, summed up with these alternative epithets: "manners and morals; manners *as* morals? Or is it morals *as* manners?" Finally, it does not matter. Moore, as Bishop describes her, is a figure both mannered—eccentric, flirtatious, self-conscious—and mannerly: decorous, tasteful, virtuous in the deepest sense, a figure committed undividedly to civilized values. In Moore, surfaces and styles of behavior are the outward shows of inner attitudes. Manners express the rock foundation of an ethical system, and aesthetics are rooted to morality. Moore's evaluative turn of mind pervades every aspect of experience, from social etiquette to modern warfare. The poetic gestures which accompany this preoccupation are those of praise, condemnation, selection, purification, transformation. She insists on these attitudes at a cost, of course, the cost of comprehensive vision. Moore's is by no means a naive vision, but she chooses not to depict (only to condemn) what is infelicitous, tragic, evil in the world. Her real toads are never repulsive. Bishop's priority of feeling over precept, of psychic authenticity over artistic transformation, of mystery and meaning over manners and morals, causes her to make a different set of poetic gestures, those of inquiry, evocation, elegy, exposure, penetration. If Moore is the poet of ethics and aesthetics, Bishop is the poet of epistemology and ontology, asking what we can know and who we are rather than what we should do and what we should admire or condemn.

Bishop learned a great deal more from her mentor than either recognized. Their friendship nurtured certain habits of mind (particularly of careful observation), certain techniques and standards (of accuracy, decorum, musical precision). But from their base of mutual interests and traditions she evolved a voice and style of her own, putting inherited instruments to use in mapping her distinctive world and defining her own aesthetic priorities. Bishop never ceased to look up to Moore, as a poet of remarkable skill and discipline, whose great confidence in the metamorphic powers of art allowed her to sustain a lively moral vision in a grim world. Bishop's own darker vision took her repeatedly away from sustaining orders, into a receding, at once cherished and ominous prospect.

Answering Anne Stevenson and perhaps qualifying an earlier warning against superficial comparisons with Moore, Bishop wrote in 1963:

> By all means say I'm a friend of Marianne's! I met her in 1934 through the college Librarian, an old friend of hers, and it was one of the greatest pieces of good fortune in my life!

This was the beginning of a literary and personal relationship which was to last until Moore's death in 1972. Usually terrified of famous people, Bishop recalled (in a letter to Anne Stevenson dated March 6, 1964) the ease she felt in getting to know Moore:

> If I really like someone well enough I don't get them [terrors]—Marianne, for example—the one "celebrity" I have ever deliberately tried to meet in my life.—We got along immediately.

Among other things, she said, she was attracted to Moore's democratic sense of people and things, and to her "wit." "Perhaps I need such people to cheer me up," she wrote to Anne Stevenson (January 8, 1964). Moore represented not only the successful career, but the successful outlook—a charmed way of being in the world.

In addition to providing serious attention to each other's work, they shared friends, concern for each other's health, success and objects, events, places. Letter after letter indulges in the mutual pleasure of tracing particulars. The subject might be Bishop's cat Minnow, sights at a circus, an art exhibition, a postcard, a feather, a shell. Their bond was based in a mutual enchantment with the play of words and things. The relationship had a practical side as well, for Moore went out of her way to help Bishop acquire grants and find publishers for her work (she arranged for her first publication in book form, in the anthology *Trial Balances* in 1935). She even typed out a few of her poems for her. In return she derived vicarious enjoyment from watching the young poet develop, from hearing about her many travels and receiving regular "tributes" from exotic places. When Bishop's self-confidence began to lag, Moore as nurturing parent would bolster her. On August 21, 1936, two years after Bishop graduated from college she wrote to Moore:

> I cannot, cannot decide what to do—I am even considering studying medicine or bio-chemistry, and have procured all sorts of catalogues, etc. I feel that I have given myself more than a fair trial, and the accomplishment has been nothing at all.

Moore replied on August 28, 1936, recalling Bishop to her natural vocation:

> What you say about studying medicine does not disturb me at all; for interesting as medicine is, I feel you would not be able to give up writing, with the ability for it that you have; but it does disturb me that you should have the *feeling* that it might be well to give it up. To have produced what you have—either verse or prose is enviable, and you certainly would not suppose that such method as goes wiith a precise and proportioning ear, is "contemporary" or usual.

Even as late as 1942 Bishop still compared her meager production with that of Moore and contemporaries, and Moore offered consoling advice (May 11, 1942):

> Don't let writing be a threat . . . it is unjust to probity to reproach oneself for lagging, when often premature and dogged struggle spoil one's ability to treat the material right at a maturer and more favorable time.

Bishop never lost the sense of being inadequate to her vocation and to Moore's example, but at the same time that example encouraged her in the worth of her own pursuits. Above all, Moore was among the first to recognize and insist that Bishop had a calling.

Bishop felt Moore's influence strongly for a long time. Sending a poem on September 15, 1936, she apologizes for "an extremely impolite, if true, display of your 'influence.' " A week later, she speaks of "your effect in one's interpretation of other poetry." A few months after this (January 5, 1937), she apologizes for having unconsciously "stolen something from 'The Frigate Pelican' " for her story "The Sea and Its Shore." She was so impressed in 1942 by Moore's essay "Humility, Concentration and Gusto" that, she said, she hummed the title all day. And years later (June 5, 1956) its impression seems to have remained: "I was interviewed by a journalist friend for a literary newspaper here, and imitating you, I'm afraid, I said *I* liked three things in poetry: Spontaneity, Accuracy, and Mystery." This last imitation of Moore is perhaps the most revealing, for while the two aphorisms look alike, they suggest important differences in emphasis. Both poets admire "accuracy" (indeed Moore often praised Bishop for her accuracy), but Moore's sense of accuracy seems more classical—located in technique, moral posture and rhetoric, in the good and the beautiful more than in the visionary true. Spontaneity and Mystery were certainly important to Moore, but they do not top her list. They tend to reflect the Romantic priorities of the seeker, placing less emphasis on skill and performance, more on imaginative experience and personal reflection.

Moore's advice and praise were most often specific to individual fastidiousness of the gentlewoman. Her concern for "neatness of finish" dominates her detailed comments on poem after poem, which point out infelicities of diction, awkward phrases, redundancies. Of "A Miracle for Breakfast," for instance, she writes (December 22, 1936): "in stanza 2, line 2, of the poem, I resist 'bitterly' and 'very' in 'very hot' in line 3; and 'gallons of' in 4th line from the end." Of "Large Bad Picture" she writes (November 16, 1943): "The *thought* in the sight of the aquatic animal is just what is needed; and in prose, 'sighing' seems high art. But here it seems not so expert as the rest? Perhaps it is the rhyme, 'air,' that seems a little facile." Moore felt especially strongly about the advantages of economy and understatement in art, attacking intensifiers—very, all, usually—mercilously. "Perhaps you would let me omit some words, the habit having fastened on me irremediably" (March 12, 1937). Moore's mother also read most of Bishop's early work, and many of the suggestions, especially ommissions of distasteful explicitness, were, Moore admitted, "contributed." Of "The Sea and Its Shore" she wrote (December 17, 1936): "Mother is a rabid advocate of the power of suggestion versus statement and wishes you need not say just at the end that he was drunk." Moore stressed the importance of sound as scintillating surface in poetry, and regularly offered suggestions on this aspect of Bishop's work, such as her comment on the sestina "A Miracle for Breakfast" (December 22, 1936): "although I tremble to say so, since you confirm the words more than once, are not 'crumb' and 'sun' almost too nearly the same sound even as a phrase of Chinese chromatics?" Of a Bishop story she writes on December 17, 1936: "The tempo and fastidious avoidance of night-riding rush makes me very apprehensive of suggested dispatch at certain points, but with a grave pace as with staccato effects, one really heightens the effect, I think, by concealed contrasts?" We see in these details a larger concern for refinement of surface, economy of style, precision of word choice as the aesthetic expressions of modesty, restraint, courtesy, judiciousness. In these instances Moore's suggestions did not challenge alternative aesthetic values. Later on, Bishop's voice developed, her own priorities of representational and experiential truth, and of inclusive vision (pain as well as pleasure addressed) would cause her to pass over some of Moore's suggestions.

Besides these matters of craft a strong sense of literary propriety (or perhaps even censorship, to use a stronger term) often determined Moore's responses. To the poet of manners and morals certain words and phrases simply did not belong in poems. After a number of suggestions about Bishop's war poem "Roosters," which Moore copied out with corrections, she writes of her objection to Bishop's use of the phrase "water closet" (October 16, 1940):

> Regarding the water-closet, Dylan Thomas, W. C. Williams, E. E. Cummings, and others feel that they are avoiding a duty if they balk at anything like unprudishness, but I say to them "I can't care about all things equally, I have a major effect to produce, and the heroisms of abstinence are as great as the heroisms of courage, and so are the rewards." I think it is to your credit, Elizabeth, that when I say you are not to say, "water-closet," you go on saying it a little (like Donald in National Velvet), and it is calculated to make me wonder if I haven't mistaken a cosmetic patch for a touch of lamp-black, but I think not. The trouble is, people are not depersonalized enough to accept the picture rather than the thought. . . . I acclaimed "the mermaid's pap" in Christopher [Smart] but few of us, it seems to me, are fundamentally rude enough to enrich our work in such ways without cost. If I tell Mother there is a feather on her dress and she says, "On my back?" I am likely to say, "No. On your rump," alluding to Cowper's hare that "swung his rump around." But in my work, I daren't risk saying, "My mother had a feather on her rump."

When specific points of revision came packaged with such firm precepts and values, they must have been very hard to resist. But perhaps Moore intended them to be resisted to some extent. By confronting Bishop with aesthetic and moral principles she forced the young poet to consider her own artistic decisions on a larger scale. Such necessary defenses played a crucial part in Bishop's development, making her more self-conscious about her artistic intentions.

> What I'm about to say, I'm afraid, will sound like ELIZABETH KNOWS BEST. . . . However, I *have* changed to small initial letters! and I have made several other of your corrections and suggestions. . . . But I can't seem to bring myself to give up the set form, which I'm afraid you think fills the poem with redundancies, etc. I feel that the rather rattletrap rhythm is appropriate—maybe I can explain it.
>
> I cherish my "water-closet" and the other sordidities because I want to emphasize the essential baseness of militarism. In the first part I was thinking of Key West, and also of those aerial views of dismal little towns in Finland & Norway, when the Germans took over, and their atmosphere of poverty. That's why, although I see what *you* mean, I want to keep "tin rooster" instead of "gold," and not to use "fastidious beds." And for the same reason I want to keep as the title the rather contemptuous word ROOSTERS rather than the more classical COCK; and I want to repeat the "gun-metal" (I also had in mind the violent roosters Picasso did in connection with his GUERNICA picture). . . .
>
> It has been so hard to decide what to do, and I know that aesthetically you are quite right, but I can't bring myself to sacrifice what (I think) is a very important "violence" of tone—which I feel to be helped by what *you* must feel to be just a bad case of the *threes*. It makes me feel like a wonderful Klee picture I saw at his show the other day, "The Man of Confusion." I wonder if you could be mesmerized across the bridge to see it again with me?

I have quoted the letter at length to indicate the detail of Moore's suggestions, and also Bishop's strong need to find reasons for every suggestion she turned down. Clearly her emerging aesthetic did not hold "neatness of finish" so high as naturalness and spontaneity of effect and did not always hold aesthetic standards above mimetic ones. Moore's magnificent surfaces and cerebral, civilized manner on the page contrast early with Bishop's rhetorical simplicity and deliberate roughness or flatness within the artistic frame. For Bishop, the language of poetry is justified by its faithfulness to the texture of experience rather than to an ideal of taste. (We may be amused by Moore's suggestion of the title "Cocks" as more classical than Roosters. Moore's imagination clearly did not entertain vulgar connotations.)

For Moore, ecstacy stimulated art, expediency determined its forms. Bishop's art emerged from a more troubled vision and its forms as well are sometimes self-consciously inexpedient. I do not want to suggest, however, that Bishop's poetics gave license to ugliness or formlessness as truer to reality. The claims of art to organize, if not ameliorate, experience were strong for Bishop (if not as strong as in Moore). Finally, too, the lesson of restraint learned from Moore served her well in finding an art that intensified truth under the pressure of artistic control.

For Moore, imaginative orders possess something like the power of salvation, however individual. Bishop was no less attracted to form, but to her aesthetic order was a means of heightening the sense of tragedy. In a letter to Anne Stevenson (March 23, 1964) she wrote:

> the *real* expression of tragedy, or just horror and pathos, lies exactly in man's ability to construct, to use form. The exquisite form of a tubercular Mozart, say, is more profoundly moving than any wild electronic wail and tells more about the famous "human condition."

The classicist upholds the standard of instruction as high as that of beauty; *dolce*, to cite Horace, must have its *utile*.

Moore was most persuasive, and most influential, when she questioned the purposiveness of Bishop's art and the depth of its moral intentions. Bishop did not always meet her standard of usefulness and instruction. In a letter of March 7, 1937, Moore writes:

> I enclose the suggestions I spoke of, about THE LABORS OF HANNIBAL. Your things have the insidiousness of creativeness, in that the after impression is stronger than the impression while reading, but you are menaced by the goodness of your mechanics. One should, of course, have the feeling, this is ingeniously contrived; but a thing should make one feel after reading it, that one's life has been altered or added to. When I set out to find fault with you, there are so many excellences in your mechanics that I seem to be commending you instead, and I wish to say, above all, that I am sure good treatment is a handicap unless along with it, significant values come out with an essential baldness. I hope the *un*essential baldness of this attack will not make it seem that I am against minutiae.

Such a letter could not but deeply affect a young poet. Another letter a year later reinforced the point and showed Moore's confidence in the possibility of holding and expressing fundamental beliefs, especially Christian ones (May 1, 1938):

> I feel that although large-scale "substance" runs the risk of inconsequence through aesthetic impotence—to whom treatment really *is* substance—I can't help wishing you would sometimes in some way, risk some unprotected profundity of experience, some characteristic private defiance of the significantly detestable. Continuously fascinated as I am by the creativeness and uniqueness of these assemblings of yours—which are really poems—I feel a responsibility against anything that might threaten you; yet fear to admit such anxiety, lest I influence you away from an essential necessity or particular strength. The golden eggs can't be dealt with theoretically, by presumptuous mass salvation formulae. But I do feel that tentativeness and interiorizing are your danger as well as your strength. . . .
>
> The wrought excellence and infectious continuity of your thinkings—the abashingly as I said above—formidable demureness, disgust me with my own bald performances, and what I have said sounds preceptorial but such clumsiness perhaps is better than the conscientious timidity which kept me from writing.

Bishop responded that she had "some severe meditations on the theme of criticism you imply so gently." But finally she is too skeptical a poet to offer wisdom in the form of a creed. Perhaps Moore's neoclassical preference for sententiae over obstinate questionings, of maxim over negative capability, blinded her from the searching vision of Bishop's descriptions. And Moore's Protestant faith provided her with certainties to which Bishop did not have access. Bishop worried a great deal throughout her career about being a "precious" poet, and did strive increasingly in her verse and fiction for such "profundity of experience." A distinct deepening occurs after 1938, most apparent in her last volume, *Geography III*, but it is *not* the deepening of moral guidelines, rather of moral inquiry. Affection for objects continues to generate the major values in her poetry, though she had a great deal of doubt about this method. In a letter to Moore (September 11, 1940), she describes this method:

> I have written a half-dozen *phrases* that I can still bear to re-read without too much embarrassment. But I have that continuous

> uncomfortable feeling of "things" in the head, like icebergs or rocks or awkwardly-shaped pieces of furniture—it's as if all the nouns were there but the verbs were lacking—if you know what I mean. And I can't help having the theory that if they are joggled around hard enough and long enough some kind of electricity will occur, just by friction, that will arrange everything.

Moore tended to balance her gyroscopic observations on a firm moral base, secured in epigram, however complex or paradoxical. Her wisdom is instructive and evaluative. She offers precepts to live by. Bishop's tendency, however, was to move toward the moral condition of uncertainty and mystery, the moral atmosphere of loss, temporality, memory and desire, the questions we live by.

Nurture requires support as much as instruction. Moore's discerning praise, which affirmed talent even where it differed from her own, may have kept Bishop writing even when self-doubt inflicted its harshest judgments. Letters like the following would have affected how Bishop viewed her own accomplishments (September 20, 1936):

> The poems are so fine, and dart-proof in every way,—especially THE WEED and PARIS, 7 AM—that they shiver my impulsive offers of helpfulness. This exteriorizing of the interior, and the aliveness all through, it seems to me are the essential sincerity that unsatisfactory surrealism struggles toward. Yet the sobriety and weight and impact of the past are also there. The great amount of care, the reach of the imagination, and the pleasure conveyed, make it hard for me not to say a great deal; but I fear to make suggestions lest I hamper you.

In reviews Moore recognizes that Bishop's strengths are tied to what in her own verse would be weaknesses. Poetry should, she wrote in one review, "pierce you to the marrow without revolting you," and we feel that while Bishop may have transgressed that border more often than her mentor liked, Moore knew that Bishop's aesthetic rested in exploring that border.

Reviewing Bishop's *North and South*, Randall Jarrell immediately perceived its indebtedness to Moore's work. And while his insights may not have pleased either poet, they are difficult to refute:

> When you read Miss Bishop's "Florida," a poem whose first sentence begins, "The state with the prettiest name," and whose last sentence begins, "The alligator who has five distinct calls: friendliness, love, mating, war, and a warning" you don't need to be

> told that the poetry of Marianne Moore was, in the beginning, an appropriately selected foundation for Miss Bishop's work.

Jarrell was pointing to their practice of description, of course, their observationists' capacity for fact, which far exceeded imagism in pursuing the path of the particular. Robert Lowell similarly matched their "elaborate descriptive technique" in his review of *North and South.* Relentless accuracy was not merely a slogan for these poets. In her 1948 essay on Moore, "As We Like It," Bishop celebrated her friend's "delight of imitation," the same quality Moore had earlier praised in Bishop's work. "As far as I know, Miss Marianne Moore is The World's Greatest Living Observer." Claiming that Moore had bettered Hopkins in "feats of description," she paid her highest compliment, for Hopkins was Bishop's literary father. Accurate description was no by-product or bonus of expression but a primary literary quality for Bishop, accompanied by a "ritualistic solemnity" even in light or ironic poems. Such solemnity (undiminished by other tones) characterizes many of her own descriptions, as this one from "At the Fishhouses": "All is silver: the heavy surface of the sea, / swelling slowly as if considering spilling over." [All lines quoted from Elizabeth Bishop's poetry are taken from *The Complete Poems 1927–1979* (New York: Farrar, Straus and Giroux, 1983).] Moore, Bishop argues in "As We Like It," seems "entirely to give herself up to the object under contemplation, to feel in all sincerity how it is to be *it*," a self-forgetfulness she would later admire in Darwin. Intention for these poets should not obscure the surface of things. Bishop sensed in Moore a "compulsion to imitation," an obsessive search for the particular beyond the support of the general or ideal. In "Questions of Travel" she examined the same compulsion in herself and concluded with a list of irresistible details which begins:

> But surely it would have been a pity
> not to have seen the trees along this road,
> really exaggerated in their beauty,
> not to have seen them gesturing
> like noble pantomimists, robed in pink.

She "goes on" just as Moore often does, if with less iridescent display.

But a comparison of their descriptive acts defines the difference between the poetry of manners and morals, on the one hand, and that of moods and mysteries on the other. Moore continually attaches value to fact, where Bishop attaches yearning, fear, uncertainty. Moore celebrates the jerboa, for instance, for its harmony of form and function in contrast to the waste of

Pharoah's Egypt. Her eye clings to the desert rat's surfaces, finding in them ideals of economy and modesty that become aesthetic standards:

> it turns its bird head—
> the nap directed
> neatly back and blending
> with the ear which reiterates the slimness
> of the body. . . .
>
> . . . It
> honors the sand by assuming its color;
> closed upper paws seeming one with the fur
> in its flight from a danger.

Bishop's eye is more likely to focus on loss, on traces of decay, on mysterious resemblances to the human which the mind cannot dissect. In "Florida," for instance, the poem Jarrell singles out for its Moorish qualities, we find a passage Moore would not have written:

> Enormous turtles, helpless and mild,
> die and leave their barnacled shells on the beaches,
> and their large white skulls with round eye-sockets
> twice the size of a man's.

Here is tragic rather than exemplary beauty. And while the passage exudes the deepest moral sadness, it affirms no particular set of values, offers no "moral." As Moore herself recognized in reviewing Bishop, it is the poetry of knowledge but not of instruction: "at last we have someone who knows, who is not didactic."

The art of personification, scorned by most modernists, is revived by these two observationists. They modernize the technique by making it an art of reciprocity rather than an imposition on things. "There are morals aplenty in animal life," Bishop writes in "As We Like It," "but they have to be studied out by devotedly and minutely observing the animal, not by regarding the deer as a man imprisoned in a 'leathern coat.' " Moore's poetry, she felt, found a balance of self and other. "With all its inseparable combinations of the formally fabulous with the factual, and the artificial with the perfectly natural, her animal poetry seduces us to dream of some realm of reciprocity, a true *lingua unicornis*." Moore's Plumet Basilisk, Pangolin, Jerboa, Frigate Pelican; Bishop's Man-Moth, Fish, Rooster, Sandpiper, Giant Toad, Strayed Crab, Giant Snail, Hanging Mouse, are only a few examples of such reciprocity at work. A regard for the otherness of what the imagination fixes on means ultimately a willingness, as Moore wrote, to "relinquish what one would keep." Moore's Plumet Basilisk dives into water and his sudden splash "Marks his temporary loss." While "victory filled up the little rented boat" Bishop must "let the fish go."

For both poets personification was as much a way of getting outside the limits of the human perspective as of imposing a human point of view, though ultimately the aim may be to find themselves anew. Bishop takes this technique farthest, locating her interest not as Moore does on the outsides of things, on their behavioral characteristics of habit and coloring, but on the inner lives of creatures. She takes on a voice of things as well as a voice for things. Moore celebrates elephants for the morals they exemplify, but hesitates to ascribe intention to them or go beyond what fact will verify. They are "a pilgrims' / pattern of revery not revenge."

> With trunk tucked up compactly—the elephant's
> sign of defeat—he resisted, but is the child
>
> of reason now. His straight trunk seems to say: when
> what we hoped for came to nothing, we revived.

Moore marks the difference between fact and association. They *seem* to say, they offer a pattern for the pilgrim. Bishop's sandpiper has a more identifiable inner life:

> The roaring alongside he takes for granted,
> and that every so often the world is bound to shake.
> He runs, he runs to the south, finical, awkward,
> in a state of controlled panic, a student of Blake.

Bishop's animals represent human fallibility as often as the possibilities for heroism. She imagines, in fact, how the world would look to us did we share the sandpiper's point of view, as figuratively we do. Yet the poem insists on particularity, and ends much as a Moore poem might, in a list of facts: "The millions of grains are black, white, tan, and gray, / mixed with quartz grains, rose and amethyst." We would see this ourselves had we the sandpiper's scale of vision. "To a Snail" and "The Man-Moth" offer a sharper contrast in their use of personification. Moore's snail, a figure for her aesthetic predilections, suggests by his appearances a "principle that is hid," but her attention is to the evaluation of surface. A figure for the marriage of manners and morals, aesthetics and ethics, he demonstrates that "contractility is a virtue as modesty is a virtue." Bishop's imaginary "man-moth," equally self-reflective, works from the inside out, exposing the secret side of the human spirit.

While Jarrell was one of the first to remark on Bishop's indebtedness to Moore, he also recognized such significant distinctions. Bishop, he said is "simpler, milder, less driven into desperate straits or dens of innocence, and taking this century of Polycarp (martyr) more for granted." Jarrell's casual remark locates a profound difference in voice which helps to explain apparently minor differences of aesthetic judgment—word choice, rhythm and phrasing. In Moore, a tone of indictment and superior irony, an inclination to pick and choose, combines with a fundamental optimism about the ties between morality and aesthetics, and about the triumph of the imagination over an imperfect world. Her intricate surfaces and her daunting intelligence give her world a strained redemptiveness. Moore culls usable bits and fragments from the flux of things, to construct a dazzling, highly idiosyncratic and independent reality. Bishop, a disarmed traveler rather than a collector, pursues an elusive image of stability, with less confidence about the self-protective value of art: "Less idiosyncratic, and less magnificent," in Lowell's words, she is also "softer, dreamier, more human and more personal" unlike the armored Moore. A philosophical and moral gloom characterizes her excursive vision. She is more impressed by the mess of life than by its neatness of finish.

These differences emerge in a comparison of Moore's "The Steeple Jack" and Bishop's "Little Exercise," both poems depicting seaside scenes from several perspectives. Both poems suggest danger glimpsed and contained. They both include interpretive metaphor and self-conscious pictorial ordering. And yet Moore, even with her irony, invests much more confidence in her elegant surface than Bishop does in her simple one. The world Moore entertains *is* safe despite its fallibility; Bishop's world is less comfortably balanced, less decorative and less pastoral.

Moore's poem depicts elements dangerous elsewhere but tamed and aestheticized in this holiday world. She describes, to use William Empson's concept of pastoral, a partial world as if it were a whole world. For "exotic serpent life" there is the "diffident little newt," "cats, not cobras, to / keep down rats." Even the storm is part of the local color, a "whirlwind fife-and-drum" which, though it "bends the salt marsh grass" and "disturbs stars in the sky and the / star on the steeple" still evokes pleasure: "it is a privilege to see so / much confusion." There is a certain mockery of this tourist response to flux, but even positive figures in the poem share the view. "Dürer would have seen a reason for living / in a town like this." To him "eight stranded whales" are objects of aesthetic contemplation, not pity. One is secure in one's point of view. Every danger, every negative element is counterbalanced or even dismissed within an overriding pictorialism. Moore does not suggest that this *is* reality, but that it is a possible way of experiencing reality. "Disguised by what / might seem the opposite, the sea- / side flowers and trees are favored by the fog." While Moore admits the place is formed in the eyes of its beholders, she never disparages such aestheticing. Each character might be "part of a novel," and each character finds a "home" in this place. The old puritan town is far from upright, its steeple (based on one in Brooklyn) is "not true," and the steeple jack, dressed in devil's red, looks for all the world like Jonathan Edwards' spider. Nevertheless, he is "placing danger signs by the church / while he is gilding the solid- / pointed star, which on a steeple / stands for hope." Hope and imagination always successfully counterbalance evil in Moore.

While Moore's last word is hope, Bishop's is "disturbed" and an atmosphere of disturbance dominates "Little Exercise." No major hurricanes shake this Florida scene, but a general agitation pervades the poem. Metaphor tends to draw out the latent danger. The storm is "roaming the sky uneasily like a dog looking for a place to sleep in" and the little palm trees are "suddenly revealed / as fistfuls of limp fish-skeletons." The pictorializing is more cinematic, the point of view moving, so that the repeated imperative to "think" does not offer a secure point of view. Neither the reassuring guide nor amused ironist directs our sight. If the storm looks like a stage set from afar, "a series / of small, badly lit battle-scenes," this does not make its effects less real. The last scene is the most telling in this respect.

> Think of someone sleeping in the bottom of a row-boat
> tied to a mangrove root or the pile of a bridge;
> think of him as uninjured, barely disturbed.

The figure in the boat is a kind of surrogate for the reader, who in being asked to "think" of him is asked in a sense of identify with him, but with the weight of superior knowledge. While "someone" sleeps in the boat we remain apprehensive, aware of the dangers just escaped, for his hold is precarious, he is "tied to a mangrove root or the pile of a bridge" and while he is "uninjured" the suggestion of injury lingers, in "barely disturbed." While Moore concludes by restoring balance, by asserting that her town "could not be dangerous" (however ironically she may mean this), Bishop closes in an atmosphere of imbalance. This little exercise has no confident moral; instead, it shakes the confidence implied in an authorial stance.

Bishop's tribute to Moore, "Invitation to Miss Marianne Moore," tell us much about the relationship between these two poets. Moore delighted in the piece and undoubtedly recognized herself in its flourish of detail (August 24, 1948): "Your magic poem—every word a living wonder—with an enfoldment that does not ever go back of itself, and the colors!"

The gesture of invitation rather than challenge or homage is itself significant in relation to an earlier poet, suggesting camaraderie above rivalry. This is also an invocation, an acknowledgment of lack and a call for support. Indeed, Moore becomes a kind of aerial spirit, bringing lightness into a drab world. The poem begins by readying the world for the visit. The ordinary world is metamorphosed in expectation, anticipating a poetic presence:

> Enter: two rivers, gracefully bearing
> countless little pellucid jellies
> in cut-glass epergnes dragging with silver chains.

Moore herself appears oxymoronically as a good witch or necessary angel, at once gracing the world with imaginative glitter and casting a moral eye upon its stains. She as a "slight censorious frown and blue ribbons," wears an austere black cape full "of butterfly wings and bon-mots." Such Mozartian conjunctions of light and dark mirror Moore's aesthetic. Bishop admires her ability to see the world as it is, without being crushed by it, admires her "natural heroism" by which she can hear a higher music and connect the good with the beautiful.

> Mounting the sky with natural heroism,
> above the accidents, above the malignant movies,
> the taxicabs and injustices at large,
> while horns are resounding in your beautiful ears
> that simultaneously listen to
> a soft uninvented music, fit for the musk deer.

Moore's art tames the brute world and raises it out of lassitude: the lions outside the library follow her through the doors to the reading rooms, the grim museums "behave like courteous male bower-birds."

But Bishop seems less confident about what ultimate impact such a "daytime comet" will have on the world. When she offers her invited guest various entertainments, they seem incommensurate with the pleasure of her company:

> We can sit down and weep; we can go shopping,
> or play at a game of constantly being wrong
> with a priceless set of vocabularies,
> or we can bravely deplore, but please
>   please come flying.

Is this Bishop's reminder about the limits of art? The options are not as arbitrary as the list makes them sound. They describe the sadness of the world, its consumerism, but also the pleasure Moore takes in picking and choosing. They describe Moore's relentless accuracy (which to Bishop, as to Stevens, may have a tragic dimension), and they describe Moore's courage.

Bishop manages to be similarly specific, in this apparently whimsical piece, about the techniques she admires in Moore, techniques which facilitate her transformations. The "inaudible abacus" is of course Moore's syllabic method, the "dynasties of negative constructions" those double negatives which render positives and those ironic reversals. Moore's poetry generates something indeed "unnebulous" (not yet obvious), but still celestial. Out of her enchanting presence, Bishop again sees the corrupt world seething underneath compelling surfaces. But her skepticism never dampens her genuine appreciation for Moore's spirit—rather, it heightens the need for it. In a remark she made later to Anne Stevenson (January 8, 1964) we can understand the place of this spirit:

> My outlook is pessimistic. I think we are still barbarians. . . . But I think we should be gay in spite of it, sometimes even giddy, to make life endurable and to keep ourselves "new, tender, quick."

Though more often than not in different parts of the world, the affection of these two women for one another and for art sustained their correspondence until Moore's death. As the older poet's own artistic energy naturally declined with her health, her admiration for the now mature Bishop, and her wish to be reunited with her, grew stronger. Her penultimate letter to Bishop, in shaky handwriting, expresses this need: "Art seems to have desisted? I still want to paint—all the fur on my bushy best paint brush eaten up by a moth. . . . Come back!" (January 3, 1969).

Living such different lives as they did, these women in many ways complemented one another. Bishop seems to have found in Marianne Moore a source of stability, vigorous enchantment, optimism, and dedication to craft. Moore found in Bishop a source of vicarious adventure and mystery, but was also drawn to her personal and artistic courage, and to the promised continuation of many of her own poetic values, in an entirely individual voice. As readers, we are fourtunate in having both poets, the gentlewoman and the seeker, who together preserve for us the good, the true and the beautiful.

JOHN M. SLATIN

"*Advancing Backward in a Circle*": *Moore as (Natural) Historian*

Moore writes in "A Grave" (1921) that "repression is not the most obvious characteristic of the sea," and we may say with equal assurance that imitation "is not the most obvious characteristic" of her work. This is hardly surprising, given the original strength of her "reluctance to be unoriginal"; but just as "repression" is a hidden characteristic of the sea, so a concern with imitation is a latent feature of Moore's work from the beginning of her career, and, as the following brief survey will indicate, it comes closer and closer to the surface as time goes on.

In her first published essay, "The Accented Syllable" (October, 1916), Moore offers implicit justification for her own increasingly sophisticated use of syllabic verse, arguing that it is virtually impossible to establish or maintain "a distinctive tone of voice" in any other medium. Prose is unacceptable because it has no defense against accidental resemblances: "written tones of voice may resemble one another and . . . a distinctive tone of voice employed by one author may resemble that same tone of voice as employed by another author." Rhymed verse, as Moore calls conventional accentual-syllabic verse, is equally unpromising, because in this "case . . . a distinctive tone of voice is dependent on naturalistic effects, and naturalistic effects are so rare in rhyme as almost not to exist." Worst of all, though, is "free verse," which not only tends naturally toward mimesis but actually encourages deliberate imitation: "So far as free verse is concerned," Moore writes, "it is the easiest

---

From *Twentieth Century Literature* 30, nos. 2/3 (Summer/Fall 1984). Originally entitled " 'Advancing Backward in a Circle': Marianne Moore as (Natural) Historian."

thing in the world to create one intonation in the image of another until finally one has assembled a bouquet of vocal exclamation points." Nowhere does she say explicitly that syllabic verse is for her the only satisfactory solution to the problem of distinctiveness; but a careful look at her earlier poems indicates quite clearly that her syllabic patterns give formal expression to what she calls in "Critics and Connoisseurs" (July, 1916) "an attitude of self-defense," enabling her to resist the temptation to do "the easiest thing" by preventing her from "creat[ing] one intonation in the image of another."

The real problem is to prevent *herself* from becoming the mere reflected image of another poet, as we see in the early poem "Blake," which I give in its entirety:

I wonder if you feel as you look at us,
As if you were seeing yourself in a mirror at the end
  of a long corridor—walking frail-ly.
I am sure that we feel as we look at you,
As if we were ambiguous and all but improbable
  Reflections of the sun—shining pale-ly.

[In quoting Moore I have followed the first published text of each poem.]

Blake, as Moore acknowledges in a letter to Pound four years later, is among "the direct influences bearing on [her] work"; here, though, she sees herself as a pale, attenuated image of him, a distant "mirror" or satellite whose poems shine as "ambiguous and all but improbable / Reflections" of his "sun."

Moore often uses words associated with *light* or *the sun* to designate writers to whom she ascribes both literary mastery and the possession of a visionary power; but her response to that light is deeply ambivalent. In a poem called "You Are Like the Realistic Product of an Idealistic Search for Gold at the Foot of the Rainbow" (later re-titled "To a Chameleon"), published in May, 1916, she praises the chameleon for its ability to conceal itself by absorbing light. But it is not always desirable to "snap the spectrum up for food" as the chameleon does; a poem originally drafted in 1915 and published in 1924 presents the sun as a piercing force to be resisted by "An Egyptian Pulled Glass Bottle in the Shape of a Fish," and here she celebrates "that / spectacular and nimble animal the fish, / whose scales turn aside the sun's sword with their polish."

Before 1921, it is far more common to find her trying actively to resist penetration by the light than to find her seeking, chameleon-like, to absorb it. In "Black Earth" (April, 1918), the poet "inhabit[s]" an "elephant skin. . . . fibred over like the shell of / The coco-nut, [a] piece of black glass through which no light // Can filter." Her pride in her imperviousness is matched by a somewhat envious scorn for the human "Tree trunk without / Roots," whom she images as the "Spiritual / Brother to the coral / Plant, absorbed into which, the equable sapphire light / Becomes a nebulous green." A few months later, in "The Fish" (August, 1918), resistance continues, but "the submerged shafts of the // Sun, split like spun / Glass," have managed to penetrate the "black jade" of the ocean's surface, with devastating results: the light reveals a "turquoise sea / Of bodies."

By the time "Picking and Choosing" appears in April, 1920, Moore has concluded that "the opaque allusion—the simulated flight // upward—accomplishes nothing," that continued resistance to the "sun's sword" is both futile and wrong. Thus in "When I Buy Pictures" (July, 1921), she proposes a new set of criteria for the successful work of art:

> It comes to this: of whatever sort it is,
> it must acknowledge the forces which have made it;
> it must be "lit with piercing glances into the life of things;"
> then I "take it in hand as a savage would take a looking-
> glass."

Rather than resist penetration by the light, the poem must now "be 'lit with piercing glances into the life of things,' " and this requirement has a twofold bearing on Moore's poetic practice. It means incorporating a larger number of quotations into the poems (as rays of light which also serve to "acknowledge the forces" to which the poem is indebted); and it means *abandoning the syllabic patterns* on which Moore has previously relied as barriers against the light. This is why the new poems which appear in various periodicals between July, 1921, and January, 1925, are in free verse—the very form Moore had rejected in 1916 on the grounds that were she to use it, "it would be the easiest thing in the world to create one intonation in the image of another."

And this is precisely what she does in the closing lines of "Novices" (February, 1923), where a group of young writers, suavely ignorant of the true nature of their craft, are

> "split like a glass against a wall"
> in this "precipitate of dazzling impressions,
> the spontaneous unforced passion of the Hebrew language—
> an abyss of verbs full of reverberation and tempestuous
> energy,"
> in which action perpetuates action and angle is at variance with
> angle
> till submerged by the general action;
> obscured by fathomless suggestions of colour,

by incessantly panting lines of green, white with concussion,
in the drama of water against rocks—this "ocean of hurrying
consonants"
with its "great livid stains like long slabs of green marble,"
its "flashing lances of perpendicular lighting" and "molten fires
swallowed up,"
"with foam on its barriers,"
"crashing itself out in one long hiss of spray."

What we see here is not only a series of quotations joined together to form a composite image of the sea in motion; it is also an effort to "create one intonation in the image of another." The quotations have been carefully arranged so as to replicate, as nearly as possible, the rhythmic effects described in George Adam Smith's analysis of *Isaiah* 17:12–13. Smith writes in *The Expositor's Bible:*

> The phonetics of the passage are wonderful. The general impression is that of a stormy ocean booming in to the shore and then crashing itself out into one long hiss of spray and foam upon its barriers. The details are noteworthy. In ver. 12 we have thirteen heavy M-sounds, besides two heavy B's, to five N's, five H's, and four sibilants. But in ver. 13 the sibilants predominate; and before the sharp rebuke of the Lord the great, booming sound of ver. 12 scatters out into a long *yish-sha 'oon*. The occasional use of a prolonged vowel amid so many hurrying consonants produces exactly the effect now of the lift of a storm swell out at sea and now the pause of a great wave before it crashes on the shore.

Returning to this passage two or three years after copying it into her reading notebook, Moore discovers in it the prescription for a rhythmic structure which may be filled out by words other than the original ones and adapted to the resources of a language other than the original Hebrew. And as we shall see, in "Bird-Witted" she adapts the principles discovered here to the resources of the syllabic patterns to which she had returned with the composition of "The Steeple-Jack" in 1932; and she will do so again later on, in translating *The Fables of La Fontaine* (1954)—the culminating product of her interest in literary mimesis.

After 1932, Moore's syllabic patterns serve a significantly different function than formerly. They no longer work to secure the distinctiveness of Moore's voice by inhibiting imitation. Instead, they work to celebrate and preserve, where possible, the innocence of the poems' *subjects*—an innocence closely allied with the distinctiveness of the subjects themselves. Because the mode of these celebrations is mimetic, however, it has been too readily assumed by Moore's critics that the poems take their own innocence—and Moore's—for granted; but this is not the case.

It is no accident that "Bird-Witted" takes its title from the writings of Sir Francis Bacon, whom Moore admired both as a literary stylist and as a scientist credited with a major role in the development of modern scientific methods based on careful, empirical observation of natural phenomenon—a development which coincides with the settling of Virginia in the late 16th and early 17th centuries. The poem invites us once more to "Observe the terse Virginian," the mocking-bird to which we are introduced in the fourth stanza of "Virginia Britannia," and to do so with an exact and scrupulous eye; we are no longer to "Behold" it as a static image, as we do in "Virginia Britannia" and in the case of Wordsworth's "child," that "six months darling of a pigmy size!" The invitation here is implicit: instead of being commanded to "Observe," we are shown a triad of young mocking-birds awaiting their mother at feeding-time. The careful observation of this family of birds in action gives an ironic twist, however, to Bacon's concern over what might happen "If a boy be bird-witted," for Moore is interested not only in the empty-headedness of the young (whose sex is of no concern to the poem) but also in the mother-wit of the adult female who has to feed and protect them.

> With innocent wide penguin eyes, three
>   grown fledgling mocking-birds below
> the pussy-willow tree,
>   stand in a row,
> wings touching, feebly solemn,
> till they see
>   their no longer larger
>   mother bringing
> something which will partially
> feed one of them.

The youth of these three birds is crucial: the first thing we learn about them is that their "eyes" are "innocent"—innocent, it will turn out, of that power of observation which would enable them to identify their enemies, and of the capacity for imitation which their mother possesses (though she does not exercise it here), and which depends in turn upon accurate observation.

The young birds are evidently capable of recognizing their mother, but the poet's powers of observation are considerably sharper. As Hugh Kenner has noted, the cries of the "fledgling mocking-birds" are caught in the reiterated double-*ee*'s of the stanza, though for a moment "their cry is muted to the final syllable of 'partially' " when "they see" their mother coming with food. As the feeding begins, their voices are "raised with a new urgency" in the rhyming "squeak" and "meek" and "beak" of the second stanza—decidedly unmusical sounds attesting to their inability to "imitate the call" of anything but broken machinery:

> Towards the high keyed intermittent squeak
>   of broken carriage-springs, made by
> the three similar, meek-
>   coated bird's-eye
> freckled forms she comes; and when
> from the beak
>   of one, the still living
>   beetle has dropped
> out, she picks it up and puts
> it in again.

This goes beyond careful attention to detail: as Kenner says, "there is affectionate mimesis in the awkward 'dropped / out' and the businesslike 'she picks it up and puts / it in again.' " The poem is similarly mimetic when, at a crucial stage later on, it stumbles slightly, with one of the birds, then regains its footing and proceeds:

>   A dangling foot that missed
>   its grasp, is raised
> and finds the twig on which it
> planned to perch.

On a casual reading, it may seem that these birds are the objects of a scrupulously neutral (if sympathetic) attention, of the sort empiricism is supposed to demand. But the eye which initially perceives the young birds' eyes as "innocent" is informed by a moral sense, a knowledge which is by definition disallowed by empirical procedures. The poet's status as observer is in fact the central issue in "Bird-Witted"—though we have no way of knowing this until the fourth stanza, where Moore turns her whole attention to the mother:

>   What delightful note
> with rapid unexpected flute-

sounds leaping from the throat
  of the astute
grown bird comes back to one from
the remote
      unenergetic sun-
      lit air before
the brood was here? Why has the
bird's voice become

harsh?

As Kenner notes, the mother's song "echoes without effort" in the stanza's alternating rhymes, and then "drops into harshness" as the poem moves into the new stanza and enters a critical new phase. But there is a considerable difference between the mimetic effort we have observed so far and the imitative work being performed here.

Uniquely, the stanza just quoted provides no visual data at all; it is wholly devoted to sound. Furthermore, in other stanzas the poem keeps time with the movements of the birds themselves; but the "delightful note . . . leaping from the throat / of the astute / grown bird" is not being sounded now: it only

    comes back to one from
the remote
      unenergetic sun-
      lit air before
the brood was here.

It is, then, a "note" sounding not in the ear but in what Wallace Stevens later called "the delicatest ear of the mind," reminding us of a moment of apparently innocent ecstasy (but see "Virginia Britannia") now past, and deliberately recalled—not by the bird, of course, but by the poet. And Moore's act of recall here is no more innocent than the one which, in the closing lines of "Virginia Britannia," balances the full burden of the poem on a single, carefully poised word out of memory.

Again Kenner alerts us to a crucial aspect of what is going on here when he suggests that "Bird-Witted" may have taken its technical inspiration from Pound's *ABC of Reading*, which had been published just over a year before "Bird-Witted" appeared in January, 1936. Pound writes that for the troubadour poets the " 'whole art' of poetry consisted in putting together about six strophes of poetry so that the words and tune should be welded together without joint and without wem"; the poet whose work best exemplified that art, he says, was "the best smith, as Dante called *Arnaut Daniel*, [who] made the birds sing IN HIS WORDS . . . for six strophes WITH the words making sense." This is exactly what Moore has sought to do in "Bird-Witted," and she has done it in a way which both confirms and extends Kenner's hypothesis. For she has used Pound's discussion of Daniel very much as she had earlier used Smith's discussion of *Isaiah*—as a technical prescription which enables her to give formal, mimetic expression to the interest in Provençal poetry which her reading of Pound's *Cantos* had engendered five years earlier. (She even follows Pound's description of the "perfect strophe" in Daniel "where the bird call interrupts the verse.") Reviewing *A Draft of XXX Cantos* for *Poetry* in October, 1931, Moore had written:

> If poetics allure, the Cantos will . . . show that in Provençal minstrelsy we encounter a fascinating precision; the delicacy and exactness of Arnaut Daniel, whose invention, the sestina form, is "like a thin sheet of flame folding and infolding upon itself." *In this tongue . . . is to be found pattern* [my italics]. And the Cantos show the troubadours not only sang poems but *were* poems . . .
>
> Mr. Pound brings to his reading, master-appreciation; and his gratitude takes two forms; he thanks the book and tells where you may see it. "Any man who would read Arnaut and the troubadours owes great thanks to Emil Levy of Freiburg," he says in *Instigations*. . . . He sings of this in Canto XX. . . .
>
> And as those who love books know, the place in which one read a book or talked of it partakes of its virtue in recollections; so for Mr. Pound the cedars and new-mown hay and far-off nightingale at Freiburg have the glamour of Provence.

Moore's syllabic reinvention of the sestina in "Bird-Witted" is a "very great feat," as Kenner says; but it is much more than a technical tour de force. It is a kind of homage to Pound; and as we shall see, it serves a specific function with respect to Moore's own complex "recollection" in "Bird-Witted" (and in "Smooth Gnarled Crape Myrtle" as well) of another "far-off nightingale." We must prepare the ground, however, by first taking up the question of memory in a more general way.

For the art of memory seems to function, in Moore's poems of the Thirties, as a prelude to, a warning of, and a shield against danger. In "The Steeple-Jack," for instance, Moore relies on the devastatingly accurate memory of the "college student / named Ambrose" to aim her own perception of dangerous untruth at the heart of a community so firmly convinced of its own innocence that its "simple people" are unable to read even the most blatant "sign" of "Danger." Ambrose, we are told, "knows" the scene "by heart," as the poet knows the mocking-bird's "delightful note"; the vision revealed by his memory serves as a standard against which to measure "the pitch / of the church // spire" and by which to prove that it is "not true." In the end, it allows us to supply the properly ironic coloring for the opening words of the final stanza: "It could not be dangerous to be living / in a town like this," but it is.

As Moore calls on Ambrose's memory in "The Steeple-Jack," so in "Virginia Britannia" she calls upon her own poetic memory for "intimation" as the poem reaches its crisis—when the forces which are to carry out the moral renovation of America have met with resistance. Memory fuels resistance to danger in "Bird-Witted," too, for here the adult bird's voice has "become // harsh" because, as the present overtakes the lilting rhymes of memory, "A piebald cat" has been "observing" her young, and it is now climbing toward them. She must act *now:*

The
parent darting down, nerved by what chills
the blood, and by hope rewarded—
of toil—since nothing fills
squeaking unfed
mouths, wages deadly combat,
and half kills
with bayonet beak and
cruel wings, the
intellectual, cautious-
ly c r e e p ing cat.

The urgency of the situation is underscored by the fact that the creatures in Moore's poems are rarely so violent, even in self-defense. The jerboa, for example, conceals itself from predators by "assuming [the] colour" of the sand; the plumet basilisk is also hidden by its coloration, that "octave of faulty / decorum"—at least until "nightfall, which is for man the basilisk whose look will kill; but is // for lizards men can / kill, the welcome dark." The frigate-pelican "hides / in the height and in the majestic / display of his art," while the pangolin, an "armoured animal," either "draws away from / danger unpugnaciously, / with no sound but a harmless hiss," or "rolls himself into a ball that has / power to defy all effort to unroll it." But the mocking-bird cannot do as the frigate-pelican does: "the majestic / display" of her mimetic "art" will not hide her now, nor will it protect her young; so she must change her tune and go on the attack in order to defend her home ground—as in "Virginia Britannia"—against an invader more coldly calculating, more "intellectual," than herself.

For the mother bird, then, to be "Bird-Witted" is to mobilize instinct against a natural antagonist, to hazard her own life in defense of her young. For the poet, however, it is deliberately to mobilize remembered emotion through the formal resources of the past, against an "intellectual . . . c r e e p ing" figure which preys upon "innocent wide penguin eye[d]" children: it is to imitate innocence in order to defend it, and to do so in full awareness that the deliberateness of poetic mimesis belies the apparent innocence of her posture. Of course the poem cannot literally protect these or any other birds against attack by a marauding cat; it can, however, mobilize its resources in a parodic defense of the mocking-bird against the kind of treatment Keats accords the nightingale in his famous "Ode."

Moore writes in "Smooth Gnarled Crape Myrtle"—the fourth and final poem in "The Old Dominion" group—that

> "The legendary white-
> eared black bulbul that sings
> only in pure Sanskrit" should
> be here—"tame clever
> true nightingale."

The " 'tame clever / true nightingale' " is not "here," of course, but to a considerable extent Moore behaves as if it were. Keats asks in the second strophe of the "Ode to a Nightingale" for "a draught of Vintage! . . . Tasting of Flora and the country-green, / Dance, and Provencal song," and Moore obliges him, in "Bird-Witted," with a poem about a mocking-bird (syllabically equivalent to the nightingale) which imitates the Provençal "pattern" of Arnaut Daniel. And she goes further: her situation as listener, in the crucial fourth stanza where the bird is invisible, closely parallels the situation in which Keats finds himself in the fifth strophe of his "Ode." He "cannot see" either his surroundings or the bird; lying in "embalmed darkness," he can do nothing in the following strophe but listen:

> Darkling I listen; and, for many a time
> I have been half in love with easeful Death,
> Called him soft names in many a mused rhyme,
> To take into the air my quiet breath;
> Now more than ever seems it rich to die,
> To cease upon the midnight with no pain,
> While thou art pouring forth my soul abroad
> In such an ecstasy!
> Still wouldst thou sing, and I have ears in vain—
> To thy high requiem become a sod.

Moore is not listening to "such an ecstasy" as Keats hears, but rather remembering a moment from the past; and her own death is not in question. Unlike Keats's "immortal Bird," however, Moore's mocking-bird and her young have indeed been "born for death," and though it is not yet their time to die, the "hungry generations" have appeared—in the form of "A piebald cat"—to "tread [them] down" as they never will Keats's bird. Just as Keats is wrenched back to his "sole self" by the sound of his own voice repeating the word "Forlorn!" as if it were "a bell," so Moore is called back to the present by the suddenly "harsh" voice of the mother bird, interrupting her memory of "ecstasy" and forcing her to attend to the emergencies of the present. "Bird-Witted" thus justifies its symbolic treatment of the mocking-bird by calling attention to the particular exigencies of its situation in a way that does not concern Keats at all; what we hear in the mocking-bird's song is the "note" of its own insistent perception of danger, rather than the personal note Keats strikes in the "Ode." The implication seems to be that Keats, for all his display of emotion, has transformed the nightingale into a merely "intellectual" symbol of his own desires, and that in doing so he has indulged in a process very similar to that which works upon the mocking-bird itself in "Virginia Britannia."

The mocking-bird enters "Virginia Britannia" in a blur of motion so fast that for a moment we are unable even to identify the "terse Virginian" as a mocking-bird. But the bird, like the reader, is soon arrested by the command to "Observe," and it comes to a stand "on the round stone- / topped table with lead cupids grouped to / form the pedestal." The mocking-bird has begun to slow, to freeze, long before the end of the stanza, however: it is likened to a statue even as it first comes clearly into focus "with head / held half away, and meditative eye as dead / as sculptured marble / eyes." Now, perched on what is explicitly termed a "pedestal" formed by "lead cupids" in a leaden mockery of loving support, it resembles a statue so closely that it is as if it had been turned to "lead" by the sheer force of the "Care" which "has formed" the scene as if for the express purpose of accommodating and subduing the bird—and by the difficult consonants that slow the rhythm of our reading. It is in this posture that the mocking-bird enters our memory, so that we are implicated with the poet in the alchemical, "intellectual" transmutation of a living creature into a base material.

"Bird-Witted" brings this faintly ominous leaden figure to life again, transforming it into a momentarily animated figure of sound. But Moore's effort to undo the effects of her own "intellectual," Keatsian treatment of the mocking-bird by parodic means is doomed to fail—for parody is a mimetic mode, and must employ Keatsian tactics. As in "Virginia Britannia," therefore, the tempo of "Bird-Witted" slows dramatically when the sentence arrives in what seems to be the present, when it comes to the "grown bird" and the predicate that places her "delightful note" in the "remote" past. The tempo slows because we are not in fact in the present, or rather because we are in a present which is bound by the Keatsian past: what we are hearing is a "ditt[y] of no tune" like those which play throughout the "Ode on a Grecian Urn"—a "note" played "Not to the sensual ear" but to "the spirit." We see the mother bird "darting down" to meet the cat, but the engagement is delayed while we are told what impels her to action ("hope . . . of toil"), and when finally she "wages deadly combat, / and half kills" her antagonist, the object of the verb is deferred until the last possible moment—deferred not only by syntax, but by typography as well. For in the first three printings of the poem the letters of the final line are more widely spaced than the rest: the mother bird

> wages deadly combat,
> and half kills
> with bayonet beak and
> cruel wings, the
> intellectual cautious-
> ly c r e e p ing cat.

The effect is to freeze the scene: the cat is transfixed as it moves toward its prey, and the mother bird is caught as it were in mid-air, just on the point of attack, by the "intellectual," "unheard" music of the "Ode on a Grecian Urn." Like Keats's "marble men and maidens," Moore's cat and bird will remain so, in the memory of art. When we see them again in "Half Deity," the third poem in the sequence, they have been slightly transformed, but they are still fixed in the same attitudes.

The almost total critical neglect of "Half Deity" may be explained by Moore's decision to omit it from both *The Collected Poems* of 1951 and *The Complete Poems* of 1967—explained, but not justified. The poem is far too important to be ignored. Only one critic, Laurence Stapleton, considers that it "has a rightful place beside the other Virginia poems," but her own treatment is too cursory to specify that "place" or to suggest the poem's crucial bearing on the sequence as a whole.

Like "Virginia Britannia" and "Bird-Witted," "Half Deity" is concerned with the relationship between childhood innocence and adult knowledge, but it explores that relationship more intensively than the others do. "Virginia Britannia" and "Bird-Witted" take the difference between innocence and experience more or less for granted; they can do so, however, only because

"Half Deity" offers a rather full account of the passage from one state to the other—an account which is complicated and intensified by Moore's insistence in "Smooth Gnarled Crape Myrtle" that the distance between innocence and guilty knowledge is almost imperceptible: there "is but a / step" between them.

The passage from innocence to experience occurs when the relationship of observer to observed becomes instead a relation between a pursuer and her prey—when, that is, observation becomes an effort not just to secure visual knowledge of a given object but also to possess that object. Or rather, the passage occurs when the observer becomes consciously aware that she is a pursuer already, and that her pursuit must fail of its object: "Half Deity" implies that observation is never innocent of the desire for possession. The difference between child and adult, therefore, is that the latter has "learned to spare" the object of her desire in a way the child has not—for observation, like imitation, has to be "learned," though it has its origin in an instinctive "curiosity." But the adult "spare[s]" the object only from the physical consequences of the possessive urge. Opting for intellectual rather than merely physical possession, the observer makes the object an object of memory instead of immediate sensory experience; she may therefore seem more innocent than the child who attempts to secure the object physically. We have seen that memory may serve as a warning of imminent danger; but it also poses a theat to the integrity of the object, for it transforms and deadens its objects by subordinating them to patterns already formed.

"A subject and an object," says Emerson in "Experience," "—it takes so much to make the galvanic circuit complete, but magnitude adds nothing. What imports it whether it is Kepler and the sphere, Columbus and America, a reader and his book, or puss with her tail?" Pursuit inevitably becomes self-pursuit, and then "the galvanic circuit" can be made "complete" only in a provisional, a metaphorical way, and then only with considerable pain. As Emerson writes earlier in the same essay, "souls never touch their objects." But when the soul *is* the object of the soul's pursuit, as it is in "Half Deity"—when the pursuer deliberately puts on the "aspect" of the innocent observer in an effort to repossess and reanimate her own childhood innocence, which is either a memory or a fiction or both—then the closing of the circle inflicts a sharper pain than the one "puss" must feel when she catches up with "her tail" and bites down. For to capture the memory of one's former innocence is to discover, simultaneously, that what one has in memory is what one has lost in fact, and so to discover the full burden of one's guilt. This, I think, is why Moore elected not to include "Half Deity" in late collections of her work: like "Black Earth" (later renamed "Melanchthon"), it is too explicitly self-revealing, and too deeply disturbing, to suit the public image she had come by then to project so successfully.

"Half Deity" begins by carefully establishing the poet in the posture of innocent observer:

Half Deity

half worm. We all, infant and adult, have
stopped to watch the butterfly—last of the
elves—and learned to spare the wingless worm
that hopefully ascends the tree.

This opening leads us to believe that when the poet stops, a few lines later, "to watch" a "peninsula-tailed" butterfly which "has been / sleeping upright on an elm," she intends only to look at it in order to confirm for herself what others have reported—for "its yellowness, / that of the autumn poplar-leaf, by day / has been observed." We assume that she will otherwise "spare" it her attentions, for unlike the sea in "A Grave," she is evidently not "a collector." We have not yet been given reason to consider that our having "learned to spare" the caterpillar, "the wingless worm / that hopefully ascends the tree," says nothing of our eventual response to the butterfly that caterpillar will become; and so we are not distressed when the poet's apparently matter-of-fact observation gives rise to pursuit, because the poet herself takes no visible part in the chase. So far as we can tell, she is the observer and reporter, not the pursuer.

That role is played by another figure, an "infant" "half deity" who appears without warning a third of the way into the poem. "Disguised in butterfly- / bush Wedgwood blue, Psyche follows" the butterfly from tree to tree—much as the mocking-bird "drives the / owl" in "Virginia Britannia"—and the action develops so quickly from this point on that we have no time for surprise at the presence in Moore's work of a figure so obviously and so conventionally poetic, no time to consider that the landscape of "The Old Dominion" has suddenly become so thoroughly Romantic that Moore, like Keats, can all "thoughtlessly" happen upon Psyche in a wood. Perhaps, though, we may explain Psyche's sudden appearance by recalling the strange, offhand comment made earlier on, that the butterfly's "yellowness . . . *by day* / has been observed" [my italics]. The phrase implies that the action of the poem takes place at night, and may in fact be a dream—a typically Romantic mode. This might help, too, to account for the specific trees to which Psyche pursues the butterfly. She goes first to a tree whose Latin name, "Micromalus," means "little apple" but suggests as well "little evil," and whose English name, "the midget / crab," calls to mind not only miniature, inedible versions of forbidden fruit but small, painfully grasping creatures as well; then she goes to "the mimosa," the central symbol of Shelley's "The Sensitive Plant," where the tree inhabits a beautiful garden, and lives in a mysterious affinity with a beautiful lady—at least for a time. For "When Winter had gone and Spring came back / The Sensitive Plant was a leafless wreck." And so Psyche leaves the wrecked mimosa and goes straight "from that, to the flowering pomegranate," the tree whose fruit was forbidden to Persephone, who ate it nonetheless and brought winter into the world.

Keats's "Ode to Psyche" begins with the poet's unexpected discovery, as he wanders "in a forest thoughtlessly," of a sleeping couple whom he recognizes as Cupid and Psyche. But Keats—who feared that "there was nothing original to be written in poetry; that its riches were already exhausted—and all its beauties forestalled"—dismisses the "winged boy" without even troubling to name him, for he has no interest in retelling the ancient legend of Cupid and Psyche's love. All his attention is on Psyche, and he revels in his discovery of a subject whose "riches" have not been "exhausted," whose "beauties" have not been "forestalled": Psyche, "latest born" of the goddesses as Moore's butterfly is "last of the elves," was born "too late for antique vows, / Too, too late for the fond believing lyre." No poet has sung her praises, nor made his name inseparable from hers; she has had

> No voice, no lute, no pipe, no incense sweet
> From chain-swung censer teeming;
> No shrine, no grove, no oracle, no heat
> Of pale-mouth'd prophet dreaming.
> (11. 32–35)

The poet begs her to "let him fill those offices; declaring, "I will be thy priest," he promises in the final strophe to build in Psyche's honor

> a fane
> In some untrodden region of my mind,
> Where branched thoughts, new grown with pleasant pain,
> Instead of pines shall murmur in the wind:
> Far, far around shall those dark-cluster'd trees
> Fledge the wild-ridged mountains steep by steep;
> And there by zephyrs, streams, and birds, and bees,
> The moss-lain Dryads shall be lull'd to sleep;
> And in the midst of this wide quietness
> A rosy sanctuary will I dress

With the wreath'd trellis of a working brain,
  With buds, and bells, and stars without a name,
With all the gardener Fancy e'er could feign,
  Who breeding flowers, will never breed the same:
And there shall be for thee all soft delight
  That shadowy thought can win,
A bright torch, and a casement ope at night,
  To let the warm Love in!

(ll. 50–67)

Keats's "Ode," ostensibly a celebratory gesture occasioned by the poet's discovery of the goddess sleeping in the wood, is transformed by his ambitious desire for originality into an attempt to displace Cupid and possess Psyche for himself. (Compare the similar but far more overt displacement in Whitman's *Song of Myself*: "I turn the bride-groom out of bed and stay with the bride myself, / I tighten her all night to my thighs and lips.") What Keats ends by building, therefore, is less "a fane" than what Moore calls in "Half Deity" a "flowering, shrewd-scented tropical / device" whose function is to secure the poet's dominion over Psyche by imprisoning her "In some untrodden region of [his] mind."

Similarly, although Psyche's pursuit of the butterfly in "Half Deity" seems to spring from a relatively uncomplicated desire "to watch" it, she soon finds herself wholly committed to trapping the elusive creature. She follows it until,

Baffled not by the quick-clouding serene gray
moon, but forced by the hot hot sun to pant,
  she stands on rug-soft grass; though "it is not
  permitted to gaze informally
    on majesty, in such a manner as might
  well happen here." The blind
    all-seeing butterfly, fearing the slight
finger, wanders—as though it were ignorant—
a step further and lights on Zephyr's palm.

Psyche, Zephyr, and the butterfly now form a tableau in which all our attention is directed to the confrontation of observer and observed, pursuer and pursued:

Small unglazed china eyes of butterflies—
  pale tobacco crown—with the large eyes of
  the Nymph on them; gray eyes that now are

black, for she, with controlled agitated glance
observes the insect's face
and all's a-quiver with significance
as in the scene with cats' eyes on the magpie's eyes
by Goya.

Psyche only "observes the insect's face" here—but the butterfly, rightly "vexed because curiosity has / been pursuing it," is unable to remain "calm." For if in "Bird-Witted" the "delightful note" of a "remote" and untroubled past is recalled as a prelude to danger, "Half Deity" recalls the "deadly combat" of "Bird-Witted" in the midst of an apparently innocent confrontation. Psyche's "curiosity" begins to look less innocent, moreover, when we recall that her marriage to Cupid was annulled when she disobeyed the divine injunction against looking upon his face. And "though 'it is not / permitted to gaze informally / on majesty, in such a manner as might / well happen' " again " 'here,' " Psyche " 'might / well' " find a certain sanction for her curiosity in the reflection that—as Alice says elsewhere—" 'A cat may look at a king.' " For that is precisely what does " 'happen here.' " The analogy to Goya's "scene with cats' eyes on the magpie's eyes" likens Psyche not to the bird (which would be dubious enough, since the magpie is a thievish bird) but rather to the "intellectual cautious- / ly c r e e p ing cat" of "Bird-Witted." And the cat is most itself in preying upon innocence, as readers of earlier poems like "Silence" (where the cat " 'takes its prey to privacy— / the mouse's limp tail dangling like a shoelace from its mouth' ") and "Peter" (where the cat is naturally inclined "to purloin, to pursue" the "hen") will recall.

All this may seem to set "Half Deity" at odds with the celebration, in "Bird-Witted," of the effort to repel the predator. But we know by now what "Smooth Gnarled Crape Myrtle" will confirm that "An aspect may deceive." We must consider, too, the poet's lament in the same poem that "Art is unfortunate. // One may be a blameless / bachelor and it is but a / step to Congreve"; for there is "but a / step" between "Bird-Witted" and "Half Deity." We have seen that "Bird-Witted" inherits from "Virginia Britannia" the memory, in statuary form, of a living creature—a memory which it reanimates by imitating the intricate aural patterns of Arnaut Daniel's verse. But at the very moment when those aural patterns are most conspicuously displayed, the fourth stanza where the poet must carry the tune alone, the imitation of Daniel coincides with the silent memory of the "Ode on a Grecian Urn"; and from then on covergent imitations sustain the formal movement of the verse while gradually returning the bird (and the cat with her) to the initial state of immobility. This is not an innocent stratagem (if there is such a thing) but a desperately conscious one. "Bird-Witted" concentrates upon presenting to the reader the more innocent "aspect" of Moore's poetic enterprise, but it is the peculiar misfortune of an art so wholly mimetic that it must imitate whatever comes into its ken. It is, therefore, only by resorting in desperation to Keats, only by forcing both the mocking-bird and the cat into conformity with the frozen statuary of the Grecian Urn, that Moore prevents herself from taking a mimetic "step further" with the " intellectual cautious- / ly c r e e p ing cat" whose movements the typography has already begun to imitate—prevents herself, that is, from giving the poem an "aspect" as predatory as Psyche's has now become. For, like the poet and the reader in "Virginia Britannia," and like Psyche here, the cat begins by "observing" the "fledgling mocking-birds."

Like the cat, moreover, Psyche is immobilized just when her barely "controlled agitated glance" reveals the true character of her interest in the butterfly. As her "large . . . gray eyes" darken to "black" with excitement, they become so opaque as to recall the "meditative eye" of the "lead- / gray . . . mocking-bird" of "Virginia Britannia"—an eye seemingly "as dead / as sculptured marble / eyes"; but there is a crucial difference between Psyche's eyes and the bird's. The "eyes of the Nymph," apparently so intensely alive, are in fact "sculptured marble," and so are Zephyr's "mirror eyes" and the "Small unglazed china eyes" of the butterfly itself. The action has been brought to a halt by the sudden assertion—apparently against the Keatsian movement of Psyche's pursuit but actually, as the conclusion of "Bird-Witted" attests, in logical confirmation of the end to which that pursuit must lead—of the poet's memory of a "Carved Marble Group by Jean Baptiste Boyer," representing "Psyche trying to capture the butterfly held out on Zephyr's palm."

That memory cannot contain the action for long, however. Reanimated as suddenly as it had been frozen, the butterfly now "springs away, [a] zebra half-deified," and in the next instant the poet takes the irrevocable "step" she had denied herself in "Bird-Witted." She thereby reveals the extent to which her own imitation of Keats, parodic though it may be, had entangled her with Psyche. Until now, the poet has preserved her status as observer of the entire episode; but now she suddenly insults the butterfly, calling after it: "Twig-veined, irascible, / fastidious, stubborn undisciplined zebra! Sometimes one is grateful to / a stranger for looking very nice." So intolerable is it that the butterfly should escape that the poet's voice turns markedly childlike, as though by acting the petulant child for a moment (and she is very like Alice just now) she could disguise a deeper, more adult sense of loss and lure the butterfly back.

But "An aspect may deceive," and "looking very nice" is not enough to satisfy the "blind / all-seeing butterfly," which has only wandered on to Zephyr's hand in the first place "*as though* it were ignorant" [my italics]. It sees, therefore, that it is "free / to leave the breeze's hand" as it would not be "free / to leave" the "half-shut" hand Psyche has extended toward it. And so, like Emily Dickinson's "Little Tippler" (Dickinson had "For Poets . . . Keats—and Mr and Mrs Browning"),

it flies, drunken with triviality
or guided by visions of strength, away till
diminished like wreckage on the sea,
rising and falling easily; mounting
the swell and keeping its true course with
what swift majesty, indifferent to
us, it's gone.

"It's gone," and the poet can only wonder: "Deaf to my / voice, or magnet-nice? as it flutters through / airs now slack, now fresh. It has strict ears," she adds ruefully, "when the / West Wind speaks." The lineation here emphasizes the possessive pronoun ("*my* / voice"), and the question brings the poet fully into the open. Psyche has served only as a mask—and not a very effective one at that. The poet's interest in the butterfly is as "intellectual," and therefore as predatory, as Psyche's has become—and she too is immobilized by the weight of her own desire.

But if the butterfly is finally "indifferent / to" anyone who might take an active interest in it, it has yet been drawn as if by a "magnet" to Zephyr, the Shelleyan "West Wind," for whose words it has such "strict ears," and whose "hand spread out was enough / to tempt the fiery tiger-horse to stand." Moore's memory of the "Ode to the West Wind" has served to rescue the poem (and the butterfly) from the impasse to which her imitation of Keats has brought it. As we have seen, what Keats attempts in the "Ode to Psyche" is the attainment of mastery, an ambition which his professed desire to serve the goddess and worship as "priest" at her "fane" cannot conceal; by contrast, in the "Ode to the West Wind" Shelley acknowledges the wind as *his* master. He seeks not to possess its power for himself but rather to be possessed by it as a prophet is possessed by the divine afflatus. His concern, unlike Keats's, is less for himself than for the "unawakened earth": he wants to borrow the the wind's "power" and make it speak his "words," but he wants it not to glorify himself but rather to "quicken a new birth," to arouse the world from its "Winter" sleep to a revolutionary "Spring."

Moore is not, I think, especially concerned with the particular features of the revolution Shelley had in mind, and in fact must have found his doctrines thoroughly incompatible with her own conservative views; but his doctrines are not the issue here. The nature of Moore's interest in Shelley is most clearly indicated by the words of her friend Scofield Thayer, former editor of *The Dial* and a great admirer of Moore and her work, who wrote of Shelley in 1913 that while "many of the poet's ideals now appear scarcely comprehensible, the integrity of his purpose is not the less patent." Thayer's remarks (which Moore transcribed into her reading notebook in November, 1928) have a clear bearing on Zephyr's success in attracting the butterfly though he makes no apparent effort to do so. His "hand" is "spread out," giving assurance of "the integrity of his purpose"—an assurance which the "blind / all-seeing butterfly" recognizes, and by which it distinguishes between the Shelleyan Zephyr and the Keatsian Zephyr: Zephyr has "no net," and makes no such attempt as Psyche's to "capture the butterfly" in a "half-shut / hand." Nor is Zephyr more "comprehensible" than Shelley: "many of the poet's ideals now appear scarcely comprehensible," says Thayer—and so, Moore writes, Zephyr's "talk was as strange as my grandmother's muff."

Moore's "talk" is "strange," too; but her struggle to "overcome [her] reluctance to be unoriginal"—which has led her actively to pursue "possible comparisons and coincidences" with other writers—has betrayed her into what she perceives as a loss of "integrity." Significantly, Moore does not imitate Shelley in "Half Deity"; rather, she captures the erratic, fluttering movement of the butterfly by parodying the loosely Pindaric form of Keats's "Ode to Psyche." But parody is only another form of imitation, and even in parody Moore is possessed by the Keatsian obsession with originality which she is struggling to "overcome." Inevitably, then, she becomes Psyche, straining after the butterfly which is the emblem of her own soul, and seeing in her inability to capture it the extent to which, unlike the butterfly, she has departed from her own "true course"—seeing, that is, a loss of self, a loss of innocence and "integrity of purpose." "They that have wings must not have weights," she says early in the poem—but she has no wings. On the contrary, she is so weighted down by memory and desire that, like Psyche, she is immobilized, turned to stone. Even the self whose emblem she strains after is only a memory. The closing line, delivered as an artlessly inconsequent throwaway, lodges the entire poem in the past, reminding us that the poet, for all that she "look[s] very nice" "Disguised in butterfly- / bush Wedgwood blue," is not a child but an adult remembering a dream of a childhood long since past: "His talk was as strange as my grandmother's muff."

"Such a life as [Shelley's,]" writes Scofield Thayer, "resembles the sepulchar slab in the pavement of an ancient church; the impertinences of name and insignia are worn away by the feet of time, but the crossed arms remain." The grave thus becomes the image of an inscrutable and anonymous integrity, for Thayer immediately goes on to insist that the incomprehensibility of Shelley's ideals leaves "the integrity of his purpose . . . not the less patent." And so we circle back to "Virginia Britannia," where in the "typical ivied-bower-and-ruined-tower churchyard" of the opening stanza we find that

A deer-
track in a church-floor
brick and Sir George Yeardley's
coffin tacks and
tomb remain.

This image is so specific that it bears no obvious relation to Thayer's discussion of Shelley; in the final version, however, the resemblance is much closer. For the identity of the "great sinner" who "lyeth here under the sycamore" is no longer "known": the "impertinences" of Yeardley's "name and insignia" have been "worn away" by revision, leaving only the "deer- / track" and "a fine pavement tomb with engraved top."

But the original image is more fully informed by Thayer's odd analogy than it seems. Yeardley was the only knighted member of the Jamestown colony, and he received his title in recognition of his work in aiding the community to establish itself. Apparently, then, his "tomb" functions in an ironic capacity as an image of justly rewarded integrity, and thus strikes the keynote not only for "Virginia Britannia" but for "The Old Dominion" as a whole. It is "integrity of purpose" that concerns Moore most deeply as she explores what Thayer calls, in the subtitle of his essay on Shelley, "The Poetic Value of Revolutionary Principles." Like Emerson's nature, the landscape of colonial Virginia "offers all her creatures to [the poet] as a picture-language" which, under Moore's scrutiny, reveals the principles inherent in the original "colonizing" of the New World and the subsequent history of America as a nation which owes its existence to the practical application of revolutionary ideals.

We must bear in mind, however, that "An aspect may deceive." For we shall find as the poem proceeds that the "picture-language" of "Virginia Britannia" spells out not a linear history of simple integrity but rather a history of principles perverted in the application and from the start. The history of America as this poem tell us is (to borrow a phrase from "Marriage," but which is originally from Sir Francis Bacon) a history " 'of circular traditions and impostures, / committing many spoils.' " "Virginia Britannia" is an attempt to rectify that history, to set America back on the "true course" of integrity; as we shall see, however, it works by the apparently paradoxical method of "advancing back- / ward in a circle"—a revolutionary method in the strictest etymological sense of the word "revolution," a method which requires that Moore accept the very perversions she is trying to correct and that she accept them not only in principle but in practice as well. Like Whitman, then—a poet for whom she felt a profound distaste—Moore identifies the form of poetry with the form of America itself, which is the form of its history. For those perversions, those " 'circular traditions and impostures' " and their " 'many spoils,' " are inseparable from the principles to which they give visible expression: they are the history of America. Nowhere is the paradoxical intertwining of principle and perversion, the backward-circling movement of advance, more powerfully evident than in the deliberate use of the word "intimation" to mark the boundary separating the mature poet from the figure of the innocent child and to confess the poet's participation in the circular logic of American history.

The "picture-language" of the Virginia landscape is all the more revealing because it is not entirely the language of nature. As we have seen [elsewhere], the landscape which the poem purports to describe has been "formed" by the "Care" of an anonymous gardener or gardeners, in painstaking and nostalgic imitation of the landscape the colonists had left behind. What remains for us, however, is a monumental and wholly inadvertent parody, "an almost English" landscape dominated not by the " 'tame clever / true nightingale' " which "should be here" to suit the tastes of " 'one who dresses // in New York but dreams of / London' " (as "Smooth Gnarled Crape Myrtle" puts it), but rather by the hostile, mimetic, statuesque mocking-bird.

The gardeners' efforts to turn Virginia into an earthly Paradise have gone awry, have ended by producing a "Rare unscent- / ed, provident- / ly hot, too sweet, inconsistent flower- / bed" in which "serpentine shadows star- / tle strangers" while the inhabitants remain curiously oblivious. The grotesquely thickened "stem" of "the white wall-rose," however, is itself a sign of danger: for the "wide-spaced great blunt alternating os- / trich-skin warts that were thorns" signify the " 'many spoils' " which have been committed by "the predatory hand" against which, in "Roses Only" (1917), the rose's thorns provide the only measure of "proof." Nothing is safe here: the "poor unpoisonous terrapin likes to / idle near the sea-top" where it makes easy prey; soon "Terrapin / meat and crested spoon / feed the mistress" of that "everywhere open / shaded house on Indian / named Virginian / streams, in counties named for English lords!"

The history of "Virginia Britannia," then, is the history not of integrity stoutly maintained but of "tobacco-crop / gains" memorialized on "church tablets," of mixed motives and cross purposes working "on / The Chickahominy"—one of those "Indian / named Virginian / streams"—to establish "the Negro (opportunely brought) to / strengthen protest against tyranny." It is a history founded on appropriation:

> Strangler fig, pale fiercely
> unpretentious North American, and Dutch
> trader, and noble
> Roman, in taking what they
> pleased—colonizing as we say—
> were not all intel-
> lect and delicacy.

The Virginia landscape is more than a natural historical record: it is a work of art predicated upon the colonists' (and their descendants') having combined the strength to "tak[e] what they / pleased" with an intense longing "to be unoriginal," to use what they took as the material from which to construct a simulacrum of the English landscape as a permanent monument to England and the past—an enormous mortuary sculpture, as it were. So powerful is that combination of strength and longing that it can assimilate to its grand design even those native elements which, in breaking the silence of the grave, threaten to overwhelm the memory of home with their mockery. Thus the mocking-bird, though as it enters the scene it "drives the / owl from tree to tree and imitates the call / of whippoorwill or / lark or katydid," falls silent and turns to "lead" under the spell of the gardeners' "Care": it is left frozen in its place, "still standing there alone / on the round stone-topped table with lead cupids grouped to / form the pedestal."

Nor may we omit Moore's name from the roster of those who have made "Virginia Britannia" what it is by "taking what they / pleased—colonizing as we say." For the poem which discovers in the landscape the long history of appropriation is itself not only the most recent product of that history, but a "colonizing" power in its own right.

> The slowmoving glossy
> saddle-cavalcade
>
> of buckeye brown surprising
> jumpers; the contrasting work-mule and
> show-mule and witch-cross door and "strong sweet prison"
> are a part of what
> has come about, in the black
> idiom, from advancing back-

ward in a circle;
      from taking the Potomac
   cowbirdlike; and on
The Chickahominy
establishing
the Negro (opportunely brought) to
strengthen protest against
      tyranny.

Here Moore registers her own "protest against" the "tyranny" to which Blacks in America have been and are subject; but in "strengthen[ing] that "protest" with a phrase "opportunely brought" into the poem from "the Black / idiom" she knowingly implicates herself in the very "tyranny" she condemns. The availability of that "idiom" depends, of course, on the institution of slavery, under which "the Negro" was brought to America to sustain the outmoded economy of the South and its "tyrant taste." But Moore uses "the Negro" in a similar way, deliberately appropriating his language to define and sustain the economy of "Virginia Britannia" itself—to enact and "strengthen" the circular logic of its opportunistic history.

Thus Moore is not simply describing a landscape, as she seems to be. Rather, she is extending the method we have seen her use in "Novices" and "Bird-Witted," finding in the construction of the landscape itself the technical principles of composition by which she now composes her own imitative reconstruction of a landscape which is already, in her words, "one of America's most undeniable poems." She is not so much writing "Virginia Britannia," then, as rewriting it, and correcting as she goes (much as she does in revising her own poems, including this one); and she is working along the lines laid down almost a century earlier by Emerson, who writes in "The Poet" (1844) that

> poetry was all written before time was, and whenever we are so finely organized that we can penetrate into that region where the air is music, we hear those primal warblings and attempt to write them down, but we lose ever and anon a word or a verse and substitute something of our own, and thus miswrite the poem.

The original settlers of Virginia, forced to "substitute something of [their] own" for the missing "words" of the English original, have "miswrit[ten] the poem" of Jamestown—and as Emerson tells us a few pages later, "herein is the legitimation of criticism, in the mind's faith that the [poem is] a corrupt version of some text in nature with which [it] ought to be made to tally."

Moore's initial response to the colonists' inadvertently parodic miswriting is to counter with a deliberately parodic reconstruction of that parody which both reveals and corrects it. From the outset she intertwines various elements—natural and artificial, domestic and foreign—so thoroughly that all seem equally out of place in the end, and equally at home as well. In the first stanza, for instance, the alternating pattern formed by "the redbird, / the red-coated musketeer, / the trumpet-flower, the cavalier," seems to accommodate "the parson, and the / wild parishioner" without strain; but here Moore has already extended the poem well beyond the temporal and chronological limits of what we call Colonial Virginia. In the early seventeenth century "New England was called Northern Virginnia," as she points out; and the presence in this closely patterned landscape of "the parson, and the / wild parishioner" points not only to the "deer- / track in a church-floor / brick" but also, and more problematically, to a permanent reminder of just how "unEnglish" this "almost English" scene really is. The pairing is a reminder, too, of just how far America has strayed from its "true course," for it recalls the most celebrated adulterous union in nineteenth-century American fiction—the forest meeting between "The Pastor and His Parishioner" in which Hester Prynne persuades Arthur Dimmesdale to join her in fleeing the oppressive strictures of Puritan Boston.

Following Hawthorne's ironic design (for of course Hester and Dimmesdale are foiled by her devilish, cuckolded husband), Moore binds these figures permanently into the American landscape. And she does so with the same "Care" with which she "has formed, a- / mong" the "unEnglish insect sounds" of stanzas which "should sound like a kind of inexhaustible bumble-bee" (as she put it later), "the white wall-rose" with the grotesquely thickened American "stem" whose missing "thorns" are no longer "proof" against "the predatory hand" that governs the landscape. In "Virginia Britannia," however, the "observing" eye does the work of the hand—and "observing" is a very "predatory" activity, as we have had ample occasion to discover.

We cannot gauge the full extent of the eye's rapacity until we consider that it is the poet's simultaneous observance of the forms of the past and of the present which impels her to cast "Virginia Britannia" as a syllabic imitation of the Immortality Ode and, at crucial moments, so complicate that willingness "to be unoriginal" by combining with it the strength to take what she pleases. In doing so—in "colonizing as we say"—Moore reveals the full extent of her unoriginality, of her willingness to let herself be influenced by other writers. For her definition of "colonizing" ("taking what they / pleased") is very nearly identical in phrasing to the definition of influence which Eliot had advanced in his esay "In Memory" of Henry James (1918)—an essay on which Moore relies in "Picking and Choosing," which redefines the complementary relationship between criticism and poetry along the lines of Eliot's discussion: "To be influenced by a writer," says Eliot, "is to have a chance inspiration from him; or to take what one wants." It is Eliot himself who, at a crucial moment in "Virginia Britannia," provides Moore with "a chance inspiration," and it is from his most recent work that she takes "what [she] wants." The mocking-bird to which we have already devoted so much time may be indigenous to Virginia, but like virtually everything in "Virginia Britannia" it has been imported, "opportunely brought" in from elsewhere. It comes from Eliot's short poem "Virginia," one of several small landscapes published under the heading "Words for Music" in the *Virginia Quarterly Review* in April, 1934:

> Red river, red river,
> Slow flow heat is silence
> No will is still as a river
> Still. Will heat move
> Only through the mocking-bird
> Heard once?

The mocking-bird belongs to the immediate present; but though it "drives the / owl from tree to tree," it cannot overcome the full burden of the English past. Having been forcefully appropriated by a poet ever-observant of her contemporaries' work, it is introduced into a scene so rigidly determined by the past that the bird is struck dumb and cast in lead. For the scene owes its form to Moore's parodic effort to "Observe" the form of the Immortality Ode—an effort which perpetuates, in turn, the awkward attempts of the original colonists to "Observe" the cherished forms of their own history.

As Moore's corrective measures take effect, as the present begins apparently to free itself from the bonds of the past, there is a corresponding change in the character of Moore's parody. By the penultimate stanza, parody has become anticipatory as well as reminiscent:

> The song-
> bird wakes too soon, to enjoy
> excellent idleness, destroy-
> ing legitimate
> laziness, the unbought toy
> even in the dark
> risking loud whee whee whee
> of joy, the car-

away-seed-spotted sparrow perched on
the dew-drenched juniper
        beside the window-ledge;
        the little hedge-
sparrow that wakes up seven minutes
   sooner than the lark

they say.

But there is no escape from the past. In the final stanza, the delighted, gently mocking anticipation of Shelley's Skylark shades into a much more straightforwardly honorific imitation of the Immortality Ode, and though the anticipatory note remains it has been muted. For "The clouds that gather round the setting sun / Do take a sober colouring from an eye / That hath kept watch o'er man's mortality," and when the poem encounters a group of stationary figures whom even the flaming sunset "can / not move," Moore resorts directly to Wordsworth. This time, in a final, desperate acknowledgement of her own complicity in and responsibility for the American historical process, she takes liberties not only with Wordsworth's formal patterns, but with his language and, most importantly, with his central symbol as well.

Like the "solid- / pointed star" which "stands for hope" at the end of "The Steeple-Jack," like Zephyr in "Half Deity," the child, receiving "an intimation" which she does not seek, seems to hold out the "hope" of escape from the long history of "colonizing" which the poem has developed. But as Moore writes in "The Hero"—one of two companion pieces to "The Steeple-Jack"—hope is not hope "until all ground for hope has / vanished." The child is mother to the woman, an "*historic* metamorphoser" [my italics] like the butterfly in "Half Deity"—and so she is doomed to undergo a process of growth which will invert precisely the transformation of "the wingless worm / that hopefully ascends the tree" into a "weightless" butterfly. The child is already "historic," as Psyche is—a figure caught by poetic memory in the attitude from which, like the butterfly from its cocoon, the predatory, "intellectual" adult emerges into history to stand rooted and grasping in "endless imitation" of an innocence which has already receded into the "remote" past and which she knows from the outset to be permanently lost. "Art is unfortunate."

Chronology

1887 Marianne Moore is born on November 15 in Kirkwood, near St. Louis, Missouri, to John Milton and Mary (Warner) Moore. Her father suffers a nervous breakdown.

1894 After the death of Moore's grandfather, the Reverend John Riddle Warner, Moore and her mother and brother move to Carlisle, Pennsylvania.

1896–1905 Moore is educated at the Metzger Institute, Carlisle.

1905–9 Attends Bryn Mawr College; Hilda Doolittle is a fellow student. Moore's first published poetry appears in Bryn Mawr journals.

1910 Moore graduates from Carlisle Commercial College.

1911 Moore travels with her mother in England and France. Begins teaching commercial subjects at the United States Indian School in Carlisle.

1915 First poems appear in the *Egoist* (London), *Poetry* (Chicago), and *Others* (New York).

1916 Moore moves to Chatham, New Jersey, with her mother to keep house for her brother, John Warner Moore, a Presbyterian minister.

1918 Moore moves to Greenwich Village, New York City, with her mother. Works as a secretary and private tutor. Meets Alfred Kreymborg, William Carlos Williams, Wallace Stevens, Kenneth Burke.

1920 Moore's poems begin to appear in *The Dial*.

1921 *Poems* is published by The Egoist Press, London.

1921–25 Moore works part-time at the Hudson Park Branch of the New York Public Library.

1923 "Marriage" is published separately.

1924 *Observations* is published by Dial Press. Moore receives the Dial Award for 1924.

1925 Moore becomes acting editor of *The Dial* magazine.

1926 Appointed editor of *The Dial.*

1929 *The Dial* ceases publication. Moore and her mother move to Brooklyn. Moore devotes her full time to writing.

1932 Receives the Helen Haire Levinson Prize for Poetry.

1934 First meets Elizabeth Bishop.

1935 *Selected Poems* is published in New York and in London with an introduction by T. S. Eliot. Moore receives the Ernest Hartsock Memorial Prize.

1936 *The Pangolin and Other Verse* is published.

1940 Moore receives the Shelley Memorial Award.

1941 *What Are Years?* is published.

1944 *Nevertheless* is published. Moore receives the Harriet Monroe Poetry Award.

1945 Moore receives a Guggenheim Fellowship. Translates, with Elizabeth Mayer, Adalbert Stifter's *Rock Crystal, A Christmas Tale.*

1947 Moore is elected to the National Institute of Arts and Letters. Her mother dies.

1949 "A Face" is published separately.

1951 *Collected Poems* is published. Moore receives the Pulitzer Prize for Poetry, the National Book Award, and the Bollingen Prize.

1953 Moore serves as visiting lecturer at Bryn Mawr College. Receives the M. Carey Thomas Award and the National Institute of Arts and Letters Gold Medal for Poetry.

1954 Moore's translation of *The Fables of La Fontaine* is published. *Gedichte*, a bilingual edition of poems, is published in Germany.

1955 *Predilections* (selected essays) and the *Selected Fables of La Fontaine* are published. Moore is elected member of the American Academy of Arts and Letters.

1956 *Like a Bulwark* is published.

1957 Moore participates in the First Bollingen Poetry Festival at The Johns Hopkins University.

1958 *Idiosyncracy and Technique: Two Lectures* is published.

1959 *O to Be a Dragon* is published.

1961 *A Marianne Moore Reader* is published.

1962 *The Absentee: A Comedy in Four Acts* is published.

1963 Moore translates and adapts three tales by Charles Perrault: "Puss in Boots," "The Sleeping Beauty," and "Cinderella."

1966 Moore moves to Manhattan.

1967 *The Complete Poems* is published. Moore receives the Edward MacDowell Medal and the Poetry Society of America's Gold Medal.

1968 Moore is awarded the National Medal for Literature. Throws out first baseball of the season at Yankee Stadium.

1972 Moore dies on February 5.

1981 *The Complete Poems*, definitive edition with the author's final revisions, is published.

Contributors

HAROLD BLOOM, Sterling Professor of the Humanities at Yale University, is the author of *The Anxiety of Influence*, *Poetry and Repression*, and many other volumes of literary criticism. His forthcoming study, *Freud: Transference and Authority*, attempts a full-scale reading of all of Freud's major writings. A MacArthur Prize Fellow, he is general editor of five series of literary criticism published by Chelsea House.

HUGH KENNER, Professor of English at The Johns Hopkins University, is our leading critic of American modernist literature. His books of criticism include *Gnomon*, *The Pound Era*, and *A Homemade World: The American Modernist Writers*.

PAMELA WHITE HADAS teaches at Washington University. She is the author of several volumes of poetry and the critical study *Marianne Moore: Poet of Affection*.

MARIE BORROFF is William Lampson Professor of English at Yale University and the author of *Language and the Poet: Verbal Artistry in Frost, Stevens, and Moore* and *Sir Gawain and the Green Knight: A Stylistic and Metrical Study*.

HELEN VENDLER is Professor of English at Boston University. She is the author of *Yeats'* Vision *and the Later Plays*, *On Extended Wings*, *The Poetry of George Herbert*, and *Part of Nature, Part of Us: Modern American Poets*.

BONNIE COSTELLO is Associate Professor of English at Boston University and the author of *Marianne Moore: Imaginary Possessions*.

DAVID BROMWICH is Professor of English at Princeton University. He is the author of *Hazlitt: The Mind of a Critic*.

JOHN M. SLATIN is Assistant Professor of English at the University of Texas at Austin. He is the author of *The Savage's Romance: The Poetry of Marianne Moore*.

Bibliography

Abbott, Craig S. *Marianne Moore: A Descriptive Bibliography*. Pittsburgh: University of Pittsburgh Press, 1977.

———. *Marianne Moore: A Reference Guide*. Boston: G. K. Hall and Co., 1978.

Ashbery, John. "Jerboas, Pelicans, and Pee Wee Reese." *New York World Journal Tribune Book Week* 4 (October 30, 1966): 1.

———. "Straight Lines over Rough Terrain." *New York Times Book Review* (November 26, 1967): 1.

Auden, W. H. "Marianne Moore." In *The Dyer's Hand and Other Essays*, 296–305. New York: Random House, 1962.

Bar-Yaacov, Lois. "Marianne Moore: An 'In-Patriot.' " *The Hebrew University Studies in Literature* 3 (Autumn 1975): 165–95.

Blackmur, R. P. "The Method of Marianne Moore." In *The Double-Agent: Essays on Craft and Elucidation*, 141–71. New York: Arrow Editions, 1935.

Bogan, Louise. *A Poet's Alphabet: Reflections on the Literary Art and Vocation*, 254–57, 303–6. New York: McGraw-Hill, 1970.

Borroff, Marie. *Language and the Poet: Verbal Artistry in Frost, Stevens, and Moore*. Chicago: The University of Chicago Press, 1979.

Burke, Kenneth. "Motives and Motifs in the Poetry of Marianne Moore." In *A Grammar of Motives*, 485–502. New York: Prentice-Hall, 1945.

Coffman, Stanley K. *Imagism: A Chapter for the History of Modern Poetry*. Norman: University of Oklahoma Press, 1951.

Cole, Thomas. "The Revised Poems of Marianne Moore." *Imagi* 6, no. 1 (1952): 11–12.

Costello, Bonnie. *Marianne Moore: Imaginary Possessions*. Cambridge: Harvard University Press, 1981.

Culler, Jonathan. *Structuralist Poetics: Structuralism, Linguistics, and the Study of Literature*, 150–51. Ithaca: Cornell University Press, 1975.

Davenport, Guy. "Marianne Moore." In *The Geography of the Imagination*, 114–23. San Francisco: North Point Press, 1981.

Dembo, L. S. "Marianne Moore: Unparticularities." In *Conceptions of Reality in Modern American Poetry*. Berkeley: University of California Press, 1966.

Dickey, James. "Marianne Moore." In *Babel to Byzantium: Poets and Poetry Now*, 156–64. New York: Farrar, Straus & Giroux, 1968.

Engel, Bernard. *Marianne Moore*. New York: Twayne Publishers, 1964.

Fowlie, Wallace. "Marianne Moore." *Sewanee Review* 60 (July 1952): 537–47.

Fuller, Roy B. "An Artifice of Versification." In *Owls and Artificers: Oxford Lectures on Poetry*, 44–68. London: Andre Deutsch, 1971.

Gross, Harvey. "Marianne Moore." In *Sound and Form in Modern Poetry*, 112–17. Ann Arbor: University of Michigan Press, 1964.

Hadas, Pamela White. *Marianne Moore: Poet of Affection*. Syracuse: Syracuse University Press, 1977.

Hall, Donald. *Marianne Moore: The Cage and the Animal*. New York: Western Publishing Co., 1970.

Hayes, Ann L. "On Reading Marianne Moore." In *A Modern Miscellany*, 1–19. Pittsburgh: Carnegie-Mellon University, 1970.

Hecht, Anthony. "Writers' Rights and Readers' Rights." *The Hudson Review* 21 (Spring 1968): 207–9.

Jarrell, Randall. "Two Essays on Marianne Moore." In *Poetry and the Age*, 162–87. New York: Vintage-Knopf, 1953.

Kennedy, X. J. "Marianne Moore." *The Minnesota Review* 2 (Spring 1962): 369–76.

Kenner, Hugh. "Artemis and Harlequin." *The National Review* 19 (December 26, 1967): 1432–33.

———. *A Homemade World: The American Modernist Writers*. New York: Alfred A. Knopf, 1975.

———. *The Pound Era*. Berkeley and Los Angeles: University of California Press, 1971.

Kunitz, Stanley. *A Kind of Order, a Kind of Folly: Essay and Conversation*, 220–27. Boston: Little, Brown, 1975.

Leavis, F. R. "Marianne Moore." *Scrutiny* 4, no. 1 (1935): 87–90.

Levin, Harry. *Grounds for Comparison*. Cambridge: Harvard University Press, 1972.

McCormick, John. *The Middle Distance: A Comparative History of American Literature 1919–1932*. New York: Free Press, 1971.

Marianne Moore Newsletter, 1977–

Monroe, Harriet. "Symposium on Marianne Moore." *Poetry* 19 (January 1922): 208–16.

Nitchie, George. *Marianne Moore: An Introduction to the Poetry*. New York: Columbia University Press, 1969.

Parkin, Rebecca Price. "Certain Difficulties in Reading Marianne Moore: Exemplified in Her 'Apparition of Splendor.' " *PMLA* 81 (June 1966): 167–72.

———. "Some Characteristics of Marianne Moore's Humor." *College English* 27 (February 1967): 403–8.

Pearce, Roy Harvey. "Marianne Moore." In *The Continuity of American Poetry*, 366–75. Princeton: Princeton University Press, 1961.

Phillips, Elizabeth. *Marianne Moore*. New York: Frederick Ungar, 1982.

Plimpton, George. "The World Series with Marianne Moore: Letter from an October Afternoon." *Harper's* 229 (October 1964): 50–58.

Poesis: A Journal of Criticism 6, nos. 3/4 (1985). Special Moore/H.D. issue.

Quarterly Review of Literature 4, no. 2 (1948). Special Marianne Moore issue.

Rexroth, Kenneth. *American Poetry in the Twentieth Century*. New York: Herder & Herder, 1971.

Sprague, Rosemary. "Marianne Moore." In *Imaginary Gardens: A Study of Five American Poets*, 183–208. Philadelphia: Chilton Book Co., 1969.

Stapleton, Laurence. *Marianne Moore: The Poet's Advance.* Princeton: Princeton University Press, 1978.

Stevens, Wallace. "About One of Marianne Moore's Poems." In *The Necessary Angel: Essays on Reality and the Imagination,* 93–103. New York: Alfred A. Knopf, 1951.

———. "A Poet that Matters." In *Opus Posthumous,* 247–54. New York: Alfred A. Knopf, 1957.

Sutton, Walter. "Marianne Moore." In *American Free Verse: The Modern Revolution in Poetry,* 103–17. New York: New Directions, 1973.

Tambimuttu, Thurairajah, ed. *Festschrift for Marianne Moore's Seventy-seventh Birthday.* New York: Tambimuttu & Mass, 1964.

Therese, Sister Mary. *Marianne Moore: A Critical Essay.* Grand Rapids, Mich.: William Eerdmans, 1969.

Tomlinson, Charles. "Abundance, Not Too Much: The Poetry of Marianne Moore." *Sewanee Review* 65 (Autumn 1957): 677–87.

———, ed. *Marianne Moore: A Collection of Critical Essays.* Englewood Cliffs, N.J.: Prentice-Hall, Inc., 1969.

Vonalt, Larry P. "Marianne Moore's Mediums." *Sewanee Review* 78 (Fall 1970): 669–78.

Waggoner, Hyatt H. "Marianne Moore." In *American Poets: From the Puritans to the Present,* 364–68. Boston: Houghton Mifflin, 1968.

Wasserstrom, William, ed. *A Dial Miscellany.* Syracuse: Syracuse University Press, 1973.

———. *The Time of the Dial.* Syracuse: Syracuse University Press, 1963.

Weatherhead, A. Kingsley. *The Edge of the Image: Marianne Moore, William Carlos Williams and Some Other Poets.* Seattle: University of Washington Press, 1967.

Winters, Yvor. "Holiday and Day of Wrath." *Poetry* 26 (April 1925): 39–44.

Zabel, Morton Dauwen. "A Literalist of the Imagination." *Poetry* 47 (March 1936): 326–36.

Acknowledgments

"The Experience of the Eye" (originally entitled "The Experience of the Eye: Marianne Moore's Tradition") by Hugh Kenner from *The Southern Review* 1 (October 1965), © 1965 by The Louisiana State University, © 1968 by Hugh Kenner. Reprinted by permission.

"Treading Chasms" (originally entitled "Fighting Affections") by Pamela White Hadas from *Marianne Moore: Poet of Affection* by Pamela White Hadas, © 1977 by Syracuse University Press, Reprinted by permission of the publisher. Syracuse, New York.

"Marianne Moore's Promotional Prose" (originally entitled "Marianne Moore's Promotional Prose: A Poem's Guise at Last") by Marie Borroff from *Language and the Poet: Verbal Artistry in Frost, Stevens, and Moore* by Marie Borroff, © 1979 by The University of Chicago. Reprinted by permission of The University of Chicago Press.

"Marianne Moore" by Helen Vendler from *Part of Nature, Part of Us: Modern American Poets* by Helen Vendler, © 1980 by the President and Fellows of Harvard College. Reprinted by permission of Harvard University Press.

"The 'Feminine' Language of Marianne Moore" by Bonnie Costello from *Women and Language in Literature and Society*, edited by Sally McConnell-Ginet, Ruth Borker, and Nelly Furman, © 1980 by Praeger Publishers. Reprinted by permission.

"Emphatic Reticence" (originally entitled "Marianne Moore's Poems") by David Bromwich from *Poetry* 139, no. 6 (March 1982), © 1982 by The Modern Poetry Association. Reprinted by permission of the author and the Editor of *Poetry*.

"Marianne Moore and Elizabeth Bishop: Friendship and Influence" by Bonnie Costello from *Twentieth Century Literature* 30, nos. 2/3 (Summer/Fall 1984), © 1984 by Hofstra University Press. Reprinted by permission.

" 'Advancing Backward in a Circle': Moore as (Natural) Historian" (originally entitled " 'Advancing Backward in a Circle': Marianne Moore as (Natural) Historian") by John M. Slatin from *Twentieth Century Literature* 30, nos. 2/3 (Summer/Fall 1984), © 1984 by Hofstra University Press. Reprinted by permission.

Index

REDEFINING

EQUALITY

REDEFINING EQUALITY

Edited by
Neal Devins
&
Davison M. Douglas

New York Oxford
OXFORD UNIVERSITY PRESS
1998

Oxford University Press

Oxford New York
Athens Auckland Bangkok Bogota Bombay Buenos Aires
Calcutta Cape Town Dar es Salaam Delhi Florence Hong Kong
Istanbul Karachi Kuala Lumpur Madras Madrid Melbourne
Mexico City Nairobi Paris Singapore Taipei Tokyo Toronto Warsaw

and associated companies in
Berlin Ibadan

Published by Oxford University Press, Inc.
198 Madison Avenue, New York, New York 10016

Library of Congress Cataloging-in-Publication Data
Redefining equality / edited by Neal Devins and Davison M. Douglas.
p. cm.
Includes index.
ISBN 0-19-511664-X; ISBN 0-19-511665-8 (pbk.)
1. Equality—United States. 2. Equality before the law—United States. I. Devins, Neal E. II. Douglas, Davison M.
JC575.R43 1997
323.42'0973—dc21 97-1884

1 3 5 7 9 8 6 4 2

Printed in the United States of America
on acid-free paper

To Our Siblings

Alicia, Marc, and Joyce

N. D.

John M. Douglas, Jr., and James O. Douglas

D. D.

Acknowledgments

A great many people contributed to the completion of this book. First and foremost, we would like to thank the contributors, who worked with us as we tried to mold this group of essays into a book that will help shape the ongoing dialogue about equality. We would also like to thank our research assistants Allison Cox, Amy Laderberg, Ken Mahieu, Catherine Rogers, and Chris Wesser for their tireless work in tracking down elusive sources and proofreading the final text, and Adrienne Parker for preparing the index. Della Harris and Felicia Burton of the William and Mary Law School provided wonderful clerical support. The William and Mary Law School also provided financial assistance. Helen McInnis and Paula Wald of Oxford University Press offered important encouragement along the way. Finally, we would like to thank the editors of the *William and Mary Law Review* for hosting two symposia on equality. Not only did several of the contributors to this volume participate in these symposia, but the idea of assembling a multidisciplinary collection of essays on equality emerged from these symposia.

Williamsburg, Virginia
August 1997

N. D.
D. D.

Contents

Contributors

KATHRYN ABRAMS is a professor of law at Cornell Law School. She has written many works in the area of feminist jurisprudence, including articles in the *Yale Law Journal, Stanford Law Review, Michigan Law Review*, and *Columbia Law Review*.

ERWIN CHEMERINSKY is Legion Lex Professor of Law at the University of Southern California Law Center. He writes widely in the areas of constitutional law and civil rights law and is the author of *Constitutional Law: Principles and Policies* (1997); *Federal Jurisdiction* (1994); and *Interpreting the Constitution* (1987).

DREW S. DAYS III is Alfred M. Rankin Professor at Yale Law School. From 1993 to 1996, he was Solicitor General of the United States. He writes in the area of race relations law and has published articles in the *Yale Law Journal, Texas Law Review, Vanderbilt Law Review*, and *William and Mary Law Review*.

RICHARD DELGADO is Charles Inglis Thomson Professor of Law at the University of Colorado. He is the author of many books and articles on critical race theory, including *The Rodrigo Chronicles: Conversations about America and Race* (1995); *Critical Race Theory: The Cutting Edge* (1995); *The Price We Pay: The Case against Racist Speech, Hate Propaganda, and Pornography* (1995); and *Failed Revolutions: Social Reform and the Limits of Legal Imagination* (1994) (with Jean Stefancic).

NEAL DEVINS is a professor of law and a lecturer in government at William and Mary. He writes in the area of constitutional law and politics and is the author of *Shaping Constitutional Values: Elected Government, the Supreme Court, and the*

Abortion Dispute (1996); *Political Dynamics of Constitutional Law*, 2d ed. (1996) (with Louis Fisher); and *Public Values, Private Schools* (1989).

DAVISON M. DOUGLAS is a professor of law and Director of the Institute of Bill of Rights Law at William and Mary Law School. He writes in the area of race and American law and is the author of *Reading, Writing, and Race: The Desegregation of the Charlotte Schools* (1995) and *School Busing: Constitutional and Political Developments* (1994).

DAVID J. GARROW is a Presidential Distinguished Professor at Emory University. He has written several books on the modern civil rights movement, including the Pulitzer Prize–winning book *Bearing the Cross: Martin Luther King, Jr., and the Southern Christian Leadership Conference* (1986) and *Protest at Selma: Martin Luther King, Jr., and the Voting Rights Act of 1965* (1978). He is also the author of *Liberty and Sexuality: The Right to Privacy and Making of* Roe v. Wade (1994).

HUGH DAVIS GRAHAM is Holland N. McTyeire Professor of History at Vanderbilt University. He has written several books on modern American history, including *The Civil Rights Era: Origins and Development of National Policy, 1960–1972* (1990); *The Uncertain Triumph: Federal Education Policy in the Kennedy and Johnson Years* (1984); and *Southern Politics and the Second Reconstruction* (1975) (with Numan Bartley).

JENNIFER L. HOCHSCHILD is a professor of politics and public affairs at Princeton University. She is the author of several books on equality, including *Facing Up to the American Dream: Race, Class, and the Soul of the Nation* (1995); *The New American Dilemma: Liberal Democracy and School Desegregation* (1984); and *What's Fair: American Beliefs about Distributive Justice* (1981).

JEREMY RABKIN is an associate professor of government at Cornell University. He writes about American politics and is the author of *Judicial Compulsions: How Public Law Distorts Public Policy* (1989) and *The Fettered Presidency: Legal Constraints on the Executive Branch* (1989) (with Gordon Crovitz).

GERALD N. ROSENBERG is an associate professor of political science and a lecturer in law at the University of Chicago. He spent the 1995–96 academic year as a visiting fellow in the Law Program of the Research School of Social Sciences at the Australian National University. He writes widely in the area of courts and politics and is the author of *The Hollow Hope: Can Courts Bring about Social Change?* (1991, 1994).

CHRISTINE H. ROSSELL is a professor of political science at Boston University. She is the author of numerous publications dealing with school desegregation, including *The Carrot or the Stick for School Desegregation Policy* (1990) and *The Consequences of School Desegregation Policy* (1983) (with Willis Hawley).

REVA B. SIEGEL is a professor of law at Yale Law School. She is the author of numerous publications dealing with legal history and feminist jurisprudence, including articles in the *Yale Law Journal, Stanford Law Review*, and *Georgetown Law Journal*.

JEAN STEFANCIC is a research associate at the University of Colorado Law School. She writes on legal scholarship and law reform and is the author of *Failed Revolutions: Social Reform and the Limits of Legal Imagination* (1994) (with Richard Delgado).

DAVID A. STRAUSS is Harry N. Wyatt Professor of Law at the University of Chicago Law School. He is also coeditor of the *Supreme Court Review*. He writes widely in the area of constitutional law and jurisprudence and has published articles in the *Yale Law Journal, Columbia Law Review*, and *University of Chicago Law Review*.

REDEFINING

EQUALITY

1

Introduction

The Pursuit of Equality

DAVISON M. DOUGLAS
NEAL DEVINS

The notion of equality is central to American civic life. Enshrined in two of the nation's central documents—the Declaration of Independence ("We hold these truths to be self-evident, that all men are created equal") and the U.S. Constitution ("No state shall . . . deny to any person within its jurisdiction the equal protection of the laws")—equality is one of the basic foundations of our national life.

Yet in the most diverse nation on the planet, the notion of equality has proved elusive. A cursory survey of American history reveals the many ways in which Americans have not been treated equally under the law. We need think only of the treatment of African Americans in slavery and later in Jim Crow segregation, of women and their lack of full civil and political equality until the recent past, of the genocide and repression of this country's native population, of the variety of indignities suffered by gays and lesbians, and of the exclusionary treatment of a vast array of immigrant groups for us to realize that equality has been denied to many Americans.

In the 1990s, the issue of equality—for whites as well as for racial minorities, for men as well as for women—continues to bedevil our civic life. Cries of unequal treatment continue to be heard in both public discourse and the courts. America is far from having reached consensus over the meaning of equality and whether we have in fact achieved it. Competing views of what constitutes equality have erupted into a cultural conflict that looms large in contemporary American politics. As we move toward the twenty-first century, the debate over affirmative action, for example, promises to become an ever more explosive political issue that brings theoretical conversations about equality into the living rooms and polling places of America. Our ongoing struggle to define equality is far more than an exercise in legal definition. The conflict over the meaning of equality is in reality a battle for the soul of America. How we as a nation ultimately choose to define equality will dramatically shape our social and political life.

This book contributes to this growing debate. By presenting an array of views about the meaning of equality and the ways in which we have sought to achieve it, this volume provides new perspectives for the ongoing debate over equality. In particular, by bringing together lawyers, historians, social scientists, and political theorists from across the ideological spectrum, this collection presents a range of opinions and insights that speak to America's ability to find a common language—let alone a common ground—in sorting out the equality riddle.

Defining Equality

Part of what is troubling about our national conversation about equality is that it is difficult to reach agreement about what equality actually means. Equality has often been characterized as the elimination of formal legal barriers of exclusion based on certain immutable characteristics such as race and gender. This view of equality, sometimes referred to as "the antidiscrimination principle," is reflected in contemporary calls for a "color-blind" society. According to this view, equality is measured in terms of equal opportunity, not equal results, and thus broad disparities in economic and political power do not necessarily reflect a failure of equality.

Yet this view of equality has been attacked for precisely this reason. Pointing, for example, to the roadblocks that stand in the way of a minority child raised in an urban ghetto with limited economic and educational opportunities, many civil rights leaders condemn this notion of equality for failing to take into account that many Americans do not possess equal opportunity to compete for economic and political power. Indeed, the failure of antidiscrimination prohibitions to address vast disparities in power and wealth helps explain the emergence of a broad array of social policies and legislative initiatives that use race and gender in a "benign" manner. Affirmative action programs in employment and education have given preference to women and members of certain racial minority groups. Race-conscious pupil assignments coupled with school busing have been used to achieve racially mixed urban schools. Racially gerrymandered electoral districts have sought to increase the number of black and Hispanic elected officials.

America, however, has never reached consensus about the desirability of such race-conscious programs. In part, these measures have been opposed as violative of the principle of "color-blindness"—that race (and gender) should be irrelevant in public and private decisionmaking. Opponents have also dubbed these initiatives counterproductive—doing little to narrow the income, education, and political gap between minorities and nonminorities and doing much to exacerbate racial tension. Thus, at the root of the current equality debate is a fundamental disagreement about how to achieve equality. This book seeks to illustrate the broad range of views about the meaning and pursuit of equality.

Kathyrn Abrams, in "Equality and Impasse: Mobilizing Group-Based Perspectives in an Era of Group-Blindness," argues that gender-and race-neutral policies often mask more subtle forms of exclusion. A staunch advocate of legal doctrines that allow the affirmative use of race, such as affirmative action and racially gerrymandered electoral districts, Abrams derides recent Supreme Court decisions for placing color-blindness ahead of the interests of the victim-outsider. Abrams blames courts—even the more liberal Warren Court—for failing to appreciate the experience of discrimination from the perspective of the outsider and argues that therefore judicial decisions that appear ''neutral'' are often not.

Building on this theme, Reva Siegel's ''Civil Rights Reform in Historical Perspective: Regulating Marital Violence'' offers a concrete example of the way in which neutral legal standards can mask inequality. Siegel traces both the demise of the doctrine of chastisement, which permitted a husband to ''chastise'' or beat his wife with impunity, and the concurrent emergence of the doctrine of marital privacy, which provided certain tort and criminal immunities within the context of marriage. Although seemingly neutral, the marital privacy doctrine in fact allowed the continuation of physical beating, and hence gender inequality, inside the marital unit.

David Strauss, in ''The Illusory Distinction between Equality of Opportunity and Equality of Result,'' goes much further than do Abrams and Siegel in attacking the color-blind vision of equality. Whereas Abrams and Siegel implicitly embrace the notion that equality doctrine is properly concerned with the provision of equal opportunity for outsider groups—as defined in racial, ethnic, or gender terms—Strauss contends that equality doctrine should be concerned with eradicating inequality on a far broader scale.

Strauss invites us to consider a notion of equality of opportunity that takes into account barriers to opportunity over which a person has no control—in addition to race and gender—such as talents, abilities, and family wealth. If the foundation for antidiscrimination prohibitions is an abhorrence of exclusion due to factors outside our control, then, asks Strauss, should we not be equally disturbed over the disfavoring of individuals who have limited talents and abilities and family wealth to employ in their pursuit of material and political success? Strauss's argument is all the more provocative given that the effect of limited talents and abilities has become far more dramatic than ever before, as the gap between the ''haves'' and ''have-nots'' has progressively widened.[1] Abrams, Siegel, and Strauss—with different emphases—invite us to consider whether the elimination of formal barriers to full participation in America's social and economic life is in fact sufficient to create a society in which there is equal social and economic opportunity. Each suggests that formal equality does not translate into true equality.

Jeremy Rabkin offers a vastly different vision of equality in ''Racial Divisions and Judicial Obstructions.'' Pointing to the role that affirmative action and other Great Society programs have had in exacerbating the divide between black and white America, Rabkin endorses the color-blind view of equality and argues that defining equality in any other way invites intrusive governmental regulation that in fact undermines minority interests. Hence, Rabkin implicitly questions the assumption of Abrams, Siegel, and Strauss that equality should be measured by equality of result.

Finally, Jennifer Hochschild, in ''The Word 'American' Ends in 'I Can': The

Ambiguous Promise of the American Dream,'' explores the ideology of ''the American dream''—the promise of unlimited opportunity for economic and social advancement for all Americans and its relationship to equality. Hochschild argues that although the possibility of such unlimited advancement holds a powerful allure, in fact the ''dream'' is not attainable by all Americans and the ''losers'' often suffer unwarranted and corrosive denigration at the hands of the ''winners.''

Minority Attitudes toward Equality

Part of the difficulty in defining equality is the widespread belief that the meaning and content of equality vary among racial groups. Several of the authors in this volume attempt to assay the attitudes of minority groups toward equality. Some observers have assumed that racial minorities have a monolithic view of what constitutes equality. Certainly, as Hugh Graham notes in ''The Politics of Clientele Capture: Civil Rights Policy and the Reagan Administration,'' the civil rights establishment has sought to convey such a sense of unanimity in its political advocacy. Yet the minority community's views on affirmative action, school busing, and other equality issues are far more diverse and nuanced than the views often represented in the political process. For example, many African Americans have increasingly questioned the value of affirmative action or school busing.[2]

Two of the essayists in this volume address this topic by examining the issue of busing to desegregate urban schools. In ''The Convergence of Black and White Attitudes on School Desegregation Issues,'' Christine Rossell challenges the assumption that African Americans generally support race-conscious pupil assignments coupled with school busing to overcome racially identifiable schools. Relying on extensive empirical surveys of the attitudes of African American parents, Rossell concludes that a majority of African American parents in fact favor neighborhood schools or voluntary magnet schools. Black support for these alternative arrangements has significantly increased since the mid-1980s, suggesting that for many in the African American community, equality is not contingent on racial mixing but on greater educational and economic opportunity.

Drew Days, in ''*Brown* Blues: Rethinking the Integrative Ideal,'' argues that much of the decline in black support for racial mixing in the public schools is due not to an embrace of racial isolation but rather to the recognition that African Americans have borne so much of the cost of school desegregation in terms of both the loss of black values and institutions and the tangible burdens of blacks' being forced to assimilate into white environments. Hence, Days explains the decline in black support for school integration not in terms of a rejection of racial mixing and embrace of neighborhood schools, as Rossell might suggest, but rather in terms of minority support for policies that minimize the burdens African Americans have been obliged to assume in the wake of desegregation initiatives.

The divergence between Days and Rossell reveals the different perspectives that Americans bring to the concept of equality and suggests the difficulty in assessing racial attitudes concerning both the meaning of equality and the desirability of race-conscious remedies. Needless to say, if it is this difficult to assess attitudes toward equality, there is little hope of reaching consensus in America about the meaning of equality.

Do Courts Matter?

Consensus over the mechanisms by which government can secure equality also seems impossible, as suggested by the ever-increasing divide over the propriety of court-ordered social change. Many observers have heralded the courts for playing *the* central role in the quest for equality during certain periods of American history. In particular, during the 1950s and 1960s, the Supreme Court issued a broad range of decisions that struck down various governmental and private arrangements that excluded certain minority groups from economic and political benefits. The most celebrated of these decisions—the Supreme Court's 1954 decision in *Brown v. Board of Education*—is testament to a Supreme Court willing to challenge a long-standing governmental practice that enjoyed broad and intense political support.

But in recent years, fundamental questions have been raised about the extent to which the courts have actually delivered equality.[3] Concluding that those interested in gaining racial and gender equality should pursue their goals in the political process, many liberal scholars now argue that the main gains of racial equality in this country's history have come not through the courts but through the political process: the abolition of slavery by statute, the Reconstruction amendments to the U.S. Constitution, and the civil rights legislation of the Reconstruction era and the 1960s. Conservatives also advocate a diminished judicial role but for quite different reasons. Claiming that court-ordered reform is little more than the exercise of raw power by judges and civil rights leaders, conservatives decry judicial activism for standing in the way of innovative democratic solutions to equality.

Several of the essayists in this volume address the vital issue of the role of the courts in the quest for equality. Siegel offers the view that equality gains secured by courts often mask the retention of inequality under new legal standards. She examines the way in which legal elites have preserved their status privileges in the face of "pro-equality" court decisions. As Siegel concludes, civil rights reform can alter legal rules, but the new legal doctrines often leave in place the original inequalities as legal elites subvert the new changes in their own favor.

Critical race theorists Richard Delgado and Jean Stefancic, in "The Social Construction of *Brown v. Board of Education*: Law Reform and the Reconstructive Paradox," also express skepticism about the ability of courts to engage in meaningful reform in the face of political and cultural opposition. Specifically, Delgado and Stefancic conclude that decisions of courts—including the Supreme Court's *Brown* decision—have had far less impact in securing equality than we have previously suspected because courts are inherently constrained by broader political and cultural factors.

This "limited" view of courts—and particularly of the *Brown* Court—has much to recommend it. The *Brown* decision in fact did not lead to widespread southern school desegregation. Most southern schools remained segregated for the next decade. Not until Congress and the president sought to make *Brown* a reality by enacting the Civil Rights Act of 1964 did black children enter white southern schools in appreciable numbers.

Indeed, Gerald Rosenberg demonstrates that most Americans are unaware of the actions of the Court and that its decisions on equality have had limited effect on public opinion. For this reason, Rosenberg, in "The Irrelevant Court: The Supreme Court's Inability to Influence Popular Beliefs about Equality (or Anything Else)," concludes that courts are far less able than we have previously suspected to trigger widespread social reform. Public attitudes toward racial and gender equality have changed dramatically during the past forty years, but the Supreme Court's role in that change has been relatively minor.

Along the same lines, Neal Devins, in "The Judicial Role in Equality Decisionmaking," cautions that there are inherent limits on judicial authority and argues that the laments of judicial activists about the failure of the courts to extend the rights of women and minorities do not fully appreciate the institutional limits that courts face. To Devins, courts are confronted with a broad range of competing interests that require balancing, and as a result, courts are constrained by broader social and political concerns. Thus, courts cannot champion equality interests to the extent that judicial activists might hope for. In this sense, Devins agrees with Rosenberg, Delgado, and Stefancic in their view of the inherent limits on courts in securing racial change.

The Role of Courts

Increasing skepticism over the potency of judicial action, however, has hardly quieted liberal defenders and conservative critics of interventionist judicial review. Erwin Chemerinsky, in "Can Courts Make a Difference?" delivers an impassioned defense of judicial activism. While conceding that African Americans continue to lag behind other groups in their struggle for a greater share of the American dream, Chemerinsky claims that the failure of courts to achieve certain equality goals is not simply a function of the inherent limits of judicial power but rather is a function of judicial unwillingness, particularly with the Burger and Rehnquist Courts, to wield this power. Similarly, Abrams champions the role that courts can play in securing meaningful equality but concludes that courts have failed to exercise such power because of inattentiveness to victim-outsider concerns.

David Garrow, in "The Supreme Court's Pursuit of Equality and Liberty and the Burdens of History," agrees in part with Chemerinsky's and Abrams's view of the inherent power of courts to affect the struggle for equality. Garrow examines the Supreme Court's decisions affecting equality and liberty interests of the post-*Brown* era and concludes that the Court aggressively pursued equality and liberty interests not because the requisite constitutional doctrines required such decisions but because the Court wished to achieve policy goals it deemed morally compelling. In this way, the Court proved to be an important protector of equality interests and helped reshape attitudes in America about the rights of women and racial minorities. Garrow, for example, concludes that the Court's decision in *Brown* is not supported by history but that because of the compelling nature of the black litigants' claims in the case, the Court decided not to remain tethered to traditional understandings of the meaning of equal protection and hence proceeded to strike down segregated schools.

As both Chemerinsky and Garrow argue, certain court decisions have obviously had a profound impact on American life, even if those decisions failed, as Rosenberg suggests, to reshape public attitudes. The most obvious examples are those court decisions designed to desegregate schools in America's cities. Courts throughout the nation ordered urban school systems during the 1970s to adopt mandatory pupil reassignment plans coupled with extensive school busing notwithstanding vigorous opposition to such plans. Although these busing orders prompted strong reaction in both Congress and the executive branch and triggered a number of legislative efforts to restrict the use of busing to desegregate urban schools, such remedies would remain an important method of desegregating urban schools for the next two decades. Certainly the courts' busing decisions did not favorably influence public opinion—indeed, they inspired spirited opposition—but notwithstanding that failure, those decisions had a profound impact on both urban public school systems and the meaning of equality in America's cities.

Although most scholars, including several in this volume, celebrate the role of the courts, particularly the Supreme Court, in vindicating the equality concerns of minority groups in the face of majoritarian hostility, Rabkin argues that courts have undermined equality of opportunity for minority groups through a number of decisions that have misapplied constitutional doctrines. In Rabkin's view, the courts in many instances have been so unduly solicitous of perceived violations of individual rights that they have harmed the interest of the broader community. Rabkin contends that despite judicial and legislative activism during the past thirty years, the minority underclass suffers as much as ever and that such activism has had a negative effect on the struggle for equality of opportunity.

Although not as directly critical of modern judicial activism as is Rabkin, Hugh Graham also suggests that the courts have the ability to subvert the popular political process and have done so on certain equality issues, particularly school desegregation and affirmative action. In particular, Graham calls attention to the ways in which the courts have blocked elected governmental reforms by becoming the willing captive of civil rights interests.

Equality and Politics

Skepticism of the courts' role in the modern struggle for equality is well founded. Although the Supreme Court in the *Brown* case articulated a dramatic shift in equal protection constitutional doctrine, perhaps the central achievements in the struggle for racial and gender equality of the last half century have been two acts of Congress: the Civil Rights Act of 1964, directed at eliminating racial discrimination in employment, public accommodations, and education, and the Voting Rights Act of 1965, directed at enfranchising African American voters. Although the 1964 Act failed to eliminate much racial and gender discrimination, it did constitute a major affirmation of the principle of equality at a time when segregation and overt discrimination were widespread. Over the course of the next few years, as a result of the 1964 Act, initial steps were made toward eliminating discrimination in the workplace and dramatic gains were made in desegregating southern schools and public accommodations. During the same period, black voter registration significantly increased throughout the South in response to the Voting Rights Act and the number of black elected officials in the South substantially increased in the late 1960s and early 1970s.

In time, the antidiscrimination measures of the 1960s gave way to race-conscious initiatives. In 1969, the Nixon administration ordered racial preferences in hiring at federally assisted construction projects. Following this executive order, the use of affirmative action in education and employment in both the public and the private sector increased. Subsequently, in the early 1980s, Congress approved the use of racially gerrymandered electoral districts to assist the election of minority candidiates.

These various legislative and executive initiatives occurred as a result of cultural and political support for improving the status of certain outsider groups—racial and ethnic minorities and women—that had traditionally been excluded from full participation in America's civic and economic life. At the same time, political and social divisiveness followed this shift away from strict equality of opportunity. The 1980 election of Ronald Reagan was testament to this emerging fault line in the equality debate. Reagan (and George Bush after him) vehemently opposed affirmative action, proclaiming: "We must not allow the noble concept of equal opportunity to be distorted into federal guidelines or quotas which require race, ethnicity, or sex—rather than ability and qualifications—to be the principal factor in hiring or education."[4] From 1980 to 1992, however, limited action was taken to reverse governmental affirmative action policies. Graham, in his essay on the Reagan administration, helps explain why. In doing so, Graham reveals much about the politics of equality in America.

According to Graham, the civil rights establishment wielded significant influence over federal agencies and departments charged with administering affirmative action programs. As a result, the heads of those agencies and departments successfully lobbied the president for the retention of their affirmative action programs. In effect, Graham blames the difficulties in altering civil rights policies on interest-group politics in which advocacy groups have become highly skilled at using the political process—and the courts—to prevent rollbacks in certain civil rights programs that might otherwise enjoy popular support.

Rabkin likewise holds the civil rights establishment responsible for the failure of elective politics in the quest for equality. To Rabkin, many policy initiatives might help the underclass—such as welfare reform, crime-fighting measures, and public support of private schools—but they have foundered because of aggressive opposition by civil rights groups and restrictive court decisions.

The politics of equality, however, have changed during the past decade. The minority community, as Rossell, Days, and others have suggested, is not monolithic in its support of race-conscious remedies. Moreover, with growing dissatisfaction among white voters with affirmative action, politicians are increasingly willing to risk the opprobrium of the civil rights establishment by opposing affirmative action.

As a result, the politics of equality has once again exploded with a new fury. Populist initiatives on affirmative action launched in California and elsewhere promise to accelerate the debate on the continued wisdom and viability of government-sponsored affirmative action programs. Attacks on race-conscious pupil assignments are ongoing, and proposals for voluntary methods of desegregating urban schools proliferate. And racially gerrymandered electoral districts are under increasing fire from both the courts and the politicians. The political debate over equality will certainly continue prominently into the next century, particularly as the economic gap between black and white in America remains broad.

Whence Equality?

The essays in this volume are intended to contribute to our national conversation about equality in America. But at the same time, the broad range of perspectives and basic disagreements about the core meaning of equality reflected in these essays reveals the profound difficulty in resolving one of this nation's central dilemmas. For proponents of the color-blind theory, we should establish neutral rules and let the resulting inequalities be addressed through individual and private initiative. But for others, neutrality imposed on a society with the history of this nation in its treatment of racial and ethnic minorities cannot be meaningful, and more aggressive measures are thus required.

The fight over equality is about much more than whether color-blindness or group consciousness should prevail. It is also about the capacity of courts to mandate change, the danger of elected officials' being captured by interest groups, and the difficulty of sorting out minority attitudes toward governmental action. Answers to these concerns are as much about values and life experiences as anything else. Complicating matters further, historians, social scientists, economists, lawyers, and political theorists see these questions through different lenses. Indeed, if the essays in this volume demonstrate anything, they demonstrate the broad range of perspectives about this most difficult issue.

Equality concerns, of course, will continue to play a major role in American politics and social debate. Although broad consensus about the meaning and content of equality will continue to be elusive, it is crucial that the conversation continue, that the assumptions of various perspectives on the issue be set forth with clarity. It is with this purpose that the editors have assembled this volume of essays, that it might contribute to our nation's ongoing debate over equality.

NOTES

1. See, e.g., Philip Cook and Robert Frank, *The Winner Take All Society* (New York: Free Press, 1995).

2. See, e.g., Thomas Sowell, *Civil Rights: Rhetoric or Reality* (New York: W. Morrow, 1984); Glenn C. Loury, *One by One from the Inside Out: Essays and Review on Race and Responsibility in America* (New York: Free Press, 1995).

3. Gerald N. Rosenberg, *The Hollow Hope: Can Courts Bring About Social Change?* (Chicago: University of Chicago Press, 1991); Michael J. Klarman, ''*Brown*, Racial Change, and the Civil Rights Movement,'' *Virginia Law Review* 80 (1994): 7–150.

4. Quoted in Gary L. McDowell, ''Affirmative Inaction: The Brock-Meese Standoff in Federal Racial Quotas,'' *Policy Review* 48 (Spring 1989): 32.

2

Equality and Impasse

Mobilizing Group-Based Perspectives in an Era of Group-Blindness

KATHRYN ABRAMS

For more than a decade, critical legal commentators have observed a tension between doctrinal understandings of equality and the perspectives of outsider, or victim, groups.[1] This tension has grown into frank divergence as ''color-blindness'' has become a constitutional sword, used to dismantle governmental programs from state and federal set-asides to ''safe'' minority electoral districts. Underlying this tension is a conflict not simply about the nature of discrimination but about a range of related concepts: namely, the meaning, dynamics, and consequences of group membership, in which ''group'' connotes those connected by race, sex, or other largely inalienable characteristic that has assumed social salience. This essay will trace the escalating tension between doctrinal understandings and outsiders' understandings of these concepts. It will then ask how the law might accommodate outsiders' understandings of ''group-ness'' and group-based discrimination, at a time when mainstream constitutional doctrine prevents institutional actors from considering the social consequences—indeed the very fact—of group membership.

Early Equal Opportunity: A Dominant View and an Alternative

Discrimination as Erroneous Ascription of Difference

A doctrine broad enough to include constitutional claims, as well as federal employment and electoral law, is inevitably complex. Yet it is possible to identify themes that unify federal equality doctrine, creating coherence in its approach to discrimination and the groups it affects. In the period between the judicial assault on school desegregation and the more recent retrenchment in areas such as affirmative action, a dominant strain in this doctrine has characterized discrimination as the erroneous ascription of difference. In this view, discrimination occurs when decisionmakers ascribe differences to socially marginalized groups, in which no such differences exist.[2] This flawed ascription of difference most often results from ignorance or prejudice, which leads decisionmakers to see traits such as race or gender as affecting a range of qualities and capabilities. These erroneous judgments operate to restrict the access of affected groups to public goods, such as political participation or employment. For example, decisionmakers might reason that women are not physically or emotionally capable of serving as firefighters or that blacks are of sufficiently distinct abilities or "social station" that it is not appropriate to grant them the franchise or educate them with whites. The misstep is to believe that outsider group membership entails differences that it does not entail and to allocate valuable opportunities on this basis.

This view of discrimination has often been described as part of a "perpetrator perspective."[3] This label seems appropriate for several reasons. First, the analysis posits particular agents—decisionmakers, "perpetrators"—as the determinative force behind discrimination. This focus on the decisions of individual agents arises partly from the premises of liberal theory—liberal assumptions about responsibility, agency, and causation have made it easier for us to think about social phenomena as arising from the acts of individuals. It arises partly from the solipsism of often-privileged legal thinkers who tend to identify more readily with those agents who might be held responsible for discriminatory decisions than with those who might suffer because of them. However, the premise that analysis of discrimination should begin with the agent, and the agent's process of judgment, rather than with the target and the effect of the agent's judgment on the target's life, means that many forms of group-based discrimination are largely excluded from analysis. For example, how discriminatory decisions or judgments set in motion patterns that continue to produce group disadvantage without renewed differentiating decisionmaking or how group-specific insensitivity that does not rise to the level of a differentiating judgment can produce disadvantage are matters that are rarely discussed within this conceptual paradigm.

A second reason that this view of discrimination might be labeled "perpetrator"-oriented is that it reflects a skeletal conception of what it means to be a member of a victim group, a conception more typically of perpetrators than of group members themselves. First, the wrong implicit in actionable "discrimination" is viewed from the perspective of the decisionmaker rather than from the perspective of the group subject to the negative characterization. For example, an employer's judgment that women should not hold particular jobs because they will inevitably abandon them to have children is described as wrong because it is incorrect as applied to many women. It is not relevant, from the standpoint of doctrine, that this judgment stigmatizes women workers or limits their professional opportunities.

Second, and more important, the dominant view embodies a simplified notion of how the characteristics associated with group identity operate in the lives of members. The characteristics that define group-ness, in the leading statutory and constitutional cases, are thought to be biologically transmitted and static rather than socially constructed, complex, or malleable. Although the cases acknowledge the fact that not all members of a group are identical or fungible—there are, for example, women of different races, as well as African Americans or Asians of both sexes—this fact has only limited salience for the operation of doctrine. The cases do not highlight hierarchies or antagonisms that arise within a group, making group-based identity more complex for its subjects. Nor, in their general focus on perpetrators' cognitive errors, do the cases describe the ways that discrimination may operate differently across different subsets of a group's members, reflecting diverse stereotypes and judgments. For example, the stereotypes and epithets through which women are harassed in the workplace may vary according to the race, age, and demeanor of the targeted woman. Even the comparatively flexible sexual harassment law that has emerged under the 1964 Civil Rights Act's Title VII prohibition of employment discrimination has had difficulty accommodating this fact.[4] This lack of descriptive nuance may arise from the fact that the leading cases regard group membership as incidental to the essential human nature of any legal subject. Group membership is not a sufficiently rich or variable influence to play a determinative role in shaping the consciousness of individuals, and it is likely to lead to erroneous categorization when decisionmakers take it into account. Guided by such assumptions, legal decisionmakers have often viewed group-based characteristics as qualities that are best overlooked.

Results Analysis as a Partial Alternative

Despite the prevalence of this early conceptualization, it was not the only available framework for understanding discrimination. A distinct understanding of discrimination, and how it operates in the lives of victim groups, emerged from those portions of antidiscrimination doctrine that found discrimination in disparate "effects" or "results." This alternate focus, which did not require a specific perpetrator, let alone a flawed ascription of difference, came about in a variety of ways. Scrutiny of actual results first began as a means of measuring remedial compliance with strong, if amorphous, equal protection mandates. Analyzing the extent of racial integration in a school operating under a desegregation decree, for example, helped to determine whether the district was acting appropriately to eliminate segregation "root and branch." *Washington v. Davis*,[5] a 1976 Supreme Court decision best known for its refusal to constitutionalize discriminatory effect as an independent index of discrimination, generated an instrumental use for "results" analysis: racially disparate effects could function as evidence of the pivotal, but often elusive, discriminatory intent.[6]

In still other cases, the practice of scrutinizing results operated less as a means of identifying or rectifying agent-based discrimination than as a distinct way of understanding discrimination. In federal employment discrimination law,[7] courts determined that equality for covered groups could be undermined by "built-in headwinds": tests, selection norms, or other institutional practices that operated to the disadvantage of race or gender groups, without being structured by a specific discriminatory mindset. In the frankest departure from the predominant approach, the amended section 2 of the Voting Rights Act required an analysis of "results" that cut the assessment of minority vote dilution loose from questions of agent-centered judgment or intent. Moreover, the early section 2 cases established the ''opportunity to elect the candidates of [one's] choice'' as the index of an undiluted vote—a standard that often required the construction of race-conscious (or ''safe'' minority) districts.[8]

Voting rights was not, of course, the only context in which an analytic framework that focused on results began to go hand-in-hand with explicit race-conscious remediation. In the school desegregation context, as noted above, results analysis became an instrument of race-conscious remediation. Moreover, in the workplace and in higher education, race-conscious programs gained prominence as a prophylactic measure, which seemed consistent with a result-centered analysis.

This alternate approach to identifying discrimination correlated more strongly with the way that outsider groups understood their own circumstances, leading some commentators to describe it as ''victim-oriented.''[9] It shifted the focus of judicial scrutiny, demonstrating that the salient thing about discrimination was not the flaws in decisionmakers' reasoning but the barriers that differential results created to the livelihood, education, or civic participation of politically marginalized groups.[10] In so doing, this approach characterized as discrimination those practical consequences that outsider groups were most likely to find burdensome or oppressive in their own lives. From this perspective, it was also possible to glimpse aspects of discrimination, often perceived by victim groups, that had been erased or obscured by the dominant view. Effects analysis made clear that discrimination could be associated with apparently benign, impersonal practices, as well as prejudiced human motives. And in its more various, nuanced portrait of the way in which outsider groups are disadvantaged, this approach encouraged legal actors to view discrimination as a variable, institution-specific phenomenon rather than a pattern of misapprehension that is repeated from context to context.

Some elements of this view of discrimination also pointed to a richer conception of group membership. The development of a view distinct from the agent-centered perspective—a vantage point informed by, or at least consistent with, the experience of suffering discrimination—highlighted the affirmative, constitutive role of group membership. Group membership was not simply an incidental characteristic, capable of misleading biased or ignorant decisionmakers. Whether through the shared experience of discrimination or through other elements of group culture, group membership shaped ways of seeing the world that had distinctive, affirmative value. The role of group membership in forming the individual consciousness of group members was also underscored by the arguments in favor of group-conscious remedies. The diversity that was invoked as a justification for affirmative action in the educational setting and the emphasis on the shared political perspectives of minority groups in the context of the Voting Rights Act made clear that group membership affected the political preferences and substantive contributions of those socialized in a particular group context.

In other respects, however, this body of doctrine disturbed few of the dominant understandings about group membership. Groups were still defined biologically, even if group membership was understood as reflecting a cultural or social overlay. And groups were most often characterized as unitary rather than marked by subgroup variations and tensions. It was during this period, for example, that several leading Title VII cases declined to recognize the distinctive injuries suffered by black women.[11] This reluctance among legal decisionmakers of the period to see group experience as embodying both similarities and differences among members—as in the sexual harassment example above—prevented them from seeing the full variability and contextualization of discrimination.

It is partly for this reason that the first two decades of antidiscrimination decisions reflected a subtle tension rather than a stark divergence between the agent, or ''perpetrator,'' focus prevailing in mainstream doctrine and the ''outsider,'' or ''victim,'' focus that surfaced intermittently in approaches such as disparate impact or results analysis. The two approaches shared several conclusions about the nature of group membership. Moreover, the punctuation of the dominant approach with ventures into results analysis suggested to outsiders that their perspectives were not wholly excluded from equality doctrine.[12] In the past fifteen years, however, two developments have rendered the tension between these analytic approaches both sharper and more visible.

The first is the steady erosion of the outsider focus in federal antidiscrimination doctrine. This focus has been curtailed in part by doctrinal changes in Title VII that have narrowed the scope of disparate impact analysis. But it has been most effectively undermined by a group-blind interpretation of equal protection, which has been applied to educational and employment settings as well as to the context of the Voting Rights Act. These changes have resulted not simply in the triumph of the ''perpetrator'' perspective as outlined above but in its metamorphosis toward a broad constitutional right to individualized (i.e., group-blind) treatment.

Paradoxically, however, this more decisive submergence of the victim perspective in antidiscrimination law has been coupled with a burgeoning of outsiders' perspectives on discrimination in feminist, critical race, and gay legal theory. This second development, with its emphasis on experiential epistemology, has generated fuller, more concrete, accounts of how discrimination operates in the lives of its victims. More important, perhaps it has generated more sophisticated understandings of how groups themselves are constituted. It has demonstrated how multiplicity within acknowledged groups not only creates hierarchies among group members but also alters and pluralizes the dynamics of discrimination itself.

Contemporary Equality Doctrine: A Tension Amplified

The rejection of victim-oriented analysis has come about in a variety of ways. One of the subtler, and perhaps less indelible, forces of erosion has been the judicial revision of burden of proof rules under Title VII. In some cases, defendants have been permitted considerable vagueness in their articulation of nondiscriminatory reasons, to the point at which they have sometimes prevailed on the basis of accounts that do not explain why another applicant was given a particular job rather than the plaintiff.[13] Plaintiffs, on the other hand, have increasingly been held to the specificity of a smoking gun in arguing that defendants' ostensibly legitimate reasons constituted a pretext for discrimination. For example, a recent holding that even a showing that the defendant lied about his nondiscriminatory reasons was insufficient to prove pretext set a high watermark in interpreting the plaintiff's burden of persuasion.[14]

By making it more difficult for plaintiffs to prevail under a disparate impact standard, these cases have reduced the extent to which this approach provides an independent basis of recovery. More important, they have threatened the conceptual distinctness of this claim by requiring something perilously close to a demonstration of discriminatory judgment in proving pretext. Yet they may in the long run do less damage than the second salient doctrinal development of this period: an effort to curtail group-conscious governmental programs with a group-blind interpretation of the equal protection clause.[15] The Title VII decisions, as judicial efforts at statutory interpretation, may still be subject to congressional revision, a power that has been used on several occasions to limit judicial interpretations of this statute. Moreover, while these cases limit the scope of one victim-oriented framework (the disparate impact approach), they neither directly delegitimate it nor undo gains achieved under it in earlier contexts. The constitutional attack on race-conscious remedies—or affirmative action—has achieved these more ambitious objectives as well. The challenge it poses to the assumptions of the victim-oriented model, and the ways in which it expands even the earlier ''perpetrator'' perspective, may be seen by examining three conceptual shifts that this line of cases has brought about.

The first has been the separation of the equal protection clause from its historic role as the instrument for protecting blacks and, by analogy, other oppressed groups. In a series of decisions, beginning with the landmark *Bakke* case of the late 1970s,[16] the equal protection clause has been interpreted to protect an individual's right to equal treatment rather than to secure particular, politically marginalized groups against unfair or oppressive governmental action. The justification has been partly historical—the nation has passed the point at which it can maintain a ''two-class'' structure of protection for blacks only[17]—but it has also been largely pragmatic. If the Court acknowledged a right to group-based protection in this context, some justices have argued, they would be deluged with a complex, shifting mass of claims that the Court, as a principle-bound, apolitical body, is not suited to distinguish.[18] This redefinition of the equal protection clause, as the ''neutral'' arbiter of individual rights, is underscored by the Court's decision, previewed in the early cases and consolidated by a majority in 1989,[19] to apply strict scrutiny to all race-based classifications, including ''benign'' plans that favor members of socially marginalized groups. The justices assert that it is virtually impossible to distinguish benign from discriminatory programs and that even the best-intended plans may have highly prejudicial consequences, both for the whites asked to bear the burden and for their intended beneficiaries.[20] The decoupling of the equal protection clause from the vindication of minority opportunity is also clear in a final feature of these cases: the increasing stringency with which the Court has viewed any state justifications for departing from group-blind treatment. In early cases, such as *Bakke*, the Court accepted justifications including compensation for past discrimination and cultivation of diversity in a university's student body and endorsed race-conscious programs such as Harvard University's admissions program as instruments for advancing these goals.[21] In subsequent cases, the Court became increasingly exacting in the showings of institutional discrimination that it judged sufficient to justify a race-conscious remedial plan.[22] In the most recent cases, epitomized by *Shaw v. Reno*, the Court has evinced skepticism about many apparently strong justifications for race-conscious state action, including compliance with the Justice Department's interpretation of the Voting Rights Act.[23]

These cases also reflect an increasing distance, on the part of the Court, from the perspectives and perceptions of victims of group-based discrimination. The justices' concern about the institutional difficulty of mediating among multiple group-based claims has often seemed to overshadow their concern about rectifying the injustices represented by those claims—a clear retreat from the viewpoint of the victim toward the mindset of the governmental decisionmaker. Moreover, the Court's insistence on the possibility—indeed, the justice—of considering individuals from all groups similarly situated disregards the concrete, experiential knowledge of outsider groups. These "individuals" do not perceive themselves to be similarly situated in their access to public benefits or their need for governmental protection; in their view, the distinctions among groups that the Court has despaired of making can be grounded in broad social, or more particularized local, patterns of interaction. The Court's insistence on abstracting from these life-defining circumstances reflects a frank rejection of outsider claimants' experientially based knowledge. In addition to its insistence on the similar situation, for constitutional purposes, of all racial groups, the Court has often provided its own "counternarratives" to contest outsiders' claims that their circumstances reflect remediable discrimination. In its 1989 repudiation of the minority business set-aside plan in Richmond, Virginia, for example, the Court hypothesized that the low numbers of minority business enterprises in local contractors' associations—a circumstance the state had offered as evidence of discrimination—might well be attributable to lack of interest by minority group members in the construction industry.[24] The Court also flouted the expressed perspectives of many minority voters in *Shaw v. Reno* by suggesting that the state's assumption that minority voters shared salient political interests was a stereotype-laden insult to those voters' independence and heterogeneity.[25]

The affirmative action cases, in the end, do more than dispute outsiders' knowledge: they also reflect a subtle change in the mainstream, perpetrator-oriented understanding of discrimination. Cases involving race-conscious remedies—unlike those involving straightforward discrimination—raise no inferences about the abilities of the excluded, or disadvantaged, contenders. Whether the justification is compensation for past discrimination or cultivation of diversity, these plans' preference for members of minority groups reflects no judgment that whites are incompetent or unable to compete.[26] Hence one might plausibly say that these cases are less about protection from erroneous differentiating judgments than about protection from judgments that reflect or produce any group-based differentiation at all. Equal protection seems to establish one's presumptive entitlement to be treated simply as an individual or as an exemplar of universal, rather than group-specific, human characteristics.[27]

The Development of Outsider Perspectives on Groups and Group-ness

Paradoxically, however, even as antidiscrimination doctrine was being purged of group-based claims and other conceptualizations reflecting outsider perspectives on discrimination, these perspectives were undergoing a renaissance in the domain of legal theory. The 1980s saw the dramatic growth and development of a critical jurisprudence aimed at elaborating the vantage point of politically oppressed or marginalized groups. This work was stimulated in part by a methodological shift in the social sciences: a critique of objectivity and objectivist epistemologies that gradually worked its way into law.[28] The critique challenged the traditional view of legal principles as natural, necessary, or inevitable means to govern social life. These principles, like any other ideas or ''truths,'' were partial, contingent, and the product of situated perspectives. It was the authority—the privileged social and professional positions—of those who pronounced them, critics contended, that permitted legal decisionmakers to characterize these partial perspectives as natural or universal. One strategy that critics used to contest the universality of legal principles was to make visible the alternative understandings that had been excluded by legal decisionmakers. Often using the tool of experiential narrative—which supplied the stories that law had rendered marginal and emphasized the role of one's perspective in shaping one's view of the proper legal standard—outsider scholars reconceptualized discrimination in terms informed by their own experience. Thus, Catharine MacKinnon argued that gender discrimination is not the flawed estimation of the similarities and differences between men and women: women's stories suggest, instead, that discrimination consists in the inequalities men impose on women through sexualized dominance and other forms of power.[29] And Derrick Bell challenged the ostensible tension between affirmative action and academic merit in his ''Chronicles''—quasi-fictional dialogues in which he and Geneva Crenshaw, an intrepid black female interlocutor, interrogate conventional antidiscrimination doctrine.[30]

These jurisprudential perspectives placed the phenomenon of discrimination in a new light. First, they set out in palpably concrete terms what it means to be a target of group-based discrimination, supplying, in some respects, an antidote to the perpetrator focus of mainstream doctrine. Intentional discrimination is described not as an inaccurate ascription of difference by decisionmakers but as a stigmatizing, devaluative characterization that erodes the self-conception and subtly constricts the life possibilities of the victim. When Patricia Williams describes her exclusion from Bennetton's by an impassive, gum-chewing, buzzer-wielding salesperson, she does not dwell on his error in assuming she had no resources for making a purchase; she focuses instead on her confusion, humiliation, and fury in being excluded.[31] Moreover, the emphasis, in this literature, on the practical and personal consequences of discriminatory treatment has also challenged mainstream doctrine's exclusive focus on intentional forms of discrimination, highlighting as well discrimination perpetuated by a range of ''neutral'' institutional practices and selective insensitivities. Patricia Williams's account of how an ''aesthetic of uniformity'' kept black women out of the Rockettes[32] or Charles Lawrence's description of how an interviewer's elaborate praise of a Latino candidate's English was perceived as a condescending and hurtful slight[33] vividly document these patterns and support the group-affirming corrective of race-conscious remedies.

While this literature has mounted an explicit challenge to elements of the "perpetrator" approach, it has also introduced perspectives not entirely comprehended by the kind of "victim" orientation reflected in results analysis. Feminist and critical race scholarship have characterized discrimination as a force that is not only institutionally particularized, as some disparate impact accounts suggest, but also capable of metamorphosing over time or in relation to altered circumstances. Accounts of how sexual harassment often follows the end of formal exclusion of women from professions and trades,[34] for example, demonstrate not just the multiplicity but also the durability and adaptability of discriminatory practices. Such accounts also suggest a sense of entitlement among perpetrators—a belief in the legitimacy of their privilege—that explains features of discrimination unelaborated by earlier accounts: how practices thought to be neutral might operate discriminatorily or how those in positions of power might respond with naked animus when their sense of control is called into question. Finally, while these outsider accounts of discrimination highlight the ways in which discrimination restricts public opportunities, such as in employment and political participation, they also underscore a number of other consequences that are less frequently remarked in antidiscrimination doctrine. The devaluation of sexual harassment, for example, might result in the denial or forfeiture of a job but might also make the conditions of the job more onerous or make it difficult to perform at the level expected.[35] The devaluative assumptions applied to single black motherhood, to take another example, might result in the denial of welfare or health care benefits but might also result in more intrusive governmental surveillance.[36] These insights create a more comprehensive, complex picture of how discrimination operates and what it means for the life circumstances of those who suffer it.

Yet even more dramatically revisionary than outsider jurisprudence's account of discrimination is its understanding of group-ness and group membership. In contrast to the proponents of the dominant doctrinal view, outsider scholars have not described group-ness as an incidental overlay on a shared, essential humanity. Wary of the marginalizing power of the ostensibly universal, and convinced that one's life narrative is given shape by one's particularity, these scholars have seen group membership as defining and constitutive for outsiders. Although this insight reflects some similarity with the premises of result-based doctrinal approaches, this scholarship in many respects offers a more sophisticated analysis of the dynamics of group membership than has yet been manifested in any facet of antidiscrimination doctrine.

First, group membership is rarely viewed as a function of simple biological transmission. The color of one's skin, for example, may begin as a function of heredity, but even the identity that would seem to be conferred by biology is less predictable and stable than one might suspect. Judy Scales-Trent, for example, writes about the experience of being a "black person who looks white in a world that doesn't tolerate ambiguity very well."[37] Her accounts of "passing" as white, "coming out" as black, and trying to carve out an identity amid the confusion of those around her suggest that even the categories we view as most polar and biologically ordained do not always declare themselves with unambivalent clarity.[38] The extent to which the perceptions of others in Scales-Trent's life render malleable and contingent an identity that is biologically consistent illustrates a second point: the role of social construction in shaping the boundaries of group membership. Patricia Williams writes tellingly of a debate among her colleagues over whether she was "really black."[39] Kimberle Crenshaw describes how Anita Hill was "de-raced" by her defenders' resort to the conventional "rape trope" of sexual harassment and by Clarence Thomas's invocation of the "high-tech lynching" metaphor.[40] None of these interpretations prevailed because the woman in question was too light-skinned to be immediately identifiable as black. They transpired because, as both authors conclude, race is invested with a variety of sometimes-conflicting social meanings, and those more privileged than the bearer of the disputed characteristics often enjoy the power to decide how those meanings will be assigned and how a particular person will be placed within the operative categories.

The Anita Hill example points to a third insight communicated by these theorists: that group membership is not singular or monolithic but multiple and intersecting. Even a single group-based element of a person's identity may not have a predictable or consistent effect on his or her experience or political commitments. But more important, within each "group" are members with diverse, intersecting characteristics. This intersectionality means that there is not only variation but also hierarchy and exclusion within groups. Lesbian feminists and feminists of color, for example, have explained in compelling terms how feminist accounts have marginalized their subgroup members and posited a "universal woman" who is actually white and heterosexual.[41] Intersection of multiple group-based characteristics also means that particular individuals may integrate those characteristics differently from one context to another. A particular woman may identify primarily with her gender in one setting, with her race in another, or with her parental status or sexual orientation in a third. Influencing the way in which a given outsider integrates her multiple characteristics are the perceptions of a society that has difficulty comprehending complexity and that may understand certain group-based characteristics in ways that effectively erase intersections. One reason Anita Hill's supporters resorted to a "rape trope" patterned on the experiences of white women, Crenshaw explains, was because dominant society had such difficulty conceptualizing life at the intersection of race and gender discrimination.[42]

These observations, in turn, highlight dynamics of discrimination—sources of variability and complexity—that were not made visible even by "victim-oriented" doctrinal approaches, such as disparate impact. They reveal that intentional discrimination may take forms that are different for different subgroups of the targeted category, as in the sexual harassment example provided above. Yet this intragroup differentiation does not make the discrimination that occurs any less "gender" or "race" discrimination: it simply means that perpetrators take into account the fact that there are, for example, several racial variants of the gender female and that perpetrators can be insulated from legal reach if decisionmakers take one subgroup's experience of discrimination as a groupwide norm. These outsider insights also suggest that discrimination that operates through "neutral" practices or otherwise without intent may have differential impact across different subgroups of a protected category. For example, the practice of employing only those applicants known to an incumbent employee may favor men over women, but it may also favor white women over women of color. Finally, recent outsider scholarship makes clear that social and institutional decisions about who is considered to be a member of a particular group can themselves be a source of harm—in the way that Anita Hill was harmed by being de-raced—because they often operate on the basis of unjustified stereotypes and allocate important institutional and legal opportunities in disparate ways.

Mobilizing at the Impasse: Strategies for Instilling Group-Based Perspectives in Antidiscrimination Law

Antidiscrimination law has thus reached a peculiar impasse: outsider theorists have developed increasingly sophisticated understandings of group membership and group-based discrimination at the same time that antidiscrimination doctrine has required legal and other institutional actors to abstract from the very fact of group membership. One must next ask whether there are any potential legal vehicles through which outsider groups might resist the effort to drive group consciousness from equality doctrine and express their increasingly complex views of group identity and discrimination. What bodies of law might permit outsiders to describe discrimination as a variable phenomenon that encompasses intentional devaluation, selective insensitivity, neutral practices with disparate effects, and flawed ascription of difference; that erodes self-esteem or enhances institutional surveillance as well as diminishes public opportunities; that finds and exploits the distinctive characteristics of subgroups as well as impedes the group as a whole?

Some efforts might be made, in the first instance, to limit the move toward group-blindness in leading areas of antidiscrimination law. One can scarcely deny the fact that recent doctrinal changes have made many of these areas far less hospitable venues for the implementation of group-based perspectives. Yet it may be possible not only to strike group-preserving compromises but also to use the courts' suspicion of strict race-based programs, for example, to create classifications that highlight the complexity and contingency of race and other categories. Outsiders might support affirmative action programs that combine racial characteristics with indices of economic disadvantage, as is being contemplated in some government contractor programs.[43] This strategy reflects some acquiescence in the paradoxical development that characteristics not viewed as suspect may be less vulnerable to challenge than the long-protected characteristic of minority race. But it also continues to protect the professional opportunities of many minority contractors, while highlighting the extent to which race-based disadvantage has a palpable class-related component.

A second goal might be to identify claims that can serve as the successors to "results" analysis or affirmative action doctrine, in the sense that they incorporate in law a view of discrimination and group membership that corresponds more closely to outsider perspectives. One plausible candidate lies squarely within federal antidiscrimination doctrine: the Title VII claim for sexual or racial harassment. The nature of the harassment claim, and the ways in which it has been elaborated over the past fifteen years, underscore many of the points made by feminist and critical race scholars about group membership and discrimination. It reveals, first and foremost, that discrimination arises not only from flawed perceptions of difference but also from the insensitivity born of privilege and from the willful imposition of unequal power. The harasser injects into a professional setting prejudiced responses to group membership that have no place there. He may do it willfully, to keep the target off balance in a professional context new to racial minorities or women. He may do it ignorantly, because he is unable to think of minority or female employees as anything but members of those groups and his privilege has protected him from having to think critically about this mental habit. Both dynamics convey crucial insights about discrimination that can be usefully highlighted by this claim.

Second, because harassment has the virtue, if one may call it that, of making the prejudiced conceptions of the perpetrator vividly clear, it can demonstrate discrimination's variable, contextualized character, particularly in relation to heterogeneous groups. A perpetrator's language may show, for example, that he devalues only some subgroups; or devalues several subgroups but demeans them through distinctive subgroup-specific language; or targets only those whose biological sex or race coincides or conflicts with their social characteristics. Highlighting these variable patterns underscores the diversity within what we sometimes take to be monolithic groups and reveals that "race" or "gender" discrimination may comprise a number of prejudiced attitudes toward subgroups, which have both common and disparate themes.

Finally, because harassment is on the boundary between discrimination that produces denial of access to public opportunities and discrimination that produces other, less-familiar kinds of injuries, it may be used to highlight those categories of harm that need to be brought to public attention: harm to self-esteem, or impediments to the effective performance of one's job, or disproportionate official surveillance.

A third way in which outsiders might mobilize group-based perspectives is to employ disparate impact analysis as a political, rather than a legal, tool. Many forms of discrimination that subject their victims to increased governmental intervention or surveillance, rather than to more traditional denials of opportunity, operate by producing a disparate impact on outsider groups. Governmental intervention in the fertility or parenting of minority women is a prime example.[44] The prescription of Norplant as part of the resolution of child-neglect claims, or the pressure to undergo sterilization imposed by medical practitioners or welfare policies, or the reporting of suspected substance abuse by pregnant women are all policies that embody no explicit group-based classifications. These policies impose an automatic disparate impact on women, given the biology of human reproduction. But they also produce a disparate impact on the basis of race, with nonwhite women being targeted for such intervention more frequently than white women and black women being targeted most frequently of all.[45] Increasingly, outsider scholars have decried this effect as an unattended form of discrimination in the operation of welfare and family programs.[46] This critique might serve as a model for other outsider scholars and advocates. Discussion of the sources of disparate impact illuminates the many forms of discrimination that fail to conform to the model of flawed ascription of difference. Moreover, the political pressure applied by such arguments may be sufficient to terminate newly commenced or particularly controversial programs; even in settings in which such claims lack the legal power or political influence necessary to end the challenged practices, they keep the necessity of considering group-based impact on the public agenda.

This last benefit points to a final, long-term strategy for proponents of outsider perspectives on discrimination. The very act of elaborating these perspectives is a critical resource in their translation or incorporation into law. Scholarship and political discourse embodying these views preserve and develop them for a time when courts may be more willing to incorporate group-based perspectives in antidiscrimination doctrine. They may, more important, play an indirect role in bringing that time about—a role that is not unprecedented in antidiscrimination law. One force that contributed to the revolution of *Brown* was the development of a body of views, drawing both on social science[47] and on individual narrative,[48] that made clear the effect of segregation as it was perceived and experienced by black children. In the face of this persistent, concrete testament, legal fictions of a separation that communicated no disrespect to either group ultimately had to give way. Proponents of group-based perspectives, confronting a legal world of presumptively equally situated individuals, could do no better than to heed this example.

NOTES

I would like to thank Henry Shue for numerous conversations on the subject of this chapter and Neal Devins and Davison Douglas for helpful comments on an earlier draft.

1. ''Outsider'' is a term that is frequently used in the critical jurisprudential literature to refer to socially and politically marginalized groups. See, e.g., Richard Delgado and Jean Stefancic, ''Images of the Outsider in American Law and Culture,'' in Richard Delgado, ed., *Critical Race Theory: The Cutting Edge* (Philadelphia: Temple University Press, 1995), 217. In this chapter, I use the term primarily to refer to people of color, particularly blacks, and women; but others have also used the term to refer to gays and lesbians, members of minority religious groups, and people with disabilities.

2. This understanding is reflected in the equal protection premise that like entities must be treated alike or in the requirement that differentiating legislative classifications must be justified by rationales that characterize groups as unlike or describe specific instances of dissimilar treatment as relating to an important public purpose. This assumption also informs Title VII disparate treatment doctrine, which permits differential treatment of statutorily covered groups only when authorized by a ''bona fide occupational qualification.''

3. The first person to use the term ''perpetrator perspective'' in the literature on race appears to have been Alan Freeman in his article ''Legitimizing Racial Discrimination Through Anti-Discrimination Law: A Critical Review of Supreme Court Doctrine,'' *Minnesota Law Review* 62 (1978): 1049. Catharine MacKinnon used a similar expression in her early articles on gender inequalities, when she wrote that rape law in this society embodies the view of the ''reasonable rapist.'' See Catharine MacKinnon, ''Feminism, Marxism, Method, and the State: Toward Feminist Jurisprudence,'' *Signs* 8 (1983): 635.

Implicit in the term ''perpetrator perspective'' is the assumption that what is to be known about discrimination is not a single truth, or a universal constant, but rather varies, depending on the perspective of the observer or knower. This epistemological assumption is sometimes at odds with the positions taken by the courts in discrimination cases, in which they assert or project the understanding that there is a single appropriate way of characterizing discrimination or an alleged discriminatory incident. The most notorious example of this judicial view is the Supreme Court's opinion in *Plessy v. Ferguson*, in which the majority stated that "separate but equal" is a badge of inferiority, "solely because the colored race chooses to put that construction upon it." 163 U.S. 537 (1896).

4. A fuller description of this difficulty is contained in Kathryn Abrams, "Title VII and the Complex Female Subject," *Michigan Law Review* 92 (August 1994): 2479.

5. 426 U.S. 288 (1976).

6. See *Village of Arlington Heights v. Metropolitan Housing Development Corp.*, 429 U.S. 252 (1977).

7. See *Griggs v. Duke Power Co.*, 401 U.S. 424 (1971).

8. See, e.g., *Thornburg v. Gingles*, 478 U.S. 30 (1986) (describing "opportunity to elect the candidates of [one's] choice" as the core value protected by section 2 of the Voting Rights Act); *Ketchum v. Byrne*, 740 F.2d 1398 (7th Cir. 1984), cert. denied sub nom *City Council of Chicago v. Ketchum*, 471 U.S. 1135 (1985) (affirming importance of supermajority or "safe" minority districts in remedying Voting Rights Act Violations).

9. See, e.g., Freeman, "Legitimizing Racial Discrimination"; D. Marvin Jones, "No Time for Trumpets: Title VII, Equality, and the Fin de Siecle," *Michigan Law Review* 92 (August 1994): 2311.

10. The imposition of race-or gender-conscious remedies, grounded sometimes on a generalized showing of societal discrimination, demonstrated that correcting entrenched and often complex patterns of injustice was as compelling a mandate as identifying the specific agent responsible for a particular practice.

11. For a compelling discussion of these cases, see Kimberle Crenshaw, "Demarginalizing the Intersection of Race and Sex: A Black Feminist Critique of Antidiscrimination Doctrine, Feminist Theory, and Antiracist Politics," *University of Chicago Legal Forum* (1989): 139.

12. In fact, the strong beachheads established by "results" analysis in statutory areas, such as Title VII and the Voting Rights Act, gave their proponents reason to hope that they might one day become predominants or at least be incorporated into constitutional doctrine—a hope that may have triggered the Court's constitutional rejoinder in *Washington v. Davis*, 426 U.S. 229 (1976), and its more recent effort to neutralize the power of the Voting Rights Act in *Shaw v. Reno*, 113 S. Ct. 2816 (1993).

13. *Texas Dep't of Community Affairs v. Burdine*, 450 U.S. 248 (1981).

14. *St. Mary's v. Hicks*, 113 S. Ct. 2742 (1993). The lower courts are divided on whether evidence of lying is sufficient to support a jury verdict; the Supreme Court held only that it is not sufficient to justify finding liability without the trial court's submitting the case to a jury.

15. The same may be said of a development on which I do not comment here: the Court's refusal to constitutionalize the "effects" approach in *Washington v. Davis*, 426 U.S. 229 (1976). Although *Washington v. Davis* prevented the "effects" approach from becoming ascendant, the cases of the type I am going to discuss undercut its rationale and force in contexts in which it has previously been well established.

16. *Regents of Univ. of California v. Bakke*, 438 U.S. 265 (1978).

17. Justice Lewis F. Powell, Jr., noted cryptically in *Bakke* that it is "far too late to argue that the guarantee of equal protection to all persons permits the recognition of special wards entitled to a degree of protection greater than that accorded others." Ibid. at 295. To my

mind, the abrogation of a role for the clause that dates back to the end of the Civil War requires more explanation than Justice Powell offers in this opinion.

18. The prototype of this argument may be found in Justice Powell's opinion in *Bakke*, 438 U.S. at 295–97. It is also offered by Justice Sandra Day O'Connor in *City of Richmond v. J. A. Croson Co.*, 488 U.S. 469, 505–6 (1989).

19. See *City of Richmond*, 488 U.S. 469.

20. *City of Richmond*, 488 U.S. at 493; *Bakke*, 438 U.S. at 298.

21. *Bakke*, 438 U.S. at 316–18.

22. *City of Richmond*, 488 U.S. at 493-506.

23. *Shaw*, 113 S. Ct. at 2830–31.

24. *City of Richmond*, 488 U.S. at 503.

25. *Shaw*, 113 S. Ct. at 2827.

26. On the contrary, opponents of race-conscious remedies frequently express concern that these programs will cast negative aspersions on the capabilities of their beneficiaries. See, e.g., *Bakke*, 438 U.S. at 298.

27. This reasoning reaches a high watermark in recent cases such as *Shaw v. Reno*, 113 S. Ct. 2816 (1993), a case challenging the constitutionality of race-conscious electoral districting, in which the Court refers to a "right to participate in a color-blind electoral process," ibid. at 2824, and asserts that even the black voters whose electoral opportunity is enhanced by the districts are disserved by the state's operating assumption that black voters share political interests, ibid. at 2827.

28. The works that helped bring this critique to law include Derrick A. Bell, Jr., *And We Are Not Saved: The Elusive Quest for Racial Justice* (New York: Basic Books, 1987); Martha Minow, *Making All the Difference: Inclusion, Exclusion, and American Law* (Ithaca, N.Y.: Cornell University Press, 1990); Joseph Singer, "The Player and the Cards: Nihilism and Legal Theory," *Yale Law Journal* 94 (November 1984): 1–70; Kimberle Crenshaw, "Race, Reform, and Retrenchment: Transformation and Legitimation in Anti-Discrimination Law," *Harvard Law Review* 101 (May 1988): 1331; Richard Delgado, "The Imperial Scholar," *University of Pennsylvania Law Review* 132 (March 1984): 561; MacKinnon, "Feminism, Marxism, Method, and the State." This critique is not entirely unprecedented in law, as certain of its elements were previewed in the work of legal realists. For a thought-provoking discussion of the relation between legal realism and critical legal theory, see Joseph Singer, "Legal Realism Now," *California Law Review* 76 (March 1988): 465, 531.

29. See Catharine MacKinnon, *Feminism Unmodified* (Cambridge: Harvard University Press, 1987), 32–45.

30. Bell, *And We Are Not Saved.* The chronicle in which Bell challenges this tension most explicitly is "The Chronicle of the DeVine Gift"; the ostensible tension between affirmative action and meritocracy is only one of the many premises of conventional anti-discrimination doctrine contested in this pathbreaking book.

31. Patricia Williams, "Spirit-Murdering the Messenger: The Discourse of Fingerpointing as the Law's Response to Racism," *Miami Law Review* 42 (September 1987): 127.

32. Patricia Williams, "The Obliging Shell: An Informal Essay on Formal Equal Opportunity," *Michigan Law Review* 89 (August 1989): 2128.

33. Charles Lawrence, "The Id, the Ego, and Equal Protection: Reckoning with Unconscious Racism," *Stanford Law Review* 39 (January 1987): 317.

34. See Vicki Schultz, "Telling Stories about Women and Work: Judicial Interpretations of Sex Segregation in the Workplace in Title VII Cases Raising the Lack of Interest Defense," *Harvard Law Review* 103 (June 1990): 1749.

35. Both Justice O'Connor's majority opinion and Justice Ruth Bader Ginsburg's con-

currence in the recent *Harris* case support this view of the harm of sexual harassment. See *Harris v. Forklift Systems*, 114 S. Ct. 367 (1993).

36. See generally Dorothy Roberts, ''Punishing Drug Addicts Who Have Babies: Women of Color, Equality, and the Right of Privacy,'' *Harvard Law Review* 104 (May 1991): 1419.

37. Judy Scales-Trent, ''Commonalities: On Being Black and White, Different, and the Same,'' *Yale Journal of Law and Feminism* 2 (Spring 1990): 305.

38. Similar insights have been communicated by scholars writing about gender, sexuality, and sexual orientation. They suggest that categories such as male/female, gay/straight are far more ambivalent than antidiscrimination doctrine, or mainstream political views, suggest. See, e.g., Katherine Franke, ''The Central Mistake of Sex Discrimination Law: The Disaggregation of Sex from Gender,'' *University of Pennsylvania Law Review* 144 (November 1995): 1; Mary Anne Case, ''Disaggregating Gender from Sex and Sexual Orientation: The Effeminate Man in the Law and Feminist Jurisprudence,'' *Yale Law Journal* 105 (October 1995): 1; Francisco Valdez, ''Queers, Sissies, Dykes, and 'Tomboys' Deconstructing the Conflation of 'Sex,' 'Gender,' and 'Sexual Orientation' in Euro-American Law and Society,'' *California Law Review* 83 (January 1995): 1; Abrams, ''Title VII and the Complex Female Subject.'' See generally Ruth Colker, ''Bi,'' *Ohio State Law Journal* 56, no. 1 (1995): 1.

39. Patricia Williams, *The Alchemy of Race and Rights* (Cambridge: Harvard University Press, 1990).

40. Kimberle Crenshaw, ''Whose Story Is It Anyway? Feminist and Antiracist Appropriations of Anita Hill,'' in *Race-ing Justice, Engender-ing Power*, ed. Toni Morrison (New York: Pantheon, 1992).

41. See, e.g., Crenshaw, ''Demarginalizing the Intersection of Race and Sex''; Patricia Cain, ''Feminist Jurisprudence: Grounding the Theories,'' *Berkeley Women's Law Journal* 4, no. 2 (1989–90): 191.

42. Crenshaw, ''Whose Story Is It Anyway?''

43. For an interesting discussion of the pros and cons of pure class-based affirmative action, see Joanne Barkin, ''Symposium: Affirmative Action,'' *Dissent* 42 (Fall 1995): 461, 462–63.

44. See Roberts, ''Punishing Drug Addicts Who Have Babies''; Michelle Oberman, ''Sex, Drugs, Pregnancy, and the Law: Rethinking the Problems of Pregnant Women Who Use Drugs,'' *Hastings Law Journal* 43 (March 1992): 505.

45. Roberts, ''Punishing Drug Addicts Who Have Babies,'' 1434.

46. See ibid.; Oberman, ''Sex, Drugs, Pregnancy, and the Law.''

47. See *Brown v. Board of Education*, 347 U.S. 483 (1954) (n. 11).

48. See Charles L. Black, ''The Lawfulness of the Desegregation Decisions,'' *Yale Law Journal* 69 (1960): 421.

3

Civil Rights Reform in Historical Perspective

Regulating Marital Violence

REVA B. SIEGEL

In the nineteenth century, and again in the twentieth century, the American feminist movement has attempted to reform the law of marriage so as to secure for wives equality with their husbands. In each century, the movement's efforts have produced significant changes in the law structuring marriage. The status of married women has improved, but wives still have not attained equality with their husbands—if we measure equality as the dignitary and material "goods" associated with the wealth wives control, or the work they perform, or the degree of physical security they enjoy. The legal system continues to play an important role in perpetuating these status differences, although, over time, the role that law plays in enforcing status relations has become increasingly less visible.

As this essay will show, efforts to reform a status regime do bring about change—but not always the kind of change advocates seek. When the legitimacy of a status regime is successfully contested, lawmakers and jurists will both cede and defend status privileges—gradually relinquishing the original rules and justificatory rhetoric of the contested regime and finding new rules and reasons to protect such status privileges as they choose to defend. Thus, civil rights reform can breathe "new life" into a body of status law by pressuring elites to translate it into a more contemporary, and less controversial, social idiom. I call this kind of change in the rules and rhetoric of a status regime "preservation through transformation," and I illustrate this modernization dynamic in a case study of domestic assault law as it evolved in rule structure and rationale from a law of marital prerogative to a law of marital privacy.

The Anglo-American common law originally provided that a husband, as master of his household, could subject his wife to corporal punishment or "chastisement" as long as he did not inflict permanent injury on her. During the nineteenth century, an era of feminist agitation for reform of marriage law, courts in England and in the United States declared that a husband no longer had the right to chastise his wife. Yet for a century after courts repudiated the right of chastisement, the American legal system continued to treat wife beating differently from other cases of assault and battery. Although authorities denied that a husband had the right to beat his wife, they rarely intervened in cases of marital violence; a husband who assaulted his wife was granted various formal and informal immunities from prosecution in order to protect the privacy of the family and to promote domestic harmony.

As the nineteenth-century feminist movement protested a husband's marital prerogatives, it helped bring about the repudiation of chastisement doctrine; but in so doing, the movement also precipitated changes in the regulation of marital violence that "modernized" this body of status law. Instead of reasoning about marriage in the older, hierarchy-based norms of the common law, lawmakers began to justify the regulation of domestic violence in the language of privacy and love associated with companionate marriage in the industrial era. Once translated from an antiquated to a more contemporary gender idiom, the state's justification for treating wife beating differently from other kinds of assault seemed reasonable in ways the law of chastisement did not.

As the evolution of domestic violence law illustrates, political opposition to a status regime may bring about changes that incrementally improve the welfare of subordinated groups. With the demise of chastisement law, the situation of married women improved—certainly, in dignitary terms, and perhaps materially as well. At the same time, the story of chastisement's demise suggests that there is a price for the dignitary and material gains that civil rights reform may bring. If a reform movement is at all successful in advancing its justice claims, it will bring pressure to bear on lawmakers to rationalize status-enforcing state action in new and less socially controversial terms. This process of adaptation can actually revitalize a body of status law, *enhancing* its capacity to legitimate social inequalities that remain among status-differentiated groups. Examined from this perspective, the reform of chastisement doctrine can teach us much about the dilemmas confronting movements for social justice in America today.

Reforming Spousal Assault Law: From Prerogative to Privacy

The Right of Chastisement and Its Critics

Until the late nineteenth century, Anglo-American common law structured marriage to give a husband superiority over his wife in all aspects of the relationship. By law, a husband acquired rights to his wife's person, the value of her paid and unpaid labor, and most property she brought into the marriage. A wife was obliged to obey and serve her husband, and the husband was subject to a reciprocal duty to support his wife and represent her within the legal system. According to the doctrine of marital unity, a wife's legal identity "merged" with her husband's, so that she was unable to file suit without his participation, whether to enforce contracts or to seek damages in tort. The husband was in turn responsible for his wife's conduct—liable, under certain circumstances, for her contracts, torts, and even some crimes.[1]

As master of the household, a husband could command his wife's obedience and subject her to corporal punishment or "chastisement" if she defied his authority. In his treatise on the English common law, William Blackstone explained that a husband could "give his wife moderate correction,"

> [f]or, as he is to answer for her misbehaviour, the law thought it reasonable to intrust him with this power of restraining her, by domestic chastisement, in the same moderation that a man is allowed to correct his apprentices or children; for whom the master or parent is also liable in some cases to answer. But this power of correction was confined within reasonable bounds, and the husband was prohibited from using any violence to his wife.[2]

As Blackstone suggested, the right to give corporal punishment was subject to legal and customary limits. The master of the household might chastise his wife (or children or servants), but he could not inflict permanent injury on them without risking indictment for assault and battery.

Blackstone's *Commentaries* played an important role in shaping American legal culture;[3] and early American law treatises described chastisement as one of the husband's marital prerogatives.[4] Records of chastisement law in America are scant, however. The practice of wife beating was more frequently addressed in popular culture than in published judicial decisions of the era. Yet cases in a number of states, particularly in the southern and mid-Atlantic region, recognized a husband's prerogative to chastise his wife.[5]

By the middle of the nineteenth century, a variety of political and economic forces had begun to erode the common law of marital status in which the right of chastisement was situated.[6] Two of the most powerful reform movements of nineteenth-century America, the movements against slavery ("abolition") and alcohol ("temperance"), gave rise to the first organized movement for women's rights. Although membership in this new reform movement was relatively small, it was well connected to social elites both within and without government. In 1848, when the "woman's rights" movement held its first convention, it denounced the law of marriage in a formal "Declaration of Sentiments":

> He has made her, if married, in the eye of the law, civilly dead.
> He has taken from her all right in property, even to the wages she earns.
> . . . *In the covenant of marriage, she is compelled to promise obedience to her husband, he becoming, to all intents and purposes, her master—the law giving him power to deprive her of her liberty, and to administer chastisement.*[7]

By mid-century, legislatures in a number of states had begun to enact statutes that modified the common law of marital status; these first statutes typically allowed wives to hold property in their own names. Passage of the married women's property acts inaugurated a gradual process of reform that continues to the present day. At no point was there a categorical repudiation of the doctrine of marital unity; rather, with feminists continually protesting the law of marital status, legislatures and courts modified the common law in piecemeal fashion, giving wives the right to hold property in marriage, the right to their earnings, and the rudiments of legal agency: the right to file suit in their own names and to claim contract and tort damages.[8]

During this period, the right of chastisement was subject to two kinds of criticism. Criticism of the prerogative began indirectly. As the temperance movement protested the social evils of alcohol, it drew public attention to the violence that drunken husbands so often inflicted on their families. The movement's conventions, newspapers, poems, songs, and novels featured vivid accounts of women and children who had been impoverished, terrorized, maimed, and killed by drunken men.[9] Temperance protest was simultaneously radical and conservative in tenor. Condemning alcohol provided reformers an outlet for criticizing the social conditions of family life, in the name of protecting the sanctity of family life. Initially, at least, temperance activists preached one remedy for the family violence they so graphically depicted: prohibiting the sale of alcohol.

The woman's rights movement differed from the temperance movement, both in its diagnosis of family violence and in the social remedies it proposed. As woman's rights advocates attacked the hierarchical structure of marriage, they challenged the husband's authority over his wife, which the prerogative to chastise practically and symbolically embodied. The woman's rights movement thus broke with the temperance movement by depicting wife beating as a symptom of fundamental defects in the structure of marriage itself. The movement's 1848 "Declaration of Sentiments" identified chastisement as part of a political system of male dominance, an analysis that feminists continued to elaborate in the ensuing decades.

For woman's rights advocates, a structural diagnosis of male violence against women dictated a structural remedy. In the 1870s, one of the movement's newspapers argued that domestic violence exposed the "fiction of Woman's protection by man" and thus demonstrated "the necessity that women should have increased power, social, civil, legal, political and ecclesiastical, in order to protect themselves."[10] "These horrors," another writer contended, "result inevitably from the subjection and disfranchisement of women, just as similar outrages used to result from the subjection and disfranchisement of negroes. Equal Rights and Impartial Suffrage are the only radical cure for these barbarities."[11] But some in the movement proposed more immediate remedies. Beginning in the 1850s, a vocal minority in the temperance and woman's rights movement argued that wives should be allowed to divorce drunken, violent husbands.[12]

Formal Repudiation of the Right of Chastisement

The American legal system did respond to these criticisms of chastisement law—but it did so in complex ways. Decades of protest by temperance and woman's rights advocates, combined with shifting attitudes toward corporal punishment and changing gender mores, worked to discredit the law of chastisement. By the 1870s, there was no judge or treatise writer in the United States who would defend the right of chastisement. Thus, when wife beaters were charged with assault and battery, judges refused to entertain the claim that a husband had a legal right to strike his wife. Instead judges pronounced chastisement a "quaint" or "barbaric" remnant of the past and allowed the criminal prosecution to proceed. As an Alabama court explained in 1871: "The wife is not to be considered as the husband's slave. And the privilege, ancient though it be, to beat her with a stick, to pull her hair, choke her, spit in her face or kick her about the floor, or to inflict upon her like indignities, is not now acknowledged by our law."[13] In several states, legislatures enacted statutes specifically prohibiting wife beating; three states even revived corporal punishment for the crime, providing that wife beaters could be sentenced to the whipping post.[14]

Thus the law governing wife beating began to change. But if lawmakers and jurists unanimously repudiated the law of chastisement, they did not adopt legal rules that would necessarily constrain wife beating.

For example, during the late nineteenth century, the legal system remained largely unresponsive to feminist demands for reforms that might assist battered wives in protecting themselves. Feminist efforts to secure for the battered wife the right to separate from her husband, or to divorce him, were largely unsuccessful: reform proposals of this sort were disparaged as threatening the sanctity of marriage and family. In this period, states did begin to grant divorce on grounds of cruelty, but the standards for securing such a divorce were quite difficult to satisfy. Typically, a battered wife was required to prove that her husband acted with "extreme" and "repeated" cruelty.[15] Moreover, the evidence required to prove "extreme cruelty" varied by class, on the assumption that violence was a common, and normal, part of life among the married poor.[16] At the same time, a husband could defeat his wife's divorce petition either by showing that she misbehaved in some way that "provoked" his violence or by showing that she delayed petitioning for divorce and so forgave and "condoned" his violence.[17] In short, the law of divorce still assumed that a wife was obliged to endure various kinds of violence as a normal—and sometimes deserved—part of married life.

Just as marriage law changed to allow divorce on grounds of cruelty while continuing to tolerate significant amounts of violence in the marital relationship, so the criminal law also changed to prohibit chastisement while continuing to allow much violence in marriage to go unchecked. Here, too, class played an important role in discourses about marital violence. In the closing decades of the nineteenth century, commentators regularly depicted wife beating as the practice of lawless or unruly men of the "dangerous" classes. More particularly, they demonized the wife beater as a racial "other," whom authorities needed to control in order to secure social stability. Statistics on arrests and convictions for wife beating during this era demonstrate that criminal assault law was enforced against wife beaters only sporadically and then most often against African Americans and immigrant ethnic groups.[18]

The reforms of the 1870s did not mark the beginning of more fundamental change. Instead, for the ensuing century, the American legal system continued to tolerate violence in marriage as it did not in other relationships. As we will see, it was possible for lawmakers and jurists to condone wife beating even as they condemned the chastisement prerogative because lawmakers and jurists had begun to reason about the regulation of marital violence in a new conceptual framework.

Regulating Domestic Violence in an Era of Companionate Marriage

In the world of Blackstone's *Commentaries*, marriage was a hierarchical relationship in which a husband ruled over his wife and other members of the household. Yet by the nineteenth century, this authority-based conception of marriage had begun to lose its persuasive power—a development that clearly contributed to the demise of the chastisement prerogative. For example, treatise author James Schouler observed in 1870 that there was a tension between the hierarchical premises of chastisement doctrine and contemporary conceptions of marriage: "In a ruder state of society the husband frequently maintained his authority by force. . . . *But [in recent times] the wife has been regarded more as the companion of her husband*; and this right of chastisement may be regarded as exceedingly questionable at the present day. *The rule of love has superseded the rule of force*."[19] The shift in popular understandings of marriage that Schouler's treatise registers had important consequences for the way in which jurists reasoned about a husband's marital authority. Nineteenth-century jurists did not deny that a husband had authority over his wife; instead, as Schouler's treatise illustrates, they insisted that a husband rule his household by love rather than by force. This mingling of authority and affect-based conceptions of marriage shaped the body of marital status law that emerged in the wake of chastisement's demise.

As jurists began to reason about domestic violence within the discourse of companionate marriage, they developed a new framework for analyzing the regulation of wife beating. Judges who would no longer defend the husband's right to inflict corporal punishment on his wife began instead to emphasize that the law should promote *domestic harmony* between husband and wife and protect the *privacy* of the marriage relationship.

THE DISCOURSE OF AFFECTIVE PRIVACY IN DOMESTIC ASSAULT LAW

The discourse of affective privacy, a new mode of reasoning about the regulation of marital violence, made its earliest appearance in American case law as a *justification* for the right of chastisement. For example, when North Carolina upheld the right of chastisement in *State v. Black*,[20] the court justified the prerogative on two grounds: the husband's authority over his wife ("[a] husband is responsible for the acts of his wife, and he is required to govern his household") and the need to shield domestic conflicts from public scrutiny ("the law will not invade the domestic forum or go behind the curtain").[21] In *Black*, the traditional hierarchy-based rationale for chastisement law was intermingled with new rationales couched in the discourse of affective privacy: "public exhibition in the court-house of such quarrels and fights between man and wife widens the breach, makes reconciliation almost impossible, and encourages insubordination."[22]

Such arguments began to play an even more prominent role in the regulation of marital violence when North Carolina repudiated the doctrine of chastisement in the 1868 case of *State v. Rhodes*.[23] In *Rhodes*, the North Carolina Supreme Court declined to enforce an assault and battery charge against a man who assaulted his wife. The court repudiated the chastisement prerogative but then granted the wife beater immunity from criminal prosecution, justifying this new immunity policy in the rhetoric of affective privacy:

> [H]owever great are the evils of ill temper, quarrels, and even personal conflicts inflicting only temporary pain, they are not comparable with the evils which would result from raising the curtain, and exposing to public curiosity and criticism, the nursery and the bed chamber. Every household has and must have, a government of its own, modelled to suit the temper, disposition and condition of its inmates. Mere ebullitions of passion, impulsive violence, and temporary pain, affection will soon forget and forgive; and each member will find excuse for the other in his own frailties. But when trifles are taken hold of by the public, and the parties are exposed and disgraced, and each endeavors to justify himself or herself by criminating the other, that which ought to be forgotten in a day, will be remembered for life.[24]

As the court summed up the new doctrine six years later in a much-quoted opinion: "If no permanent injury has been inflicted, nor malice, cruelty nor dangerous violence shown by the husband, *it is better to draw the curtain, shut out the public gaze, and leave the parties to forget and forgive.*"[25] Thus, North Carolina courts abrogated a husband's prerogative to chastise his wife but supplanted it with an immunity from prosecution that coincided with the scope of the former prerogative. The law of chastisement was thus translated into a body of doctrine that comported with the logic of companionate marriage.

The concern for privacy that appears in these North Carolina cases does not seem to have played a significant role in the development of criminal law in the late nineteenth century—perhaps because criminal prosecution of wife beaters during this era was focused on controlling men of the "lower classes," men whose privacy needs elites scarcely recognized, much less sought to protect. But privacy-based reasoning about domestic violence did shape the development of private law in the late nineteenth century, playing a key role in the law of intentional torts as it emerged from reform by the married women's property acts. It was in the law of torts that privacy-based reasoning about marital violence flourished before returning to shape the criminal law during the early twentieth century.

PRIVACY IN THE EMERGING LAW OF INTERSPOUSAL TORT IMMUNITY

While it was clear by the second half of the nineteenth century that wife beating was a crime, it was not at all clear that this same conduct constituted a tort. A criminal prosecution for wife beating was brought against a husband by the state, whereas a tort claim was prosecuted by the married woman herself. Could a battered wife bring suit against her husband in order to vindicate her own injuries without depending on the state to intervene and protect her? The question was startling to those versed in common-law understandings of marriage. The same body of common law that vested a husband with the prerogative to chastise his wife also denied a married woman the right to file suit without her husband's consent and joinder.[26] Interspousal litigation violated fundamental precepts of the doctrine of marital unity.

But if the prospect of a wife's suing her husband contravened the most basic common-law concepts of marriage, it was also an inevitable outgrowth of common-law reform in the mid-nineteenth century—a period when the doctrine of marital unity was undergoing statutory modification under the pressure of feminist advocacy. Courts asked to determine whether wife beating was a tort had to interpret the marriage reform legislation whose enactment the woman's rights movement had advocated. Among the many rights these laws gave married women was the right to file suit without their husbands' joinder and the right to collect tort damages for injuries to their persons and property. Under these reform statutes, could a wife now bring a tort suit against a husband who assaulted her and collect money damages? The question presented women as agents of their own vindication in a dual sense: a plaintiff sought redress for her injury without relying on the state to protect her, and she did so under the authority of legislation enacted in response to feminist advocacy.

The law of torts differed from the criminal law in one other respect relevant to our analysis of the development of modern domestic assault law. A wife was likely to bring a suit for money damages against a husband who assaulted her only in circumstances in which there were assets to redistribute within the family. Thus, as jurists would surely recognize, it was married men of the middle and upper classes who might face tort claims for wife beating—precisely those men who were unlikely to face criminal prosecution for wife beating during the late nineteenth century.

With these gender- and class-salient features to recommend it, the new tort claim was not well received. Regardless of whether a husband beat, choked, stabbed, or shot his wife, all courts that heard such tort claims initially rejected them. (This doctrine of "interspousal tort immunity" survived well into the twentieth century and still remains law in a number of states today.)[27]

The Supreme Court of Maine was one of the first to synthesize the "domestic harmony" and "privacy" rationales in a tort case decided in 1877. In *Abbott v. Abbott*, a woman sued her ex-husband in tort, alleging that he violently assaulted her. The Maine court ruled that the plaintiff could not recover tort damages from her ex-husband. The court acknowledged that "there has been for many years a gradual evolution of the law going on, for the amelioration of the married woman's condition, until it is now undoubtedly, the law of England and of all the American states that the husband has no right to strike his wife, to punish her, under any circumstances or provocation whatever."[28] Yet, after repudiating the right of chastisement, the court declared that a husband was immune from tort liability for assaulting his wife. To support this view, the court quoted an opinion of the North Carolina Supreme Court explaining why a husband should be immune from criminal prosecution for beating his wife : " '[I]t is better to draw the curtain, shut out the public gaze, and leave the parties to forget and forgive.' "[29] Asserting that a tort remedy was not "desirable" as a wife could seek relief in the criminal courts, or seek a divorce on grounds of cruelty, the court observed that "[i]t would be a poor policy for the law to grant the remedy asked for in this case," for "[t]he private matters of the whole period of married existence might be exposed by suits'' and ''this would add a new method by which estates could be plundered.''[30]

When the U.S. Supreme Court construed the District of Columbia's married woman's property act in 1910, it invoked both a ''privacy'' and a ''domestic harmony'' rationale for interspousal tort immunity.[31] The Court asserted that Congress had not intended to give spouses the capacity to sue each other;[32] it then observed that allowing intramarital suits would ''open the doors of the courts to accusations of all sorts of one spouse against the other, and bring into public notice complaints for assault, slander and libel'' and questioned whether ''the exercise of such jurisdisction would be promotive of the public welfare and domestic harmony.''[33] By the early twentieth century, numerous state supreme courts had barred wives from suing their husbands for intentional torts typically on the grounds that ''the tranquility of family relations'' would be ''disturbed by dragging into court for judicial investigation at the suit of a peevish, fault-finding husband, or at the suit of the nagging, ill-tempered wife, *matters of no serious moment, which if permitted to slumber in the home closet would silently be forgiven or forgotten.*''[34]

It is important to observe that courts developed the doctrine of interspousal tort immunity in response to the *reform* of the common law. As the common law was slowly modified by statute and judicial decision, courts had to explain anomalies in the law of marital status that simply did not exist before. At common law, a wife lacked capacity to sue anyone without her husband's joinder, so her inability to sue her husband was hardly in need of explanation. But once a married woman was granted the right to sue in tort for injuries to property or person, courts had to decide whether she could sue her husband and, if not, to explain why not. All courts that faced the claim initially ruled against it, with some explaining the emergent law of interspousal tort immunity by invoking the doctrine of marital unity. But because the doctrine of unity was itself under attack, courts sought *new* grounds on which to justify the immunity bar. ''Privacy'' supplied grounds on which to justify interspousal tort immunity—grounds that were seemingly independent of the increasingly discredited language of marital hierarchy. And so the discourse of marital status began to shift from the rhetoric of ''marital unity'' to the rhetoric of ''privacy'' and ''domestic harmony.''

Thus, judges seeking to explain the modified structure of marital status law increasingly drew upon gender concepts of the industrial era to explain the law of marriage in more contemporary and socially credible terms. Rather than represent marriage in the biblical discourse of ''one flesh,'' as a relation that ''merged'' wife with husband, courts instead discussed marriage as it was understood in nineteenth-century America: as a companionate relationship based on an affective bond that flourished best in a sphere separate from civil society. Some judges even went so far as to depict the marriage relation as situated in a home with heavily curtained windows: thus, a court would not hear a wife's suit for damages against a husband who battered her because public policy counseled that ''it is better to draw the curtain, shut out the public gaze, and leave the parties to forget and forgive.''[35] With this shift to privacy talk, a husband's marital prerogatives could be preserved in new juridical form—as legal immunities.

Once courts ceased to rely on the rhetoric of marital unity and began to discuss marriage in the language of privacy and affect, they no longer had to explain the law of marriage as enforcing relations of hierarchy. Instead, courts could explain the law of marriage as preserving relations of *altruism*. If a wife suffered a beating at the hands of her husband, "it is better to . . . leave the parties to forget and forgive."[36] As the North Carolina Supreme Court observed: "[The law] drops the curtain upon scenes of domestic life, preferring not to take cognizance of what transpires within that circle, to the exposure of public prosecution. It presumes that acts of wrong committed in passsion will be followed by contrition and atonement in a cooler moment, and forgiveness will blot it out of memory."[37] In short, it was no longer necessary to justify a husband's acts of abuse as the lawful prerogatives of a master. Rather, the state granted a husband immunity to abuse his wife in order to foster the altruistic ethos of the private realm. In this way, laws that protected relations of domination could be justified as promoting relations of love. The regulation of marital violence was thus translated into the language of companionate marriage prevailing during the industrial era.

PRIVACY IN THE CRIMINAL LAW OF DOMESTIC ASSAULT

By the beginning of the twentieth century, this new mode of reasoning about marital violence traveled from tort law to criminal law and found institutional expression in the criminal justice system. During this period, cities began to establish special domestic relations courts staffed by social workers to handle complaints of marital violence; by 1920 most major cities had such courts. The family court system sought to decriminalize marital violence. The underlying theory of this special court system, a New York City judge explained, was that "domestic trouble cases are not criminal in a legal sense."[38] Rather than arrest or punish those who assaulted their partners, the judge and social workers urged couples to reconcile, providing informal or formal counseling designed to preserve the relationship whenever possible. Battered wives were discouraged from filing criminal charges against their husbands, urged to accept responsibility for their role in provoking the violence, and encouraged to remain in the relationship and rebuild it rather than attempt to separate or divorce. The police adjusted their arrest procedures to accord with the new philosophy of the domestic relations courts, channeling family violence cases out of the criminal justice system and into counseling whenever possible. In this institutional framework, physical assault was not viewed as criminal conduct; instead, it was viewed as an expression of emotions that needed to be adjusted and rechanneled into marriage.

Regulation of marital violence continued in this "therapeutic" framework for much of the twentieth century. There was no formal immunity rule as in tort law, but the criminal justice system developed a set of informal procedures for handling marital violence—which it justified in the discourse of affective privacy. In the 1960s, for example, the training bulletin of the International Association of Chiefs of Police offered the following instructions for handling "family disturbances":

> For the most part these disputes are personal matters requiring no direct police action. However, an inquiry into the facts must be made to satisfy the originating complaint. . . . Once inside the home, the officer's sole purpose is to *preserve the peace . . . [a]ttempt to soothe feelings, pacify parties* . . . [s]uggest parties refer their problem to a church or a community agency. . . . In dealing with family disputes *the power of arrest should be exercised as a last resort. The officer should never create a police problem when there is only a family problem existing.*[39]

Until the last decade, this set of instructions was quite typical of police procedure in American cities. For example, in California, the Oakland Police Department's 1975 "Training Bulletin on Techniques of Dispute Intervention" asserted that "*[t]he police role in a dispute situation is more often that of a mediator and peacemaker than enforcer of law*. . . . Normally, officers should adhere to the policy that that arrests shall be avoided . . . but when one of the parties demands arrest, you should . . . encourage the parties to reason with each other."[40]

It was not until the late 1970s that the contemporary women's rights movement mounted an effective challenge to this regime. Today, after numerous protest activities and lawsuits, there are shelters for battered women and their children, new arrest procedures for police departments across the country, and even federal legislation making gender-motivated assaults a civil rights violation.[41] Yet as the U.S. surgeon general recently found, battering of women by husbands, ex-husbands, and lovers remains the single largest cause of injury to women in the United States today.[42]

Notwithstanding profound changes in the laws and mores of marriage since the turn of the century, Americans still reason about marital violence in terms of privacy. O. J. Simpson invoked this tradition in 1989 when he shouted at police who had responded to his wife's call for help: "The police have been out here eight times before, and now you're going to arrest me for this? *This is a family matter.* Why do you want to make a big deal out of it when we can handle it?"[43] The chief justice of the United States invoked this discourse of the private when he objected to provisions in the new Violence against Women Act[44] that create a federal cause of action for gender-motivated violence. The bill's "broad definition of criminal conduct is so open-ended, and the new private right of action so sweeping," Chief Justice William H. Rehnquist complained, "that the legislation *could involve the federal courts in a whole host of domestic relations disputes.*"[45]

Civil Rights Reform and the Modernization of Status Discourse

In this essay I have attempted to demonstrate that some kinds of privacy talk are properly understood as modern expressions of the putatively discredited doctrine of marital unity. There is no necessary connection here, only a historically contingent one. But the connection is terribly important to observe for just that reason. Status talk is mutable and remarkably adaptable: it will evolve as the rule structure of a status regime evolves. In the ensuing sections I reflect briefly on the significance of this observation for our understanding of civil rights reform, both historical and contemporary.

Historical Perspectives

Status regimes are not static but dynamic—revitalized from time to time as they are reshaped by diverse political forces and draw on evolving social mores. For example, in the decades after the Civil War, a regime of racial status built on the law of chattel slavery evolved in rule structure and rhetoric into the form of American apartheid known as "Jim Crow." The law of de jure segregation differed from chattel slavery in its constitutive rules (so that former slaves were subject to a different set of labor codes and restrictions on their civil liberties); it is less commonly observed that the law of de jure segregation also differed from chattel slavery, at least in part, in the rhetorics employed to justify its constitutive rules. During the aptly named "Reconstruction" era, overtly hierarchy-based justifications offered for chattel slavery began to give way to justifications for apartheid that drew upon racial discourses of the private. Thus, in *Plessy v. Ferguson*, the Supreme Court upheld racial segregation under the Fourteenth Amendment by reasoning that racial equality did not require "an enforced commingling of the two races":[46]

> The object of the amendment was undoubtedly to enforce the absolute equality of the two races before the law, but in the nature of things it could not have been intended to abolish distinctions based upon color, or to enforce social, as distinguished from political equality, or a commingling of the two races upon terms unsatisfactory to either. . . . If the two races are to meet upon terms of social equality, it must be the result of natural affinities, a mutual appreciation of each other's merits and a voluntary consent of individuals.[47]

The racial discourse of the private that the Court invoked in *Plessy* differed from the discourses of affective privacy employed to rationalize elements of marital status law during the same period but functioned in strikingly similar ways: to explain laws enforcing status privileges, once justified in overtly hierarchy-based discourses, with reference to other, less contested, social values.

There were significant differences in the rules and rhetoric that were employed to enforce racial status relations under chattel slavery and under Jim Crow. Yet it plainly would be wrong to overlook the elements of continuity between regimes. During Reconstruction, the legal system still played a significant role in maintaining the differences in material and dignitary privilege that constituted "the two races," although it now did so by means of a new cluster of rules and rhetorics. In short, Jim Crow was a successor to chattel slavery that enforced the status relations we call "race" by somewhat less formalized means. I call this dynamic of preservation through transformation in the structure of a status regime "deformalization" or "modernization."

Modernization of a status regime occurs when a legal system enforces social stratification by means that change over time. One commonly recognized way that law enforces social stratification is by according groups hierarchically differentiated entitlements and obligations. In antebellum America, the law of slavery and marriage enforced race and gender hierarchy by such overt means. But by the Reconstruction era, the law of race and gender status had begun, slowly, to evolve, in diverse ways eschewing the overtly hierarchical forms of the antebellum period. In this era, the legal system continued to draw distinctions on the basis of race and gender, but it now began to emphasize formal equality of entitlements in relationships once explicitly organized as relationships of mastery and subordination and to repudiate openly caste-based justifications for such group-based distinctions as the law continued to enforce. While the American legal system continued to distribute social goods and privileges in ways that favored whites and males, it now began self-consciously to disavow its role in doing so. The new interest in rule equality and the energy devoted to explaining law without recourse to overtly caste-based justifications mark an important shift in the mode of regulating race and gender relations, a deformalization and concomitant modernization of status law.

Civil rights agitation plays a significant role in precipitating the modernization of status regimes. Abolitionist protest (and a civil war) contributed to the modernization of racial-status law during the Reconstruction era, just as the woman's rights protest contributed to the modernization of gender-status law during this same period. If successful, protest of this sort will draw the legitimacy of a status regime into question and so bring pressure to bear on lawmakers and other legal elites to cede status privileges. In such circumstances, legal elites may begin to cede status privileges, but they will also defend them. They will initially defend privileges within the traditional rhetoric of the status regime—but because the traditional rhetoric of the status regime is now socially contested, they will begin to search for "new reasons" to justify those status privileges they choose to defend. As reform of the common-law marital-status rules illustrates, this process of ceding and defending status privileges will result in changes in the constitutive rules of the regime and in its justificatory rhetoric—with the result that, over time, status relationships will be translated from an older, socially contested idiom into a newer, more socially acceptable idiom. In short, civil rights reform is an important engine of social change. Yet civil rights reform does not simply abolish a status regime; in important respects, it modernizes the rules and rhetoric through which status relations are enforced and justified.

The dynamic of preservation through transformation that I am describing need not arise through the conspiratorial or malevolent motivations of the legal elites directing reform. Indeed, we can posit for purposes of argument that the legal elites who implement these changes in the constitutive rules and rhetoric of a status regime are acting in "good faith." For example, I assume that the judges who repudiated marital chastisement, yet developed the interspousal tort immunity doctrine to constrain interpretation of the married women's property acts, did not snicker in the robing room in gleeful appreciation of their interpretive sophistry. They could well have harbored the good-faith conviction that privacy and domestic harmony were important social values that required protection as they superintended the marriage relation through a period of turbulent legal transformation. Thus, as judges contemplated the question of whether the reform statutes granting married women a tort claim for injury to their persons and property should be construed to enable wives to sue their husbands, judges could well have decided, in all sincerity, that considerations of ''public policy'' warranted interpreting the statutes to bar the claim.

Yet it also seems clear that, as educated, propertied men, judges reasoned about this question within certain legal traditions and from a certain social position that predisposed them to certain legal conclusions. Judges who initially adopted the tort immunity rule openly embraced it as preserving elements of the doctrine of marital unity; only as the doctrine of marital unity was progressively discredited did courts come to rely exclusively on justifications couched in the discourse of affective privacy. Moreover, given the social position from which judges reasoned about ''public policy,'' they were far more likely to appreciate the benefits of the tort immunity rule (to propertied husbands) than to register its costs (to battered wives)—a phenomenon Paul Brest has elegantly dubbed ''selective sympathy and indifference.''[48] Of course, we can assume that at least some of these judges had the critical faculties to discern, and thus to correct for, the biases to which their deliberative processes were subject. Sometimes, however, critical oblivion is bliss, especially when it is interest-convergent.

Does this inquiry into the modernization of status regimes turn out to be a story about stasis after all? Is Jim Crow slavery by another name and the network of formal and informal immunities for wife beating that emerged during Reconstruction the functional equivalent of chastisement? As I indicated at the outset of this discussion, I believe that the dynamic I am describing can fairly be called one of preservation through transformation or characterized in any way that indicates that elements of continuity *and* change are at stake in the process. A body of status law is modernized when its rules and rhetoric are reformed, and yet the law continues to distribute material and dignitary privileges in ways that maintain the distinctions constituting the regime (e.g., ''race'' or ''gender'') in relatively continuous terms. Modernization of a status regime may nonetheless bring about perceptible, even significant, changes in status relations. For example, we can posit that African Americans were ''better off'' under a regime of Jim Crow than a regime of chattel slavery, certainly in terms of dignitary values and possibly in terms of their material welfare as well. Similarly, we can posit that married women were ''better off'' under a regime of formal and informal immunities for wife beating, certainly in terms of dignitary values and possibly in terms of their material welfare as well.

There is, however, one way in which members of each group were indisputably worse off: in their capacity to achieve further, welfare-enhancing reform of the status regime in which they were subordinated. By the mid-nineteenth century, slavery and marital-status law (chastisement, in particular) were socially contested and substantially discredited practices. They lacked legitimacy in the eyes of many. But once racial-status law and marital-status law were reformed in the Reconstruction era, each status regime gained substantially in legitimacy. As each regime was translated from contested rules and rhetorics into more contemporary rules and rhetorics, each was again ''naturalized'' as just and reasonable, in significant part because each was now formally and substantively distinguishable from its contested predecessor: each could be justified in terms of social values that were distinct from the orthodox, hierarchy-based norms that characterized its predecessor (slavery, marriage) as a regime of mastery. Considered from this perspective, we can see that civil rights reform may alleviate certain dignitary or material aspects of the inequalities that subordinated groups suffer; *but we can also see that civil rights reform may enhance the legal system's capacity to legitimate residual social inequalities among status-differentiated groups.*

Of course, struggle persists, and oftentimes subordinated groups can exploit the semantic instability of status discourses for their own resistance purposes. After many decades, the rhetoric of separate but equal was turned against Jim Crow, and the discourse of privacy developed a constitutional life that would have startled the nineteenth-century judiciary. It might seem that such developments would tend ultimately to destabilize regimes of race and gender status. Yet the dynamic runs in both directions. Protest or resistance discourses are semantically unstable as well, with the result that rhetorics employed by recent civil rights movements to challenge laws enforcing race-and gender-status relationships are now being turned to *status-preserving* ends. As the recent life of the color-blindness trope illustrates, civil rights rhetoric can supply "legitimate," "nondiscriminatory" reasons for opposing affirmative action and other group-conscious initiatives intended to remedy racial and gender inequalities. This change in the political valence of civil rights discourse—a phenomenon Jack Balkin calls "ideological drift"[49]—occurs as those who oppose current efforts to rectify race and gender stratification seek to justify their opposition in terms that can be differentiated from a naked interest in preserving race and gender stratification. Although many justifications might suffice for these purposes, claiming fidelity to principles of equality would seem to provide an unimpeachable reason for opposing group-conscious efforts to rectify race and gender stratification. The language of color-blindness can now be appropriated for these purposes, because the rule structure of contemporary race- and gender-status law has changed in response to demands for color-and sex-blindness that have been advanced by the civil rights movement over the last several decades, and government rarely employs race-and gender-conscious regulation any more, except for the purpose of alleviating social stratification. Under such circumstances, old protest discourses (such as color-blindness) are especially susceptible to capture, "drift," or co-optation, as they justify adherence to the status quo in terms that are especially difficult to impugn. As I observed at the outset of this discussion, status talk is mutable and remarkably adaptable and will evolve as the rule structure of a status regime evolves.[50]

Contemporary Perspectives

To what extent is the legal system responsible for the continuing race and gender stratification of American society? Today it is commonplace to distinguish between de jure and de facto discrimination—and to attribute some aspects of race and gender stratification to state action and others to "social" factors that might reflect "the continuing effects of past discrimination." Largely unarticulated in such accounts of de jure and de facto discrimination is any theory about what kinds of state action are discriminatory, or status enforcing. Most often it is tacitly assumed that race- or gender-specific state action is status enforcing, whereas so-called facially neutral state action is not.

This way of reasoning about the de jure–de facto distinction has its roots in equal protection doctrines requiring "heightened scrutiny" of race- or gender-specific state action. Under the pressure of this constitutional requirement, laws that only recently were cast in race- or gender-specific terms have been revised so that they are now cleansed of any race- or gender-specific references. As a consequence, the persisting race and gender stratification of American life is commonly (and often legally) attributed to "the continuing effects of past discrimination" rather than to current, "facially neutral" forms of state action.

There is little in contemporary equal protection doctrine that challenges this view. The Court will hear arguments that race- or sex-based state action is discriminatory; otherwise it requires plaintiffs to prove that facially neutral state action is motivated by a discriminatory purpose.[51] Yet the Court has construed "discriminatory purpose" to be a state of mind akin to malice,[52] and, as the Court itself has acknowledged, it is exceedingly difficult to prove "discriminatory purpose" once it is defined in this way: lawmakers can always articulate socially benign (or at least nonmalicious) reasons for policies they adopt that may "incidentally" perpetuate status inequalities among groups. Cumulatively, this body of equal protection doctrine has given lawmakers a strong incentive to change the rule structure of policies that long enforced racial or gender stratification and to articulate "legitimate, nondiscriminatory reasons" for those policies in order to immunize them from further equal protection challenge.

Thus, the civil rights revolutions of the 1960s and 1970s precipitated a shift in the rule structure and justificatory rhetoric of laws that long played a role in enforcing race- and gender-status relations. Given that today most state action has been cleansed of race- and gender-specific references, can we assume, as both the Supreme Court and the American public seemingly have, that by virtue of these reforms, the state has generally withdrawn from the business of enforcing race- and gender-status relations?

We might consider this question by examining how equal protection doctrines of heightened scrutiny have affected law enforcement policies regulating marital violence. Although general criminal assault statutes were often used to regulate "domestic disturbances," it was also commonplace for judicial opinions, statutes, and law enforcement policies to refer to the conduct as "wife beating" or otherwise to discuss the parties involved in gender-specific terms. After 1976, when the Court decided in *Craig v. Boren*[53] that sex-based state action would be subject to a heightened or intermediate standard of review under the equal protection clause of the Fourteenth Amendment, all this began to change. Residual gender-specific references were deleted from the law and replaced with gender-neutral language, with the result that the conduct is now generally referred to as "spousal assault" or "domestic violence." (To be sure, in this era many feminists advocated the use of gender-neutral language in domestic violence policies, *in the course of seeking reform of their substantive norms*; lawmakers readily adopted the gender-neutral language and moved far more slowly to revise the constitutive norms and procedures of their domestic violence policies.)

Now, when litigants challenge law enforcement policies providing lesser degrees of protection to victims of domestic violence, they have great difficulty proving that the policies are sexually discriminatory—despite the fact that it is women who are overwhelmingly the targets of assaults between intimates.[54] A number of federal circuit courts have ruled that facially neutral spousal assault policies are not subject to heightened standards of review under the equal protection clause (although such policies may constitute discrimination against married persons or cohabitants, subject to more deferential or "rational relation" review).[55] Because such policies are couched in gender-neutral terms, plaintiffs seeking to prove that the policies were animated by a sexually discriminatory purpose would have to show that they were adopted "at least in part because of, and not merely in spite of," their impact on women.[56] Similar problems in proving sex discrimination occur with equal protection challenges to the doctrine of interspousal tort immunity (which, as we have seen, was couched, from the outset, in formally gender-neutral terms), or to the exemption for "spousal" rape, or to rules giving "spouses" rights to the value of labor performed in the household.

In this way, modern doctrines of equal protection are effacing the gender-specific (or race-specific) antecedents of state policies that in their current, facially neutral form may well continue to enforce relations of gender or racial inequality. While modern equal protection law has served to disestablish certain forms of status-enforcing state action, in many cases, the changes equal protection doctrines effected were at best superficial.[57]

Consider the domestic violence policies we have examined. The threat of equal protection litigation prompted the deletion of gender-specific references from the law; once "sanitized" in this way, such policies have become exceedingly difficult to challenge with existing constitutional tools, even when their historically rooted norms remain intact and substantially unquestioned. Under the case law we have just surveyed, a municipality defending a facially neutral domestic violence policy against an equal protection claim need show only that the policy is rationally related to some legitimate state purpose and was not adopted "because of" its "adverse effects" on women. To say the least, this showing does not require municipalities to make significant changes in the structure of their policies—even if the facially neutral policies continue to treat victims of assaults by intimates differently than other victims of assault. In *Siddle v. City of Cambridge*,[58] the court found that the city's proffered justifications did in fact pass the rational-basis test:

> The state puts forth several justifications for any differences that may exist. These justifications fulfill the rational basis test, and reach the level of an important state objective. *The first is that the criminal area may not be the best place to resolve marital problems of this sort. The government needs flexibility so that all of its resources, including mental health agencies, can rectify the situation.* Often criminal sanctions alone are ineffective. *Moreover, domestic violence situation [sic] are different from other forms of criminal behavior in their complex emotional causes of behavior.* . . . The government need not treat cases as the same, because it would be unproductive, and possibility counter-productive, to do so.[59]

The justifications accepted by this court as satisfying the rational relation (and even intermediate scrutiny) test should be quite familiar. The reasons supplied are conventional expressions of the discourse of affective privacy, which has been used to justify criminal law policies on domestic violence since the Progressive Era—*reasons for affording informal immunity to assaults between intimates that would not obtain in other contexts.* The analytical framework of equal protection cases such as these merely serves to rationalize a body of laws whose normative roots can be traced to the ancient doctrine of marital chastisement. For close to two decades now, the modern feminist movement has protested the inadequacy of domestic violence policies but, in the course of this work, has received considerably less assistance from the Constitution's promise of equal protection of the laws than the lineage of the policies would seem to warrant.

There are certain modifications to equal protection doctrine that could make it supple enough to police for bias in the new forms of "facially neutral" state action it has helped bring into being. For instance, the Court might revise the doctrinal criteria that define race-and sex-based state action for purposes of triggering heightened scrutiny. Given the lineage of "spousal" assault policies, why should the mere use of gender-neutral language immunize the policies from heightened scrutiny? Or the Court might revise the much-criticized doctrines of discriminatory purpose that plaintiffs must use to challenge facially neutral policies and practices. Given the history of marital violence regulation, why must a plaintiff show that a facially neutral spousal assault policy was adopted "because of" its "adverse effects" on women? This requirement seems especially perverse in an "equal rights" era, when policymakers conventionally supply "legitimate, nondiscriminatory" reasons for their actions.

Unfortunately, as currently constituted, the Court shows scant interest in revising equal protection doctrines of heightened scrutiny and discriminatory purpose. This body of constitutional law once served to dismantle status-enforcing state action, but, because of its very success in precipitating the reform—*and modernization*—of status-enforcing state action, the doctrines often serve to rationalize rather than scrutinize the new, facially neutral forms of status-enforcing state action they helped bring into being.

Conclusion

As this essay has demonstrated, status law is dynamic and evolves in rule structure and rhetoric under the pressure of civil rights reform. In the nineteenth century, when judges repudiated a husband's common-law prerogative to chastise his wife, they began to grant wife beaters a variety of formal and informal immunities from public and private prosecution. Just as the doctrine of chastisement was rationalized by rhetorics of hierarchy, this new regime of immunity rules was rationalized by rhetorics of interiority: by a discourse of affective privacy that invoked the feelings and spaces of domesticity to justify the law of marital status in an era of companionate marriage.

In short, as this essay has illustrated, emotions have a history, and their discursive roots can be traced—if only in small part—to the nineteenth-century courtroom, where the discourse of affective privacy served to make "reasonable" marital-status doctrines when talk of marital unity no longer could. There, judges invoking the discourse of affective privacy translated the hierarchy-based chastisement doctrine into immunity rules couched in a more modern idiom: "If no permanent injury has been inflicted, nor malice, cruelty nor dangerous violence shown by the husband, *it is better to draw the curtain, shut out the public gaze, and leave the parties to forget and forgive.*"[60] The American antidiscrimination tradition pays scant attention to these chameleon-like qualities of status talk; it has reified the phenomena it calls "sex discrimination" and "race discrimination," without attending to their dynamic character. But this study of marital violence law demonstrates that status discourse is mutable, evolving as it is contested over the course of the centuries. If civil rights reform is to be effective, civil rights law must continually adapt, striving to remain in critical dialogue with the evolving rules and rhetoric of any status regime it aspires to disestablish.

NOTES

This chapter is drawn in part from "'The Rule of Love': Wife Beating as Prerogative and Privacy," *Yale Law Journal* 105 (1996): 2117–2207.

1. William Blackstone, *Commentaries*, vol. 1 (Chicago: University of Chicago Press, 1979), 441; see, e.g., Norma Basch, *In the Eyes of the Law: Women, Marriage, and Property in Nineteenth-Century New York* (Ithaca: Cornell University Press, 1982), 51–52.
2. Blackstone, *Commentaries*, 444.
3. See Daniel Boorstin, *The Mysterious Science of the Law: An Essay on Blackstone's Commentaries* (Cambridge, Mass.: Harvard University Press, 1941), 1.
4. See, e.g., James Kent, *Commentaries on American Law*, vol. 2 (New York: E. B. Clayton, 1840), 180; Francis Wharton, *A Treatise on the Criminal Law of the United States* (Pittsburgh: James Kay, Jr. & Brother, 1846), 314.
5. For early American cases recognizing the right of chastisement, see *Helms v. Franciscus*, 2 Bland 544, 562 n. (Md. Ch. 1840) (quoting *Bread's Case*, Chancery Proceedings, lib. C.D. fol. 319 [1681]; *Bradley v. State*, 1 Miss. (Walk.) 156, 158 (1824); *State v. Black*, 60 N.C. 262 (1864); *State v. Buckley*, 2 Del. (2 Harr.) 552 (1838); *Richards v. Richards*, 1 Grant's Cases 389, 392–93 (Pa. 1856); *Adams v. Adams*, 100 Mass. 365, 369–70 (1868).
6. For an overview of the historiography on the reform of marital status law in nineteenth-century America, see Reva Siegel, "The Modernization of Marital Status Law: Adjudicating Wives' Rights to Earnings, 1860–1930," *Georgetown Law Journal* 82 (1994): 2127, 2132–41.
7. *Report of the Woman's Rights Convention, Held at Seneca Falls, N.Y., July 19 & 20, 1848* (Rochester, N.Y.: John Dick, 1848), 6 (emphasis added).
8. For an illustration of the slow progress of common-law reform, see Siegel, "Marital Status Law," 2149–57; Reva Siegel, "Home As Work: The First Woman's Rights Claims Concerning Wives' Household Labor, 1850–1880," *Yale Law Journal* 103 (1994): 1073, 1167–77.
9. Jerome Nadelhaft, "Wife Torture: A Known Phenomenon in Nineteenth-Century America," *Journal of American Culture* 10 (1987): 39, 42.
10. C. C. H. of East Orange, New Jersey, "Crimes against Women," *Woman's Journal* (December 25, 1875): 413.
11. Henry B. Blackwell, "Crimes of a Single Day," *Woman's Journal* (January 29, 1876): 34.
12. Elizabeth Pleck, *Domestic Tyranny: The Making of American Social Policy against Family Violence from Colonial Times to the Present* (New York: Oxford University Press,

1987), 100; Elizabeth Pleck, ''Feminist Responses to 'Crimes against Women,' 1868–1896,'' *Signs* 8 (1983): 451, 462–65.

13. *Fulgam v. State*, 46 Ala. 143, 146 (1871).

14. Elizabeth Pleck, ''The Whipping Post for Wife Beaters, 1876–1906,'' in *Essays on the Family and Historical Change*, ed. David Levine et al. (College Station: Texas A&M University Press, 1983), 127.

15. See, e.g., Chester Vernier, *American Family Laws*, vol. 2, sec. 66 (London: Oxford University Press, 1932) (quoting, by state, statutory definitions of cruelty as grounds for divorce).

16. See, e.g., *Bailey v. Bailey*, 97 Mass. 373, 379 (1867) (''Among the lower classes, blows sometimes pass between married couples who in the main are happy, and have no desire to part. Amidst very coarse habits . . . a word and a blow go together'') (quoting Shelford, *Marriage and Divorce*, sec. 764, at 428).

17. On the defense of provocation, see, e.g., *Knight v. Knight*, 31 Ia. 451 (1871). On the defense of condonation, see, e.g., *Davies v. Davies*, 37 N.Y. 45, 46, 48 (1869).

18. See, e.g. Pleck, ''The Whipping Post,'' 135–36. For more extended discussion of race and class bias in the prosecution of wife beaters in this era, see Reva B. Siegel, '' 'The Rule of Love': Wife Beating as Prerogative and Privacy,'' *Yale Law Journal* 105 (1996): 2117, 2134–41.

19. James Schouler, *A Treatise on the Law of Domestic Relations; Embracing Husband and Wife, Parent and Child, Guardian and Ward, Infancy, and Master and Servant* (Boston: Little, Brown & Co., 1870), 59 (emphasis added).

20. 60 N.C. 262 (1864).

21. Ibid.

22. Ibid.

23. 61 N.C. (Phil. Law) 453 (1868).

24. Ibid. at 457.

25. *State v. Oliver*, 70 N.C. 60, 61–62 (1874) (emphasis added).

26. See Joseph Story, *Commentaries on Equity Pleadings, and the Incidents Thereof, According to the Practice of the Courts of Equity, of England and America*, 7th ed. (Boston: Little, Brown & Co., 1865), 54–55.

27. Carl Tobias, ''Interspousal Tort Immunity in America,'' *Georgia Law Review* 23 (1989): 359, 383.

28. 67 Me. 304, 307 (1877).

29. Ibid. (quoting *State v. Oliver*, 70 N.C. 60, 61–62 [1874]).

30. Ibid. at 308.

31. *Thompson v. Thompson*, 218 U.S. 611 (1910).

32. Ibid. at 617.

33. Ibid. at 617–18.

34. *Drake v. Drake*, 177 N.W. 624, 625 (Minn. 1920) (emphasis added).

35. *Abbott v. Abbott*, 67 Me. 304, 307 (1877) (quoting *State v. Oliver*, 70 N.C. 60, 61–62 [1874]).

36. Ibid.

37. *State v. Fulton*, 63 S.E. 145, 145 (N.C. 1908) (quoting *State v. Edens*, 95 N.C. 693) (spousal tort immunity for slander).

38. Pleck, *Domestic Tyranny*, 137 (quoting Judge Bernhard Rabbino of New York City Court of Domestic Relations).

39. International Association of Police Chiefs, *Training Key No. 16, Handling Disturbance Calls* 1968–69), 94–95, quoted in Sue E. Eisenberg and Patricia L. Micklow, ''The Assaulted Wife: 'Catch 22' Revisited,'' *Women's Rights Law Reporter* 3 (1977): 138, 156 (emphasis added).

40. Del Martin, *Battered Wives* (1981), 93–94 (emphasis added).

41. See Violence Against Women Act, Pub. L. No. 103-322, 108 Stat. 1796 (1994) (codified at 42 U.S.C. § 13,981 [1994]).

42. Joan Zorza, "The Criminal Law of Misdemeanor Domestic Violence, 1970–1990," *Journal of Criminal Law and Criminology* 83 (1992): 46, 46 (quoting Nikki R. Van Hightower and Susan A. McManus, "Limits of State Constitutional Guarantees: Lessons from Efforts to Implement Domestic Violence Policies," *Public Administrative Review* 49 [1982]: 269, 269).

43. Josh Meyer, "Police Records Detail 1989 Beating That Led to Charge; A Bloodied Nicole Simpson, Hiding in Bushes after 911 Call, Told Officers: 'He's Going to Kill Me.' Judge Overruled Prosecutors' Request That Simpson Serve Jail Time," *Los Angeles Times*, 17 June 1994, pt. A, 24 (emphasis added).

44. 42 U.S.C. § 13,981 (1994).

45. William Rehnquist, "Chief Justice's 1991 Year-End Report on the Federal Judiciary," *Third Branch*, January 1992, 3 (emphasis added), quoted in "Developments in Law: Legal Responses to Domestic Violence," *Harvard Law Review* 106 (1993): 1498, 1545–46.

46. 163 U.S. 537, 551 (1896).

47. Ibid. at 544, 551.

48. Paul Brest, "The Supreme Court, 1975 Term—Foreword: In Defense of the Antidiscrimination Principle," *Harvard Law Review* 90 (1976): 1, 7–8.

49. J. M. Balkin, "Ideological Drift and the Struggle over Meaning," *Connecticut Law Review* 25 (1993): 869, 872–73.

50. Of course, nothing in the account of modernization I offer requires that new status discourses be generated out of co-opted protest discourses. On the other hand, my account of the modernization of status regimes does explain why old protest discourses are especially attractive candidates for co-optation into status discourses. As I indicate in the text, old protest discourses provide seemingly unimpeachable grounds for defending the structure of a status regime when its legitimacy is under attack.

51. See *Washington v. Davis*, 426 U.S. 229 (1976).

52. See *Personnel Adm'r v. Feeney*, 442 U.S. 256, 279 (1979).

53. 429 U.S. 190 (1976).

54. The Justice Department has estimated that 90% to 95% of domestic violence victims are women. "Laws Mandating Reporting of Domestic Violence: Do They Promote Patient Well-Being?" *Journal of the American Medical Association* 273 (1995): 1781 (quoting U.S. Department of Justice, Bureau of Justice Statistics, *Violence between Intimates* [1994]).

55. The leading case in this area is *Hynson v. City of Chester Legal Dep't*, 864 F.2d 1026, 1031 (3d Cir. 1988).

56. See *Personnel Adm'r v. Feeney*, 442 U.S. 256, 279 (1979).

57. Making a race- or gender-specific law facially neutral may have very different consequences, depending on a variety of factors, including the nature of the law, the nature of the social practice it regulates, and the ways in which the regulated practice allocates dignitary and/or material privileges. Although the topic is far too vast to explore in the present context, the following examples should suffice to illustrate my point. Removing racial distinctions from a school assignment policy may facilitate the integration of a school system but will have less of an integration effect if the policy endorses "neighborhood" school assignments under conditions of residential segregation. Removing gender distinctions from a law conscripting persons for military service will facilitate the integration of the armed forces but will have less of an integration effect if the conscription policy specifies height, weight, and strength requirements that relatively few women can meet. Removing gender

distinctions from the law of rape will not much alter the social conditions under which rapes are practiced; nor will removing gender distinctions from domestic violence law much alter the practice of "spouse beating." Making such laws facially neutral does not alter the constraints on men who assault women; rather it extends the scope of the prohibition to include women. Presumably this reform will have a marginal deterrent effect on women's conduct but none on men's conduct. Nor is it clear what "symbolic" message is communicated by making gender-specific laws regulating gender-salient practices into gender-neutral laws. To disrupt the subordinating practice in these cases, it is necessary to alter the norms of the laws that regulate it. In short, formal equality will disrupt certain subordinating practices and leave others relatively undisturbed—possibly even masking the nature of the harm they are inflicting.

58. 761 F. Supp. 503 (S.D. Ohio 1991).

59. Ibid. at 512 (emphasis added).

60. *State v. Oliver*, 70 N.C. 60, 61–62 (1874) (criminal immunity case) (emphasis added), quoted in *Abbott v. Abbott*, 67 Me. 304, 307 (1877) (tort immunity case).

4

The Illusory Distinction between Equality of Opportunity and Equality of Result

DAVID A. STRAUSS

"Our society should guarantee equality of opportunity, but not equality of result." The idea is a familiar one. Usually it is offered as part of a general attack on government measures that redistribute wealth. The idea appears to be that the government's role is to ensure that everyone starts off from the same point, not that everyone ends up in the same condition. If people have equal opportunities, what they make of those opportunities is their responsibility. If they end up worse off, the government should not intervene to help them.[1]

I want to suggest that the distinction between equality of opportunity and equality of result is not a useful one. I do not mean to say that the notion of equality of opportunity is an empty one; on the contrary, it is potentially a powerful and important ideal. It is, however, much more complex than the proponents of the distinction between "opportunity" and "result" acknowledge.

The most natural conception of equality of opportunity, which I discuss in the second section of this chapter, is that equality of opportunity requires the elimination of barriers to advancement that are in some sense arbitrary. This conception of equality of opportunity, however, requires large-scale redistributions of resources—perhaps not literal equality of results, in the sense that every person must have the same resources, but a much closer approximation to that state than the advocates of "equality of opportunity, not result" might suspect (and probably much closer than anyone would desire). The central idea is familiar: talents and abilities, the qualities that (ideally) are responsible for inequalities in results, are in an important sense no less arbitrary than the barriers that any advocate of equality of opportunity would want to eliminate.

In the third section, I will discuss a different conception of equality of opportunity, one that is perhaps closer to what the advocates of "equality of opportunity, not result" have in mind. This conception sees equality of opportunity as a meritocratic principle that allows, roughly speaking, the free operation of the market. According to this view, government actions that alter outcomes produced by the market derogate from equality of opportunity and can be viewed only as efforts to promote equality of result.

My argument is that the market-oriented meritocratic conception of equality of opportunity, although a coherent view, is an ideal of equality only in a limited and somewhat counterintuitive sense. More important, the form of equality that characterizes well-functioning market processes also characterizes well-functioning democratic processes. Therefore, in principle, there is no difference between the equality manifested in market-oriented meritocracy (so-called equality of opportunity) and the equality characteristic of a well-functioning democracy that alters market outcomes (so-called equality of result). It follows that the distinction between opportunity and result is an unhelpful and misleading way to categorize social institutions.

Equality of Opportunity as the Elimination of Arbitrary Barriers to Advancement

Formal Equality of Opportunity

One indisputable aspect of equality of opportunity is what might be called formal equality of opportunity.[2] I believe that those who rely on the distinction between equality of opportunity and equality of result have this principle in mind as at least the minimum content of equality of opportunity.

The principle of formal equality of opportunity holds, in the classic formulation, that careers should be open to talents.[3] The law should not bar a person from an occupation or a position of prestige just because—as the principle would have been stated at a time when it was more controversial than today—that person was born into a family that does not belong to the aristocracy.[4] Today the equivalent example would probably be not birth into a nonaristocratic family but birth into a certain racial group. A law that bars members of a racial minority from certain jobs, for example, denies them equality of opportunity.

Why are formal barriers to opportunity unacceptable? Perhaps the most obvious reason is the intuition that a person's fortunes should not depend on such arbitrary circumstances as race or family background. These are accidents of birth that are beyond an individual's control. It is therefore unfair to the individual to allow these factors to be so influential. There are other plausible arguments against formal barriers, of course. For example, one might say that formal equality of opportunity is desirable not because it is fairer to the individual but because it maximizes social well-being. I consider those arguments below. At least the most obvious and immediate argument for equality of opportunity is based on the idea that it is unfair to allow arbitrary factors to have a dramatic effect on a person's life.

This argument for equality of opportunity, however, quickly leads to arguments for much more than the elimination of formal barriers. The call for "equality of opportunity, not equality of result'' is sometimes offered as a reason for opposing welfare state measures.[5] But if the basis of equality of opportunity is the unfairness of allowing arbitrary factors to affect a person's chances in life, it is immediately apparent that equality of opportunity might require extensive government welfare and redistribution programs.[6] This is an important theme of John Rawls's *Theory of Justice*—that the principles that justify well-established liberal institutions, such as toleration, also entail substantial redistribution of resources.

The reasoning is familiar. Even without formal barriers, a person with as much talent and initiative as another may not do as well if he or she has had, for example, an inferior education or inferior health care. Indeed, because family background has such a powerful influence on people's fortunes, true equality of opportunity probably would require a degree of intervention into the family that we would find unacceptable.[7] For example, parents' willingness to play an active role in their children's education surely affects the children's prospects in life. But having parents interested in one's welfare is as much an arbitrary factor as having parents descended from King Arthur. Therefore, the idea of equality of opportunity as elimination of arbitrary barriers, if extended logically, would require that the interests and abilities of parents be equalized among families. No one would accept that conclusion.

The government might, however, do many things short of that to equalize opportunity. It could ensure, for example, equal schooling and equal access to health care without unacceptably interfering in the family. The notion of equal schooling is more complex than it might appear at first: some might dispute, for example, whether the government should provide the same resources to all or special educational benefits to those with special needs.[8] In any event, this conception of equality of opportunity would still require substantial government activity, in the nature of welfare state measures.

It does not follow that the distinction between equality of opportunity and equality of result is useless. It is plausible and coherent to say that the government should ensure that no one's fortunes in life will suffer because he or she did not have access to health care or education as good as anyone else's but that if opportunities are equalized in that way, the government must not correct any differences in results. Those differences, it might be said, are caused by differences in talent or initiative, not differences in opportunities.

Talents and Abilities as Accidents of Birth

The difference between equality of opportunity and equality of result begins to collapse when one recognizes that differences in talent are as much an accident of birth as skin color or aristocratic pedigree.[9] Of course, people can develop their talents through initiative and determination. But it is not obvious that such qualities as initiative and determination should be considered to be within an individual's control. Even assuming that those qualities are not considered accidents of birth, and even taking the most expansive view of how much people can develop, there is undeniably a substantial component of ability that a person cannot, on any view, control.[10] It is the result not just of heredity but of childhood and other environmental influences that cannot be plausibly attributed to the individual any more than race can be.

If equality of opportunity means that people's fortunes should not be determined by factors over which they have no control, then allowing their talents to affect their fortunes violates equality of opportunity. "There is no more reason to permit the distribution of income and wealth to be settled by the distribution of natural assets than by historical and social fortune. . . . From a moral standpoint the two seem equally arbitrary."[11] Once we take this step, however, the difference between equality of opportunity and equality of result begins to disappear. Differences in talent and ability, to the considerable extent that they are not within a person's control, should no more be permitted to affect a person's fortunes than differences in race or social class.

Three related objections might be made to this argument.

FORMAL VERSUS INFORMAL BARRIERS

First, it might be said that distinctions based on race or family status create explicit formal barriers. By contrast, no law says that untalented people may not seek certain positions. People with lesser talents, unlike the victims of formal barriers, are free to seek their fortunes as best they can. They will not do as well, but that is not the result of barriers erected by the government. It is just the result of "the way the world is"—specifically, it is the result of a multitude of decisions made by private individuals and reflected in the operation of various markets. Certain attributes are rewarded; others are not. But that is different from the government's decreeing that some categories of people will be barred entirely from certain opportunities.

This distinction is an important one for many purposes. Indeed, there must be some difference between a market system that rewards the untalented less than the talented and a system of formal barriers that excludes, for example, racial minorities: there is strong public consensus against the latter,[12] but few people entirely oppose the former.

But this difference between the formal barriers of racially exclusionary laws and the market barriers to those lacking certain talents has nothing to do with whether the influential factor is an accident of birth. The only difference is that one appears as an explicit legal barrier and the other seems to be an incident of the operation of a market economy. In both instances, society has made a decision to allow an arbitrary factor to affect a person's fortunes. A market, no less than a formal barrier, is created and maintained by the government: the government defines and maintains property rights, punishes theft and fraud, and so on. The government can do those things in a way that rewards talents (as it does, in a sense, when it maintains a market economy); or it can do those things in a way that rewards some other characteristics, of a kind we do not think should be rewarded. Those two kinds of action by the government are obviously not equally justifiable. But they are both actions by the government, even if only one consists of what we would call a formal barrier.[13] In either case, the government's action results in a person's fortune being determined by an accident of birth.

THE SUPPOSED INEVITABILITY OF INEQUALITY IN TALENTS

The second objection is that talents, unlike such things as education or health care, cannot be distributed equally. Talents have already been distributed unequally by nature. (Indeed, that is the foundation of the argument that foreclosing opportunities on the basis of talents is no less arbitrary than foreclosing them on the basis of race or family background.) Barriers resulting from formal exclusionary laws can be eliminated by the stroke of a pen. Barriers resulting from unequal education, health care, and the like are more difficult to eliminate, but the government can at least ameliorate them. Talents cannot be equalized even in theory. Indeed, the objection would continue, the government cannot even reduce the differences in talent. Therefore, the barrier to equal opportunity resulting from unequal talents cannot be compared to either formal barriers or unequal education.

To be sure, the objection would conclude, some day we might be able to engineer people genetically so as to equalize talents. Then we would have to face the question whether it would be worth doing so in order to equalize opportunity. The answer would surely be no, but at least we would be aware that we were overriding the interest in equality of opportunity in favor of more fundamental values. But until we can do such things, it might be said, inequalities of talent simply do not raise the question of equality of opportunity because there is nothing we can do about them.

This argument, too, is mistaken, for two reasons. First, although we cannot transplant talents, it does not follow that nothing can be done to equalize them. People might be educated differentially so as to minimize disparities in talent.[14] Equality in education does not necessarily mean that everyone receives the same education; it might mean that educations should be tailored for those with special needs (as is required in certain cases by the Individuals with Disabilities Education Act).[15] Or the idea of ''special needs'' might be generalized: equal education might mean that education is tailored for the talents of each person (or, more realistically, each category of people) so as to minimize the effects of inequalities of talent. There are many possible arguments against such an approach to education.[16] But for present purposes, it is enough that such a form of education is theoretically possible. That possibility shows the error of saying that inequalities in talent are simply a given that cannot be altered.

The notion that nothing can be done about inequalities of talent is mistaken for a further reason. Equality of opportunity, according to the conception I am discussing, requires that people's fortunes in life not be affected by arbitrary factors over which they have no control. One way to achieve this is to eliminate or equalize the arbitrary factors. But if those factors cannot be eliminated, another way of providing equality of opportunity is to ensure that those factors do not affect people's chances in life. Racial differences, like differences in talent, cannot be eliminated: the way we ensure equality of opportunity in the face of racial differences is to have institutions that eliminate the influence of race.

At this point, however, equality of opportunity collapses more or less completely into equality of result. Talent is an arbitrary factor; nature distributes it unequally, and, let us assume, education cannot equalize it. But equality of opportunity requires that arbitrary factors not determine people's fortunes. The only way to satisfy equality of opportunity, therefore, is to equalize people's fortunes so that they do not reflect the irreducible inequalities of talent—that is, to bring about equality of result. If we do not take major steps toward equality of result, then the arbitrary difference in talents will produce a difference in fortunes. Therefore equality of opportunity, faithfully pursued, requires substantial equalization of results.

This argument does not establish that equality of opportunity requires complete equality of result: the difference in fortunes is partly the result of what individuals have done with their talents, and there might be a sense in which that is under their control. Of course it is unclear—and a very complex question—exactly what it means for something to be under a person's control.[17] But even if we gave the largest plausible scope to the category of factors that are thought to be under people's control, many of the things that determine people's fortunes would still not be under their control. Equality of opportunity, understood as the requirement that fortunes not be determined by arbitrary factors, would still require a great equalization of results, even if not complete equality. Indeed, even assuming that the objective of a regime of equality of opportunity is to prevent only those factors that are unquestionably beyond people's control from affecting their fortunes in life, that regime would require the elimination of inequalities of fortune on a massive scale. It would require something approaching equality of result far more closely than the critics of the welfare state would like.

If this argument is correct, distinguishing equality of opportunity from equality of result serves no purpose. Equality of opportunity entails, if not complete equality of result, substantial equality of result. The interesting question is not the choice between equality of opportunity and equality of result. It is how much equality of opportunity we want. To what extent do we want the leveling entailed by the proposition—which I am taking to be definitional of equality of opportunity—that fortunes should not depend on arbitrary circumstances? That is a difficult question in many ways. But the claim that equality of opportunity is superior to equality of result does not help resolve it.

ESSENTIAL VERSUS INESSENTIAL ATTRIBUTES

The third objection to the view that talents and abilities are factors just as arbitrary as race or aristocratic background is related to the quite different conception of equality of opportunity that I discuss in the section below. The objection is that talents and abilities are different because they are essential rather than incidental to the individual. They are constitutive of an individual's identity in a way that race and social class are not.[18] Genetic engineering to equalize talents and abilities is an unthinkable invasion of individual autonomy. Redistributing the fruits of those talents and abilities is obviously less invasive but, in principle, suffers from a similar flaw: it amounts to depriving a person of something that is an essential aspect of his or her identity.

The difficulty with this argument lies in the justification offered for its central claim about the constituents of personal identity. Some societies regard race as a central constituent of a person's identity.[19] (Some would say it is so regarded in our society.) Historically, some societies regarded social class as far more central to one's identity than talents or abilities as we define them.[20] Race is as unalterable as ability, and in some cultures, social class is no more easily alterable. Nothing inherent in any of these qualities suggests that one is more central to human identity than the other. Different societies define the constituents of human identity differently.

Again, there are good reasons for considering ability to be more central to a person's identity than family background. But those reasons concern the consequences of doing so. In particular, talents and abilities, at least in a market-oriented society, relate to the capacity of people to produce goods and services that satisfy others' desires. But talents and abilities remain arbitrary factors in the sense that they are beyond the person's control, and allowing them to determine the person's fortunes remains inconsistent with equality of opportunity (as I have defined that term for now). There are good reasons for departing from equality of opportunity in this respect, but a departure from equality of opportunity is exactly what is involved. To the extent we do not depart from equality of opportunity, we are necessarily committed to trying to bring about a large measure of equality of result.

Equality of Opportunity as a Meritocratic Principle

The Meritocratic Conception

Equality of opportunity might be understood in a fundamentally different way. The barriers that must be eliminated, according to this understanding, are arbitrary not in the sense that they are beyond people's control but in the sense that we cannot give adequate reasons for them.[21] There is no good reason to allow a person's fortunes to turn on race or social class. But talents and abilities are not arbitrary in the crucial sense because they correspond to the capacity to produce value in society. Rewarding them, therefore, is not inconsistent with equality of opportunity.

By contrast, barriers based on factors like race and social class diminish the amount of value produced in society and therefore should be eliminated. Those barriers are arbitrary in the sense that they are irrational; no good reason can be given for them, and a good reason can be given for eliminating them. When such a formal barrier prevents talented people from reaching the positions for which they are best suited, society loses the benefits of their talents.[22] Multiplied across a large number of people held back by formal barriers, the effects on the total well-being of society can be enormous. Formal barriers based on race or class are arbitrary in this sense of being unreasoned, not in the sense that those factors are accidents of birth.

The point of equality of opportunity, on this view, is to guarantee that people go as far as their abilities, talents, initiative, and dedication take them. (I refer simply to "merit" to denote that complex of characteristics; later I discuss the complexities of the notion of merit.) So understood, equality of opportunity appears to be a principle that justifies, and perhaps requires, inequality of results. There should be equality among those people with the same level of merit, but there is no reason for equality among those with different levels of merit. Because abilities differ, as do the willingness and capacity to use them, results will differ. Equality of result seems antithetical to this conception of equality of opportunity because equality of result seems to call for leveling the differences in condition that are produced by different levels of merit. I refer to this conception of "equality of opportunity, not equality of result" as the meritocratic conception; those with the most merit ought to do better.

The Justification for the Meritocratic Conception

Part of the intuitive appeal of this conception of "equality of opportunity, not equality of result" stems from the analogy that can be drawn to a game.[23] If a game is well designed and its rules are enforced, each of the competitors can be said to have an equal opportunity to win even though some will have more of the requisite abilities. To insist that the results be equalized to compensate for differences in abilities among the competitors would be inconsistent with the whole idea of playing the game.

As the analogy suggests, however, we must justify the game that is being played. In our society, people who succeed in the marketplace, roughly speaking, are rewarded. But why should we play the market-oriented game to which we are accustomed instead of, for example, a game that rewards physical strength and courage or hereditary ties to famous families? Those games would be lost by many people who win the market game and would be won by many people who do not succeed in the market.

Today the most common justification for the market game is consequentialist. On this view, "merit" is rewarded because it makes society better off. We reward people who produce things that other people value; people succeed according to their abilities to satisfy others' desires. That is what "merit" is. There is no fixed catalog of capacities that are rewarded, and no one is rewarded for the mere possession of an unexercised capacity. It all depends on what will benefit society. The "barriers" that face the untalented simply reflect their lack of the capacities that bring value to others in society.

According to the meritocratic conception, then, equality of opportunity exists when everyone is allowed to compete equally to satisfy others' desires, as those desires are revealed in the market. When the government alters the results of that competition, it promotes equality of result, not equality of opportunity.[24] There is much to say, of course, about the justification for the market game. Most would agree today, I believe, that market mechanisms should play an important role in distributing wealth, but few would say that market distributions are inviolate. My purpose here, however, is to analyze the conception of equality of opportunity that corresponds to this game and to determine its relationship to the notion of equality of result. My argument is that the kind of *equality* involved in the market-oriented meritocratic regime of equality of opportunity is not meaningfully distinguishable from the kind of equality involved in government actions to "equalize results" by altering the distributions produced by the market.

THE NATURE OF MERITOCRATIC EQUALITY

Leaving aside the distinction between opportunity and result for a moment, it is not clear why a market-oriented meritocracy should be characterized as one of equality at all, in anything but a Pickwickian sense. In a game, everyone has an equal opportunity to succeed only if "equality" is defined by the rules of the game. In a sport, a person lacking the relevant athletic ability obviously does not have the same opportunity to succeed as an athletically gifted person.[25] Why should not the market-oriented meritocratic regime be characterized as one of *in*equality of opportunity? People with certain talents have a much better chance to succeed than others. The inequality of opportunity may be justified by the way in which the market operates to satisfy desires. But inequality of opportunity remains a more accurate description.

Suppose, for example, there were a society that valued not the satisfaction of desires as revealed in the market but the production of human specimens of great physical beauty and strength; suppose that society showered riches on the few people who had such characteristics because it thought that doing so would propitiate the gods. We would not regard such a society as one characterized by equality of opportunity. If we did so regard it, then any society could be so regarded. But in what sense does that society have less equality of opportunity than a market-oriented meritocratic society? Anyone who became extremely strong or beautiful could succeed spectacularly; in that sense there would be equality of opportunity. Of course, characteristics beyond people's control would powerfully affect their chances of success. But that is true of the meritocratic conception as well. As in the meritocratic society, people in the society that valued beauty and strength could do something to improve their chances. Some might be able to "pull themselves up by the bootstraps" and succeed despite being born without the greatest natural attributes of beauty or strength. Most others who lacked good fortune would not succeed, no matter how hard they worked. There would be differences from a modern market economy but only differences in degree.

In this light, there is something puzzling about the association of market regimes with any kind of equality. Nonetheless, there is a persistent intuition that a market-oriented meritocratic regime is characterized by equality of opportunity in a way that is not true of other regimes, such as the hypothetical one I just described or an aristocratic regime. Three related aspects of the market regime seem to account for this.

First, in the market regime many people have the impression that they have a significant degree of control over whether they succeed. Many people feel that even though they may in the end be defeated by their lack of talents, their fate is in their own hands to some degree. If they work hard and are enterprising, they have a chance. Obviously not everyone holds this view, and in significant ways it is an illusion. Nevertheless, it is a commonly held view and may account to some degree for the perception that a market-oriented regime is one of equality of opportunity.

Second and related, in a market regime there may be a sense, within certain classes, that almost anyone can succeed. All a person has to do is to figure out a way to appeal to large numbers of people—to build a better mousetrap—and that person will succeed. In an aristocratic regime, by contrast, it will be clearer for many more people at an early point in their lives that they are destined not to succeed because they were born into the wrong family.

Third, in a market-oriented regime the specific criteria of value are fluid. The path to success is not obvious and can change overnight. In addition, no single person has the power to determine which capacities will be rewarded. Value is the result of a multitude of private decisions. All of these factors contribute to the sense that few people are permanently closed out. Moreover, failure will seem, even to someone who failed, to be the result of that person's own shortcomings rather than the fiat of another person. In a regime of equality of opportunity, the explanation for failure is: "I had a chance, but I wasn't good enough." In a regime with unequal opportunity, the complaint is: "I never had a fair chance; so-and-so [a person or group] closed the door on me."

Of course, each of these intuitions about a market regime is to a significant extent incorrect. People often do not have control in any meaningful sense (even leaving aside controversial questions about what "control" might mean) over whether they succeed in the market. While we cannot identify winners and losers at birth to the same degree we can in certain other regimes, we do know from the outset that many people will be losers. (And we can probably identify more market losers at birth than the official rhetoric would acknowledge.) Finally, in a market regime the criteria of value are, in fact, dictated by others, of course; the only reason we might think they are not is that the others are numerous, and they dictate through a large number of decisions that are often visible only in the aggregate.

At the same time, however, these intuitions reveal something significant about the notion of equality of opportunity—something that begins to give some content to the notion of equality of opportunity, although it undermines any effort to draw an easy contrast between equality of opportunity and equality of result. The apparent fluidity and unpredictability of markets are a result of what might be described as their democratic character. In a market-oriented meritocracy, the forces that determine success or failure are democratic in the sense that they are the products of a multitude of personal decisions, not the act of a dictatorial person or group. The intuition that this is a regime of equality derives from the sense that everyone is subject to these forces; no one person can control them, and no one is exempt from them.

It is in this sense that the market-oriented meritocratic regime can be said to be one of equality of opportunity. It is manifestly untrue that everyone has an equal chance to succeed or that everyone has an equal chance to control his or her destiny. It is true, however, that no identifiable person or, if the markets are operating as they should, self-conscious group of persons can dictate another's fate.[26]

Democratic Equality in Markets and Governments

In the end, therefore, the so-called equality of opportunity in a market-oriented meritocratic regime is not that everyone has an equal chance to succeed but that no one has a greater chance than anyone else to determine who will succeed. In practice, of course, this will often not be true; some individuals will have power in the market. But the meritocratic conception is an ideal: there is equality of opportunity when markets operate perfectly. There is inequality only to the extent that markets are imperfect.

This understanding of equality of opportunity begins to give some definite content to that notion, in the face of the Rawlsian challenge that all factors producing inequality are as arbitrary as the formal barriers that everyone agrees are inconsistent with equality of opportunity. Equality of opportunity exists if identifiable individuals do not determine one's fortunes. On this account, there is an important sense in which equality of opportunity might be said to exist in a market-oriented society but not in an aristocratic regime.

But the distinction between equality of opportunity and equality of result is not yet rehabilitated. The claim of those who contrast equality of opportunity and equality of result is that equality of opportunity, conceived as a market-oriented meritocratic principle, is different from equality of result, understood as a government action designed to offset the effects of the market. In fact, however, the kind of equality involved in the two cases is, potentially at least, the same.

Once we understand that the equality of a meritocracy is equality not in the chance to succeed but in the chance to influence others' abilities to succeed, there is nothing distinctive about meritocracy. The same democratic characteristics that arguably make a meritocracy a regime of equality are present elsewhere. Most notably, of course, these characteristics are present in a well-functioning democratic government. In a well-functioning democracy, as in a well-functioning market economy, decisions are impersonal in the sense that they are not the products of the will of an identifiable individual.

Specifically, in a well-functioning democracy, every person has an equal opportunity to succeed by persuading fellow citizens to provide him or her with benefits—in the same sense that, in a well-functioning market economy, every person has an equal opportunity to create a new mousetrap. In both cases, some will fail. But in both cases, success will be determined by apparently impersonal forces rather than by the will of an identifiable individual. This is the only sense in which markets provide equality of opportunity. Democratic decisionmaking provides equality in exactly the same sense. The same kind of equality that is a characteristic of well-functioning markets is present in well-functioning democracies as well.

What does it mean to refer to a "well-functioning" democracy? Under either of two conceptions of democracy, democratic decisions (including decisions that equalize results) afford the same kind of equality as the so-called equality of opportunity that characterizes market-oriented meritocracy. It is not necessary to assume that a democratic system always pursues the public interest or to reject "public choice" accounts that treat political outcomes as the products of self-interested behavior.[27] If democracy is a pluralist struggle among self-interested groups, then democratic decisions will provide the same kind of equality as a market, as long as no one group or coalition can entrench itself in power.[28] Indeed, the pluralist view is deliberately modeled after the theory of the market.[29]

Alternatively, if democratic politics is characterized by an effort to promote the public interest, conceived in a way that treats everyone fairly, then this form of equality of opportunity is again present.[30] Specifically, in either of these forms of democratic society, people will have an opportunity to persuade their fellow citizens to advance their interests—just as in the market, people have an opportunity to succeed by satisfying others' desires. Some efforts at persuasion will fail—some will be doomed from the start—but that is true of efforts in the market as well. In a well-functioning democracy, under either the pluralist or public-interest model, outcomes are not dictated by individuals or cohesive groups of individuals. Outcomes are the result of forces that cannot be identified with any individual: either the market-mimicking dynamic of pluralist democracy or the disinterested inquiry into the public interest.

Of course, democracy can function badly in a variety of ways. ''Equality of result'' might be imposed by a dominant group. Then the kind of equality found in well-functioning markets will be absent. But markets can also be imperfect—not just when there is concentration in an industry but in more routine cases of agency and information costs that allow, for example, a bureaucratic superior to exercise unwarranted power over a subordinate. This problem is commonplace in employment markets: sexual harassment is a notorious example.

There is much room for debate (and of course much debate) over whether the market or democracy is more likely to malfunction, how often, and how badly. Those are complex questions that depend heavily on empirical knowledge. But the dichotomy—equality of opportunity is characteristic of market-oriented meritocracy, while equality of result is characteristic of democratic decisionmaking—is misconceived. When markets function well, they are characterized by something that can plausibly be called equality of opportunity. But that same kind of equality is present in well-functioning democratic decisionmaking. When both markets and democratic governments function correctly, the kind of equality displayed in the markets is also present in the government.

Conclusion

Equality of opportunity is a powerful ideal. It is, however, more complex than it first appears, and the contrast between equality of opportunity and equality of result is not a useful one. Understood in perhaps the most natural sense—as a requirement that a person's fortunes not be determined by accidents of birth or other factors over which he or she has no control—equality of opportunity has very powerful implications. It calls for the large-scale equalization of results.

Understood in a different sense—as a characteristic of a market-oriented meritocratic regime—equality of opportunity does not necessarily call for such dramatic measures. But the meritocratic conception of equality of opportunity is a conception of equality only in a very specialized way. People have equal opportunities only in the sense that their chances for success are not dictated by identifiable others. The same kind of equality inheres in well-functioning democratic political arrangements that bring about equality of result by altering market outcomes. Arguments for equality of opportunity and equality of result rest on the same foundations, and the rhetoric that contrasts them is more misleading than valuable.

NOTES

I thank Neal Devins, Elana Kagan, Lawrence Lessig, Geoffrey Stone, and Cass Sunstein for their helpful comments on earlier drafts. The Russell Baker Scholars Fund and the Lee and Brena Freeman Faculty Research Fund at the University of Chicago Law School provided financial support.

1. The literature on equality of opportunity is of course very extensive. For a recent exchange, see *Boston Review* 20 (April/May 1995): 3–16. Recent collections on the subject include Ellen Frankel Paul et al., eds., *Equal Opportunity* (Cambridge: Basil Blackwell, 1987); Norman Bowie, ed., *Equal Opportunity* (Boulder: Westview Press, 1988). For the use of the ''equality of opportunity, not result'' slogan to oppose welfare state measures, see, e.g., Michael Novak, *The Spirit of Democratic Capitalism* (New York: S & S Trade, 1982), 123–25 (1982); Thomas Sowell, *Civil Rights: Rhetoric or Reality?* (New York: W. Morrow, 1984), 37–60.

2. This principle has been stated by many. For a prominent example, see Henry Sidgwick, *The Methods of Ethics*, 7th ed. (Indianapolis: Hackett Publishing, 1907), 285 n.1.

3. Ibid.

4. For a well-known account of the historical development of this principle, see Richard H. Tawney, *Equality*, 4th ed. (New York: Barnes & Noble, 1964), ch. 3, sec. 2.

5. See, e.g., Novak, *Democratic Capitalism*, 123–25; Sowell, *Civil Rights*, 37–60.

6. This is a familiar point. See, e.g., John Rawls, *A Theory of Justice* (Cambridge, Mass.: Belknap Press, 1971); Robert Haveman, *Starting Even* (New York: S & S Trade, 1988); see also Robert Nozick, *Anarchy, State, and Utopia* (New York: Basic Books, 1974), 235–38 (criticizing equality of opportunity on ground that it requires redistribution).

7. This is a principal theme of James Fishkin, *Justice, Equal Opportunity, and the Family* (New Haven: Yale University Press, 1983). See ibid., 1–10.

8. See text accompanying notes 14–16.

9. See Rawls, *Theory of Justice*, 73–74; see also Douglas Rae, *Equalities* (Cambridge: Harvard University Press, 1981), 64–81.

10. See Rae, *Equalities*, 70; Sidgwick, *Methods of Ethics*, 285 n.1.

11. Rawls, *Theory of Justice*, 74–75; see also Bernard Williams, ''The Idea of Equality,'' in *Problems of the Self* (Cambridge: Cambridge University Press, 1973), 230, 239–49.

12. Even opponents of the antidiscrimination laws acknowledge this point. See, e.g., Richard A. Epstein, *Forbidden Grounds* (Cambridge: Harvard University Press, 1992), 1–9.

13. See, e.g., Cass R. Sunstein, *The Partial Constitution* (Cambridge: Harvard University Press, 1993), especially ch. 3; Robert L. Hale, ''Coercion and Distribution in a Supposedly Non-Coercive State,'' *Political Science Quarterly* 38 (1923): 470–74.

14. See Amy Gutmann, ''Distributing Public Education in a Democracy,'' in *Democracy and the Welfare State*, ed. Amy Gutmann (Princeton: Princeton University Press, 1988), 107, 110–111 (discussing Fishkin, *Justice, Equal Opportunity, and the Family*).

15. 20 U.S.C. §§ 1400–1485.

16. See, e.g., Gutmann, *Democracy and the Welfare State*, 111–12.

17. This problem is addressed by John E. Roemer, "Equality and Responsibility," *Boston Review* 20 (April/May 1995): 3, and by many of the responses to Roemer's article in that issue of the *Boston Review*. See, in particular, Samuel Scheffler, "Another Unfunded Mandate," *Boston Review* 20 (April/May 1995): 10.

18. This position is suggested by writers disparate in their ultimate views, e.g., Michael Sandel, *Liberalism and the Limits of Justice* (Cambridge: Cambridge University Press, 1982), and Nozick, *Anarchy, State, and Utopia.*

19. See, e.g., Louis Dumont, *Homo Hierarchius*, trans. Mark Sainsbury et al. (Chicago: University of Chicago Press, 1970), 33–200 (discussing caste system in India); Donald L. Horowitz, *Ethnic Groups in Conflict* (Berkeley: University of California Press, 1985), 95–288 (discussing ethnic conflict generally).

20. See, e.g., Stanley I. Binn and Richard S. Peters, *The Principles of Political Thought* (New York: Free Press, 1965), 132.

21. On the connection between equality and the ability to give reasons for differences among people, see Williams, *Problems of the Self*, 240–41.

22. See ibid., 242–45.

23. This analogy is in the nontechnical sense of a game played for amusement, not in the more technical sense in which "game" is used in microeconomics to refer to certain kinds of interactions between people. See, e.g., Rae, *Equalities*, 65–66.

24. For this conception, see Daniel Bell, "On Meritocracy and Equality," *Public Interest* 29 (1972): 29, 40–41.

25. These points are advanced to support a different conclusion in Peter Westen, "The Concept of Equal Opportunity," *Ethics* 95 (1985): 837.

26. In fact, even if markets operate as they should, they reward people only for satisfying desires as those desires are revealed in the market. Many important kinds of desires are not adequately accounted for in the market. For a well-known discussion, see Amartya K. Sen, "Rational Fools: A Critique of the Behavioral Foundations of Economic Theory," *Philosophy and Public Affairs* 6 (1977): 317.

27. See generally Dennis C. Mueller, *Public Choice II* (Cambridge: Cambridge University Press, 1989).

28. A well-known description of this form of pluralist democracy is found in Robert A. Dahl, *A Preface to Democratic Theory* (Chicago: University of Chicago Press, 1956).

29. See, e.g., Anthony Downs, *An Economic Theory of Democracy* (New York: Harper Collins, 1957); Joseph A. Schumpeter, *Capitalism, Socialism and Democracy*, 5th ed. (New York: Harper Collins, 1950), chs. 21–23.

30. See, e.g., Rawls, *Theory of Justice*, 359–61.

5

The Word "American" Ends in "I Can"

The Ambiguous Promise of the American Dream

JENNIFER L. HOCHSCHILD

[I]n the beginning," wrote John Locke, "all the world was America."[1] Locke was referring specifically to the absence of a cash nexus in primitive society, but the sentence evokes the unsullied newness, infinite possibility, limitless resources that are commonly understood to be the essence of "the American dream." The idea of the American dream has been attached to everything from religious freedom to a home in the suburbs, and it has inspired emotions ranging from deep gratification to disillusioned fury. Nevertheless, the phrase elicits for most Americans some variant of Locke's fantasy—a new world where anything can happen and good things might.

Millions of immigrants moved to America and internal migrants moved around within it in order to fulfill their version of the American dream.[2] By objective measures and their own accounts, many came astonishingly close to success.[3] Just as many were probably defeated and disillusioned.[4] My purpose is to examine what the American dream has done for and meant to various migrants, focusing especially on African Americans, who did not come to America to fulfill their dreams. The American dream is, however, an ideology whose power extends far beyond my particular interests in race. It has been Americans' dominant ideology at least since the early nineteenth century. Americans' beliefs about happiness, freedom, personal and collective responsibility, and equality can all be understood in the context of the American dream and perhaps only in that context. Opponents, embittered former believers, and boosters alike all shape their assumptions and actions in response, one way or another, to the enticing promise of the dream.

In this chapter I provide an extended definition of the American dream and discuss its virtues and drawbacks as a dominant ideology. I conclude by drawing implications for the ideal and practice of equality, American style.

The Meaning of Success

What is the American dream? It consists of tenets about achieving success. Let us first explore the meaning of ''success'' and then consider the rules for achieving it.

Former president Ronald Reagan stated, ''[W]hat I want to see above all is that this country remains a country where someone can always get rich. That's the one thing that we have and that must be preserved.''[5] Most people agree with President Reagan that success means a high income, prestigious job, and economic security. Material well-being, however, is only one form of accomplishment. People seek success in arenas ranging from the pulpit to the stage of the Metropolitan Opera House, from membership in the newest and hottest dance club to membership in the Senate. Indeed, if we believe oral histories, people define success as ''a right to say what they wanta say, do what they wanta do, and fashion a world into something that can be great for everyone''[6] as often as they think of it in terms of wealth and status.

Different kinds of success need not, but often do, conflict. A classic plot of American family sagas is the children's rejection of the parents' hard-won wealth and social standing in favor of some ''deeper,'' more meaningful form of accomplishment.[7] The conflict need not be intergenerational, however, and the rejection may work in reverse, as Cotton Mather sadly reported:

> There have been very fine settlements in the north-east regions; but what is become of them? I have heard that one of our ministers once preaching to a congregation there, urged them to approve themselves a religious people from this consideration, ''that otherwise they would contradict the main end of planting this wilderness''; whereupon a well-known person, then in the assembly, cryed out, ''Sir, you are mistaken: you think you are preaching to the people at the [Plymouth] Bay; our main end was to catch fish.''[8]

Mather ''wished, that something more excellent had been the main end of the settlements in that brave country,''[9] but the ideology of the American dream itself remains agnostic on the definition of ''excellent.''

No matter what it consists of, success can be measured in three ways, the choice among which results in profoundly different normative and behavioral consequences. First, success can be absolute. In this case, achieving the American dream implies reaching some threshold of well-being, perhaps higher than where one began but not necessarily dazzling. One of the first American civil engineers thus explained westward migration: ''Every man will endeavor to improve his circumstances by a change of occupation or by a change of place. He fixes a standard mark of enjoyments by comparison of his present situation with what the new and unpeopled district holds out to him.''[10] Rock star Bruce Springsteen provided a more recent instance: ''I don't think the American dream was that everybody was going to make . . . a billion dollars, but it was that everybody was going to have an opportunity and the chance to live a life with some decency and some dignity and a chance for some self-respect.''[11]

In the ideology of the American dream, absolute success is in principle equally available to everyone although guaranteed to no one. As Springsteen continued, "I dreamed something and I was lucky. A large part of it came true. But it's not just for one; it's gotta be for everyone, and you've gotta fight for it every day."[12] To the degree that a society makes it possible for most people to become better off—to achieve absolute success, in my terms—the society is structured to promote equality of results without any hint of identity of results.

Second, success can be relative. By this measurement, the American dream means becoming better off than some point of comparison. That point may be one's own childhood, people in the old country, one's neighbors, a character from a book, another race or gender—anything or anyone that one chooses to measure oneself against. Relative success implies no threshold of well-being and may or may not entail continually changing the comparison group as one achieves a given level of accomplishment. Memoirist James Comer captured a benign version of relative success in his depiction of a "kind of competition . . . we [his parents] had . . . going on" with "the closest friends that we had":[13]

> When we first met them, we had a dining room and they didn't. They went back and they turned one of their bedrooms into a dining room. . . . After that we bought this big Buick car. And we came to their house and they had bought another car. She bought a fur coat one year and your dad bought me one the next. But it was a friendly thing, the way we raced. It gave you something to work for, to look forward to. Every year we tried to have something different to show them what we had done, and they would have something to show us.[14]

In 1736, William Byrd II articulated a more malign version: slaves "blow up the pride, and ruin the industry of our white people, who seeing a rank of poor creatures below them, detest work for fear it should make them look like slaves."[15]

As Byrd suggested, relative success implies a rather different understanding of equality than does absolute success. It contains no hint of equality of outcomes; rather it calls for, at most, equal chances for all to do better than some standard. It implies, in short, a "soft" form of equal opportunity.

A third form of success is competitive. Success in this context consists not of reaching a threshold or doing better than some standard but of achieving victory over someone else. My success implies at the least your lack of success and, at the most, your failure. One's competitors are usually people, whether known and concrete as opponents in a tennis match or unknown and abstract as all other applicants for a job. For example, *U.S. News and World Report*, in an article celebrating success in the roaring '80s, pictured a businessman with flying tie and bulging briefcase striding over four prone colleagues, with the caption, "Like it or not, success often means stepping over others."[16] One's opponent may, however, be entirely impersonal—a hurricane, a disease, or a mountain. John Henry, "the steel-drivin' man," is famed for beating a machine, and Paul Bunyan, for taming the primeval forest. This form of success rejects equality of results, and competitors generally do not worry about whether their opponent starts with an equal chance for victory. Thus competitive success implies, at most, a "hard" form of equal opportunity.

Rules for Achieving Success

Success can be material, spiritual, or otherwise; it may be available to all or a few. One person's success may enable the success of others or come at their expense. How is it to be sought and achieved? The bundle of commonly understood, even unconsciously assumed, tenets about achieving success are what make up the ideology of the American dream.

As I construe it, the ideology has four related but distinct premises. They answer the questions: *Who* may pursue the American dream? In *what* does the pursuit consist? *How* does one successfully pursue the dream? And *why* is the pursuit worthy of our deepest commitment? The answer to "who" in the standard ideology is "everyone, regardless of ascriptive traits, family background, or personal history." The answer to "what" is "the reasonable anticipation, though not the promise, of success, however it is defined." The answer to "how" is "through actions and traits under one's own control." The answer to "why" is "true success is associated with virtue." Let us consider each rule in turn.

The first tenet, that all people may always pursue their dreams, is the most direct connotation of Locke's statement that "in the beginning, all the world was *America*."[17] The idea extends, however, beyond the image of a pristine state of nature waiting for whoever "discovers" it; even in the distinctly nonpristine, nonnatural world of Harlem in New York City and Harlan County, Kentucky, anyone can pursue a dream. A century ago, one moved to the frontier to hide a spotted past and begin afresh. As one woman from that period put it, Montana frontierswomen "never ask[ed] women where they [had] come from or what they did before they came to live in our neck of the woods. If they wore a wedding band and were good wives, mothers, and neighbors that was enough for us to know."[18] Today one appeals to the Equal Employment Opportunity Commission to overturn racial, gender, or age discrimination. In effect, Americans believe they can create in their own lives a ministate of nature that will allow them to slough off the past and invent a better future.

The second tenet, that one may reasonably anticipate success, suggests a more guarded promise. After all, "reasonable anticipation" is far from a guarantee, as all children on the morning of their birthdays know. Reasonable anticipation, however, is also much more than simply longing; most children are not silly or crazy to expect at least some of what they wish for on their birthdays. Immigrants most clearly articulate this hope: "All my life I am thinking to come to this country. For what I read in the magazines, and the movies. . . . I would have a beautiful castle in the United States. I will have a thousand servant. I will have five Rolls-Royces in my door. . . . We thinking everybody has this kind of life. . . . I have this kind of dream."[19]

The third premise, that success results from action's under one's own control, explains how one is to achieve the success that one anticipates. Ralph Waldo Emerson is uncharacteristically succinct on the point: "There is always a reason, in *the man*, for his good or bad fortune, and so in making money."[20] Lest we smile at the quaint optimism, or crude propaganda, of our ancestors, consider a recent advertisement from Citicorp Bank. It shows a carefully balanced group of shining faces—young and old, male and female, black, Latino, WASP, and Asian—all gazing starry-eyed at the middle distance over the words:

> FROM SEA TO SHINING SEA, THE WILL TO SUCCEED IS PART OF THE AMERICAN SPIRIT. The instant you become an American, whether by birth or by choice, you are guaranteed . . . the freedom to succeed. You are free to dream your own dream of success, to study, to work, to create and discover and build, for yourself and your children, the success you want.[21]

Implicit in this flow of oratory is the fourth tenet of the American dream, that the pursuit of success warrants so much fervor because it is associated with virtue. "Associated with" has at least four more precise meanings: virtue leads to success, success makes a person virtuous, success indicates virtue, or apparent success is not real success unless one is also virtuous. Benjamin Franklin provides the most famous aphorisms on this point: "[N]o Qualities were so likely to make a poor Man's Fortune as those of Probity & Integrity." Conversely, "Proverbial Sentences, chiefly such as inculcated Industry and Frugality," are included in *Poor Richard's Almanack* as "the Means of procuring Wealth and thereby securing Virtue, it being more difficult for a Man in Want to act always honestly, as . . . *it is hard for an empty Sack to stand upright*."[22]

If we consider these four premises of the American dream in light of the varying meanings of success described earlier, we can see the full richness—and seductiveness—of the ideology. Different understandings of success do not much affect the first tenet, the norm of universal participation and endless chances to start over. However, such understandings do affect the other three tenets.

If success is defined as achieving some absolute threshold of well-being, the ideology portrays America as a land of plenty and Americans as "people of plenty."[23] Hard work and virtue (combined through most of our history with plenty of purportedly uninhabited land in the West) allow everyone to anticipate success even in the face of continued adversity. This is the great theme, of course, of one of the most powerful children's sagas ever written in America, Laura Ingalls Wilder's *Little House in the Big Woods* series. Many years—and eight volumes—of grasshopper plagues, ferocious blizzards, cheating and cowardly railroad bosses, and even hostile Indians cannot prevent Pa and his girls from eventually "winning their bet with Uncle Sam" and becoming prosperous homesteaders.[24]

If success is defined competitively, however, the ideology portrays a rather different America. Hard work and virtue combined with scarce resources produce winners who are successful and good and losers who have failed and are bad. This theme appears in John Rockefeller's Sunday school address: "The growth of a large business . . . is merely a survival of the fittest.. . . .The American Beauty rose can be produced in the splendor and fragrance which bring cheer to its beholder only by sacrificing the early buds which grow up around it. This is not an evil tendency in business. It is merely the working out of a law of nature and a law of God."[25]

As the perennial popularity of the *Little House* series indicates, Americans prefer the self-image of universal achievement to the self-image of a few stalwarts triumphing over weaker contenders. However, more important than any single image are the enormous elasticity and range of the ideology of the American dream. People can encourage themselves with softer versions, congratulate themselves with harder ones, and exult with the hardest, as their circumstances and characters warrant.

Thus, the American dream is in many ways an enormously successful ideology. It has for centuries lured people to America and moved them around within it and has kept them striving in horrible conditions against impossible odds. Most Americans celebrate it unthinkingly, along with apple pie and motherhood; criticism typically is limited to imperfections in its application. But like apple pie and motherhood, the American dream upon closer examination turns out to be less than perfect. Let us turn, then, to flaws intrinsic to the dream.

Defects in the American Dream

The First Tenet: Equal Participation

Each premise, and the overall dream, is problematic.[26] The first tenet, that everyone can participate equally and can always start over, is troubling to the degree that it is not true. It is, of course, never true in the strongest sense because people cannot shed their existing selves as snakes shed their skin. So the myth of the individual ministate of nature is just that—a fantasy to be sought but never attained.

Nothing is wrong with fantasies as long as people understand that that is what they are. For that reason, a weaker formulation of the first tenet—people start the pursuit with varying degrees of advantage, but no one is barred from the pursuit—is more troubling because its falsity is much less clear. For most of American history, being a woman, Native American, Asian, black, or pauper has barred people from all but a very narrow range of possible futures. The constraints of ascriptive traits arguably have weakened over time, but until recently no more than about a third of the population was able to take seriously the first premise of the American dream.

This flaw has implications beyond the evident ones of racism and sexism. The emotional potency of the American dream has made people who *were* able to identify with it the norm for everyone else. White men, especially European immigrants able to ride the wave of the Industrial Revolution to comfort or even prosperity, became the epitomizing demonstration of America as the bountiful state of nature. Those who did not fit the model disappeared from the collective self-portrait. Thus the irony doubles: not only have most Americans been denied the ideal of universal participation, but also our national self-image denies the very fact of this denial.

This double irony creates deep misunderstandings and correspondingly deep political tensions. Consider as an example racial discrimination. Whereas the proportion of whites who believe that racial discrimination is declining rose from three-tenths to nine-tenths over the past twenty-five years, the analogous proportion of blacks *declined* from between 50 and 90 percent in the mid-1960s to between 20 and 45 percent by the 1990s.[27] To cite only one specific instance of these dramatically different perceptions, in 1995, 72 percent of blacks but only 38 percent of whites agreed that past and present discrimination is a "major reason" for the problems faced by African Americans.[28] About the same proportions agreed that "racism is a big problem in our society today."[29]

Most blacks, in short, do not believe that the first tenet of the American dream applies to them. Most whites deny this disbelief.[30] As a consequence of these very different starting points, blacks and whites typically disagree on the policies needed to enable blacks to realize the claim of the first tenet of the American dream. The most vocal disagreement is over affirmative action policies, but debates over spending on urban infrastructure, management of social welfare, access to higher education, and other topics all stem from divergent assumptions about whether the premise of equal access to the dream really holds true.

The Second Tenet: Reasonable Anticipation of Success

The flaws of the second tenet of the American dream, the reasonable anticipation of success, stem from the close link between anticipation and expectation. That link presents little problem as long as enough resources and opportunities exist so that everyone has a reasonable chance of having some expectations met. Indeed, panegyrists of the American dream always expound on the bounty and openness of the American continent. For example, South Carolina governor James Glen typified the eighteenth-century entrepreneurs of colonization by promising:

> Adventurers will be pleased to find a Change from Poverty and Distress to Ease and Plenty; they are invited to a Country not yet half settled, where the Rivers are crouded with Fish, and the Forests with Game; and no Game-Act to restrain them from enjoying those Bounties of Providence, no heavy Taxes to impoverish them, nor oppressive Landlords to snatch the hard-earned Morsel from the Mouth of Indigence, and where Industry will certainly inrich them.[31]

These fantasies are innocuous as long as the resources roughly balance the dreams for enough people enough of the time. If, however, they do not—or worse, if they used to but do no longer—then the dream rapidly loses its appeal. The particular circumstances that cause resources to no longer balance dreams vary, ranging from the closing of the frontier to an economic downturn to a rapid increase in the number of dreamers. The general point, though, always holds: no one promises that dreams will be fulfilled, but the distinction between the right to dream of success and the right to succeed is psychologically hard to maintain. Maintaining the distinction is especially hard because the dream sustains Americans against daily nightmares only if they believe that they have a significant likelihood, not just a formal chance, of reaching their goals.

In short, the right to aspire to success works as an ideological substitute for a guarantee of success only if it begins to approach a guarantee. When it becomes clear that chances for success are slim or getting slimmer, the whole tenor of the American dream changes dramatically.

The general problem of scarcity varies slightly depending on what form of success people anticipate. It is most obvious and acute for those focused on competitive success, in which, by definition, resources and opportunities are insufficient to satisfy all dreamers. Scarcity may, however, be more problematic for those who look forward to relative success, if only because there are more such people and because they have no a priori reason to assume that many will fail. Thus, journalists worry that "for the first time in living memory, America's children have less hope of attaining a higher standard of living than their parents did."[32] The problem of scarcity may be most devastating for people anticipating absolute success because they have the least reason to expect that some will fail.[33] Losers of this type have an unmatched poignancy: "I don't dream any more like I used to. I believed that in this country, we would have all we needed for the decent life. I don't see that any more."[34]

Conversely, the availability of resources and opportunities may shape the kind of success that people dream of. If resources are profoundly scarce as in a famine, or inherently limited as in election to the presidency, people almost certainly envision competitive success. If resources are moderately scarce, people will be concerned about their positions relative to those of others, but they will not necessarily see another's gain as their loss. When resources and opportunities seem wide open—anyone can achieve salvation, get an "A" on the exam, claim 160 acres of western prairie—people are most free to pursue their own dreams and measure their achievements by their own absolute standards.

This logic suggests a dynamic: as resources become tighter, people are likely to shift their hopes for success from absolute to relative to competitive. For example, before the 1980s, according to one journalist, "there was always enough to go around, plenty of places in the sun. It didn't even matter much about the rich—so long as everyone was living better, it seemed the rich couldn't be denied their chance to get richer." But "today that wave [of prosperity] has crested. . . . Now when the rich get richer, the middle class stagnates—and the poor get decidedly poorer."[35]

The risks of anticipating success do not stop with anticipation. Attaining one's dreams can be surprisingly problematic as well. From Jane Austen to Theodore Dreiser to John Updike, writers have limned the loneliness of being at the top, the spiritual costs of cutthroat competition, the shallowness of a society that rewards success above all else. Alexis de Tocqueville characteristically provided one of the most eloquent of these admonitions: "[Americans] never stop thinking of the good things they have not got. It is odd to watch with what feverish ardor the Americans pursue prosperity and how they are ever tormented by the shadowy suspicion that they may not have chosen the shortest route to get it."[36] Tocqueville continued by pointing out that the obsession with ever more success threatens not only the individual soul but also the body politic, noting that "[t]hey find it a tiresome inconvenience to exercise political rights which distract them from industry. . . . The role of government is left unfilled."[37]

The problems of success, however, pale beside the problems of failure. Because success is so central to Americans' self-image, and because they expect as well as hope to achieve it, Americans are not gracious about failure. Others' failure reminds them that the dream may be just that—a dream, to be distinguished from waking reality. Their own failure confirms that fear. Assistant professors denied tenure thus report contracting a sudden case of "leprosy"; their friends back away from them, and their own bodies betray their internal selves. Once Dreiser's G. W. Hurstwood loses his job as manager of Chicago's most fashionable saloon, he cannot prevent himself from sinking into lethargy, sloth, and utter destitution.

Furthermore, the better the dream works for other people, the more devastating failure is for the smaller and smaller proportion of people left behind. Thus in World War II, members of military units with a high probability of promotion were less satisfied with advancement opportunities than were members of units with a much lower probability of promotion because failure to earn promotion in the former case was both more salient and more demonstrably a personal rather than a systemic flaw.[38] In short, the ideology of the American dream includes no cushion for failure; a failed dream denies the loser not only success but even a shred of dignity to cover or soften the loss.

The Third Tenet: Success Is within One's Own Control

The nakedness of failure is made more stark by the third premise of the American dream—the belief that success results from actions and traits under one's own control. Logic does not support the reasoning that if success results from individual volition, then failure results from lack of volition. All one needs in order to see the logical flaw here is the distinction between "necessary" and "sufficient." But that distinction is not obvious or intuitive, and in any case the psycho-logic of the American dream differs from strict logic. In the psycho-logic, if one may claim responsibility for success, one must accept responsibility for failure.

Americans who do everything they can and still fail may come to understand that effort and talent alone do not guarantee success, but they have a hard time persuading others. After all, they are losers—why listen to them? Will we not benefit more by listening to winners, who seldom challenge the premise that effort and talent breed success? Americans are thus much less willing than Europeans to ascribe poverty to structural flaws or wealth to the prior ownership of wealth. For example, in 1985 only 31 percent of Americans agreed that "[i]n America what you achieve in life depends largely on your family background,"[39] compared with 51 percent of Austrians, 52 percent of Britons, and 63 percent of Italians.[40] Germans resemble Americans on this question; only 35 percent agreed.[41] However, three-quarters of American respondents compared with only half of the Germans agreed that "differences in social standing between people are acceptable because they basically reflect what people made out of the opportunities they had."[42] Similarly, 85 percent of Americans and 72 percent of Germans agreed that "America (Germany) has an open society. What one achieves in life no longer depends on one's family background, but on the abilities one has and the education one acquires."[43] In short, people who fail not only challenge the implicit promise of the American dream, but also are stigmatized because they presumably manifest—to winners more than to losers, to be sure—weakness of will or lack of talent.

The Fourth Tenet: Success Equals Virtue

The final blow to people who fail to achieve their dreams comes from the ideology's fourth tenet, the association of success with virtue. By the psycho-logic just described, if success implies virtue, failure implies sin.

American history and popular culture are replete with demonstrations of the connection between failure and sin. In the 1600s, indentured servants—kidnapped children, convicts, and families impoverished by the enclosure movement alike—were met on the shores of the New World with the assumption that they were all "strong and idle beggars, vagabonds, egyptians, comon and notorious whoores, theeves, and other dissolute and lousy persons."[44] A century later, even revolutionaries assumed that "only the 'shiftless, diseased, or vicious' were 'labourers, . . . who look to the earning of today for the subsistence of tomorrow.' " Members of nineteenth-century reform societies concurred, stating that fallen women were typically "the daughters of the ignorant, depraved and vicious part of our population, trained up without culture of any kind, amidst the contagion of evil example, and enter upon a life of prostitution for the gratification of their unbridled passions, and become harlots altogether by choice."[45]

Small wonder that by the late twentieth century, even the poor blame the poor for their condition. Despite her vivid awareness of exploitation by the rich, an aging cleaning woman insists that many people are poor because they "make the money and drink it all up. They don't care about the kids or the clothes. Just have a bottle on that table all the time."[46] In 1985, 60 percent of poor people, compared with 61 percent of the nonpoor, agreed that often "welfare encourages husbands to avoid family responsibilities."[47] Even more startling, 64 percent of the poor, but only 44 percent of the nonpoor, agreed that often "[p]oor young women have babies so they can collect welfare."[48]

The association of success with virtue obviously harms losers. The association, though, creates equally important if less obvious problems for winners. On the one hand, if I believe that virtue produced my success or that success has made me even more virtuous, I am likely to become insufferably smug. That may not bother me much, but the fact that people around me feel the same way will. In addition, this equation raises the stakes very high for further rounds of endeavor. If I continue to win, all is well; if I falter, I lose my amour propre as well as my wealth or power. On the other hand, if I recognize that my success is due partly to my lying to a few clients, evading a few taxes, or cheating a few employees, then I am likely to take on considerable guilt. This guilt might induce reform and recompense, but it may just as well induce drinking to assuage the unease, persecution of other nonvirtuous winners, attempts to show that losers are even more sinful, or simple hypocrisy.

These problems intensify when patterns of group success rather than the idiosyncrasies of individual success are at issue. If members of one group are seen as disproportionately successful, that group acquires a halo of ascribed virtue. For example, consider an article titled "The Great Jewish Invasion" that appeared in *McClure's Magazine* in 1907.[49] The author's ethnicity, the publication, the date, and the article's title all lead one to expect an anti-Semitic diatribe, at best only thinly veiled. The first few pages seem to confirm that expectation, pointing out that the success of New York's Jews is "remarkable" because most Jewish New Yorkers "are not what are commonly regarded as the most enlightened of their race,"[50] being from eastern rather than western Europe.[51] After all "[n]o people have had a more inadequate preparation, educational and economic, for American citizenship."[52] The article, nevertheless, goes on to describe in careful and admiring detail how these dirt-poor, ignorant, orthodox immigrants work, save, cooperate, sacrifice for their children—and end up wealthy beyond anyone's wildest imaginings.[53] In his highest possible accolade, the author even insists that the Russian Jew's "enthusiasm for America knows no bounds. He eagerly looks forward to the time when he can be naturalized."[54] In short, in one generation the East European Orthodox Jewish immigrant had gone from an unassimilable, bovine drag on the American spirit to the epitome of all of the American virtues. Nothing succeeds like success.

The contemporary equivalent of Burton Hendrick's "amazing" Jews are Southeast Asians. A half century ago, Americans could hardly derogate Chinese and Japanese immigrants enough. Now, newspapers have a seemingly endless supply of rags-to-riches stories about the daughter of destitute boat people who became the high school valedictorian a scant five years after arriving in the United States and is now in a premed program at Stanford. Such success is inevitably due to hard work, self-discipline, family support, and refusal to follow the bad example set by American-born peers.[55] This journalistic trend has become so powerful that spokespeople for Asian immigrants feel impelled to insist publicly that not *all* Asians escape poverty, crime, and discrimination and that even the most successful pay a heavy emotional cost.[56]

To argue that excessive praise is as bad as racism or ethnic slurs would be churlish. The problem is that the newly anointed group is often used to cast aspersions, implicit or explicit, on some other equally despised group that has not managed to fulfill the American dream. In Hendrick's case, the main negative reference group is the Irish, who drink and gamble, yield their productive jobs to Jews, and, worst of all, band together in labor unions, in the "Irish vote," and in political party machines.[57] In the case of immigrant Asians, the usual—if slightly more subtle—message is, "Why can't American blacks do the same thing? After all, they at least speak English when they start school." This dynamic adds yet another component to the nightmare of a failed American dream. Members of a denigrated group are disproportionately likely to fail to achieve their goals; they are blamed as individuals, and perhaps blame themselves, for their failure; and they carry a further stigma as members of a group that cannot help itself as other groups have done.

Defects in the Overall Dream

Finally, consider several problems inherent in the ideology of the American dream as a whole rather than in any single tenet. The American dream need not, but often does, take on a radically individualist cast. Achievers mark their success by moving away from the tenement, ghetto, or "holler" of their impoverished and impotent youth, thus speeding the breakup of their ethnic community. This is a bittersweet phenomenon. The freedom to move up and out is desirable, or at least desired; however, certainly those left behind, probably those who leave, and arguably the nation as a whole lose when groups of people with close cultural and personal ties break those ties in the pursuit of "the bitch-goddess, success."[58] The line between autonomy and atomism is hard to draw.

American culture is full of stories about the ambivalent effects of success on communities and their residents. A Polish folksong tells of a man who emigrated to America, worked for three years in a foundry, returned home with "gold and silver,"[59] but found that "my children did not know me, [f]or they fled from me, a stranger."[60] The emancipated children may be as distressed as the abandoned parents. In 1933 five brothers complained to the *Jewish Daily Forward*: "Imagine, even when we go with our father to buy something in a store on Fifth Avenue, New York, he insists on speaking Yiddish. We are not ashamed of our parents, God forbid, but they ought to know where it's proper and where it's not."[61]

The second problem is more conceptual than behavioral. The American dream need not be individualistic in the narrow sense, given that one can under its rubric pursue success for one's family or community as well as for oneself. But it is highly *individual*, in that it leads one to focus on people's behaviors rather than on economic processes, environmental constraints, or political structures as the causal explanation for social orderings. That focus is not itself a flaw; it is simply an epistemological choice with methodological implications for the study of American politics. But to the degree that the focus carries a moral message, it points to a weakness at the very heart of the dream.

The idea of the blank slate in the first tenet, the almost-promise of success of the second, the reliance on personal attributes in the third, the association of failure with sin in the fourth—all of these elements of the dream make it extremely difficult for Americans to see that everyone cannot simultaneously attain more than absolute success. Capitalist markets require some firms to fail; elections require some candidates and policy preferences to lose; status hierarchies must have a bottom in order to have a top. But the optimistic language of and methodological individualism built into the American dream *necessarily* deceive people about these societal operations. We need not invoke hypocrites out of Mark Twain or "blue-eyed white devils" in order to understand why some people never attain success; hypocrisy and bias only enter the picture in determining *who* fails. Our basic institutions are designed to ensure that some fail, at least relatively, and the dream does nothing to help Americans cope with or even to recognize that fact.

A final problem of the American dream results from its very dominance. Americans have few models and little historical sanction for simply opting out of the drive for wealth, status, or power. We do not lack for eloquent arguments against the success drive. Henry David Thoreau's *Walden* has, ironically, become an icon. At the height of the Jacksonian celebration of opportunities for the common man, James Fenimore Cooper sniffed, "A people that deems the possession of riches its highest source of distinction, admits one of the most degrading of all influences to preside over its opinions."[62] Even in the "me-decade" of the 1980s, George Will based a thriving journalistic career on the claim of being among the last of the old-time Tories, expounding on "the disappointment many people feel about affluence. Envy has increased while society has become more wealthy."[63]

Most Americans, however, honor this alternative vision more in the breach than in the observance, if then. We have no powerful ascetic tradition comparable to that of Hindus, Buddhists, and Native Americans. We have instead Thoreau, the Shakers, and 1960s hippies—curiosities from whom we take aphorisms, furniture, and hair styles once they are distant enough not to challenge our daily lives. We have similarly little in our ideological tool kit to help us see "small is beautiful" and "social limits to growth" as attractive alternatives rather than dystopias to be staved off as long as possible. Socialism has never enjoyed more than a tiny foothold among the American electorate.

Conclusion

Tocqueville assured his readers that "up to now the Americans have happily avoided all the reefs I have just charted."[64] Arguably we continue, 150 years later, to sail free, and perhaps we always will. If the United States does hit the reefs, however, the ideology of the American dream will not be of much help. Just as individuals whose dreams fail are left with precious few emotional and material resources, so a society that stakes so much on a dream of ever-expanding success is deeply vulnerable to natural, social, or demographic boundaries.

This point brings us back to the beginning—the meaning of the American dream and its implications for Americans' belief in and practice of equality. In the end, the ideology boils down to a profession of hope. It is profoundly egalitarian in at least three ways: it offers that hope to all individuals, at every point in their lives; it posits that all have the means at hand to realize their hopes; and it accepts all wishes as equally deserving and equally precious. It is, however, profoundly inegalitarian also. Its endorsement of inequality is most obvious when success is defined competitively, but the endorsement does not stop there. Losers, whether individuals or groups, have no value in the ideology except insofar as they are object lessons or potential winners sometime in the future. The harshness of this judgment has always been masked by the fact that most people win at least a little bit or are simply written out of the game as nonplayers. The draconian judgment is never far from the profession of hope, however, and one cannot understand the profoundly ambiguous nature of the American dream unless both its egalitarian and inegalitarian sides are kept simultaneously in view.

NOTES

I would like to thank Deborah Baumgold, Albert Hirschman, Kristie Monroe, Noah Pickus, and members of the 1991–92 School of Social Sciences Seminar at the Institute for Advanced Study for their help on earlier drafts of this chapter. Support for this research was provided in part by the Spencer Foundation, the Center for Advanced Study in the Behavioral Sciences, and the Institute for Advanced Study. This chapter is a revision of chapter 1 of

Facing Up to the American Dream: Race, Class, and the Soul of the Nation (Princeton: Princeton University Press, 1995).

1. John Locke, *Second Treatise of Government*, ed. Thomas P. Peandon (New York: Macmillan Co., 1952), 29.

2. Immigration Act of 1990, Pub. L. No. 101-649, § 101, 104 Stat. 4978, 4981–82 (1990) (codified at 8 U.S.C. § 1151 [Supp. II 1990]) (limiting number of legal immigrants to 700,000 for 1992–94 and to 675,000 thereafter).

3. For example, Andrew Carnegie, who immigrated to America from Scotland in 1848, became a millionaire and patron of the arts. See Burton J. Hendrick, *The Life of Andrew Carnegie* (New Brunswick, N.J.: Transaction Publishers, 1932).

4. See generally Upton Sinclair, *The Jungle* (New York: Airmont, 1906) (telling the story of exploited immigrants); George C. Harring, ''America and Vietnam: The Unending War,'' *Foreign Affairs* 70 (Winter 1991): 104 (noting that many Vietnamese immigrants remain unassimilated and live below the poverty line).

5. Ronald Reagan, *Weekly Compilation of Presidential Documents* 19 (28 June 1983), 938, 943.

6. Studs Terkel, *American Dreams: Lost and Found* (New York: Ballantine Books, 1980), 236 (quoting Ed Sadlowski, son of Polish immigrants, who became the youngest district director of United Steel Workers of America).

7. Two recent examples are David Chandler and Mary Chandler, *The Binghams of Louisville: The Dark History behind One of America's Great Fortunes* (New York: Crown, 1987), and Adam Hochschild, *Half the Way Home: A Memoir of Father and Son* (New York: Viking Penguin, 1987).

8. Cotton Mather, *Magnalia Christi Americana*, ed. Raymond J. Cunningham and Frederick Ungar (1702; reprint, New York: Continuum, 1970), 27.

9. Ibid., 27–28.

10. Loammi Baldwin, *Thoughts on a Study of Political Economy* (New York: Kelley, 1809), 15, quoted in Stanley Lebergott, *The Americans: An Economic Record* (New York: Norton, 1984), 85.

11. Quoted in Dave Marsh, *Glory Days: Bruce Springsteen in the 1980s* (New York: Dell, 1984), 264.

12. Ibid.

13. James P. Comer, *Maggie's American Dream: The Life and Times of a Black Family* (New York: NAL-Dutton, 1988), 83–85. James Comer is an African American raised in poverty in Barbour County, Indiana, who became a physician. His book recaptures the life and dreams of his mother, Maggie Comer.

14. Ibid.

15. Byrd II to Lord Egmont, 12 July 1736, in *American Historical Review* 1 (1985): 88–90, quoted in Michael Greenberg, ''William Byrd II and the World of the Market,'' *Social Studies* 16 (1977): 454.

16. Lawrence D. Maloney, ''SUCCESS! The Chase Is Back in Style Again,'' *U.S. News and World Report*, 3 October 1983, 60.

17. See Locke, *Treatise on Government*, 29.

18. Quoted in Julie R. Jeffrey, *Frontier Women: The Trans-Mississippi West 1840–1880* (New York: Hill & Wang, 1979), 141.

19. Miguel Cortéz, quoted in Terkel, *American Dreams*, 131.

20. Ralph Waldo Emerson, ''Wealth,'' in *The Conduct of Life* (Boston: Ticknor & Fields, 1860), 71, 86.

21. Citicorp advertisement, *Time*, 21 August 1989, 44–45.

22. Benjamin Franklin, *Autobiography, in Writings*, ed. J. A. Leo Lemay (New York: Library of America, 1987), 1392, 1397.

23. David M. Potter, *People of Plenty: Economic Abundance and the American Character* (Chicago: University of Chicago Press, 1954).

24. See, e.g., "Pa's Song": "I'm sure in this world there are plenty of good things enough for us all. . . . It is only by plodding and striving . . . that you'll ever be thriving, which you'll do if you've only the will." Laura Ingalls Wilder, *The Long Winter* (New York: Harper & Row, 1940), 334.

25. W. J. Ghent, *Our Benevolent Feudalism* (New York: Macmillan, Co. 1902) (quoting Rockefeller).

26. For an earlier formulation of the defects of the American dream, see Jennifer L. Hochschild, "The Double-Edged Sword of Equal Opportunity," in *Power, Inequality, and Democratic Politics*, ed. Ian Shapiro and Grant Reeher (Boulder: Westview Press, 1988), 168–200.

27. See William Brink and Louis Harris, *Black and White: A Study of U.S. Racial Attitudes Today* (New York: Simon & Schuster, 1966), 222–31; Thomas E. Cavanagh, *Inside Black America* (Washington, D.C.: Joint Center for Political Study, 1985), 3; CBS News/ New York Times Poll, *The Kerner Commission—Ten Years Later* (New York: New York Times, 1978), 8; Philip E. Converse et al., *American Social Attitudes Data Sourcebook, 1947–1978* (Cambridge: Harvard University Press, 1980), 79; Louis Harris et al., *A Study of Attitudes toward Racial and Religious Minorities and toward Women* (New York: Louis Harris & Associates, 1978), 56; Gary T. Marx, *Protest and Prejudice: A Study of Belief in the Black Community* (New York: Harper and Row, 1967), 5–11, 220; Media General/ Associated Press, *Public Opinion Poll*, at tables 1, 2 (New York: Associated Press, 1988); Howard Schuman et al., *Racial Attitudes in America* (Cambridge: Harvard University Press, 1988), xiii, xiv, 118–27, 141–43; "Black and White: A Newsweek Poll," *Newsweek*, 7 March 1988, 18, 23; Washington Post, *Washington Post Poll: Race Relations* (Washington, D.C.: Washington Post, 1992); Los Angeles Times, *Judge Thomas, Race Relations, and Ronald Reagan*. Poll #259, (Los Angeles: Los Angeles Times, 1991); Washington Post/ Harvard University/Kaiser Foundation, *Survey on Race* (Washington, D.C.: Washington Post, 1995); *Gallup Poll Social Audit on Black/White Relations in the United States*, http: //www.gallup.com/poll/special/race/, 10 June 1997.

28. Washington Post, *Survey on Race*, 1995.

29. Ibid.

30. For more extensive analyses of how perceptions of racial discrimination differ by race, see Jennifer L. Hochschild and Monica Herk, " 'Yes, but . . .' ": Principles and Caveats in American Racial Attitudes," in *Nomos: Majorities and Minorities*, no. 32, ed. John W. Chapman and Alan Wertheimer, (New York: New York University Press, 1990), 308; and Hochschild, *Facing Up to the American Dream*.

31. Message from James Glen (1749), quoted in Warren B. Smith, *White Servitude in Colonial South Carolina* (Colombia: University of South Carolina Press, 1961), 51. A half a century later, J. Hector St. John de Crevecoeur was less instrumental, but no less extravagant: "After a foreigner from any part of Europe is arrived and become a citizen; let him devoutly listen to the voice of our great parent, which says to him, 'Welcome to my shores, distressed European; bless the hour in which thou didst see my verdant fields, my fair navigable rivers, and my green mountains! If thou wilt work, I have bread for thee; if thou wilt be honest, sober, and industrious, I have greater rewards to confer on thee—ease and independence. . . . Go thou and work and till; thou shalt prosper, provided thou be just, grateful, and industrious.' " J. Hector St. John de Crevecoeur, *Letters from an American Farmer* (1782; reprint, New York: Penguin Books, 1981), 89–90.

32. Mark L. Goldstein, "The End of the American Dream?" *Industry Weekly*, 4 April 1988, 77. See also Katherine Newman, *Declining Fortunes: The Withering of the American Dream* (New York: Basic Books, 1993).

33. See notes 10–13 above and accompanying text (defining absolute success).

34. Terkel, *American Dreams*, 116 (quoting Florence Scala, daughter of Italian immigrants who led the fight against city hall to save her old neighborhood on Chicago's near west side).

35. Goldstein, "End of the American Dream," 77.

36. Alexis de Tocqueville, *Democracy in America*, ed. J. P. Mayer and Max Lerner, trans. George Lawrence (1835; reprint, New York: Doubleday & Co., 1966).

37. Ibid., 512.

38. Samuel Stouffer et al., *The American Soldier: Adjustment during Army Life* (Princeton, N.J.: Princeton University Press, 1949), 1.

39. Tom W. Smith, "The Welfare State in Cross-National Perspective," *Public Opinion Quarterly* 51 (1987): 404, 411. All results combine "Agree strongly" and "Agree" categories.

40. Ibid.

41. Ibid.

42. Tom W. Smith, "Public Opinion and the Welfare State: A Cross-National Perspective" (paper presented at the Annual Meeting of the American Sociological Association [1987]).

43. Ibid., 39.

44. Gary B. Nash, *Red, White, and Black: The Peoples of Early America* (New York: Prentice Hall, 1982), 217.

45. Magdalen Society, "First Annual Report of the Executive Committee (1830)," in *The Reform Impulse, 1825–1850*, ed. Walter G. Hugins (Columbia: University of South Carolina Press, 1972), 41–42.

46. Quoted in Jennifer L. Hochschild, *What's Fair? American Beliefs about Distributive Justice* (Cambridge: Harvard University Press, 1981), 113.

47. I. A. Lewis and William Schneider, "Hard Times: The Public on Poverty," *Public Opinion* (June–July 1985): 2, 7.

48. Ibid.

49. Burton J. Hendrick, "The Great Jewish Invasion," *McClure's* 28 (1907): 307.

50. Ibid., 310.

51. Ibid.

52. Ibid., 311.

53. Ibid., 312–21.

54. Ibid., 320–21.

55. E.g., Fox Butterfield, "Why Asians Are Going to the Head of the Class," *New York Times*, 3 August 1986, Education Section, 18–23.

56. See, e.g., Reed Ueda, "False Modesty," *New Republic*, 3 July 1989, 16–17 (noting that group success has led to a model minority image that hides many of the problems currently afflicting Asian American societies).

57. Hendrick, "The Great Jewish Invasion," 321.

58. William James to H. G. Wells, in *The Letters of William James* (Boston: Atlantic Monthly, 1920), 2:260.

59. John J. Bukowczyk, *And My Children Did Not Know Me: A History of the Polish-Americans* (Bloomington: Indiana University Press, 1987): frontispiece.

60. Ibid.

61. Quoted in Loren Baritz, *The Good Life: The Meaning of Success for the American Middle Class* (New York: Knopf, 1989), 136.

62. James Fenimore Cooper, *The American Democrat* (Indianapolis: Liberty Fund, 1838), 138.

63. George Will, ''The Hell of Affluence,'' in *The Pursuit of Happiness and Other Sobering Thoughts* (New York: Harper Collins, 1978), 97, 98.

64. Tocqueville, *Democracy in America*, 513.

6

Racial Divisions and Judicial Obstructions

JEREMY RABKIN

Historians may well look back on 1995 as the year that marked the end of "the civil rights era." It began with the transfer of power in Washington to new conservative majorities in Congress, promising substantial cutbacks in federal interference in American society. Before the year was out, the nation's capital played host to a Million Man March, organized by Nation of Islam leader Louis Farrakhan, a purveyor of hate against Jews, Asian Americans, and whites. It was a fearful counterpart to Rev. Martin Luther King's celebrated March on Washington in the summer of 1963, at the outset of the civil rights era: whereas King had preached to a multiracial crowd on behalf of federal enforcement of civil rights, Farrakhan preached a message of black self-help to an exclusively black crowd—and Farrakhan drew two or three times as large a crowd as King.

Both white and black Americans, in quite different ways, expressed an impatience to move beyond the failed liberal policies of the past three decades. The country must do much soul-searching and rethinking in the years to come. On that, almost everyone is agreed. The rethinking, if it is to succeed, must extend to courts as well. Federal judges were seen as central actors in the early stages of the civil rights struggle, as the landmark decision in *Brown v. Board of Education* launched a long tedious struggle for school desegregation, not only in the South but eventually in the urban school districts of the North as well. In more recent times, debates over affirmative action and racial-preference policies have returned again and again to the federal courts, which have been cast as the ultimate arbiters of racial justice.

But all this may now be past—and well past. It would be a considerable exaggeration to depict federal courts as the main cause of failed social policies in the past generation. But it is no exaggeration to say that social policies of the past generation have indeed failed in their central challenge—the healing of racial divisions in the United States. It is simply a fact that courts have been deeply implicated in the elaboration of those failed policies. Fresh thinking about public policy must return to thinking about judicial policies because many judicial policies threaten to derail promising new policy initiatives, if courts do not "rethink their priorities" (to borrow the phrase that so intimidated judges and other political figures in the 1960s).

Two disclaimers are worth emphasizing at the outset. First, the issue is not whether the courts will uphold constitutional guarantees. That is a piece of childish rhetoric designed to appeal to only the very partisan or the very naive. Fairly put, the issue is whether courts will continue to pursue the particular slant given to constitutional interpretation in the past thirty years—most of it marking a considerable leap beyond earlier interpretation and almost all of it guided by policy visions then in fashion. The issue is not even whether courts will adhere to original intent but whether they will insist on adhering to failed intent of the past generation.

Second, in worrying over judicial obstacles to new policy directions, one must necessarily engage in speculation about potential threats. Policy innovations that have not yet been enacted have not yet been tested in the courts. Policy experiments that are still in their early stages have not received definitive judgment from the Supreme Court. And if one thing is sure, it is that courts have been quite unpredictable in their response to new trends in policy—sometimes jumping on the bandwagon of popular policy ideas, sometimes seeking to console the losers in policy debates by imposing new roadblocks. When we are dealing with jurisprudence that has no serious constitutional anchor—as is so plainly true of most doctrines on civil liberties and civil rights—we cannot predict how restrictive or accommodating the doctrine will prove to be in particular cases. The point is to sound a warning of what may prove troublesome, unless courts do undertake more fresh thinking.

At a higher level of generality, however, some things can be said with some confidence. In what follows, I will elaborate three main arguments. First, the ongoing debate about racial preferences and affirmative action—in which courts have been expected to play a central decisional role—is largely irrelevant to our current problems because these civil rights remedies have not touched the problem of the black underclass, which is at the heart of our current racial discord. Second, new approaches must center on local initiatives, to which law and courts have little to contribute—except to prune earlier doctrines that may inhibit or forestall local initiatives. Third, that the threat to new approaches in older doctrines reflects not just the predictable bias of federal courts—toward legalistic, procedural, and uniform national standards—but also the particular bias of New Deal and Great Society liberalism, which expected to deal with moral, spiritual, and human problems by redistributing material resources under the ongoing supervision of Washington bureaucracies.

The Irrelevance of Traditional Remedies

Having denounced racial segregation in the South during the 1950s, the federal courts played a leading role in the late 1960s and early 1970s in demanding that governments must, after all, take account of race—for "benign" purposes. Since the mid-1970s, the Supreme Court has wrestled with the vexing question of how far racial classification or racial-preference schemes can be pressed before they cease to be "benign."[1] As courts have assumed such a central role in past phases of the debate on civil rights, it is natural to think that courts will ultimately play the decisive role in determining the proper bounds of "affirmative action." It is natural to think this way, but it is almost surely mistaken.

To start with, the Supreme Court has vacillated with such regularity on these issues that vacillation, itself, has come to seem the Court's settled policy.[2] Just on the issue of affirmative action set-asides—by which some portion of contracts or benefits are "set aside" for minorities, outside the normal process of competitive bidding—the Court has landed on every side of the issue over the past fifteen years. It was in favor of federal set-asides for construction contracts in 1980;[3] then it struck down in 1987 a virtually identical program initiated by the city of Richmond;[4] then in 1990 it endorsed a fixed system of racial preferences in the awarding of broadcast licenses by the Federal Communications Commission.[5] The confusion reached a fitting culmination in 1995, as the Court ruled that "strict scrutiny" must be imposed on racial set-aside schemes in the awarding of federal construction contracts, but the Court's opinion hastened to add that such programs might well survive such scrutiny.[6]

The Court's hesitations are understandable. Passions run high on both sides of the general issue. It is hard to say that groups that have long been the victims of discrimination should, at some arbitrary stopping point, suddenly forfeit all claims to special governmental solicitude. It is equally hard to deny that individuals who do not belong to a favored minority group may have a legitimate sense of grievance when the accident of their birth works against them in the bestowal of governmental benefits. So the Court has been threading its way carefully—and indecisively.

But even if the Court steels itself to a more consistent repudiation of the most explicit racial-preference programs, judicial rulings are unlikely to quiet the larger debate about racial favoritism. Very few individuals from the favored minority groups own companies that can bid for governmental contracts or licenses, anyway. Indeed, very few white individuals are in a position to be affected in any direct way by such programs. On the other hand, most employment opportunities and opportunities for higher education, affecting tens of millions of people, are very much affected by existing civil rights regulation. And these nondiscrimination programs have a built-in momentum toward racial favoritism that is most unlikely to be affected by tinkering at the margin with affirmative action programs.

The basic reason is that since the late 1960s, the federal government has tracked racial breakdowns in employment, as well as in admissions to institutions of higher education. These figures may then be used to make out a prima facie case of discrimination. Reliance on a "neutral" decision criterion—such as the presence of a high school diploma—may be challenged unless it is proved to be a "bona fide" qualifying criterion.[7] Proving that any normal indicator is a valid predictor of future performance is a daunting (and extremely costly) effort. Employers and admissions committees are thus under constant pressure to make their resulting numbers look right to governmental monitors. Their behavior can be called "nondiscrimination,'' but the effect is not different from the racial preferences demanded by more explicit affirmative action programs.

Even if the Supreme Court reverses ground and becomes more solicitous of ''reverse discrimination'' claims—something that should not be relied on—this tendency to hire and admit by the numbers will be with us for a long time. The reason is that affirmative action is now deeply ingrained in the internal culture both of big business and of most academic institutions. Even if the federal government relaxed its pressure for numerical results, much of the business world and many public employers, at federal, state, and local levels, would probably continue to operate some informal system of affirmative action. So would most academic institutions. They would continue with affirmative action because managers in private companies, public agencies, and educational institutions have all become accustomed to operating in this way and remain fearful of accusations—even when divorced from legal sanctions—that they are ''racist'' or guilty of ''institutional racism.''[8] So a great many institutions will simply rearrange their decisionmaking criteria to ensure that they produce the desired racially balanced results.[9] To enforce truly color-blind decisionmaking, it would be necessary for governmental agencies (or courts) to decide the precise decisionmaking standards appropriate for a neutral decision. And almost no one favors the radical extension of governmental control that this approach would entail.

Thus, when the California Board of Regents, at the urging of Governor Pete Wilson, issued a directive prohibiting affirmative action preferences within the state's higher education system, the policy was protested by faculties and leading administrators within the University of California system—but most observers predicted it would not make much difference in the end.[10] When a citizens' group tried to launch a ballot initiative in California to impose a wider prohibition on any racial preference in state contracting or state employment, it found much public support in opinion polls—and a nearly total refusal by the business community to provide funding for the task of gathering enough signatures to place this initiative on the state ballot.[11] In Congress, the most ''radical'' measure to reform racial preferences, a bill sponsored by Republican representative Charles T. Canady in the House in 1995,[12] would prohibit courts from enforcing explicit quotas to remedy past discrimination but would not revise the way ''discrimination'' is defined or judged in federal litigation.

My own view is that efforts to reduce the extent of race-conscious remedies in the law are worthwhile because the law is a teacher as well as an enforcer. The more explicit the race-conscious element in law, the more it teaches whites that blacks cannot compete on their own and the more it teaches blacks that whites are too irredeemably racist to afford fair treatment to all races without coercion.

But the larger point is that, whatever the prospects for reducing race-conscious remedies, we are likely to retain a good deal of race-conscious policy throughout society. Defenders of this approach, like President Bill Clinton, may argue that it is necessary to ensure that white America does not relax its efforts to ensure equality and to ensure that minority citizens do not give up hope. And yet, as even President Clinton has recognized, it has become not only an intractable conflict but also an increasingly marginal one. Racial-preference programs cannot promise an end to racial tensions. Nor is it plausible, on the other hand, that abandoning such programs will put an end to racial tensions.

Even President Clinton, while insisting that racial-preference programs must be retained, acknowledged in a major speech—delivered on the same day as the Farrakhan march—that affirmative action was not reaching the deepest roots of division.[13] "Blacks," he said, "are right to think something is terribly wrong when . . . almost one in three African American men in their 20s are either in jail, on parole or otherwise under the supervision of the criminal justice system—nearly one in three." The comparable figure for white males is about 7 percent—that is, little more than one-fifth the rate for young blacks. President Clinton did not, however, pretend that whites, for their part, were wrong to draw fearful conclusions from these statistics. Rather, he rightly called on blacks to "understand and acknowledge the roots of white fear in America. There is a legitimate fear of the violence that is too prevalent in our urban areas; and . . . too often [it] has a black face."

The larger truth is that the problems of the inner city have gotten worse, not better, during the civil rights era of the last thirty years. As President Clinton said, we have witnessed "a generation of deepening social problems that disproportionately impact black Americans."

Crime is only the most dramatic expression of a larger pattern of social breakdown. As late as the mid-1960s, 75 percent of black households with children under eighteen years old were headed by married couples; by the mid-1980s, more than half of such black families were headed by women on their own. At the start of the 1960s, fewer than 25 percent of total births among black mothers were out of wedlock; by the mid-1980s, some 60 percent of black babies were born out of wedlock (compared to 12.5 percent among whites).[14] By the early 1990s, the illegitimacy rate among blacks was nearly 70 percent (while the rate among whites climbed to 22 percent).[15]

For decades, it has been conventional wisdom among liberal policymakers to trace problems of crime and family breakdown to economic dislocation. No doubt, there is truth in the warnings that cities do not offer the abundance of well-paying manufacturing jobs for unskilled labor that attracted black migrants to the North in the 1940s and 1950s. But it is equally clear that family breakdown makes it far more difficult to seize the opportunities that do exist. Children of unwed mothers are far more likely to drop out of school, to repeat the pattern of unwed pregnancy, and to fall into trouble with drugs and with crime.[16]

Thirty years of civil rights enforcement has proved sadly unequal to dealing with these worsening problems. Affirmative action may well have provided a useful leg up for many blacks. But the persistence of a black underclass continues to have a poisoning effect on race relations.

This trend is well documented in Jennifer Hochschild's 1995 book, *Facing Up to the American Dream*. During the 1960s, pollsters continually found optimism among black Americans about the prospects for increasing racial equality, with anywhere from 50 percent to 80 percent of black respondents professing to see racial equality on the increase. By the 1980s, similar polls found that only 20 percent to 45 percent of black respondents saw themselves on a trajectory toward increased equality, and up to half in some polls claimed that the situation of blacks had actually worsened.[17]

Hochschild's most striking and dismaying finding, however, is what she describes as "the paradox of succeeding more and enjoying it less." It is precisely the black middle class—whether defined by education or by income—that has become more embittered and disillusioned. And this is not simply because more worldly people always lose some illusions on their way up in life. Throughout the 1960s, "lower status blacks perceived more white hostility than did their higher-status counterparts," but "that discrepancy was reversed by the end of the 1970s." Polls since then consistently find more "bitterness about white intentions" among higher-status blacks.[18]

The extent of the disaffection among middle-class blacks has generated some alarming responses. A 1990 poll, for example, found that 67 percent of black college graduates (compared with 42 percent of blacks with less than a high school education and 16 percent of whites) thought it was either "true" or "might be true" that "the Government deliberately makes sure that drugs are easily available in poor black neighborhoods in order to harm black people." Asked to consider whether the AIDS virus was "deliberately created in a laboratory in order to infect black people," 40 percent of black college graduates thought this was "true" or "might be true" (compared with 18 percent of blacks with less than a high school education and 5 percent of whites).[19]

What can account for disaffection so severe as to make even such paranoid fantasies seem plausible? How can it be that those who have benefited most from increasing opportunities are so relentlessly suspicious? Hochschild offers a very plausible interpretation: "Many middle-class blacks feel an acute responsibility to their history, their poorer fellows, their race, and each other. That sense of responsibility may not be growing, but the sense that American society will not allow them to fulfill their responsibility despite new-found wealth and power clearly *is* growing. The new frustration leads to bitterness against other Americans and eventually against the American dream."[20]

After such experience, it is very hard to believe that a redoubled commitment to affirmative action will actually take us on a path to further racial healing.

New Approaches, Old Roadblocks

Racial divisions may add urgency to dealing with the plight of inner cities. But the desperation of inner-city conditions would have an urgent claim on public policy in any case. Because the problems are not distinctively racial, solutions can be framed in nonracial terms. Some may arouse opposition in particular communities more than others. But most things that can be done need to be done at the local level, anyway. There is room for and indeed a basic need for trying different approaches in different places. But in one area after another there are common threats from restrictive court rulings.

Crime control is a good place to start. The prevalence of criminal violence in inner cities may frighten whites. But the main victims tend to be nonwhites, and the toll is staggering. In 1992, for example, African Americans, though only 12 percent of the population, constituted almost half of all murder victims (and 94 percent of their killers were also black).[21] Black males were seven times more likely to be victims of murder than their white counterparts, and the life expectancy of black men in central Harlem was calculated, in the early 1990s, to be lower than that of men in Bangladesh.[22]

Professor John DiIulio of Princeton University, one of the leading scholars on crime control, emphasizes that, beyond the tragedy of the immediate victims, the consequences of such carnage destabilize and demoralize entire communities, so it is hard to be hopeful about anything else in inner cities if we cannot put a decisive check on street violence.[23] DiIulio's main prescription, seeking longer and more predictable sentences, does seem to be bearing results. It is expensive to provide prisons on the necessary scale, however, and there is constant pressure on available capacity. Some judges have responded by demanding more facilities for prisoners, driving up the costs. Others have actually ordered prison release programs to ease crowding. There is certainly a legitimate role for courts in preventing the most abusive prison conditions. It is at least fair to ask, however, whether the rights of prisoners should be purchased at the expense of potential victims of prematurely released criminals.[24] Some judges do not seem to take this question at all seriously. Proposals have been put before Congress, therefore, to limit the power of federal judges to order prison releases,[25] but whether such measures would be accepted by courts remains in question.

But even the staunchest advocates of incarceration do not pretend it is a panacea. Prisons may be cost-effective in reducing the social cost of crime, but the cost of prison construction and maintenance still provokes resistance from weary taxpayers (all the more so because the affluent, who pay more taxes, actually do better at protecting themselves, through various private measures, from the burdens and costs of unchecked violent crime). Moreover, the current scale of incarceration has already begun to generate significant political resistance, especially from minority leaders protesting the extremely disproportionate presence of blacks and Hispanics in the nation's prisons. Yet demographic projections suggest that we are in for a new surge of violent crime over the next few years, as a larger cohort of young people enters the most crime-prone period of life.[26]

Some analysts argue that although it is important to have tough sentences, to put a heavy "price" on crime, it is even more important to make criminal justice swift and certain. So the issue is not just the capacity of prisons but the efficiency of police and of the criminal courts. Critics have argued for some decades that court-imposed burdens on the criminal justice system may significantly inhibit police effectiveness. Evidence is certainly disputed. But it is indisputable that some constitutional doctrines—like the "exclusionary rule" that prohibits the use of improperly obtained evidence in criminal trials—impose burdens that have no direct relation to the primary question of whether the defendant is, in fact, guilty as charged.[27] Whatever reformers may have imagined in the 1960s, it is now a much more urgent question whether the multiplication of technical objections—which rich defendants can exploit and ordinary defendants cannot, in practice, afford to pursue—has actually helped to enhance public confidence in the criminal justice system or simply exacerbated public cynicism.[28]

But even a streamlined criminal justice system and an expanded role for official policing cannot be expected, in themselves, to restore order to communities where violence has become endemic. So advocates of tougher measures—along with those who shrink from tougher measures—also put stress on preventive measures. In particular, there has been renewed interest in mobilizing community efforts to help restore order to chaotic and violent neighborhoods.

An obvious beginning is to make streets safer so that more people are willing to move around openly and to make violent criminals more hesitant to act where there will be more witnesses and perhaps more good Samaritans coming to the aid of potential victims. James Q. Wilson, one of the leading analysts of crime-control policy, has urged that police make periodic sweeps of neighborhoods to disarm criminals. He urges that criminals be frisked and disarmed on the streets.[29] The idea is appealing and seems more promising than gun-control schemes that try to prevent the flow of guns into the community in the first place. The notion is that even though it may be difficult to prevent access to guns, carrying them in the streets can be made dangerous.

One difficulty with this approach, however, is that courts may not stand for it. The Supreme Court held in 1968 that police must have probable cause to make searches of suspects.[30] Courts might apply this in lenient ways, as some seem to have done. But others have been rather strict. Courts can be a serious obstacle if they determine to be. In 1994, for example, the U.S. Court of Appeals for the Seventh Circuit overturned a conviction for illegal firearms possession: Milwaukee police had received an anonymous tip about a suspicious car (a Cadillac with tinted windows) and, when they approached the passengers, found a gun barrel protruding from the defendant's coat. Neither the tip nor the suspicious appearance of the car was sufficient, according to the court, to justify the subsequent successful firearms search.[31] Similar rulings are not hard to find.[32]

A related proposal, urged by Wilson, among others, suggested that cities experiment with "perimeter control" to block off streets in hopes of cutting down on through traffic and making neighborhoods more self-contained.[33] The idea is to provide urban neighborhoods with some of the benefits associated with private gated communities for the affluent. In fact, such measures have been taken in California and a few other places to considerable local satisfaction.[34]

But again there are potential legal obstacles. The Supreme Court ruled in 1972 that state "vagrancy" laws are unconstitutionally vague.[35] The opinion by Justice William O. Douglas rhapsodized about Walt Whitman, drawing poetic inspiration from idling through the streets. It is not likely to be a view that commends itself to people in poor neighborhoods, where drifters are more likely to be armed drug dealers than idling poets. But some judges have been extremely solicitous of drifters. In 1990 a judge ruled that there is a constitutional right to be a panhandler in the New York City subways.[36] In a similar case, a court ruled that an unwashed, muttering homeless person had a constitutional right to remain an "annoying" presence in a public library.[37] Courts have also embraced challenges to laws prohibiting loitering for the purpose of begging.[38] It will not be easy to control access to secured neighborhoods if judges of this sort continue to impose their will on struggling communities.

One finds this inclination over and over among contemporary judges, however. The Bush administration tried to evict drug dealers from federally funded housing projects. The Fourth Circuit ruled that this program violates the due process rights of the drug dealers, who must be allowed to stay in public housing—continuing to deal crack cocaine to children and pregnant women—until given an opportunity to defend themselves in a formal hearing.[39]

If judges are hesitant about going after drug dealers, they may be equally uneasy about going after drug users in systematic ways. James Q. Wilson has urged that routine, frequent drug testing be imposed on former users to ensure that they stay away from drugs. He may be right that legal problems can be avoided by focusing on those with previous drug convictions. But again, notions of "probable cause" and "expectations of privacy" can be quite elastic. A majority of the Supreme Court expressed outright opposition or great uneasiness at a school district's policy of imposing mandatory drug testing on high school athletes.[40]

People with financial means have increasingly sought to insulate themselves from crime by retreating to guarded private enclaves. The poor would face obstacles in trying to follow this example, even if the government or charitable donors helped them to secure some of the necessary resources. Some cities, for example, have experimented with private conservancy groups to care for public parks. The experiment might be extended to private parks, private police. But again, court doctrines from earlier times cast a shadow. Courts remain divided on whether even private property, such as shopping malls, should be considered a "public forum," subject to First Amendment restrictions on regulation.[41] Efforts to impose certain standards of polite behavior in private parks may well run afoul of such doctrines.[42] Hiring private police? One of the most ready sources—church volunteers—may raise First Amendment objections if any government money is involved.[43] But government money may be essential when dealing with public housing projects. A rigorous application of recent doctrines, in other words, may make the poor singularly captive to constitutional fashion.

Schools, Families, Judges

What is true for crime control is equally true for education. Dissatisfaction with public schools is widespread and for understandable reasons. So there is great interest in increasing choice. Middle-class families can escape public schools. Why not provide more choice to poor families? Milwaukee attempted to do just this—and was promptly sued. A federal court declared a school choice program unconstitutional for allowing students into religious schools. But 93 of Milwaukee's 130 private schools happen to be religious schools. Parents participating in the choice program were overwhelming black and Hispanic. Non-Catholic parents were still eager for the discipline and morale available in Catholic schools. They certainly had reason to shun the public schools, where fewer than half the students graduate from high school. The dropout rate is seven times the average for the state of Wisconsin, and of those remaining, 79 percent failed the math-proficiency test required for graduation.[44] But although the public schools were demonstrably failing, a federal judge decided that the students simply could not be allowed an alternative: offering students and their parents a choice would be a threat to civil liberty![45]

The Milwaukee case is simply the most recent and most dramatic illustration of a long-established pattern. Across the country, public school systems have been woefully unsuccessful in teaching reading, spelling, or basic math to inner-city children.[46] Careful studies have long confirmed that parochial schools do much better at teaching basic skills, even while spending much less per pupil than public schools. Evidently parochial schools are better equipped to impart the discipline and self-respect needed for orderly learning. They do better, even with inner-city students, even when they are Catholic schools trying to inspire students from non-Catholic families.[47]

Yet state governmental efforts to subsidize parochial education—aimed at making it more widely available—have repeatedly been struck down by the Supreme Court on the grounds that such subsidies would constitute an establishment of religion, somehow violating the rights of ardent secularists. The Court managed to persuade itself that aid to religious colleges could be squared with its reading of the First Amendment, but aid to elementary and secondary parochial schools—which would be far more relevant to the plight of children in the inner cities—must remain unacceptable.[48] The Court, which was prepared to embark on such bitterly divisive measures as mandatory busing programs for school integration, claimed that aid to religiously affiliated schools (at the elementary and secondary level) would be too "divisive."[49] In an era when almost all other forms of governmental spending are insulated from constitutional challenge, the Court has pursued its opposition to assisting religious schools with relentless energy.[50]

Opponents of subsidizing private schools insist that drawing more ambitious students into private schools will undermine the quality of public schools. Of course, the obvious response is to let public schools compete more effectively. But those who emphasize the need for reforms in the public schools may encounter a new set of judicial obstacles.

One of the main problems is reasserting discipline in public schools. Recently, the president of the American Federation of Teachers, the nation's second largest teacher's union, proposed a series of reforms to make American public schools as effective as their European counterparts. The "first essential element" on his list was "the refusal to tolerate disruptive student behavior that regularly interferes with education." Albert Shanker notes that efforts to remove disruptive students from the classroom are infrequent: "When they occur, advocacy groups mount lengthy, expensive legal challenges. And courts are apt to side with the 'repentant' offender rather than the unseen victims—the other students."[51]

Courts are indeed apt to side with the "repentant" offender. A few years ago, for example, a federal court reviewed the twenty-nine-day suspension of a student who, all parties stipulated, "engaged in verbal and physical temper tantrums which included kicking and scratching teachers and hitting other students." The court, acceding to the parents' insistence on making a federal case out of a temporary suspension, ordered the student reinstated.[52]

Of course, beyond removing the most disruptive students, public schools need to cultivate orderly habits and a sense of academic discipline among the ordinary students. Some educators have urged that it would be helpful to separate boys and girls, particularly in early grades, because boys tend to be much more restless and aggressive, becoming frustrated and repelled by the orderly classroom routines to which girls adapt so readily.[53] Experiments of this kind have shown some promise. But it may not be possible to pursue them. A court has already held that mandatory segregation based on sex is unconstitutional.[54]

Other educators have urged the need for more-restrictive dress codes to discourage distracting competition over styles of dress. There have even been proposals to have public schools require standardized school uniforms, as has been done by many private schools and by public schools in other countries. It might help to encourage a sense of discipline. It might promote a sense that school is serious and not a setting for flamboyant personal display.[55] It might also be held unconstitutional because some courts have held that students have a constitutional right to dress as they like.[56]

If schools venture beyond outward displays of discipline to direct efforts to promote moral training, they will again risk judicial scrutiny and interference. Public schools can be slapped down for even the most indirect reference to religious authority. The Supreme Court itself ruled in 1980 that display of the Ten Commandments in public schools would be constitutionally intolerable pedagogy.[57] Even a moment of silent reflection at the beginning of the day was judged by the Supreme Court to be intolerably burdensome to the religious liberty of students.[58] The Court not only condemns such indirect acknowledgment of religious authority but also has condemned straightforward educational decisions—like removing books from school libraries—when it suspects a religious motivation.[59] So lower courts have gotten into the business of determining which books need to be on the shelves of public school libraries and even which school practices, suspected of having been banned by religiously motivated school boards, must be restored to public schools under the banner of assured secularism.[60]

The point hardly requires belaboring. Federal courts have displayed remarkable confidence in their ability to dictate the proper path of public education. Some of the school districts most closely managed by federal judges have deteriorated most dramatically. After more than a decade of micromanaging public schools in Boston, a federal court left the school system more racially segregated than before, while reading and math scores had also fallen lower.[61] Kansas City had much the same experience after decades of judicial management of its public schools.[62] There is much legitimate disagreement about the proper approach to educating poor children with low motivation or inadequate parental support. There needs to be much experiment. Experience suggests, however, that judges are the very last people from whom to expect any constructive help. If they make things worse, after all, they can simply shrug their shoulders, walk away, and chalk it all up to the obligations of "the law." Schools will do better when they are more accountable to parents rather than to judges.

Improving the capacities of parents is surely the most important and most difficult challenge facing public policy. But here, too, judges figure mostly as potential obstacles to necessary reforms.

The most obvious and immediate way to improve parenting is to increase the number of people involved: two is almost always better than one. Single-parent households—meaning, in practice, children reared by unwed mothers—have become the norm in inner cities. It is difficult to know how to break this dreadful pattern at such an advanced stage. It is always difficult to influence private, intimate behavior. It is particularly difficult when policymakers have to worry about not punishing children for the sins of their parents. But serious efforts must be made.

One obvious place to start is with the welfare system. Though the point is certainly disputed among social scientists, there is growing recognition that the welfare system has offered perverse incentives to illegitimacy. Many scholars argue that the generous terms of the Aid to Families with Dependent Children Act (together with related services, such as Medicaid and food stamps) offer more reward than minimum-wage employment, encouraging motherhood as a sort of career—from which the fathers are, by the rules of the system, excluded.[63] It is certainly true that without this "safety net," very young women would have to be vastly more cautious about becoming pregnant without a reliable breadwinning partner—as women were, in black communities and elsewhere in America, before the 1960s.

We are now entering an era in which a Republican Congress seeks to offer much wider discretion to the states to experiment with new approaches to welfare. It remains to be seen whether courts will go along. An early experiment in New Jersey, denying additional financial support to families that have additional children while on welfare, has been upheld by a lower court,[64] but the litigation continues. And it is surely only the beginning. Conditions attached to welfare eligibility may require intrusive monitoring and subjective or contentious judgments by local officials regarding individual cases. (Was the client *genuinely* trying to stay in a training program, *genuinely* trying to take proper care of the children, and so on?) The Supreme Court held in 1970 that welfare payments are an entitlement, requiring comparable procedural protections as private property.[65] Although the doctrine has been subject to considerable erosion, it might well resurface as the instrument by which activist judges seek to put brakes on state experiments in welfare reform.

Other experiments in trying to restore the strength of family obligation will generate even more controversy and more litigation. Congressman Newt Gingrich stirred much controversy when he urged that states and localities might want to reopen orphanages for children who were intolerably neglected by the parents. In fact, the suggestion made by James Q. Wilson was for state-run "homes" for mothers and children, providing a structured program along with food and shelter.[66] Could assignment to such a "home" be made compulsory? We don't yet know.

Some states are seeking to impose financial obligations on fathers of minor children, even if they have not married the mother and even if they have never previously assumed financial responsibility for the mother. Can the mother be forced to identify the father? Can suspected fathers be forced to submit to blood tests and DNA tests? Can their earnings be forcibly garnished until the children have reached adulthood? What happens to the mothers in the meantime? Can more extreme sanctions—such as imprisonment—be applied if the fathers fail to generate any earnings to meet their financial obligations? Litigation is certain. Only the ultimate attitude of the courts is not.

Other efforts may be made to stigmatize unwed motherhood more directly. Only a few decades ago, it was routine to remove pregnant students from schools or at least from regular classes with other students. The idea was to remove a bad example and to stigmatize it. Whether this would still be helpful in discouraging teen pregnancy may be debated. It is at present illegal, under federal regulations interpreting a statute prohibiting sex discrimination.[67] If the regulations are lifted by federal authorities, some local school districts may want to experiment with a return to older approaches. But lower courts have found constitutional objections to discrimination against unwed mothers.[68] Other means of stigmatizing unwed motherhood—or providing special acknowledgment for married mothers—will face similar hurdles.

No one can be sure how courts will respond to such policies. But less than a decade ago, four justices of the Supreme Court insisted that the Constitution guaranteed the right to participate in homosexual practices—or, rather, guaranteed a wide sphere of autonomy for sexual conduct between consenting adults.[69] More recently, the Supreme Court held that it was not ''rational'' to exclude ''homosexual orientation'' from the personal attributes covered by state or local antidiscrimination measures, prompting speculation that the Court is now prepared to proclaim broad constitutional protection for homosexual conduct.[70] The Court has repeatedly reaffirmed a broad right to abortion. It is certainly possible to argue that government may not interfere in ''reproductive choice'' and to argue at the same time that once the choice to have children is made, the government has considerable authority to enforce parental standards of proper care for children. It is certainly possible to argue that single individuals should have broad autonomy to conduct their sex lives as they see fit, but that special burdens or restrictions may apply to parents. It is possible to argue such things. But cases affirming a constitutional right to sexual freedom certainly generate a doctrinal momentum that militates against stern restrictions in the name of protecting family life. And over the past two decades, the Supreme Court has on a number of occasions expressed mistrust of governmental measures that seem to enshrine a particular definition of ''the family'' (as the traditional two-parents-with-children family).[71]

As with crime-control measures and with educational reform measures, we cannot be sure what will work in policies to restore the primacy of family life, what will receive public support, and what will have serious influence on behavior. We cannot be sure how much will be achieved by symbolic measures, aimed at rallying salutary opinion and reinforcing sound moral convictions. We may never be able to gauge the contribution of particular policies or gestures, amid a mass of other policies. But we will never gain any clarity at all without trying new approaches. And we will not be able to do even much of that if courts insist on blocking the way.

Judicial Pride and Inner-City Despair

One might charitably interpret these court decisions as reflecting the judicial commitment to civil liberty. One might say, that is, that an overriding regard for civil liberty has motivated courts to resist efforts at crime control, to oppose efforts to expand school choice and tighten school discipline, and to hobble efforts to revive public morals.

Even when viewed in these terms, however, the stance of the courts is not easy to defend. The Constitution speaks of securing "the blessings of liberty." The framers were perfectly aware, however, that when taken to extremes, liberty could be something quite other than a blessing. *The Federalist* notes that chaotic government "poisons the blessings of liberty, itself."[72] Indeed, *The Federalist* warns, quite explicitly, that "liberty may be endangered by the abuses of liberty as well as by the abuses of power; and . . . the former rather than the latter is apparently most to be apprehended by the United States."[73] In fact, the thought is not altogether alien to the current Supreme Court. The Court is quite comfortable sanctioning abridgments of commercial liberty, including those once thought to have been protected by the Constitution, in order to secure what is conceived to be the greater good.

The truth is that the central thrust of contemporary jurisprudence has only been incidentally concerned with liberty. Rather, it has been most of all concerned with a certain view of equality. Ronald Dworkin, one of the most celebrated legal commentators of the past generation, argued quite explicitly that the main constitutional principle must be equality rather than liberty. And he argued that the constitutional promise of equality must be understood as an obligation of government to provide "equal concern and respect": government "must not constrain liberty on the ground that one citizen's conception of the good life . . . is nobler or superior to another's."[74]

For some decades, the federal courts have pursued a vision of "equality" that is reasonably well captured in Dworkin's formulations. The Court has sanctioned a vast amount of intrusive governmental constraints on private activity. But it has sought to reassure itself that in all of this, government is simply controlling harmful effects and never expressing moral approbation for one way of life over another. It is hard to explain the Court's allergic response to public acknowledgment of religion—and its general resistance to public assistance to religious schools—except in terms of some formula such as this: religion makes the most authoritative claims about the right way of life; government may therefore spend public funds with no serious constitutional check—except when it comes to religion.[75]

On occasion, the justices themselves put aside legal technicalities to proclaim the vision quite openly. Only recently, three justices—then viewed as the very center of the Court—signed their names to the following declamation: "At the heart of liberty is the right to define one's own concept of existence, of meaning, of the universe, and of the mystery of human life."[76] Liberty, to these justices, has no necessary or intrinsic connection with independence, with personal responsibility, or even with human dignity or the sacredness of the human person. "*At the heart of liberty*'' is the cosmic freedom to reconceive the universe in any way one likes—with government and the broader community entirely on the sidelines.

No justice of the Supreme Court, of course, actually has the foolhardy courage of this sophomoric conviction. Were it true that this credo represented ''the heart of liberty,'' it would follow that laws against pornography and narcotics, for example, would be unconstitutional because their main purpose and effect are to stigmatize the view of ''meaning'' and ''the universe'' that identifies empty orgasms and drug-induced stupors with the aim of human ''existence.'' There are highly respectable legal commentators who argue that a proper view of the Constitution does entail a constitutional right to all manner of sexual satisfactions (at least among consenting adults) and all manner of narcotic consumption. Suicide, too, has been defended as a constitutional right—as it is a most logical response to a certain despairing concept of ''existence'' and of ''the mystery of human life.''[77]

It may be that such consistency is a luxury of tenured professors that judges, even with life tenure of their own, cannot quite afford. More likely, the justices do not have the time or inclination to reflect on the full implications of their own (or their young law clerks') rhetoric. To some extent, they are, like all politicians, prisoners of the phrasemakers. But once set in play, the logic of the doctrine has a certain irresistible force—even though for all that, it frequently is resisted, whether from political necessity or unreflective habit. Much that the Court does can only be explained by the current liberal view that government must never prefer one way of life to another or one moral outlook to another.

Such relentless moral relativism is totally at odds with the common sense of the ordinary citizen. The ordinary citizen thinks it is very wrong to have children when you cannot care for them, very wrong to desert your children and the mother of your children, very wrong to drop out of school and become dependent on governmental handouts. The ordinary citizen would not dream of saying that such ''ways of life'' are entitled to ''equal concern and respect.'' Of course, it would be dangerous or impractical to give government the power to force everyone to lead a fully virtuous life. But it defies common sense to suppose that government should be indifferent to whether citizens will try to lead more responsible and productive lives.

Why do courts so often set themselves against common sense? One reason, surely, is that it strikes them as too common. For decades, liberal opinion has puffed itself with pride at being more ''understanding'' than the common person. Judges seem to be particularly tempted by such moral vanity. If judges were not more ''understanding'' than the ordinary person, after all, why would they be given such large powers with such little accountability? There is the additional consideration that such superior ''understanding'' has been deployed to justify ever-larger claims of power by federal judges: if the views of ordinary citizens were more to be trusted, there would be less excuse for judges to exert control over schools, prisons, and a range of other institutions, previously left to the good judgment of elected local officials.

It is not a straight line from the formulaic, academic nihilism of the professors and the judges to the nihilistic self-destructiveness of real life in the inner cities.

But there is surely a connection. The crisis of the inner cities is primarily a moral and spiritual crisis. In the depths of the Great Depression, even amid segregation and open racism, there was nothing like the pattern of violence and family breakdown that is reflected in current statistics. There was not the same level of violence and moral anarchy because there was not the same level of utter despair.

For some decades, liberal judges have hewed to the philosophy that shrugs off moral despair as nothing much to worry about—nothing that can't be cured with a little more welfare spending. So the Supreme Court did its best to impose national standards for welfare support in 1969 on the premise that welfare handouts are essential to life.[78] Almost simultaneously it embarked on a program of containing religious education as dangerous and divisive, while raising questions about family obligations at every turn.

In such stances, the courts reflected a strong current of elite opinion, and no doubt they helped to give it more confidence and wider effect.[79] By now, the failure of liberal policy prescriptions has vastly reduced the number of elected officeholders who still adhere to this outlook. One can be sure that the liberalism of the 1960s and 1970s is doomed. One can even be sure that it will be in retreat (as it may already be) within the courts and must eventually give way to sounder views. But one cannot be sure it will happen soon.

Vast social problems will not soon be remedied, in any case. But it remains a matter of some interest whether judges will continue to contribute to the problem. Unlike elected politicians, judges may perpetuate delusions through a life term on the bench.

NOTES

1. Andrew Kull, *The Color-Blind Constitution* (Cambridge: Harvard University Press, 1992), offers a useful survey of the Court's move into "benign" racial remedies in the late 1960s and its struggles to place some limits on racial-preference measures ever since.

2. As Kull remarks, "In the constitutional cases on affirmative action . . . the Court has produced—at enormous length—a record of its inability to agree on any decisive legal principle." Ibid., 207–8. For a detailed review of the Court's recent vacillations, see Neal Devins, "*Adarand Constructors, Inc. v. Pena* and the Continuing Irrelevance of Supreme Court Affirmative Action Decisions," *William and Mary Law Review* 37 (Winter 1996): 673.

3. *Fullilove v. Klutznick*, 448 U.S. 448 (1980).

4. *City of Richmond v. J. A. Croson Co.*, 448 U.S. 469 (1989).

5. *Metro Broadcasting, Inc. v. FCC*, 497 U.S. 547 (1990).

6. *Adarand Constructors, Inc. v. Pena*, 515 U.S. 200 (1995).

7. The development of this system and the operational premises behind it are usefully described in Nathan Glazer, *Affirmative Discrimination* (New York: Basic Books, 1978). A more recent survey concludes that the system holds employers guilty of "discrimination" when their "only sin is hiring the best employees they can find." Stuart Taylor, "Clinton and the Quota Game," *Legal Times*, 28 December 1992, 23.

8. See Anne B. Fisher, "Businessmen Like to Hire by the Numbers," *Fortune*, 16 September 1985, 26 (describing internal affirmative action officers who monitor corporate compliance with proportional hiring goals and nurture internal constituencies for maintaining

such policies). Similar officers exist at all universities. For a more recent survey confirming corporate complacency about proportional hiring programs, see Steven A. Holmes, "Affirmative Action Plans are Part of Business Life," *New York Times*, 22 November 1991, sec. A, 20. For the counterpart tendencies among local government employers, see Stephen Engelberg, "Attack on Quotas Opposed by Cities," *New York Times*, 4 May 1985, sec. A, 1.

9. For an account of how this was done by the University of Texas (Austin) School of Law in response to a reverse discrimination suit demonstrating explicit racial admissions quotas, see Michael Greve, "Segregation Now," *Weekly Standard*, 15 December 1995, 31–35.

10. Bill Small, "Wilson Steps Up Attack on Affirmative Action," *Los Angeles Times*, 19 July 1995, sec. A, 3.

11. John Miller and Abigail Thernstrom, "Losing Race," *New Republic*, 26 June 1995, 17.

12. Equal Opportunity Act of 1995, H.R. 2128, introduced 27 July 1995 (with 72 cosponsors), 104th Congress.

13. Remarks by the president to the Carpenter Lectureship in the Humanities and Sciences, University of Texas, Austin, October 16, 1995.

14. Gerald D. Jaynes and Robin M. Williams, Jr., eds., *A Common Destiny: Blacks and American Society* (Washington: National Research Council, 1989), 518, 528.

15. Bureau of the Census, *Statistical Abstract of the United States 1994* (Washington, D.C., 1994), 80.

16. For a review of the evidence, see Irwin Garfinkel and Sara S. McLanahan, *Single Mothers and Their Children: A New American Dilemma* (Washington, D.C.: Urban Institute Press, 1989).

17. Jennifer Hochschild, *Facing Up to the American Dream* (Princeton: Princeton University Press, 1995), 60–61.

18. Ibid., 74–75.

19. Ibid., 106.

20. Ibid., 140.

21. U.S. Department of Justice, *United States Crime Reports 1993* (Washington, D.C.: Government Printing Office, 1993), 17.

22. Bob Herbert, "Who Will Help the Black Man?" *New York Times Magazine*, 4 December 1994, 74.

23. John DiIulio, "The Question of Black Crime," *Public Interest*, no. 117 (Fall 1994): 4.

24. See John DiIulio, *Courts, Corrections, and the Constitution: The Impact of Judicial Interventions on Prisons and Jails* (New York: Oxford University Press, 1990).

25. Stop Turning Out Our Prisoners Act, H.R. 554, introduced 18 January 1995, 104th Congress.

26. James Q. Wilson, "Crime in America," *Commentary* (February 1995): 20.

27. See, e.g., the recent book by Judge Harold J. Rothwax of New York arguing that the exclusionary rule requires considerable modification to avoid perverse results in the criminal justice system: *Guilty: The Collapse of the Criminal Justice System* (New York: Random House, 1996).

28. Richard Parker, "The Coming Legal Backlash," *New Republic*, 20 March 1995, 21.

29. James Q. Wilson, "Just Take Away Their Guns," *New York Times*, 6 March 1994, sec. G, 47; James Q. Wilson, "Why Falling Crime Statistics Don't Make Us Feel More Secure," *Los Angeles Times*, 25 September 1994, sec. M, 1.

30. *Terry v. Ohio*, 392 U.S. 1 (1968).

31. *United States v. Packer*, 15 F.3d 654 (1994).

32. See, e.g., *United States v. Scopo*, 814 F. Supp. 292 (E.D.N.Y. 1993) (suppressing

evidence of handgun possession because police, after trailing defendant from a stakeout of site used by Colombo crime family, had stopped defendant's car for failing to signal a lane change and then found handgun on his person after frisking him—but not, the court ruled, with "adequate cause").

33. James Q. Wilson, "Human Nature and Social Progress" (paper presented at Bradley Lecture, American Enterprise Institute [1991]).

34. R. Marshall Elizer and Nazir Lalani, "Facing Up to a Street Closure Epidemic," *Public Works* 125 (May 1994): 38, reviews some examples, noting that "increasing crime rates have triggered moves by cities in Southern California to close streets to reduce gang and drug related activities from being conducted in residential neighborhoods," but such efforts sometimes generate local protests for increasing traffic congestion. See also Ronald Brownstein, "The Mean Streets: Cities Are Reclaiming Besieged Areas by Erecting Traffic Barriers and Cracking Down on Panhandlers and Loitering; Some Fear Loss of Freedom," *Los Angeles Times*, 4 May 1994, sec. A, 1 (noting that local residents have praised such efforts but "civil libertarians and homeless advocates" have denounced them in places as "authoritarian").

35. *Papachristou v. City of Jacksonville*, 405 U.S. 156 (1972). See the similar ruling in *Palmer v. City of Euclid*, 402 U.S. 544 (1971), and the parallel reasoning in *Kolender v. Lawson*, 461 U.S. 352 (1983). On the basis of these and similar federal precedents, a New York state court held the state's antiloitering law unconstitutional in *People v. Bright*, 520 N.E.2d 1355 (N.Y. Ct. App. 1988).

36. *Young v. New York City Transit Authority*, 729 F. Supp. 341 (S.D.N.Y. 1990), *rev'd on other grounds*, 903 F.2d 146 (2d Cir. 1990).

37. *Kreimer v. Bureau of Police*, 765 F. Supp. 181 (D.N.J. 1991), *rev'd*, 958 F.2d 1242 (3d Cir. 1992).

38. *Loper v. New York City Police Dep't*, 766 F. Supp. 1280 (S.D.N.Y. 1991).

39. *Richmond Tenant Organization v. Kemp*, 956 F.2d 1300 (4th Cir. 1992).

40. *Veronica School District v. Acton*, 115 S. Ct. 2386 (1995). Justices John Paul Stevens III, Sandra Day O'Connor, and David H. Souter dissented outright; Justices Ruth Bader Ginsburg and Stephen Breyer expressed reservations about extending the testing program in a concurring opinion.

41. See Curtis J. Berger, "Pruneyard Revisited: Political Activity on Private Lands," *New York University Law Review* 66 (June 1991): 633.

42. See, e.g., the New Jersey state court ruling in *State v. Kolz*, 276 A.2d 595 (1971) (holding that courts must enforce First Amendment guarantees against a private retirement village lest they "create a political 'isolation booth' "). Ibid. at 600. For an extended argument for the applicability of constitutional restrictions to private residential associations, see "Note: The Rule of Law in Residential Associations," *Harvard Law Review* 99 (December 1985): 472.

43. Contracts with the Nation of Islam, to provide security patrols in public housing projects, have generated grateful support from local residents and charges from outside advocacy groups that they threaten the separation of church and state. See Clarence Page, "Should the CHA Turn for Security to Nation of Islam?" *Chicago Tribune*, 16 February 1994, 17; Brian Blomquist, "City Praised for Involving Nation Security; Police to Work with Farrakhan's Men," *Washington Times*, 13 October 1995, sec. C, 7; Meyer Eisenberg, "Statement of Anti-Defamation League on Federally Funded Security Services Provided by Affiliates of the Nation of Islam," in *Hearing before Committee on Banking and Financial Services, Subcommittee on General Oversight and Investigations*, U.S. House of Representatives, 2 March 1995.

44. George F. Will, "What School Choice Could Do in Milwaukee," *Washington Post*,

10 September 1995, sec. C, 7; John Norquist, " 'Choice' about Parental Power," *Wisconsin State Journal*, 26 February 1995, 2B.

45. Kimberly J. McClarin, "Court Bars Voucher Plan in Religious Schools," *New York Times*, 26 August 1995, sec. 1, 8.

46. John Chubb and Terry Moe, *Politics, Markets, and America's Schools* (Washington, D.C.: Brookings Institution, 1990), offers much statistical evidence on these tragic patterns.

47. James S. Coleman, *High School Achievement: Public, Catholic, and Parochial Schools Compared* (New York: Basic Books, 1982), 186–91.

48. Compare *Tilton v. Richardson*, 403 U.S. 672 (1971), with *Lemon v. Kurtzmann*, 403 U.S. 602 (1971).

49. *Lemon*, 403 U.S. at 622 ("[P]olitical division along religious lines was one of the principal evils against which the First Amendment was intended to protect. . . . [Debate over religious issues would] tend to confuse and obscure other issues of great urgency").

50. In *Aguilar v. Felton*, 473 U.S. 402 (1985), for example, the Court found that even allowing public school reading teachers to offer special remedial services in parochial schools would constitute excessive governmental "entanglement" with religion. It appears, however, that governmental fire departments will still be allowed to put out fires in religious schools. Only educational services to students in religious schools rattle the Court.

51. Albert Shanker, "Education Contract with America," *Wall Street Journal*, 15 September 1995, sec. A, 14.

52. *John Doe, Jr. v. Rockingham County School Board*, 658 F. Supp. 403 (W.D. Va. 1987). A recent study concludes that "the amount of litigation on the issue in recent years suggests continuing uncertainty as to precisely what process is due students facing possible expulsion." James W. McMasters, "Mediation: New Process for High School Disciplinary Expulsions," *Northwestern University Law Review* 84 (Winter 1990): 737. Twenty years ago, the cost of a formal proceeding for expulsion was calculated at about half the cost of a total year's education for one pupil. David Kirp, "Proceduralism and Bureaucracy: Due Process in the School Setting," *Stanford Law Review* 28 (May 1976): 859–60.

53. For recent endorsements of this view, see Jon Glass, "Separated, Boys and Girls May Learn Better; Controversial Approach Limits Intimidation, Classroom Distractions," *Virginian-Pilot* (Norfolk), 4 January 1995, sec. A, 1; Eric Wee, "School Board Approves Experiments; Same-Sex Classes to Expand," *Washington Post*, 4 May 1995, 6; Richard Rothstein, "Single Sex Schools: Why Ruin Good Experiments with Politics?" *Los Angeles Times*, 21 January 1996, sec. M, 6; Richard Cowen, "Experimental Class," *Record* (Bergen County, N.J.), 29 April 1994, sec. C, 1; Daniel Gardnswartz, "Public Education: An Inner City Crisis! Single Sex Schools: An Inner City Answer?" *Emory Law Journal* 42 (Spring 1993): 591; Sharon K. Mollman, "The Gender Gap: Separating the Sexes in Public Education," *Indiana Law Journal* 68 (Winter 1992): 149; "Note: Inner-City Single-Sex Schools: Educational Reform or Invidious Discrimination?" *Harvard Law Review* 105 (May 1992): 1741.

54. *Vorchheimer v. School District*, 532 F.2d 880 (3d Cir. 1976), upheld a *voluntary* program of single-sex high schools, but the ruling was upheld by only a 4–4 vote of the Supreme Court. 430 U.S. 703 (1977). A mandatory program of this kind was held unconstitutional in *United States v. Hinds School Board*, 560 F.2d 619 (5th Cir. 1977).

55. The suggestion was endorsed by President Clinton in his January 1996 State of the Union Address.

56. See, e.g., *Arnold v. Carpenter*, 459 F.2d 939 (7th Cir. 1972) (striking down school hair-code requirements); *Bannister v. Paradis*, 316 F. Supp. 185 (D.N.H. 1970) (striking down prohibition on dungarees); *Johnson v. Joint School District No. 60*, 508 P.2d 547 (Idaho 1973) (striking down requirement for girls to wear dresses).

57. *Stone v. Graham*, 449 U.S. 39 (1980).

58. *Wallace v. Jaffree*, 472 U.S. 38 (1985).

59. *Island Trees v. Pico*, 457 U.S. 853 (1982).

60. See, e.g., *Virgil v. School Board of Columbia City*, 677 F. Supp. 1547 (M.D. Fla. 1988) (upholding removal of works by Aristophanes and Chaucer from school curriculum); *Brown v. Woodland Joint Unified School District*, 27 F.3d 1373 (9th Cir. 1994) (upholding use of books on "witchcraft" and "voodoo" in school curriculum); *Delcarpio v. St. Tammany Parish School Board*, 865 F. Supp. 350 (E.D. La. 1994) (ordering school district to reverse policy under which it removed books on voodoo spells from school library); *Clayton v. Place*, 690 F. Supp. 850 (W.D. Mo. 1988) (ordering restoration of school dances, allegedly discontinued by school authorities based on religious objections to dancing).

61. Allan Gold, "Boston Schools Set to Overhaul Busing Policies," *New York Times*, 28 December 1988, sec. B, 6.

62. See *Missouri v. Jenkins*, 495 U.S. 33 (1995).

63. For a recent, quite accessible symposium of social scientists on the connections between welfare eligibility standards, family breakdown, and the culture of poverty, see "Sex, Families, Race, Poverty, and Welfare," *American Enterprise*, January 1995.

64. *C. K. v. Shalala*, 883 F. Supp. 991 (D.N.J. 1995) (denying motions for summary judgment).

65. *Goldberg v. Kelly*, 397 U.S. 254 (1970).

66. Wilson, "Crime in America." A similar suggestion by John DiIulio calls for government-sponsored "boarding schools," which "would be formally connected to churches and be frankly and unapologetically religious in character." He says, "Let perverted civil libertarians and others who have worked to prevent inner-city blacks from target-hardening their communities (erecting concrete barriers, metal detectors in high schools, automatically evicting drug dealers from public housing) scream bloody murder about the church-state issues this ostensibly poses." "White Lies about Black Crime," *Public Interest*, no. 118 (Winter 1995): 40.

67. Title IX, Education Amendments of 1972, codified at 20 U.S.C. § 1681 (1972); regulations governing "marital or parental status" (including "pregnancy and related conditions") at 10 C.F.R. § 1040.43 (1972).

68. See, e.g., *Andrews v. Drew School District*, 507 F.2d 611 (5th Cir. 1975) (striking down, on constitutional grounds, school-district rule against employing parents of illegitimate children); *Moore v. Board of Education of Chidester School District No. 59*, 448 F.2d 709 (8th Cir. 1971) (disallowing, on constitutional grounds, dismissal of teacher on grounds of unwed pregnancy); *Ordway v. Hargraves*, 323 F. Supp. 1155 (D. Mass. 1971) (overruling, on constitutional grounds, exclusion of unwed mother from regular attendance at public high school); *Perry v. Grenada Mun. School District*, 300 F. Supp. 748 (N.D. Miss. 1969) (overturning, on constitutional grounds, school-board policy excluding unwed mothers from admission to high school).

69. *Bowers v. Hardwick*, 478 U.S. 186 (1986).

70. *Romer v. Evans*, 116 S. Ct. 1620 (1996).

71. See, e.g., *Moore v. East Cleveland*, 431 U.S. 494 (1977) (overturning local ordinance restricting residency to "families" related by blood or marriage); *New Jersey Welfare Rights Organization v. Cahill*, 411 U.S. 619 (1973) (overturning statute limiting welfare benefits to families in which parents are "ceremonially married"); *U.S. Dep't of Agriculture v. Moreno*, 413 U.S. 508 (1973) (overturning federal statute excluding food stamp eligibility from households with unrelated individuals).

72. James Madison, *The Federalist, No. 62*, ed. Jacob Cooke (Middletown, Conn.: Wesleyan University Press, 1961), 421.

73. Ibid., *No. 63*, 428.

74. Ronald Dworkin, *Taking Rights Seriously* (Cambridge: Harvard University Press, 1977), 273.

75. Compare the decision granting standing to taxpayers complaining of governmental aid to religious schools in *Flast v. Cohen*, 392 U.S. 83 (1968), with subsequent denials of taxpayer standing to challenge any other sort of spending on the basis of any other putative constitutional restriction on spending, as, for example, in *United States v. Richardson*, 418 U.S. 166 (1974) (complaining of secret appropriations for the Central Intelligence Agency, contrary to the requirement in Article I, Section 9, that "a regular statement and account of . . . expenditures of all public money shall be published from time to time").

76. Opinion of Justices Souter, O'Connor, and Kennedy, *Planned Parenthood of Southeastern Pennsylvania v. Casey*, 505 U.S. 833, 851 (1992). It should be noted that this was not a throwaway line in a marginal decision. It was a central part of the argument by which the three centrist justices (all Reagan or Bush appointees) sought to put an end to ongoing national debate about abortion in what they themselves characterized as a decision of "rare importance."

77. For examples of all three positions, see David Richards, *Drugs, Sex, Death, and the Law: An Essay on Human Rights and Overcriminalization* (Totowa, N.J.: Rowan & Littlefield, 1982).

78. *Shapiro v. Thompson*, 394 U.S. 618 (1969) (holding that waiting period to go on welfare after moving to another state would deny "right to travel" to the indigent).

79. For one attempt to sketch the line from liberal opinion—through court rulings—to inner-city demoralization, see Myron Magnet, *The Dream and the Nightmare: The Sixties' Legacy to the Underclass* (New York: Morrow & Co., 1993).

7

The Politics of Clientele Capture

Civil Rights Policy and the Reagan Administration

HUGH DAVIS GRAHAM

This chapter uses the Reagan administration as a case study of national policymaking in the post-1960s American state. Specifically examined is the attempt by conservative Republican policymakers during Reagan's presidency to narrow the reach of federal civil rights enforcement. As a presidential candidate opposing Jimmy Carter in 1980, Ronald Reagan declared: "We must not allow the noble concept of equal opportunity to be distorted into federal guidelines or quotas which require race, ethnicity, or sex—rather than ability and qualifications—to be the principal factor in hiring or education."[1] The 1980 Republican platform criticized "bureaucratic regulations which rely on quotas, ratios, and numerical requirements to exclude some individuals in favor of others."

Reagan conservatives, claiming a national mandate that in 1981 gave Republicans control of the White House and the Senate and, consequently, effective control of appointments to the federal courts, objected to the expansion since 1964 in all three branches of government of civil rights policies that privileged some Americans over others on the basis of traits they were born with. To conservatives, the development during the 1970s of affirmative action requirements based on minority preferences violated both the letter and spirit of the Civil Rights Act of 1964, which prohibited discrimination against any individual on account of race, national origin, or sex. Consequently the Reagan administration launched a counterattack to narrow the range of governmental intrusion in all three branches—the federal agencies, the judiciary, and the Congress. In the executive agencies, where White House control was greatest, Reagan conservatives replaced Carter appointees and attempted to limit the authority of Washington bureaucrats over business firms, state and local governments, and educational institutions. In the federal courts, Justice Department officials held that the Constitution was color-blind and required equal treatment of all citizens irrespective of their race or ethnicity. In the legislative branch, the Reagan White House asked Congress to loosen Washington's regulatory grip not only over airlines, trucking, and banking—a policy of economic deregulation begun by the Carter administration—but also over employers burdened by affirmative action requirements in hiring and promotions. By the end of the 1980s, when President Reagan left office, the results were mixed, but most of Reagan's counteroffensive had been defeated.[2]

This chapter examines civil rights policies during the Reagan presidency not to assess their efficacy in reversing policies inherited from the Carter administration but rather to illuminate the underlying structure of the American regulatory state as it relates to equality that developed following the Civil Rights Act of 1964. Despite internal divisions and policy ambivalence, the Reagan administration launched an ideological counterattack without precedent against the affirmative action regime built during the presidencies of Lyndon Johnson, Richard Nixon, Gerald Ford, and Jimmy Carter. As this list of presidents implies, the construction of a coherent system of race-conscious remedies was a bipartisan effort, with Nixon providing the breakthrough initiatives and Carter presiding over administrative consolidation. The Reagan assault against the affirmative action regime, like explosives detonated in searching for oil deposits, sent shock waves echoing through the substrata of government, the productive economy, and the institutions of civil society. Their refraction, viewed from the perspective of the late 1990s, clarifies foundation structures and fault lines in the new regulatory order that previously had remained hidden.

In the civil rights policies developed by the elected branches of government from the Civil Rights Act in 1964 to the election of a Republican congressional majority in 1994, one finds more policy continuity than change consequent to the Reagan revolution. The Reagan counterattack against the affirmative action regime was spirited, but it was overwhelmed by the deeper forces driving the tide of civil rights regulation during 1964–94. Behind the accumulation and clutter since 1964 of specific civil rights statutes, executive orders, court decisions, and agency regulations, three new developments in the American regulatory state combined to increase the power of the civil rights coalition and weaken the hand of conservative opponents. This chapter examines all three in the light cast by Reagan's battle against them.

The first was the expansion of public law litigation, a new form of policymaking pioneered by the National Association for the Advancement of Colored People (NAACP) in *Brown v. Board of Education.* In public law litigation, the policy process is driven not by elected and appointed government officials but instead by private, public-interest organizations (such as the NAACP). To force change, they sue government agencies (school boards, cabinet departments) on behalf of class-action clients (minority schoolchildren, people with disabilities) to win court-ordered remedies (school desegregation orders, minority-hiring directives). The second new development was a pattern of policy replication developed by Congress in the 1970s, a kind of legislative cloning process, whereby Congress copied the statutory language of Title VI of the Civil Rights Act of 1964, used by agencies during the Johnson and Nixon administrations to develop affirmative action programs for African Americans, and applied it to benefit new advocacy groups.

Third was a new pattern of clientele capture. Federal agencies created to deal with civil rights policy—for example, the Civil Rights Commission, the Equal Employment Opportunity Commission (EEOC), and new offices of civil rights regulation in the Departments of Justice, Labor, and Health, Education, and Welfare (HEW)—developed close coalition ties with benefiting clientele groups. Conservatives complained that regulatory agencies, like courts, should not be captured by advocacy groups that benefited from their decisions. These three paths of institutional development in civil rights enforcement were complex, gradual, and obscure. They were parallel and interdependent yet followed no blueprint. They depended so heavily on processes largely unknown to voters but familiar to insiders—lobbyists for advocacy groups, lawyers for public-interest law firms, policy entrepreneurs in legislative committees—that they were difficult for Reagan conservatives to attack through populistic appeals to voter resentment.

Civil Rights Regulation: The Carter Legacy

The minority-preference policies that most offended Reagan conservatives traced their origins to the affirmative action language attached to federal nondiscrimination requirements in the 1960s.[3] In 1964 the Civil Rights Act banned discrimination on account of race, and the Johnson administration, in enforcing Titles VI (contract compliance) and VII (job discrimination), avoided minority preferences. In the wake of the urban riots of 1965–68, however, the Nixon administration shifted the emphasis of equal employment policy to minority-conscious remedies. Most controversial was the Philadelphia Plan of 1969, which attacked labor union discrimination by requiring proportional representation of workers in federally assisted construction projects. By 1972 federal agencies were enforcing a new regimen of civil rights regulation in contract compliance keyed to the "adverse impact" standard championed by the Leadership Conference on Civil Rights.[4] This standard prohibited any employment test or job requirement, such as a high school diploma, that produced a disproportionately negative impact on minorities unless the test or requirement was justified by employers as a business necessity.

During the 1970s, presidents of both parties in the White House cooperated with Congress in an additive process that extended the remedies designed for African Americans to a widening array of mobilized rights-based groups, including women, Hispanics, Asians, Native Americans, people with disabilities, and the elderly. From 1977 to 1981 the Carter administration reorganized and enlarged the federal enforcement machinery, consolidating regulatory responsibilities and jurisdiction under a strengthened EEOC and Office of Federal Contract Compliance Programs (OFCCP) in the Labor Department.[5] During this period, moreover, an accumulation of appellate decisions under the Burger Court rationalized and codified the requirements of affirmative action enforcement.[6] By 1980 the Leadership Conference, widely respected for its lobbying effectiveness, defended the liberal legacy of the Warren and Burger Courts in civil rights policy as "settled law."[7]

The Reagan Counterattack against Civil Rights Regulation

In 1981 the Reagan administration inherited a maturing system of civil rights regulation. Given the margin of Reagan's victory over Carter, including Republican control of the Senate, the Reagan revolutionaries in 1981 planned sharp changes in civil rights policy. As conservative reformers, the Reagan revolutionaries faced three routes to changing regulatory policy: (1) changing priorities and procedures in the enforcement agencies; (2) changing the federal judges who interpreted the law and the Constitution; and (3) changing the law in Congress. The first route, changing enforcement leaders and policies, is the shortest and quickest, but successor regimes may find it easiest to reverse. Reagan was most successful, especially during his first term when Republicans controlled Senate confirmations, in appointing conservatives to senior posts in the regulatory and mission agencies.[8] Although environmental and consumer deregulation claimed priority under Reagan, the deregulatory campaign included civil rights components. But the well-organized civil rights coalition, contesting each initiative, exacted a high price for limited changes.

In pursuing the first route, which offered employers immediate administrative relief from affirmative action regulation, the Reagan administration was moderately successful in curbing civil rights regulation by the two main enforcement agencies—the EEOC, especially under the chairmanship of Clarence Thomas, and the obscure but more potent OFCCP in the Labor Department. Both agencies shifted enforcement emphasis from class-action proceedings to conciliation and lawsuits seeking make-whole relief for identified victims of discrimination. In both agencies the shift in regulatory strategy was accomplished not through formal, notice-and-comment procedures but through internal policy directives.[9] In addition, the administration slowed regulatory activity by cutting the agency budgets and by requiring agencies to obtain clearance from the president's Office of Management and Budget (OMB) before proposing regulations in the *Federal Register*. These measures, however, were inherently vulnerable to reversal by successor administrations. More significant was the prospect of changing the civil rights regulations administratively. In the Reagan presidency, this effort centered on revising Executive Order No. 11246, the Johnson directive of 1965 that Nixon had used in the Philadelphia Plan to authorize minority-preference requirements in governmental contracts.

The second pathway to conservative reform, changing the ideological makeup of the federal judiciary, was a high priority for the Reagan administration but one that offered the least immediate payoff. The third pathway, changing civil rights statutes in Congress, was the most difficult because Democrats retained large majorities in the House and because the Leadership Conference had built effective majority coalitions in both chambers.[10] The opportunity for change arose in 1984, partly as a consequence of Reagan's judicial appointments, when the Supreme Court's opinion in *Grove City College v. Bell* triggered a legislative battle that Reagan could not avoid and thus sought to turn to his own advantage.

The Campaign to Rewrite the Affirmative Action Executive Order

Reagan's smashing electoral victory in 1980 meant that rewriting the affirmative action order, at least theoretically, could be accomplished shortly after the inauguration—with the proverbial stroke of a pen. The drive to revise Executive Order 11246 was led by William Bradford Reynolds, assistant attorney general for civil rights, and supported by Edwin Meese III, White House counselor during Reagan's first term and, after February 1985, Reagan's attorney general. In January 1984 Reynolds, frustrated by the unwillingness of Labor secretaries Raymond J. Donovan (1981–85) and, after April 1985, William E. Brock III to abandon minority-preference policies inherited from the Carter administration, launched a major campaign to revise the executive order.[11] Meese, who chaired the Domestic Policy Council of the cabinet, won support for revising the executive order from Secretaries Donald Hodel (Interior), William J. Bennett (Education), and John Herrington (Energy) and from OMB director James C. Miller III.

Leading the cabinet-level opposition to rewriting Executive Order 11246 was Labor secretary Brock, whose department had risen in authority and esteem since 1965 largely on the strength of its status as the government's leading agency in contract compliance. Joining Brock in defending the affirmative action status quo within Reagan's cabinet were Secretaries George Shultz (State), James Baker (Treasury), Margaret Heckler (Health and Human Services), Elizabeth Dole (Transportation), and Samuel Pierce (Housing and Urban Development).[12] Brock's resistance stemmed partly from within the Labor Department bureaucracy, where the rights revolution of the 1960s and 1970s, by adding the Office of Federal Contracts (OFCC) in 1965 and the Occupational Safety and Health Administration (OSHA) in 1970, had transformed a once-feeble mission agency into a powerful, two-fisted engine of social regulation. Shultz, as Nixon's first Labor secretary, had led the campaign to adopt the Philadelphia Plan.[13] Dole and Heckler had political ties to organized women's groups; Pierce, the lone African American in Reagan's cabinet, was attentive to urban constituencies.

Resistance in Reagan's cabinet to changing the executive order had political as well as bureaucratic origins. It reflected Republican uneasiness over attacking affirmative action, reinforced by the reluctance of the nation's large employers to plunge into unknown legal waters.[14] The Associated General Contractors and the U.S. Chamber of Commerce supported Reynolds and his conservative battalion in the campaign for color-blind antidiscrimination enforcement. But the National Association of Manufacturers supported Brock. Big business, strongly Republican and supporting deregulation elsewhere, preferred the known routines of underutilization analysis and minority hiring requirements to the unknown perils of reverse-discrimination lawsuits.[15]

At a cabinet meeting on 22 October 1985, Brock mounted a stout defense against the revisionists. He argued that the Labor Department's goals were not quotas, that enforcement abuses inherited from the Carter years were being corrected administratively, and that a political war over affirmative action would damage Republicans in the 1986 and 1988 elections. Meese, a supporter of cabinet government, was unwilling to take directly to the president an issue on which his cabinet was so deeply divided. Nor was White House chief of staff Donald Regan, who screened President Reagan from the entire dispute. In March 1986 Reynolds released a report documenting alleged quota requirements from OFCCP correspondence with contractors. This action, however, only stiffened the resistance of Brock and his allies, who resented such intramural attacks from the Justice Department. When Congress recessed for the 1986 elections, Reynolds's campaign was dead.[16]

Appointing Conservatives to the Federal Courts

The second pathway to curbing affirmative action enforcement, appointing youthful conservatives to the federal courts, was a priority of the Reagan revolution. In his first year in the White House, Reagan appointed Sandra Day O'Connor, the first woman to sit on the high bench, to replace retiring Associate Justice Potter Stewart. In 1986, on the retirement of chief justice Warren E. Burger, Reagan won confirmation of William H. Rehnquist as Chief Justice and Antonin Scalia as associate justice. In 1987, Democrats regained control of the Senate and rejected Reagan's nomination of Robert H. Bork, a conservative he earlier named to the appellate court. Reagan subsequently won Senate confirmation for Anthony M. Kennedy to fill the vacancy created by the retirement of Justice Lewis F. Powell, Jr. By the end of his eight years in the White House, Reagan had filled 338 judgeships on the district and appeals courts—about half the total.[17]

The payoff, however, was slow in coming. Reagan's conservative judicial appointments did not turn the tide against the Warren Court legacy until after Reagan left the White House. Despite the claims of Reynolds in the Justice Department that the Supreme Court had confined affirmative action remedies to actual victims of illegal discrimination, the Court in a series of civil rights opinions during Reagan's second term continued by a narrow margin to support the claims of minority and female plaintiffs.[18] Conservatives were disappointed by the Supreme Court's unwillingness during the Reagan years to overturn liberal precedents, especially in constitutional interpretation, involving affirmative action, abortion rights, school prayer, and rights of the criminally accused. On certain statutory issues, however, the Supreme Court provided better leverage for attacking the growth of regulation from Washington.

The Storm over Grove City College

The third way for the Reagan administration to reduce civil rights regulation, changing the law itself, was opened unexpectedly in February 1984 by the Supreme Court in the *Grove City College* decision. The dispute began in 1977 when Grove City College, a private, coeducational institution in Pennsylvania dedicated to providing a liberal arts education within a Christian framework, refused to sign form 639A, an assurance of compliance sent by HEW officials. These were blank-check promises routinely required by contract-compliance officials, whether acting under the authority of Executive Order 11246, as in the Labor or Defense Department, or of Title VI, as in HEW's Office of Civil Rights (OCR), policing federal grants to colleges and universities or state and local governments. School officials who signed form 639A, for example, agreed to comply with Title IX of the Education Amendments of 1972 "and all applicable requirements imposed by or pursuant to the Department's regulation" to the end that "no person in the United States shall, on the basis of sex, be . . . subjected to discrimination under any education program or activity for which [it] receives or benefits from Federal financial assistance from the Department."[19]

Jealous of its independence from public authorities, Grove City College had never accepted financial assistance from the government, including direct student tuition grants and loans that most American colleges and universities routinely processed through their financial aid offices. Grove City College did, however, enroll students who themselves obtained tuition grants from government offices or loans from banks with government guarantees.[20] Faced with Grove City College's refusal, federal education officials in 1978 obtained from an administrative law judge an order suspending all aid to Grove City students. The college and four students whose aid was terminated (two women and two men) then filed suit against HEW secretary Patricia Roberts Harris.[21] Throughout the six-year process of trial and appeal, all courts rejected Grove City's contention that indirect aid through students did not constitute federal financial assistance and hence did not bring the college under OCR regulations. The courts disagreed, however, on whether the "education program or activity" losing federal funds was the entire college or only the program receiving the aid—in Grove City's case, the financial aid office.[22]

Grove City College appealed to the Supreme Court, which decided the case on 28 February 1984. Agreeing with Solicitor General Rex Lee of the Reagan administration, the Court in a 6–3 opinion upheld the circuit court ruling that indirect aid triggered Title IX coverage and that the department could terminate the students' tuition grants.[23] But the majority in *Grove City* rejected the view, previously supported by U.S. government officials but not by Reagan's solicitor general, that the entire college was the "education program or activity" receiving the federal financial assistance. By ruling in *Grove City* that indirect aid triggered institutional coverage but that aid to one program did not bring entire institutions under regulation, the Supreme Court in 1984 expanded the reach of Title IX regulations to virtually every school and college in the country, while limiting its effect to the particular educational program aided.

The victory for the Reagan Justice Department in *Grove City* prompted a great outcry from the civil rights coalition. The Leadership Conference on Civil Rights, speaking for 165 member organizations, took the lead in coordinating a bipartisan congressional drive to overturn *Grove City* legislatively, attacking the decision as a radical shift that reversed twenty years of enforcement practice under the Civil Rights Act. Liberal critics claimed that *Grove City* stripped away federal protections against discrimination in campus departments of history or athletics because they did not receive earmarked federal aid. In June 1982 the Democratic-controlled House easily passed a bill (by a vote of 375–32) stipulating that a dollar of federal assistance to any program brought the entire institution under federal regulatory control. But a parallel bill remained stalled in the Republican-controlled Senate when the 98th Congress adjourned for the elections of 1984.[24]

Early in 1985 a split developed within the civil rights coalition over the obligation of educational institutions to include abortion services in their medical care coverage. The U.S. Catholic Conference of Bishops, a pillar of the coalition when the rights of racial and ethnic minorities were at issue, opposed any legislation that might extend abortion rights coverage to Catholic hospitals and educational institutions. As a result, neither chamber could pass a bill that the civil rights coalition called a "restoration" bill. In January 1988, with the reluctant concurrence of the Leadership Conference, the Senate accepted an amendment by Republican John Danforth of Missouri that nullified existing regulations requiring educational institutions to provide abortion as well as pregnancy and childbirth services under health insurance and leave policies. This compromise, though opposed by the National Organization of Women (NOW), defused the abortion issue sufficiently to permit passage by both houses in 1988 of the Civil Rights Restoration Act.

Reagan, claiming that the bill greatly extended the reach of civil rights regulation before *Grove City* rather than merely restoring it, vetoed the bill. In this claim Reagan was partly correct. Under the guise of "restoration," the Leadership Conference and its allies in Congress had broadened the scope of federal regulation. The Grove City bill narrowed exemptions involving religious schools and smaller businesses, for example, and extended to the housing industry a presumption of governmental regulatory jurisdiction. For four years the Reagan administration and its congressional allies, led in the Senate by Republican Orrin G. Hatch of Utah, marshaled a parade of horribles to discredit the Grove City bill. White House aide Michael Horowitz, one of the more creative of the conservative alarmists, warned that under the Restoration Act, farmers and ranchers receiving agricultural subsidies, churches and synagogues running day-care centers, and mom-and-pop grocers participating in the food stamp program would all fall under the boot heel of civil rights bureaucrats.[25]

Voters, however, remained unmoved by and uninterested in conservative horror stories about abuses in federal contract compliance, argued in the arcane language of the *Federal Register*. In March 1988 Congress overrode the president's veto by margins humiliating to Reagan—73–24 in the Senate and 292–133 in the House.[26] Of the Senate's forty-five Republicans, twenty-one abandoned their president in the showdown over the Grove City bill.[27] The Reagan revolution, so effective in building majorities for new tax and defense policies, was swept aside by three deeper currents when challenging the post-1964 regulatory state.[28] The first of these, the development of public law litigation, was spawned by the civil rights revolution itself.

Public Law Litigation

Unlike traditional disputes in the civil law involving private parties, in public law litigation, advocacy groups sue the government on behalf of public-interest clients. As public-interest advocacy groups multiplied in the 1960s, courts were drawn deeply into the policymaking process, often trumping the decisions of elected officials. Appointed judges, sheltered from political pressures associated with raising and spending tax funds, offered quick results. Public law litigation exploded during the 1970s, led by race-centered lawsuits like the *Adams* suit over school desegregation. In *Adams* a federal district judge in Maryland for twenty years negotiated school desegregation regulations between the OCR, an expanding list of plaintiffs and intervenors, and state and local officials representing thousands of school districts and higher education systems. Begun by the NAACP Legal Defense and Educational Fund (LDF) in 1970, the *Adams* case soon drew in the Mexican American Legal Defense and Education Fund (MALDEF), the Women's Equity Action League (WEAL), and other public-interest organizations. In addition to civil rights constituencies—racial minorities, women, language minorities, children, people with disabilities, the elderly—*Adams* in its remarkable twenty-year lifespan included public-interest plaintiffs suing on behalf of environmental protection, consumer rights, workplace and transportation safety, and other causes.

Public law litigation pulled the courts into ongoing policy negotiations between plaintiffs' lawyers, federal and state mission agencies, federal regulatory agencies, and trial judges. Presidential control of executive agencies, weakened by the thickening of bureaucracy that accompanied the growth of government programs following World War II, was further weakened by the encroachments of courts, where court-ordered injunctions and court-approved consent decrees bound agencies and preempted presidential authority. Lawsuits like *Adams*, lasting far longer than any presidency, limited the ability and often the willingness of agency officials to follow the president's policy directives.

In such a closed, expert-oriented process, voter awareness is curtailed and public accountability is blurred. In recent studies of the *Adams* case, viewed from different perspectives by political scientist Stephen Halpern and historian William A. Link, presidents, congresses, and cabinet secretaries come and go, remote from the quadrilateral bargaining between plaintiffs' lawyers, enforcement officials in federal agencies, state and local government officials, and federal district judges.[29] Such an insider game, following paths forged by the LDF, MALDEF, the American Civil Liberties Union, Nader's Raiders, the Environmental Defense Fund, and similar organizations, offered little leverage during the 1970s and 1980s for conservatives attempting to shift the direction and shrink the control of government.

Cloning Title VI

A second source of advantage for the civil rights coalition was the congressional practice, adopted quietly during the 1970s, of using the contract-compliance language of Title VI, originally designed for African Americans, to provide similar, adverse impact remedies for other rights-based groups. By the end of the 1960s the OCR, backed by federal courts, had demonstrated the leverage provided by cross-cutting regulations. These rules obliged recipients of federal dollars for whatever purpose (antipoverty, clean water, school lunches) to comply with regulations serving other purposes (school desegregation, bilingual education, birth-control counseling). The effectiveness of the Title VI model of cross-cutting regulation in winning impressive gains in employment and education for racial and ethnic minorities was not lost on the leaders of other movements, most notably feminist groups, people with disabilities, and the elderly. By 1975 advocacy groups representing all four of these constituencies had persuaded Congress to borrow the language of Title VI and apply it to their own regulatory needs.[30]

Feminist groups such as NOW and WEAL, having persuaded President Johnson in 1967 to include sex discrimination in the executive order program enforcing Title VI, won similar inclusion of women from the OFCC in its Revised Order No. 4 in 1971. In 1972 Congress by voice vote passed Title IX, amending the education statutes to bar federal financial assistance to any educational program or activity that practiced sex discrimination. The following year, 1973, Congress in section 504 of the Rehabilitation Act reshaped the familiar language of Title VI to read as follows: "No otherwise qualified handicapped individual in the United States shall, solely by reason of his handicap, be excluded from participation in, be denied the benefits of, or be subject to discrimination under, any program or activity receiving Federal financial assistance."[31] In the Age Discrimination Act of 1975, Congress again borrowed the language of Title VI and filled in the modifier blank with "age" discrimination.

These extensions of the Title VI device during the 1970s differed from the pioneering efforts of the 1960s in several respects. In each instance a far-reaching expansion of cross-cutting regulation occurred with little grassroots pressure from constituency movements, little attention in the media, little congressional debate, and little opposition. Working quietly with advocacy-group lobbies, policy entrepreneurs in Congress extended Title VI's cross-cutting formula to protect new groups, often "with virtually no discussion or debate about the similarities and differences in the forms of discrimination faced by different groups and the types of remedies that might prove most effective in dealing with them."[32] Section 504 of the Rehabilitation Act, taken almost verbatim from Title VI and enacted without hearings, demonstrated an important difference between regulatory laws on behalf of civil rights constituencies (racial and ethnic minorities, women, the elderly, people with disabilities) and legislation governing other forms of social regulation (consumer fraud, health and safety, environmental protection).

In the detailed statutes governing the Enviromntal Protection Agency (EPA) or OSHA, for example, Congress stipulated precise standards for agency enforcement. In the protected-class extensions based on Title VI, on the other hand, Congress delegated wide discretion to the enforcement agencies. In section 504 of the Rehabilitation Act, for example, Congress surely did not mean what it appeared to say (that blind individuals could drive taxis as long as they were "otherwise qualified").[33] What section 504 *did* require would be decided later, mainly by staff lawyers in the OCR and the OFCC, working in consultation with disability rights organizations. By 1980 their regulations, following the path of federal aid, would cover every school system in the country, most colleges and universities, more than 200,000 private businesses and nonprofit organizations, and 23 million employees.

By the time Reagan entered the White House, the additive or cumulative model of civil rights regulation had built a muscular coalition of protected-class constituencies. The roster of the Leadership Conference, listing more than 165 member organizations, read like a Who's Who of organized African Americans, women,

Hispanics, labor unions, Protestant denominations, the Roman Catholic hierarchy, Jewish civic groups, disability rights organizations, and so on. The *Grove City* decision, and Reagan's legislative campaign to defend it, threatened and hence united them. In an inside-the-beltway contest like the Grove City contest, with the general public largely disengaged, victory went to the best organized coalition of interest groups. In that kind of competition, the Leadership Conference, led by the able Ralph Neas, had no peer.[34] By comparison, the organized interests supporting President Reagan—the U.S. Chamber of Commerce, the Associated General Contractors, the American Farm Bureau Federation, the National Apartment Association, the American Association of Bible Colleges—were badly outnumbered and outgunned.

The New Clientele Capture

The third institutionalized process advancing the regulatory agenda of the civil rights coalition was a new form of a traditional phenomenon—agency capture. The practice is as old as Jacksonian democracy, in which party patronage ruled the civil service and mission agencies were expected to cater to the needs of their organized constituencies—farmers, veterans, laborers, educators, businesspeople. Federal regulatory agencies, however, unlike traditional mission departments, were designed by reformers to remain independent and represent the public interest. In the original, pessimistic model of capture, developed from studies of the independent regulatory agencies created by the progressives and the New Dealers, the industries to be regulated—railroads, shippers, airlines, broadcasters, and power companies—tended to win control of the commissions or boards designed to regulate economic behavior in the public interest. In the new civil rights regulation of the 1960s, however, capture took a different twist. Routinely, newly created regulatory offices, such as the EEOC, OCR, and OFCC, were dominated not by the employers and organizations being regulated but by representatives of the constituencies being served. Redistributionist policies enforced by the new regulatory agencies for civil rights would benefit the protected-class designees—African Americans in the 1960s and Latinos, women, people with disabilities, and other groups in the 1970s.[35]

By time-honored practice in American government, interest groups have sought a dominant voice in programs and agencies that affect their welfare—farmers in the Department of Agriculture, veterans in Veterans Affairs, ranching, mining, and timber interests in Interior, unions in Labor, and small business in Commerce. What was new about the social regulation of the 1960s and 1970s, however, was that the benefits of affirmative action affected the entire economy and hence all government departments, not just targeted program sectors. The legislation of 1964–68 mandating equal opportunity in a society deeply rooted in discriminatory norms had made civil rights enforcement a rapid growth field. In 1970 the civil rights bureaucracies in Washington included the Civil Rights Division (including its Voting Rights Section) in the Justice Department; an independent investigatory commission, the Civil Rights Commission; an independent regulatory commission, the EEOC; twenty-seven contract-compliance offices in the mission agencies, including most notably the OFCC in Labor and the OCR in HEW; and the Office of Minority Business Enterprise (OMBE) in the Department of Commerce. Outside the Washington bureaucracy and its regional outposts were overlapping layers of equal opportunity offices in state, county, and municipal jurisdictions; in public school districts and higher education systems; in foundations and nonprofit organizations; and in large business and professional firms.

The simple-capture notion has always lent itself to caricature and misuse. Of particular significance, one of the most striking changes in the politics of policy and regulation in the post-1964 era was seen in the schizophrenic behavior of capture in the new social regulation. In the 1970s the pessimism of liberal reformers over agency capture and regulatory decay gave way to optimism that the new social regulation was structurally resistant to capture. The new agencies of environmental and consumer protection did not seem threatened by capture. But in a development that has not received sufficient scholarly attention, the civil rights component of the new social regulation diverged from this trend. The explanation for this difference between civil rights regulation on the one hand and environmental, consumer, and safety regulation on the other lies in the way outside interests are arrayed in the political environment. In James Q. Wilson's analysis of the politics of regulation, the political environment surrounding most forms of environmental, consumer protection, and transportation safety regulation is characterized by widely distributed benefits (clean air and water, safe drugs and highways) and narrowly concentrated costs (pollution abatement equipment, toxic waste disposal, air-bag requirements).[36] This kind of regulation is popular with consumers and voters, but its concentrated costs bring strong resistance from regulated industries hostile to its goals. In social regulation of occupational health and safety, in which both costs and benefits are highly concentrated, agencies such as OSHA are subject to competing pressures from rival interest groups—organized labor seeking expensive improvements in the workplace environment and business firms resisting costs not tied to productivity. In these political environments, agency capture by regulated interests is difficult. Regulation cuts widely across industrial sectors (environmental protection, pure food and drugs, transportation safety) or rival interests (business, labor) to keep the agency erect (OSHA, National Labor Relations Board).

In modern civil rights regulation, however, benefits (jobs, promotions, admissions, contract set-asides) are narrowly concentrated among protected-class clienteles (racial and ethnic minorities, women, people with disabilities) while costs are widely distributed. Agencies in this environment face a dominant interest group or coalition of advocacy groups favoring its goals. Wilson calls this pattern *client* politics. It is long familiar to us in the folklore of economic regulation, in which regulated industries (railroads, shippers, airlines, motor carriers) captured "client agencies" (Interstate Commerce Commission [ICC], Civil Aeronautics Board [CAB], Federal Communications Commission). The mechanistic metaphors of agency capture and self-serving "iron triangles" linking agencies, legislative committees, and beneficiary groups have always oversimplified institutional and interest-group relationships, and space does not permit addressing that complexity here. Nonetheless, the deregulation movement of the late 1970s built a formidable empirical case against the cozy environment of client protection found at agencies like the CAB and the ICC. Similarly, by the 1970s, clientele groups representing the interests of minorities, women, and people with disabilities (the NAACP, MALDEF, NOW, WEAL, the American Coalition of Citizens with Disabilities) lobbied intensely and effectively to shape the regulatory agenda of agencies like the EEOC, OFCC, OCR, Voting Rights Section in the Justice Department, Office of Bilingual Education and Minority Language Affairs, and their counterpart agencies in thousands of federal, state, county, and municipal governments.

The political power of advocacy groups within the civil rights enforcement agencies, backed by the lobbying of the Leadership Conference in Congress and generally supported by the federal courts into the middle 1980s, pushed the agencies to adopt aggressive compliance standards. The OCR's desegregation guidelines, the OFCC's affirmative action program, the EEOC's guidelines on employee selection procedures and race-normed test scores, and the Justice Department's standards for "minority-majority" electoral districts highlight the power of civil rights interests over executive agencies. Agencies such as the OCR, whiplashed between aggressive clientele groups, congressional oversight committees, federal courts in semipermanent lawsuits like the *Adams* case, the political pressures of election campaigns, and shrinking budget resources, often had difficulty pleasing any constituency.[37] Nonetheless, the success of the civil rights coalition in controlling the legislative agenda during the Reagan and Bush administrations, reversing in Congress the Supreme Court's restrictive statutory rulings—in *Grove City College v. Bell* as well as in significant voting rights and employment discrimination decisions[38]—testifies to the advantages of the client model in the politics of regulation.

1994: End of a Thirty-Year Era?

The passage of the Civil Rights Act of 1991 and the election of Bill Clinton in 1992, returning the presidency and Congress to Democratic control in 1993, suggested for a season that the post-1964 regime of rights regulation had weathered the counterattack of the Reagan years.[39] Indeed, in the congressional elections of 1994, the Republican "Contract with America," a ten-point credo of conservative policy goals, nowhere mentioned civil rights. Then came the earthquake of 1994: insurgent Republicans led by House minority leader Newt Gingrich won control of Congress; California voters, resenting the burden of immigration entitlements in a deteriorating economy, passed Proposition 187; Republican leaders with records supporting affirmative action, most notably Senate majority leader Bob Dole and California governor Pete Wilson, attacked minority-preference programs. Equally significant, a conservative majority on the Supreme Court shocked the civil rights coalition in 1995 by narrowing federal minority set-aside programs (*Adarand Constructors, Inc. v. Pena*) and racial gerrymandering in legislative districts (*Miller v. Johnson*).

With hindsight we can see premonitory symptoms of the conservative revolt of the mid-1990s. In 1985, Democratic pollster Stanley Greenberg reported growing disaffection in Michigan among white working-class voters over minority job preferences. Subsequent national surveys by Gallup, ABC News–*Washington Post*, the

University of Michigan's Institute for Social Research, the *New York Times*, and NBC News–*Wall Street Journal* showed growing resentment of affirmative action among whites of both sexes.[40] In *The Scar of Race*, Paul Sniderman and Thomas Piazza found whites by increasing margins supporting not only antidiscrimination policies but also governmental programs to provide income, services, and training to improve the economic and social circumstances of blacks. But on issues of school busing for racial balance and affirmative action preferences, white Americans of both sexes were massively opposed.[41]

Resentment of group-based preference policies was fanned by economic stress—falling real wages, polarizing income distribution, declining job security—and by massive immigration. Following the family reunification reforms of 1965, 25 million immigrants came to the United States. Three quarters of them were from Latin America or Asia and hence qualified under many affirmative action programs for protected-class status on the basis of ancestry. During the 1970s and 1980s the Small Business Administration, for example, in its 8(a) program of subsidized loans and grants, approved minority-preference status for individuals on the basis of ancestry from Indonesia, Sri Lanka, India, Pakistan, China, and Japan, ethnic communities whose history in the United States varies widely but whose average family income and education by the 1990s considerably exceeded that of "white" families.[42]

It is too early to draw conclusions about the direction of change in the mid-1990s. Conservative majorities on the Supreme Court and Republican majorities in Congress are changing the ground rules that governed the 1964–94 era. President Clinton, reelected in 1996, was the first Democrat reelected to the White House since Franklin Roosevelt. Yet his campaign featured issues and proposals (family values, free trade, welfare reform, balancing the budget, policing crime) previously emphasized by Republicans.

We can begin to draw conclusions, however, about the dynamics of the era that seems to be passing. Paradoxically, as the power of the civil rights coalition and the security of affirmative action programs increased, the perceived legitimacy of minority-preference remedies decreased. As the civil rights coalition grew by extending protected-class status to an expanding array of advocacy groups, it purchased insider bargaining power at the price of weakening public claims to fairness. The tension between power and legitimacy thus produced a kind of equilibrium cycle. By populating the federal judiciary with a generation of young conservatives, Reagan and Bush ultimately transformed the face of civil rights enforcement. Reagan's civil rights counterrevolution, however, did not bring with it a fundamental change in policies and programs. As a result, the Reagan revolution did little to deflect the shift of civil rights regulation from individual to group-based claims during 1964–94.

NOTES

1. Quoted in Gary L. McDowell, "Affirmative Inaction: The Brock-Meese Standoff in Federal Racial Quotas," *Policy Review* 48 (Spring 1989): 32.
2. Norman C. Amaker, *Civil Rights and the Reagan Administration* (Washington, D.C.:

The Urban Institute Press, 1988); Robert R. Detletsen, *Civil Rights under Reagan* (San Francisco: Institute for Contemporary Studies, 1991).

3. Hugh Davis Graham, *The Civil Rights Era: Origin and Development of National Policy, 1960–1972* (New York: Oxford University Press, 1990); Hugh Davis Graham, "Race, History, and Policy: African-Americans and Civil Rights since 1964," *Journal of Policy History* 6 (1994): 12–39.

4. Hugh Davis Graham, "Richard Nixon and Civil Rights: Explaining an Enigma," *Presidential Studies Quarterly* 26 (Winter 1996): 93–106.

5. U.S. Commission on Civil Rights, *The Federal Civil Rights Enforcement Budget: Fiscal Year 1983* (Washington, D.C: Government Printing Office, 1982), 14–54.

6. See Paul Brest, "Race Discrimination," *The Burger Court: The Counter-Revolution That Wasn't*, ed. Vincent Blasi (New Haven: Yale University Press, 1983), 113–31.

7. Michael Pertschuk, *Giant Killers* (New York: Norton, 1986), 148–80.

8. Jeremy Rabkin, "The Reagan Revolution Meets the Regulatory Labyrinth," in *Do Elections Matter?* ed. Benjamin Ginsberg and Alan Stone (Armonck, N.Y.: M. E. Sharpe, 1986), 221–39.

9. See Alfred W. Blumrosen, *Modern Law: The Law Transmission System and Equal Opportunity* (Madison: University of Wisconsin Press, 1993), 267–74.

10. Although Republicans gained 33 House seats in the 1980 elections, Democratic majorities in the 97th Congress (1981–83) were 243–192 and in the 98th Congress (1983–85), 269–165.

11. James C. Miller III to Orrin G. Hatch, 14 September 1981, White House Office files (WHORM), HU 011-12, Ronald Reagan Library (RRL), Simi Valley, Calif.; Augustus F. Hawkins to the President, 16 October 1984, WHORM PE 002, RRL; William Bradford Reynolds to Mayor W. Wilson Goode, 12 December 1985, WHORM HU 010, RRL; memo, Ralph G. Neas to members of the press, "Update on the Executive Order on Affirmative Action," 15 February 1986, Leadership Conference on Civil Rights Papers (LCCRP), Manuscript Division, Library of Congress, Washington, D.C.

12. *Newsweek*, 30 December 1985; Daniel Seligman, "It Was Foreseeable," *Fortune*, 22 July 1985; McDowell, "Affirmative Inaction," 32–37.

13. Hugh Davis Graham, *Civil Rights and the Presidency* (New York: Oxford University Press, 1992), 150–69.

14. Memo, Mel Bradley to Jack Svahn, 23 October 1984, WHORM PE 002, RRL; memo, John G. Roberts to Diana G. Holland, 10 April 1986, WHORM PQ 341, RRL.

15. Daniel Seligman, "Affirmative Action Is Here to Stay," *Fortune*, 19 April 1982; Anne B. Fisher, "Businessmen Like to Hire by the Numbers," *Fortune*, 16 September 1985; Steven A. Holmes, "Affirmative Action Plans Are Part of Business Life," *New York Times*, 22 November 1991.

16. Memo, Robert M. Kruger to Peter J. Wallison, 7 April 1986, Kruger files OA 18389, RRL.

17. Walter F. Murphy, "Reagan's Judicial Strategy," *Looking Back on the Reagan Presidency*, ed. Larry Berman (Baltimore: Johns Hopkins University Press, 1990), 207–37.

18. Neal Devins, "Affirmative Action after Reagan," *Texas Law Review* 68 (December 1989): 353.

19. *Grove City College v. Bell, Secretary of Education*, 465 U.S. 555, 560–61 (1984).

20. At the time of the suit, Grove City College enrolled approximately 2,200 students, 140 of whom received federal tuition grants and 342 of whom had obtained federally guaranteed (and interest-subsidized) tuition loans. All parties to the Grove City dispute agreed that the college, half of whose students were women, had not engaged in discrimination by sex, race, or any other form prohibited by federal or state law.

21. *Grove City College v. Harris*, 500 F.Supp. 253 (W.D. Pa. 1980).

22. *Grove City College v. Harris*, 687 F.2d 684 (1982).

23. *Grove City College v. Bell*, 465 U.S. 555 (1984).

24. Robert Pear, "Bill Draws Criticism from Administration," *New York Times*, 23 May 1984; Nadine Cohodas and Janet Cook, "Civil Rights Bill Approved by Two House Committees," *Congressional Quarterly Weekly Report*, 26 May 1984, 1229; Spencer Rich, "Administration Accused of Trying to Sidetrack Key Rights Bill," *Washington Post*, 14 August 1984.

25. See, e.g., memo, Mike Horowitz to David Stockman et al., 4 May 1984, Christena Bach files, OA 12739, RRL.

26. Mark Willen, "Congress Overrides Reagan's Grove City Veto," *Congressional Quarterly Weekly Report*, 26 March 1988, 774–76; Courtney Leatherman, "Congress Overrides President's Veto of Civil Rights Bill," *Chronicle of Higher Education*, 30 March 1988.

27. Liberal Republicans, though shrinking in numbers, were prominent supporters of the Civil Rights Restoration Bill. Senators Lowell P. Weicker (Connecticut) and Bob Packwood (Oregon) joined Democrat Edward Kennedy as cosponsors. Robert Dole of Kansas, Senate majority leader in the 99th Congress, campaigned against Reagan's Grove City policy from the outset, and Senator Pete Wilson of California voted to overturn Reagan's veto.

28. Charles O. Jones, *The Presidency in a Separated System* (Washington, D.C.: Brookings Institution, 1994), 140–43.

29. Stephen C. Halpern, *On the Limits of the Law: The Legacy of Title VI of the Civil Rights Act* (Baltimore: Johns Hopkins University Press, 1995); William A. Link, *William Friday: Power, Purpose, and American Higher Education* (Chapel Hill: University of North Carolina Press, 1995), 249–337.

30. U.S. Advisory Commission on Intergovernmental Relations, *Regulatory Federalism* (Washington, D.C.: ACIR, 1984), 70, 91. In 1970, Hispanic advocacy groups persuaded the OCR under its Title VI authority to issue the "May 25 Memorandum" requiring federally aided school districts to provide bilingual education plans. See Coleman Brez Stein, Jr., *Sink or Swim: The Politics of Bilingual Education* (New York: Praeger, 1986), 36–44.

31. Edward D. Berkowitz, "A Historical Preface to the Americans with Disabilities Act," in *Civil Rights in the United States*, ed. Hugh Davis Graham (University Park: Pennsylvania State University Press, 1994), 102–3.

32. U.S. Advisory Commission on Intergovernmental Relations, *Federal Regulation of State and Local Governments: The Mixed Record of the 1980s* (Washington, D.C.: ACIR, 1993), 9.

33. On section 504, see Richard K. Scotch, *From Goodwill to Civil Rights* (Philadelphia: Temple University Press, 1984); Edward D. Berkowitz, *Disabled Policy: America's Programs for the Handicapped* (New York: Cambridge University Press, 1987).

34. See letter, Benjamin L. Hooks and Ralph G. Neas to members of Congress, 25 April 1984, LCCRP. Among the more than 160 member organizations of the Leadership Conference were the NAACP, National Council of Churches, AFL-CIO, League of Women Voters, ACLU, National Urban League, United Auto Workers, NOW, American Jewish Congress, MALDEF, National Education Association, Children's Defense Fund, American Coalition of Citizens with Disabilities, National Catholic Conference for Interracial Justice, and American Council of the Blind.

35. James Q. Wilson, ed., *The Politics of Regulation* (New York: Basic Books, 1980); Michael Reagan, *Regulation: The Politics of Policy* (Boston: Little, Brown & Co., 1987).

36. James Q. Wilson, *Bureaucracy* (New York: Basic Books, 1989), 72–89; Wilson, *Politics of Regulation*, 357–94.

37. In a few celebrated instances (school desegregation guidelines for Mayor Richard

Daley's Chicago, school dress codes and hair-length codes, school-busing requirements for racial balance), OCR regulations were repudiated even by Democratic-controlled Congresses. In others (banning boys choirs and father-daughter school dinners), public ridicule forced bureaucratic retreat. See, e.g., Joseph A. Califano, *Governing America* (New York: Simon & Schuster, 1981), 219–26; Jeremy Rabkin, *Judicial Compulsions* (New York: Basic Books, 1989), 147–81.

38. *City of Mobile, Alabama v. Bolden*, 446 U.S. 55 (1980) (voting rights); *Grove City College v. Bell*, 465 U.S. 555 (1984); *Ward's Cove Packing Co. v. Antonio*, 109 S. Ct. 2115 (1989) (employment discrimination).

39. See, e.g., William C. Berman, *America's Right Turn: From Nixon to Bush* (Baltimore: Johns Hopkins University Press, 1994).

40. Seymour Martin Lipset, "Equal Chances versus Equal Rights," *Annals* 523 (September 1992): 63–74; Seymour Martin Lipset, "Affirmative Action and the American Creed," *Wilson Quarterly* (Winter 1992): 52–62.

41. Paul M. Sniderman and Thomas Piazza, *The Scar of Race* (Cambridge, Mass.: Belknap Press, 1993), 5.

42. George R. LaNoue, "Split Visions: Minority Business Set-Asides," *Annals of American Academy of Political and Social Science* 523 (September 1992): 104–16; George R. LaNoue and John C. Sullivan, "Presumptions for Preferences: The Small Business Administration's Decisions on Groups Entitled to Affirmative Action," *Journal of Policy History* 6 (1994): 439–67.

8

The Convergence of Black and White Attitudes on School Desegregation Issues

CHRISTINE H. ROSSELL

In its pursuit of racial equality in the schools in the four decades since *Brown v. Board of Education*, the civil rights leadership has made various assumptions about the attitudes and policy preferences of black and white parents. From 1968 to the present, the plaintiffs' attorneys initiated class-action suits on behalf of black students and their parents that demanded the achievement of racial balance throughout the school system by means of mandatory reassignments. In addition, the plaintiffs' attorneys argued that white opposition to mandatory reassignment should be ignored by the courts because it was caused by racism. Most federal district courts appear to have been convinced by these arguments since, from 1968 through 1981, they overwhelmingly ordered the implementation of the mandatory reassignment plans demanded by the attorneys who claimed to be representing the interests of black students and their parents. The opinion data offered in this chapter, however, show that these suppositions about the attitudes and opinions of black and white parents have been wrong and suggest that the civil rights establishment has not always reflected the views of its constituency. Contrary to popular belief, black attitudes toward mandatory reassignments are not very favorable and never have been. In addition, there is considerable evidence calling into question the assumption that white opposition to busing stems solely from racism. In short, the civil rights leadership's almost singleminded pursuit of mandatory reassignment plans in school desegregation litigation from the late 1960s through the early 1990s has either ignored or disregarded the attitudes of ordinary parents. It is thus time to rethink our policies on equality in education because, at least with regard to school desegregation, they have been out of sync with what black parents, and indeed parents of all races, actually believe and want for their children.

The Evolution of School Desegregation Plans

From 1954 to 1968, the criterion for convicting a school district of intentional segregation was the existence of government-mandated segregation, and the only remedy required was that states rescind their segregation laws and that school districts stop assigning children to schools solely on the basis of their race. Neighborhood schools were considered a legitimate desegregation tool because they were race neutral—that is, students were assigned to schools on the basis of their residence, not their race. In the *Brown* litigation, the court explained that although one of the schools in Topeka was "inhabited entirely by colored students, no violation of any constitutional right results because they are compelled to attend the school in the district in which they live."[1] Nevertheless, in the South of the 1950s, neighborhood schools were considered quite revolutionary and thus were fiercely resisted since they could result in black children attending the same school with white children.

As an alternative to race-neutral assignment policies such as neighborhood schools, school districts in the South during the 1950s and early 1960s adopted court-approved "pupil placement laws" and "freedom of choice" plans that were generally believed to be delaying tactics. If these devices were delaying tactics, they appear to have worked; southern schools remained racially imbalanced throughout most of the 1960s. Intellectuals and the courts believed this lack of integration was due solely to the coercion of blacks. It was simply taken for granted that most, if not all, blacks wanted to go to school with whites, even if it meant crosstown busing or other inconveniences. Civil rights advocates did not bother to ask black parents—the injured parties—if this was the remedy they wanted, nor did they question the assumption that busing would achieve more integration than neighborhood schools or any voluntary techniques.

The 1968 Supreme Court decision in *Green v. County Board of Education*[2] marks a watershed in southern desegregation plans because it required that school districts not only stop discriminating but also actually achieve integrated schools. As a result of this decision and subsequent court decisions—in particular the Supreme Court's 1971 decision in *Swann v. Charlotte-Mecklenburg Board of Education*,[3] which established the principle of racial balance and approved crosstown busing to achieve it—the public schools of the Deep South were substantially integrated between 1970 and 1972 by court orders that, at least on paper, reassigned students within a district so that the racial composition of each school was roughly equal to that of the school district as a whole. These plans, popularly called "forced busing," produced protests and white and middle-class flight of varying intensity in every school district in which they were implemented.

As a result of these unintended negative outcomes, by the mid-1970s courts began permitting a second type of voluntary desegregation plans that included such incentives as magnet schools. These magnet-voluntary desegregation plans allowed students to stay at their neighborhood schools if they chose to do so but tried to entice them to opposite-race schools by means of special programs called magnets. Typically, the options to transfer also included a majority to minority (M to M) transfer program in which any student in the school district could transfer from any school in which his or her race was in the majority to any school in which his or her race was in the minority.[4] In general, only minority students participated in the majority to minority program because even today whites will not voluntarily transfer to schools in minority neighborhoods without an incentive in the form of a magnet program.[5]

Controlled choice is the third of the three basic types of desegregation plans (mandatory reassignment, voluntary magnet, and controlled choice) implemented. Controlled-choice plans came into existence in the early 1980s as mandatory reassignment plans grew out of favor with the courts, other policymakers, and minority parents. The academics and policymakers who embraced controlled choice were those who remained uneasy over the freedom of parents in voluntary plans to keep their children in neighborhood schools. Controlled choice thus represents a compromise desegregation strategy partway between mandatory reassignment plans that reassign everyone and completely voluntary plans that allow students to remain in their neighborhood schools if they so desire.

The basic foundation of all controlled-choice desegregation plans is that, at a minimum, parents of entering students or those changing schools are *required* to rank a number of schools in the school system in order of preference and no one is guaranteed a neighborhood school or any other school. The school administration, while trying to give parents their first-choice school, reserves the right to assign students to any school it wants them to go to (typically one where their attendance will satisfy racial-balance requirements). Anywhere from 10 to 40 percent of students do not receive their first-choice school, and more important, many parents refuse to stick around to see if they get a good school assignment in the lottery. Thus, these same plans have produced significant white flight.[6]

The voluntary and controlled-choice plans are virtually the only new plans implemented in the last decade. Indeed, since 1981, only two new mandatory reassignment plans have been ordered by courts, both in Mississippi.[7] This dearth of mandatory reassignment plans has not been a retreat from school desegregation and the pursuit of equality in education, however, since there have been numerous desegregation plans implemented in the last decade and a half, and virtually every school district charged with intentional school segregation has been convicted. Rather, the lack of mandatory reassignment plans represents a retreat from one type of desegregation plan—the type that produces the most opposition and white flight.

Thus, school segregation remedies have almost come full circle. Although the voluntary plans implemented after *Brown* were considered ineffective because no whites ever transferred to black schools—prompting the courts to approve only mandatory reassignment plans from 1968 to 1975—these courts did occasionally point out that voluntary plans per se were not unconstitutional and were to be evaluated in terms of their results. When freedom of choice offered a *real* promise of achieving a unitary, nonracial system, there was no objection to it. What has changed in the years since *Swann* is the willingness of the courts to entertain the possibility that voluntary plans might ultimately achieve more integration at less social cost than mandatory plans. This shift in the courts is thus not a retreat from the principle of equality of education but a retreat from a strategy that came to be viewed as an inefficient and counterproductive means of achieving equality.

Attitudes toward Desegregation

Most people now agree that white attitudes toward desegregation strategies, like white behavioral response, appear to be influenced by two characteristics of plans: the extent of parental choice and the right to remain at one's neighborhood school. The plaintiffs arguing on behalf of mandatory reassignment plans, however, have assumed that these issues were *not* important to black parents. Indeed, with few exceptions, it has been an almost unquestioned assumption of intellectual writing and court opinions in the 1970s that black parents were demanding the mandatory reassignment plans that forced them out of their neighborhood schools to opposite-race schools across town. During this period, while almost universally ordering the plaintiffs' mandatory reassignment plans to be implemented, few courts questioned the plaintiffs' attorneys on whether black parents really wanted to abandon the race-neutral assignment policies of *Brown* for the race-conscious assignment policies of *Green* and *Swann*.

Attitudes on Principles

The *Brown* decision was made at a time when whites were evenly split on the principle of school integration. Only 50 percent believed that white and black students should go to the same school.[8] By 1963, one year before the Civil Rights Act, a clear majority of whites—64 percent—believed in the principle of integration. By 1982 fully 90 percent of whites believed in the principle of integration. By 1985 this belief had reached its peak of 93 percent, causing the National Opinion Research Center (NORC) to stop asking the question because there was so little variation on it. This broad white support for the principle of integration has continued since 1985.[9] One could easily believe that only the lunatic fringe—about 6 percent of the white population—is opposed to the principle of school integration.

This support for the principle of school integration is also true of blacks. Indeed, the only difference between blacks and whites on this issue is that blacks have always had high support for the principle of school integration, at least since they were first asked this question in a national poll in 1972. By 1991 there was only a 2 percentage point difference between whites and blacks in their attitudes toward school integration, with more than 90 percent of both blacks and whites supporting school integration. Thus, despite dire predictions of a resurgence of segregationist attitudes among blacks and whites, these data show no retreat on this principle.

Figure 8.1 elaborates on parental attitudes toward integration by demonstrating the willingness of parents to send their children to integrated schools of three different racial mixtures: a few blacks, half black, and majority black. Although in 1959 more than 70 percent of southern whites objected to sending their children to a school with a few blacks, in contrast to fewer than 10 percent of nonsouthern

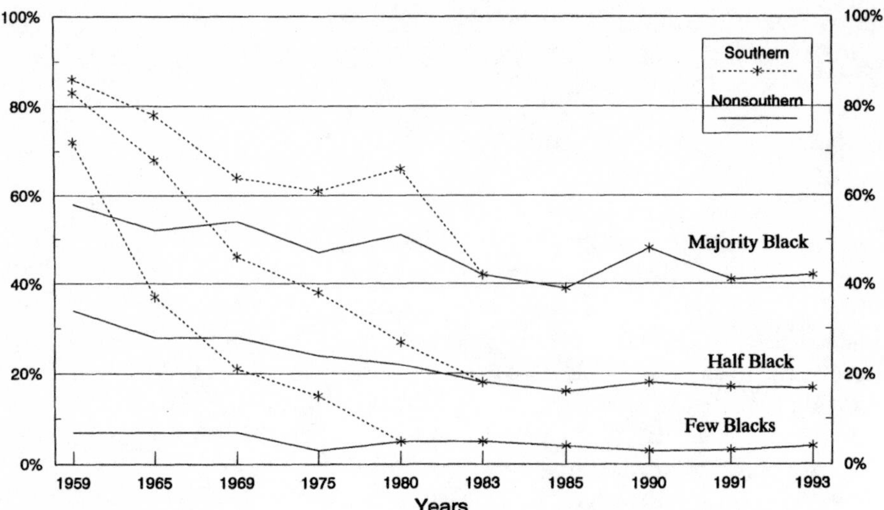

Sources: Gallup Polls, 1959–80, by region; NORC General Social Science Survey, 1983–93.
Note: No regional breakdown was available for NORC survey, 1983–93.

FIGURE 8.1. Percentage of Whites Objecting to Schools with a Few Blacks, Half Black Schools, Majority Black Schools

whites, by 1980 there was no regional difference and by 1993 only 4 percent of whites objected to sending their children to a school with a few blacks.[10]

In 1968 almost 85 percent of southerners and 35 percent of northerners objected to sending their children to a school that was half black. In 1980, the last year a regional breakdown was available, southerners were only 5 percentage points more likely than northerners to object to sending their children to a school that is half black. By 1993, only 17 percent of whites objected to sending their children to a school that was half black, despite the fact that nationally blacks are only 12 percent of the population.

The changes over time in white parents' willingness to send their children to an integrated school that is majority black are even more extraordinary. Although in 1968 almost 90 percent of southerners and 60 percent of northerners objected to sending their children to a school that was majority black, by 1980 there was only a 15 percentage point difference between southerners and northerners. By 1993, only 42 percent of whites objected to sending their children to a school that was majority black.

The national surveys can be criticized on the grounds that they are a random sample of adults, most of whom either do not have children or do not live in a school district with a sizable black population. Thus for many of these respondents, questions regarding the racial composition of a school they would be willing to send their children to are abstract or irrelevant.

Armor and Rossell conducted surveys of public school parents in school districts around the United States faced with adopting a school desegregation plan under court order.[11] The parent survey data, however, show similar results. From 1977 to 1991, on average, only 13 percent of white parents (4 percentage points fewer than in the NORC national survey) and as much as 5 percent of black parents objected to sending their children to their neighborhood schools if they became half black/Hispanic. Moreover, only 33 percent of white parents (8 percentage points fewer than in the NORC national survey) and as much as 14 percent of black parents objected to sending their children to their neighborhood schools if they became predominantly black/Hispanic.

Given the fact that this question taps issues of power and control, not just race, it is quite remarkable that a majority of white adults and white public school parents do not object to having their children in schools where their race is not in the majority as long as they are their neighborhood schools. It is also interesting that a 50–50 racial composition is more desirable to black parents than is a predominantly minority composition, although the increase in objection to a predominantly minority school is less than is the white increase in objection.

Thus, these data suggest that the civil rights movement has been extraordinarily successful in achieving its symbolic goals. Almost no one is upset if there are a few blacks in his or her child's school. The Little Rock crisis and others like it, in which angry white mobs protested a handful of black children entering their schools, are gone forever. More surprisingly, most white parents do not object to their children being in a racial minority in their neighborhood schools. Blacks are no longer "official pariahs" and racial prejudice in the old-fashioned sense is simply, for all but a tiny minority of whites and blacks, socially unacceptable. This change is a remarkable revolution in white attitudes that must be credited to the moral leadership of the civil rights movement.

Attitudes on Implementation Techniques

At the same time that racial intolerance and support for segregation were declining, however, post-*Swann* mandatory reassignment plans were producing an increase in white enrollment losses in the North from an average annual 2.4 percent loss before desegregation to a 10 percent loss with the implementation of a plan.[12] In the South, white enrollment losses increased from an average 0.8 percent loss predesegregation to a 7.5 percent loss with implementation of a plan.[13] The southern loss is even more dramatic because it occurred in the kinds of school districts thought to be most immune to white flight—countywide districts already encompassing the suburban areas to which whites would normally be expected to flee.

White flight is not inconsistent with white attitudes. Although whites support the principle of integration, they overwhelmingly oppose the most widely used method of desegregating schools—mandatory reassignment or "busing." The Institute for Social Research (ISR) at the University of Michigan asked the following question in 1972, 1974, 1976, 1980, and 1984:[14]

> There is much discussion about the best way to deal with racial problems. Some people think achieving racial integration of schools is so important that it justifies busing

children to schools out of their own neighborhoods. Others think letting children go to their neighborhood schools is so important that they oppose busing. Where would you place yourself on this scale, or haven't you thought much about this?

1. Bus to achieve integration (1–4)
2. Keep children in neighborhood schools (5–7)
3. Haven't thought much about this.

As shown in figure 8.2, the ISR survey demonstrates a consistent lack of support for busing to achieve integration on the part of whites—rarely greater than 10 percent—when the alternative is keeping children in their neighborhood schools. Black respondents are, however, not exactly supportive of the concept of busing to achieve integration. Indeed, they are clearly split on this issue with only a minority or a bare majority supporting mandatory reassignment. By 1984, only 40 percent of blacks supported busing for integration over neighborhood schools.

Figure 8.2 also shows the Armor and Rossell parent survey results for the years 1977, 1981, 1986, 1988, 1989, 1990, and 1991 in school districts considering desegregation plan alternatives. The question was worded differently from the ISR survey question in that parents were asked only whether they support a mandatory reassignment plan for their school districts. They were not asked to compare such a plan directly to neighborhood schools as in the ISR survey.[15] When black *parents* were asked about a mandatory reassignment plan for the school system in which their children were enrolled, however, there was, on average, about the same lack of support as in the ISR national surveys of black adults.

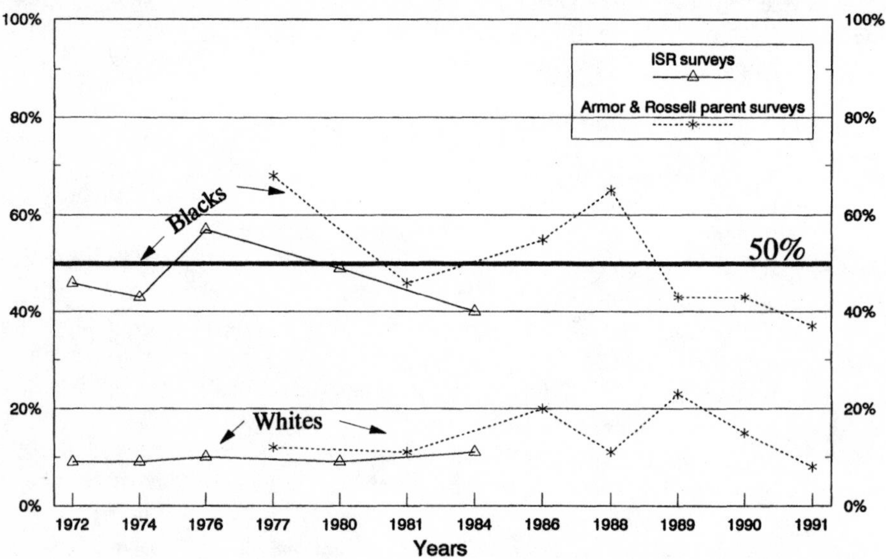

Sources: Institute for Social Research (ISR) surveys, 1972–84; Armor and Rossell district parent surveys, 1977–91.

FIGURE 8.2. Percentage Supporting Busing for Integration rather than Neighborhood Schools

The parent surveys generally show declining support for mandatory reassignment among black parents from a high of almost 70 percent in Los Angeles in 1977 to a low of less than 40 percent in Knox County, Tennessee, in 1991. The exception to this trend is the 65 percent support in Natchez, Mississippi, in 1988. In comparison to the national surveys, however, the low percentage in Knox County is only slightly lower than the percentages shown by the ISR surveys in every year except 1976. Therefore, black support for mandatory reassignment not only has declined since 1972 but also has rarely enjoyed majority support.

White support for mandatory reassignment shows a different trend. Although there is some fluctuation depending on the district or year, the level of white support for mandatory reassignment varies from 10 to 20 percent and there seems to be no trend over time as with black support.

As shown in figure 8.3, on average, black and white parents agree that the most desirable desegregation policy alternative for their districts is neighborhood schools with choice[16] followed by the redrawing of attendance zones of adjacent schools ("Change Zones").[17] What they least want for their children is a mandatory reassignment plan—although controlled choice has even less support among black parents. Interestingly, only a minority of parents of both races support controlled-choice plans, although they provide a lot of choice, perhaps because the plans do not guarantee children the right to attend their neighborhood schools or to be assigned to their first-choice schools.[18] Thus, the inclusion of choice and neighborhood schools explains not only white (and middle-class black) behavioral responses (e.g., protest and white flight) to school desegregation plans but also both black and white attitudinal support for desegregation alternatives.

Figure 8.4 shows the behavioral intentions of black and white public school

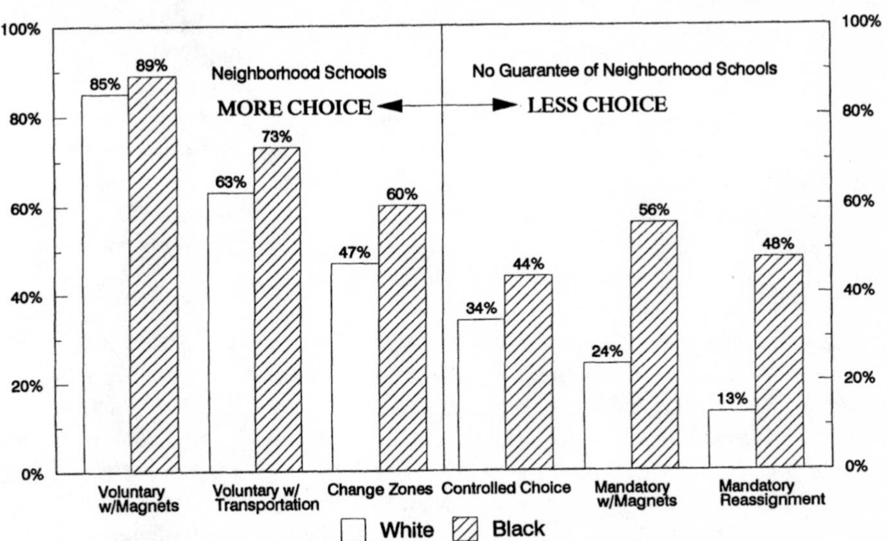

Sources: Armor and Rossell surveys, 1986, 1988, 1990, 1991; Armor survey, 1989.

FIGURE 8.3. Percentage of Parents Supporting Alternative Desegregation Plans

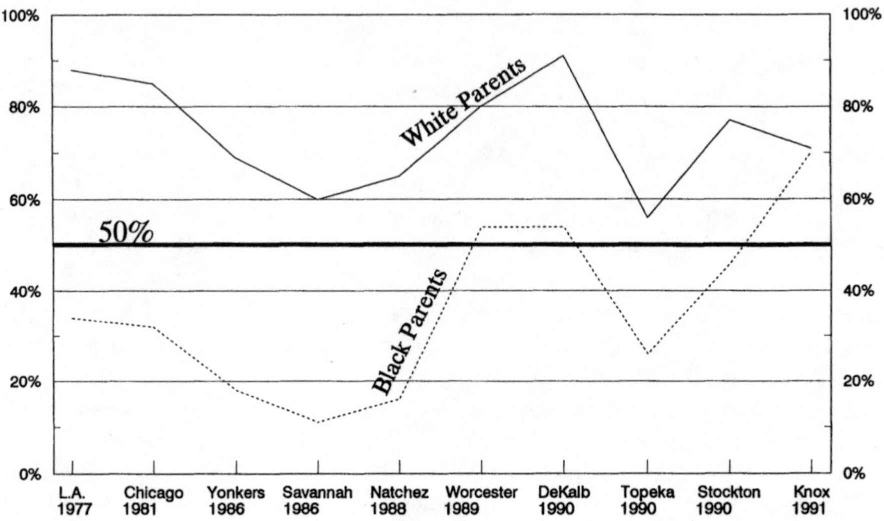

Sources: Armor surveys, 1977, 1981, 1989; Armor and Rossell surveys, 1986, 1988, 1990, 1991.

FIGURE 8.4. Percentage of Parents Not Going Along With Mandatory Reassignment of Own Child

parents if a mandatory reassignment plan were adopted in their school districts and their children were reassigned to an opposite-race school. The percentage of white parents who would not go along with a mandatory reassignment plan declines over time but increases for black parents until, by 1991 in Knox County, Tennessee (which at the time of the survey was about 85 percent white), 71 percent of white parents and 70 percent of black parents would not go along with a mandatory reassignment plan that assigned their children to an opposite-race school.

Even more surprising is the low willingness of black parents to transfer their children voluntarily out of their own schools to an opposite-race school, even when that school has a special magnet program. Given all of the publicity about the poor quality of black schools and the high level of support for neighborhood schools with magnets, it is surprising that only 33 percent of black parents, on average, would definitely choose to transfer their children to a magnet school in an opposite-race neighborhood.

These findings are, however, consistent with black parents' perceptions of the extent of racial "discrimination" in education that exists in their districts. On average, only 35 percent of black parents believe that black students get a worse education in their public schools than do white students.[19] Thus, contrary to the assumption of most of the court decisions of the 1970s and the academic writing on this subject, only a minority of black Americans support mandatory reassignment and a majority would not go along with a mandatory reassignment of their own children to an opposite-race school. Most black parents, like most white parents, prefer their neighborhood schools to being bused out to a school they did not choose, and even more surprising, a large majority of black parents prefer their neighborhood schools to a special school that they could choose, perhaps because most of them believe that black children are currently receiving an education that is at least as good as white children receive.

Given these survey results, it is not unreasonable to ask why the civil rights community has ignored black parents and their preferences. In "Serving Two Masters," Derrick Bell, a black law professor at New York University,[20] concludes that it is because the National Association for the Advancement of Colored People (NAACP) Legal Defense and Educational Fund (LDF), the major plaintiffs' attorney in school desegregation cases, have a conflict of interest. The LDF ignores its clients' preferences because it has to answer to the middle-class blacks and whites who provide financial support for the organization and who not only believe fervently in school integration but also believe in a kind of "domestic domino theory" in which failure on the busing issue would trigger a string of defeats in other civil rights arenas. Its local clientele, black parents, have little or no contact with the LDF once it has solicited them as plaintiffs for litigation. Ron Edmonds, another black educational expert and scholar, agrees with Bell on this point.[21]

Nathaniel Jones, NAACP general counsel, defends the group's behavior with the argument that "it would be absurd to expect that each and every black person should be polled before a lawsuit is filed, or a plan of desegregation is proposed."[22] In a private conversation, Jones said that he did not need to ask black parents about their preferences because he himself was black and could draw on his own life experiences.[23] But he cannot possibly know his clients' preferences, which is precisely the problem with class-action suits—lawyers are a highly educated, highly paid, elite group who, regardless of their origins, are not capable of knowing what their clients want without asking them.[24]

One watchdog group charges that the reason class-action suits often do not represent the preferences of the attorneys' clients is not just because of a conflict of interest but because of egotism. Class-action suits "have the capacity to provide large sources of narcissistic gratification . . . and the psychological motivations which influence the lawyer in taking on 'a fiercer dragon' through the class action may also underlie the tendency to direct the suit toward the goals of the lawyer rather than the client."[25]

Indeed, it is interesting to note that in the Chicago, Yonkers, Worcester (Massachusetts), and Stockton (California) cases, the legal counsel for the plaintiffs offered a mandatory reassignment plan supported by only a minority of black parents, and in none of the desegregation court cases in the school districts noted in Figure 8.4 did the plaintiffs' attorneys offer the plan most supported by black parents—a neighborhood school plan with magnets—despite being given the results of the parent surveys showing that the attorneys were not representing the preferences of their "clients."[26]

Explanations for Rejection of Busing and Acceptance of Integration

What accounts for the preferences of black and white parents, in particular the high level rejecting busing and supporting neighborhood schools? Unfortunately, because of the fascination with white racism in America and the disinterest of the intelligentsia in the opinions of ordinary black parents,[27] almost all of the research and writing have focused on an explanation for white attitudes and opinions.

Black Attitudes

I know of only a few social scientists, most notably Howard Schuman, Charlotte Steeh, and Lawrence Bobo[28] and Lee Sigelman and Susan Welsh,[29] who have even acknowledged, let alone analyzed, declining black support for mandatory reassignment and other governmental strategies for forcing racial equality in American society. Schuman, Steeh, and Bobo offer two hypotheses to explain this phenomenon. Their first hypothesis is that after the incredible energy blacks put into the civil rights movement of the 1960s, there had to be some ''natural falling away during the 1970s as the salience of these issues decreased.''[30] They see this decline as part of a cyclical psychological pattern—a burst of energy must be followed by exhaustion and alienation. Their second hypothesis is that some blacks may have retreated from the use of federal force for desegregation because of their perception that it was so intensely opposed by whites as to be impractical. In short, white opposition to busing and its resulting flight and protest, rather than blacks own preferences, may have caused the decline in black support.[31]

But Schuman, Steeh, and Bobo admit they find neither explanation satisfactory, and there is little evidence to support either hypothesis. At the very least, however, they believe the gap between blacks' support for the principle of school integration and their opposition to or conflict over *forcing* people to integrate can help us interpret white trends. They conclude: ''In their attitudes, as in their lives more generally, blacks and whites in the United States are inescapably connected in many ways, and these connections are easily missed when only one group is considered at a time.''[32] Sigelman and Welch agree that the fact that the rejection of busing occurred in tandem for whites and blacks makes it difficult to interpret it as an indication of growing prejudice against blacks. They argue there are some good reasons why black parents might reject busing. For one thing, it diverts attention from what is most important to them: the quality of education of their children. In addition, it is inconvenient, deprives black parents of choice, contravenes the principle of neighborhood schools, and may lower their child's self-esteem. ''Thus, many blacks have good reason to suspect that busing to integrate may harm their children.''[33]

White Attitudes

Two major theories of the determinants of political attitudes and behavior have been used to explain white opposition to busing. The first theory is that whites are motivated by diffuse attitudes formed in early childhood. In other words, racism explains white opposition to busing. This theory has been offered in several guises—one Schuman, Steeh, and Bobo[34] call ''superficial tolerance'' from the works of Mary Jackman,[35] and the other they call ''symbolic racism'' from the work of David Sears and his colleagues and John McConahay.[36]

Jackman's "superficial tolerance" theory argues that the "implementation" questions demonstrate a genuine commitment to integration, whereas the "principle" questions show only a superficial commitment to integration. The problem with her argument, however, is that it ignores the fact that implementation techniques can have varying success in achieving the goals of the civil rights movement and that both blacks and whites might be capable of perceiving this. It also ignores the very real change in white tolerance for half black, and even majority black, schools in their own neighborhoods—a level that is now so high it can hardly be called "superficial" tolerance.

The "symbolic racism" theory in general argues that white racial attitudes are formed in early childhood, but because racism is less socially acceptable today, this racism is expressed covertly in opposition to busing, to a black candidate, or to preferential treatment for blacks. Thus, these opinions on issues are symbolically related to deep-rooted attitudes regarding the racial inferiority of blacks or to fear of them and their effect on society. The evidence for the symbolic racism theory is that in national surveys of white adults, opposition to busing is moderately correlated with a variety of more obvious measures of prejudice (such as support for segregation in general), and it has little relationship to whether an adult has a school-age child—presumably a measure of self-interest.

The major problems with the symbolic racism research[37] are that (1) the absolute levels of opposition to busing are so high that virtually the entire white population must be labeled racist,[38] which ignores not only the change in and currently high level of tolerance for half black and majority black schools but black opposition to busing as well; (2) although opposition to busing is correlated with prejudice, prejudice does not need opposition to busing as a vehicle for expression, as demonstrated by the 6 percent of the white population that still maintains that white and black students should go to separate schools and the 70 percent that at one time maintained it; (3) the size of the correlation between the researchers' racial intolerance scale and a seven-point antibusing item is .36, leaving much of the variation unexplained so that one might reasonably conclude that all racists may oppose busing but not everyone opposed to busing is a racist; and (4) the researchers' definition of self-interest is too narrow in assuming that busing has no cost to those without children, a fact that the childless residents of cities beset by protest, white flight, and unhappy neighbors, relatives, and friends would probably dispute. Indeed, if one thinks of self-interest in terms of collective as well as individual interest, it is quite possible for a group that thinks of itself as distinct to view as a personal threat something that happens to only some members of the group.[39]

Moreover, if whites do lie on surveys, the fact that they feel they now have to lie, not just in public but in a semiprivate situation, and that prior to *Brown* they could openly express blatant racist opinions suggests a fundamental change in American norms that cannot be ignored. Indeed, the only question is exactly how much this enormous social change has truly affected individual attitudes. It would be hard to imagine that it has had no effect.

The second general theory explaining white opposition to busing is that whites express attitudes and behave in ways that are in their own self-interest. In other words, white parents oppose busing because it entails real costs and burdens for them and their children (or their future children and current friends, relatives, and neighbors' children) and the benefit does not appear to be greater than the cost. Self-interest can also be expressed in terms of the kind of society one wants to live in. For example, Seymour Lipset and William Schneider reviewed a wide range of survey questions and concluded that there is a powerful consensus in American society against discrimination that disappears when issues of compulsory integration or preferential treatment are raised because the former is viewed as a threat to freedom and the latter is seen as another form of discrimination.[40]

In short, there is a basic conflict between two important values held by Americans—individual freedom and egalitarianism—that are at the core of our conception of a good society. This value-conflict theory would suggest that most blacks are opposed to busing not only because of the costs in terms of white resentment but also because they, too, resent being forced to go to a school they did not choose by a government they do not particularly trust for an ideal they are not sure produces the benefits claimed for it using a strategy that obviously has some serious costs.

Indeed, Derrick Bell, a black legal scholar, personifies this when he writes:

> Yet, the remedies set forth in the major school cases following *Brown*—balancing the student and teacher populations by race in each school, eliminating one-race schools, redrawing school attendance lines, and transporting students to achieve racial balance—have not in themselves guaranteed black children better schooling than they received in the pre-Brown era. . . . Plans relying on racial balance to foreclose evasion have not eliminated the need for further orders protecting black children against discriminatory policies, including resegregation within desegregated schools, the loss of black faculty and administrators, suspensions and expulsions at much higher rates than white students, and varying forms of racial harassment ranging from exclusion from extracurricular activities to physical violence. . . . The educational benefits that have resulted from the mandatory assignment of black and white children to the same schools are also debatable. If benefits did exist, they have begun to dissipate as whites flee in alarming numbers from school districts ordered to implement mandatory reassignment plans.[41]

Conclusions

The survey data reviewed above strongly suggest that most blacks perceive busing as not in their self-interest. If that is true, then why is this not also possible for whites who have seen trumpeted in the media allegations by the plaintiffs' attorneys that black schools are inferior and that white racists will ensure that desegregation is accompanied by protest and violence and who furthermore were raised to believe that neighborhood schools are the best kind of schools because they allow local control and parent participation in the education of their children? In short, there are some real benefits to neighborhood schools and real costs to mandatory reassignment out of one's neighborhood to a school not of one's choice that both black and white parents are probably capable of perceiving.

Moreover, the superiority of mandatory reassignment plans in simply achieving integration is just not evident. By the fall of 1996, the Boston public schools, for example, were 83.2 percent minority twenty-two years after the original mandatory reassignment order. Indeed, there was almost half the interracial exposure in 1996—14.9 percent white in the average minority child's school—than the 24 percent white in the average minority child's school that existed before the first mandatory reassignment plan was implemented in 1974. Nor is this an isolated occurrence. Most of the big cities of the United States that implemented mandatory reassignment plans have almost no whites left in the public schools. Although their desegregation plans only caused, on average, about half of the long-term decline in white enrollment, few people seem able or willing to make this distinction. They see the ''forced busing'' plans as completely responsible for the fact that there are few whites, or middle-class parents of other races, left in the public schools of these big cities.

Nor do the national trends demonstrate the superiority of mandatory reassignment plans. As shown in Rossell and Armor (1996), school districts that had never had a formal desegregation plan continue to have greater interracial exposure—that is, a higher proportion white in the average black child's school—than school districts that implemented a formal desegregation plan.[42] In addition, school districts that only implemented a voluntary desegregation plan (neighborhood schools with majority to minority transfer programs or magnet options or freedom of choice) have greater interracial exposure than school districts that implemented mandatory reassignment plans, although they had no initial advantage in the percentage of white students[43] or interracial exposure. Controlled choice seems to have had no effect at all on interracial exposure.[44]

Thus, after forty years of desegregation plans, many of them massive racial balance/busing schemes with serious costs not only to communities but also to individuals, particularly the poorest families who do not have the alternatives available to the affluent, there is no evidence to support the conclusion that mandatory reassignment plans do a better job of achieving school integration than doing nothing formal (beyond not discriminating or modifying attendance zones of adjacent schools or placing new schools so they will be racially balanced) or letting people stay in their neighborhood schools and offering them the chance to transfer to an opposite-race school if they so choose. While white and black parents may not have the image in their minds of national trends in desegregation outcomes when they respond to survey questions regarding their desegregation preferences, they do have a sense, thanks to the national media and their own experiences, of the probability that mandatory reassignment plans will drive out whites and middle-class blacks and produce little or no benefits in the places where blacks are most likely to live—medium and large cities.

It would thus seem that the validity of the racism explanation is diminished and that of the self-interest explanation increased by the lackluster empirical evidence on positive outcomes and the current agreement between black and white parents on desegregation implementation strategies and their behavioral intentions if forced to desegregate. If black parents overwhelmingly support neighborhood schools with voluntary magnet options and would not go along with the mandatory reassignment of their own children to an opposite-race school and if only a minority even want to voluntarily transfer to a magnet school in a white neighborhood or believe that whites are getting a better education, then why is white sentiment along these lines suspect?

Paul M. Sniderman and Thomas Piazza argue that too many cynics have missed the fact that race is today largely (although not completely) an issue of politics. In the years after *Brown*, intellectuals and civil rights activists had come to believe that Americans' reactions to public policies dealing with blacks reflected how they felt about blacks. After four decades of experimenting with public polices aimed at overcoming the evils of slavery and segregation and achieving a just and decent society, however, we have learned enough to be able to have rational disagreements about what policies work best.[45] Indeed, the evidence presented in this chapter suggests that disagreements over the desirability of busing or affirmative action do not have to be covert racism; they can be rational and realistic assessments of the efficiency, effectiveness, and equity of alternative strategies in achieving the principle of a just and color-blind society. The agreement between black and white parents on principles and strategies of school integration evidenced in both the national trend data and our parent surveys in districts considering desegregation plans suggest that Sniderman and Piazza are correct when they conclude that although "prejudice is part of the politics of race . . . a larger part is politics itself. . . . Today there *is* a politics to issues of race. Racial policies themselves—the specific goals they are intended to serve, and the particular means by which they propose to accomplish those goals—define significantly the structure of conflict over race."[46]

And that is the legacy of *Brown*—black Americans are no longer a subject of public debate; it is policies designed to *help* them that are the subject of debate. Even if whites are lying about their feelings about blacks, the fact that they feel they have to lie demonstrates an enormous change in social norms since *Brown*. This is not to say, however, that we have even come close to solving the race problem in the United States; but only that we have made substantial progress in agreeing on goals, and in one policy area—integrated schools—on the means. School integration should be voluntary, and neighborhood schools should be maintained.

Unfortunately, these research findings make the public policy arena enormously complex because they mean that if we want school integration, we are going to have to accomplish it indirectly, and thus slowly, by the elimination of the social class and cultural differences between blacks and whites that still keep us largely in different neighborhoods and, at least part of the time, in different worlds. The solution is no longer simple, but perhaps it will actually achieve the goals black Americans had in 1954 of *freedom*, dignity, and equality in American life. At the very least we will be focused on the cause, not the symptom, of black/white inequality. Moreover, if nothing else is achieved, these survey data suggest that black parents will be happier.

NOTES

I am indebted to Dr. David Armor, the original creator of the school district parent surveys in 1976, for his pioneering work in this field and his generosity in collaborating with me on these projects beginning in 1986. He is also the coprincipal investigator of the national survey of school districts, ''Magnet Schools and Desegregation, Quality, and Choice'' (May 1993), cited in this chapter. I am also grateful to Tom Smith of the National Opinion Research Center for his generous willingness to do special computer runs to provide me with the most up-to-date survey findings.

1. *Brown v. Board of Education*, 139 F. Supp. 468, 470 (D. Kan. 1955).
2. 391 U.S. 430 (1968).
3. 402 U.S. 1 (1971).
4. Some school districts, particularly those that are predominantly of one race, use as their standard for the sending school whether a student's race is above the district percentage. Similarly, the standard for the receiving school is whether a student's race is below the district percentage.
5. Christine H. Rossell, ''The Carrot or the Stick for School Desegregation Policy?'' *Urban Affairs Quarterly* 25, no. 3 (1990): 474–99; Christine H. Rossell, *The Carrot or the Stick for School Desegregation Policy: Magnet Schools vs. Forced Busing* (Philadelphia: Temple University Press, 1990).
6. See Christine H. Rossell and David Armor, ''The Effectiveness of School Desegregation Plans, 1968–1991,'' *American Politics Quarterly* 24 (July 1996): 267–302; Christine H. Rossell, ''Controlled Choice Desegregation Plans: Not Enough Choice, Too Much Control?'' *Urban Affairs Review* (formerly *Urban Affairs Quarterly*) 31 (September 1995): 43–76.
7. These plans are in the Hattiesburg School District and the Natchez-Adams School District. In the latter case, a parent survey was introduced into evidence showing that black parents overwhelmingly preferred neighborhood schools with voluntary integration techniques over mandatory reassignment. The plaintiffs and the court in ordering mandatory reassignments ignored the survey.
8. The question was ''Do you think white students and black students should go to the same schools or to separate schools?'' This question was asked by the National Opinion Research Center (NORC) at the University of Chicago from 1942 through 1985 in their General Social Science Survey. The NORC data for 1942 through 1982 are from Howard Schuman, Charlotte Steeh, and Lawrence Bobo, *Racial Attitudes in America* (Cambridge: Harvard University Press, 1985), 74–75. Data for 1984 and 1985 are provided by Tom Smith at the National Opinion Research Center.
9. The data after 1985 come from the Armor and Rossell parent surveys in individual districts asking a question identical to the NORC one. The districts in which parents were asked this question are DeKalb, Georgia (1990); Topeka, Kansas (1990); Stockton, California (1990); and Knox County, Tennessee (1991).
10. The question was ''Would you yourself have any objection to sending your children to a school where a few of the children are (Negroes/blacks)?'' Gallup and NORC used the following definition of the South: Alabama, Arkansas, Delaware, Florida, Georgia, Kentucky, Louisiana, Maryland, Mississippi, North Carolina, Oklahoma, South Carolina, Tennessee, Texas, Virginia, West Virginia, and the District of Columbia.
11. Armor and Rossell parent survey results are from Los Angeles, California (1977); Chicago, Illinois (1981); Worcester, Massachusetts (1989); DeKalb, Georgia (1990); Topeka, Kansas (1990); Stockton, California (1990); Knox County, Tennessee (1991).

12. This loss is calculated as follows: white enrollment in one year is subtracted from white enrollment the previous year, and that sum is divided by white enrollment the previous year. This figure is then multiplied by 100 to produce a percentage. These data come from Christine Rossell, "Assessing the Unintended Impacts of Public Policy: School Desegregation and Resegregation" (report to the National Institute of Education, Washington, D.C., 1978).

13. Ibid.

14. The Institute for Social Research (ISR) responses from 1972 through 1980 are quoted in Schuman, Steeh, and Bobo, *Racial Attitudes in America*, 88–89, 144–47. The ISR responses for 1984 are cited as the American National Election Study (ANES)—the opinion study directed by the ISR—in Lee Sigelman and Susan Welsh, *Black Americans' Views of Racial Inequality: The Dream Deferred* (New York: Cambridge University Press, 1991), 124.

15. The question asked in the parent surveys from 1986 on varies slightly from district to district but generally informs public school parents that the school district is considering options or ideas for school desegregation and wants their opinions of these options. For each desegregation alternative, parents were asked whether they strongly support, somewhat support, strongly oppose, or somewhat oppose the described alternative. In the case of mandatory reassignment plans, the question usually asked was how they feel about mandatory busing of students in order to attain racial integration.

16. The question generally began with wording similar to the following: "As you may know the ______ public schools are considering ways to improve school integration. I am going to read you a few ideas that could improve school integration in the ______ public schools, and I would like you to tell me if you strongly support, support somewhat, oppose somewhat, or strongly oppose each idea." The voluntary techniques described were "What about voluntary transfers to other schools to improve racial integration, with free transportation?" "What about a voluntary program in which children can attend integrated schools with special programs like intense computer or science studies, which are called magnet schools?"

17. The question was "What about improving integration by changing attendance boundaries of adjacent schools?"

18. The question was generally worded: "Another method for racial and ethnic integration is called a controlled-choice plan. In this type of plan, all neighborhood attendance zones are eliminated and no one is guaranteed a neighborhood school. Instead, all parents choose what schools they would like their children to attend, which could include your current neighborhood school. The administration would make school assignments, and it would try to give everyone their first choices. But it would also have to make sure each school was integrated, so some students would be assigned to schools their parents did not choose. Free transportation would be provided if you chose or were assigned to a school other than your neighborhood school."

19. Armor and Rossell parent survey results.

20. Derrick A. Bell, Jr., "Serving Two Masters: Integration Ideals and Client Interests in School Desegregation Litigation," *Yale Law Journal* 85 (March 1976): 470–516.

21. Ron Edmonds, "Advocating Inequity: A Critique of the Civil Rights Attorney in Class Action Desegregation Suits," *Black Law Journal* 3 (1974): 178, quoted in Bell, "Serving Two Masters," 490.

22. Nathaniel Jones to Derrick A. Bell, Jr., 31 July 1975, cited in Bell, "Serving Two Masters," 492.

23. Nathaniel Jones, conversation with author, Williamsburg, Virginia, 17 May 1994.

24. Nor is listening to parent activists a good substitute. As any political scientist knows, activists have different attitudes and opinions from ordinary citizens.

25. Council on Legal Education for Professional Responsibility, Inc., *Lawyers, Clients & Ethics*, ed. M. Bloom, 101 (1974), quoted in Bell, ''Serving Two Masters,'' 493.

26. In Stockton, an 80% minority school district, the plaintiffs' attorneys finally agreed after months of negotiations to enter into a settlement agreement offering educational enhancements but only because the changing demographics of the school district eventually caused them to conclude that desegregation was no longer achievable, not because it was not supported by their ''clients.'' In Knox County the plaintiff organization was not a black civil rights legal defense group but the Office for Civil Rights, and its position on mandatory reassignment was not very clear. The only thing that was clear was that the district's prior majority to minority transfer plan and other voluntary efforts were considered inadequate.

27. It is telling that the first national survey of the attitudes of black Americans on the principle of school integration and their opinions on school desegregation implementation techniques was in 1972, eighteen years after *Brown*, four years after *Green*, and one year after *Swann*, all court decisions that produced major innovations in legal principles governing school segregation and, in *Swann*, innovations regarding strategies to eliminate it. These innovations apparently did not need to be informed by information regarding what black parents wanted. Indeed, I am not aware of *any* advocate of mandatory reassignment who has polled black parents on this issue.

28. See Schuman, Steeh, and Bobo, *Racial Attitudes in America.*

29. See Sigelman and Welch, *Black Americans' Views of Racial Inequality.*

30. See Schuman, Steeh, and Bobo, *Racial Attitudes in America*, 159.

31. Ibid.

32. Ibid., 161.

33. See Sigelman and Welch, *Black Americans' Views of Racial Inequality*, 126.

34. See Schuman, Steeh, and Bobo, *Racial Attitudes in America*, 171–88.

35. Mary R. Jackman, ''General and Applied Tolerance: Does Education Increase Commitment to Racial Integration?'' *American Journal of Political Science* 22 (1978): 302–24; Mary R. Jackman, ''Education and Policy Commitment to Racial Integration,'' *American Journal of Political Science* 25 (1981): 256–69; Mary R. Jackman and Michael J. Muha, ''Education and Intergroup Attitudes: Moral Enlightenment, Superficial Democratic Commitment, or Ideological Refinement,'' *American Sociological Review* 49 (1984): 751–69.

36. Donald R. Kinder and David O. Sears, ''Prejudice and Politics: Symbolic Racism vs. Racial Threats to the 'Good Life,' '' *Journal of Personality and Social Psychology* 40 (1981): 414–31; David O. Sears et al., ''Self-Interest vs. Symbolic Politics in Policy Attitudes and Presidential Votings,'' *American Political Science Review* 74 (1980): 670–84; David O. Sears, Carl P. Hensler, and Leslie K. Speer, ''Whites' Opposition to 'Busing': Self-Interest or Symbolic Politics?'' *American Political Science Review* 73 (1979): 369–84; John B. McConahay, ''Self-Interest versus Racial Attitudes as Correlates of Anti-Busing Attitudes in Louisville,'' *Journal of Politics* 44 (1982): 692–720; John B. McConahay, Betty B. Hardee, and Valerie Batts, ''Has Racism Declined in America? It Depends on Who Is Asking and What Is Asked,'' *Journal of Conflict Resolution* 25 (1981): 563–79.

37. Much of my discussion here draws on Schuman, Steeh, and Bobo's criticisms, *Racial Attitudes in America*, 178–79.

38. Moreover, it produces a variable that is so skewed that what Sears and his colleagues are really measuring is symbolic ''antiracism.''

39. As Schuman, Steeh, and Bobo point out, almost all blacks were opposed to the Reagan administration and its policies, but only a few of them were directly affected by those policies. Schuman, Steeh, and Bobo, *Racial Attitudes in America.*

40. Seymour Martin Lipset and William Schneider, ''The *Bakke* Case: How Would It Be

Decided at the Bar of Public Opinion?'' *Public Opinion* (March/April 1978): 38–44, quoted in Schuman, Steeh, and Bobo, *Racial Attitudes in America.*

41. Derrick A. Bell, Jr., ''*Brown v. Board of Education* and the Interest-Convergence Dilemma,'' *Harvard Law Review* 93 (1980): 531.

42. Rossell and Armor, ''Effectiveness of School Desegregation Plans.''

43. In 1968 both the districts with voluntary and those with mandatory plans had 69% white students. The districts that never had a plan had 80% white students, and those with a controlled-choice plan had 78% white students.

44. The lack of superiority of the mandatory reassignment plans or controlled choice is not due to the fact that they were less extensive than the voluntary plans. Indeed, there is almost no difference between voluntary and mandatory plan districts in their 1991 racial imbalance, and the controlled choice plans have a bit less racial imbalance. See also Rossell, ''Controlled Choice Desegregation Plans.''

45. Moreover, as Sniderman and Piazza demonstrate in some experiments alternating the order of questions, the mere mention of policies that are thought of as fundamentally unfair, such as affirmative action, can actually increase white prejudice against blacks. In short, rather than racism causing opposition to policies designed to help blacks, policies designed to help blacks can increase racist attitudes. Paul M. Sniderman and Thomas Piazza, *The Scar of Race* (Cambridge: Harvard University Press, 1993).

46. Ibid., 175.

9

Brown Blues

Rethinking the Integrative Ideal

DREW S. DAYS III

More than forty years have passed since the Supreme Court's *Brown v. Board of Education*[1] decision, declaring unconstitutional state-imposed segregation of public schools. One would have thought that by now American society would have arrived at a consensus with respect to the substance and scope of *Brown*. The truth is otherwise. Even in the education sector of our national life that *Brown* specifically addressed, deep differences remain over what changes that decision was designed to effect.

Of course, opposition to *Brown* by whites committed to the maintenance of racial segregation in public education has been a daily reality from the moment the decision was announced. Over the years, that opposition has taken a variety of forms both simpleminded and sophisticated. However, it was generally thought that one group, African Americans, was uniformly supportive of *Brown* and committed to its full implementation in education. After all, *Brown* was the culmination of a long campaign by the National Association for the Advancement of Colored People (NAACP) to overturn the ''separate but equal'' doctrine. It also ushered in, without doubt, more than a generation of court decisions and legislation that eradicated all vestiges of formal segregation in America. Blacks seemed to agree with the Supreme Court's pronouncement in *Brown* that children are unlikely to function effectively in America's pluralistic society unless they live and learn with people of different races from an early age.[2]

Several developments in recent years suggest, however, that growing numbers of blacks may be turning away from this integrative ideal. Four examples of this shift are worth noting: first, black parents now express support for school board efforts to end desegregation plans that involve busing, favoring instead a return to neighborhood schools, even though this would result in increases in the number of virtually all-black schools in the inner city;[3] second, at the urging of black parents, school boards in a number of major cities have attempted to create all-black male academies;[4] third, black administrators, faculty, students, and alumni of historically black colleges in the South have joined state officials in opposition to court-ordered higher education desegregation plans;[5] and fourth, black students on predominantly white college campuses have urged administrators to provide special facilities for black students' social and cultural events.[6] Some critics have dismissed these developments as perverse efforts by blacks to return to a "separate but equal" regime. In fact, these developments raise serious and complex questions about the future of race relations in America that deserve careful analysis, not simplistic characterization. This chapter is an attempt to contribute constructively to that process.

Blacks and Neighborhood Schools

The school desegregation process has not been unproblematic, to say the least. More than forty years after *Brown*, there is still active litigation alleging constitutional violations. There is no gainsaying, however, that as a result of *Brown* and its progeny, thousands of black, white, and Hispanic children have been able to receive integrated educations and develop both educational and social skills that will stand them in good stead in later life. At the very least, the mandatory presence of white children has saved some black and other minority children from the physically inferior facilities—and inferior resources—to which they had been assigned under segregation.

Acknowledging the important gains of desegregation, however, should not blind us to the continuing legacy of segregation within desegregated systems. In many schools, racially segregated classes make it unlikely that children of different races will have meaningful interaction during the school day. Moreover, the black community has paid, in some instances, a high price for desegregation. For example, schools that served not only as educational institutions but also as community centers in predominantly black neighborhoods have been closed;[7] the burden of busing has fallen disproportionately on black children;[8] black teachers and administrators have been dismissed and demoted disproportionately;[9] and black students have encountered increased disciplinary action in recently desegregated schools.[10]

Most important, perhaps, given the initial hope that desegregation would increase the quality of educational opportunity for black students, is the fact that the desegregation process has not necessarily brought about improvements. Indeed, in some cases, desegregation has limited opportunity. For example, where magnet schools offering innovative educational programs have replaced formerly all-black facilities, black student enrollment in the special programs has been limited by the need to maintain racial balance.[11] This record establishes, contrary to common assumptions, that desegregation has not been an unmitigated benefit to previously segregated black students, teachers, and administrators.

We need not conclude that these negative consequences are the inevitable result of desegregation, however, and that the black community might have been better off seeking to improve educational opportunities within a segregated system. The more plausible explanation is that the same racist tendencies in America that created and maintained segregated schools did not disappear overnight once desegregation was mandated. Rather, they merely found new opportunities in this new arrangement to disadvantage the black community.

Whatever the pros and cons of desegregation, however, the reality is that demographic changes in the United States since 1954 have produced a pattern of residential segregation.[12] This makes further progress in school desegregation in certain areas difficult to envision. Urban centers across the nation are predominantly black and Hispanic; the suburbs and rural areas are predominantly white.[13] Even in those cities where the white population exceeds the minority, the public school populations are predominantly black and Hispanic. This latter phenomenon can be explained by the presence of childless white couples, older white couples, and white families with children enrolled in private and parochial, rather than public, schools.

Although some litigation efforts to achieve metropolitan-wide desegregation have been successful, the Supreme Court's 1974 decision in a Detroit school desegregation case[14] effectively limited the availability of that remedy in most urban areas. A few large cities have adopted voluntary desegregation plans involving urban and suburban communities,[15] but their impact on inner-city segregation has been modest, largely because those participating in such programs have been disproportionately black. The result has been, therefore, a one-way rather than a two-way process, with urban blacks heading out to suburban schools but relatively few suburban whites coming into the city.[16]

It is true that some predominantly black and Hispanic school districts have been able to obtain significant resources from their states based on a second Supreme Court ruling involving Detroit schools.[17] Still, the educational experiences of many black and Hispanic students in America will occur in one-race schools in poorly funded urban communities that have been abandoned by large numbers of white—as well as middle-class black—families.[18] Even in those districts where it is still possible for blacks and whites to attend school together, some members of the black community have begun to question whether the result achieved is worth the time and expense that desegregation entails.

There is also a sense among some blacks that although some desegregation plans no longer produce meaningful numbers of whites and blacks studying together, the plans are maintained because of the mistaken belief that blacks cannot learn unless whites are sitting next to them in class. The blacks who challenge the continuation of such plans argue that a return to neighborhood school assignment makes more sense because parental and community involvement in the schools would be more likely to increase. Moreover, governmental resources expended on busing could be redirected to increasing the quality of materials and instruction available at those schools.

Blacks and whites who oppose efforts to roll back desegregation plans do so for a variety of reasons. First, they fear that such proposals are yet another attempt by school boards guilty of past intentional segregation to escape any further role in avoiding resegregation. Second, they suspect blacks who support such rollbacks of acting more in their own political and economic interests than in the interests of black children. What roll-back proponents seek, in fact, are more and better jobs for black administrators and teachers in exchange for reduced pressure for increasing or maintaining desegregation levels. Third, roll-back opponents fear that a return to all-black schools will result in "benign neglect" of those schools in terms of resources allocated for facilities, materials, and personnel.[19]

This debate, although perhaps the subject of greater media focus in recent years, is not a new one. Blacks, having seen the bad, along with the good, of desegregation, have for some time questioned whether the process should be extended to the limits that the Supreme Court precedents allowed. This attitude has been particularly prevalent with respect to desegregation plans that require extensive busing. These voices of restraint often had no effective forum, however, because they were often white school boards correctly viewed as inherently untrustworthy spokespersons for this point of view. The major civil rights organizations representing the plaintiffs in desegregation cases, on the other hand, strongly reject any thought of stopping short of what the Constitution would permit.

The debate has taken on a new dimension, however, because black mayors, city council members, and school superintendents have begun to express similar concerns about the wisdom of what they see as "desegregation at any cost." Courts are justifiably perplexed over how to evaluate the views of this group because their authority, as elected and appointed blacks, to speak for the black community certainly is equal to, if not greater than, that of plaintiffs and their lawyers in school desegregation cases. Although some might dismiss their views as perversely malevolent toward black students, the positions of black elected and appointed officials deserve an evaluation as expressions of concern about the most effective approach to educating black children under daunting circumstances.

For these and other reasons, blacks increasingly support efforts by school districts under court desegregation orders to return to neighborhood school arrangements, even though such modifications inevitably will return certain facilities in the black community to largely one-race status.[20] Of course, we must not lose sight of the fact that constitutional rights are individual. Whether a school district has satisfied its responsibility under *Brown* and its progeny to dismantle a dual system is not subject to resolution by referendum. The difficult legal question, one with which the Supreme Court continues to grapple, is how we determine whether the dual system is still in place.[21] Meanwhile, debates over modifications of desegregation plans continue.

Proponents of modification argue that once the school board has done all it can to eradicate the vestiges of its previously dual system, it has satisfied constitutional requirements. Continued segregation, they contend, is not the school board's fault but rather the consequence of residential segregation caused by private choice and market forces. Opponents of rolling back desegregation plans argue that the school board has a duty to continue making adjustments until the results of the pattern of segregation it created have been eradicated. They take the position that demographics cited by the board as an explanation of continued segregation are not adventitious but rather the consequence of past school board practices. Under current Supreme Court doctrines, the proponents of modification are likely to prevail because the Court consistently has refused to consider the extent to which segregative actions by governmental agencies other than school boards might justify maintenance of desegregation plans when modification would result in resegregation. Consequently, school desegregation plaintiffs are left with a wrong in search of a remedy.[22] As they witness schools that were all black before desegregation return to that status once the board's modifications go into effect, it must seem to them that years of effort have been in vain.

Schools for Black Males

Media attention and public debate over the past few years have also focused on proposals to establish public schools or programs exclusively for black male students.[23] In Milwaukee, for example, the school board planned to designate two schools as all-black or virtually all-black facilities in which special attention would be given to the educational and developmental needs of black males. These "immersion schools" would offer features unavailable in other Milwaukee facilities: school days one hour longer and less rigidly structured than normal, a multicultural curriculum, and mandatory Saturday classes held in cooperation with the local branch of the Urban League. Weekend sessions would focus on nonacademic subjects, such as "what it means to be a responsible male," "how to save and invest money," and "the practicalities of cooking and cleaning." The students would also be required to wear uniforms.

As a result of actual or threatened litigation, Milwaukee's proposal and similar ones in other urban school districts were modified to include female and white students who wished to participate.[24] The legal and political debate continues, however. At the core of the controversy is the question of whether a school that admits only blacks is any more constitutional than the ones that *Brown* outlawed because they admitted only whites.

At one level, they clearly are not comparable. The system of state-imposed racial segregation in public education that *Brown* declared unconstitutional was designed to ensure that blacks remained a second-class, subjugated race in American society. Schools established for black males, in contrast, are not designed to subjugate whites or deny them first-class citizenship. Rather, they address what most people would acknowledge is the critical plight of young black males in urban America. The premise of the theory is that "one of the most obvious psychosocial deficits in the environment of inner-city black boys is the lack of consistent, positive, literate, black *male* role models."[25]

At another level, however, our history counsels us to be wary of *any* racial classifications. For that reason, the Supreme Court has mandated that any use of racial criteria by government must be for the purpose of achieving a compelling interest and must be necessary to achieve that purpose. Dual school systems under segregation failed that test because maintaining segregation of the races did not constitute a compelling governmental interest. All-black academies, in contrast, concededly are designed to meet a compelling interest—saving black males from educational and social disaster.[26] However, the case has not been made persuasively that this is an interest that *necessarily* requires the exclusion of whites.

The fact that the school district might be able to achieve its goals more efficiently employing a racially exclusive approach is no justification for such a system. Expedience cannot legitimize racial segregation. Even taking the proponents of all-black academies at their word, there is little evidence to support the view that mentoring, counseling, extended school days, small classes, and a curriculum that gives proper recognition to the contributions of blacks to American society will improve black male educational and social functioning *only* in a racially segregated setting. Such an enriched educational environment is likely to produce positive effects *irrespective* of the racial setting.

Proponents may contend that only experimentation will determine the effectiveness of such programs. Racial classifications, however, are not proper subjects for experimentation. Of course, in many urban settings, the likelihood that whites will be enrolled in center-city schools and thereby be displaced to accommodate the all-black academies is slim. Similarly, whites likely will not apply to attend such schools. Under these circumstances, as a practical matter, school districts can set up programs for all-black student bodies without imposing any bar to whites.

Proposals to create all-black male academies have attracted adherents largely in those districts where a number of schools in the center city, as in Milwaukee, cannot feasibly be desegregated. Under these circumstances, it is hard to fault black parents and sympathetic school officials who do not believe that black male students can await the integration millennium. Consequently, they have joined forces to develop a structure that they hope will save black males. Such approaches clearly reflect disenchantment with the *Brown* integrative ideal and may be educationally misguided. However, to the extent that whites and females may participate, the programs would not appear to violate constitutional limits.

Historically Black Colleges and Universities

Lawyers for the NAACP prepared for their ultimate assault on the "separate but equal" doctrine in *Brown* by challenging successfully the exclusion of blacks from all-white graduate and professional schools.[27] Indeed, it was in one of those earlier cases that the Supreme Court acknowledged the "intangible" inequality caused by segregation that would figure so prominently in its 1954 decision.[28] The Court made clear shortly after *Brown II*,[29] the desegregation implementation decision in 1955, that southern higher education officials could not delay opening their institutions by invoking the "all deliberate speed" doctrine.[30] Consequently, efforts by blacks to enroll in previously all-white colleges and universities during the late 1950s and early 1960s found support in the courts, as well as in the executive branch. In a few instances, the government even called out troops to ensure the admission of blacks.[31]

Meanwhile, almost no attention was being given to the fact that southern and border states were continuing to operate dual systems of higher education. This arrangement was dictated, in large part, by the federal government's promotion in 1862, under the First Morrill Act,[32] of state land grant colleges for whites and then in 1890, under the Second Morrill Act,[33] parallel institutions for blacks. Thereafter states systematically discriminated against black institutions in the allocation of funds for a period that extended well beyond 1954.[34]

The historically black institutions, as a group, nevertheless, achieved remarkable success educating students from segregated and inferior secondary schools. They developed programs that provided their students with instruction and nurturing sufficient to prepare them to function effectively in society after graduation. In many cases, their graduates have pursued graduate and professional training at prestigious universities in the North and West.

Early attempts to challenge dual systems of higher education produced court orders that seemed to embrace a "freedom-of-choice" approach. State officials successfully argued that college students were not assigned to institutions but rather were free to select a college or university based on considerations of curriculum, location, cost, and admissions requirements. Consequently, as long as states did not preclude students from attending an institution because of their race, the courts determined that dual systems did not offend the Constitution.

In the early 1970s, however, black plaintiffs initiated litigation in *Adams v. Richardson*, charging federal officials with illegally providing funds to states that maintained dual systems of higher education.[35] As a result of this suit, the court ordered the Department of Health, Education, and Welfare (HEW)—and later the Department of Education—to launch an enforcement campaign to dismantle those systems. Central to that campaign was the premise that the states in question had a constitutional duty to act affirmatively to remedy the conditions that created and perpetuated separate black and white institutions at the postsecondary level.[36]

Unlike earlier court decisions, federal administrative directives rejected the notion that "freedom of choice" was the proper remedial model.[37] They recognized that students' choices were shaped powerfully by the effects of long-standing mandated segregation and discriminatory resource allocations between black and white institutions. One example of this was the placement of new institutions with parallel curricula in communities where previously only historically black public institutions existed. These parallel institutions effectively provided white students with segregated alternatives.[38]

Black higher-education groups were at odds with federal agencies and the NAACP Legal Defense and Educational Fund, which brought the *Adams* suit, regarding the wisdom of pressing desegregation of public colleges and universities.[39] Black college presidents, faculty, and alumni were undoubtedly mindful of the burdens the black community had been forced to bear during desegregation of public primary and secondary systems. They feared that desegregation of higher education would result, at best, in whites displacing black teachers and administrators, as well as black students. At worst, given the relative inferiority of their institutions, desegregation might result in the closing of schools or the absorption of traditionally black institutions into historically white schools. In either event, institutions important to the black community would lose their identity, and opportunities in higher education for black administrators, faculty, and students would be significantly diminished.

Despite similar concerns, however, proponents of desegregation in higher education believed that both litigation and administrative enforcement could increase resources available to historically black institutions. Reducing program duplication and forcing the states to locate especially attractive academic programs at traditionally black schools would also enhance the schools' long-term viability.[40]

It is fair to say that this desegregation effort has not been very successful. Significant segregation between historically black and white institutions is still apparent. Since 1973, state officials have effectively utilized the administrative process to delay meaningful change. Ultimately, the Court of Appeals for the District of Columbia Circuit dismissed the *Adams* litigation on technical grounds.[41] As a result, the federal government is able to decide on the nature, scope, and timing of enforcement largely free of court oversight.

Two higher-education desegregation efforts, one involving Louisiana and the other Mississippi, were severed from the *Adams* administrative process and referred by HEW to the Justice Department for judicial enforcement. Little systemic desegregation has occurred in either case over the many years they have been in court. The Supreme Court recently ruled on Mississippi's higher-education desegregation case.[42]

The case presented the Court with an opportunity to define a state's constitutional duty to dismantle formerly dual systems of higher education, a question that had produced conflicting answers in the lower federal courts. Some courts had taken the position that higher-education authorities had an affirmative responsibility, similar to that imposed on school boards in the case of primary and secondary school desegregation, to eradicate the vestiges of their dual systems.[43] Like the HEW in the *Adams* proceedings, these courts believed that this responsibility must be discharged by addressing a variety of practices that affect students' decisions about which institutions they attend, such as admissions standards, program duplication, institutional resources, and governance.[44] Other courts rejected the notion that primary and secondary school desegregation doctrines had any applicability to higher education, principally because college and university attendance is not mandated by the state but depends on individual student choice.[45] Consequently, these courts—including both the trial and appellate courts in the Mississippi case—concluded that a state's constitutional responsibility ends once the state has removed all racial bars to students' attending the college or university of their choice.[46]

In *United States v. Fordice*,[47] the Supreme Court essentially embraced the former "affirmative duty" doctrine and reversed the lower courts' determination that Mississippi had met its constitutional responsibility. The Court found that in at least four areas—admission standards, program duplication, institutional mission assignments, and continued operation of all eight public universities—the state had failed to show that the "policies and practices traceable to its prior system that continue to have segregative effects" had "sound educational justification" and could not "be practicably eliminated."[48] The case was then returned to the lower courts for evaluation of the Mississippi system against the Court's newly articulated standard.

The Court's decision leaves in limbo, however, the future of Mississippi's three historically black institutions. Although the Court acknowledged that "closure of one or more institutions would decrease the discriminatory effects of the present system,"[49] it declined to find such action constitutionally required. However, it flatly rejected the notion that Mississippi had a constitutional duty to upgrade the historically black institutions, as such. Rather, it left to the lower courts the question of whether "an increase in funding is necessary to achieve a full dismantlement."[50] Given this ambiguity, the possibility exists that Mississippi will be able to achieve a unitary higher-education system by closing those institutions.[51]

It is this fear that black institutions will be the inevitable casualties of higher-education desegregation that has complicated the dismantling of dual systems. Take, for example, the ostensibly odd alignment of parties in the Louisiana case. After concluding that Louisiana's desegregation plans were inadequate, the federal court commissioned its own strategy. That plan envisioned, among other things, merging the traditionally black Southern University Law Center into the law school of Louisiana State University (LSU), the state's traditionally white flagship institution.[52] The two law schools are located in Baton Rouge, only a few miles apart.

That the state opposed the merger plan was not surprising. However, it was joined by the Southern University Board of Supervisors, which viewed the court's order as a step backward, rather than forward, for black education in Louisiana.[53] The board claimed that blacks, the victims of the state's history of segregation and discrimination in higher education, were being required to bear a disproportionate burden in rectifying that situation.[54] Specifically, the board contended that the merger of Southern University's law school with LSU's would undoubtedly displace black faculty and staff and curtail opportunities for blacks seeking legal education.[55] The court's plan did not envision LSU's absorbing Southern University's faculty and staff, nor did it require LSU to expand to ensure against a net loss of law school seats for black students after the merger.

In defense of its plan, the court took the position that the merger was required by the Constitution and was in the long-term interests of the citizens of Louisiana, black and white.[56] But for the state's creation and maintenance of segregated higher education, the court pointed out, there would not still be two public law schools in the same city, one white and the other black. The court concluded that desegregation could occur only if one of the institutions closed. Moreover, the court observed that in a fiscally strapped state, maintaining two law schools in Baton Rouge made no economic sense.

Southern University's law school had been denied adequate state support because of its status as a black institution. The condition of its physical plant and the quality of its educational program were, as a result, inferior to those of LSU. Consequently, the court concluded that Southern University's law school should be the one to close.[57] In response to the Southern University Board of Supervisors' concerns about the desegregation process, the court suggested that the board was interested in protecting the jobs of Southern University faculty and administrators rather than in improving educational opportunities for blacks.

This controversy delineates starkly the dilemma confronting proponents of higher-education desegregation. The court clearly was correct that the maintenance of dual, segregated law schools in one city makes no legal or fiscal sense and that merging the institutions would require blacks and whites to study law together rather than apart. But the black opponents of the merger also have compelling arguments. Absent the state's history of discriminatory treatment of Southern University Law Center, the school's facilities and program probably would not be so inferior to those of LSU. Had there been "tangible" equality over the years between the two institutions, white students might have opted to attend Southern University rather than LSU based on "intangible" considerations, such as the presence of particular faculty members or curricular emphases. Moreover, there is no reason why Southern University's board should apologize for seeking to protect the jobs of faculty and administrators. They, too, are victims of the state's segregative practices.

Finally, Southern University Law Center and LSU Law School have different admissions criteria. As a consequence, Southern University has been able to admit some black students who, based on objective indicators such as grade point average and Law School Admission Test scores, would not be competitive candidates at LSU. Southern University, nevertheless, has been able to train and graduate generations of black lawyers who provide competent legal services to poor and minority communities in the state. Unless LSU ensured that black students whom Southern University would have admitted would find seats at LSU, the merger would represent a net loss of educational opportunities for black students in Louisiana.

The Louisiana case eventually was dismissed in light of the Fifth Circuit's ruling in the Mississippi case.[58] Solving the dilemma in Louisiana and in other states where higher-education desegregation is under way will not be easy now that the Supreme Court has vacated that decision.[59] The solution cannot be achieved overnight, however. It must operate within the twin constraints of constitutional requirements and economic reality. At the same time, it must address responsibly the displacement effects of the desegregation process and the ironic price that the black community must pay for desegregation.

Blacks on White Campuses

The proposed merger of Southern University Law Center with LSU undoubtedly raised concerns in the minds of black students about the reception they were likely to receive upon enrolling at LSU. Would the administration be supportive? Would faculty members nurture their intellectual development? Would white students accept them as colleagues and peers? These are questions that many black applicants likely ask when considering a predominantly white college or university anywhere in the country. The alternative for these students is to attend one of a group of public and private historically black institutions with proven track records of providing students with excellent preparation for postgraduate employment or education.

These are not idle concerns. Blacks have always encountered difficulties in predominantly white institutions, as accounts of the "best and brightest" of pioneer black students at prestigious northern institutions attest.[60] They had to overcome both social isolation and a lack of evenhanded administrative and faculty support in order to excel. Even though black enrollment in these institutions has increased over the years, the schools generally have not succeeded in retaining and graduating blacks in proportions equal to those for white students.[61]

Explanations for this disparity range from the failure of such institutions to provide adequate financial support to the academic deficiencies of the students. One of the major variables, however, appears to be black students' perception of the degree to which the institutions will offer supportive environments within which they can grow academically and socially.[62] This concern is not unique to blacks, of course. Students from other racial or ethnic minorities, public school graduates, southerners going north, and northerners going south want to know whether they are going to feel at home in the institutions they are considering. The stakes just seem to be higher for blacks.

The number of black students attending traditionally white institutions surpassed token levels in the late 1960s, largely through a combination of more aggressive recruiting of candidates clearly meeting normal admissions criteria, as well as the establishment of affirmative action programs for qualified but less competitive students. This development was not an unalloyed advance, however, in efforts to increase educational opportunities for black students and reduce racial segregation in higher education. Black students on predominantly white campuses began to express concern about the difficulties of their adjustment, unlike their predecessors, who usually opted to suffer in silence. With varying degrees of insistence, black students asked that college administrators provide facilities specifically to allow them opportunities for greater social interaction than the institutions were affording them.

These requests prompted a range of reactions from blacks and whites, many quite hostile to the idea of black "Afro-Am houses" on campus. Some blacks and whites who had fought to end segregation viewed such developments as striking at the very heart of what *Brown* symbolized. Some administrators wondered why blacks had sought admission to their predominantly white institutions in order to segregate themselves from their white classmates. Whites who would have preferred not to see any black students on campus pointed cynically to the demands for special "houses" to justify their support for social groups, such as Greek societies or eating clubs, that excluded blacks.[63]

These considerations, even the cynical claims of racists, highlight the difficulty of defending university support for racially *exclusive* social clubs and living arrangements that bar nonblacks irrespective of their backgrounds or interests.[64] Blacks-only clubs or dormitories are bad social policy in that they reinforce racial stereotypes and most likely are unconstitutional. Ensuring that a hostile campus environment does not force black students to terminate their studies before graduation may well qualify as a compelling interest that justifies the establishment of such clubs and dormitories. As in the case of all-black academies, however, it is not clear that racially exclusive facilities within the university are *necessary* to achieving that goal.

In contrast, administrative support for *nonexclusive* facilities to benefit black students is sound social policy. They may provide black students with a "safe harbor" from stormy weather, particularly for those who are encountering a predominantly white environment for the first time.[65] When special facilities for blacks first appeared on campuses, some sympathetic observers thought, perhaps naively, that blacks would have decreasing need for such refuges as time passed. However, the ongoing debate over affirmative action issues—from the legality of minority scholarships to whether blacks are stigmatized by such efforts—and the growth of hate speech on college campuses[66] have surely caused black students on predominantly white campuses to feel more embattled than ever before. Black students should not have to subject themselves to undue psychological and emotional stress in order to enjoy the prestige, rich resources, outstanding academic programs, and influential alumni networks that top, predominantly white institutions provide their students. ''Afro-Am houses,'' properly handled, need not be the source of racial divisiveness. Rather, they can serve to promote the healthy integration of black students and black culture into the life of predominantly white institutions. Such integration does not demand black assimilation but instead reflects respect for cultural diversity.

Conclusion

The *Brown* decision and the integrative ideal that it embraced have opened opportunities for black advancement that were previously unthinkable. *Brown* also transformed our entire society in other ways too numerous to recite under these circumstances. As the four developments discussed above suggest, however, the increasing racial polarization and residential segregation in America have put the integrative ideal to the test. Concerns about the burdens blacks have had to carry in the desegregation process, the degree to which integration requires assimilation and rejection of black values and institutions, and the seemingly intractable problems presented for largely black school systems in educational *extremis* are causing growing numbers of blacks to rethink *Brown*'s integrative ideal. These are admittedly difficult questions. Nevertheless, they deserve to be asked—indeed, they cannot be avoided. They must also be answered, although the answers may be uncomfortable and disappointing, at least in the short run, for those of us who hoped that we would see a different America forty years after *Brown*.

NOTES

1. 347 U.S. 483 (1954).
2. Martin Luther King, Jr., ''The Ethical Demands for Integration,'' in *A Testament of Hope: The Essential Writings of Martin Luther King, Jr.*, ed. James M. Washington (New York: Harper Collins, 1986), 117.
3. See, e.g., Gary Orfield and Susan E. Eaton, *Dismantling Desegregation: The Quiet Reversal of Brown v. Board of Education* (1996), 73–114; Steven A. Holmes, ''At N.A.A.C.P., Talk of a Shift on Integration,'' *New York Times*, 23 June 1997, sec. A, 1; and Michel Marriott, ''Louisville Debates Plan to End Forced Grade School Busing,'' *New York Times*, 11 December 1991, sec. B, 13.
4. Dirk Johnson, ''Milwaukee Creating Two Schools for Black Boys,'' *New York Times*, 30 September 1990, sec. A, 1.
5. Peter Applebome, ''Separate but Equal Goes Back to Court—A Special Report; Epilogue to Integration Fight: Blacks Favor Own Colleges,'' *New York Times*, 29 May 1991, sec. A, l.
6. ''Cornell: Opposition Blocks Plan to Improve Dorm Racial Mix,'' *New York Times*, 12 April 1992, sec. A, 51.
7. See *Bell v. West Point Mun. Separate School District*, 446 F.2d 1362 (5th Cir. 1971).

8. U.S. Commission on Civil Rights, *Fulfilling the Letter and Spirit of the Law* (Washington, D.C.: U.S. Commission on Civil Rights, 1976), 202–6.

9. Senate Select Committee on Equal Education Opportunity, *Desegregation under the Law*, 91st Cong., 2d sess., 1970, 1006–7, 1082–144.

10. U.S. Commission on Civil Rights, *Fulfilling the Letter and Spirit of the Law*, 255–69.

11. Jennifer L. Hochschild, *The New American Dilemma: Liberal Democracy and School Desegregation* (New Haven: Yale University Press, 1984), 77.

12. Gerald D. Jaynes and Robyn M. Williams, Jr., eds., *A Common Destiny: Blacks and American Society* (Washington, D.C.: National Research Council, 1989), 88–91.

13. This pattern of residential segregation has been affected somewhat by decisions of African American urban dwellers to locate in all-black upscale suburban communities. See David J. Dent, "The New Black Suburbs," *New York Times*, 14 June 1992, sec. 6, 18.

14. *Milliken v. Bradley*, 418 U.S. 717 (1974).

15. See, e.g., *Liddell v. Missouri*, 731 F.2d 1294, 1300 (8th Cir.) (en banc), *cert. denied*, 469 U.S. 816 (1984) (discussing a voluntary plan for St. Louis and suburbs).

16. See *Liddell*, 731 F.2d at 1301–2.

17. See *Milliken v. Bradley*, 433 U.S. 267 (1977). But see also *Missouri v. Jenkins*, 115 S. Ct. 2038 (1995) (limitation on further state funding of educational enrichment programs).

18. See William J. Wilson, *The Truly Disadvantaged: The Inner City, the Under-Class, and Public Policy* (Chicago: University of Chicago Press, 1987), 56–58, 102–4, 135–36.

19. See Gary Orfield and Carole Ashkinaze, *The Closing Door: Conservative Policy and Black Opportunity* (Chicago: University of Chicago Press, 1991), 105–12.

20. See David Montgomery and Terry M. Neal, "In P.G., a New School of Thought: Evolving Views on Race, Segregation Lead to Busing Consensus," *Washington Post*, 28 July 1996, sec. B, 1.

21. See *Freeman v. Pitts*, 112 S. Ct. 1430 (1992); *Board of Education v. Dowell*, 111 S. Ct. 630 (1991).

22. See *Swann v. Charlotte-Mecklenburg Board of Education*, 402 U.S. 1, 22–23, 31–32 (1971). For a more complete treatment of this issue, see Drew S. Days III, "School Desegregation Law in the 1980's: Why Isn't Anybody Laughing?" *Yale Law Journal* 95 (July 1986): 1737.

23. Tom Dunkel, "Self-Segregated Schools Seek to Build Self-Esteem," *Washington Times*, 11 March 1991, sec. E, 1.

24. Carol Innerst, "School Geared to Black Boys Attracts Girls," *Washington Times*, 3 September 1991, sec. A, 3; Patrice M. Jones, "A Place All Their Own: Detriot Uses Special Academies to Help Black Boys Overcome Challenges," *Plain Dealer*, 23 April 1996, sec. A, 1.

25. Spencer H. Holland, "A Radical Approach to Educating Young Black Males," *Education Week*, 25 March 1987, 24.

26. In Milwaukee, for example, 50% of the black males entering high school do not graduate. Dunkel, "Self-Segregated Schools," sec. E, 1. Black males make up 27.6% of the school population but account for half of all students suspended. Ibid. In 1990, out of 5,716 black males in the city's public high schools, only 125 had grade point averages above 3.0. Ibid.

27. See Mark V. Tushnet, *The NAACP Legal Strategy against Segregated Education, 1925–1950* (Chapel Hill: University of North Carolina Press, 1987), 105–37.

28. *Sweatt v. Painter*, 339 U.S. 629, 634–35 (1950).

29. *Brown v. Board of Education*, 349 U.S. 294 (1955).

30. *Florida ex rel. Hawkins v. Board of Control*, 350 U.S. 413, 413–14 (1956); see also Charlayne Hunter-Gault, *In My Place* (New York: Farrar Straus Giroux, 1992).

31. James H. Meredith, *Three Years in Mississippi* (Bloomington: Indiana University Press, 1966), 207–14.

32. Ch. 130, § 4, 12 Stat. 503, 504 (1862) (codified as amended at 7 U.S.C. §§ 301–305, 307–308 (1988)).

33. Ch. 841, 26 Stat. 417 (1890) (codified as amended at 7 U.S.C. §§ 321–326, 328 [1988]).

34. For a general review of the Morrill Acts and underfunding of historically black institutions, see Gil Kujovich, "Equal Opportunity in Higher Education and the Black Public College: The Era of Separate but Equal," *Minnesota Law Review* 72 (October 1987): 29, 40–64.

35. 480 F.2d 1159 (D.C. Cir. 1973) (en banc) (per curiam).

36. See ibid. at 1163–65; *Geier v. University of Tennessee*, 597 F.2d 1056, 1065 (6th Cir. 1979).

37. See, e.g., *Federal Register* 43, "Revised Criteria Specifying the Ingredients of Acceptable Plans to Desegregate State Systems of Public Higher Education," 95th Cong., 15 February 1978, 6658–59, 6661 (hereafter cited as "Revised Criteria").

38. See *Geier v. Blanton*, 427 F. Supp. 644 (M.D. Tenn. 1977) (mandating merger of parallel institutions because desegregation was not occurring), *aff'd sub nom. Geier v. University of Tennessee*, 597 F.2d. 1056 (6th Cir. 1979).

39. For a full discussion of these concerns, see Jean L. Preer, *Lawyers v. Educators: Black Colleges and Desegregation in Public Higher Education* (Westport, Conn.: Greenwood Press, 1982), 182–232.

40. "Revised Criteria," 6658–64.

41. *Women's Equity Action League v. Cavazos*, 906 F.2d. 742 (D.C. Cir. 1990).

42. *United States v. Fordice*, 505 U.S. 717 (1992).

43. See *United States v. Louisiana*, 718 F. Supp. 499, 532–35 (E.D. La. 1989).

44. See, e.g., *Geier v. Blanton*, 427 F. Supp. 644, 657–60 (M.D. Tenn. 1977), *aff'd sub nom. Geier v. University of Tennessee*, 597 F.2d 1056 (6th Cir. 1979).

45. See *Allain*, 674 F. Supp. at 1553–54.

46. *Ayers v. Allain*, 914 F.3d 676, 687 (5th Cir. 1990) (en banc), *vacated and remanded, sub nom. United States v. Fordice*, 505 U.S. 717 (1992); *Allain*, 674 F. Supp. at 1554.

47. 505 U.S. 717 (1992).

48. Ibid. at 731.

49. Ibid. at 742.

50. Ibid.

51. Both Justice Thomas, ibid. at 747–48 (Thomas, J., concurring), and Justice Scalia, ibid. at 758–60 (Scalia, J., concurring in judgment and dissenting in part), expressed concern in *Fordice* over the future of historically black institutions.

52. *United States v. Louisiana*, 718 F. Supp. at 514.

53. Marilyn Milloy, "Black School Fights Desegregation," *Newsday*, 19 November 1989, 6.

54. See *United States v. Louisiana*, 718 F. Supp. at 533.

55. See ibid.

56. Ibid. at 532–35; see also ibid. at 508, 513–14 (explaining the need to end duplication of law schools in order to end dual system).

57. Ibid. at 513–14.

58. *United States v. Louisiana*, 751 F. Supp. 606 (E.D. La. 1990), *vacating* 692 F. Supp. 642 (E.D. La. 1988).

59. *United States v. Fordice*, 505 U.S. 717 (1992), *vacating Ayers v. Allain*, 914 F.2d 676 (5th Cir. 1990). For further proceedings in the Louisiana case, see *United States v. Louisiana*, 9 F.3d 1159 (5th Cir. 1993) (remanding it for further proceedings in light of *Fordice*).

60. See, e.g., Gilbert Ware, *William Hastie: Grace under Pressure* (New York: Oxford University Press, 1984), 12–20 (accounting William Hastie's college experience at Amherst in the 1920s). Hastie graduated Phi Beta Kappa, made the *Law Review* at Harvard, and later became the first black federal judge.

61. See Walter R. Allen, ''The Color of Success: African-American College Student Outcomes at Predominantly White and Historically Black Public Colleges and Universities,'' *Harvard Education Review* 62 (1992): 26, 27. See generally Jacqueline Fleming, *Blacks in College* (San Francisco: Jossey-Bass, 1984) (presenting comprehensive study of black students' intellectual development in various settings).

62. Richard C. Richardson and Elizabeth F. Skinner, *Achieving Quality and Diversity: Universities in a Multicultural Society* (Phoenix: Oryx Press, 1991), 33–46.

63. See ''University of Minnesota Will Not Recognize or Support Group That Promotes 'White Culture,' '' *Chronicle of Higher Education*, 18 March 1992, A34.

64. See ''Campus Life; Syracuse: Blacks-Only Group May Soon Forfeit Status and Money,'' *New York Times*, 9 December 1990, sec. A, 62; Mary Jo Hill, ''Do Theme Dorms Sanction Self-Segregation?'' *Christian Science Monitor*, 15 July 1996, 12.

65. Carnegie Foundation for the Advancement of Teaching, *Campus Life: In Search of Community* (New York: Carnegie Foundation, 1990), 25–32.

66. See Robert Demmons, '' 'We Won't Go Back': The First and Second Assaults on Affirmative Action,'' in *We Won't Go Back: Making the Case for Affirmative Action*, ed. Charles R. Lawrence III and Mari J. Matsuda (Boston: Houghton Mifflin, 1997). For a collection of campus incidents, see Mari J. Matsuda, ''Public Response to Racist Speech: Considering the Victim's Story,'' *Michigan Law Review* 87 (August 1989): 2320, 2370–73 nn.245–56; see also Carnegie Foundation, *In Search of Community*, 26–34 (giving examples of racial harassment).

10

The Social Construction of *Brown v. Board of Education*

Law Reform and the Reconstructive Paradox

RICHARD DELGADO
JEAN STEFANCIC

Fundamental to so much discussion about equality in America has been the Supreme Court's 1954 decision in *Brown v. Board of Education*[1] declaring racially segregated schools unconstitutional. Yet critics have differed as to the success of the Court's *Brown* decision in actually achieving equality in American life. Broadly speaking, there are two views about *Brown*. The conventional view holds that *Brown* is one of the two or three most important cases in American legal history. According to this interpretation, *Brown* supplied the impetus for the modern civil rights movement, demonstrated that courts, at least at times, can assert moral leadership, and emphasized that African Americans are entitled to live in the United States on terms equal to whites.[2]

The other view, that of the revisionists, holds that *Brown* accomplished relatively little, in either the short or the long run.[3] Revisionists argue that *Brown* is the product of a momentary convergence between white and black interests that began to fade soon thereafter.[4] Some argue that landmark cases like *Brown* may even impair the cause of black rights by inducing a mood of unwarranted euphoria among supporters while stiffening resistance on the part of diehards and white supremacists.0[5] Revisionists and conventionalists are apt to differ not only in their understanding of *Brown* but also in their interpretation of how social change occurs. In general, revisionists hold that social reform is difficult to achieve, especially through law, and that gains have a way of slipping back.[6] The more sanguine conventionalists argue that if *Brown* has not brought about racial justice by itself, we can at least move closer to this goal through further effort. *Brown* has certainly helped; and if it has fallen short, what we need is a *Brown III* or a *Brown IV*.[7]

Although these and other differences separate the revisionists and the conventionalists, in one respect they both approach *Brown* in the same manner. Each examines the situation that prevailed before and after *Brown* and asks: Did the landmark decision make a difference? Were the forces that led to the 1960s-era reforms already in motion before *Brown*? Did *Brown* benefit white elites more than it benefited blacks? If it benefited blacks, did it help mostly middle-class blacks, leaving the underclass as badly off as before? Both groups, in short, examine *Brown* longitudinally and temporally, looking for evidence of causation or its lack. The argument has what we might call a vertical character: one lines up the situation that prevailed before *Brown* and after and looks for signs that *Brown* brought about changes.

In this chapter, we argue that an ignored, and equally vital, axis is horizontal.[8] To understand *Brown*'s role, and that of law reform cases generally, one must attend to contemporaneous events in society at the time *Brown* was decided. Focusing on this other dimension enables us to understand why *Brown* was seen as a breakthrough case, even though it failed to have much effect outside the narrow area of school desegregation,[9] and even there, less than one might have hoped.[10] Moreover, focusing on this horizontal dimension allows us to understand law's limitations in propelling social change in general.

We begin by summarizing what *Brown* was and was not able to accomplish, doctrinally and conceptually, employing as our principal illustration the debate over campus hate-speech rules.[11] We argue that society's resistance to reform in this area is just one example of a backward drift in matters of race, and the decisions whose narratives more aptly characterize our time are not *Brown* but the nineteenth-century Supreme Court cases—*Plessy v. Ferguson*,[12] the *Civil Rights Cases*,[13] and *Dred Scott v. Sandford*.[14] Finally, we put forward a *reconstructive paradox* that names and explains why, despite evidence to the contrary, we continue to believe the legal system can bring about significant change in areas such as race when it is in fact capable of bringing about very little.[15]

How *Brown* Failed to Generalize

Many critics have pointed out that *Brown* accomplished relatively little in the way of school desegregation, except in the Deep South, and that black children are as likely today as they were forty years ago to attend predominantly black schools.[16] To this, one could add doctrinal retrenchment in closely related areas. Although subsequent courts have left *Brown* standing, in the sense that they did not expressly overrule it, they have done much to cut back its effect. School districts may not enact metropolitan desegregation plans, at least in the absence of a showing of prior discrimination.[17] Education is not a fundamental interest,[18] nor is poverty a suspect class.[19] States have no obligation to fund property-rich and property-poor districts similarly.[20] Segregation that results from white flight is essentially irremediable.[21] Black male academies are unconstitutional,[22] minority scholarships are under fire,[23] and affirmative action that takes the form of reserving slots in state-funded professional schools is illegal.[24]

Why did *Brown* end up having so little effect, even in the area of school reform? Elsewhere, we have put forward the thesis that social reform through law is relatively ineffective because law's scope is so narrow.[25] Because every social practice is part of an interlocking system of other practices, meanings, and interpretations, changing just one element (e.g., student-assignment rules) leaves the rest unchanged.[26] Thus, when the Supreme Court decided *Brown*, its principle was soon robbed of much effect when, in a myriad of decisions, school officials, lower courts, sheriffs, and others interpreted *Brown* against the familiar background.[27] "Of course, the Supreme Court didn't mean *that*," they would reason in close cases. It is as though legal decisions take place against a gravitational field, with the pull being toward the familiar, toward stasis.[28] Because *Brown* set out to change just one element, leaving the force field itself intact, its effect quickly eroded. For social reform to happen, "everything must change at once," but in the law, doctrines such as stare decisis, standing, mootness, ripeness, and political question mean that the law cannot change everything at once.[29] It can decide only the case before it.

Disbelieving or obstructionist officials are not the only forces that act to rob landmark decisions of much of their effect. If they were, all that would be necessary would be vigilance and determined enforcement. Rather, such decisions fail to establish themselves in the wider legal culture, so that even those who are generally sympathetic to reform fail to see their applications in closely related areas.

Consider, for example, the debate over campus hate-speech rules.[30] Beginning about a decade ago, college and university administrators began noticing an upsurge in the number of racist insults, graffiti, and name-calling taking place on their campuses.[31] At some institutions, the number of students of color began to drop as parents decided to send their sons and daughters elsewhere.[32] Many campuses responded by enacting anti-hate-speech rules that punished certain forms of racial or sexual taunting or name-calling.[33] The rules sparked immediate resistance.

Brown at least had some effect. Today, a school official who might be tempted to assign all the black children to one school and the white ones to another would likely think, "I had better not do that, at least unless I disguise what I am doing." Today's opponents of hate-speech rules, however, show little such hesitation; they proceed as though *Brown* had not taken place at all.[34] Hate-speech rules are in many respects like student-assignment rules.[35] Yet opponents make the same arguments against them, the same rhetorical moves, that we witnessed with the classic resistance to school desegregation.

Under *Plessy v. Ferguson*,[36] schemes that allocated benefits along racial lines were upheld, as long as the benefit blacks received was roughly comparable to that received by whites. In *Plessy*, blacks were forced to ride in one railroad car, whites in another.[37] The Supreme Court upheld the railroad's rule: separate but equal. Whites and blacks were equally disadvantaged: neither could ride in the other's car. A similar situation prevailed in the schools of Topeka, Kansas, at the time *Brown* was decided. Indeed, shortly after the decision was announced, a famous constitutional scholar was prompted to wonder if the decision was principled: Why should the rights of blacks to associate with whites trump that of whites *not* to associate with blacks?[38] One right balanced another, one claim against its perfect reciprocal.

In the debate about hate speech, we find a strikingly similar structure. The white person insists on a right to say whatever is on his or her mind. The black person demands protection when what is on the white's mind is a direct face-to-face racial insult. One claims a right to do *X*, the other the right not to have *X* done to him or her. One right emanates from one part of the Constitution—the First Amendment—one, from another—the Fourteenth Amendment.[39] As with separate but equal, today's debate over hate speech features commentators insisting that the black's injury is all in his or her head.[40] This perspective parallels early cases in which the Supreme Court told blacks that the indignity of being herded into separate railroad cars is offensive only if they put that construction on it.[41] Today's opponents of hate-speech rules dismiss the black's injury as merely dignitary and not a real harm.[42] One well-regarded constitutional scholar recently rejected the "silencing" argument by pointing out that it requires mental mediation—the victim decides to remain silent.[43] As with *Brown*, the opposition to hate-speech rules portrays itself as highly principled. It is not in favor of hate speech (heaven forbid). Rather, there are other, higher principles at stake here.[44]

Why *Brown* Failed to Generalize

Brown effected little change in terms of doctrine, consciousness, or the realities of life for black schoolchildren. Yet society has constructed the decision as a breakthrough of momentous proportions. We believe the two observations are related. *Brown*'s sharp departure from the past caused it to stand out, to seem a breathtaking advance. This departure also assured that it would fail to "take"—would succumb to what we called earlier a kind of social gravity.[45] In this section, we spell out in greater detail what that gravity is. We conclude by describing a "reconstructive paradox" that afflicts all reform movements, especially those that rely heavily on the law and litigation.

The Forces That Swallow Social Reform Decisions Like Brown

What we have described as a kind of social gravity that affects all novel social claims, especially legal ones, has at least three components. As we previously mentioned, it includes the system of meanings and interpretations against which the new rule must operate.[46] It also includes a set of narratives, or "stock stories," with which the new ruling is required to harmonize.[47] Last, it includes a set of social practices with which the new command must contend.[48] Each of these components mitigates the new decision's effect. Each is an aspect of what we called the horizontal dimension[49] of a case, that which was taking place in society at the time the case was adjudicated.

MEANINGS AND SOCIAL INTERPRETATIONS

Any text, including legal ones, is interpreted against a background of meanings, presumptions, and preexisting understandings.[50] If a parent tells a child, "Clean up your room," the terms "clean" and "room" have relatively well agreed-on meanings. The child knows he or she is not expected to launder the drapes or vacuum the attic space above the room. If an adolescent tells the parent, "I'll be back by midnight," both understand that "midnight" means tonight, not next week, and that "back" means inside the house. The same is true of legal commands. Thus, when *Brown* ordered school districts to desegregate "with all deliberate speed,"[51] southern officials interpreted the decree in terms of their common sense. In hundreds of close cases, they construed *Brown* to mean the only thing it could mean, consistent with their experience: integration that went not too far and not too fast and that left the school system as intact as possible.[52] Operators of public beaches, restaurants, colleges, and other facilities interpreted *Brown* as a case affecting only schools. Some school officials even took the position that it bound only the districts before the court.[53] To recalcitrant officials, *Brown* looked like an exception, an improbable edict that should naturally be interpreted in that light. The only way to harmonize it with common sense was to construe it narrowly: "Of course, the Supreme Court did not mean that blacks and whites are strictly equal," they told themselves. "It surely didn't mean that we would have to do *this*" (assign black principals to white schools, provide college counseling to all, adopt due process protections in school discipline cases affecting black children facing expulsion, and so on). Because *Brown* was interpreted against the background of a myriad of such understandings, traditions, and expectations and because, unlike a parent, the Supreme Court was not instantly available to clarify what it meant, the case had relatively little impact. It did change one thing, student-assignment rules, but the rest of society remained essentially the same.[54] The gain in this one area was quickly swallowed up by interpretive effects emanating from all of the others.[55]

SOCIAL PRACTICES

A second component of what we have called the gravitational field against which new legal rules must operate is the set of preexisting social practices, most of which the Supreme Court is powerless to change. These practices include friendship patterns, the way a teacher looks at or responds to a black child, and that child's own self-concept and expectations with respect to treatment from whites. They include the ways in which librarians, bus drivers, shop owners, and landlords deal with the young black schoolchild and his or her family. They determine who is chosen for student-body president, the debate team, and the cheerleading squad. If all of these practices remain the same while only student-assignment rules change, a black child's life will not be greatly improved after *Brown* (and may be considerably worse).[56]

Of course, a forced change in one social practice theoretically could prompt reconsideration of all of the others. Because white schoolchildren now are required to attend school in a building that will house some blacks, the other social practices we have mentioned might begin to change. But everything we know about cognitive dissonance and resistance to the unfamiliar suggests the opposite.[57] New practices that are discordant with old ones are resisted and adopted, if at all, slowly and grudgingly.[58] New reasons are found to justify now disputed social practices.[59]

THE ROLE OF NARRATIVES

A final component of the social milieu that affects the reception of a legal decision or rule is the backdrop of narratives or stories against which the new element will be forced to operate.[60] Narratives are the simple, scriptlike interpretive structures—"he hit first," "I didn't know it was yours," "majority rules," or "I've been here longer"—that we use to order our understanding of the world.[61]

In the school desegregation setting, court decrees confront a whole host of narratives and social perceptions that generate resistance. Such narratives include: "neighborhood schools are best"; "who are these outsiders trying to tell us what to do?"; "blacks were happy until . . ."; "black people just want to push into where they are not wanted"; "they want things they don't deserve and haven't earned"; "integration might be okay, but the schools should remain predominantly white, and the curriculum, teachers, and so on, roughly as they are now"; and so on.[62]

As with meanings and social practices, these and other narratives could theoretically change. A person who holds a stock of hundreds of such narratives regarding minority people, neighborhood schools, and "the way things are" could radically revise his or her worldview when confronted by the image of a surprisingly nice, intelligent, reasonable black individual at a school or workplace. But narratives change very slowly, in part because we interpret new experiences and new narratives in terms of the old ones—the ones we hold.[63] These old narratives, indeed, form the basis for understanding new experiences, including that of our first close black associate. It is far easier to pronounce the black an "exception" than to revise one's entire stock of beliefs.

Eventually, of course, social stories and practices change but much more slowly than we like to think.[64] And when they do, courts and decrees play little role in bringing about the change.[65] Courts are usually distant institutions. Unlike flesh-and-blood persons, they cannot follow up an exchange by saying, for example: "No, he is not an exception; most of them are like that if you take the trouble to get to know them." Courts are not in a position to engage society in the kind of continuing dialogue that could in theory change meanings and practices.[66] Courts can only change one practice at a time. Everything else—the entire system of practices, traditions, and meanings—remains the same, exerting its gravitational tug toward the familiar. In giving obedience to the new decree—something the courts *are* in a position to enforce—hundreds of lower-level bureaucrats, state officials, and lower-court judges will interpret the ringing words according to their commonsense understandings about persons, about relations, and about what is just and deserved.[67]

The Reconstructive Paradox

The combined effect of the forces just mentioned means that any reform measure other than the smallest and most incremental will meet predictable resistance, reinterpretation, and obstruction in ways that the legal system is ill equipped to manage and counter.[68] One perspective from which to view these horizontal forces is in terms of what we call the "reconstructive paradox." After defining the paradox,[69] we illustrate its operation by demonstrating that the current approach to race and race remedies shows the influence of the nineteenth-century cases, especially *Plessy v. Ferguson,* more than that of their more famous twentieth-century rival, *Brown v. Board of Education.*[70]

DEFINING THE RECONSTRUCTIVE PARADOX

Much of what we have said so far can be summarized in the following six steps, constituting what we call the reconstructive paradox:

1. The greater a social evil (e.g., black subordination) the more it is apt to be entrenched in our national life.[71]
2. The more entrenched the evil, the more massive the social effort that will be necessary to eradicate it.[72]
3. The harm of an entrenched evil will be invisible to many because it is embedded and ordinary.[73]
4. The massive social effort will inevitably collide with other social values and things we hold dear (e.g., settled expectations, religion, the family, privacy, and the southern way of life). It will entail dislocations, shifts in spending priorities, new taxes, and changes in the way we speak and relate to each other.[74]
5. These efforts, by contrast, will be highly visible and will spark resistance and accusations that the backers are engaging in totalitarian tactics, siding with big government, dislodging innocent whites, operating in derogation of the merit principle, elevating group over individual relief, reviving old grudges, whipping up division where none existed before, and so on.[75]
6. Resisting these latter complaints will feel right and proper, for the other side will appear to be callously sacrificing real liberty, real security, and real resources for a nebulous goal.[76]

Therefore, reconstruction will always strike many in a society as unprincipled, unwarranted, and wrong. Little surprise, then, that few take up its cause, persist for long in the face of the resistance it calls forth, or even frame their programs and objectives broadly enough so that if they are adopted, they have a chance of remaining in place and achieving some real effects.

BACK TO *PLESSY*: PRESENT-DAY RHETORIC AND EVIDENCE OF THE RECONSTRUCTIVE PARADOX OPERATING IN OUR TIME

Reform through *law alone*, as we mentioned, is apt to have little effect, because legal decrees succumb silently and painlessly to interpretation and other forms of cultural weight.[77] Even when, as happened with the civil rights revolution of the 1960s, legal reform operates in concert with broader social forces to produce undeniable and much-needed gains, resistance is apt to set in at some point. Consider how today we no longer talk in terms of separateness as an inherent injury, of black schoolchildren as victims, or of racism as a harm whose injury "is unlikely ever to be undone." Instead, we speak of the need for formal neutrality, of the dangers affirmative action poses for innocent whites, and of the need for black Americans to look to their own resources.[78] Moderates and conservatives alike have rolled back affirmative action[79] and challenged university and college theme houses, special curricula, and ethnic studies departments,[80] which they see as violations of the merit principle and fair and equal treatment policies. Courts are quick to strike down set-aside programs and affirmative action plans as "quota systems" likely to discriminate against "innocent whites."[81] The narrative of *Plessy v. Ferguson*[82] more aptly characterizes our attitudes with respect to race than do the stirring words of *Brown*.

In *Plessy*, Supreme Court Justice Henry B. Brown could not see anything wrong with a system that required blacks to sit in separate railroad cars and overlooked the unmistakable damage inflicted on blacks' sense of dignity by such a discriminatory system. Indeed, he wrote: "We consider the underlying fallacy of the plaintiff's argument to consist in the assumption that the enforced separation of the two races stamps the colored race with a badge of inferiority. If this be so, it is not by reason of anything found in the act, but solely because the colored race chooses to put that construction upon it."[83]

In a 1981 case, *City of Memphis v. Greene*,[84] Justice John Paul Stevens III declared that a municipal decision to separate a white neighborhood from a black one by allowing the construction of a wall between them to regulate traffic flow was fair and not motivated by an intention to discriminate against blacks but rather by an "interest in protecting the safety and tranquillity of a residential neighborhood."[85] Echoing the earlier opinion of Justice Brown in *Plessy*, Stevens wrote:

> Because urban neighborhoods are so frequently characterized by a common ethnic or racial heritage, a regulation's adverse impact on a particular neighborhood will often have a disparate effect on an identifiable ethnic or racial group. To regard an inevitable consequence of that kind as a form of stigma so severe as to violate the Thirteenth Amendment would trivialize the great purpose of that charter of freedom.[86]

In both cases, separated by nearly a century, during which much progress in race relations was said to have been made, blacks have been presented with a rhetorical legerdemain that tests both their ability to participate in societal self-deception and their inclination to prevail in the face of it.

Other modern-era cases show the same tendency to disregard blacks' longstanding predicament or whites' contribution to it. Because *Brown* only addressed the effects of segregated education on black schoolchildren, remaining silent on the issue of white responsibility, it was perhaps inevitable that the question of fault would become the next hurdle to blacks struggling to achieve social gains. *Washington v. Davis*[87] is perhaps the most well known example, but a number of others vie for consideration. In *Arlington Heights v. Metropolitan Housing Development Corp.*,[88] the Court held that certain zoning regulations that had the effect of excluding blacks were constitutionally valid because they were not enacted with that purpose in mind.[89] In *San Antonio Independent School District v. Rodriguez*,[90] a school finance scheme that caused a great disparity in funding tax-rich and tax-poor schools was upheld despite its serious impact on poor and minority children.[91] And, as mentioned earlier, a traffic control measure that took the form of a wall between white and black neighbors in Memphis was deemed just that, a traffic control measure, despite the way in which it physically and symbolically separated the races.[92]

Each of these cases foreshadows a retreat from the ringing words of *Brown*; each in many ways is reminiscent of the crabbed neutrality and unrealistic refusal to see discrimination that characterized *Plessy*. Not only has our time implicitly resurrected *Plessy* in its approach to racial justice, but a second notorious nineteenth-century case's star is rising as well: the *Civil Rights Cases*.[93] In the *Civil Rights Cases*, the Supreme Court wrote that blacks who were demanding equal access to various types of public accommodation were seriously overstepping and in effect demanding to be afforded special treatment. The Court wrote:

> When a man has emerged from slavery, and by the aid of beneficent legislation has shaken off the inseparable concomitants of that state, there must be some stage in the progress of his elevation when he takes the rank of a mere citizen, and ceases to be the special favorite of the laws, and when his rights as a citizen, or a man, are to be protected in the ordinary modes by which other men's rights are protected.[94]

Cases in our time show much the same attitude. Blacks' demands for justice are considered themselves unjust because they are a form of asking for special treatment and because they encroach on white privilege and settled expectations. One example is *Regents of University of California v. Bakke*.[95] There, the Supreme Court upheld the challenge of a white applicant to a state-sponsored medical school.[96] The plurality opinion cast him in the role of victim. The medical school's affirmative action program, which reserved a small number of slots for African Americans, unconstitutionally violated the rights of applicants such as Bakke.[97] The university's program operated unfairly against "innocent persons in respondent's position."[98] The state's interest in remedying past discrimination was not sufficiently compelling to justify the "special treatment" black candidates received. In language reminiscent of Justice Joseph P. Bradley's in the *Civil Rights Cases*, the plurality opinion painted the university's affirmative action program to increase the number of black doctors as coddling and favoritism.[99] Other recent affirmative action cases have taken a similar position and employed rhetoric nearly as unsympathetic as that of *Bakke*.[100]

The most startling parallel is found in *City of Richmond v. J. A. Croson Co.*,[101] in which the Court struck down a minority set-aside program in the construction industry that had been adopted by the Richmond city council.[102] The majority opinion found the council's action a potential case of "simple racial politics."[103] A concurring opinion went even further, warning that society should be watchful against those who might attempt to "even the score" at the expense of whites.[104]

Societal rhetoric follows suit. A host of commentators today rail against multicultural programs on university campuses;[105] minority-only scholarships are under fire;[106] welfare programs are under sustained attack as disguised giveaways to undeserving, unambitious, and oversexed blacks; and the use of code words like "political correctness" indicates that many in our society believe that blacks have gone too far.[107] They think blacks are now receiving special, not just equal, treatment and that it is time to put a stop to it, just as it is time to begin closing our borders to immigration from Mexico, Haiti, Cuba, and other societies of color.[108]

We believe, then, that dispassionate examination of today's dominant narratives shows that the themes of *Plessy* and the *Civil Rights Cases* are in ascension. We put forward an even more somber prediction: without concerted action or a sharp change in national circumstances, one final step will be taken. Just as the clock of time seems to be rolling backward, a final narrative may soon regain prominence: that of *Dred Scott v. Sandford.*[109]

In *Dred Scott*, the Supreme Court, in a case concerning a runaway slave, held that African Americans have "no rights which the white person is bound to respect."[110] The claim of an African American to citizenship was absurd, both historically and legally: blacks simply were not citizens because they never were such and the framers of the Constitution, "great men," never regarded them that way.[111] *Dred Scott* constitutes, certainly, the nadir of American law's treatment of African Americans, a blot on the record of the American legal conscience. Yet its narrative retains vitality today. We see growing evidence of it in Supreme Court opinions and in popular culture.[112]

Chief Justice Roger B. Taney's opinion depicted blacks as subhumans.[113] Is this shocking portrayal of other races so far from today's range of possibilities? Is the story of the primitive bestial black or Mexican completely missing in today's narratives, both in popular culture and in judicial opinions? Unfortunately, we believe not. Indeed, we believe this account of groups of color is undergoing a resurgence.

Consider, for example, the revival of race-IQ theories, some seconded by well-regarded scientists and writers such as Charles Murray, Richard Herrnstein,[114] Arthur Jensen,[115] and William Shockley.[116] Consider the number of books, such as Ben Wattenberg's *Birth Dearth*,[117] and reports that have urged renewed attention to the question of selective breeding: our "best" citizens have too few children and minorities and the poor, too many, so that the gene pool in the United States is declining. Consider the resurgence of nativism and movements to close the nation's borders particularly to brown-skinned immigrants.[118] Consider also the English-only movement.[119] Much of this attitude is fueled by the conviction that "those people" are not fit to reside here; that their language, customs, and morals are inferior; and that they are and always will be second-class citizens. All of these cultural strands converge around the idea that this is a white country and that nonwhite persons, genes, ideas, languages, and culture are inferior to European ones, a principal theme in *Dred Scott.*

Nor has the legal system been totally divorced from the return of the *Dred Scott* mentality. In the Rodney King case, a Los Angeles–area jury acquitted police officers who were videotaped beating a black motorist while he lay unresisting on the ground.[120] Testimony by the police and later interviews with the jurors showed that the motorist, King, was *seen* as the kind of being who might resist, who might at any moment strike out with tremendous force, and who, because he was caught speeding, deserved whatever penalty the police chose to inflict.[121]

Supreme Court decisions also contain hints of *Dred Scott* and its brusque dismissal of African American humanity. In *McCleskey v. Kemp*,[122] the Supreme Court considered a challenge to Georgia's infliction of the death penalty, which fell disproportionately heavily on blacks, particularly ones whose victims were white.[123] The Court rejected McClesky's claim, at the same time reprimanding him and his lawyers for even having brought it.[124] Such claims, based on statistical disparities, might be raised in virtually any setting, the Court reasoned, resulting in repetitive demands "based upon any arbitrary variable."[125] Cases brought by poor women—*Wyman v. James*[126] (the welfare-search case), *Maher v. Roe*,[127] and other abortion-funding cases—show the same thinly veiled exasperation on the part of the Court. These decisions stop barely short of telling poor women that they do not know their places and what is expected of them—to be as quiet, prudent, nondemanding, and nonsexual as possible. The demand for privacy in the face of a welfare inspection or for an abortion from a state-funded clinic appears outrageous. The women are chastised for the effrontery of wanting to live life on their own terms.[128]

Many earlier eras, of course, witnessed similar patterns of advance followed by retrenchment. During Reconstruction, African Americans made great gains, but these were followed by an era of lynching and Jim Crow laws.[129] *Brown v. Board of Education* was followed by new resistance in the South.[130] In Europe the broadened vistas and relaxed worker-migration policies of the early European community years soon were followed by xenophobia, a resurgence of Nazism, and tightened controls on immigration.[131] We believe the United States is in the middle of such a retrenchment today. Indeed, it is as though the arrow of time has reversed. We see the nineteenth-century cases appearing in modern guise before our eyes—first the *Plessy* line of cases, then the notorious *Civil Rights Cases*, and finally, in the wings, *Dred Scott v. Sandford.*

What *Brown* and the Reconstructive Paradox Mean for Activists and Reformers: Summary and Suggestions

Brown, like all law reform cases, confronted built-in resistances that deprived it of the efficacy its supporters hoped for it. Social reform proceeds, if at all, in small increments; the pendulum swing is as apt to be backward at any given time as forward. *Brown*'s relatively slight effect is part of a broader form of social response—the reconstructive paradox—which holds that the greater the evil, the greater the need for reform; the greater the reform effort, the more unprincipled and unjust the effort will seem and the greater the resistance it will call up. Even more than other avenues for reform, law is handicapped by its inability to engage in dialogue with the group whose values and practices need changing. Except in criminal law, which can put violators in jail, law has little ability to provide the constant reinforcement necessary to change attitudes or behavior. Indeed, law is always outnumbered; doctrines such as standing ensure that any wide-ranging legal edict appears incomprehensible and wrong, evoking the reaction: surely the court didn't mean *that.*

If we are right, reformers should hesitate to place much faith in the legal system as the primary instrument for their agendas.[132] Law is relatively powerless to effect social revolutions as both theory and history, including the case of *Brown*, demonstrate. Everything must change at once, so that a far greater focus than the merely legal is necessary before reform begins to be possible. Because the reconstructive paradox has greatest force with respect to courts, reformers ought to reserve judicial activism for the later stages of a revolution, using courts for the final mopping-up steps to secure a social advance that society has already begun to accept.

Litigation is expensive and frustrating if resorted to at the wrong time. We urge that reformers reconsider the appropriate time to use it. If employed too early, as it arguably may have been with *Brown*, it leads to false celebration, then disillusionment by persons who, like African Americans, have waited too long to see their just demands met—then betrayed.

Conclusion

Society has constructed *Brown v. Board of Education* as a great case. Yet as we have seen, the opinion failed to generalize and accordingly exercised little influence outside the area of school desegregation. Even within that arena, it brought about relatively few improvements in the lives of black schoolchildren, most of whom today attend schools that are just as segregated and in even greater disarray than the ones they attended in *Brown*'s time.

We believe the two observations are related, indeed dependent on one another. We saw *Brown* as a startling, extraordinary decision—which it was—for the very reasons that brought about its demise, namely, the way in which it challenged and departed from current culture and orthodoxy. Every law reform decision, we pointed out, takes place against a background of beliefs, narratives, meanings, and social practices that constitute a kind of social gravitational field. This field causes the exceptional case to erode quickly, to be resisted, interpreted away, and increasingly ignored. This dissipation has visited *Brown*. Although we afford it lip service and pay attention to its ringing, aspirational message on celebratory occasions, other narratives have turned out to have greater vitality. These more-lasting narratives are those of the nineteenth-century cases, ones that celebrate white superiority and that depict blacks as inferior, subhuman, demanding, and unjustified. As a culture, and as a legal profession, we are rapidly returning to the regime of *Plessy v. Ferguson*'s separate but equal doctrine and the *Civil Rights Cases'* view of blacks as imposers and whiners because they desire to live in American society on the same terms as whites. Moreover, we find some frightening straws in the wind—indications that ought to give pause to any defender of freedom and minority rights. We have reviewed evidence that society generally, and the legal system in particular, are beginning to regress in one final, decisive quantum jump. American society, without the spur of Cold War competition or the need for minority labor or soldiers, is in serious danger of quietly, implicitly readopting a familiar standard from another era: that of *Dred Scott v. Sandford*, in which blacks and other minorities of color have no rights that white Americans are bound to respect.

NOTES

1. 347 U.S. 483 (1954).

2. Books in this general vein include Richard Kluger, *Simple Justice* (New York: Knopf, 1976); Juan Williams, *Eyes on the Prize* (New York: Viking, 1987). For a discussion of the conventional view and its alleged weaknesses, see Michael J. Klarman, "*Brown*, Racial Change, and the Civil Rights Movement," *Virginia Law Review* 80 (February 1994): 7–150.

3. On the revisionist view of *Brown*, see, for example, Klarman, "*Brown*, Racial Change, and the Civil Rights Movement," 7–150. On the revisionist view of law reform generally, see Gerald N. Rosenberg, *The Hollow Hope: Can Courts Bring About Social Change?* (Chicago: University of Chicago Press, 1991); see also Derrick A. Bell, Jr., "*Brown v. Board of Education* and the Interest-Convergence Dilemma," *Harvard Law Review* 93 (January 1980): 518.

4. See, e.g., Bell, "*Brown v. Board of Education*," 3.

5. See Derrick A. Bell, Jr., *And We Are Not Saved: The Elusive Quest for Racial Justice* (New York: Basic Books, 1987), 3, 111; Klarman, "*Brown*, Racial Change, and the Civil Rights Movement," 85 (discussing the way *Brown* inspired a wave of southern resistance).

6. See, e.g., Bell, *And We Are Not Saved*; Richard Delgado and Jean Stefancic, *Failed Revolutions: Social Reform and the Limits of Legal Imagination* (Boulder: Westview Press, 1994).

7. See, e.g., Williams, *Eyes on the Prize*, 2.

8. That is to say, an axis that examines events contemporaneous with a key event rather than ones that came earlier or later.

9. See notes 16–44 below and accompanying text.

10. See notes 16–24 below and accompanying text.

11. See notes 30–44 below and accompanying text. For writing on the issue of hate speech, see, e.g., Mari Matsuda et al., *Words That Wound* (Boulder: Westview Press, 1993); Nadine Strossen, "Regulating Racist Speech on Campus: A Modest Proposal," *Duke Law Journal* (1990): 484.

12. 163 U.S. 537 (1896).

13. 109 U.S. 3 (1883).

14. 60 U.S. 393 (1856).

15. For an earlier treatment of a related mechanism, the *empathic fallacy*, see Richard Delgado and Jean Stefancic, "Images of the Outsider in American Law and Culture: Can Free Expression Remedy Systemic Social Ills?" *Cornell Law Review* 77 (September 1992): 1258.

16. See, e.g., Klarman, "*Brown*, Racial Change, and the Civil Rights Movement," 11–12, 76–86; see also Andrew Hacker, *Two Nations: Black and White, Separate, Hostile, Unequal* (New York: Ballantine Books, 1992); *The Words of Martin Luther King, Jr.*, ed. Coretta S. King (New York: Newmarket, 1987) (hereafter cited as *MLK*); Jerome M. Culp, Jr., "Water Buffalo and Diversity: Naming Names and Reclaiming the Racial Discourse," *Connecticut Law Review* 26 (Fall 1993): 209, 246–47 (discussing the situation in law schools).

17. See, e.g., *Milliken v. Bradley*, 433 U.S. 267 (1977).

18. *San Antonio Indep. School District v. Rodriguez*, 411 U.S. 1 (1973).

19. *James v. Valtierra*, 402 U.S. 137 (1971).

20. *Rodriguez*, 411 U.S. 1; see also *Valtierra*, 402 U.S. 137 (upholding state constitutional provision requiring low-rent housing projects to be approved by a majority of qualified electors).

21. Metropolitan desegregation plans are permissible only if the segregation results from official action, not the aggregate of individual decisions by white families to move to the suburbs. See *Milliken*, 433 U.S. 267.

22. On the difficulties of establishing such schools with public funds, see Jacqueline Conciatore, "Detroit Must Admit Girls to Public All-Male Academies, Judge Says," *Black Issues in Higher Education*, 29 August 1991, 8; "Whites in Detroit Teach Students at Black School a Fourth R: Racism," *New York Times*, 2 December 1992, sec. B, 6.

23. See, e.g., Michael A. Olivas, "Federal Law and Scholarship Policy: An Essay on the Office for Civil Rights, Title VI, and Racial Restrictions," *Journal of College and University Law* 18 (Summer 1991): 21 (articulating the position of the recent Republican administration on this issue).

24. *Regents of Univ. of California v. Bakke*, 438 U.S. 265 (1978).

25. See Delgado and Stefancic, *Failed Revolutions*, 6; see also *MLK*.

26. See, e.g., Delgado and Stefancic, *Failed Revolutions*, 6; Delgado and Stefancic, *Images of the Outsider*, 15.

27. See notes 51–55 below and accompanying text.

28. See Bell, *And We Are Not Saved*, 3 (discussing the way racial breakthroughs erode soon thereafter); see also Richard Delgado, "Derrick Bell and the Ideology of Racial Reform: Will We Ever Be Saved?" *Yale Law Journal* 97 (April 1988): 23 (elaborating on this process); *MLK*, 118–19 (on resistance to civil rights decrees).

29. On these doctrines and the way they limit the range of cases and issues courts may consider, see Ronald D. Rotunda, *Modern Constitutional Law*, 3d ed. (St. Paul: West Publishing Co., 1989), 1026–73.

30. On the problem of hate speech in general, see Matsuda, *Words That Wound*, and Strossen, "Regulating Racist Speech." On campus hate speech, see Richard Delgado, "Campus Antiracism Rules: Constitutional Narratives in Collision," *Northwestern University Law Review* 85 (Winter 1991): 343.

31. Delgado, "Campus Racism Rules," 348–58.

32. Ibid., 376, 386 n.354.

33. For a discussion of some campuses where rules have been enacted, see ibid., 358–61.

34. See notes 40–43 below and accompanying text.

35. For a discussion of these parallels, see Charles R. Lawrence III, "If He Hollers Let Him Go: Regulating Racist Speech on Campus," *Duke Law Journal* (1990): 431; Richard Delgado and Jean Stefancic, "Overcoming Legal Barriers to Regulating Hate Speech on Campuses," *Chronicle of Higher Education*, 11 August 1993, B1; notes 38–44 below and accompanying text.

36. 163 U.S. 537 (1896).

37. Ibid. at 537–39.

38. Herbert Wechsler, "Toward Neutral Principles of Constitutional Law," *Harvard Law Review* 73 (November 1959): 1.

39. For a discussion of these and other similarities, see Delgado, "Campus Antiracism Rules," 345–48; Lawrence, "If He Hollers Let Him Go," 438–40.

40. See Dinesh D'Souza, *Illiberal Education: The Politics of Race and Sex on Campus* (New York: Free Press, 1991), 132–36, 156; Nat Hentoff, *Free Speech for Me but Not for Thee* (New York: Harper Collins, 1992) (stating that minorities are ready to complain of imagined or exaggerated slights).

41. See *Plessy v. Ferguson*, 163 U.S. 537, 551 (1896).

42. See, e.g., Strossen, "Regulating Racist Speech," 498 (characterizing the injury to minorities as merely suffering an unpleasant environment).

43. Cass R. Sunstein, "Words, Conduct, Caste," *University of Chicago Law Review* 60 (Summer/Fall 1993): 795.

44. Strossen, "Regulating Racist Speech" (observing that debate implicates our grand national commitment to free speech, academic freedom, the *true* interests of minorities, and other high-sounding values).

45. See note 28 above and accompanying text.

46. See notes 28–29 above and accompanying text.

47. See Delgado and Stefancic, "Images of the Outsider"; Gerald Lopez, "Lay Lawyering," *UCLA Law Review* 32 (October 1984): 1 (discussing the role of narratives and stock stories in constructing social reality and guiding what we do and do not see).

48. See, e.g., Girardeau Spann, "Pure Politics," *Michigan Law Review* 88 (June 1990): 1971 (discussing the role of social practices in confining the effect of legal decrees).

49. For an explanation of our use of this term, see note 8 above and accompanying text.

50. These background elements often reflect the operation of social power and tradition. See Stanley Fish, *Is There a Text in This Class? The Authority of Interpretive Communities* (Cambridge: Harvard University Press, 1980); Richard Delgado, "Shadowboxing: An Essay on Power," *Cornell Law Review* 77 (May 1992): 813.

51. *Brown v. Board of Education*, 349 U.S. 294, 300 (1955).

52. See, e.g., Derrick A. Bell, Jr., *Race, Racism, and American Law*, 3d ed. (Boston: Little, Brown, & Co., 1992), 552–54, 565–607 (discussing the process of interpretation); Klarman, "*Brown*, Racial Change, and the Civil Rights Movement," 12, 76–85.

53. Bell, *Race, Racism, and American Law*, 118–20, 565–607.

54. See notes 17–26 above and accompanying text; notes 78–81 and 84–92 below and accompanying text.

55. Bell, *Race, Racism, and American Law*; see also Klarman, "*Brown*, Racial Change, and the Civil Rights Movement"; Rosenberg, *Hollow Hope*; Bell, *"Brown v. Board of Education."*

56. See *MLK*, 6 (observing that the costs of racial remedies generally are exacted from blacks); Spann, "Pure Politics."

57. See Leon Festinger, *A Theory of Cognitive Dissonance* (Stanford, Calif.: Stanford University Press, 1962).

58. Ibid.

59. Ibid.

60. See, e.g., Delgado and Stefancic, "Images of the Outsider" (discussing the role of narratives in shaping how we see the world); Delgado, "Campus Antiracism Rules."

61. See, e.g., Delgado and Stefancic, "Images of the Outsider."

62. See Klarman, "*Brown*, Racial Change, and the Civil Rights Movement" (discussing this resistance).

63. See Delgado and Stefancic, "Images of the Outsider," 1259–60 (defining "empathic fallacy" as the belief that we can change our own, and each other's, belief systems quickly and easily by presenting new arguments, stories, or accounts).

64. Ibid.

65. See Rosenberg, *Hollow Hope*; Delgado and Stefancic, *Failed Revolutions*.

66. Communities (large collectivities), by contrast, are essential to the process of forming and sharing meanings. See, e.g., Frank I. Michelman, "Foreword: Traces of Self-Government," *Harvard Law Review* 100 (November 1986): 4; see also Fish, *Is There a Text*? 278–81 (illustrating one court's limited ability to communicate the meaning of statutory language). Federal judges are situated too distantly and remotely to effect rapid change in social meanings.

67. See notes 27–29 and 50–53 above and accompanying text.

68. See Delgado and Stefancic, "Images of the Outsider," 1258–59 (observing that speech and dialogue can effectively correct small, clearly bounded, but not systemic error).

69. See text accompanying notes 71–77.

70. See text accompanying notes 78–130.

71. See, e.g., Delgado, "Shadowboxing"; Delgado and Stefancic, "Images of the Outsider."

72. Racism, for example, is generally agreed to consist of a complex of attitudes and practices that permeate institutions and individuals. See, e.g., *The Sociology of Race Relations: Reflection and Reform*, ed. Thomas F. Pettigrew (New York: Free Press, 1980); Charles R. Lawrence III, "The Id, the Ego, and Equal Protection: Reckoning with Unconscious Racism," *Stanford Law Review* 39 (January 1987): 317 (reconsidering the doctrine of discriminatory purpose).

73. See Derrick A. Bell, Jr., "Racial Realism," *Connecticut Law Review* 24 (Winter 1992): 363 (suggesting that racial equality is unobtainable because of the entrenched racism of Americans).

74. Ibid.; see also Bell, *And We Are Not Saved* (doubting that society will ever undertake such an effort).

75. Bell, "Racial Realism"; Richard Delgado, "Rodrigo's Chronicle," *Yale Law Journal* 101 (April 1992): 1357.

76. Richard Delgado and Jean Stefancic, "Imposition," *William and Mary Law Review* 35 (Spring 1994): 1025.

77. See notes 50–67 above and accompanying text.

78. Delgado and Stefancic, "Imposition" (collecting and evaluating examples of judicial and social rhetoric regarding blacks and other minorities); Thomas Ross, "Innocence and Affirmative Action," *Vanderbilt Law Review* 43 (March 1990): 297.

79. See, e.g., *Bakke*, 438 U.S. 265 (holding that admissions program that reserved positions in medical school class for disadvantaged minority students was unconstitutional). For a discussion of this retrenchment, see Joel Dreyfuss and Charles Lawrence III, *The* Bakke *Case: The Politics of Inequality* (New York: Harcourt Brace Jovanovich, 1979).

80. See, e.g., D'Souza, *Illiberal Education* (discussing the academic and cultural revolution at American universities).

81. See, e.g., *City of Richmond v. J. A. Croson Co.*, 488 U.S. 469 (1989) (striking down plan requiring city construction contracts to subcontract 30% of each contract to minority-owned businesses); Thomas Ross, "The Richmond Narratives," *Texas Law Review* 68 (December 1981): 381.

82. 163 U.S. 537 (1896).

83. Ibid. at 551.

84. 451 U.S. 100 (1981).

85. Ibid. at 119–20.

86. Ibid. at 128.

87. 426 U.S. 229 (1976) (holding that a test administered to black applicants for employment as police officers was not unconstitutional because the purpose was not discriminatory even though the impact may have been).

88. 429 U.S. 252 (1977).

89. Ibid. at 268–70.

90. 411 U.S. 1 (1973).

91. Ibid. at 54–55.

92. See notes 84–86 above and accompanying text (discussing *City of Memphis v. Greene*, 451 U.S. 100 [1981]).

93. 109 U.S. 3 (1883).

94. Ibid. at 24–25.
95. 438 U.S. 265 (1978).
96. Ibid.
97. Ibid. at 320.
98. Ibid. at 298 (plurality opinion of Powell, J.).
99. Ibid. at 295, 298–99.
100. E.g., *Wygant v. Jackson Board of Education*, 476 U.S. 267, 274–76 (1986) (rejecting role-model argument for affirmative action as dangerous, unproven, and potentially unbounded).
101. 488 U.S. 469 (1989).
102. Ibid.
103. Ibid. at 493.
104. Ibid. at 527–28 (Scalia J., concurring).
105. E.g., D'Souza, *Illiberal Education.*
106. See Olivas, "Federal Law and Scholarship Policy."
107. For examples of various social texts, ranging from editorials to conservative treatises, see Delgado and Stefancic, "Imposition."
108. Ibid., 1032 (discussing immigration issues); Gerald L. Neuman, "Back to *Dred Scott,*" *San Diego Law Review* 24, no. 2 (1987): 485 (reviewing Peter Shuck and Roger Smith, *Citizenship without Consent: Illegal Aliens in the American Polity* [New Haven: Yale University Press, 1985]).
109. 60 U.S. 393 (1856). For other discussions of the rhetorical parallels between *Dred Scott*, other nineteenth-century cases, and today's cases, see Ross, "Innocence and Affirmative Action"; Thomas Ross, "The Rhetorical Tapestry of Race: White Innocence and Black Abstraction," *William and Mary Law Review* 32 (Fall 1990): 1.
110. *Dred Scott*, 60 U.S. at 404–07.
111. Ibid. at 410.
112. See notes 122–28 below and accompanying text.
113. *Dred Scott*, 60 U.S. at 405–10 (depicting history of blacks as chattels).
114. Richard J. Herrnstein, *IQ in the Meritocracy* (London: Allen Lane, 1973); Richard Herrnstein and Charles Murray, *The Bell Curve* (New York: Free Press, 1994).
115. Arthur Jensen, "How Much Can We Boost IQ and Scholastic Achievement?" *Harvard Education Review* 39 (1969): 1.
116. For a discussion of the Nobel Prize–winning scientist's controversial views on race and IQ, see Richard Delgado et al., "Can Science Be Inopportune? Constitutional Validity of Governmental Restrictions on Race-IQ Research," *UCLA Law Review* 31 (October 1983): 128.
117. Ben J. Wattenberg, *The Birth Dearth* (New York: Pharos Books, 1987).
118. E.g., Neuman, "Back to *Dred Scott.*" On the history of U.S. nativism, see *Nativism, Discrimination, and Images of Immigrants*, ed. George Pozzetta (New York: Garland, 1991).
119. For a discussion of this and similar language-purification efforts, see Delgado and Stefancic, "Imposition," 1035; Juan Perea, "Demography and Distrust: An Essay on American Language, Cultural Pluralism, and Official English," *Minnesota Law Review* 77 (December 1992): 269.
120. For a collection of essays on the Rodney King case and the Los Angeles disturbances that followed, see "Symposium, Los Angeles, April 29, 1992 and Beyond: The Law, Issues, and Perspectives," *Southern California Law Review* 66 (May 1993): 1313.
121. Ibid.; see Jerome M. Culp, Jr., "Notes from California: Rodney King and the Race Question," *Denver University Law Review* 70, no. 2 (1993): 199.
122. 481 U.S. 279 (1987).

123. Ibid.

124. Ibid. at 319 ("McCleskey's arguments are best presented to the legislative bodies").

125. Ibid. at 317.

126. 400 U.S. 309 (1971).

127. 432 U.S. 464 (1977).

128. Delgado and Stefancic, "Imposition," 1033.

129. Bell, *Race, Racism and American Law*, 39–46; Eric Foner, *Reconstruction: America's Unfinished Revolution* (New York: Harper & Row, 1988).

130. E.g., Klarman, "*Brown*, Racial Change, and the Civil Rights Movement," 12–13, 76.

131. E.g., European Parliament Committee of Inquiry on Racism and Xenophobia, *Report on the Findings of the Inquiry* (Luxembourg: Office for Official Publications of the European Communities, 1991); Commission of the European Communities, *Legal Instruments to Combat Racism and Xenophobia* (Brussels: Directorate General, Employment, Industrial Relations and Social Affairs, 1992); "Italians Examine Fascist History," *Denver Post*, 9 April 1994, 21A.

132. Compare our conclusion with similar ones drawn by Girardeau A. Spann, *Race against the Court* (New York: New York University Press, 1993) (observing that Supreme Court litigation is of limited use as an instrument of racial reform), and Bell, *And We Are Not Saved*, 526–50; see also *MLK*, 5 (similar observation about romantic view of law and law's efficacy).

11

The Irrelevant Court

The Supreme Court's Inability to Influence Popular Beliefs about Equality (or Anything Else)

GERALD N. ROSENBERG

American citizens are riveted to certain events. Championship games in sports, for example, are talked about endlessly. Professional football's Super Bowl, played every January, draws enormous television-viewing audiences. Real-life dramas, like O. J. Simpson's 1995 criminal trial or the 1994 California highway chase leading to his arrest, create endless conversations. Autumn debates between the major presidential candidates can catch the attention of large percentages of Americans. When Americans care about an event and the media give it extensive coverage, it can become an important part of the political, social, and cultural life of the United States.

The focus of this chapter is the ability of the U.S. Supreme Court to win the attention of the American public and increase its support for racial and gender equality. When the Court issues opinions about equality, how do Americans react? Are they aware of the decisions? Do they talk about them? Does their thinking about equality change? Or does little change? Are Americans basically unaware of what the Court does, even in landmark cases? Do they form opinions about equality from sources other than the Court? Are their opinions about equality relatively fixed or susceptible to change from Court-induced reflection?

There are good reasons for expecting the Supreme Court to have the power to change people's views. First, the Supreme Court is generally considered the most powerful court in the world. The justices hold their positions for life and exercise the power to invalidate the acts of governmental officials (judicial review). Second, the nine justices are formally independent of electoral constraints and political pressure. Unlike other governmental officials, they are not politically beholden, they can't be thrown out of office for unpopular decisions, and they do not run for reelection. Third, they operate in the world of rights and principles, not policy and preferences. The questions they address are not whether a law or act is good policy or an appropriate response to interest-group demands but whether the law or act is consistent with constitutional requirements or existing legislation. The ''above-politics,'' independent, and principled nature of much Supreme Court decision-making may give Supreme Court decisions a powerful legitimacy.[1]

Many scholars who have written about the Supreme Court emphasize its ability to change opinions. Courts, one writer suggests, can provide ''a cheap method of pricking powerful consciences.''[2] For Professor Eugene V. Rostow, the Supreme Court is an ''educational body, and the Justices are inevitably teachers in a vital national seminar.''[3] Professor Alexander Bickel noted that courts have the ''capacity to appeal to men's better natures, to call forth their aspirations, which may have been forgotten in the moment's hue and cry''; courts, he suggested, are a ''great and highly effective educational institution.''[4] More recently, the Supreme Court of the mid-and late twentieth century is generally understood to have played a leading role in creating a more equal America. From civil rights to women's rights, the Court's decisions are widely believed to have led to greater equality. As Aryeh Neier puts it, ''[S]ince the early 1950s, the courts have been the most accessible and, often, the most effective instrument of government for bringing about the changes in public policy sought by social protest movements.''[5]

In contrast, there are some who believe that courts are epiphenomenal to the process of social change. Perhaps the most celebrated exponent of this view is Alexander Hamilton, who wrote in *The Federalist* of the ''natural feebleness of the judiciary,'' arguing that the courts were by far the weakest of the three branches of government.[6] In more recent times, some writers have stressed the broader environment in which courts exist. In this view, court decisions are part of a social, political, economic, and cultural milieu that gives them meaning. In and of themselves, they are unlikely to change anything or even to be noticed.[7]

Consider, for example, the Supreme Court's infamous *Dred Scott* decision (1857), which denied that African Americans were citizens, invalidated the Missouri Compromise, and upheld the constitutionality of slavery. Since it was delivered as the nation was approaching the Civil War, evidently an aim of its authors was to avoid war by treating the issue of slavery in the territories as a constitutional matter and settling it legally. By all accounts, the decision was a dismal failure. It changed no opinions, and rather than settling the issue, it fanned the flames. Not surprisingly, it was popular in the South but unpopular in the North, where it was widely referred to as a ''stump speech.''[8] Horace Greeley editorialized that the decision is ''entitled to just so much moral weight as would be the judgment of a majority of those congregated in any Washington bar-room.''[9] The *New York Independent* wrote, ''If the people obey this decision they disobey God.''[10] When emotions run high, as they do over issues of equality, one might think it unlikely that the Court's decisions would change opinions.

One reason for skepticism about the view of courts as powerful promoters of equality is that there is little or no evidence that the Court's decisions change people's views. Typically, the effect is simply assumed. But claims about the real world require evidence. If the claims are right, supportive evidence will make them that much stronger. However, if the evidence doesn't support the claims, then they ought to be treated cautiously or rejected.

The Supreme Court and Public Opinion

The modern view sketched above is that courts play an important role in alerting Americans to social and political grievances. According to one defender of the claim, "without the dramatic intervention of so dignified an institution as a court, which puts its own prestige and authority on the line, most middle-class Americans would not be informed about such grievances."[11] For this claim to hold, for courts to affect behavior, directly or indirectly, people must be aware of what courts do. Although this does not seem an onerous responsibility, survey researchers report that most Americans have little knowledge about courts and pay little attention to them. This holds true even for the Supreme Court, the most visible and important American court.

In general, surveys have shown that only about 40 percent of the American public, at best, follows Supreme Court actions, as measured by survey respondents having either read or heard something about the Court. In 1966, for example, nearly 40 percent of the American public could not identify Earl Warren, despite a decade of Court activism in which the chief justice was both loudly praised and vilified. And in 1989, while more than 25 percent of survey respondents identified Judge Joseph Wapner of television's *People's Court*, fewer than 10 percent could name the chief justice of the United States, William Rehnquist. Also, in 1966, despite important Supreme Court decisions on race, religion, criminal justice, and voting rights, 46 percent of a nationwide sample could not recall *anything at all* that the Court had recently done. And when prompted with a list of eight "decisions," four of which the Court had recently made and four of which it had never made, and asked to identify which, if any, the Court had made, only 15 percent of a 1966 sample made four or more correct choices. More recently, despite a "barrage" of media coverage of President Ronald Reagan's nomination of Judge Robert H. Bork for a seat on the U.S. Supreme Court, "surprisingly few citizens expressed concern or formed opinions on the issue."[12]

Among Americans who have some awareness of what the Court does, there is little evidence that its decisions change opinions. That is, people aware of what the Court does may disagree with it. In fact, the more knowledgeable a person is about the Supreme Court, the more likely he or she is to disagree with it. In reviewing the literature, David Adamany writes of the "Court's *incapacity* to legitimize governmental action."[13] Evidence for this conclusion comes from the work of Walter Murphy and Joseph Tanenhaus, who found that only 13 percent of the American public has the knowledge and beliefs about the Court necessary for it to legitimate action.[14] This includes the belief that the Court is a proper, impartial, and competent interpreter of the Constitution. Thus, the potential pool of people who could be influenced by a Supreme Court decision is small. The point is that although in principle law may be a powerful legitimating force in American society capable of changing opinions, in practice, courts, including the Supreme Court, are weak legitimaters.

A possible way in which this general lack of knowledge and barrier to the Court's effectiveness could be overcome is through heightened press coverage. Despite the general findings of the literature, the Supreme Court could influence

Americans through the press. The trouble with this line of reasoning is that there is little evidence that Supreme Court decisions increase press coverage. Numerous studies have documented the media's lack of interest in providing the kind of in-depth and continuous coverage that could lead to greater public awareness and influence opinions about equality. For example, Charles Franklin and Liane Kosaki examined network television news coverage of the Supreme Court over the nineteen-month period from January 1989 to July 1990. On average, there were 0.25 stories per day involving the Supreme Court (about one every four days), compared to 2.1 stories per day on the president and 1.0 stories per day on Congress.[15] As Franklin and Kosaki put it, the "episodic nature of Court decisions and the irregular coverage it receives means that substantial portions of the public will fail to hear of many decisions."[16] This combination of little interest and knowledge in what the Court does and the lack of media interest in overcoming it suggests that the Court is highly unlikely to play much of a role in influencing views on equality.

In the bulk of this chapter, I examine the question of whether Supreme Court decisions involving issues of racial and gender equality influence the opinions Americans hold on these issues. By bringing together public opinion data from a variety of fields, a coherent picture appears. And it's a picture that may surprise the reader.

Racial Equality

When the Supreme Court unanimously condemned racial segregation in public elementary and secondary schools in *Brown v. Board of Education*[17] in 1954, it marked the first time since 1875 that one of the three branches of the federal government spoke strongly in favor of civil rights on a fundamental issue. "Separate educational facilities," Chief Justice Earl Warren wrote for a unanimous Supreme Court, "are inherently unequal."[18] Surely this principled statement of constitutional requirements affected the thinking of Americans about racial equality. "*Brown,*" it is claimed, "launched the public debate over racial equality."[19] In the following section I explore the evidence that the Supreme Court through *Brown* increased support for equality.

One important way in which the Court may have changed thinking about racial equality is through inducing increased press coverage of it and balanced treatment of African Americans. However, overall, there is no evidence of such an increase or major change in reporting in the years immediately following *Brown*. In general, newspaper coverage of civil rights was poor until the massive demonstrations of the 1960s. In the South, for example, a study by the Southern Regional Council (SRC) of "representative" white newspapers concluded that they constituted "the greatest single force in perpetuating the popular stereotype of the Negro." The problem, the SRC found, was that "the average white editor believes, rightly or wrongly, that readers want little mention of the Negro which does not fit in with their own concept of colored persons."[20] Numerous studies support this conclusion. C. A. McKnight, executive director of the Southern Education Reporting Service, found that in the years following *Brown*, Supreme Court treatment of segregation received "minimum coverage."[21] This was particularly true in the South, where there was a "paucity" of coverage and where the wire services "seldom reported the story in its full dimensions and meaning."[22] And *Time* magazine criticized southern newspapers for doing a "patchy, pussyfooting job of covering the region's biggest running story since the end of slavery."[23]

The most powerful way to determine if there was a sustained increase in press coverage of civil rights in response to *Brown* is to actually count press stories over time. If the Supreme Court affected thinking about equality, then one would expect to see a sustained increase in media coverage of civil rights. The evidence is presented in figure 11.1. Although press coverage of civil rights, as measured by the number of stories dealing with the issue in the *Reader's Guide to Periodical Literature*, increased moderately in 1954 over the previous year's total, by 1958 and 1959, coverage actually dropped below the level found in several of the years of the late 1940s and early 1950s![24] In addition, if one examines the largest-circulations magazines of the 1950s and early 1960s, *Reader's Digest, Ladies Home Journal, Life*, and the *Saturday Evening Post*, the same general pattern is found. And it was not until 1962 that *TV Guide* ran a story having to do with civil rights. Thus, changes in press coverage provide no evidence that the Court's decision influenced the press to give attention to civil rights.

It is possible, of course, that public opinion is formed more by elites than by ordinary citizens. Thus, it may be that the magazines most likely read by elites, the *New York Times Magazine, Newsweek, Time*, and the *New Republic*, would provide increased coverage of civil rights in the wake of the Court's decision. But this is not the case; these magazines show the same pattern. Even though most did contain more civil rights articles in 1956 and 1957 than in the years before *Brown*,

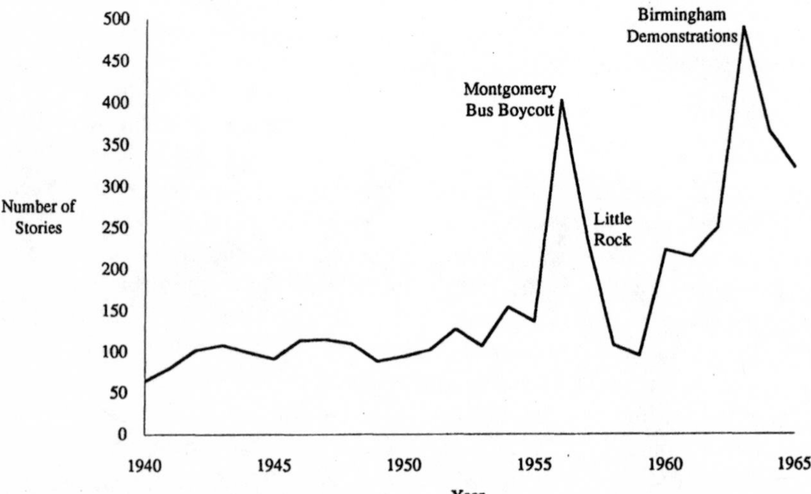

FIGURE 11.1. Magazine Coverage of Civil Rights, 1940–1965 (Reprinted by permission from Gerald N. Rosenberg, *The Hollow Hope: Can Courts Bring About Social Change*? [Chicago: The University of Chicago Press, 1991], © 1991 by The University of Chicago)

this increased coverage is most plausibly due to the factors identified above. In fact, for each of these magazines there was as much, if not more, coverage of civil rights in several of the years of the 1940s as in 1958 or 1959. The same general pattern holds for civil rights coverage in the *New York Times* as measured by the proportion of pages in the *Times Index* devoted to discrimination. In 1952 there was actually more coverage than in 1954 or 1955. Further, coverage in the years 1954, 1955, 1958, and 1959 was barely equal to or actually less than the coverage allotted to civil rights in four of the years of the 1940s! Here again, there is no evidence that the Court's action influenced views of equality by putting civil rights on the political agenda through the press.

Public Opinion

The most straightforward way to examine the Court's ability to influence thinking about racial equality is to examine public opinion. As one scholar has put it, the Supreme Court ''pricked the conscience''[25] of white America by pointing out both its constitutional duty and its shortcomings. ''Except for *Brown*,'' Aryeh Neier contends, white Americans ''would not have known about the plight of blacks under segregation.''[26]

One place to look for evidence is in responses to survey questions about racial equality in general and support for *Brown* in particular. Surprisingly, and unfortunately, there appear to be no polls addressing knowledge of *Brown*. There are, however, polls charting the reaction to *Brown* by southerners over time. In July 1954, just a few months after the decision, 24 percent of *all* southerners approved of the decision and of integrated schools and 71 percent disapproved. Nearly seven years later, in June 1961, the numbers were virtually identical, with 24 percent approving and 69 percent disapproving. Among white southerners, in February 1956, only 16 percent approved. When white southerners were asked in July 1954 whether they would object to sending their children to integrated schools, only 15 percent responded that they would not object. By 1959, support for desegregation actually dropped, with only 8 percent of white southerners responding that they would not object.[27] Given the lack of positive change over time, it is entirely possible that supportive respondents were supportive before the Court acted. If not, then at most the Court influenced about one-quarter of all southerners and about one-sixth of white southerners. But since there was at least some support for desegregated schools in the South before the Court acted, it seems fair to assume that the actual influence was less.

If there is little evidence that *Brown* increased support for school desegregation in the South, perhaps it helped change white opinions more generally. Indeed, a main argument for the Court's influence is that the Court's action pricked the conscience of white America and changed racial attitudes. Ideally, to answer this question, one would look to time-series data on white opinions about civil rights. Support for the Court's influence would be found if there was a sharp increase in supportive attitudes about racial equality after *Brown* or if the rate of change of supportive attitudes increased. Unfortunately, the data are not ideal. Questions were not asked regularly, and the pre-1954 data are sketchy. That being said, throughout the period from the beginning of World War II to the passage of the 1964 Civil Rights Act, whites became increasingly supportive of civil rights. Writing in 1956, Herbert Hyman and Paul Sheatsley found that the changes in attitude were ''solidly based'' and ''not easily accelerated nor easily reversed.''[28] Reviewing the available data in 1964, they noted the ''unbroken trend of the past twenty years.''[29] Further, they found that the changes were not due to any specific event, such as President John Kennedy's assassination or a Supreme Court decision. They found that changes in national opinion ''represent long-term trends that are not easily modified by specific—even by highly dramatic—events.''[30]

Another way of examining the Court's influence on how Americans view racial equality is to look at how the sensitivity of white Americans to civil rights changed generally. According to one scholar, the ''*Brown* decision was central to eliciting the moral outrage that both blacks and whites were to feel and express about segregation.''[31] If the Court served this role, it would necessarily have increased awareness of the plight of African Americans. The evidence, however, shows no sign of such an increase. Survey questions about whether most African Americans were being treated fairly resulted in affirmative responses of 66 percent in 1944, 66 percent in 1946, and 69 percent in 1956.[32] By 1963, when Gallup asked if any group in America was being treated unfairly, 80 percent said no. Only 5 percent of the sample named ''the Negroes'' as being unfairly treated, and 4 percent named ''the whites.''[33] This result and the change over time hardly show an America whose conscience was aroused.

This lack of sensitivity to the plight of African Americans can be seen most poignantly in the 1957 crisis involving the Court-ordered admission of nine African American children to the all-white Central High School in Little Rock, Arkansas. Governor Orval Faubus of Arkansas gained national attention by repeatedly defying court orders and blocking the desegregation. In December 1958, when Gallup asked its usual question about the most admired men in the world, Governor Faubus was among the top ten![34] If the Court pricked the conscience of white Americans, the sensitivity disappeared quickly. Thus, there does not appear to be evidence supporting the claim that the massive change in the opinions of white Americans about civil rights was an effect of the Court's action. As Burke Marshall, head of the Justice Department's Civil Rights Division, put it, ''[T]he Negro and his problems were still pretty much invisible to the country . . . until mass demonstrations of the Birmingham type.''[35]

In sum, in several areas in which the Supreme Court would be expected to increase support among white Americans for racial equality, evidence of the effect has not been found. Most Americans neither follow Supreme Court decisions nor understand the Court's constitutional role. It is not surprising, then, that change in public opinion about racial equality appears to be unrelated to the Court.

African Americans

The preceding section focussed on general poll data. In so doing, it left out the possible effect of the Supreme Court on African Americans. Here, a plausible claim is that *Brown* was the spark that ignited the African American revolution. By recognizing and legitimating African American grievances, the public pronouncement by the Court could have provided African Americans with a new image and encouraged them to act. *Brown* "begot," one legal scholar tells us, "a union of the mightiest and lowliest in America, a mystical, passionate union bound by the pained depths of the black man's cry for justice and the moral authority, unique to the Court, to see that justice realized."[36] If this is the case, then there are a number of places where evidence should be found.

For *Brown* to have played this role, African Americans must have known about the decision and approved both of its holdings and of the Court's constitutional role. As discussed earlier, there is little evidence that Americans, black or white, credit the Court with a legitimating role. Further, it is not entirely clear that knowledge of *Brown* was widespread. For example, during the school desegregation crisis in Clinton, Tennessee, in the fall of 1956, a team of social scientists interviewing people found that "a number" had "never heard of the U.S. Supreme Court decision against segregation."[37] A decade after *Brown*, a white volunteer teaching in a Mississippi Freedom School during the summer of 1964 wrote in a letter: "My students are from 13 to 17 years old, and not one of them had heard about the Supreme Court decision of 1954. . . . [T]hey are surprised to hear that the law is on their side."[38]

Part of the reason for this lack of knowledge is clearly Americans' general ignorance of Supreme Court decisions. Part is also due to poor newspaper coverage, as has been discussed. But another possibility is that many African Americans did not approve of the decision. In November 1955, a special Gallup poll found that barely half of southern African Americans (53 percent) approved of *Brown*.[39] Although such poll data should be approached cautiously, a poll taken just a few weeks later found that 82 percent of southern African Americans approved of an Interstate Commerce Commission ruling prohibiting segregation in transportation.[40] The large difference between the two approval percentages is striking. Knowledge of, and support for, *Brown* may not have been high.

Brown was not greeted with an outpouring of public support by African Americans. Overall, the reaction within the African American community to *Brown* was muted. After *Brown*, "there were no street celebrations in Negro communities"[41] and no "grand celebrations."[42] Ralph Abernathy understood the lack of public response this way: "[M]ost blacks in the Deep South states looked with curiosity at what was going [on] in the high courts, shrugged their shoulders, and went back to their day-to-day lives. . . . After all, they had waited a lifetime and seen no change at all."[43]

Another possible explanation for the generally moderate response may lie with the African American press. Its coverage of the cases preceding *Brown* showed "understandable caution" and was sometimes "optimistic, though not ecstatic."[44] After *Brown*, responses varied. In some states, like Texas, the decision was strongly supported.[45] In others, like Mississippi, little was said. Although Mississippi is undoubtedly an extreme case, a book-length compilation of studies of the African American press in the eleven southern states and Missouri had only six references to *Brown*.[46] Thus, it is possible that the African American press did not fill in where the white press failed.

Affirmative Action

In the last several decades of the twentieth century, many universities and employers throughout the United States practiced some form of affirmative action. The idea behind affirmative action is that because of both past and present prejudice, members of certain minority groups (and women) are at a disadvantage in competing with others for jobs and admissions. In evaluating qualifications of applicants, educational institutions and employers with affirmative action plans have kept this background in mind and admitted or hired individuals whose test scores or other application materials would normally not have been sufficient.

The Supreme Court entered the area in 1978 in *Regents of University of California v. Bakke*.[47] In *Bakke*, which involved an affirmative action plan at the medical school of the University of California at Davis, the Court upheld the use of race as one factor among many in admissions. Whereas the decision invalidated the use of racial quotas (and invalidated the Davis program), it found nonquota affirmative action plans constitutional. *Bakke* was followed by other decisions like *United Steel Workers v. Weber* (1978),[48] which upheld an affirmative action plan adopted by the United Steel Workers and Kaiser Aluminum, and *Fullilove v. Klutznick* (1980),[49] which upheld the minority set-aside provision of the Public Works Employment Act of 1977.

Because affirmative action is aimed at the disadvantaged, it is seen by its supporters as an equality issue. Its aim is to undo the past and present effects of discrimination, to equalize opportunity, and to help produce greater equality in the United States. If the Court has the power to increase support for equality, then the data should show an increase in support for affirmative action as a result of the Court's action. Table 11.1 presents the data.

In measuring the beliefs of Americans about affirmative action, Gallup asked the following question: "Some people say that to make up for past discrimination, women and members of minority groups should be given preferential treatment in getting jobs and places in college. Others say that ability, as determined by test scores, should be the main consideration. Which point comes closest to how you feel on this matter?" The data show no change in the wake of Supreme Court decisions supportive of affirmative action. White Americans are overwhelmingly opposed to affirmative action plans before and after the Court's decisions. Non-

TABLE 11.1. Support of Affirmative Action

	Whites		Nonwhites	
Date	Ability	Preference to Minorities	Ability	Preference to Minorities
May 1977	86%	8%	64%	27%
November 1977	84	9	55	30
April 1979*	85	10	49	38
May 1981	87	7	57	29
August 1991	84	8	60	24

Source: George H. Gallup, *The Gallup Poll: Public Opinion* (Wilmington, Del.: Scholarly Resources, Inc., 1978–92).

*The 1979 survey was given to "full-time students representing 60 campuses."

whites show a similar but less pronounced pattern. Eight percent of white respondents supported affirmative action in 1977, before the Court's action, and 8 percent of white respondents did so in 1991. Among nonwhites the change was only 3 percentage points (and it moved against affirmative action!). Once again, the data provide no support for the claim that Supreme Court decisions create support for racial equality among Americans.

In sum, while support for racial equality on most issues has grown over time, there is little evidence that the Supreme Court contributed much to this change. But perhaps this finding is unique to racial equality. In order to determine that, the next section explores gender equality.

Gender Equality

The role of women in American society and the opportunities open to them have changed a great deal over the last several decades. Although discrimination continues to exist, many women today have choices that their mothers lacked. On a formal level, the Supreme Court has added to women's equality. In a series of decisions starting in 1971, the Supreme Court struck down many laws that discriminated against women. In 1973, in *Roe v. Wade*,[50] it struck down most prohibitions on abortions. Did these decisions increase support for gender equality?[51]

Salience

It is entirely possible that litigation in abortion and women's rights changed perceptions of the position of women in American society. Indeed, many groups involved in women's rights litigation believe that "litigation, because it attracts television, newspaper, and magazine attention, is critical in raising the consciousness of the American public."[52] If this is the case, then increased press coverage of women's rights and abortion should be seen after the Court entered the field.

Starting with abortion, figure 11.2 shows that while there was a major increase in magazine coverage, it came in 1970 and 1971, well before the Court's action. There was actually less coverage of abortion in the *Reader's Guide* in 1973, the year of the Court's decisions, than in the years 1972, 1971, and 1970! With the nation's largest-circulation magazines, there was no large increase in 1973. Large increases did occur in 1970 and 1971, before the Court's action. And coverage in the *New York Times* shows the same pattern. With women's rights, figure 11.3 reports similar data. A steep increase is recorded, but it is in 1970 and 1971, before any major action by the Court. As with abortion, the major change in large-circulation magazine coverage of women's rights occurred in the years 1970 and 1971, before the Court's action. Again, *New York Times* coverage is similar.

Turning to the four magazines most likely read by political elites, the pattern repeats. There was no increase in abortion coverage in 1973, the year of the Court's decisions. In fact, all four magazines had more abortion stories in previous recent years than in 1973. With women's rights, there was no large increase in coverage in the years 1973 and beyond. The change that did occur came in 1970 and 1971.

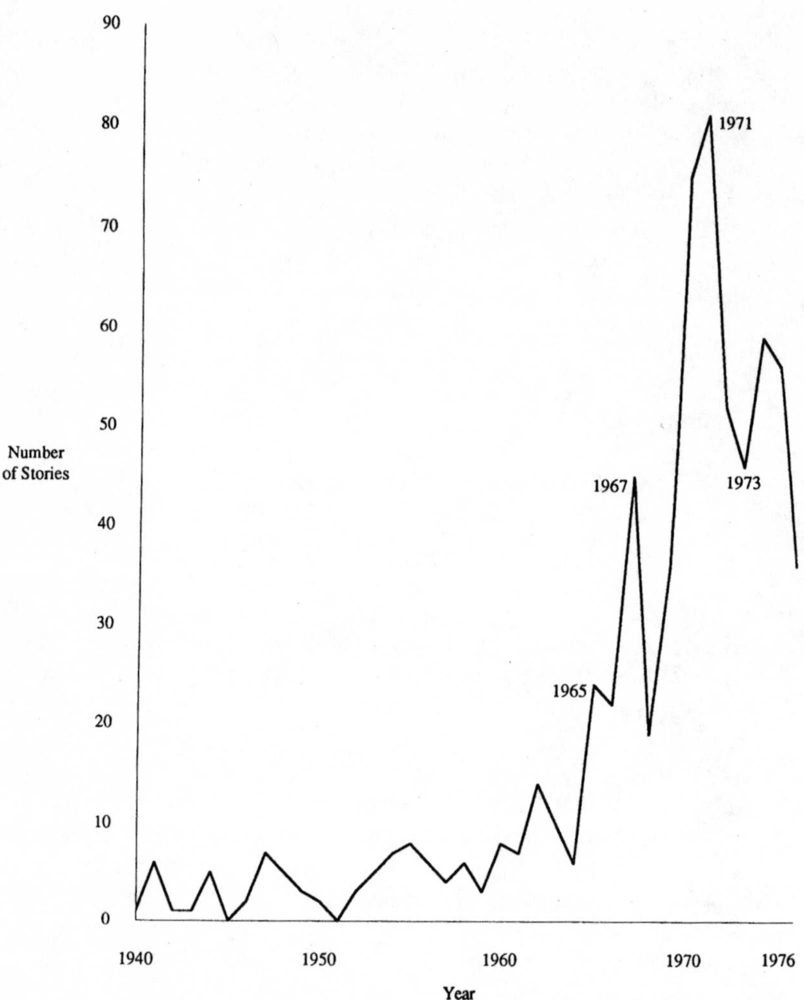

FIGURE 11.2. Magazine Coverage of Abortion, 1940–1976 (Reprinted by permission from Gerald N. Rosenberg, *The Hollow Hope: Can Courts Bring About Social Change*? [Chicago: The University of Chicago Press, 1991], © 1991 by The University of Chicago)

This pattern is particularly pronounced in coverage of the women's liberation movement. The point is clear: the Court's decisions on abortion and women's rights did *not* result in greater coverage of these issues. The argument that the Court's action gave women's rights and abortion salience lacks evidence.

Public Opinion

Media coverage aside, it is still possible that litigation in abortion and women's rights increased support for gender equality. A good place to look for evidence of this is in changes in public opinion. Fortunately, some data are available.

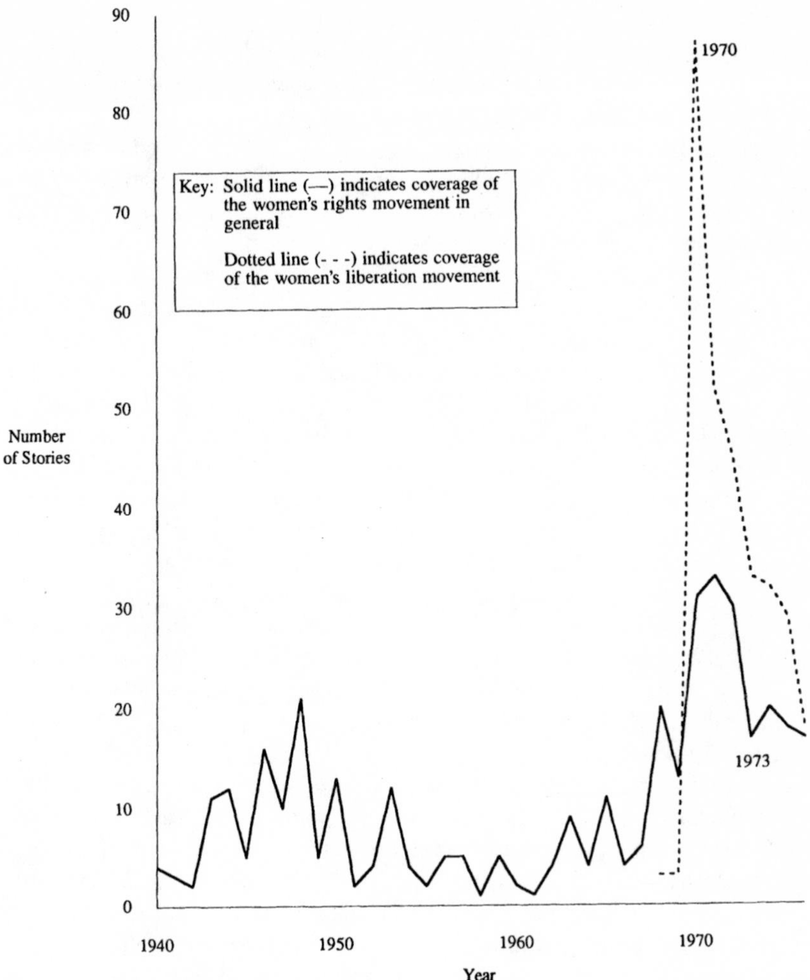

FIGURE 11.3. Magazine Coverage of Women's Rights, 1940–1976 (Reprinted by permission from Gerald N. Rosenberg, *The Hollow Hope: Can Courts Bring About Social Change*? [Chicago: The University of Chicago Press, 1991], © 1991 by The University of Chicago)

Abortion

Abortion is about the equality of women. If women lack the power to control their fertility, they lack the power to control their lives. Regardless of one's view of the constitutionality or the morality of abortion, one can explore changes in public opinion in the wake of Supreme Court decisions. If the Court plays an important role in increasing support for gender equality, then surely the Supreme Court's finding of a constitutional right to choose an abortion increased support for abortion choice.

The evidence does show large increases in support for a woman's right to choose but *before* the Court acted. By the eve of the Court's decisions in 1973, public opinion had dramatically shifted from opposition to abortion in most cases to substantial, if not majority, support. Indeed, in the decades that have followed, opinion on abortion has remained remarkably stable.

Why didn't public opinion change after the Court found a constitutional right for women to choose to terminate their pregnancies? To start, in order for the Court to affect views, people must know about its decisions. However, it appears that many Americans are unaware that the Supreme Court has issued an opinion on the constitutionality of abortion. In 1975, two years after *Roe*, a Gallup poll found that "less than half of American adult respondents were informed about the 1973 decisions."[53] In 1982, nearly a decade after the decisions and two years into the Reagan administration and its loudly proclaimed commitment to end legal abortion, 59 percent of a national survey sample answered either "don't know" or "no" to a question whether the Supreme Court had issued an opinion permitting abortion in the first three months of pregnancy.[54] These results were highlighted in 1990 by eleven teenage focus groups held around the country by the Center for Population Options in Washington, D.C. Summing up their findings, Rebecca Stone and Cynthia Waszak reported: "Many of the participants thought it [abortion] was illegal in most states, although participants seemed to know that abortion was legal in their own state. No participants said that abortion was legal in all 50 states (many were surprised to learn the truth), and only a few of the teenagers could identify *Roe v. Wade* or explain its significance."[55] These data suggest that knowledge of the Court's decisions is low. If citizens don't know that the Court has acted, the Court can't influence their views.

The data support this conclusion of little influence. Summarizing the literature, Judith Blake concludes, "None of our time series on public views regarding abortion indicates that the Supreme Court decisions had an important effect on opinion."[56] Table 11.2 provides data starting in 1975, two years after the decision. The data show that public opinion remained essentially constant for more than a decade until 1989, when it started to move in a more supportive direction.

What happened in 1989 to cause this growth in opinion supportive of abortion choice? Perhaps the Supreme Court issued an abortion decision? Indeed it did, but the Supreme Court's 1989 abortion decision (*Webster v. Reproductive Health Services*)[57] put restrictions on the right! That is, although the Court limited the right to abortion, there was a small but significant growth in pro-choice support. In other words, the Court's pro-choice decisions did not increase public support for abortion choice, but the Court's decision limiting the right seemed to create more, not less, support for it.

These findings may appear startling to many. But they are in line with what students have learned about the Supreme Court and public opinion. Data are lacking on knowledge of other women's rights issues, but it seems likely that if more than half the American public didn't know about *Roe*, then at least that percentage wouldn't know about other, less famous, Court decisions.

In sum, the Supreme Court has not been able to influence the views Americans hold about abortion. Even though there has been major increase in support for legal abortion, it occurred principally before the Court acted. The small change occurring after the Court's action has flowed counter to the Court's decision. That is, when

TABLE 11.2. Support of Abortion: Conditions under Which It Should Be Legal

Year	Always Legal	Legal in Certain Circumstances	Always Illegal
1975	21%	54%	22%
1977	22	55	19
1979	22	54	19
1980	25	53	18
1981	23	52	21
1983	23	58	16
1988	24	57	17
1989 (July)	29	51	17
1990	31	53	12
1991	33	49	14
1992 (July)	34	48	13

Source: Frank Newport and Leslie McAneny, ''Whose Court Is It Anyhow? O'Connor, Kennedy, Souter Position Reflects Abortion Views of Most Americans,'' *Gallup Poll Monthly,* no. 322 (July 1992): 51, 52.

Note: ''No opinion'' omitted.

the Court narrowed the right to choose abortion in *Webster*, the public grew somewhat more supportive of the broader right. With abortion, as with the other issues I have examined, the Court appears unable to increase support for equality.

Women's Rights

Another area to examine for evidence of the Court's ability to increase public support for equality is the change in public opinion on women's rights issues other than abortion. Although there is no firm demarcation line, as with abortion, the 1973 abortion decisions are a rough breaking point. If the Court can change views, then major changes in support for gender equality should occur after these dates. However, if change is being driven by other forces, then it should be seen before major Court decisions.

There has been substantial change in public opinion about women's rights, but much of it occurred before the Court's action. Writing in 1972, Lou Harris found that ''a swing in attitude—and a dramatic one—is taking place among women in America today.''[58] This ''dramatic swing'' occurred in the late 1960s and early 1970s, before the Court's action.

One area in which the swing was pronounced was in opinions about the place of women in American society. In 1970, for example, 40 percent of women and 42 percent of a national sample favored efforts to strengthen and change women's status in society. By 1972, there was an eight-point gain in the percentage of women supporting efforts for change (48 percent) and a six-point gain in the percentage of the national sample (48 percent).[59] A similar pattern is found with college-educated women in questions of sex-role beliefs. Using surveys from the

1960s and 1970s, Karen Mason, John Czajka, and Sara Arber found that the period 1964–70 saw "rather sizable attitude shifts" among these women. By 1970, they found that "large majorities held relatively egalitarian beliefs about women's dependency on men's plans, about the consequences of maternal employment for children's well-being, and about the differential socialization of boys and girls."[60] The attitudes of college-educated men also appeared to be changing. In 1972, for the first time, fewer than one-half of entering male college freshmen accepted the notion that a woman's place is in the home.[61] Finally, as early as 1962, a Gallup poll found that 90 percent of housewives surveyed did not want their daughters to lead the same type of life they led.[62]

Another indication of growing support for gender equality is found in opinions about married women working. In 1936 only 18 percent of Gallup's respondents said yes to the question "Should a married woman earn money if she has a husband capable of supporting her?"[63] By 1967, opinions had changed a great deal, with 44 percent of the sample responding positively to a similar Roper question.[64] Just two years later, however, the percentage of respondents approving of married women earning money increased to 55 percent.[65] This eleven-point increase in two years was nearly half the increase recorded in the thirty-one years between 1936 and 1967. And it was recorded before any major Court action. Although support has continued to grow, reaching 86 percent in 1993, the pace of change has remained steady, suggesting that it was driven by structural factors within the society.

In sum, in the area of public opinion, abortion, and women's rights, major increases in support for gender equality predate Court action. With women's rights, support did continue to grow in the 1970s, but it "did not occur at a consistently faster pace after 1970 than before."[66] Again, evidence for the Court's ability to increase support for gender equality is lacking.

Equality and Sexual Preference

A final aspect of gender equality to be considered is sexual preference. Unlike the other equality areas that I have examined, the Supreme Court has not been supportive of equality for homosexuals.[67] Indeed, in 1986 in *Bowers v. Hardwick*,[68] the Court denied constitutional protection to consenting adults to engage in private homosexual relations. If the Court's views on equality carry weight with the American public, then one would expect to see growing opposition to equality for gays.

The data that exist do show change, but in the opposite direction from *Bowers*. That is, the American public is becoming more supportive of equality for homosexuals despite the Court's ruling. For example, Gallup has repeatedly asked its respondents the following question: "In general, do you think homosexuals should or should not have equal rights in terms of job opportunities?" In 1977, 56 percent of respondents said "yes" and 33 percent said "no." By 1992, support had increased to 74 percent, with 18 percent opposing. And, in 1993, the percentage of supporters increased again, with 80 percent supporting equality and only 14 percent opposing it.[69]

Most useful for this analysis was a question concerning legalizing homosexual relations. On several occasions Gallup asked respondents whether "homosexual

TABLE 11.3. Support for Legalization of Homosexual Relations between Consenting Adults

Date	Should Be Legal	Should Not Be Legal
July 1977	43%	43%
December 1985	44	47
October 1989	47	36
June 1992	48	44

Source: George H. Gallup, *The Gallup Poll: Public Opinion* (Wilmington, Del.: Scholarly Resources, Inc., 1978–93).

relations between consenting adults'' should or should not be made legal—the very question the Court addressed in *Bowers*. Table 11.3 presents the results.

The data show a small increase of 5 percentage points in supportive responses over a fifteen-year period (1977–92) and essentially no change in negative responses. The key point is that despite the Court's denial of equality in *Bowers*, over time the American public has become more supportive of equality, not less. And this increase has occurred in the context of concern, if not hysteria, about the AIDS virus.

In sum, the Court's antigay views do not appear to have influenced the public. The American public has increased its support of equality regardless of sexual preference despite the Court's reading of the Constitution to deny that equality. This, perhaps, is a bit of good news for believers in equality. The Court may not be able to increase support for equality, but perhaps it can't lessen support either.

Conclusion

This chapter has examined the ability of the Court to influence the views of Americans on equality. The findings are consistent: there is no evidence supporting the power of the Court to increase support for racial or gender equality. Those looking to influence how Americans think about equality need to look elsewhere.

This conclusion should not be surprising. As I suggested at the beginning of this chapter, courts are only one among many institutions, and their decisions compete with other events for the public's attention. Further, to the extent that their decisions are heard, they are heard by people deeply enmeshed in powerful social and cultural networks, be they ethnic, racial, religious, and so on. As anyone who has ever debated issues of racial or gender equality can attest, opinions on such issues are often deeply held. It is naive to expect an institution seen as distant and unfamiliar, shrouded in mystery, and using arcane language and procedures to change people's views. Perhaps what is most surprising is not that the Supreme Court appears unable to increase support for equality but that anyone thinks that it can.

The findings of this chapter also suggest that claims about the real-world effects of court decisions need empirical testing. To debate the merits of judicial opinions is certainly appropriate, but when the discussion turns to the effects of such opinions, those effects must be measured. Sometimes measurement is hard and data are unavailable. What that means to the scholar as opposed to the ideologue is that claims must be put in the form of hypotheses to be tested, tentative suggestions about how people might behave. There is much to be said for principled beliefs, but to confuse them with reality is both bad scholarship and bad politics. And for those of us committed to furthering both equality and scholarship, this confusion is a double mistake.

NOTES

Ronna Landy and Julie Alig provided superb research assistance in the preparation of this chapter.

1. Owen Fiss, ''The Forms of Justice,'' *Harvard Law Review* 93 (1979): 1.

2. Note, ''Implementation Problems in Institutional Reform Litigation,'' *Harvard Law Review* 91 (1977): 428, 463.

3. Eugene V. Rostow, ''The Democratic Character of Judicial Review,'' *Harvard Law Review* 66 (1952): 193, 208.

4. Alexander M. Bickel, *The Least Dangerous Branch: The Supreme Court at the Bar of Politics*, 2d ed. (New Haven: Yale University Press, 1962, 1986), 26.

5. Aryeh Neier, *Only Judgment: The Limits of Litigation in Social Change* (Middletown, Conn.: Wesleyan University Press, 1982), 9.

6. Alexander Hamilton, *The Federalist, No. 78*, ed. Jacob Cooke (Middletown, Conn.: Wesleyan University Press, 1961).

7. For an in-depth exploration of the inability of courts to further equality by producing significant social reform, see Gerald N. Rosenberg, *The Hollow Hope: Can Courts Bring About Social Change?* (Chicago: University of Chicago Press, 1991).

8. Walter F. Murphy, *Congress and the Court* (Chicago: University of Chicago Press, 1962), 30 (discussing *Dred Scott v. Sandford*, 60 U.S. 393 [1856]).

9. Quoted in ibid., 31.

10. Ibid.

11. Neier, *Only Judgment*, 239.

12. Gregory A. Caldeira, ''Courts and Public Opinion,'' in *The American Courts: A Critical Assessment*, ed. John B. Gates and Charles A. Johnson (Washington, D.C.: Congressional Quarterly Press, 1990), 327 n.1. Caldeira bases this conclusion on Gallup poll surveys.

13. David Adamany, ''Law and Society: Legitimacy, Realigning Elections, and the Supreme Court,'' *Wisconsin Law Review* (1973): 791, 807.

14. Walter F. Murphy and Joseph Tanenhaus, ''Public Opinion and the Supreme Court: A Preliminary Mapping of Some Prerequisites for Court Legitimation of Regime Change,'' *Law and Society Review* 2 (1968): 357.

15. Charles H. Franklin and Liane C. Kosaki, ''Media, Knowledge, and Public Evaluations of the Supreme Court,'' in *Contemplating Courts*, ed. Lee Epstein (Washington, D.C.: Congressional Quarterly Press, 1995), 356–57.

16. Ibid., 370.

17. 347 U.S. 483 (1954).

18. Ibid. at 495.

19. Neier, *Only Judgment*, 241–42.

20. Southern Regional Council, *Race in the News* (Atlanta: Southern Regional Council, n.d.), 2.

21. Quoted in Reed Sarratt, *The Ordeal of Desegregation* (New York: Harper & Row, 1966), 263.

22. Pat Watters and Reese Cleghorn, *Climbing Jacob's Ladder* (New York: Harcourt, Brace and World, 1967), 73 n.10.

23. "The Press—Dilemma in Dixie," *Time*, 20 February 1956, 76.

24. The enormous increases in 1956 and 1957 are most persuasively explained not by the Court's action but rather by the Montgomery bus boycott, the violence in Clinton, Tennessee, and the presidential election campaign in 1956, as well as the Little Rock crisis in 1957.

25. Loren Miller, "Very Deliberate Speed," in *The Segregation Era 1863–1954*, ed. Allen Weinstein and Frank Otto Gatell (New York: Oxford University Press, 1970), 281.

26. Neier, *Only Judgment*, 239.

27. American Institute of Public Opinion poll, in Hazel Gaudet Erskine, "The Polls: Race Relations," *Public Opinion Quarterly* 26 (1962): 140, 141.

28. Herbert H. Hyman and Paul B. Sheatsley, "Attitudes toward Desegregation," *Scientific American* (December 1956): 39.

29. Herbert H. Hyman and Paul B. Sheatsley, "Attitudes toward Desegregation," *Scientific American* (July 1964): 23.

30. Ibid., 17.

31. Henry M. Levin, "Education and Earnings of Blacks and the *Brown* Decision," in *Have We Overcome? Race Relations Since* Brown, ed. Michael V. Namorato (Jackson: University of Mississippi Press, 1979), 110.

32. Hyman and Sheatsley, "Attitudes toward Desegregation" (December 1956): 39.

33. George H. Gallup, *The Gallup Poll: Public Opinion 1935–1971*, 3 vols. (New York: Random House, 1972), 3:1825.

34. Ibid., 2: 1548.

35. Quoted in Adam Fairclough, *To Redeem the Soul of America: The Southern Christian Leadership Conference and Martin Luther King, Jr.* (Athens: University of Georgia Press, 1987), 135.

36. Harvie J. Wilkinson III, *From Brown to Alexander: The Supreme Court and School Integration, 1954–1978* (New York: Oxford University Press, 1979), 5.

37. Glen Robinson, "Man in No Man's Land," in *With All Deliberate Speed*, ed. Don Shoemaker (New York: Harper and Brothers, 1957), 183.

38. Quoted in Elizabeth Sutherland, ed., *Letters from Mississippi* (New York: McGraw-Hill, 1965), 93.

39. Gallup, *The Gallup Poll*, 2: 1402.

40. Ibid.

41. Taylor Branch, *Parting the Waters: America in the King Years, 1954–1963* (New York: Simon & Schuster, 1988), 112.

42. Juan Williams, *Eyes on the Prize: America's Civil Rights Years, 1954–1965* (New York: Viking, 1987), 351.

43. Ralph David Abernathy, *And the Walls Came Tumbling Down* (New York: Harper & Row, 1989), 114.

44. Bill Weaver and Oscar C. Page, "The Black Press and the Drive for Integrated Graduate and Professional Schools," *Phylon* 43 (1982): 15, 21, 27.

45. James Smallwood, "Texas," in *The Black Press and the South, 1865–1979*, ed. Henry Lewis Suggs (Westport, Conn.: Greenwood Press, 1983).

46. Ibid.

47. 438 U.S. 265 (1978).

48. 443 U.S. 193 (1978).

49. 448 U.S. 448 (1980).

50. 410 U.S. 113 (1973).

51. This discussion is based on Rosenberg, *Hollow Hope*, especially ch. 8.

52. Karen O'Connor, *Women's Organizations Use of the Courts* (Lexington: Heath, 1980), 120.

53. Judith Blake, "The Supreme Court's Abortion Decisions and Public Opinion in the United States," *Population and Development Review* 3 (1977): 45, 57–59.

54. "Americans Evaluate the Court System," *Public Opinion* 5 (August/September 1982): 25.

55. Rebecca Stone and Cynthia Waszak, "Adolescent Knowledge and Attitudes about Abortion," *Family Planning Perspectives* 24 (1992): 52, 55.

56. Blake, "The Supreme Court's Abortion Decisions," 57.

57. 492 U.S. 490 (1989).

58. Louis Harris and Associates, "The 1972 Virginia Slims American Women's Poll" (n.p., n.d.), 1.

59. Connie De Boer, "The Polls: Women at Work," *Public Opinion Quarterly* 41 (1977): 268–69; Harris, "1972 Virginia Slims American Women's Poll," 2.

60. Karen Oppenheimer Mason, John L. Czajka, and Sara Arber, "Change in U.S. Women's Sex-Role Attitudes, 1964–1974," *American Sociological Review* 41 (1976): 573, 587.

61. Maren Lockwood Carden, *The New Feminist Movement* (New York: Sage, 1974), xiii n.11. The survey, done by the American Council on Education, also found that only about a quarter of women entering college held the notion.

62. Cited in Barbara S. Deckard, *The Women's Movement*, 3d ed. (New York: Harper and Row, 1983), 319.

63. Gallup, *The Gallup Poll*, 1: 39.

64. Hazel Gaudet Erskine, "The Polls: Women's Role," *Public Opinion Quarterly* 35 (1971): 275, 285.

65. Nancy E. McGlen and Karen O'Connor, *Women's Rights* (New York: Praeger, 1983), 217.

66. Mason, Czajka, and Arber, "Change in U.S. Women's Sex Role Attitudes," 594.

67. Although the Supreme Court's 1996 decision in *Romer v. Evans* removed a recently enacted obstacle to homosexuals' political participation, it did no more than return to the status quo. Unlike its actions in the other areas I have considered in this chapter, the Court did not create a new equality right.

68. 478 U.S. 186 (1986).

69. George H. Gallup, *The Gallup Poll: Public Opinion, 1972–1977*, 2 vols. (Wilmington: Del.: Scholarly Resources, Inc., 1978); *The Gallup Report*, No. 244–245 (January–February 1986): 3; *The Gallup Report*, No. 289 (October 1989): 13; *The Gallup Report*, No. 321 (June 1992): 2.

12

Can Courts Make a Difference?

ERWIN CHEMERINSKY

The 1990s are a time of skepticism about the ability of government to solve serious social problems. The Republican victory at the polls in the 1994 congressional elections is explained, in part, by frustration with government and its efforts at social improvement. Therefore, it is not surprising that doubts are being expressed about the ability of courts to make a difference. Nor is it surprising that academics, those most familiar with the judicial process and its impact, are raising the issue.

Prominent academics such as political scientist Gerald Rosenberg[1] and Professor Cass Sunstein,[2] as well as Supreme Court Justice Ruth Bader Ginsburg,[3] have strongly challenged the ability of constitutional litigation to achieve social change. Some of the chapters in this collection echo this viewpoint. Rosenberg, who has argued elsewhere that litigation "seldom bring[s] reform any closer,"[4] argues here that courts are inherently limited in their ability to influence popular opinion.[5] Political scientist Jeremy Rabkin goes even further and contends that courts are obstructing necessary social change.[6] He suggests, for instance, that Supreme Court decisions limiting aid to parochial schools undermine effective inner-city education and that criminal procedure protections prevent effective neighborhood policing.[7]

There is, of course, a tension between these positions. Scholars such as Rosenberg argue that courts make little difference; scholars such as Rabkin believe that courts make a difference but that it is a negative one. Put together, the conclusion is frightening and profound: courts can have little positive effect but can do serious damage.

The conclusion has potentially significant implications. At the very least, the conclusion means that liberals have no reason to be upset at their recent losses in the Supreme Court because victories would have meant little. More generally, such scholarship suggests that groups seeking social change should not invest their resources in the courts and litigation but should look elsewhere for reform.[8] It also encourages great judicial restraint by judges.

I strongly disagree with the conclusions of these scholars. I believe that courts can make a difference and change the law and that reforming the law can alter society. In part, the problem with such scholarship is that it fails to clearly and consistently articulate criteria for evaluating whether court decisions are successful. Also, the scholarship generalizes from a few areas to broad conclusions about the role of courts. It is a logical fallacy to say that because in some areas the judiciary has had limited impact, the courts usually fail to make much difference. Moreover, the failure in specific areas might be a result of the limitations of particular decisions and not an indication of the inherent limits of the judicial process.

My goal here, however, is not to fully explore the ability of courts to affect social change. Rather, I want to explore how the impact of courts might be assessed. How can scholars systematically assess the effects of judicial decisions? The conclusion that emerges is a relatively narrow one: courts can sometimes make an enormous difference. Analysis must be contextual, not categorical; in some circumstances, courts can have profound effects, but in other circumstances, court decisions will have little effect. It is worth considering what variables determine the effectiveness of judicial actions.

The first section of this chapter explores how the effectiveness or ineffectiveness of courts might be evaluated. The second section responds to the claim that the judiciary ultimately undermines effective social reforms.

How Can the Work of Courts Be Appraised?

Analyzing the Question

The analytical enterprise must begin by clarifying the question. Gerald Rosenberg's *Hollow Hope*, in its subtitle, asks, "Can courts bring about social change?" Several things about the question need to be noted. First, it focuses just on courts. The question could be asked even more broadly whether laws can bring about social change. For example, Professor Rabkin laments that despite all of the court decisions concerning equal protection, economic conditions for blacks are relatively unchanged.[9] Over the past thirty-five years, major civil rights statutes have been adopted. The failure to improve economic circumstances for African Americans obviously reflects inadequacies not just of the courts but also, and perhaps even more significantly, of legislatures.[10]

The point is to ask whether it makes sense to evaluate the ability of courts to make a difference apart from the general ability of the law to make a difference. Scholars and policymakers who assert that it is better to direct efforts at social reform at legislatures rather than at courts incorrectly assume that legislatures would be successful in areas in which they perceive court failure.

Second, to ask whether courts can bring about social change is to assume that it is possible to measure causation. Causation obviously is often enormously complex. Change is often a long-term process. The more profound the social change, the longer it is likely to take and the more variables that are likely to be involved. Great care needs to be taken in articulating how causation and change will be observed and measured. If changes are noted, how can we determine whether they result from the courts, from other legal changes, or from other social phenomenan?

Third, the question assumes that litigation and decisions are to be evaluated in terms of the social change that results. At the very least, this evaluation requires deciding what social changes are relevant as a measure of success. Professor Rabkin argues that antidiscrimination laws have not succeeded because of the continuing wealth disparities based on race. The assumption is that the success of these laws in terms of social change is to be measured by the gap between the income of whites and that of blacks. But why assume that income is the only measure of success? Antidiscrimination laws surely succeed if they mean less discrimination and more jobs being available for minorities, even if the black-white wealth gap continues.

Also, for many reasons, focusing on whether court decisions cause social change is an incomplete inquiry. Even if court decisions brought about no social change, they still might serve enormously important ends. Perhaps, most important, court decisions can provide redress to injured individuals. Even if laws forbidding employment discrimination are shown to have had little net effect in eradicating workplace inequalities, the statutes still serve a crucial purpose if they provide compensation to the victims of discrimination. Similarly, even if tort law does not succeed in deterring dangerous products and practices, it can be successful in compensating innocent victims.

Moreover, the redress might be noneconomic. Court decisions can provide vindication to those who have suffered from unconstitutional or illegal practices. *Brown v. Board of Education* was an enormously important statement of equality even if little school desegregation resulted. Richard Kluger eloquently described this impact of *Brown*:

> Every colored American knew that *Brown* did not mean that he would be invited to lunch with the Rotary the following week. It meant something more basic and more important. It meant that black rights had suddenly been redefined; black bodies had been reborn under a new law. Blacks' value as human beings had been changed overnight by declaration of the nation's highest court. At a stroke, the Justices had severed the remaining cords of *de facto* slavery. The Negro could no longer be fastened with the status of official pariah. No longer could the white man look right through him as if he were, in the title words of Ralph Ellison's stunning 1952 novel, *Invisible Man*. No more would he be a grinning supplicant for the benefactions of the master class; no more would he be a party to his own degradation. He was both thrilled that the signal for demise of his caste status had come from on high and angry that it had taken so long and first exacted so steep a price in suffering.[11]

Finally, and most important, court decisions upholding the Constitution can protect key values and thus have great social importance, even if no social change can be linked to the rulings. For instance, court decisions safeguarding freedom of speech protect the rights of individuals to express themselves and lead to a better-informed citizenry, even if no better policies can be linked to the decisions. Allowing the Pentagon Papers to be published did not bring about social change, but it was a crucial vindication for an important constitutional value.[12] Stopping governmental aid to parochial schools does not change society, but it enforces the establishment clause and the separation of church and state.

The point is that the question posed by Professor Rosenberg assumes that courts should be evaluated in terms of their success in bringing about social change. Evaluating the success and importance of courts requires a much broader inquiry than just their ability to effect social change.

Furthermore, it is important to note that courts can play a hugely important role in preventing social change. During the first third of this century, a conservative Supreme Court invalidated progressive legislation protecting workers and consumers, such as laws prohibiting child labor and requiring a minimum wage.[13] Is there any doubt that these decisions prevented significant social change? Likewise, in the current era, Supreme Court decisions invalidating voluntary affirmative action programs and efforts prevent a form of social change.[14] In fact, Professor Rabkin's essay suggests that current constitutional doctrines are now frustrating necessary social change in many areas.[15]

If the impact of courts is to be assessed, the evaluation must account for how courts facilitate and how they impede social change. And it is essential to separate the descriptive and the normative questions. Whether the Supreme Court's decisions limit affirmative action is descriptive; whether that is good or bad is a distinct issue requiring separate consideration.

False Starts

None of the above is meant to imply, however, that it is irrelevant to consider whether courts can bring about social change. Certainly, litigation is often initiated for that purpose, and courts sometimes act with that as a goal. The question then becomes how "social change" is to be defined and measured.

Two measures that often are used seem particularly unhelpful. One is whether courts bring about changes in popular attitudes. For instance, Professor Rosenberg's chapter in this book focuses on whether the Supreme Court's decisions influence popular beliefs about equality. Indeed, assuming that this is a crucial factor in assessing the institutional significance of the Supreme Court, he titles his chapter "The Irrelevant Court: The Supreme Court's Inability to Influence Popular Beliefs about Equality (or Anything Else)." The title suggests that if the Court does not influence popular beliefs, the Court is irrelevant.

This notion seems clearly wrong. If the Court successfully changes the law and if the reform alters society, it should make little difference whether popular beliefs are affected. It is not at all clear why court decisions should be appraised in terms of their effect on public opinion.

Perhaps the argument is that social change is impossible without changing social attitudes. But this is a claim that needs to be supported and not simply asserted. Although sometimes court reform is unlikely to succeed without changes in popular beliefs, there is no reason to believe that it is always the case. Consider the impact of the Court's decisions invalidating Jim Crow laws—the statutes in the South that mandated segregation of restaurants, hotels, parks, and almost everything else. The decisions, by any measure, were successful in desegregating public facilities. Ultimately, the "whites only" signs were taken off restrooms and water fountains and parks and beaches. If this occurred without a change in attitudes, it still was valuable and important. Perhaps, too, it caused a change in attitudes over time. Either way, there was an effect, and few would deny that it was positive.

Public opinion seems an especially inappropriate criterion to use in evaluating the judiciary. Federal judges are not elected and do not face review at the polls. Their insulation from the political process is based on the hope that it will enhance the enforcement of the Constitution. The Constitution is an inherently antimajoritarian document; it limits the ability of contemporary social majorities to act. Therefore, it is inappropriate to evaluate a politically insulated judiciary that is charged with enforcing an antimajoritarian instrument based on how much it pleases and persuades the public.

Also, evaluating the Court based on public opinion seems inherently problematic. Changes in social attitudes likely occur over a long period. Measurement is difficult and depends on the instrument.[16] Also, public opinion—whether measured by opinion polls, press coverage, or textbook content—is a product of countless factors. Methodologically, will it ever be possible to assess the role of the courts in this mix?

A second false start in evaluating courts focuses on whether social changes would have occurred anyway even without judicial decisions. In other words, the analyst concedes that social change happened and that it followed a Supreme Court decision but then argues that the reform would have occurred even without the Court's ruling. For example, Justice Ginsburg attacked *Roe v. Wade* for short-circuiting pro-choice initiatives in several state legislatures.[17]

The difficulty with such arguments is that they are projections of a world that never existed. There certainly are possible scenarios in which legislatures might have done what courts accomplished. Although it is conceivable that state legislatures would have loosened restrictions on access to abortion if *Roe* had not invalidated such laws, it also is conceivable that as pro-choice forces gained political strength, antiabortion groups would have mobilized, just as they did after *Roe*. All sorts of scenarios can be imagined supported by analysis of trends. It is questionable what is gained by the exercise or how much it can ever demonstrate that court action is unnecessary.

Also, a key problem with such projections is that they often fail to account for time or geography. *Roe v. Wade* made abortion legal in 1973 for the entire country. How long would it have been before abortion was legal everywhere in the nation without this decision?

The point is that little is to be gained by guessing how the political process might have come to the same result without judicial action. There never is any way to know.

Courts and Legal Change

In evaluating the ability of the judiciary to change society, two interrelated questions must be addressed. One is whether the Supreme Court's constitutional decisions succeed in changing the government's conduct.[18] The other is whether changing the government's actions makes a difference in society. Although generally these questions are merged, analytically they are distinct. Sometimes the complaint of scholars such as Professor Rosenberg is that Supreme Court decisions are not implemented by governmental officials or are circumvented by them. Sometimes the argument is that other social forces undermine any effect of the decisions.

Consider the example of reapportionment. In *Reynolds v. Sims*, the Supreme Court articulated the rule of one person, one vote.[19] All election districts for any elected body must be approximately equal in population size. This was a dramatic change in the law. The first question is whether this Court decision changed government. The answer is unequivocally "yes"; reapportionment of state legislatures occurred throughout the country. The second question, then, is whether changing the composition of legislatures made a difference in society. This is a much harder question because causation is so difficult to know and measure.[20] Can particular laws be traced to the reapportioned legislatures, and which laws should be regarded as significant enough to be deemed "social change"?

Assessing the ability of Court decisions to bring about change thus requires analysis of when the judiciary is likely to be successful in altering governmental conduct and also analysis of when that is likely to make a difference in society.

WHEN CAN COURTS CHANGE GOVERNMENTAL ACTIONS?

In evaluating the ability of Court decisions to change governmental conduct, several different types of situations exist. First, there are those instances when a court's decision is essentially self-executing; no further action of any governmental official or even of the courts is necessary. The most obvious example is when a court refuses to issue a ruling. For instance, in the Pentagon Papers case, the Supreme Court refused to enjoin the publication of a study of U.S. involvement in the Vietnam War.[21] No further action of any governmental official was necessary, and yet governmental policy was changed.

Second, there are those instances when a court's decision can be fully enforced by the judiciary through its power to dismiss future cases. For example, if the Supreme Court declares unconstitutional a criminal statute, the judiciary can enforce that decision simply by dismissing any future prosecutions brought under the law. The Court, by definition, has changed governance by altering the law and by ending a set of criminal prosecutions. A simple illustration is the Supreme Court's 1995 decision in *United States v. Lopez* invalidating the federal law that made it a crime to have a firearm within 1,000 feet of a school.[22] No longer will the federal government use that statute. If the government tried, the case would be dismissed by the courts.

The Supreme Court's decisions invalidating laws prohibiting the use of contraceptives[23] and forbidding abortion[24] could be enforced by the judiciary. The courts simply could dismiss any future prosecutions brought under these laws.

Third, some Supreme Court decisions upholding the constitutionality of laws or governmental practices encourage governmental action. For instance, a Supreme Court decision upholding a local ordinance might encourage other cities to adopt similar laws. In that way, the Court's ruling will change government. If the Court had upheld the affirmative action program in Richmond, Virginia, the Court might have encouraged other cities to adopt similar set-aside programs.[25] If the Supreme Court had upheld Colorado's Amendment 2, which forbade state or local legal protections for gays and lesbians, other cities and states might have adopted similar laws.[26] I would regard this as a terrible change in government, but it undoubtedly would be a change as a result of the Court's decision.

Fourth, there are Court decisions that require compliance by others in government but that the judiciary can enforce through its contempt power, typified by the classic negative injunction. The court issues an injunction, and violations are punished by contempt. Usually, the threat of contempt is sufficient to gain compliance by the government. If an employer is sued for using a racially discriminatory test in hiring, the court, upon finding a violation of the law, can enjoin future use of the test. If the employer is recalcitrant and continues to use the test, the court can hold the employer in contempt of court.

Fifth, Court decisions enforced through the award of money damages are likely to change governmental conduct. An obvious example is the law of the takings clause. If the Supreme Court were to hold that a taking occurs whenever a governmental regulation decreases the value of a person's property, the judiciary could enforce this ruling by awarding money damages in the future. There is no doubt that such a holding would profoundly alter government because it would have to pay compensation for a wide array of laws, from zoning statutes to environmental regulations.

More generally, damages can deter wrongful governmental conduct. Section 1983 litigation has as part of its purpose to deter government from violating constitutional rights. For instance, the possibility of money damages for sexual harassment provides strong encouragement for governmental employers to refrain from such behavior.

Sixth, some Court decisions require substantial actions by government in compliance and implementation and, therefore, continuing judicial monitoring and enforcement. The most obvious example is the school desegregation litigation. Changing governmental laws that segregated parks or water fountains simply required taking down the "whites only" sign. If the government failed to do this, contempt could be imposed. But desegregating schools was a far more daunting challenge because it required affirmative steps ranging from changing pupil assignments to redrawing attendance zones to busing.

The above six categories are not exhaustive, but they are instructive of the many ways in which courts can change government. In some of the categories, there is a very high likelihood that judicial action will succeed in altering governmental conduct. Denying the government an injunction or invalidating a criminal statute virtually always will succeed in changing governmental behavior. In some of the categories, governmental compliance is less certain. When the Court awards money damages against the government, particularly against the federal government, there is relatively little that the judiciary can do except hope for voluntary compliance. When the Court issues an affirmative injunction, such as for school desegregation, compliance might be a more lengthy and uncertain process.

Those who criticize the impact of Court decisions tend to pick their examples from the most problematic categories. Recognizing the range of situations in which the judiciary can change government helps in properly assessing the ability of courts to make a difference.

WHEN DOES CHANGING GOVERNMENT ACTIONS CHANGE SOCIETY?: LESSONS FROM SCHOOL DESEGREGATION

A distinct, although certainly related, question concerns whether changing governmental conduct really has any effect on society. This inquiry is much more difficult to assess because there are not clear criteria for assessing or measuring social change. "Social change" connotes an overall noticeable effect on society. Yet, few Court decisions possibly could have such an effect. For example, Supreme Court decisions concerning prisoners' rights might be enormously important for those imprisoned, but they are unlikely to cause "social change." Likewise, Court decisions preventing discrimination against nonmarital children might be very significant in the lives of those individuals, but the rulings cannot be assessed in terms of social change.[27]

Therefore, care has to be taken in assessing which cases should be evaluated in terms of their ability to achieve social change. Assuming that such cases are properly identified, then care must be taken to construct a meaningful measure of social change to use in evaluating the impact of the decisions.

There also is another pitfall in this analysis: seeing the ineffectiveness of a particular decision or judicial strategy as proving an inherent weakness of the courts. It certainly is possible to try to assess whether a specific decision or set of rulings brought about certain results. A conclusion that the decisions failed may reflect a general weakness of courts or it may reveal only a misguided approach in those cases.

Those who argue that judicial action can have little impact on society especially point to school desegregation and the legacy of *Brown v. Board of Education*.[28] For instance, Alexander Bickel characterized court-ordered busing as sheer folly, arguing that "no policy that a court can order, and a school board, a city or even a state has the capacity to put into effect, will in fact result in the foreseeable future in racially balanced schools. Only a reordering of the environment . . . might have an appreciable impact."[29]

Yet the story of school desegregation and whether it succeeded is a complicated one and not one that lends itself to a yes or no answer. Some school desegregation was achieved, although much of the promise of *Brown* remains unfulfilled. Some of the failure may have been inherent to judicial actions, but a great deal of it may be because the Court did not implement the proper remedies. Examining the topic of school desegregation is instructive in evaluating claims about the inherent limits of courts in bringing about social change.

It certainly is true that in the years immediately following *Brown*, little desegregation was achieved. In the South, just 1.2 percent of black schoolchildren were attending school with whites a decade after *Brown*.[30] In South Carolina, Alabama, and Mississippi, not one black child attended a public school with a white child in the 1962–63 school year.[31] In North Carolina, only 0.026 percent of black students attended desegregated schools in 1961, and the figure did not rise above 1 percent until 1965.[32] Similarly, in Virginia, in 1964, only 1.63 percent of blacks were attending desegregated schools.[33]

Yet the persistent efforts at desegregation ultimately had an impact. One by one the obstructionist techniques were defeated. Finally, by the mid-1960s, desegregation began to proceed. By 1968, the integration rate in the South rose to 32 percent, and by 1972–73, 91.3 percent of southern schools were desegregated.[34] To point to one example of success, the federal court's desegregation order in Oklahoma City effectively eliminated one-race schools and meant that few blacks or whites were attending schools that were more than 90 percent of one race. Indeed, it was demonstrated that eliminating the court's desegregation order would cause the resegregation of the Oklahoma City schools.[35]

Yet there is no doubt that despite forty years of judicial action, school segregation continues. Indeed, racial segregation in American schools has been increasing over the past decade. A study by the National School Boards Association found "a pattern in which impressive progress toward school integration among blacks and whites in the 1970s petered out in the 1980s."[36] The report predicted that in the 1990s, "large-scale resegregation could be the order of the day in much of the country."[37]

In virtually every area of the country, racial separation in schooling is increasing. In the Northeast, for example, half of the black students in the region attend schools with fewer than 10 percent whites, and a third go to schools that are 99 percent or more minority.[38] At the opposite end of the country, in Los Angeles, the percentage of white students in the public schools has fallen from 40 to 13 percent since the mid-1970s.[39] In Philadelphia, the percentage of white students has dropped from 32 to 23 percent.[40] In St. Paul, Minnesota, the percentage of white students in public schools has gone from 85 to 55 percent.[41]

In 1980, 63 percent of black students and 66 percent of Hispanics were in segregated schools, that is, schools with more than half minority enrollment.[42] Today, nationally, two-thirds of all black children attend schools that are more than 50 percent black.[43] The reality is that most children in the United States are educated with only children of their race, and the separation is increasing.

The key question is why. It is easy to say that the judiciary failed to achieve school desegregation, but is that because courts inherently were impotent in this area or is it because the Supreme Court failed to craft needed remedies? I strongly believe the latter.[44] Two Supreme Court decisions dramatically limited the ability of the judiciary to formulate effective remedies for segregated schools.

First, in *Milliken v. Bradley*, the Court, by a 5–4 margin, dramatically limited the ability of courts to impose interdistrict remedies in school desegregation cases.[45] In *Milliken*, the federal district court ordered fifty-three suburban school districts to participate in the desegregation of the Detroit public schools.[46] On appeal, the Sixth Circuit recognized that "any less comprehensive a solution than a metropolitan plan would result in an all-black system immediately surrounded by practically all-white suburban school systems."[47] The court of appeals held that since "school district lines are simply matters of political convenience . . . they may not be used to deny constitutional rights."[48]

The Supreme Court reversed the imposition of a metropolitan-wide remedy. The Court reasoned that suburban school districts could not be included in the desegregation plan absent proof that they committed a constitutional violation. The Court, in an opinion by Chief Justice Warren E. Burger, held that the metropolitan-wide remedy violated the equitable principle that "the scope of the remedy is determined by the nature and the extent of the constitutional violation."[49] The Court declared that "[t]o approve the remedy ordered would . . . impose on the outlying districts, not shown to have committed any constitutional violation, a wholly impermissible remedy."[50]

Although the Court did not completely rule out the possibility of a judicially created metropolitan relief in all cases, the Court made it clear that such a remedy was to be allowed only in extraordinary circumstances in which there was proof of interdistrict violations. The reality, however, is that effective desegregation often requires an interdistrict remedy. The sad fact of American metropolitan areas is that cities are predominately black and that surrounding suburban areas are predominately white. Desegregation obviously requires the ability to combine these students in integrated schools. *Milliken* generally precludes this.

If *Milliken* had been decided differently—not a fanciful possibility since it was a 5–4 decision—there could be much more desegregation of American public education. Therefore, the dismal statistics about current segregation are less an indication of the inherent failure of the judiciary and more a reflection of the Court's choices.

The second decision that limited effective desegregation, especially in northern cities, was *Keyes v. Denver*.[51] There the Court held that proof of segregation was not sufficient to establish a constitutional violation; rather, there must be proof that segregation resulted from intentionally discriminatory policies.

Segregation is often the product of a multitude of factors. Establishing governmental culpability often is difficult, if not impossible. If *Keyes* had been decided differently, then courts could have fashioned desegregation remedies if there was proof of a discriminatory impact. Requiring a showing of discriminatory intent dramatically limited the ability of the federal courts to order desegregation of de facto segregated northern city school systems.

The point is that great care has to be taken in assessing why a judicial policy failed. Scholars such as Professor Rosenberg see the failure to achieve social change as reflecting inherent limitations of courts. But equally or more plausible is the possibility that the Court might have been more successful if it had made different choices. In the area of school desegregation, the reality is that the Burger Court, dominated by four justices appointed by President Richard Nixon, made crucial decisions limiting remedies. It certainly is plausible to imagine different decisions and different results if only the Warren Court had continued for a few more years.

In conclusion, the ability of courts to bring about social change is undoubtedly a product of many factors. What is the nature of public opinion on the subject? *Roe v. Wade* was not overruled by constitutional amendment, and abortion remains legal, in part, because most people favor legalized abortions. To what extent can the Court implement its rulings regardless of public opinion? Redistricting as a result of reapportionment could be mandated and enforced by the courts on their own if necessary. To what extent can governmental officials circumvent Court decisions? School prayers were largely eliminated by the Supreme Court, but they probably continued to exist in some places because teachers ignored the decisions and no parents complained. To what extent can people circumvent or undermine Court rulings? Desegregation was frustrated, in part, by white flight to private schools and to suburban areas.

These are just some of the factors that influence whether Court decisions will have social impact. My ultimate conclusion is that analysis must always be contextual. In some areas, courts can dramatically change government and society. In other areas, courts are likely to have very limited success. Categorical statements about the ability, or lack of ability, of courts to bring about social change are misguided because so much depends on the particular area of law and the social circumstances surrounding the decisions.

Do Court Decisions Preclude Needed Social Change?

The new wave of court bashing goes further than just arguing that the judiciary is largely useless in bringing about social reforms. Scholars such as Professor Rabkin argue that the courts are preventing needed and desirable social changes.[52] Professor Rabkin contends, for example, that parochial schools "tend to do a much better job in imparting the discipline and self-respect needed for orderly learning" but laments that the Supreme Court's decisions prevent governmental subsidies of parochial education, "which might make it more widely available."[53] Similarly, he suggests that criminal procedure protections and procedural due process rights limit the ability of the government to combat drug abuse.[54]

It is tempting to debate each of these examples with Professor Rabkin, but he simply mentions them in passing, and a detailed discussion is beyond the scope of his or my chapter. The issue here is how to evaluate claims, by those such as Professor Rabkin, that courts are obstructing desirable reforms. Although I disagree with each of Professor Rabkin's examples, I certainly agree that courts have the capacity to frustrate needed social changes.

Therefore, I suggest that analysis focus on three questions in assessing whether Court decisions are, in fact, preventing desirable reforms by government. First, would a particular policy, on balance, be desirable? In other words, before ever considering the institutional question about the judicial role, the policy must be evaluated on its own merits. As an example, Professor Rabkin suggests that governmental subsidies of parochial schools would be desirable. Before criticizing the courts for preventing these subsidies, there needs to be consideration of whether they really would be desirable. I certainly think not. They would divert resources from the public schools. They would probably intensify segregation. Most of all, they would mean substantial governmental subsidies for religious institutions, which would breach the wall that should separate church and state. In a debate over the issue, each of these points would need to be developed. The point here is simply that criticizing the courts for preventing subsidies assumes their desirability.

Second, if it is established that the Court is preventing needed social change, the next question must be why. Is it that the Court has weighed the competing policies and simply has made the wrong choice? For example, the current Court is dramatically limiting governmental affirmative action efforts because of its value choices about race and equal protection. In the first third of this century, the Court prevented needed legislation to protect workers and consumers because of its commitment to a laissez-faire economy. The criticism of the Court, therefore, must focus on its value choices.

There are other reasons why the Court might frustrate needed social reforms. Is it that the Court is not sufficiently aware of the problem or the needed solution? Even the most basic constitutional rights are not absolute, and the government can prevail if it meets strict scrutiny, proving that a particular law is necessary to achieve a compelling interest. It may be that the Court does not recognize the importance of the interest or the need for the particular means. Is it that the Court is following outdated precedents?

The third and final question is whether it is possible that the Court will change its approach or whether there are ways to achieve the result regardless of the judiciary's approach. Sometimes the Court will shift course because of apparent social needs or changes in its membership. The dramatic shift in constitutional jurisprudence in the late 1930s probably reflected both the recognition of a need to defer to governmental economic regulations and ultimately the ability of President Franklin D. Roosevelt to change the composition of the Court. Sometimes there are ways of circumventing Court decisions and achieving change despite the judicial impediments.

Court decisions can bring about changes, and those changes might be good or bad. Court decisions can frustrate changes, and those changes, too, might be good or bad. There is no inherent reason why courts, or any other institution, are more likely to succeed or fail. Therefore, discussion about whether courts are preventing needed social change must also be contextual and focus on particular areas of law. Generalizations are worthless.

Conclusion

I have primarily discussed the writings of Professors Rosenberg and Rabkin because they have written chapters in this volume. My goal has not been to write a detailed reply to their chapters but, instead, to regard their writing as representative of a current wave of scholarship that questions whether courts can do good for society.

I must confess that I always have been perplexed by the point of this scholarship. Do any scholars really believe that *Brown v. Board of Education* was a mistake and that the Court should have affirmed the policy of separate but equal?

If the scholarship is making the limited point that courts sometimes fail in their efforts, I agree. It is certainly worthwhile to assess the performance of courts and try to figure out when they are most likely to succeed.

But my sense is that scholarship of this sort often seems to be making a more sweeping point about the role of courts and the futility of litigation. It is here that I strongly disagree. There are times when only courts are likely to succeed, and there are times when only legislative action is likely to be effective. There are times when the actions of both together are essential and times when neither, alone or together, can make a difference. My hope is that the writings of scholars like Professors Rosenberg and Rabkin will be understood as an invitation for such contextual analysis and not as the basis for categorical statements about the role or ability of the courts.

NOTES

I am grateful to Melanie Petross and Cheryl Watkins for their research assistance.

1. Gerald N. Rosenberg, *The Hollow Hope: Can Courts Bring About Social Change?* (Chicago: University of Chicago Press, 1991). For an excellent review of this book, see Neal Devins, "Judicial Matters," *California Law Review* 80 (July 1992): 1027.
2. Cass Sunstein, *The Partial Constitution* (Cambridge: Harvard University Press, 1993).
3. Ruth Bader Ginsburg, "Some Thoughts on Autonomy and Equality in Relation to *Roe v. Wade*," North Carolina Law Review 63 (January 1985): 375.
4. Rosenberg, *Hollow Hope*, 343.
5. See Rosenburg, chapter 11, in this volume.
6. Jeremy Rabkin, "Racial Progress and Constitutional Roadblocks," *William and Mary Law Review* 34 (Fall 1992): 75; see also Rabkin, chapter 6, in this volume.
7. Rabkin, "Racial Progress and Constitutional Roadblocks," 81, 85.
8. Rosenberg makes this point expressly in *Hollow Hope*, 342.
9. See chapter 6.
10. See, e.g., Richard Epstein, *Forbidden Grounds: The Case against Employment Discrimination Laws* (Cambridge: Harvard University Press, 1992). I have criticized Epstein's thesis in a debate with him that is published in "Forum: Should Title VII of the Civil Rights Act of 1964 Be Repealed?" *Southern California Interdisciplinary Law Journal* 2 (Fall 1994): 349, 445.
11. Richard Kluger, *Simple Justice* (New York: Knopf, 1975), 749.
12. *New York Times v. United States*, 403 U.S. 713 (1971).
13. See, e.g., *Lochner v. New York*, 198 U.S. 45 (1905) (invalidating a state law limiting hours that bakers could work); *Hammer v. Dagenhart*, 247 U.S. 251 (1918) (invalidating a federal law prohibiting the shipment in interstate commerce of goods made by child labor); *Adkins v. Children's Hospital*, 261 U.S. 525 (1923) (invalidating a state law that required a minimum wage for women).
14. See, e.g., *Miller v. Johnson*, 115 S. Ct. 2475 (1995) (limiting affirmative action in drawing election districts); *City of Richmond v. J. A. Croson Co.*, 488 U.S. 469 (1989) (invalidating a city's set-aside of public works contracts for minority-owned businesses).
15. Rabkin, "Racial Progress and Constitutional Roadblocks," 80–81.
16. Professor Rosenberg, for example, focuses on the number of press stories about civil rights and the content of textbooks. But these factors seem imprecise, at best, in measuring popular beliefs.
17. Ginsburg, "Some Thoughts on Autonomy and Equality in Relation to *Roe v. Wade*."
18. My focus here is on constitutional litigation, and, therefore, because of the state action requirement—prohibiting the filing of constitutional claims against private actors—the de-

fendant usually will be the government. A similar set of questions, of course, can be asked about the ability of the courts to change private conduct when private actors are named as defendants.

19. 377 U.S. 533 (1964).

20. Rosenberg questions whether significant laws were passed as a result of reapportionment in *Hollow Hope*, 296.

21. *New York Times*, 403 U.S. 713.

22. 115 S. Ct. 1624 (1995). The law was invalidated as exceeding the scope of Congress's commerce-clause authority.

23. See, e.g., *Griswold v. Connecticut*, 381 U.S. 479 (1965).

24. *Roe v. Wade*, 410 U.S. 113 (1973).

25. See *City of Richmond*, 488 U.S. 469.

26. *Romer v. Evans*, 116 S. Ct. 1620 (1996).

27. See, e.g., *Jiminez v. Weinberger*, 417 U.S. 628 (1974) (invalidating a section of the Social Security Act that disadvantaged nonmarital children).

28. 347 U.S. 483 (1954).

29. Alexander M. Bickel, *The Supreme Court and the Idea of Progress* (New Haven: Yale University Press, 1978), 132.

30. Michael Klarman, "*Brown*, Racial Change, and the Civil Rights Movement," *Virginia Law Review* 80 (January 1994): 7, 9.

31. Ibid., 9.

32. Ibid.

33. Ibid.

34. Klarman, "*Brown*, Racial Change, and the Civil Rights Movement," 10.

35. See *Board of Education v. Dowell*, 111 S. Ct. 630 (1991) (the Court held that once unitary status has been achieved in a school system, the desegregation order should be lifted, even if it will result in the resegregation of the public schools).

36. Larry Tye, "Social Racial Gaps Found Nationwide," *Boston Globe*, 8 January 1992, 3.

37. Ibid.

38. Larry Tye, "U.S. Sounds Retreat in School Integration," *Boston Globe*, 5 January 1992, 1.

39. Ibid., 45.

40. Ibid.

41. Ibid.

42. "Illinois Schools Most Segregated," *Chicago Sun Times*, 5 September 1982, 6.

43. Tye, "Social Racial Gaps Found Nationwide," 45.

44. I have developed this argument more fully in "Lost Opportunity: The Burger Court and the Failure to Achieve Equal Educational Opportunity," *Mercer Law Review* 45 (Spring 1994): 999.

45. 418 U.S. 717 (1974).

46. *Bradley v. Milliken*, 338 F. Supp. 582 (E.D. Mich. 1971), *aff'd*, 484 F.2d 215 (6th Cir. 1973), *rev'd*, 418 U.S. 717 (1974).

47. *Milliken v. Bradley*, 484 F.2d 215, 245 (6th Cir. 1973), *rev'd*, 418 U.S. 717 (1974).

48. 484 F.2d at 244.

49. 418 U.S. at 744.

50. Ibid. at 745.

51. 413 U.S. 189 (1973).

52. Rabkin, "Racial Progress and Constitutional Roadblocks," 80–82.

53. Ibid., 80.

54. Ibid., 83–84.

13

The Supreme Court's Pursuit of Equality and Liberty and the Burdens of History

DAVID J. GARROW

The Supreme Court's decision in *Brown v. Board of Education*[1] is commonly regarded as the signal event in the modern quest for racial equality. Confronted with widespread racial segregation of schoolchildren by reason of state law, the Court in *Brown* held that such segregation violated the equal protection clause of the Fourteenth Amendment.

The Court's *Brown* decision, however, did far more than simply declare school segregation unconstitutional. The decision also transformed the Court's role in the modern quest for equality. In its unyielding search for the morally correct result in *Brown*, the Court interpreted the Fourteenth Amendment in a manner that demonstrated that the Court would not be tethered by the burdens of history. In effect, the Court determined that the moral imperative of racial desegregation trumped fidelity to the uncertain intentions of the framers of the Fourteenth Amendment.[2] In so doing, the Court, with the *Brown* decision, unleashed a new era in constitutional jurisprudence.

In the wake of *Brown*, the Court issued a number of other decisions dealing with both equality and personal liberty that reflect the Court's willingness to fashion a Fourteenth Amendment jurisprudence that is not tightly moored to that amendment's demonstrable historical intentions.[3] In the process, the Court has helped transform the modern quest for both equality and personal liberty in ways that have served well the pursuit of justice in America.

Many people have grown up believing that while *Marbury v. Madison*[4] is of course *the* formative U.S. Supreme Court decision of all time, that the Supreme Court's decisions of 1937[5]—perhaps in conjunction with Chief Justice Harlan F. Stone's (or Louis Lusky's) famous 1938 footnote in *Carolene Products*[6]—signal the beginning of the judicial modern age.

But that belief, which was inculcated among at least two successive generations of American judicial scholars, is now all but indisputably out-of-date, for *Brown*, rather than the "constitutional revolution" of 1937, not only demarcates our modern era but, just as important, also paved the way for the Warren Court's two other landmark *antihistorical* rulings—*Baker v. Carr*[7] and *Griswold v. Connecticut*[8] (and for their even better-known progeny, *Reynolds v. Sims*[9] and *Roe v. Wade*[10])—which dramatically expanded the constitutional scope of the Fourteenth Amendment. Absent *Brown*, decisions with *Baker*'s and *Reynolds*'s muscularity are difficult to imagine; absent the most important of *Brown*'s own immediate progeny—namely, *Cooper v. Aaron*,[11] the Warren Court's *Marbury*—much of the post-1954 Court's understanding of its own role, which at present has culminated in *Planned Parenthood of Southeastern Pennsylvania v. Casey*,[12] would have evolved in a decidedly different fashion. In short, *Brown I*, in tandem with *Cooper*, not only marks the beginning of modern America's official condemnation of racial discrimination but also marks the beginning of a wide-ranging transformation of modern American life brought about by a host of high Court decisions that have relied on the justices' dramatically expansive—and aggressively antihistorical—reading and application of the Fourteenth Amendment's equal protection and due process clauses. From schooling to electoral districting to abortion, modern America is to a significant degree the product of muscular judicial utilization of the Fourteenth Amendment; it is also the product of constitutional analysis that has jettisoned the constraints of history. From *Brown* to *Baker* and *Reynolds*, and to *Griswold, Roe*, and *Casey*, I believe we can persuasively argue that it is a *better* America precisely because of how the Court *has ignored* the Constitution's historical limitations in fashioning a Fourteenth Amendment jurisprudence that is responsive to the present-day rather than to the institutional burdens of history.[13]

Careful students of *Brown* can, of course, easily recall that the Supreme Court initially hoped—and sought—to find clear Fourteenth Amendment historical support for resolving the fundamental question that *Brown* and its companion cases[14] presented. Following the first oral arguments in the *Brown* cases, the Court formally propounded five questions to the parties' attorneys. The first two questions asked for historical evidence regarding whether the framers of the Fourteenth Amendment intended or did not intend for it either to prohibit or to allow for the future prohibition of racially segregated public schooling. The third question, however, voicing a presumption that the answers to the first two would "not dispose of the issue," posed the core issue bluntly: "[I]s it within the judicial power, in construing the [Fourteenth] Amendment, to abolish segregation in the public schools?"[15] Eleven months later, on 17 May 1954, the Court baldly, but compellingly, declared that indeed it was.

As we now know, the National Association for the Advancement of Colored People (NAACP) Legal Defense and Educational Fund litigators and their many scholarly collaborators were at first deeply (and justifiably) concerned by the Court's preliminary focus on historical queries whose answers would not hasten, and might well hinder, judicial acceptance of the NAACP's basic contention.[16] But by the time of *Brown* et al.'s rearguments in December 1953, the justices themselves privately no longer regarded the answers to those two historical queries as being potentially determinative. Justice Felix Frankfurter had had one of his outgoing law clerks, Alexander M. Bickel, prepare an exhaustive historical research memorandum, and Frankfurter had distributed the impressive product to his colleagues. Although counsel at the time were quite unaware that Bickel's handiwork had firmly directed the justices away from any potential history-based solution to their American dilemma, we nowadays—thanks in part to Mark Tushnet's careful analysis—can fully appreciate that by December the historical questions "were no longer that important" to the Court itself.[17]

Even though there was—thanks to Robert Jackson and particularly Stanley Reed—no internal consensus on *how* to decide *Brown* when the justices met for their decisive conference on 12 December 1953, there nonetheless *was* an unspoken consensus that the fundamental question before them was last June's "question three": "[I]s it within the judicial power . . . to abolish segregation in the public schools?"[18] And when Chief Justice Earl Warren delivered the Court's impressively unanimous opinion in *Brown* five months later, there again, and now for the whole country to see, was an explicit consensus that the core of this question, like others yet to come, concerned not evidence or documentation of "historical intent" but, instead, the nature and reach of "the judicial power."

Warren's opinion, in two early paragraphs that understandably are not among *Brown*'s best-remembered passages but that latter-day scholars should not overlook, deftly but decisively dismissed the decisional relevance of the Fourteenth Amendment's own history. Warren noted how *Brown*'s reargument "was largely devoted to the circumstances surrounding" the Fourteenth Amendment's 1868 adoption. "It covered exhaustively consideration of the Amendment in Congress, ratification by the states, then existing practices in racial segregation, and the views of proponents and opponents of the Amendment. This discussion and our own investigation convince us that, although these sources cast some light, it is not enough to resolve the problem with which we are faced. At best, they are inconclusive."[19] "An additional reason for the inconclusive nature of the Amendment's history" vis-à-vis school segregation, Warren added, was the relatively undeveloped state of public education, especially in the South but also in the North, in 1868. "As a consequence, it is not surprising that there should be so little in the history of the Fourteenth Amendment relating to its intended effect on public education."[20]

So ended the *Brown* Court's analysis—and dismissal—of whether its constitutional adjudication of governmentally imposed racial segregation in public schools was or should in any way be bound by the constraints of history. Most readers pass over these two paragraphs without attributing any special import to them, and such an evaluation, within the four actual corners of the *Brown* opinion, is perfectly appropriate. In a more long-range frame of reference, however—one that encompasses particularly the years from 1962 (*Baker*) through 1973 (*Roe*)—the *Brown* Court's affirmative jettisoning of the Fourteenth Amendment's historical tielines marked the onset of a period of judicial freedom and, some correctly would say, judicial *sovereignty* that dramatically transformed American life for the better.[21]

In 1954 itself, nothing highlighted the Court's Farragut-like approach to mandating constitutional rights[22] more than its companion ruling in the fifth of the *Brown* family of cases, *Bolling v. Sharpe* from Washington, D.C. Since the Fourteenth

Amendment applied its equal protection clause only to the states and not to the federal government, the *Brown* Court found itself having to identify some non–Fourteenth Amendment constitutional grounds for avoiding the utterly incongruous paradox of striking down *state*-mandated school segregation while not being able to void identical governmental policy imposed by *federal* authorities. With a doctrinal dexterity that again may be more significant in historical retrospect than it appeared to be in 1954, the Court—lacking any federally applicable equal protection language—unanimously turned to the Fifth Amendment's due process clause. "[T]he concepts of equal protection and due process, both stemming from our American ideal of fairness, are not mutually exclusive," Chief Justice Warren wrote. While " 'equal protection of the laws' is a more explicit safeguard of prohibited unfairness than 'due process of law' . . . discrimination may be so unjustifiable as to be violative of due process."[23]

Without expressly acknowledging that the due process clause's key word was of course "liberty," the *Bolling* opinion, while conceding that the Court to date had not defined " 'liberty' with any great precision," nonetheless went on to emphasize that the concept was "not confined to mere freedom from bodily restraint. Liberty under law extends to the full range of conduct which the individual is free to pursue, and it cannot be restricted except for a proper governmental objective. Segregation in public education is not reasonably related to any proper governmental objective, and thus it imposes on Negro children in the District of Columbia a burden that constitutes an arbitrary deprivation of their liberty in violation of the Due Process Clause."[24] Any commentators inclined to allege that the new era—or "Second Reconstruction"—of substantive due process first began to rear its assertedly ugly head only in *Griswold v. Connecticut*[25] had best be reminded that as early as May 1954, *Bolling*'s quite uncontroversial language signaled that a highly expansive approach to due process–based constitutional liberty could well go forward hand in hand with *Brown*'s heralding of a new era of equal protection.[26]

Even more so than anything in *Brown* itself, the almost explicit point of *Bolling* is that the traditions and niceties of doctrine *do not matter*—or, at the very most, matter for relatively little—when and where the Court becomes convinced that a fundamental, moral holding needs to be made. But *Brown* and *Bolling* historically should not be weighed or evaluated apart from their most immediate and important progeny, namely the unprecedented "joint" opinion in the 1958 Little Rock school case of *Cooper v. Aaron*.[27] But just as we ought to remind each other today that 1992's *Planned Parenthood of Southeastern Pennsylvania v. Casey*[28] was not *just*, or perhaps even *principally*, about abortion, likewise we need to remember that *Cooper* was not just, or primarily, about school desegregation. Instead, *Cooper*, like *Casey*—and, I think one can argue, also like *Brown*—was fundamentally about the constitutional authority *and* the political role of the Supreme Court itself.

Cooper's most important paragraph spoke to what the Court called "some basic constitutional propositions which are settled doctrine."[29]

> Article VI of the Constitution makes the Constitution the "supreme Law of the Land." In 1803, Chief Justice Marshall, speaking for a unanimous Court, referring to the Constitution as "the fundamental and paramount law of the nation," declared in the

notable case of *Marbury v. Madison*, 1 Cranch 137, 177, that "It is emphatically the province and duty of the judicial department to say what the law is." This decision declared the basic principle that the federal judiciary is supreme in the exposition of the law of the Constitution, and that principle has ever since been respected by this Court and the Country as a permanent and indispensable feature of our constitutional system. It follows that the interpretation of the Fourteenth Amendment enunciated by this Court in the *Brown* case is the supreme law of the land, and Art. VI of the Constitution makes it of binding effect on the States "any Thing in the Constitution or Laws of any State to the Contrary notwithstanding."[30]

Cooper is arguably the Court's most important declaration of its own authority and role since *Marbury*, but, among at least a small fringe of critical commentators, even some who cannot bring themselves to publicly attack *Brown* or *Bolling* nonetheless feel able to denounce *Cooper*—and particularly that crucial passage in *Cooper*—as one of the Warren Court's "most troubling opinions" because of how it posited "a radical new notion of the status of judicial decisions."[31] *Cooper*, these critics allege, "was not the fulfillment of *Marbury* but rather its perversion,"[32] but the contrarian novelty of such a facially fallacious contention may best be understood as having more to do with *Cooper*'s own most important progeny—namely the 1992 "trio" opinion of Justices Sandra Day O'Connor, Anthony M. Kennedy, and David H. Souter in *Casey*[33]—than perhaps with *Cooper* itself.

But the substantive expansiveness of *Brown*'s application of equal protection was merely the first installment in a new, multipart constitutional scenario. *Colegrove v. Green*[34] should perhaps not be spoken of in the same sentence as *Plessy v. Ferguson*,[35] but if any decision since 1954 can be seen as equal to *Brown* in long-term historical significance, then—as Chief Justice Warren himself repeatedly said[36]—*Baker v. Carr*[37] is certainly *the* case. Justice William J. Brennan, Jr.'s, opinion for the *Baker* Court undeniably took far greater care in clearing away the preexisting judicial underbrush than had Warren's in *Brown*, but the full flowering of equal protection application to the principle of "one person, one vote"—and the Court's explicit citation of *Brown* as helpful precedent for that holding[38]—only came two years later in Warren's opinion for the Court in *Reynolds v. Sims*.[39] The equal protection clause, Warren and five of his colleagues held in *Reynolds*, "guarantees the opportunity for equal participation by all voters in the election of state legislators. Diluting the weight of votes because of place of residence impairs basic constitutional rights under the Fourteenth Amendment just as much as invidious discriminations based upon factors such as race, *Brown v. Board of Education*, 347 U.S. 483 . . ."[40]

Baker, Reynolds, and *Reynolds*'s companion cases[41] all strive far more assiduously than *Brown* and *Bolling* to comport themselves in seeming accommodation with existing precedents. But both textually and historically, *Baker* and *Reynolds*—and perhaps *Reynolds* all the more so, in light of its unwillingness to accept or apply a "federal analogy" whereby only the lower chamber of a bicameral legislature would have to be apportioned into equally populated districts[42]—stand in even more undeniable tension with any intent-based reading of the Fourteenth Amendment's equal protection clause than does *Brown*.[43]

But if critical acceptance of *Brown* is now universal and approval of *Baker* and

Reynolds is widespread but not unanimous,[44] dissent with regard to *Bolling*'s best-known (but rarely if ever acknowledged) descendant, *Griswold v. Connecticut*, is still treated with professional respect, if only because of the undeniable line of derivation that then leads from *Griswold* to *Roe v. Wade*. *Griswold*, like *Brown* and *Baker*, is accepted as *morally* correct even by those who reject its doctrinal grounding, but *Griswold*'s mottled reputation is largely the result not of Justice William O. Douglas's widely recognized compositional shortcomings[45] but of a far more significant jurisprudential legacy—namely the ignominious heritage of *Lochner v. New York*[46]—that until recently only *Bolling*, of all the new, noneconomic substantive due process liberty decisions of the past forty years, has escaped from unscathed.

This issue may well be *the* most important and indeed defining constitutional question of the present age, the question that ought to, and, it is hoped, will, separate this present generation of commentators—namely people who have come to academic maturity in the years since 1973—from the two generations (both children of 1937) that have preceded them.

Perhaps the rudest way in which to pose the question is also the most revealing: Why for more than a half century has *Lochner v. New York* been almost universally viewed as a far more infamous constitutional precedent than, say, *Korematsu v. United States*?[47] *Lochner*, as almost everyone well knows, is widely accepted as *the* symbolic ruling of the "old" conservative Court that prevailed from at least as early as 1895[48] through 1936[49] until being vanquished in the early months of 1937.[50] *Lochner* and its many progeny were resoundingly routed by the constitutional revolution of 1937 (or, more correctly, by the constitutional revolution that began in 1937 and culminated in 1941–42),[51] but the universally acknowledged *ghost* of *Lochner* survived in buoyant health well into the 1960s.[52] Only perhaps in 1973, and then far more certainly in 1992, did clear and convincing evidence finally appear that *Lochner*'s ghost was no longer badly frightening the occupants of America's most exalted judicial corridors.

In *Griswold*, of course, the Court in form, if not in substance, shied away from any prospect of encountering *Lochner*'s ghost in language that epitomizes how powerful and long lasting the jurisprudential overreaction of the 1937 revolution proved to be. "Coming to the merits," Justice Douglas warned, "we are met with a wide range of questions that implicate the Due Process Clause of the Fourteenth Amendment. Overtones of some arguments suggest that *Lochner v. New York* . . . should be our guide. But we decline that invitation as we did in *West Coast Hotel Co.* . . . We do not sit as a super-legislature to determine the wisdom, need, and propriety of laws that touch economic problems, business affairs, or social conditions."[53]

In *Griswold*, however, Connecticut's anticontraception statute "operate[d] directly on an intimate relation of husband and wife and their physician's role in one aspect of that relation,"[54] and hence Douglas, along with six of his eight colleagues, fled from *Lochner*'s ghost only in form rather than in substance. But even eight years later, in *Roe v. Wade*, only one member of *Roe*'s seven-justice majority, Potter Stewart (a *Griswold* dissenter), was willing to explicitly concede the self-obvious point that *Griswold*, of course, was and always had been a substantive due process liberty decision.[55] While Justice Douglas, a true child of 1937 if ever there was one, still sought to deny what was self-obviously undeniable,[56] the *Roe* majority simply chose to elude the point.[57]

Hence only two decades later, in 1992's *Planned Parenthood of Southeastern Pennsylvania v. Casey*,[58] did a Supreme Court majority directly and explicitly confront the fundamental doctrinal issue that had been sidestepped in both *Griswold* and *Roe*. The *Casey* "trio" opinion of Justices O'Connor, Kennedy, and Souter—joined also in its major parts by Justices Harry A. Blackmun and John Paul Stevens—indicated no hesitation whatsoever and no lingering fear of *Lochner*'s ghost in straightforwardly announcing that "Constitutional protection of the woman's decision to terminate her pregnancy derives from the Due Process Clause of the Fourteenth Amendment." Stressing that "[t]he controlling word in the cases before us is 'liberty,' " the *Casey* majority noted that "[a]lthough a literal reading of the Clause might suggest that it governs only the procedures by which a State may deprive persons of liberty, for at least 105 years, since *Mugler v. Kansas*, 123 U.S. 623, 660–61 (1887), the Clause has been understood to contain a substantive component as well, one 'barring certain government actions regardless of the fairness of the procedures used to implement them.' *Daniels v. Williams*, 474 U.S. 327, 331 (1986)."[59]

Quoting both Justice Louis Brandeis's 1927 concurrence in *Whitney v. California*[60] and Justice John M. Harlan's now-famous 1961 dissent in *Poe v. Ullman*[61] in further support of that point, the *Casey* majority went on to explain that "[i]t is a promise of the Constitution that there is a realm of personal liberty which the government may not enter. We have vindicated this principle before. Marriage is mentioned nowhere in the Bill of Rights and interracial marriage was illegal in most States in the 19th century, but the Court was no doubt correct in finding it to be an aspect of liberty protected against state interference by the substantive component of the Due Process Clause in *Loving* v. *Virginia*, 388 U.S. 1, 12 (1967)."[62]

Most centrally of all, the *Casey* majority forthrightly held that "[n]either the Bill of Rights nor the specific practices of States at the time of the adoption of the Fourteenth Amendment marks the outer limits of the substantive sphere of liberty which the Fourteenth Amendment protects,"[63] a holding that of course spoke not only to the elusions of *Roe* and *Griswold* but also to the substantive essences of *Brown* and *Bolling*. Quoting again twice at some length from the Harlan dissent in *Poe*, the *Casey* majority willingly acknowledged that "[t]he inescapable fact is that adjudication of substantive due process claims may call upon the Court in interpreting the Constitution to exercise that same capacity which by tradition courts always have exercised: reasoned judgment. Its boundaries are not susceptible of expression as a simple rule. That does not mean we are free to invalidate state policy choices with which we disagree; yet neither does it permit us to shrink from the duties of our office," as some of the century's best-known jurists, such as Learned Hand and Felix Frankfurter, no doubt would have advised.[64]

Led by Justice Souter, the *Casey* majority presented perhaps the Court's most extended discussion of the concept of precedent in this century, reviewing not only how *West Coast Hotel Co.*, by overruling *Adkins v. Children's Hospital*,[65] had "signaled the demise of *Lochner*"[66] but also the manner in which *Brown* had vanquished *Plessy*. The heart of Souter's analysis, and the heart of *Casey* itself, however, focused on the institutional and historical grounds as to why *Roe v. Wade* should not and *could not* be overruled. Any such reversal, Souter warned, "would seriously weaken the Court's capacity to exercise the judicial power and to function as the Supreme Court of a Nation dedicated to the rule of law. To understand why this would be so it is necessary to understand the source of this Court's authority, the conditions necessary for its preservation, and its relationship to the country's understanding of itself as a constitutional Republic."[67]

Alluding to the old saw that the judiciary commands neither the purse nor the sword, the *Casey* majority reiterated that the Court's actual power lies largely "in its legitimacy, a product of substance and perception that shows itself in the people's acceptance of the Judiciary as fit to determine what the Nation's law means and to declare what it demands."

> The Court must take care to speak and act in ways that allow people to accept its decisions on the terms the Court claims for them, as grounded truly in principle, not as compromises with social and political pressures having, as such, no bearing on the principled choices that the Court is obliged to make. Thus, the Court's legitimacy depends on making legally principled decisions under circumstances in which their principled character is sufficiently plausible to be accepted by the Nation.[68]

Then, in a core section that actually spoke more about *Brown* than *Roe*, Souter and his *Casey* colleagues put forward in five paragraphs the most institutionally important statement by the Court since *Cooper* and the most substantively significant declaration about the role and function of the U.S. Supreme Court since the time of John Marshall.

> Where, in the performance of its judicial duties, the Court decides a case in such a way as to resolve the sort of intensely divisive controversy reflected in *Roe* and those rare, comparable cases, its decision has a dimension that the resolution of the normal case does not carry. It is the dimension present whenever the Court's interpretation of the Constitution calls the contending sides of a national controversy to end their national division by accepting a common mandate rooted in the Constitution.
>
> The Court is not asked to do this very often, having thus addressed the Nation only twice in our lifetime, in the decisions of *Brown* and *Roe*. But when the Court does act in this way, its decision requires an equally rare precedential force to counter the inevitable efforts to overturn it and to thwart its implementation. Some of those efforts may be mere unprincipled emotional reactions; others may proceed from principles worthy of profound respect. But whatever the premises of opposition may be, only the most convincing justification under accepted standards of precedent could suffice to demonstrate that a later decision overruling the first was anything but a surrender to political pressure, and an unjustified repudiation of the principle on which the Court staked its authority in the first instance. So to overrule under fire in the absence of the most compelling reason to reexamine a watershed decision would subvert the Court's legitimacy beyond any serious question. Cf. *Brown v. Board of Education*, 349 U.S. 294, 300 (1955) (*Brown II*) . . .[69]

The *Casey* majority took note of the costs imposed upon those who were closely identified with controversial watershed decisions.

> The price may be criticism or ostracism, or it may be violence. An extra price will be paid by those who themselves disapprove of the decision's results when viewed outside of constitutional terms, but who nevertheless struggle to accept it, because they respect the rule of law. To all those who will be so tested by following, the Court implicitly undertakes to remain steadfast, lest in the end a price be paid for nothing. The promise of constancy, once given, binds its maker for as long as the power to stand by the decision survives and the understanding of the issue has not changed so fundamentally as to render the commitment obsolete. From the obligation of this promise the Court cannot and should not assume any exemption when duty requires it to decide a case in conformance with the Constitution. A willing breach of it would be nothing less than a breach of faith, and no Court that broke its faith with the people could sensibly expect credit for principle in the decision by which it did that.[70]

"Like the character of an individual," the *Casey* majority warned,

> the legitimacy of the Court must be earned over time. So, indeed, must be the character of a Nation of people who aspire to live according to the rule of law. Their belief in themselves as such a people is not readily separable from their understanding of the Court invested with the authority to decide their constitutional cases and speak before all others for their constitutional ideals. If the Court's legitimacy should be undermined, then, so would the country be in its very ability to see itself through its constitutional ideals. The Court's concern with legitimacy is not for the sake of the Court but for the sake of the Nation to which it is responsible.

"The Court's duty in the present case is clear," they concluded.

> In 1973, it confronted the already divisive issue of governmental power to limit personal choice to undergo abortion, for which it provided a new resolution based on the due process guaranteed by the Fourteenth Amendment. Whether or not a new social consensus is developing on that issue, its divisiveness is no less today than in 1973, and pressure to overrule the decision, like pressure to retain it, has grown only more intense. A decision to overrule *Roe*'s essential holding under the existing circumstances would address error, if error there was, at the cost of both profound and unnecessary damage to the Court's legitimacy, and to the Nation's commitment to the rule of law. It is therefore imperative to adhere to the essence of *Roe*'s original decision, and we do so today.[71]

Casey, of course, vindicated *Roe v. Wade*, committing the Court to constitutional protection for abortion in a manner unlikely ever to be undone. *Casey* also offered an extended and significantly intensified reprise of *Cooper* and the powerful historic legacy of *Marbury* and went at least a very long way toward fully elevating *Roe* to the tiny pantheon of American constitutional precedents that perhaps otherwise is peopled only by *Marbury, Brown*, and, possibly, *Baker*.

But in elevating *Roe* to *Brown*-like stature, *Casey* also did, or ratified, something even far more significant as well, something that so far—now more than five years after the event—has received stunningly little attention or discussion. The *Casey*

Court formally and explicitly buried *Lochner*'s ghost. Substantive due process *is*, as it *should be*, a fundamental and fully accepted aspect of present-day American constitutional doctrine.

Casey may well represent the culmination (and conclusion) of a constitutional era that began so dramatically with *Brown* and *Bolling*. Although some conservative scholars now seek to make *Brown* into a badly miscast constitutional poster child for their jurisprudence of "original intent,"[72] such efforts to rebut the interpretive (and doctrinal) radicalism of *Brown* (and *Bolling*) are unlikely to win many followers outside certain narrow precincts. *Brown* heralded not only the Court's explicit freeing of itself from the constraints of historically bounded constitutional "originalism" but also a newly expansive application of the Fourteenth Amendment that energetically encompassed both equal protection and due process. *Brown* opened the institutional door for *Baker*'s and *Reynold*'s revolutionary expansiveness involving equal protection, and *Bolling v. Sharpe* represented the first salvo in a reconstruction of fundamental due process liberty that quietly prepared the doctrinal ground for *Griswold* and for the eventual burial of *Lochner*'s ghost in *Roe* and *Casey.*

Brown and *Casey* are hence bookends to the double-barreled rereading that the Court has accorded the Fourteenth Amendment—both in *Brown* (and in *Baker*) with regard to the equal protection clause and in *Casey* (as in *Griswold* and *Roe* before) with regard to a new rebirth of the due process clause—over these past forty years. If we justifiably celebrate the political revolution(s) heralded by *Brown* (and *Baker*) and if we further celebrate or at least accede to the way in which the *Brown* Court reached above and beyond the Fourteenth Amendment's historical fetters to blot the stain of *Plessy*, so too does *Casey* call on us to acknowledge if not applaud the manner in which the modern Court has similarly expanded due process—like equal protection before it—to hasten another revolution as well. As *Brown* and *Casey* both signify, the modern-day meanings of American constitutional protections should not be, and happily are not, fettered by the burdens and limitations of history.

NOTES

A somewhat different version of this essay, entitled "From *Brown* to *Casey*: The U.S. Supreme Court and the Burdens of History," appears in Austin Sarat, ed., *Race, Law, and Culture: Reflections on* Brown v. Board of Education (New York: Oxford University Press, 1997), 74–88.

1. 347 U.S. 483 (1954).
2. For a survey of conceptual distinctions and specifications concerning "intent," see John G. Wofford, "The Blinding Light: The Uses of History in Constitutional Interpretation," *University of Chicago Law Review* 31 (Spring 1964): 502–3; and Charles A. Miller, *The Supreme Court and the Uses of History* (Cambridge: Harvard University Press, 1969), 20–28, 153–55, 165–66.
3. See *Baker v. Carr*, 369 U.S. 186 (1962); *Reynolds v. Sims*, 377 U.S. 533 (1964); *Griswold v. Connecticut*, 381 U.S. 479 (1965); *Roe v. Wade*, 410 U.S. 113 (1973).

4. 5 U.S. 137 (1803).

5. *West Coast Hotel Co. v. Parrish*, 300 U.S. 379 (1937); *National Labor Relations Board v. Jones & Laughlin Steel Corp.*, 301 U.S. 1 (1937).

6. *United States v. Carolene Products Co.*, 304 U.S. 144, 152 n.4 (1938); see also Alpheus T. Mason, *Harlan Fiske Stone: Pillar of the Law* (New York: Viking Press, 1956), 513–14; Louis Lusky, *By What Right?* (Charlottesville, Va.: Michie Co., 1975), 108–12; Louis Lusky, *Our Nine Tribunes* (Westport, Conn.: Praeger, 1993), 119–32, 177–90.

7. 369 U.S. 186 (1962).

8. 381 U.S. 479 (1965).

9. 377 U.S. 533 (1964).

10. 410 U.S. 113 (1973).

11. 358 U.S. 1 (1958).

12. 505 U.S. 833 (1992).

13. See also generally William E. Nelson, *The Fourteenth Amendment: From Political Principle to Judicial Doctrine* (Cambridge: Harvard University Press, 1988), 4–11; Judith A. Baer, "The Fruitless Search for Original Intent," in *Judging the Constitution*, ed. Michael W. McCann and Gerald L. Houseman (Glenview, Ill.: Scott, Foresman, 1989), 49–71; Mark V. Tushnet, "The Warren Court as History: An Interpretation," in *The Warren Court in Historical and Political Perspective*, ed. Mark V. Tushnet (Charlottesville: University Press of Virginia, 1994), 17–18.

14. See *Brown v. Board of Education*, 98 F. Supp. 797 (D. Kan. 1951); *Briggs v. Elliott*, 103 F. Supp. 920 (E.D. S.C. 1952); *Davis v. County School Board*, 103 F. Supp. 337 (E.D. Va. 1952); *Gebhart v. Belton*, 91 A.2d 137 (Del. Sup. Ct. 1952); cf. *Bolling v. Sharpe*, 347 U.S. 497 (1954).

15. *Brown v. Board of Education*, 345 U.S. 972 (1953); see also Richard Kluger, *Simple Justice* (New York: Knopf, 1976), 614–16.

16. See Kluger, *Simple Justice*, 618–41; Mark V. Tushnet, *Making Civil Rights Law* (New York: Oxford University Press, 1994), 196–99; Jack Greenberg, *Crusaders in the Courts* (New York: Basic Books, 1994), 177–88. As Kluger comments, "[T]he historical evidence seemed to demonstrate persuasively that neither the Congress which framed the Fourteenth Amendment nor the state legislatures which adopted it understood that its pledge of equal protection would require the end of segregation in the nation's public schools." *Simple Justice*, 634. See also Alexander M. Bickel, "The Original Understanding and the Segregation Decision," *Harvard Law Review* 69 (November 1955): 1–65; Alfred H. Kelly, "The Fourteenth Amendment Reconsidered: The Segregation Question," *Michigan Law Review* 59 (June 1956): 1049–86; Alfred H. Kelly, "The Congressional Controversy over School Segregation, 1867–1875," *American Historical Review* 64 (April 1959): 537–63. Cf. Nelson, *The Fourteenth Amendment*, 6–7. Also note Michael W. McConnell's iconoclastic (and generally unpersuasive) argument in "Originalism and the Desegregation Decisions," *Virginia Law Review* 81 (May 1995): 947–1140.

17. Tushnet, *Making Civil Rights Law*, 203–4; see also Alfred H. Kelly, "Clio and the Court: An Illicit Love Affair," *Supreme Court Review* (1965): 142–45; Kluger, *Simple Justice*, 653–55, 668–76.

18 See Kluger, *Simple Justice*, 678–83; Tushnet, *Making Civil Rights Law*, 209–11.

19. 347 U.S. at 489.

20. Ibid. at 489, 490.

21. Cf. Robert H. Bork, *The Tempting of America* (New York: Free Press, 1990), 76–77, 81.

22. After David Glasgow ("Damn the torpedoes! Full speed ahead!") Farragut (1801–

70). See Alfred T. Mahan, *Admiral Farragut* (1897); Charles L. Lewis, *David Glasgow Farragut*, vols. 1, 2 (Annapolis: U.S. Naval Academy, 1941, 1943).

23. *Bolling v. Sharpe*, 347 U.S. 497, 499 (1954).

24. Ibid. at 499–500. ''In view of our decision that the Constitution prohibits the states from maintaining racially segregated public schools,'' the *Bolling* opinion added, ''it would be unthinkable that the same Constitution would impose a lesser duty on the Federal Government.'' Ibid. at 500.

25. 381 U.S. 479 (1965).

26. Cf. Bork, *The Tempting of America*, 83–84.

27. 358 U.S. 1 (1958); see also Daniel A. Farber, ''The Supreme Court and the Rule of Law: *Cooper v. Aaron* Revisited,'' *University of Illinois Law Review* no. 2 (1982): 387–412; Tony Freyer, *The Little Rock Crisis* (Westport, Conn.: Greenwood Press, 1984).

28. 505 U.S. 833 (1992).

29. 358 U.S. at 17.

30. Ibid. at 18.

31. Eugene W. Hickok and Gary L. McDowell, *Justice vs. Law* (New York: Free Press, 1993), 76–77, 81.

32. Ibid., 168.

33. 505 U.S. 833 (1992).

34. 328 U.S. 549 (1946).

35. 163 U.S. 537 (1896).

36. See William J. Brennan, ''Chief Justice Warren,'' *Harvard Law Review* 88 (November 1974): 3; Earl Warren, *The Memoirs of Earl Warren* (Garden City: Doubleday & Co., 1977), 306; G. Edward White, *Earl Warren* (New York: Oxford University Press, 1982); Bernard Schwartz, *Super Chief* (New York: New York University Press, 1983), 410; see also John Hart Ely, ''The Chief,'' *Harvard Law Review* 88 (November 1974): 12.

37. 369 U.S. 186 (1962).

38. See *Reynolds v. Sims*, 377 U.S. 533, 566 (1964).

39. 377 U.S. 533 (1964); see also *Gray v. Sanders*, 372 U.S. 368 (1963); *Wesberry v. Sanders*, 376 U.S. 1 (1964). On *Baker* and *Reynolds*, see especially Richard C. Cortner, *The Apportionment Cases* (New York: Norton, 1970). On *Baker*, see also Gene Graham, *One Man, One Vote*: Baker v. Carr *and the American Levellers* (Boston: Little, Brown & Co., 1972). More generally, see also Robert B. McKay, *Reapportionment: The Law and Politics of Equal Representation* (New York: Twentieth Century Fund, 1965); Robert G. Dixon, Jr., *Democratic Representation: Reapportionment in Law and Politics* (New York: Oxford University Press, 1968).

40. 377 U.S. at 566.

41. *WMCA, Inc. v. Lomenzo*, 377 U.S. 633 (1964); *Maryland Committee for Fair Representation v. Tawes*, 377 U.S. 656 (1964); *Davis v. Mann*, 377 U.S. 678 (1964); *Roman v. Sincock*, 377 U.S. 695 (1964); *Lucas v. Forty-Fourth General Assembly of Colorado*, 377 U.S. 713 (1964).

42. See *Reynolds*, 377 U.S. at 572–73.

43. See Kelly, ''Clio and the Court,'' 135–37; Miller, *The Supreme Court and the Uses of History*, 128–38; Robert H. Bork, ''Neutral Principles and Some First Amendment Problems,'' *Indiana Law Journal* 47 (Fall 1971): 18: ''The principle of one man, one vote . . . runs counter to the text of the fourteenth amendment, the history surrounding its adoption and ratification and the political practice of Americans from colonial times up to the day the Court invented the new formula.'' See also Bork, *The Tempting of America*, 84–87.

44. See Miller's accurate observation that ''the apportionment decisions . . . have been accepted as law in a way that other momentous exercises of judicial review have not been.''

The Supreme Court and the Uses of History, 119. But see Alex Kozinski, "Spook of Earl: The Spirit and Specter of the Warren Court," in *The Warren Court: A Retrospective*, ed. Bernard Schwartz (New York: Oxford University Press, 1996), 378–81.

45. See David J. Garrow, *Liberty and Sexuality* (New York: Macmillan, 1994), 245–46.

46. 198 U.S. 45 (1905); see also Paul Kens, *Judicial Power and Reform Politics: The Anatomy of* Lochner v. New York (Lawrence: University Press of Kansas, 1990), 159–65.

47. 323 U.S. 214 (1944).

48. See *United States v. E. C. Knight Co.*, 156 U.S. 1 (1895); *Pollock v. Farmers' Loan & Trust* Co., 157 U.S. 429 (1895).

49. See *Carter v. Carter Coal Co.*, 298 U.S. 238 (1936); *Morehead v. New York ex rel. Tipaldo*, 298 U.S. 587 (1936).

50. See *West Coast Hotel*, 300 U.S. 379 (1937); *National Labor Relations Board*, 301 U.S. 1 (1937).

51. See, e.g., *United States v. Darby*, 312 U.S. 100 (1941); *Wickard v. Filburn*, 317 U.S. 111 (1942).

52. See Helen Garfield, "Privacy, Abortion, and Judicial Review: Haunted By the Ghost of *Lochner*," *Washington Law Review* 61 (April 1986): 293–365.

53. 381 U.S. 479, 481–82 (1965).

54. Ibid. at 482.

55. 410 U.S. 113, 167–69 (1973).

56. *Doe v. Bolton*, 410 U.S. 179, 212 n.4 (1973) (Douglas, J., concurring).

57. 410 U.S. at 153.

58. 505 U.S. 833 (1992).

59. Ibid. at 846.

60. 274 U.S. 357, 373 (1927).

61. 367 U.S. 497, 541 (1961).

62. 505 U.S. at 847–48.

63. Ibid. at 848.

64. Ibid. at 849; see also Gerald Gunther, *Learned Hand* (New York: Knopf, 1994); David J. Garrow, "Doing Justice," *Nation*, 27 February 1995, 278–81.

65. 261 U.S. 525 (1923).

66. 505 U.S. at 861.

67. Ibid. at 865.

68. Ibid. at 865–66; see also Tom R. Tyler and Gregory Mitchell, "Legitimacy and the Empowerment of Discretionary Legal Authority: The United States Supreme Court and Abortion Rights," *Duke Law Journal* 43 (February 1994): 796–98; James Boyd White, *Acts of Hope: Creating Authority in Literature, Law, and Politics* (Chicago: University of Chicago Press, 1994), 168–83.

69. 505 U.S. at 866–67.

70. Ibid. at at 867–68.

71. Ibid. at at 868–69.

72. See McConnell, "Originalism and the Desegregation Decisions."

14

The Judicial Role in Equality Decisionmaking

NEAL DEVINS

More than forty years after *Brown v. Board of Education*, the quest for equality remains elusive. Conservatives and liberals both complain bitterly about court-imposed solutions to racial isolation. For conservatives, judicial intervention in the name of equality is counterproductive. Jeremy Rabkin, for example, speaks of courts "working with the whimsical imagery of the 1960s," making it "impossible for [inner-city] neighborhoods to cope with the daily assault on their basic security."[1] In sharp contrast, the battle cry from the left attacks the courts for being too weak-kneed. Gary Orfield, for example, laments "the development of case law permitting both the abandonment of desegregation plans and return to segregated neighborhoods schools."[2] The consequence of this supposed judicial abdication, according to Erwin Chemerinsky, is that "American schools are socially segregated and grossly unequal."[3]

Complicating this debate over the judicial role, starting with President Ronald Reagan's 1986 elevation of William Rehnquist to chief justice, the potency of judicial decisionmaking has been called into question. Flying in the face of long-standing attacks against an "imperial judiciary" by conservative critics of the Court, Gerald Rosenberg and other left-leaning political scientists and constitutional lawyers began depicting court-ordered reform as a "hollow hope." For this new wave of Court critics, meaningful reform is accomplished through social movements and elected-branch initiatives. Under this view, *Brown*—although "virtually universally credited with having brought civil rights to national attention"—is pooh-poohed for "contribut[ing] virtually *nothing* to ending segregation . . . in the Southern states."[4]

Having persisted for more than forty years and with no end in sight, the fight over the propriety and force of court-centered solutions to social problems will continue. Indeed, as the first section of this chapter will show, the Court is incapable of pleasing either progressives who plead for an activist judiciary or social conservatives who deplore such judicial interventions. Judicial decisionmaking typically involves the balancing of competing interests and values, a process that is anathema to absolutist solutions. For example, the judiciary, including the exalted Warren Court, has always engaged in interest balancing in sorting out both the violation and the remedy components of school desegregation litigation. For this reason, the failure of southern states to desegregate in the decade after *Brown* reveals as much about the Warren Court's purposeful refusal to issue a meaningful remedy as it does about the limits of judicial authority.

This point is made in some detail in the second section of this chapter. Highlighting the constitutional dialogue between courts and elected officials over school desegregation, employment discrimination, and abortion, the second section uncovers the potency (as well as the limits) of the judicial role in constitutional decisionmaking.

The question of whether courts should attempt to influence social and political norms still remains. By comparing the Supreme Court's failure to play a leadership role in the affirmative action wars with its constructive participation in the battle over abortion rights, the third section suggests that courts should be players, shaping public discourse through decisions with a nationwide impact.

Interest Balancing and Equal Educational Opportunity

The Warren Court

Today, it seems inconceivable that *Brown*'s basic declaration of racial equality tested the limits of judicial authority. When *Brown* was decided, however, segregation was so ingrained in the South that the outlawing of dual school systems promised social turmoil and massive resistance. These deep feelings were not lost either on the Court or on the Department of Justice. In an effort to temper southern hostility, Chief Justice Earl Warren sought to craft a unanimous opinion of limited reach and the Justice Department recommended that the Court *not* specify a remedy in the case. Accordingly, the Court did not issue a remedy when it ruled on *Brown* that "[s]eparate educational facilities are inherently unequal."[5] After another year, in which the public had time to contemplate a desegregated country, the Court issued *Brown II*, declaring that desegregation must proceed with "all deliberate speed."[6]

The Court's bifurcation of its merits and remedies holdings, as well as the absence of judgmental rhetoric in its segregation decision, reveals that the justices sought to improve the acceptability of their decision in *Brown I* by speaking in a single moderate voice. *Brown*, therefore, is a testament not just to the reaches but also to the limits of judicial action. By taking into account potential resistance to its decision, *Brown* also exemplifies the Court's engaging in the type of interest balancing that has set political parameters on judicial intervention in equal educational opportunity. Recognizing that "some achievable remedial effectiveness may be sacrificed *because* of other social interests" and that "a limited remedy [may be chosen] when a more effective one is too costly to other interests,''[7] the Court recognized that victims' rights must be balanced against a broad spectrum of competing policy concerns. Specifically, aside from victims' rights, the *Brown* Court valued local control of public school systems and judicial restraint. Consequently, in addition to taking southern resistance into account as a factor in crafting a remedy that would best serve plaintiffs' interests, the Warren Court slowed down the pace of school desegregation for other reasons.

This conclusion is subject to criticism, for *Brown I*'s failure to specify a remedy or condemn segregation as immoral is easily explainable as the desire to avoid ''the costs that a remedy imposes . . . when such costs actually interfere with the remedy's effectiveness.''[8] *Brown II*, however, does not lend itself to such an interpretation. Rather than require southern systems to take concrete steps to dismantle dual systems, the Court recognized in *Brown II* that ''varied local school problems'' were best solved by ''[s]chool authorities,'' that district court judges were best suited to examine ''local conditions,'' and that delays associated with ''problems related to administration'' were to be expected.[9] The inevitable result of this ''remedial'' order was inaction. As J. Harvie Wilkinson put it, ''[T]he South was audibly relieved by *Brown II*, a victory of sorts snatched from the defeat of only a year ago [in *Brown*].''[10] Indeed, southern newspapers heralded the remedial order, especially since the Court entrusted the implementation of its decision to ''[o]ur local judges [who] know the local situation.''[11]

Brown II's failure cannot be excused as the best possible remedy in the face of southern resistance. The Court's emphasis on local conditions invited tokenism and delay, and southern school officials and judges acted in kind. The Supreme Court, then, did not seek to provide the type of leadership against which one can measure changes in black-white student contact. In the decade following *Brown*, the Court's only foray into school desegregation is best understood as the Warren Court's defending its institutional self-interest. Pressed—in the Little Rock case—by Arkansas governor Orval Faubus's efforts to block school desegregation, the Court aggressively defended its turf, proclaiming itself ''supreme in the exposition of the law of the Constitution.''[12] Although a more vigorous role in school cases may have immersed the Court in a thicket that may have otherwise jeopardized its social reform objectives in criminal law and elsewhere, it is indisputable that the Warren Court ducked the school desegregation issue for a decade. In 1968 it finally demanded that school boards ''come forward with a plan that promises realistically to work, and promises realistically to work *now*.''[13]

The Warren Court's intransigence on school desegregation spanned most of its sixteen-year life. Remarkably, one decade after *Brown*, only 2 percent of black children attended biracial schools in the eleven southern states. In the 1965–66 school year, however, the percentage of black children in biracial schools rose to 6 percent. The turning point here was not hyped-up judicial enforcement; instead, the principal impetus to meaningful school desegregation was rooted in elected-branch action.

Most significant, the implementation of the Elementary and Secondary Education Act of 1965, coupled with the issuance and enforcement of guidelines for Title VI of the Civil Rights Act of 1964, marked a significant expansion in federal power over state education systems. With Title VI's demand that federal grant recipients be nondiscriminatory, Congress became willing to supply billions of dollars of aid for the compensatory education of educationally deprived children. This aid was sufficient incentive for many school systems to comply with the Office for Civil Rights' nondiscrimination standards. Furthermore, by authorizing Department of Justice participation in school desegregation litigation through its 1964 Civil Rights Act, Congress encouraged judicial intervention.

It was against this backdrop of increasing federal involvement in school desegregation that the Warren Court stepped up its own involvement. This parallelism should come as no surprise. With Congress and the White House both making equal educational opportunity a national priority and envisioning an increasing judicial role, concerns of local control and judicial restraint no longer impeded judicial action. Court intervention, instead, was consistent with judicial respect for the priorities set by coequal branches of the federal government.

The Burger and Rehnquist Courts

The Warren Court's school desegregation legacy, then, is one of visionary leadership and a good dose of caution. Against this backdrop, Erwin Chemerinsky goes too far in attacking the Burger Court for deviating from Warren Court decisionmaking. This, of course, is not to say that proponents of a vigorous judicial role in equal educational opportunity should not be critical of the Burger Court. *Milliken I*'s refusal to include suburban counties in Detroit's school desegregation plan, despite the Court's recognition that the state of Michigan was partly responsible for illegal segregation in Detroit schools, explicitly placed the interests of local control and judicial restraint ahead of equal educational opportunity.[14] Likewise, local control triumphed when the Court ruled that a school system may favor neighborhood schools irrespective of ethnically segregated residential patterns, which makes racial isolation "the foreseeable and inevitable result of such an assignment policy."[15]

The Burger Court's recognition of values outside equal educational opportunity, as the Warren Court experience suggests, is inevitable, especially since four members of the Burger Court (William Rehnquist, Lewis Powell, Harry Blackmun, and Warren Burger himself) were appointed by a president, Richard Nixon, who campaigned against judicial activism and for states' rights as part of his "southern strategy." Correspondingly, by 1969, unlike the final stages of the Warren Court, when "the President, congressional leadership, and the public all recognized that protection of the rights of black Americans was the fundamental [social and educational] issue,"[16] both the executive and legislative branches were increasingly found opposing the federal courts in school desegregation questions. Mounting concern over the extension of desegregation to districts outside the South and heightened opposition to the use of mandatory reassignments ("busing") led to increased efforts by both branches to curb federal action in school desegregation. Without the support of the coequal branches of government, judicial intervention was likely to face increasing local resistance. Concerns of the judiciary's self-interest in having its orders enforced, as well as respect owed a coequal branch, warranted a diminished judicial role and, with it, increasing attention to judicial restraint concerns.

What then seems remarkable about the Burger Court is its willingness to enter the school desegregation fray at all. In several instances, the Burger Court did just that, approving fairly broad constructs for defining both the scope of the violation and the sweep of the remedy. In 1971, *Swann v. Charlotte-Mecklenburg Board of Education* recognized the use of black-white pupil ratios and mandatory student reassignments as "starting point[s] in the process of shaping a remedy."[17] For the Burger Court, to eliminate all vestiges of an unconstitutional dual school system, desegregation remedies might have to be "administratively awkward, inconvenient, and even bizarre."[18]

Interest balancing played only a minor role in *Swann*. While not rejecting concerns of the health of children from overly long bus trips, the Court emphasized that the competing value of desegregation will almost always win out. More significant, *Swann* eschewed local control, judicial restraint, institutional self-interest in crafting a clearly workable remedy, and respect for legislative and executive branch preferences in favor of massive far-reaching judicial intervention.

Another measure of the Burger Court's acquiescence to significant judicial involvement can be seen in its refusal to resolve early 1980s challenges by school systems (and the Reagan Justice Department) to continuing judicial supervision of school systems subject to long-standing desegregation orders. Specifically, rather than consider alternatives to mandatory assignments and other intrusive remedies or specify standards defining the termination of judicial authority in this area, the Burger Court put those decisions off for another day.

With the Rehnquist Court, that day arrived. In *Board of Education v. Dowell* and *Freeman v. Pitts*, the Rehnquist Court made clear that federal courts should be willing to terminate desegregation orders, placing increasing emphasis on local control and judicial restraint and, correspondingly, deemphasizing victims' rights concerns. In *Dowell*, pointing to "[c]onsiderations based on the allocation of powers within our federal system" and extolling local control's virtues in "allow[ing] citizens to participate in decisionmaking, and allow[ing] innovation so that school programs can fit local needs,"[19] the Supreme Court approved Oklahoma City's decision to abandon mandatory transportation for students in grades K–4. *Freeman* likewise emphasized limits in the courts' remedial authority: "Returning schools to the control of local authorities at the earliest practicable date is essential to restore their true accountability in our governmental system."[20] Upholding district court authority to relinquish jurisdiction over student assignments, *Freeman* relieved Dekalb County, Georgia, of any obligation to address racial isolation caused by changing demographics.

Dowell and *Freeman*, although welcoming a diminished judicial role, neither require nor encourage district court judges to terminate school desegregation injunctions.[21] Instead, like *Brown II*, these Rehnquist Court rulings empower district court judges to take local circumstances into account in sorting out whether a school system has satisfied its desegregation obligations. *Dowell* and *Freeman* also appear less draconian when placed in their social and political contexts. With the 1980 election of Ronald Reagan, the White House proposed and Congress endorsed "new federalism" in education programs that eliminated targeted funds for minority schoolchildren subject to school desegregation remedies and put in their stead block grant programs that allowed local school systems to purchase computers and the like.

Combusting with "new federalism" initiatives, legislative riders as well as Reagan and Bush Justice Department arguments emphasized local autonomy and attacked mandatory reassignments. In addition to congressional and White House opposition to intrusive judicial remedies, opinion polls suggest that busing is disfavored by the minority community. Rather than expansive judicial intervention, minority interests typically favor magnet school programs and other education-related expenditures.[22] Given the absence of support for mandatory assignments and other intrusive remedies, it is little wonder that the courts themselves would tire of continuing judicial supervision of school systems.

That the Rehnquist Court was influenced by these concerns is as inevitable as the Warren and Burger Courts' recognition of social and political factors in their equal educational opportunity jurisprudence. The election of President Bill Clinton, moreover, has done little to change these tides. As of June 1997, the Clinton administration has left school desegregation alone.[23] Congress, too, remains disinterested in these matters. Without any push for a greater federal judicial presence, the Court is likely to do little in this area. For Erwin Chemerinsky, that is ducking the issue by declaring victory. I, however, would place a less-sinister spin on the evolution of the Court's role in this area. The Court sought to advance equal educational opportunity in fits and starts, sometimes—as in *Brown I* and *Swann*—moving aggressively, and other times—as in *Brown II, Milliken*, and *Freeman*—eschewing an activist role. In the end, the Court settled on a doctrine that roughly matched social and political conditions. Without question, the Court would have played a more aggressive role had voters placed other individuals in Congress, in the White House, and—through the appointments and confirmation process—on the bench. But to expect the Court to rise above its surroundings is unrealistic. Justice Benjamin N. Cardozo reminded us that the "great tides and currents which engulf the rest of men do not turn aside in their course and pass the judges by."[24]

Do Courts Matter?

That judicial action is shaped by social and political forces, however, does not mean that courts do not play a leadership role in affecting public policy and discourse. While it is true, as Gerald Rosenberg aptly notes, that *Brown* neither prompted meaningful school desegregation nor affected public attitudes and beliefs (in part because most Americans were unaware of the decision), it is also true that *Brown*—while limited—was consequential. Furthermore, in assessing *Brown*'s impact, it is critical to take into account what the Court set out to accomplish through its decision.

To begin with, as the first part of this chapter details, *Brown* is a testament to how interest balancing affects Supreme Court decisionmaking. By purposefully limiting the scope and sweep of *Brown*, the Court did not seek to provide the type of leadership against which we can measure changes in black-white student contact. With that said, *Brown* influenced legislative deliberations over the 1964 Civil Rights Act. On the issue of Title VI funding prohibitions, bill sponsor Senator Thomas Kuchel argued that Title VI prevented "unconstitutional" expenditures of federal funds, thereby "furthering a policy of nondiscrimination, and thus eliminating defiance of the law of the land [i.e., *Brown*]."[25] For Kuchel and others, southern resistance to *Brown* made Title VI a moral imperative; otherwise, Congress would knowingly fund blatantly unconstitutional state action. More striking, Title IV of the 1964 Act, authorizing the Justice Department to file desegregation lawsuits, seems a direct response to *Brown*. Act sponsors spoke of "expediting the decade old mandate of the Supreme Court" and noted that civil rights groups lacked the funds needed to launch separate lawsuits in each of 2,000 segregationist southern school districts.[26]

The judicial role in school desegregation, of course, extends well beyond mid-1960s reforms. Indeed, the Supreme Court's approval of busing in its 1971 *Swann* decision was the judiciary's most significant, most controversial, and most debated foray into court-ordered institutional reform. Battle lines had been drawn here, with critics and proponents spinning different tales of white flight and other forms of resegregation, educational achievement, judicial fact-finding and management, and school board compliance. Three things are not in debate, all of which speak to a significant—if not dominant—judicial role.

First, courts affect behavior. When court orders result in new budgeting processes (Boston), the imposition of a statewide tax levy (Kansas City), the building of state-subsidized housing (Yonkers), and the freezing of U.S. Department of Education accounts (Chicago), there is change.[27] More significant, in response to a school desegregation order, some parents do send their children to private schools or move to another school system, although there is typically some increase in minority-nonminority contact in the public schools.

Second, court decisions prompt legislative action. Following *Swann*, President Richard Nixon delivered a national address on the evils of busing and proposed legislation making busing a remedy of "last resort" for school segregation and then "only under strict limitations."[28] Although Congress refused to limit court remedial authority, numerous restrictions on federal financial support of mandatory busing and federal advocacy of busing have been enacted since 1972.[29]

Third, court action or the threat of court action is essential to meaningful school desegregation. In most instances, the threat of legal action prompts "voluntary" reform. Fear of overreaching court orders and the costs of litigation prod such voluntary compliance. In rare instances, school boards look to courts to impose remedies that they support but lack the political courage to endorse. In such cases, courts are far from incidental; they are a necessary conduit to legitimate socially desirable but politically costly behavior. Finally (and most visibly), in some instances, courts impose remedies on reluctant districts. The results here vary dramatically. Sometimes judges or court-appointed special masters can work with community leaders to forge a successful desegregation plan. In those cases, courts play an affirmative instrumental role. On other occasions, court orders are little more than a Pyrrhic victory for civil rights litigants. When a school system prefers resistance to compliance, court action is not likely to succeed. Whether successful compromises outnumber political debacles is an open question. What is clear is that courts can facilitate success stories but only when school systems are willing players.

On the issue of busing, it may be that "[o]nly a reordering of the environment" will result in racially balanced public schools.[30] That courts cannot accomplish that task comes as no surprise. The story of school desegregation reveals that the judiciary is only a piece in a much larger puzzle. Support or resistance from the federal government and local school authorities are also pieces of this puzzle (and perhaps larger ones at that). The Supreme Court often recognizes these limits; its decisions in *Brown* are testament to this sensitivity. That the judiciary is constrained, however, does not mean that the courts are without significant influence here.

Without question, when it comes to race and schooling, "[p]olitics and law . . . each reshape the other."[31] For this reason, just as Rosenberg overstates his case, proponents of judicial activism, too, infrequently take into account inherent limits on judicial authority. Their principal complaint, instead, is that the Court is not sufficiently progressive. Erwin Chemerinsky, for example, waxes poetic about different decisions and different results if only the Warren Court had continued for a few more years.[32]

Nonjudicial forces, whether political or social, are infrequently studied and grossly underestimated. Combined with inherent limits on the judiciary's power to manage reform, these nonjudicial forces suggest that social reform through litigation is a gamble. Along these lines, it cannot be denied that there are instances when court opinions do not bind elected government. Supreme Court decisions limiting religious observance in the public schools and prohibiting the legislative veto, for example, have been disregarded. The public school cases demand that objecting students bear the fiscal and emotional toll of challenging school systems that would prefer to heed religious beliefs ahead of Supreme Court decisions. This price is quite high, and consequently many religious practices remain unchallenged. The legislative veto is a more dramatic, more surprising case, for the affected parties are Congress and the White House rather than "backwater" school systems. Nonetheless, following the Supreme Court's 1983 repudiation of this device in *Immigration and Naturalization Service v. Chandha*, more than 300 new legislative vetoes have been enacted and countless informal arrangements have been made between oversight committees and governmental agencies. The explanation for this widespread disobedience is that neither Congress nor the White House "wants the static model of separated powers offered by the Court."[33] That the Court repudiated the legislative veto hardly matters. With both sides benefiting from legislative veto arrangements, market forces have simply driven them underground.

The legislative veto and religion cases share a common feature. Neither decision creates incentives for compliance. Compliance, instead, is a by-product of the implementing community. Consequently, when the implementing community resists, the judicial impact is muted. In other instances, however, elected government acts affirmatively in the face of a decision that is not self-implementing. When a federal appeals court directed the Federal Communications Commission to take race into account in broadcast-licensing decisions, for example, the commission not only complied with that decision but embraced other policy initiatives to increase the number of minority broadcasters.[34]

Judicial influences are more pronounced when incentives for enforcement are a natural outgrowth of the opinion. Employers now incorporate Title VII employment discrimination rulings into their hiring and promotion practices in order to avoid litigation costs. Likewise, health care providers responded to the extraordinary demand for nonhospital abortions in the wake of *Roe* by opening abortion clinics. Elected government may strengthen these self-implementing decisions. For example, employment discrimination litigation pursued by the Equal Employment Opportunity Commission and Department of Justice quickened the pace of Title VII compliance. Elected government may also oppose self-implementing decisions, which occurred when antiabortion funding restrictions prevented some poor women from seeking an abortion. Yet unlike non-self-implementing decisions, in which governmental resistance is extremely significant, self-implementing decisions can withstand governmental attack. Witness the abortion decision: despite the Supreme Court's approval of the abortion-funding ban in *Harris v. McRae*, abortion rates have remained stable.

Court decisions may also overcome the inertia that sometimes stalls legislative reform efforts. For example, when *Roe* was decided, a vigorous right-to-life movement successfully blocked pro-choice legislative reform efforts in Michigan, North Dakota, and elsewhere. Although 64 percent of Americans supported abortion rights at that time, pro-life forces proved that "[a] small but intense minority can exercise political influence disproportionate to its numbers when a diffuse and silent majority does not organize to fight back."[35] *Roe*'s recognition of abortion rights therefore validated majority preferences while it invalidated the laws of forty-six states.

Roe did more than place public opinion polls ahead of legislative majorities. *Roe* also changed the political culture of abortion. States that had been willing to validate minority preferences by enacting abortion restrictions at the behest of pro-life interest groups reversed course after the Supreme Court signaled its willingness to approve such restrictions in *Planned Parenthood of Southeastern Pennsylvania v. Casey*.

This phenomenon—of elected government's acclimating to and embracing restrictive judicial norms—is not limited to abortion. The 1991 Civil Rights Act approved disparate racial impact proofs of employment discrimination, a measure that would not have been adopted by the 1964 Congress.[36] Congress's change of heart was a direct result of a 1971 Supreme Court decision, *Griggs v. Duke Power Co.*, which recognized disparate impact proofs. In 1991, however, *Griggs* was a nullity—effectively overruled by a 1989 Supreme Court decision.[37] Although *Griggs* was a judicial creation, it was also—by 1991—a cornerstone of employment discrimination litigation. The 1991 Civil Rights Act, by formally embracing disparate proofs, validated judicially created norms.[38]

The 1993 Religious Freedom Restoration Act follows a similar pattern. After the Supreme Court's 1990 *Employment Division v. Smith* decision reversed the long-standing judicial practice of subjecting *all* governmental conduct that burdens religious exercise to exacting judicial review, Congress stepped in to statutorily mandate the Court's preexisting practice.[39] For Congress, *Smith* ran headlong into legislative expectations of vigorous protections for religious exercise, expectations created by long-standing judicial practices.

Courts matter. They matter a lot. Sometimes their orders set in motion market mechanisms that guarantee their effectiveness. Sometimes the threat of judicial action prompts either settlement or legislative initiative. Their opinions influence legislative deliberations and change the status quo. Occasionally, they trump agencies and interpose their normative views into the law. It may be that these influences sometimes exceed the proper judicial role in our system of separated powers, but they *are* judicial influences nonetheless.

Should Courts Matter?

The question of whether courts should play a positive role in shaping these social and political forces remains. For very different reasons, some progressives and many conservatives oppose judicial intervention, arguing that court-ordered " 'civil rights' remedies have not touched the problem of the black underclass, which is at the heart of our current racial discord."[40] While there is an element of truth to claims that "the predictable bias of federal courts—towards legalistic, procedural, and uniform national standards"[41]—is a partial roadblock to single-sex schools and other creative efforts to improve our ever-worsening inner cities, it is also true that the judiciary must make its voice heard on abortion, affirmative action, and other controversial topics.

Courts, especially the Supreme Court, should matter. In our three-branch scheme, the Supreme Court is expected to shape constitutional values and, in so doing, preserve the judiciary's integrity as a coequal branch of government. Along these lines, *The Federalist* papers, in supporting the Court's authority to strike down governmental conduct, spoke of the judicial branch serving as "an intermediate body between the People and the Legislature, in order, among other things, to keep the latter within the limits assigned to their authority."[42] More significant, ongoing dialogues between the courts and elected government play a constructive role in shaping constitutional values.

School desegregation and abortion are particularly vivid examples of this phenomenon. The story of school desegregation is one in which, after the Court's monumental decision in *Brown*, Congress and the executive branch have framed the debate. First, the elected branches, by giving meaning to the *Brown* mandate through mid-1960s reforms, helped to propel increasing judicial scrutiny in *Swann*. Second, after two decades of attacking mandatory reassignments (and appointing Supreme Court justices), the Court has ceded to elected-branch desires and returned much of school desegregation to the control of state and local government. This give-and-take process reveals the ways in which the courts and elected government influence each other. Specifically, while elected government's resistance to busing has tempered Supreme Court doctrine, the federal government's willingness to combat purposeful discrimination is largely rooted in the *Brown* decision.

The saga of abortion rights likewise underscores the appropriately interactive nature of constitutional decisionmaking. Like *Brown, Roe* served as a critical trigger to the recognition of abortion rights. *Roe*, too, prompted elected government into action. As with court-ordered busing, two decades of elected government's resistance (and the appointment of Supreme Court justices) resulted in the Court's returning much of this divisive issue to the states. By reaffirming "the central holding of *Roe*" and repudiating *Roe*'s stringent trimester test in favor of a more deferential "undue burden" standard,[43] 1992's *Planned Parenthood v. Casey* signaled the Court's willingness to uphold state regulation—if not prohibition—of abortion.

Casey, however, did not trigger an antiabortion revolution. Most striking, according to Allan Guttmacher Institute studies, "antiabortion legislators [have] heeded . . . [*Casey*] and curtailed their attempts to make abortion illegal."[44] In 1994, for example, no legislation was introduced to outlaw abortion. Furthermore, in the two years following *Casey*, one-third of abortion-related legislative initiatives would have guaranteed the right to abortion. Finally, of the handful of abortion regulation measures adopted since *Casey*, all involve restrictions approved by the Court: waiting periods, informed consent, and parental notification.

Casey appears to have stabilized, if not resolved, the abortion dispute. While the Supreme Court eviscerated *Roe*'s trimester standard, the post-*Casey* calm reveals that, like *Brown, Roe* shaped elected government's attitudes. Contrary to the pre-*Roe* period (when forty-six states either prohibited or severely limited abortion access), abortion rights—for better or worse—are now a secure feature of our constitutional landscape.

Attaining an equilibrium with regard to school desegregation and abortion required all three branches and all levels of government to do battle with one another. This dynamic process yielded a very nuanced, very delicate (if not very deliberate) compromise. The story of affirmative action, in contrast, reveals the pitfalls of the Court's not staking out a position and thereby limiting its role in the shaping of constitutional values.

More than two decades ago, in *DeFunis v. Odegarrd*,[45] the Supreme Court issued its first nondecision in an affirmative action case. Rather than play a leadership role and define the parameters of governmental authority over race preferences, the Court ducked the issue altogether by ruling the *DeFunis* lawsuit moot. When the Court finally spoke, in *Regents of University of California v. Bakke*,[46] it issued a decision so fractured that no member of the Court joined Justice Lewis Powell's decisive lead opinion. This pattern persists. Supreme Court affirmative action decisions are fact-specific, plurality decisions far outnumber majority decisions, and the values that underlie the Court's rulings are, at best, difficult to decipher.

Witness *Adarand Constructors, Inc. v. Pena*, a 1995 decision in which the Court—by a 5–4 vote—refused for the first time to uphold a congressionally approved affirmative action plan.[47] *Adarand* promised to be a landmark, presenting the Court with an opportunity to resolve a long-standing controversy about whether all race preferences are inherently suspect. The Court settled, instead, on a middle-ground position. Specifically, by insisting that federal, as well as state, affirmative action programs be "narrowly tailored" to serve a "compelling governmental interest," *Adarand* embraced the heretofore rigid strict scrutiny standard of review. However, rather than apply strict scrutiny review to Adarand Constructors' challenge to the government's setting aside of highway construction funds to minority businesses, the Court sent the dispute back to the district court where it had originated. More significant, *Adarand* sought to "dispel the notion that strict scrutiny is 'strict in theory,' but fatal in fact."[48] Referring to the "unhappy persistence of both the practice and lingering effects of racial discrimination," *Adarand* emphasized that "government is not disqualified from acting in response to it."[49]

Adarand's mixed message makes it a rather slippery precedent. Moreover, because the Court remanded the case rather than resolve the dispute, *Adarand* offers little guidance about the application of strict scrutiny review. By refusing to stake out a hard-line position, the Court positioned itself to ratchet up, ratchet down, or maintain its ambiguous application of strict scrutiny review. Furthermore, because the Supreme Court did not fill in the outlines of its decision before the 1996 elections, *Adarand* effectively made the 1996 presidential election a referendum on affirmative action. Specifically, since the next Supreme Court appointee could either tighten or eviscerate the strict scrutiny standard adopted by *Adarand*'s five-member majority, *Adarand*'s future was necessarily hinged to the choice of Bill Clinton (who strongly supported preferences) or Bob Dole (who was lined up against affirmative action). As such, *Adarand* reinforces the purely political nature of affirmative action decisionmaking, thereby undermining the Court's authority and the Constitution's relevance.

Although social and political forces typically play a part in defining the reaches of Supreme Court decisionmaking, Court decisions often play a large role in shaping constitutional and other dialogues that take place among the branches. *Adarand*, in contrast, places few meaningful checks on elected government's action.

Admittedly, the Court's failure to use its bully pulpit to speak about the rightness or wrongness of preferences reflects the public's division and lack of consensus on the affirmative action issue. Nonetheless, by not staking out a position, the Court has played next to no role in shaping public discourse on affirmative action. This is unfortunate—it reduces the level of respect for the Court among the other branches and weighs down the public discourse on affirmative action with meaningless legalisms. In contrast, on issues like abortion and school desegregation, the Court has proved itself a player, shaping policy through decisions that have had a nationwide impact.

Conclusion

"The genius of [our] system lies in the very tension itself, and in our ability to combine active democracy, constitutional principles, and judicial judgment."[50] For this reason, vigorous interchange between the Court, elected government, and the public results in more vibrant and enduring constitutional interpretation. School desegregation and abortion illustrate this phenomenon. In both instances, constitutional dialogues between the Court and elected government have—given both the volatility of the issue and the difficulty of finding a middle-ground solution—resulted in a workable and durable balancing of competing interests.

When it comes to affirmative action, however, the Court has failed to speak in a way that alters the political forces. It has neither defined the terms of the affirmative action debate particularly well nor used its bully pulpit to explain what values are at stake. As a result, although it is often true that "speaking no more broadly than is absolutely required avoids throwing settled law into confusion[,] doing so [on affirmative action] preserves a chaos that is evident to anyone who can read and count."[51]

Constitutional decisionmaking is a never-ending process. It requires the participation of all branches and levels of government. It requires the Court to balance competing values and interests in crafting decisions; it requires elected officials to incorporate judicial norms into their decisionmaking. Consequently, although there may be "a magnetic attraction to the notion of an ultimate constitutional interpreter," complex social policy issues are better resolved through "the sweaty intimacy of creatures locked in combat."[52]

NOTES

1. Jeremy Rabkin, "Racial Progress and Constitutional Road Blocks," *William and Mary Law Review* 34 (Fall 1992): 75, 86. See Rabkin, chapter 6, in this volume.

2. Gary Orfield, "The Growth of Segregation in American Public Schools: Changing Patterns of Separation and Poverty since 1968: A Report of the Harvard Project in School Desegregation to the National School Board Association" (paper presented December 1993), 7.

3. Erwin Chemerinsky, "Lost Opportunity: The Burger Court and the Failure to Achieve Equal Educational Opportunity," *Mercer Law Review* 45 (Spring 1994): 999. See also Chemerinsky, chapter 12, in this volume.

4. Gerald Rosenberg, *The Hollow Hope: Can Courts Bring About Social Change?* (Chicago: University of Chicago Press, 1991), 52. See also Rosenberg, chapter 11, and Delgado and Stefancic, chapter 10, in this volume.

5. 347 U.S. 483, 495 (1956).

6. 349 U.S. 294, 301 (1955).

7. Paul Gewirtz, "Remedies and Resistance," *Yale Law Journal* 92 (March 1983): 585, 589 (emphasis added).

8. Ibid., 599.

9. 349 U.S. at 299–300.

10. Harvie Wilkinson III, "The Supreme Court and Southern School Desegregation, 1955–1970: A History and Analysis," *Virginia Law Review* 64 (May 1978): 485, 490.

11. Reed Sarratt, *The Ordeal of Desegregation* (New York: Harper & Row, 1966), 200 (quoting a southern attorney).

12. *Cooper v. Aaron*, 358 U.S. 1, 18 (1958). See Garrow, chapter 13, in this volume.

13. *Green v. County School Board of New Kent*, 391 U.S. 430, 439 (1968) (emphasis added).

14. *Milliken v. Bradley*, 418 U.S. 717, 741 (1974); see Chemerinsky, "Lost Opportunity," 99.

15. *United States v. Texas Education Agency*, 532 F.2d 380, 392 (5th Cir. 1976), *rev'd, Austin Indep. School District v. United States*, 429 U.S. 990 (1976) (mem.).

16. Gary Orfield, *The Reconstruction of Southern Education* (New York: Wiley-Interscience, 1969), 339.

17. 402 U.S. 1, 25 (1971).

18. Ibid. at 28.

19. 498 U.S. 237, 248 (1991).

20. 503 U.S. 467, 490 (1992).

21. In *Missouri v. Jenkins*, 115 S. Ct. 2038 (1995), however, the Rehnquist Court concluded that educational achievement was not an appropriate goal of a desegregation order. Pointing to the values of local control and judicial restraint enunciated in both *Dowell* and *Freeman*, the Court concluded that educational achievement was too amorphous and, as such, boundless.

22. See Christine Rossell, chapter 8, and Drew S. Days III, chapter 9, in this volume.

23. In one case, *Missouri v. Jenkins*, the Clinton administration did file an amicus brief, unsuccessfully arguing that educational achievement can and should be linked to prior unlawful racial segregation.

24. Benjamin Cardozo, *The Nature of the Judicial Process* (New Haven: Yale University Press, 1921), 168.

25. *Cong. Rec.*, 88th Cong., 2d sess., 1964, 110, pt. 5:6562 (statement of Senator Kuchel).

26. Bernard Schwartz, *Statutory History of the United States: Civil Rights* (New York: Chelsea House Publishers, 1970), 1245 (statement of Senator Kuchel), 1205–6 (statement of Senator Humphrey).

27. The cases are *Morgan v. McDonough*, 540 F.2d 527 (1st Cir. 1976), *cert. denied*, 429 U.S. 1042 (1977) (Boston); *Missouri v. Jenkins*, 495 U.S. 33 (1990) (Kansas City); *United States v. Yonkers Board of Education*, 837 F.2d 1181 (2d Cir. 1987), *cert. denied*, 486 U.S. 1055 (1988) (Yonkers); *United States v. Board of Education of City of Chicago*, 567 F. Supp. 272 (N.D. Ill.), *aff'd*, 717 F.2d 378 (7th Cir. 1983) (Chicago).

28. Equal Educational Opportunities Act, H.R. 13915, 92d Cong., 2d Sess. (1972); see also *Public Papers of the Presidents of the United States: Richard Nixon, 1972* (Washington, D.C.: Government Printing office, 1972), 425–28.

29. See Louis Fisher and Neal Devins, *Political Dynamics of Constitutional Law*, 2d ed. (St. Paul: West Publishing Co., 1996), 246–49.

30. Alexander M. Bickel, *The Supreme Court and the Idea of Progress* (New Haven: Yale University Press, 1972), 132.

31. David Kirp, *Just Schools* (Berkeley: University of California Press, 1983), 70.

32. Chemerinsky, "Lost Opportunity," 1011. See also Abrams, chapter 2, in this volume.

33. Fisher, *Constitutional Dialogues* (Princeton: Princeton University Press, 1988), 228.

34. This episode is discussed in Neal Devins, "*Metro Broadcasting v FCC*: Requiem for a Heavyweight," *Texas Law Review* 69 (November 1990): 125.

35. Kathleen M. Sullivan, "Law's Labor," *New Republic*, 23 March 1994, 42, 44.

36. See Graham, chapter 7, in this volume.

37. *Wards Cove Packing Co. v. Atonio*, 490 U.S. 642 (1989).

38. See Neal Devins, "Reagan Redux: Civil Rights under Bush," *Notre Dame Law Review*, no. 5 (1993): 955.

39. The Religious Freedom Restoration Act, Pub. L. No. 103–141 (1993).

40. Rabkin, "Racial Progress and Constitutional Road Blocks."

41. *Ibid.*

42. Alexander Hamilton, *The Federalist, No. 78*, ed. H. B. Dawson (New York: Charles Scribner's Sons, 1983), 54.

43. 505 U.S. 833, 878 (1992).

44. Alan Guttmacher Institute, *State Reproductive Health Monitor* 5, no. 2 (May 1994): ii.

45. 416 U.S. 312 (1974).

46. 438 U.S. 265 (1978).

47. 115 S. Ct. 2097 (1995).

48. Ibid. at 2117.

49. Ibid.

50. John Agresto, *The Supreme Court and Constitutional Democracy* (Ithaca, N.Y.: Cornell University Press, 1984), 167.

51. *Webster v. Reproductive Health Services*, 492 U.S. 490, 535 (1989) (Scalia, J., concurring).

52. Walter F. Murphy, ''Who Shall Interpret?'' *Review of Politics* 48 (Summer 1981): 401, 417; Bickel, *The Supreme Court and the Idea of Progress*, 99.

Index